W9-CAN-083

METROPOLITAIN

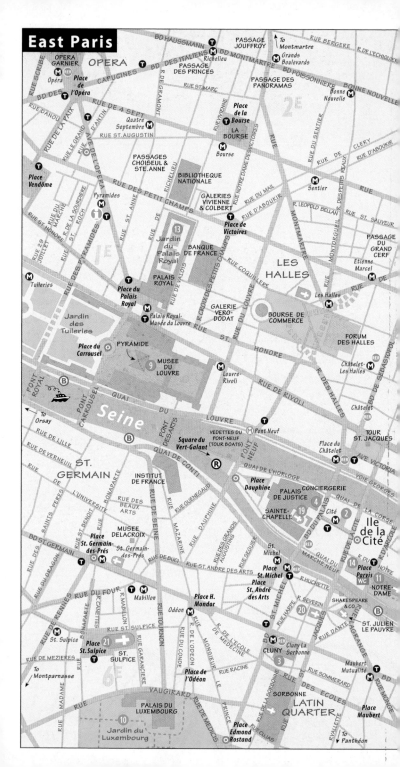

# CONTENTS

# Rick Steves'

# PARIS

Rick Steves, Steve Smith
& Gene Openshaw

# 2013

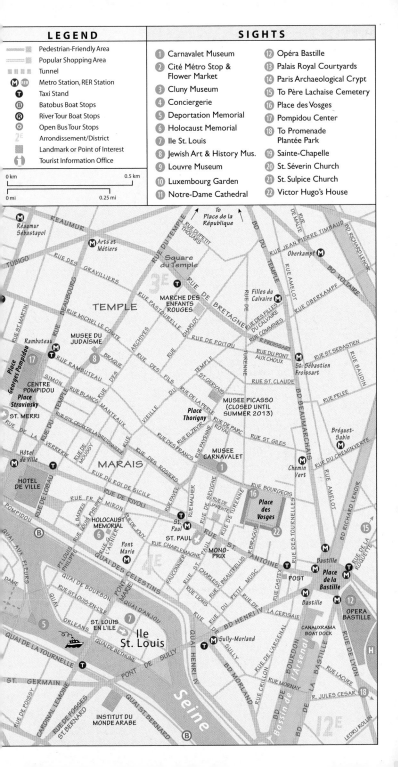

## LEGEND

- Pedestrian-Friendly Area
- Popular Shopping Area
- Tunnel
- **M** **RER** Metro Station, RER Station
- **T** Taxi Stand
- **B** Batobus Boat Stops
- **R** River Tour Boat Stops
- **O** Open Bus Tour Stops
- 2ᴱ Arrondissement/District
- Landmark or Point of Interest
- **i** Tourist Information Office

0 km          0.5 km

0 mi          0.25 mi

## SIGHTS

1. Carnavalet Museum
2. Cité Métro Stop & Flower Market
3. Cluny Museum
4. Conciergerie
5. Deportation Memorial
6. Holocaust Memorial
7. Ile St. Louis
8. Jewish Art & History Mus.
9. Louvre Museum
10. Luxembourg Garden
11. Notre-Dame Cathedral
12. Opéra Bastille
13. Palais Royal Courtyards
14. Paris Archaeological Crypt
15. To Père Lachaise Cemetery
16. Place des Vosges
17. Pompidou Center
18. To Promenade Plantée Park
19. Sainte-Chapelle
20. St. Séverin Church
21. St. Sulpice Church
22. Victor Hugo's House

# West Paris

To La Défense

MUSEE JACQUEMART-ANDRÉ

Charles de Gaulle Etoile

Place Charles de Gaulle

PEDESTRIAN UNDERPASS

ARC DE TRIOMPHE

AVE DE WAGRAM

RUE DU FAUBOURG ST HONORE

AVE HOCHE

RUE DE MONCEAU

AVE MACMAHON

BEAUJON

BALZAC

BD HAUSSMANN

AVE DE FRIEDLAND

R. DU FAUBOURG ST HONORE

AVE CARNOT

AVE DE LA GRANDE ARMEE

RUE

AVE FOCH

RUE D'ARTOIS

RUE WASHINGTON

RUE DE BERRI

St. Philippe du Roule

VICTOR HUGO

Kléber

George V

CHAMPS-ELYSEES

RUE DE COLISEE

FRANKLIN

Rond-Point des Champs-Elysées

LAURISTON

AVE KLEBER

RUE D'IENA

AVE JEAN GIRAUDOUX

RUE

RUE C. COLUMBUS

RUE QUENTIN BAUCHART

RUE PIERRE CHARRON

MARBEUF

RUE DE MARIGNAN

RUE BASSANO

Franklin D. Roosevelt

ROOSEVELT

Place des Etats-Unis

RUE GALILEE

DE

RUE FRANCOIS 1ER

RUE DE CHAILLOT

AVE MARCEAU

RUE C. MAROT

RUE DU BOCCADOR

Place François 1er

GOUJON

JEAN

BAYARD

Boissière

RUE DE LUBECK

RUE PIERRE 1ER DE SERBIE

AVE PIERRE 1ER DE SERBIE

GEORGE V

AVE MONTAIGNE

RUE

HAMELIN

RUE D'IENA

RUE FRESNEL

RUE DE CHAILLOT

RUE FREYCINET

Alma Marceau

Place de l'Alma

COURS ALBERT 1ER

R. DE LONGCHAMP

Place d'Iéna

Iéna

PRESIDENT WILSON

AVE DU

RUE DE LA MANUTENTION

RUE DE LA MANUTENTION

RUE DEBROUSSE

PONT DE L'ALMA

Seine

PONT DES INVALIDES

AVE ALBERT DE MUN

AVE DE NEW YORK

PASSERELLE DEBILLY

Pont de l'Alma

LES EGOUTS DE PARIS

QUAI D'ORSAY

AMERICAN CHURCH

Trocadéro

Jardins du Trocadéro

Place de la Résistance

RUE COGNACQ JAY

L'UNIVERSITE

RUE JEAN NICOT

RUE SURCOUF

MALAR

RUE FABOURG

QUAI BRANLY

QUAI BRANLY MUSEUM

PONT D'IENA

RUE

DE

L'UNIVERSITE

PASSAGE LANDRIEU

RUE

DOMINIQUE

RUE AMELIE

RUE J. NICOT

RUE DE LA COMETE

RUE J. COMETE

La Tour-Maubourg

TOUR EIFFEL

AVE DE LA BOURDONNAIS

RUE DE MONTTESSUY

RUE DE LA EXPO

ST DOMINIQUE

RUE CLER

RUE AUGEREAU

RUE BOSQUET

RUE AMELIE

RUE PSICHARI

RUE DUVIVIER

GRENELLE

Champ de Mars Tour Eiffel

Parc du Champ de Mars

AVE CHARLES FLOQUET

AVE JOSEPH BOUVARD

START OF BUS #69 TOUR

AVE EMILE DESCHANEL

RUE DU CHAMP DE MARS

RUE CLER

POST

RUE DE LA MOTTE PICQUET

RUE CHEVERT

BD

RUE JEAN REY

AVE DE SUFFREN

Place de l'Ecole Militaire

Ecole Militaire

RUE ST. SAENS

RUE DESAIX

RUE DE LA FEDERATION

GRENELLE

Place Joffre

ECOLE MILITAIRE

AVE DUQUESNE

AVE DE

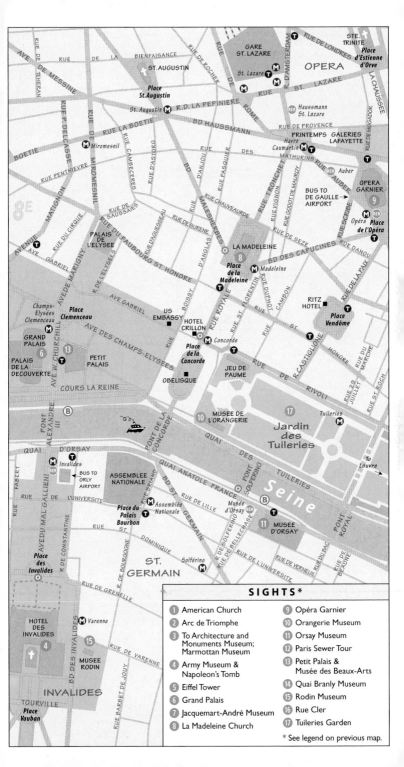

# SIGHTS*

1. American Church
2. Arc de Triomphe
3. To Architecture and Monuments Museum; Marmottan Museum
4. Army Museum & Napoleon's Tomb
5. Eiffel Tower
6. Grand Palais
7. Jacquemart-André Museum
8. La Madeleine Church
9. Opéra Garnier
10. Orangerie Museum
11. Orsay Museum
12. Paris Sewer Tour
13. Petit Palais & Musée des Beaux-Arts
14. Quai Branly Museum
15. Rodin Museum
16. Rue Cler
17. Tuileries Garden

* See legend on previous map.

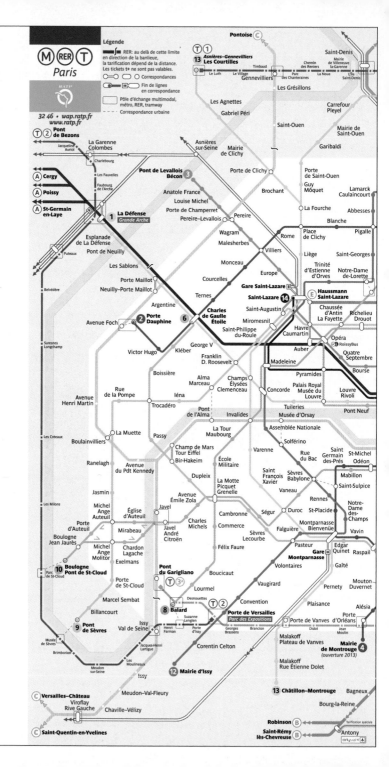

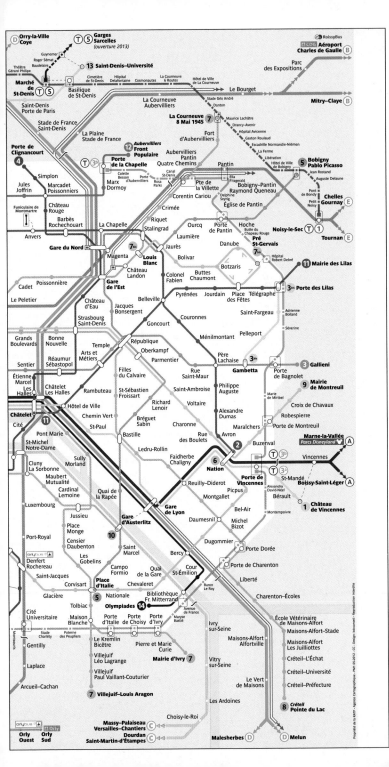

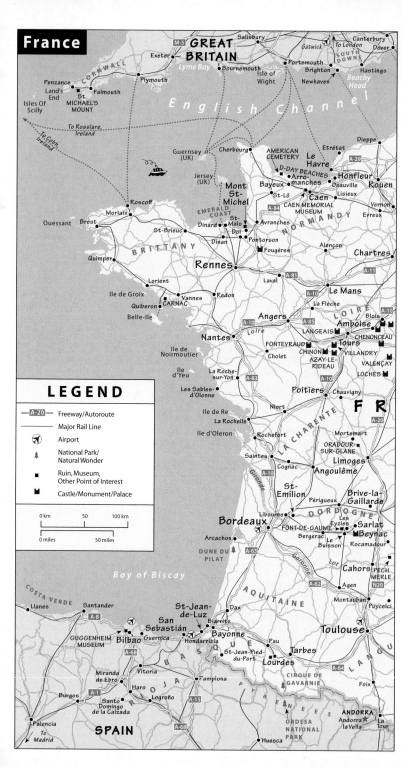

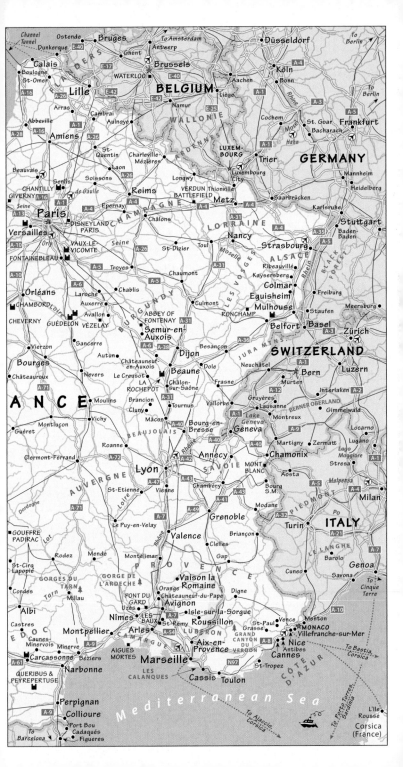

# Rick Steves'

# PARIS

## 2013

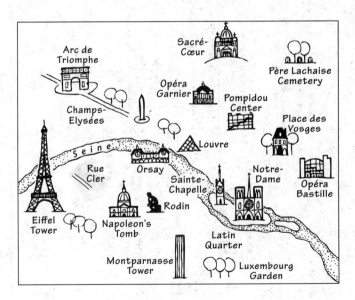

Arc de Triomphe · Sacré-Cœur · Père Lachaise Cemetery · Champs-Elysées · Opéra Garnier · Pompidou Center · Place des Vosges · Seine · Louvre · Rue Cler · Orsay · Sainte-Chapelle · Notre-Dame · Opéra Bastille · Eiffel Tower · Napoleon's Tomb · Rodin · Latin Quarter · Montparnasse Tower · Luxembourg Garden

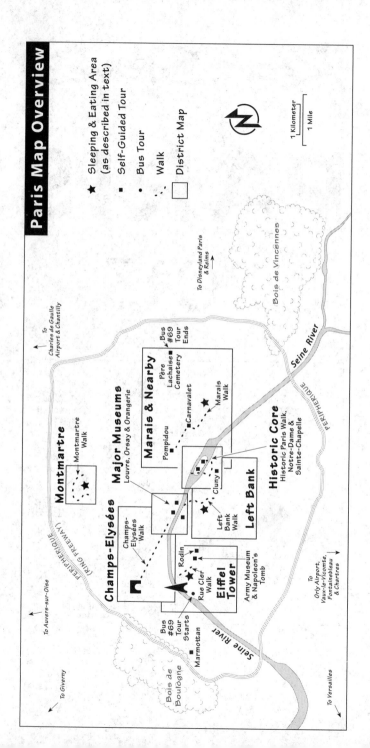

# Paris Map Overview

Legend:
- ★ Sleeping & Eating Area (as described in text)
- ■ Self-Guided Tour
- ● Bus Tour
- ··· Walk
- ☐ District Map

1 Kilometer
1 Mile

**Montmartre**
Montmartre Walk

**Champs-Elysées**
Champs-Elysées Walk

**Major Museums**
Louvre, Orsay & Orangerie

**Marais & Nearby**
- Pompidou
- Carnavalet
- Père Lachaise Cemetery
- Bus #69 Tour Ends
- Marais Walk

**Eiffel Tower**
Rue Cler Walk
Army Museum & Napoleon's Tomb
Rodin

**Left Bank**
Left Bank Walk
Cluny

**Historic Core**
Historic Paris Walk,
Notre-Dame &
Sainte-Chapelle

Marmottan
Bus #69 Tour Starts

Seine River

PÉRIPHÉRIQUE (RING FREEWAY)

Bois de Boulogne
Bois de Vincennes

To Auvers-sur-Oise
To Charles de Gaulle Airport & Chantilly
To Disneyland Paris & Reims
To Giverny
To Versailles
To Orly Airport, Vaux-le-Vicomte, Fontainebleau & Chartres

# INTRODUCTION

Paris—the City of Light—has been a beacon of culture for centuries. As a world capital of art, fashion, food, literature, and ideas, it stands as a symbol of all the fine things human civilization can offer. Come prepared to celebrate this, rather than judge our cultural differences, and you'll capture the romance and *joie de vivre* that this city exudes.

Paris offers sweeping boulevards, chatty crêpe stands, chic boutiques, and world-class art galleries. Sip decaf with deconstructionists at a sidewalk café, then step into an Impressionist painting in a tree-lined park. Climb Notre-Dame and rub shoulders with the gargoyles. Cruise the Seine, zip to the top of the Eiffel Tower, and saunter down Avenue des Champs-Elysées. Master the Louvre and Orsay museums. Save some after-dark energy for one of the world's most romantic cities.

## About This Book

*Rick Steves' Paris 2013* is a personal tour guide in your pocket. Better yet, it's actually three tour guides in your pocket: The co-authors of this book are Steve Smith and Gene Openshaw. Steve has been traveling to France—as a guide, researcher, homeowner, and devout Francophile—every year since 1985. Gene and I have been exploring the wonders of the Old World since our first "Europe through the gutter" trip together as high school buddies in the 1970s. An inquisitive historian and lover of European culture, Gene wrote most of this book's self-guided museum tours and neighborhood walks. Together, Steve, Gene, and I keep this book current (though, for simplicity, from this point "we" will shed our respective egos and become "I").

The book divides Paris up into convenient neighborhoods

INTRODUCTION

## Map Legend

| | | | | | |
|---|---|---|---|---|---|
| ⊾ | Viewpoint | ⊘ | Airport | )▬▬( | Tunnel |
| ↑ | Entrance | Ⓣ | Taxi Stand | ▬▬▬ | Pedestrian Zone |
| ⊕ | Tourist Info | ⊓ | Tram Stop | - - - - - | Railway |
| WC | Restroom | Ⓑ | Bus Stop | ⋯⋯⋯ | Ferry/Boat Route |
| ⌂ | Castle | Ⓟ | Parking | ⊢—⊣ | Tram |
| ⌂ | Church | Ⓡ | RER Train | ▮▮▮▮▮ | Stairs |
| ▪ | Statue/Point of Interest | Ⓑ | Batobus Stop | · · · · · | Walk/Tour Route |
| ⌁ | Park | Ⓜ | Métro Stope | | |
| ◎ | Fountain | )( | Mtn. Pass | - - - - - | Trail |

*Use this legend to help you navigate the maps in this book.*

(shown on "Paris Map Overview", page xiv). In this book, you'll find the following chapters:

**Orientation to Paris** includes specifics on public transportation, helpful hints, local tour options, easy-to-read maps, and tourist information. The "Planning Your Time" section suggests a schedule for how to best use your limited time.

**Sights in Paris** describes the top attractions and includes their cost and hours.

**Self-Guided Walks** cover six of Paris' most intriguing neighborhoods: Historic Paris (including Notre-Dame and Sainte-Chapelle), Rue Cler (near the Eiffel Tower), the Left Bank, the Champs-Elysées, the Marais, and Montmartre.

**Self-Guided Tours** lead you through Paris' most fascinating museums and sights: the Louvre, Orsay, Orangerie, Eiffel Tower, Rodin, Army Museum and Napoleon's Tomb, Marmottan, Cluny, Pompidou Center, Carnavalet, and Père Lachaise Cemetery. The Bus #69 Sightseeing Tour gives an inexpensive overview of the city.

**Sleeping in Paris** describes my favorite hotels in six appealing neighborhoods (plus hotels convenient to Paris' two main airports), from budget deals to cushy splurges.

**Eating in Paris** serves up a range of options, from inexpensive cafés to romantic bistros, arranged by neighborhood, plus a listing of historic cafés.

**Paris with Children** includes my top recommendations and helpful planning tips for keeping your kids (and you) happy in Paris, along with information for visiting Disneyland Paris.

**Shopping in Paris** gives you advice on shopping painlessly and enjoyably, without letting it overwhelm your vacation or bust your budget. Read up on Paris' great department stores, neighborhood boutiques, flea markets, outdoor food markets, and arcaded, Old World shopping streets.

**Entertainment in Paris** is your guide to fun, including music, bus and taxi tours, and the best night walks and river cruises. You'll also find information on how to translate *Pariscope,* the weekly entertainment guide.

**Paris in Winter** provides tips on how to enjoy the City of Light during the wonderfully untouristy holiday season and beyond.

**Paris Connections** lays the groundwork for your smooth arrival and departure, covering transportation by train (including the Eurostar to London) and plane, with detailed information on Paris' two major airports (Charles de Gaulle and Orly), a minor airport (Beauvais), and Paris' six train stations.

**Day Trips** include the great châteaux of Versailles (with a self-guided tour), Vaux-le-Vicomte, Fontainebleau, and Chantilly; Chartres' majestic cathedral (with a self-guided tour and a town walk as well); the Impressionist retreats of Claude Monet's Giverny and Vincent van Gogh's Auvers-sur-Oise; and, *finalement,* the Champagne city of Reims. For those who like to linger, I list accommodations near most of these sights.

**France: Past and Present** gives you a quick overview of the country's tumultuous history and contemporary challenges.

The **appendix** is a traveler's tool kit, with telephone tips, useful phone numbers, websites, recommended books and films, a festival list, a climate chart, a handy packing checklist, a hotel reservation form, a guide to pronouncing Parisian landmarks, and French survival phrases.

Browse through this book and select your favorite sights. Then have a *fantastique* trip! Traveling like a temporary local, you'll get the absolute most out of every mile, minute, and dollar. As you visit places I know and love, I'm happy you'll be meeting my favorite Parisians.

# Planning

This section will help you get started planning your trip—with advice on trip costs, when to go, and what you should know before you take off.

## Travel Smart

Your trip to Paris is like a complex play—easier to follow and to really appreciate on a second viewing. While no one does the same trip twice to gain that advantage, reading this book in its entirety before your trip accomplishes much the same thing.

Design an itinerary that enables you to visit sights at the best possible times. Note festivals, holidays, street-market days, and days when sights are closed. You can wait in line at the Louvre, or—with a Paris Museum Pass—zip through without breaking

# Key to This Book

## Updates

This book is updated every year—but once you pin down Paris, it wiggles. For the latest, visit www.ricksteves.com/update. For a valuable list of reports and experiences—good and bad—from fellow travelers, check www.ricksteves.com/feedback.

## Abbreviations and Times

I use the following symbols and abbreviations in this book:
Sights are rated:

 Don't miss

▲▲ Try hard to see

▲ Worthwhile if you can make it

**No rating** Worth knowing about

Tourist information offices are abbreviated as **TI**, and bathrooms are **WC**s. To categorize accommodations, I use a **Sleep Code** (described on page 378).

Like Europe, this book uses the **24-hour clock.** It's the same through 12:00 noon, then keep going: 13:00, 14:00, and so on. For anything over 12, subtract 12 and add p.m. (14:00 is 2:00 p.m.).

When giving **opening times,** I include both peak season and off-season hours if they differ. So, if a museum is listed as "May-Oct daily 9:00-16:00," it should be open from 9 a.m. until 4 p.m. from the first day of May until the last day of October (but expect exceptions).

If you see a ☉ symbol near a sight listing, it means that sight is described in far greater detail elsewhere—either with its own self-guided tour, or as part of a self-guided walk.

For **transit** or **tour departures,** I first list the frequency, then the duration. So, a train connection listed as "2/hour, 1.5 hours" departs twice each hour, and the journey lasts an hour and a half.

a sweat. Day-tripping to Versailles on Monday is bad, since it's closed—but it's not recommended on Tuesday either, when the Louvre is closed and tourist mobs storm the palace (for train tips to sights beyond Paris, see the Connections chapter). A smart trip is a puzzle—a fun, doable, and worthwhile challenge.

Be sure to mix intense and relaxed periods in your itinerary. Every trip—and every traveler—needs slack time (laundry, picnics, people-watching, and so on). Pace yourself. Assume you will return.

Reread this book as you travel, and visit local TIs. Upon arrival in a new town, lay the groundwork for a smooth departure; write down (or print out from an online source) the schedule for the train or bus that you'll take when you depart.

Get online at Internet cafés or your hotel, though I encourage you to disconnect from life back home and immerse yourself in the French experience. Carry a mobile phone (or use a phone card) to make travel plans: You can find tourist information, learn the latest on sights (special events, tour schedules, etc.), book tickets and tours, make reservations, reconfirm hotels, research transportation connections, and keep in touch with your loved ones.

Enjoy the friendliness of the French people. Connect with the culture. Learn a new French expression each day and practice it. Cheer for your favorite bowler at a *boules* match, leave no chair unturned in your quest for the best café, find that perfect Eiffel Tower view, and make friends with a crêpe stand. Slow down to appreciate the sincerity of your Parisian hosts, and be open to unexpected experiences. Ask questions—most locals are eager to point you in their idea of the right direction. Keep a notepad in your pocket for confirming prices, noting directions, and organizing your thoughts. Wear your money belt, learn the currency, and figure out how to estimate prices in dollars. Those who expect to travel smart, do.

## Trip Costs

Five components make up your trip costs: airfare, surface transportation, room and board, sightseeing and entertainment, and shopping and miscellany.

**Airfare:** A basic round-trip flight from the US to Paris can cost, on average, about $900-2,000 total, depending on where you fly from and when (cheaper in winter).

**Surface Transportation:** For a typical one-week visit, allow about $60 for Métro tickets and a couple of day trips. To budget the cost to get between Paris and either major airport, figure (for each way) an extra $85 by taxi, $30 by airport van (if splitting with another person), $22 for the airport bus, or $13 for the RER train or Roissy-Bus.

**Room and Board:** You can manage comfortably in Paris in 2013 on $170 a day per person for room and board. This allows $15 for breakfast, $20 for lunch, $40 for dinner, and $95 for lodging (based on two people splitting the cost of a $190 double room). If you've got more money, I've listed great ways to spend it. Students and tightwads can enjoy Paris on $80 a day ($40 per bed, $40 for meals and snacks).

**Sightseeing and Entertainment:** Get the Paris Museum Pass, which covers most sights in the city (for more information, see page 52). You'll pay about $50 for a two-day pass (4 days/$70, 6 days/$90). While you can buy the pass through some US travel agents, it's easy and best to buy in Paris. Without a Museum Pass, figure about $12 per major sight (Orsay $12, Louvre $14) and about $10 for others. Assume that bus tours and splurge experiences (e.g.,

# The Language Barrier and That French Attitude

You've no doubt heard that Parisians are "mean and cold and refuse to speak English." This is an out-of-date preconception left over from the days of Charles de Gaulle. Parisians are as friendly as any other people, and no more disagreeable than New Yorkers. Like many big cities, Paris is a melting pot of international cultures; your evening hotel receptionist is just as likely to speak French with an accent as not. Without any doubt, Parisians speak more English than Americans speak French. Be reasonable in your expectations: French waiters are paid to be efficient, not chatty. And Parisian postal clerks are every bit as speedy, cheery, and multilingual as ours are back home.

The biggest mistake most Americans make when traveling in France is trying to do too much with limited time. Hurried, impatient travelers who miss the subtle pleasures of people-watching from a sun-dappled café often misinterpret French attitudes. By slowing your pace and making an effort to understand French culture by living it, you're more likely to have a richer experience. With the five weeks of paid vacation and 35-hour work week that many French workers consider as nonnegotiable rights, your hosts can't fathom why anyone would rush through their vacation.

Parisians take great pride in their customs, clinging to the sense of their own cultural superiority. Let's face it: It's tough to keep on smiling when you've been crushed by a Big Mac, Mickey-Moused by Disney, and drowned in Starbucks coffee. Your hosts are cold only if you decide to see them that way. Polite and formal, the French respect the fine points of culture and tradition. In Paris, strolling down the street with a big grin on your face and saying hello to strangers is a sign of senil-

---

concerts in Sainte-Chapelle) cost $20-40. An overall average of $30 a day works for most people. Don't skimp here. After all, this category is the driving force behind your trip—you came to sight-see, enjoy, and experience Paris.

**Shopping and Miscellany:** Figure $5 per ice cream cone, coffee, or soft drink. Shopping can vary in cost from nearly nothing to a small fortune. Good budget travelers find that this category has little to do with assembling a trip full of lifelong and wonderful memories.

## When to Go

Late spring and fall bring the best weather and the biggest crowds. May, June, September, and October are the toughest months for hotel-hunting—don't expect many hotel deals. Summers are gen-

INTRODUCTION

ity, not friendliness (seriously). Parisians think that Americans, while friendly, are hesitant to pursue more serious friendships. Recognize sincerity and look for kindness. Give them the benefit of the doubt.

Communication difficulties are exaggerated. To hurdle the language barrier, start with the French survival phrases in this book (see the appendix). For a richer experience, bring a small English/French dictionary and/or a phrase book (look for mine, which contains a dictionary and menu decoder), a menu reader, and a good supply of patience. In transactions, a small notepad and pen minimize misunderstandings about prices; have vendors write the price down.

Though many French people—especially those in the tourist trade, and in big cities—speak English, you'll get better treatment if you use French pleasantries. If you learn only five phrases, learn and use these: *bonjour* (good day), *pardon* (pardon me), *s'il vous plaît* (please), *merci* (thank you), and *au revoir* (good-bye). The French value politeness. Begin every encounter with *"Bonjour* (or *S'il vous plaît), madame* (or *monsieur),"* and end every encounter with *"Au revoir, madame* (or *monsieur)."*

When you do make an effort to speak French, expect to be politely corrected—*c'est normal.* The French are linguistic perfectionists—they take their language (and other languages) seriously. Often they speak more English than they let on. This isn't a tourist-baiting tactic, but timidity on their part to speak another language less than fluently. If you want them to speak English, say, *"Bonjour, madame* (or *monsieur). Parlez-vous anglais?"* They may say *"non,"* but as you continue you'll probably find they speak more English than you speak French.

erally hot and dry; if you wilt in the heat, look for a room with air-conditioning. Rooms are usually easier to land in mid-summer (many hotels offer deals), and though many French businesses close in August, you'll hardly notice.

Paris makes a great winter getaway (see Paris in Winter chapter). Airfare costs less, cafés are cozy, and the city feels lively but not touristy. The only problem—weather—is solved by dressing correctly. Expect cold (even freezing lows) and rain (hats, gloves, scarves, umbrellas, and thick-soled shoes are essential). For specific temperatures, see the climate chart in the appendix.

## Know Before You Go

Your trip is more likely to go smoothly if you plan ahead. Check this list of things to arrange while you're still at home.

# Paris Almanac

**Population:** About 2.2 million in the city center.

**Currency:** Euro.

**Nickname:** The City of Light.

**City Layout:** Paris is the capital and largest city in France. The Seine River slices through the city, with the Right Bank to the north and the Left Bank to the south (orient yourself by looking downstream—the Left Bank is to your left, the Right Bank to your right). The city is divided into 20 municipal boroughs, called arrondissements.

**Transportation Basics:** The Métro is the most-used public transportation in Paris, with 16 colored lines, 300 stations, and nearly 5 million passengers riding each day.

**Tourist Tracks:** Paris is the world's top tourist destination, attracting more than 40 million tourists a year. Of its 3,800 historical monuments, the most popular draws within the city are the Louvre (nearly 9 million people tour it each year) and the Eiffel Tower (more than 7 million). But Mona doesn't hold a candle to Mickey—Disneyland Paris gets 15 million visitors a year.

**Favorite Open-Air Market:** The Rue Cler market, near the Eiffel Tower, has produce stands, wine shops, florists, fishmongers, and specialty shops that sell rose-petal *macarons* and lavender honey.

**Culture Count:** Most Parisians, including those of French ancestry, were born outside of the city—and roughly one in five residents of greater Paris was born outside France (and one in three has at least one immigrant parent). The city has significant populations of people from Africa, China, Eastern Europe, and the Middle East.

**Famous Residents:** Brigitte Bardot, Juliette Binoche, Carla Bruni, Sofia Coppola, Catherine Deneuve, Gérard Depardieu, Johnny Depp, Jean-Luc Godard, Rickie Lee Jones, Diane Kruger, Tony Parker, Roman Polanski, Mick Jagger, Kristin Scott Thomas, Audrey Tautou...

**Average Parisian:** Compared to the average Frenchman or Frenchwoman, the average Parisian is younger (since so many people retire in the countryside), makes more money, and is more likely to live alone or with just one other person. That said, the city has experienced a baby boom in the last several years—while most Parisian parents have just one child, the number of bigger families goes up each year.

You need a **passport**—but no visa or shots—to travel in France. You may be denied entry into certain European countries if your passport is due to expire within three to six months of your ticketed date of return. Get it renewed if you'll be cutting it close. It can take up to six weeks to get or renew a passport (for more on passports, see www.travel.state.gov). Pack a photocopy of your passport in your luggage in case the original is lost or stolen.

**Book rooms well in advance** if you'll be traveling during peak season (April through October) or any major holidays (see page 664). Some famous restaurants (but not ones I recommend) require reservations several weeks in advance.

Call your **debit- and credit-card companies** to let them know the countries you'll be visiting, to ask about fees, request your PIN (it will be mailed to you), and more. See page 13 for details.

Do your homework if you want to buy **travel insurance.** Compare the cost of the insurance to the likelihood of your using it and your potential loss if something goes wrong. Also, check whether your existing insurance (health, homeowners, or renters) covers you and your possessions overseas. For more tips, see www.ricksteves. com/insurance.

All **high-speed trains** (TGVs) in France require a seat reservation; book as early as possible, as these trains fill fast, and some routes use TGV trains almost exclusively. This is especially true if you're traveling with a railpass, as TGV passholder reservations are limited, and usually sell out well before other seat reservations do. If you're taking an overnight train (especially between Paris and Rome or Venice), and you need a *couchette* (overnight bunk)—and you *must* leave on a certain day—consider booking it in advance through a US agent (such as www.raileurope.com), even though it may cost more. (For more on train travel, see page 522 and www. ricksteves.com/rail.)

If you're planning on **renting a car** for travels beyond Paris, you'll need to bring your driver's license.

To avoid long ticket-buying lines at the **Eiffel Tower,** book an entry time in advance using its online reservation system (see page 200).

If seeing the City of Light at night from a taxi appeals to you, photocopy the **"Floodlit Paris Taxi Tour"** (in the Entertainment in Paris chapter) to bring along and give to your cabbie.

If you plan to hire a **local guide,** reserve ahead by email. Popular guides can get booked up.

If you're bringing a **mobile device,** download any apps you might want to use on the road, such as translators, maps, and transit schedules. Check out **Rick Steves Audio Europe,** featuring audio tours of major sights, hours of travel interviews on Paris, and more (via www.ricksteves.com/audioeurope, iTunes, Google Play, or the Rick Steves Audio Europe free smartphone app; for details, see page 660).

If you'll be **traveling with children,** read my pre-trip suggestions on page 463.

Check the **Rick Steves guidebook updates** page for any recent changes to this book (www.ricksteves.com/update).

Because **airline carry-on restrictions** are always changing, visit the Transportation Security Administration's website (www. tsa.gov/travelers) for an up-to-date list of what you can bring on the plane with you...and what you must check.

# Practicalities

**Emergency and Medical Help:** In France, dial 17 for English-speaking police help. To summon an ambulance, call 15. If you get sick, do as the French do and go to a pharmacist for advice. Or ask at your hotel for help—they'll know the nearest medical and emergency services.

**Theft or Loss:** To replace a passport, you'll need to go in person to an embassy or consulate (see page 655). If your credit and debit cards disappear, cancel and replace them (see "Damage Control for Lost Cards" on page 14). File a police report either on the spot or within a day or two; it's required if you submit an insurance claim for lost or stolen railpasses or travel gear, and can help with replacing your passport or credit and debit cards. For more information, see www.ricksteves.com/help. Precautionary measures can minimize the effects of loss—back up your photos and other files frequently.

**Time Zones:** France, like most of continental Europe, is generally six/nine hours ahead of the East/West Coasts of the US. The exceptions are the beginning and end of Daylight Saving Time: Europe "springs forward" the last Sunday in March (two weeks after most of North America), and "falls back" the last Sunday in October (one week before North America). For a handy online time converter, see www.timeanddate.com/worldclock.

**Business Hours:** In France, most shops are open Tuesday through Saturday (10:00-12:00 & 14:00-19:00) and closed Sunday, though many small markets, *boulangeries* (bakeries), and street markets are open Sunday mornings until noon. On Mondays, some businesses are closed until 14:00 and possibly all day.

Saturdays are virtually weekdays; Sundays have the same pros and cons as they do for travelers in the US. Special events and weekly markets pop up (usually until about noon), sightseeing attractions are generally open, while banks and many shops are closed, public transportation options are fewer, and there's no rush hour.

# Cheap Tricks in Paris

**Book good-value rooms early.** I list several well-located and comfortable hotels with rooms under €100, but you'll need to beat others to the punch.

**Enjoy picnic lunches and dinners.** You'll find tasty €5 sandwiches, to-go salads, quiches, and high-quality takeout at bakeries, charcuteries, and stands. Wine merchants sell chilled, picnic-friendly bottles that they'll happily open for you. Scenic picnic sites are everywhere.

**In cafés, stand at the bar** to sip your drink, and you'll get the lowest prices. Before ordering at a table, check out the price list *(Les Prix de Consommation)*, which is always prominently displayed. This shows the price of the most commonly ordered drinks *au comptoir* (at the counter) and *en salle* (seated at a table). I use the price of *un café* (shot of espresso) at the counter as my barometer—if the price is €1.50 or less, the place is likely to be reasonable. If given a choice between small, medium, or large size beverage, be aware that small is usually the norm and that medium drinks can be crazy pricey.

**Order only a *plat*** (main course) for dinner on some nights. And at cafés (as opposed to restaurants), it's fine to order only a soup or salad for dinner.

**Shop at grocery stores** for bottled water, drinks, and snacks, not at expensive snack stands. Refill bottles from the tap.

**Visit sights on free days** (see sidebar on page 64).

**Buy a Paris Museum Pass** and use it wisely (see page 52 for advice).

**Watt's Up?** Europe's electrical system is 220 volts, instead of North America's 110 volts. Most newer electronics (such as laptops, battery chargers, and hair dryers) convert automatically, so you won't need a converter plug, but you will need an adapter plug with two round prongs, sold inexpensively at travel stores in the US. Avoid bringing older appliances that don't automatically convert voltage; instead, buy a cheap replacement in Europe. You can buy low-cost hair dryers and other small appliances at Darty and Monoprix stores, which you'll find in most Parisian neighborhoods (ask your hotelier for the closest branch).

**Discounts:** Discounts aren't always listed in this book. However, many sights offer discounts for youths (up to age 18), students (with proper identification cards, www.isic.org), families, and groups of 10 or more. Always ask. Seniors (age 60 and over) may get the odd discount, though most require European citizenship. To inquire about a senior discount, ask, *"Réduction troisième âge?"* (ray-dook-see-ohn twah-zee-ehm ahzh).

INTRODUCTION

# Money

This section covers advice on how to pay for purchases on your trip (including getting cash from ATMs and paying with plastic), dealing with lost or stolen cards, VAT (sales tax) refunds, and tipping.

## What to Bring

Bring both a credit card and a debit card. You'll use the debit card at cash machines (ATMs) to withdraw local cash for most purchases, and the credit card to pay for larger items. Some travelers carry a third card, in case one gets demagnetized or eaten by a temperamental machine.

For an emergency reserve, bring several hundred dollars in hard cash in $20 bills. Keep in mind, though, that French banks won't exchange dollars; should you need to exchange your US bills, go to a currency-exchange booth (and be prepared for lousy rates and/or outrageous fees).

## Cash

Cash is just as desirable in Europe as it is at home. Small businesses (hotels, restaurants, and shops) prefer that you pay your bills with cash. Some vendors will charge you extra for using a credit card, and some won't take credit cards at all. Cash is the best—and sometimes only—way to pay for bus fare, taxis, and local guides.

Throughout Europe, ATMs are the standard way for travelers to get cash. Stay away from "independent" ATMs such as Travelex, Euronet, and Forex, which charge huge commissions and have terrible exchange rates.

To withdraw money from an ATM (known as a *distributeur*; dee-stree-bew-tur), you'll need a debit card (ideally with a Visa or MasterCard logo for maximum usability), plus a PIN code. Know your PIN code in numbers; there are only numbers—no letters—on European keypads. For security, it's best to shield the keypad when entering your PIN at an ATM. Although you can use a credit card for ATM transactions, it's generally more expensive (and only makes sense in an emergency), because it's considered a cash advance rather than a withdrawal. Try to withdraw large sums of money to reduce the number of per-transaction bank fees you'll pay.

Pickpockets target tourists. To safeguard your cash, wear a money belt—a pouch with a strap that you buckle around your waist like a belt and tuck under your clothes. Keep your cash, credit cards, and passport secure in your money belt, and carry only a day's spending money in your front pocket.

## Credit and Debit Cards

For purchases, Visa and MasterCard are more commonly accepted than American Express. Just like at home, credit or debit cards work easily at larger hotels, restaurants, and shops. I typically use my debit card to withdraw cash to pay for most purchases. I use my credit card only in a few specific situations: to book hotel res-ervations by phone, to cover major expenses (such as car rentals, plane tickets, and hotel stays), and to pay for things near the end of my trip (to avoid another visit to the ATM). While you could use a debit card to make large purchases, using a credit card offers a greater degree of fraud protection (because debit cards draw funds directly from your account).

**Ask Your Credit- or Debit-Card Company:** Before your trip, contact the company that issued your debit or credit cards.

• Confirm your **card will work overseas,** and alert them that you'll be using it in Europe; otherwise, they may deny transactions if they perceive unusual spending patterns.

• Ask for the specifics on transaction **fees.** When you use your credit or debit card—either for purchases or ATM withdrawals— you'll often be charged additional "international transaction" fees of up to 3 percent (1 percent is normal) plus $5 per transaction. Some banks have agreements with European partners that reduce or eliminate the transaction fee. For example, Bank of America debit-card holders can use French Parisbas-BNP ATMs without being charged the transaction fee (but they still pay the 1 percent international fee). If your card's fees seem high, consider getting a different card just for your trip: Capital One (www.capitalone.com) and most credit unions have low-to-no international fees.

• If you plan to withdraw cash from ATMs, confirm your daily **withdrawal limit**, and if necessary, ask your bank to adjust it. Some travelers prefer a high limit that allows them to take out more cash at each ATM stop (saving on bank fees), while others prefer to set a lower limit in case their card is stolen. Note that foreign banks also set maximum withdrawal amounts for their ATMs.

• Get your bank's emergency phone number in the US (but not

its 800 number, which isn't accessible from overseas) to call collect if you have a problem.

• Ask for your credit card's **PIN** in case you encounter Europe's "chip-and-PIN" system; the bank won't tell you your PIN over the phone, so allow time for it to be mailed to you.

**Chip and PIN:** If your card is declined for a purchase in Europe, it may be because Europeans are increasingly using chip-and-PIN cards, which are embedded with an electronic chip (rather than the magnetic stripe used on our American-style cards). Much of Europe is adopting this system, and some merchants rely on it exclusively. You're most likely to encounter chip-and-PIN problems at automated payment machines, such as those at train and subway stations, toll roads, parking garages, luggage lockers, and self-serve gas pumps.

But don't panic. To prevent problems, carry plenty of cash (you can always use an ATM with your magnetic-stripe debit card). It's also a good idea to memorize the PIN number of your magnetic-stripe credit card (if you don't know it, ask your bank to mail it to you before you leave home). This lets you use it at some chip-and-PIN machines—just enter your PIN when prompted. If a machine won't take your card, find a cashier who can make your card work (they can print a receipt for you to sign), or find a machine that takes cash.

If you are still concerned, you can apply for a chip card in the US (though I think it's overkill). While big US banks offer these cards with high annual fees, a better option is the no-annual-fee GlobeTrek Visa, offered by Andrews Federal Credit Union in Maryland (open to all US residents; see www.andrewsfcu.org).

**Dynamic Currency Conversion:** If merchants offer to convert your purchase price into dollars (called dynamic currency conversion, or DCC), refuse this "service." You'll pay even more in fees for the expensive convenience of seeing your charge in dollars.

## Damage Control for Lost Cards

If you lose your credit, debit, or ATM card, you can stop people from using your card by reporting the loss immediately to the respective global customer-assistance centers. Call these 24-hour US numbers collect: Visa (tel. 303/967-1096), MasterCard (tel. 636/722-7111), and American Express (tel. 336/393-1111). For another option (with the same results), you can call these toll-free numbers in France: Visa (tel. 08 00 90 11 79) and MasterCard (tel. 08 00 90 13 87). American Express has a Paris office, but the call isn't free (tel. 01 47 77 70 00, greeting in French only, dial 1 to speak with someone in English). Diners Club has offices in the US (tel. 303/799-1504, call collect) and Paris (tel. 08 10 31 41 59).

At a minimum, you'll need to know the name of the financial

institution that issued you the card, along with the type of card (classic, platinum, or whatever). Providing the following information will allow for a quicker cancellation of your missing card: full card number, whether you are the primary or secondary cardholder, the cardholder's name exactly as printed on the card, billing address, home phone number, circumstances of the loss or theft, and identification verification (your birth date, your mother's maiden name, or your Social Security number—memorize this, don't carry a copy). If you are the secondary cardholder, you'll also need to provide the primary cardholder's identification-verification details. You can generally receive a temporary card within two or three business days in Europe (see www.ricksteves.com/help for more).

If you report your loss within two days, you typically won't be responsible for any unauthorized transactions on your account, although many banks charge a liability fee of $50.

## Tipping

Tipping *(donner un pourboire)* in France isn't as automatic and generous as it is in the US, but for special service, tips are appreciated, if not expected. As in the US, the proper amount depends on your resources, tipping philosophy, and the circumstances, but some general guidelines apply.

**Restaurants:** At cafés and restaurants, a service charge is always included in the price of what you order *(service compris* or *prix net)*, but you won't see it listed on your bill. Unlike in the US, France pays servers a decent wage. Because of this, most locals never tip (credit-card receipts don't even have space to add a tip). If you feel the service was *exceptional*, it's kind to tip up to 5 percent extra. But never feel guilty if you don't leave a tip.

**Taxis:** To tip the cabbie, round up. For a typical ride, round up your fare a bit (for instance, if the fare is €13, pay €14); for a long ride, round to the nearest €10 (for a €58 fare, give €60). If the cabbie hauls your bags and zips you to the airport to help you catch your flight, you might want to toss in a little more. But if you feel like you're being driven in circles or otherwise ripped off, skip the tip.

**Services:** In general, if someone in the service industry does a super job for you, a small tip of a euro or two is appropriate...but not required. If you're not sure whether (or how much) to tip for a service, ask your hotelier or the TI.

## Getting a VAT Refund

Wrapped into the purchase price of your French souvenirs is a Value-Added Tax (VAT) of 19.6 percent. You're entitled to get most of that tax back if you purchase more than €175 (about $230) worth of goods at a store that participates in the VAT-refund scheme. Typically, you must ring up the minimum at a single retailer—you can't add up your purchases from various shops to reach the required amount.

Getting your refund is usually straightforward and, if you buy a substantial amount of souvenirs, well worth the hassle. If you're lucky, the merchant will subtract the tax when you make your purchase. (This is more likely to occur if the store ships the goods to your home.) Otherwise, you'll need to:

**Get the paperwork.** Have the merchant completely fill out the necessary refund document, *Bordereau de Vente a l'Exportation*, also called a "cheque." You'll have to present your passport. Get the paperwork done before you leave the store to ensure you'll have everything you need (including your original sales receipt).

**Get your stamp at the border or airport.** Process your VAT document at your last stop in the EU (e.g., at the airport) with the customs agent who deals with VAT refunds. Before checking in for your flight, find the local customs office, and be prepared to stand in line. It's best to keep your purchases in your carry-on for viewing, but if they're too large or dangerous to carry on (such as knives), have your purchases easily accessible in the bag you're about to check, ready to show the customs agent. You're not supposed to use your purchased goods before you leave. If you show up at customs wearing your chic new shoes, officials might look the other way—or deny you a refund.

**Collect your refund.** You'll need to return your stamped document to the retailer or its representative. Many merchants work with a service, such as Global Blue or Premier Tax Free, which have offices at major airports, ports, or border crossings (either before or after security, probably strategically located near a duty-free shop). These services, which extract a 4 percent fee, can refund your money immediately in cash or credit your card (within two billing cycles). If the retailer handles VAT refunds directly, it's up to you to contact the merchant for your refund. You can mail the documents from home, or more quickly, from your point of departure (using a stamped, self-addressed envelope or one that's been provided by the merchant). You'll then have to wait—it can take months.

## Customs for American Shoppers

You are allowed to take home $800 worth of items per person duty-free, once every 30 days. You can also bring in duty-free a liter of alcohol. As for food, you can take home many processed and packaged foods: vacuum-packed cheeses, dried herbs, jams, baked goods, candy, chocolate, oil, vinegar, mustard, and honey. Fresh fruits and vegetables and most meats are not allowed. However, canned goose, duck, and pork pâté can be imported to the US, though not beef. Any liquid-containing foods must be packed in checked luggage, a potential recipe for disaster. To check customs rules and duty rates, visit www.cbp.gov.

# Sightseeing

Sightseeing can be hard work. Use these tips to make your visits to Paris' finest sights meaningful, fun, efficient, and painless.

## Plan Ahead

Set up an itinerary that allows you to fit in all your must-see sights. For a one-stop look at opening hours, see "Paris at a Glance" (page 58). Remember, the Louvre and some other museums are closed on Tuesday, and many others are closed on Monday (see "Daily Reminder" on page 26). Most sights keep stable hours, but you can easily confirm the latest by checking their website or picking up the booklet *Musées, Monuments Historiques, et Expositions,* free at most museums. You can also find good information on many of Paris' sights online at www.parisinfo.com.

Don't put off visiting a must-see sight—you never know when a place will close unexpectedly for a holiday, strike, or restoration. On holidays (see list on page 664), expect reduced hours or closures. In summer, some sights may stay open late. Off-season, many museums have shorter hours.

Going at the right time helps avoid crowds. This book offers tips on specific sights. Try visiting very early (arrive at least 15 minutes before opening time), or very late. Evening visits are usually peaceful, with fewer crowds. The Louvre and Orsay museums are open selected evenings, while the Pompidou Center is open late every night except Tuesday (when it's closed all day).

Plan to buy a Paris Museum Pass, which can speed you through lines and save you money (for pass details, see page 52). For information on more money-saving tips, see "Affording Paris' Sights" on page 64.

Study up. To get the most out of the self-guided tours and sight descriptions in this book, read them before you visit. The Louvre is more interesting if you understand why the *Venus de Milo* is so disarming.

## At Sights

Here's what you can typically expect:

Some important sights require you to check daypacks and coats. To avoid checking a small backpack, carry it under your arm like a purse as you enter. From a guard's point of view, a backpack is generally a problem while a purse is not. If you check a bag, the attendant may ask you (in French) if it contains anything of

## How Was Your Trip?

Were your travels fun, smooth, and meaningful? If you'd like to share your tips, concerns, and discoveries, please fill out the survey at www.ricksteves.com/feedback. I value your feedback. Thanks in advance—it helps a lot.

value—e.g., camera, phone, money, passport—since these cannot be checked.

At churches—which often offer interesting art (usually free) and a cool, welcome seat—a modest dress code (no bare shoulders or shorts) is encouraged.

Flash photography is often banned, but taking photos without a flash is usually allowed. Flashes damage oil paintings and distract others in the room. Even without a flash, a handheld camera will take a decent picture (or buy postcards or posters at the museum bookstore).

Museums may have special exhibits in addition to their permanent collections. Some exhibits are included in the entry price, while others come at an extra cost (which you may have to pay even if you don't want to see the exhibit).

Expect changes—artwork can be on tour, on loan, out sick, or shifted at the whim of the curator. To adapt, pick up any available free floor plans as you enter, and ask museum staff if you can't find a particular item. Say the title or artist's name, or point to the photograph in this book and ask for its location by saying, *"Où est?"* (oo ay).

Many sights rent audioguides, which generally offer useful recorded descriptions in English (about €6, sometimes included with admission). If you bring along your earbuds, you can enjoy better sound and avoid holding the device to your ear. To save money, you can bring a Y-jack and share one audioguide with your travel partner. I've produced free downloadable audio tours for the Louvre, Orsay Museum, Versailles, and my Historic Paris Walk; see page 24.

Important sights may have an on-site café or cafeteria (usually a handy place to rejuvenate during a long visit). The WCs at sights are usually free and generally clean.

Many sights sell postcards that highlight their attractions. Before you leave a sight, scan the postcards and thumb through the biggest guidebook (or skim its index) to be sure that you haven't overlooked something that you'd like to see.

Most sights stop admitting people 30-60 minutes before closing time, and some rooms may close early (often about 45 minutes before the actual closing time). Guards usher people out, so don't save the best for last.

Every sight or museum offers more than what is covered in this book. Use the information in this book as an introduction—not the final word.

# Traveling as a Temporary Local

We travel all the way to France to enjoy differences—to become temporary locals. You'll experience frustrations. Certain truths that we find "God-given" or "self-evident," such as cold beer, ice in drinks, bottomless cups of coffee, hot showers, and bigger being better, are suddenly not so true. One of the benefits of travel is the eye-opening realization that there are logical, civil, and even better alternatives.

Paris is an understandably proud city. To enjoy its people, you need to celebrate the differences. A willingness to go local ensures that you'll enjoy a full dose of Parisian hospitality.

Europeans generally like Americans. But if there is a negative aspect to the French image of Americans, it's that we are loud, wasteful, ethnocentric, too informal (which can seem disrespectful), and a bit naive.

The French (and Europeans in general) place a high value on speaking quietly in restaurants and on trains. Listen while on the bus or in a restaurant—the place can be packed, but the decibel level is low. Try to adjust your volume accordingly to show respect for the culture.

While the French look bemusedly at some of our Yankee excesses—and worriedly at others—they nearly always afford us individual travelers all the warmth we deserve.

Judging from all the happy feedback I receive from travelers who have used this book, it's safe to assume you'll enjoy a great, affordable vacation—with the finesse of an independent, experienced traveler.

Thanks, and *bon voyage!*

# Back Door Travel Philosophy

**From *Rick Steves' Europe Through the Back Door***

Travel is intensified living—maximum thrills per minute and one of the last great sources of legal adventure. Travel is freedom. It's recess, and we need it.

Experiencing the real Europe requires catching it by surprise, going casual...."Through the Back Door."

Affording travel is a matter of priorities. (Make do with the old car.) You can eat and sleep—simply, safely, and enjoyably—anywhere in Europe for $120 a day plus transportation costs. In many ways, spending more money only builds a thicker wall between you and what you traveled so far to see. Europe is a cultural carnival, and time after time, you'll find that its best acts are free and the best seats are the cheap ones.

A tight budget forces you to travel close to the ground, meeting and communicating with the people. Never sacrifice sleep, nutrition, safety, or cleanliness to save money. Simply enjoy the local-style alternatives to expensive hotels and restaurants.

Connecting with people carbonates your experience. Extroverts have more fun. If your trip is low on magic moments, kick yourself and make things happen. If you don't enjoy a place, maybe you don't know enough about it. Seek the truth. Recognize tourist traps. Give a culture the benefit of your open mind. See things as different, but not better or worse. Any culture has plenty to share.

Of course, travel, like the world, is a series of hills and valleys. Be fanatically positive and militantly optimistic. If something's not to your liking, change your liking.

Travel can make you a happier American, as well as a citizen of the world. Our Earth is home to seven billion equally precious people. It's humbling to travel and find that other people don't have the "American Dream"—they have their own dreams. Europeans like us, but with all due respect, they wouldn't trade passports.

Thoughtful travel engages us with the world. In tough economic times, it reminds us what is truly important. By broadening perspectives, travel teaches new ways to measure quality of life.

Globetrotting destroys ethnocentricity, helping us understand and appreciate other cultures. Rather than fear the diversity on this planet, celebrate it. Among your most prized souvenirs will be the strands of different cultures you choose to knit into your own character. The world is a cultural yarn shop, and Back Door travelers are weaving the ultimate tapestry. Join in!

# ORIENTATION TO PARIS

Paris is magnificent, but it's also super-sized, crowded, and fast-paced. Use this orientation to the City of Light to help illuminate your trip. The day plans—for visits of one to seven days—will help you prioritize the many sights. You'll tap into Paris' information sources for current events. Most importantly, you'll learn to navigate Paris by Métro, bus, taxi, bicycle, or on foot. With the proper approach and a measure of patience, you'll fall head over heels for Europe's cultural capital.

## Paris: A Verbal Map

Central Paris (population 2.2 million) is circled by a ring-road and split in half by the Seine River, which runs east-west. If you were on a boat floating downstream, the Right Bank (Rive Droite) would be on your right, and the Left Bank (Rive Gauche) on your left. The bull's-eye on your map is Notre-Dame, on an island in the middle of the Seine.

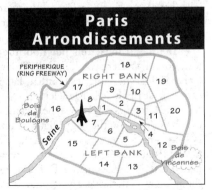

Twenty arrondissements (administrative districts) spiral out from the center, like an escargot shell. If your hotel's zip code is 75007, you know (from the last two digits) that it's in the 7th arrondissement. The city is speckled with Métro stops, and most Parisians locate addresses by the closest stop. So in Parisian jargon, the Eiffel Tower is on *la Rive Gauche* (the Left Bank) in the *7ème*

ORIENTATION TO PARIS

(7th arrondissement), zip code 75007, Mo: Trocadéro (the nearest Métro stop).

As you're tracking down addresses, these words and pronunciations will help: Métro (may-troh), *place* (plahs; square), *rue* (roo; road), *avenue* (ah-vuh-noo), *boulevard* (boo-luh-var), and *pont* (pohn; bridge).

## Paris by Neighborhood

Paris is a big city, but its major sights cluster in convenient zones. Grouping your sightseeing, walks, dining, and shopping thoughtfully can save you lots of time and money.

The **historic core** centers on the Ile de la Cité ("Island of the City"), located in the middle of the Seine. On the Ile de la Cité, you'll find Paris' oldest sights, from Roman ruins to the medieval Notre-Dame and Sainte-Chapelle churches. Other sights in this area: Archaeological Crypt, Deportation Memorial, Conciergerie, flower market, Paris Plages, and the lovely island of Ile St. Louis, with appealing shops, cafés, and restaurants. Paris' most historic riverside vendors, *les bouquinistes*, line both sides of the Seine as it passes Ile de la Cité.

The **major museums neighborhood** is just west of the historic core. It's where you'll find the Louvre, Orsay, and Orangerie. Other sights: the Tuileries Garden, Palais Royal's courtyards, and shopping at Place de la Madeleine.

The **Champs-Elysées**—the greatest of many grand, 19th-century boulevards on the Right Bank—runs northwest from Place de la Concorde to the Arc de Triomphe. Other sights: the Petit and Grand Palais, Opéra Garnier, Jacquemart-André Museum, Fragonard Perfume Museum, La Défense and La Grande Arche, and shopping at Galeries Lafayette and at Passages Choiseul and Ste. Anne.

The **Eiffel Tower** neighborhood, south of the Champs-Elysées, sits in the shadow of that famous monument, located in the Champ de Mars park. This area also boasts the colorful Rue Cler (with many recommended hotels and restaurants), the Army Museum and Napoleon's Tomb, the Rodin Museum,

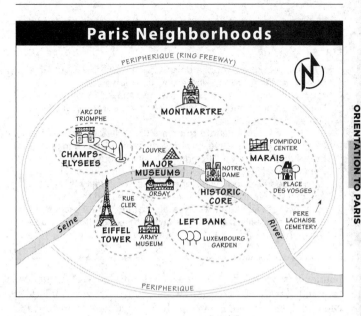

## Paris Neighborhoods

PERIPHERIQUE (RING FREEWAY)

ARC DE TRIOMPHE

MONTMARTRE

CHAMPS-ELYSEES

LOUVRE

MAJOR MUSEUMS

ORSAY

RUE CLER

NOTRE-DAME

HISTORIC CORE

POMPIDOU CENTER

MARAIS

PLACE DES VOSGES

PERE LACHAISE CEMETERY

EIFFEL TOWER

ARMY MUSEUM

LEFT BANK

LUXEMBOURG GARDEN

Seine

River

PERIPHERIQUE

and the thriving outdoor market Marché Boulevard de Grenelle (Wed and Sun mornings). Other sights: Quai Branly Museum, National Maritime Museum, Architecture and Monuments Museum, and Sewer Tour. The Marmottan Museum is west of the Eiffel Tower on the Right Bank.

The **Left Bank** is home to...the Left Bank. Anchored by the large Luxembourg Garden (near numerous recommended hotels and eateries), the Left Bank is the traditional neighborhood of Paris' intellectual, artistic, and café life. Other sights: the Latin Quarter, Cluny Museum, St. Germain-des-Prés and St. Sulpice churches, Panthéon, Montparnasse Tower, Catacombs, Delacroix Museum, and the Jardin des Plantes park. This is also one of Paris' best shopping areas (see the Sèvres-Babylone to St. Sulpice shopping stroll on page 478).

The **Marais neighborhood** has lots of recommended restaurants and hotels, shops, the delightful Place des Vosges, and artistic sights such as the Pompidou Center and Picasso Museum (currently closed for renovation until summer 2013). This area is alive with avant-garde

## Rick Steves Audio Europe

If you're bringing a mobile device, be sure to check out **Rick Steves Audio Europe,** where you can download free audio tours and hours of travel interviews (via the Rick Steves Audio Europe smartphone app, www.ricksteves.com/audioeurope, iTunes, or Google Play).

My self-guided **audio tours** are user-friendly, easy to follow, fun, and informative, covering the major sights and neighborhoods in Paris: the Historic Paris Walk, Louvre, Orsay, and Versailles Palace. Compared to live tours, my audio tours are hard to beat: Nobody will stand you up, the quality is reliable, you can take the tour exactly when you like, and they're free.

Rick Steves Audio Europe also offers a far-reaching library of intriguing **travel interviews** with experts from around the globe.

boutiques (see page 485). Other Marais sights: Jewish Art and History and Carnavalet museums, Victor Hugo's House, Holocaust Memorial, Promenade Plantée park, Père Lachaise Cemetery, the traffic-free street market on Rue Montorgueil, and markets at Bastille and Place d'Aligre.

**Montmartre,** topped by the bulbous white domes of Sacré-Cœur, hovers on the northern fringes of your Paris map. This hilltop neighborhood still retains some of the untamed rural charm that once drew Impressionist painters and turn-of-the-century bohemians. Other sights: Dalí and Montmartre museums, Moulin Rouge, Museum of Erotic Art, Pigalle, and nearby Puces St. Ouen flea market.

## Planning Your Time

In the planning sections that follow, I've listed sights in descending order of importance. Therefore, if you have only one day, just do Day 1; for two days, add Day 2; and so on. When planning where to plug in Versailles, remember that the Château is closed on Mondays and especially crowded on Sundays and Tuesdays—try to avoid these days. For other itinerary considerations on a day-by-day basis, check the "Daily Reminder" on page 26.

### Paris in One, Two, or Three Busy Days

If you want to fit in Versailles on a three-day visit, try it either on the morning of the third day or the afternoon of the second day.

### Day 1
**Morning:** Follow this book's Historic Paris Walk, featuring Ile de la Cité, Notre-Dame, the Latin Quarter, and Sainte-Chapelle.

**Afternoon:** Tour the Louvre.

**Evening:** Enjoy the Trocadéro scene and a twilight ride up the Eiffel Tower.

### Day 2

**Morning:** Follow this book's Champs-Elysées Walk from the Arc de Triomphe down the grand Avenue des Champs-Elysées to the Tuileries Garden.

**Midday:** Cross the pedestrian bridge from the Tuileries Garden, then tour the Orsay Museum.

**Afternoon:** Tour the Rodin Museum, or the Army Museum and Napoleon's Tomb.

**Evening:** Take one of the tours by bus, taxi, or retro-chic Deux Chevaux car (see page 500). (If you're staying more than two days, save this for your last-night finale.)

### Day 3

**Morning:** Ride the RER suburban train out to Versailles (tour the Château and sample the gardens).

**Afternoon:** Take this book's Marais Walk.

**Evening:** Cruise the Seine River or have dinner on Ile St. Louis, then take a floodlit walk by Notre-Dame.

## Paris in Five to Seven Days Without Going In-Seine

### Day 1

**Morning:** Follow this book's Historic Paris Walk, featuring Ile de la Cité, Notre-Dame, the Latin Quarter, and Sainte-Chapelle. If you enjoy medieval art, visit the Cluny Museum.

**Afternoon:** Tour the Opéra Garnier, and end your day enjoying the glorious rooftop views at the Galeries Lafayette and Printemps department stores.

**Evening:** Cruise the Seine River.

### Day 2

Reversing the morning and afternoon activities on this day works well because the Champs-Elysées Walk leaves you near the Louvre—but most people have more energy for museums in the morning.

**Morning:** Tour the Louvre (arrive 20 minutes before opening). Have coffee or lunch at Café le Nemours (across the street from the Louvre).

**Afternoon:** Follow this book's Champs-Elysées Walk from the Arc de Triomphe downhill along the incomparable Avenue des Champs-Elysées to the Tuileries Garden, and possibly the Orangerie Museum.

# Daily Reminder

**Sunday:** Many sights are free on the first Sunday of the month, including the Louvre, Orsay, Rodin, Cluny, Pompidou, Quai Branly, and Delacroix museums. During the winter, the Arc de Triomphe (Oct-March) and all the sights at Versailles (Nov-March) are also free. These free days at popular sights attract hordes of visitors.

Versailles is more crowded than usual on Sunday—but on the upside, the garden's fountains are running (April-Oct).

Look for organ concerts at St. Sulpice and possibly other churches. The American Church often hosts a free concert (usually classical piano and vocals, generally Sept-June at 17:00—but not every week and not in Dec). Summer brings puppet shows to Luxembourg Garden and the Champ de Mars park.

Most of Paris' stores are closed on Sunday, but shoppers will find relief along the Champs-Elysées and in the Marais neighborhood's lively Jewish Quarter, where many stores are open. Many recommended restaurants in the Rue Cler neighborhood are closed for dinner.

**Monday:** These sights are closed today: Orsay, Rodin, Marmottan, Carnavalet, Catacombs, Petit Palais, Victor Hugo's House, Quai Branly, Paris Archaeological Crypt, and Deportation Memorial. Outside of Paris, these sights are closed: all sights in Auvers-sur-Oise and all sights at Versailles. The Louvre is more crowded because of these closings. The Army Museum and Napoleon's Tomb is closed the first Monday of every month (though the tomb is open every Mon in June-Aug). Market streets such as Rue Cler and Rue Mouffetard are dead today. Some banks are closed. It's discount night at many cinemas.

**Tuesday:** Many sights are closed today, including the Louvre,

**Evening:** Enjoy dinner on Ile St. Louis, then a floodlit walk by Notre-Dame.

## Day 3
**Morning:** Tour the Orsay Museum (arrive 15 minutes before opening).

**Midday:** Tour the Rodin Museum (café lunch in gardens).

**Afternoon:** Visit the Army Museum and Napoleon's Tomb, then take this book's Rue Cler Walk and relax at a café.

**Evening:** Take one of the nighttime tours by taxi, bus, or retro-chic Deux Chevaux car.

Orangerie, Cluny, Pompidou, National Maritime, Delacroix, and Architecture and Monuments museums, as well as the châteaux of Chantilly and Fontainebleau and many sights in Auvers-sur-Oise. The Orsay and Versailles are particularly busy today; the fountains at Versailles run today from late May until late June. The Army Museum may be open until 21:00 (April-Sept).

**Wednesday:** All sights are open, and some have late hours, including the Louvre (until 21:45, last entry 21:00) and the Rodin Museum (until 20:45). The weekly *Pariscope* magazine comes out today. Most schools are closed, so many kids' sights are busy, and in summer the puppet shows play in Luxembourg Garden and the Champ de Mars park. Some cinemas offer discounts.

**Thursday:** All sights are open except the Sewer Tour. Some sights are open late, including the Orsay (until 21:45, last entry 21:00), Marmottan (20:00), and the Holocaust Memorial (22:00). Some department stores are open late.

**Friday:** All sights are open (Louvre until 21:45, last entry 21:00) except the Sewer Tour. Afternoon trains and roads leaving Paris are crowded. Restaurants are busy—it's smart to book ahead at popular places.

**Saturday:** All sights are open except the Jewish Art and History Museum and the Holocaust Memorial. The fountains run at Versailles (April-Oct), and Vaux-le-Vicomte hosts candlelight visits tonight (early May-early Oct); otherwise, avoid weekend crowds at area châteaux and Impressionist sights. Department stores are jammed today. The Jewish Quarter is quiet. Restaurants throughout Paris get packed; reserve in advance if you have a particular place in mind. Luxembourg Garden and the Champ de Mars park host puppet shows in summer.

## Day 4

**Morning:** Catch the RER suburban train by 8:00 to arrive early at Versailles (before it opens at 9:00) and tour the palace's interior. (If you get a later start, reverse today's plan by doing the gardens first and the château's interior later in the afternoon.)

**Midday:** Have lunch in the gardens at Versailles.

**Afternoon:** Spend the afternoon touring the gardens, the Trianon Palaces, and Domaine de Marie-Antoinette.

**Evening:** Have dinner in Versailles town or return to Paris. For dessert, follow this book's Left Bank Walk and end at St. Sulpice.

## Day 5

**Morning:** Follow this book's Marais Walk and tour the Carnavalet Museum. Have lunch on Place des Vosges or Rue des Rosiers.

**Afternoon:** Tour the Pompidou Center and the Jewish Art and History Museum, or wander through Les Halles and up traffic-free Rue Montorgueil.

**Evening:** Enjoy the Trocadéro scene and a twilight ride up the Eiffel Tower.

## Day 6

**Morning:** Take an Impressionist escape to Giverny or Auvers-sur-Oise, or take a day trip to historic Reims, Chartres, or Vaux-le-Vicomte. If you get back to Paris in time, consider the following options:

**Late Afternoon:** Follow this book's Left Bank Walk (featuring art galleries, boutiques, historic cafés, and grand boulevards), mix in some shopping (see the Sèvres-Babylone to St. Sulpice stroll on page 478), then relax in Luxembourg Garden or at a nearby café (see "Les Grands Cafés de Paris," page 458).

**Evening:** Join the parade along the Champs-Elysées (which offers a different scene at night than the daytime walk you enjoyed on Day 2). If you haven't hiked to the top of the Arc de Triomphe yet, consider doing it by twilight.

## Day 7

**Choose from:**

More shopping and cafés
Bus #69 tour followed by Père Lachaise Cemetery
Montmartre and Sacré-Cœur (by day)
Marmottan or Jacquemart-André museums
Day trip to Vaux-le-Vicomte and Fontainebleau
Day trip to Disneyland Paris

**Evening:** Night bus or boat tour (whichever you have yet to do).

# Overview

## Tourist Information

Paris tourist offices (abbreviated as "TI" in this book) can provide useful information but may have long lines. Pick up the free *Paris for You!* booklet. If you're looking for a map, they may charge you for it (all you really need are the freebie maps available at any hotel or in the front of this book). TIs also sell individual tickets to sights (see "Avoiding Lines with Advance Tickets" on page 31), as well as Paris Museum Passes (see page 52). If you plan to get a Museum Pass, it's quicker to buy these at participating sights (except major museums, where lines can be long).

Paris has several TI locations, including **Pyramides** (daily May-Oct 9:00-19:00, Nov-April 10:00-19:00, at Pyramides Métro stop between the Louvre and Opéra), **Gare du Nord** (daily 8:00-18:00), and two in **Montmartre,** both with a focus on their neighborhood (one on Place du Tertre, daily 10:00-18:00, tel. 01 42 62 21 21, and the other above the Anvers Métro stop, daily 10:00-18:00). In summer, TI kiosks may pop up in the squares in front of Notre-Dame and Hôtel de Ville. The official website for Paris' TIs is www.parisinfo.com.

Both **airports** have handy information offices with long hours and short lines (see the Paris Connections chapter).

*Pariscope:* The weekly €0.40 *Pariscope* magazine (or one of its clones, available at any newsstand) lists museum hours, art exhibits, concerts, festivals, plays, movies, and nightclubs. Smart sightseers rely on this for the latest listings (see page 493).

**Other Publications:** *L'Officiel des Spectacles* (€0.35), which is similar to *Pariscope,* also lists goings-on around town (in French). The *Paris Voice,* with snappy reviews of concerts, plays, and current events, is available only online at www.parisvoice.com. For a schedule of museum hours and English museum tours, get the free *Musées, Monuments Historiques, et Expositions* booklet at any museum.

**Helpful Websites:** These websites come highly recommended for local information and events: www.gogoparis.com, www.secretsofparis.com, and www.bonjourparis.com.

**American Church and Franco-American Center:** This interdenominational church—in the Rue Cler neighborhood, facing the river between the Eiffel Tower and Orsay Museum—is a nerve center for the American expat community. Worship services are held every Sunday (traditional services at 9:00 and 11:00, contemporary service at 13:30). The coffee hour after the 11:00 service and the free Sunday concerts (generally Sept-June at 17:00—but not every week and not in Dec) are a good way to get a taste of émigré life in Paris (reception open Mon-Sat 9:00-12:00 & 13:00-22:00, Sun 14:30-19:00, 65 Quai d'Orsay, Mo: Invalides, tel. 01 40 62 05 00, www.acparis.org). It's also a handy place to pick up free copies of *France-USA Contacts*, an advertisement paper with info on housing and employment for the 50,000 Americans living in Paris (www.fusac.fr).

## Arrival in Paris

For a comprehensive rundown of the city's train stations and airports, and for information on parking a car, see the Paris Connections chapter.

## Helpful Hints

**Theft Alert:** Thieves thrive near famous monuments and on Métro and RER lines that serve high-profile tourist sights. Beware of pickpockets working busy lines (e.g., at ticket windows at train stations). Pay attention when it's your turn and your back is to the crowd—keep your bag firmly gripped in front of you. In general, it's smart to wear a money belt, put your wallet in your front pocket, loop your day bag over your shoulders, and keep a tight grip on your purse or shopping bag. Muggings are rare, but they do occur. If you're out late, avoid the dark riverfront embankments and any place where the lighting is dim and pedestrian activity is minimal.

Paris is taking action to combat crime by stationing police at monuments, on streets, and on the Métro, as well as security cameras at key sights. You'll go through quick and reassuring airport-like security checks at many major attractions.

**ATM Alert:** When withdrawing money from a cash machine, use your hand to shield your PIN number from prying eyes. Don't engage with anyone who offers to "help" you use an ATM (which works just like ours do) or warns you that it isn't working properly. If that happens, cancel your operation and find a different machine.

**Tourist Scams:** Be aware of the latest scams, including these current favorites. The "found ring" scam involves an innocent-looking person who picks up a ring off the ground and asks if you dropped it. When you say no, the person examines the ring more closely, then shows you a mark "proving" that it's pure gold. He offers to sell it to you for a good price—several times more than he paid for it before dropping it on the sidewalk.

In the "friendship bracelet" scam, a vendor approaches you and asks if you'll help him with a demonstration. He proceeds to make a friendship bracelet right on your arm. When finished, he asks you to pay for the bracelet he created just for you. And since you can't easily take it off on the spot, he counts on your feeling obliged to pay up.

Distractions by a stranger—often a "salesman," someone asking you to sign a petition, or someone posing as a deaf person to show you a small note to read—can all be tricks that function as a smokescreen for theft. As you try to wriggle away from the pushy stranger, an accomplice picks your pocket.

In popular tourist spots (such as in front of Notre-Dame) young ladies ask if you speak English, then pretend to beg for money while actually angling to get your wallet.

To all these scammers, simply say "no" firmly, don't apologize, don't smile, and step away purposefully.

**Pedestrian Safety:** Parisian drivers are notorious for ignoring pedestrians. Look both ways (many streets are one-way) and be careful of seemingly quiet bus/taxi lanes. Don't assume you have the right of way, even in a crosswalk. When crossing a street, keep your pace constant and don't stop suddenly. By law, drivers are allowed to miss pedestrians by up to just one meter—a little more than three feet (1.5 meters in the countryside). Drivers calculate your speed so they won't hit you, provided you don't alter your route or pace.

Watch out for bicyclists. This popular and silent transportation may come at you from unexpected places and directions—cyclists ride in specially marked bike lanes on wide sidewalks and also have a right to use lanes reserved for buses and taxis. Bikes commonly go against traffic, as many bike paths are on one-way streets. Always look both ways.

Busy Parisian sidewalks are much like freeways, so conduct yourself as if you were a foot-fueled-car: Stick to your lane, look to the left before passing a slow-moving pedestrian, and if you need to stop, look for a safe place to pull over.

**Museum Strategies:** The worthwhile Paris Museum Pass, covering most sights in the city, is sold at museums and monuments, as well as TIs and FNAC stores (no surcharge). For detailed information, see page 52. For other museum strategies, see "Sightseeing" on page 17.

**Avoiding Lines with Advance Tickets:** If you don't purchase a Paris Museum Pass, which allows you to skip most ticket lines, you have other options. Throughout Paris, TIs and FNAC stores sell individual fast-track "*coupe-file*" tickets, letting you use the Museum Pass entrance at sights. TIs sell these tickets for no extra fee, but FNACs add a surcharge of 10-20 percent—often worth it, as these stores are everywhere, even on the Champs-Elysées (ask your hotelier for the nearest one).

For sights that can otherwise have long waits (such as the Arc de Triomphe, Opéra Garnier, Versailles, and Monet's gardens in Giverny), these tickets are a good idea. (Note that Versailles and the Arc de Triomphe are covered by the Paris Museum Pass.)

For some sights, you can book tickets online and print a receipt (either from home or at your hotel) that serves as your entry pass. This works great at the Eiffel Tower (though you must choose an entry time), Monet's gardens at Giverny, and the Jacquemart-André Museum, as well as for activities like the Bateaux-Mouches cruises and Sainte-Chapelle concerts. Increasingly, other sights are adding this helpful service. However, buying Paris Museum Passes and certain tickets online is not worth the cost or hassle because you have to either pay dearly to have them shipped to you or print vouchers and redeem them in person at a Paris TI.

**Bookstores:** Paris has many English-language bookstores, where you can pick up guidebooks (at nearly double their American prices). Most carry this book. My favorites include:

• **Red Wheelbarrow Bookstore** (in the Marais neighborhood, for sale and may be gone in 2013; if open, generally Mon 10:00-18:00, Tue-Sat 10:00-19:00, Sun 14:00-18:00; 22 Rue St. Paul, Mo: St. Paul, tel. 01 48 04 75 08).

• **Shakespeare and Company** (some used travel books, Mon-Fri 10:00-23:00, Sat-Sun 11:00-23:00, 37 Rue de la Bûcherie, across the river from Notre-Dame, Mo: St. Michel, tel. 01 43 25 40 93; described on page 108).

• **W. H. Smith** (Mon-Sat 9:00-19:00, Sun 12:30-19:00, 248 Rue de Rivoli, Mo: Concorde, tel. 01 44 77 88 99).

• **San Francisco Book Company** (Mon-Sat 11:00-21:00, Sun 14:00-19:30, 17 Rue Monsieur le Prince, Mo: Odéon, tel. 01 43 29 15 70).

**Public WCs:** Most public toilets are free. If it's a pay toilet, the price will be clearly indicated. If the toilet is free but there's an attendant, it's polite (but not necessary) to leave a tip of €0.20-0.50. Booth-like pay toilets on the sidewalks provide both relief and a memory (don't leave small children inside unattended). The restrooms in museums are free and the best you'll find. Or walk into any sidewalk café like you own the place, and find the toilet in the back. If you have to buy something, your cheapest  option is to order a shot of espresso *(un café)* standing at the bar. Keep toilet paper or tissues with you, as some WCs are poorly stocked.

**Tobacco Stands *(Tabacs):*** These little kiosks—usually just a counter inside a café—are handy and very local. They sell public-transit tickets, cards for parking meters, postage stamps (though not all sell international postage—to mail something home, use two domestic stamps, or go to a post office), prepaid phone cards, and...oh yeah, cigarettes. (For more on this slice of Parisian life, see page 196. For details on parking cards and prepaid phone cards, see pages 537 and 651.) To find one of these kiosks, just look for a *Tabac* sign and the red cylinder-shaped symbol above certain cafés. A *tabac* can be a godsend for avoiding long ticket lines at the Métro, especially at the end of the month when ticket booths get crowded with locals buying next month's pass.

## Getting Around Paris

Paris is easy to navigate. Your basic choices are Métro (in-city subway), RER (suburban rail tied into the Métro system), public bus, and taxi. (Also consider the hop-on, hop-off bus and boat tours, described under "Tours," later.)

You can buy tickets and passes at Métro stations and at many *tabacs*. Staffed ticket windows in stations are gradually being phased out in favor of ticket machines, so expect some stations to have machines only—be sure to carry coins or small bills of €20 or less (not all machines take bills and none take American credit cards). If a ticket machine is out of order or if you're out of change, buy tickets at a *tabac*.

**Public-Transit Tickets:** The Métro, RER, and buses all work on the same tickets. You can make as many transfers as you need on a single ticket, except when transferring between the Métro/RER system and the bus system, which requires using an additional ticket. A **single ticket** costs €1.70. To save money, buy a *carnet* (kar-nay) of 10 tickets for €12.70 (cheaper for ages 4-10). *Carnets* can be shared among travelers.

**Passe Navigo:** You can buy a chip-embedded card, called the Passe Navigo (though for most tourists, *carnets* are a better deal). You pay a onetime €5 fee for the Navigo card itself (which also requires a postage stamp-size photo of yourself—bring your own, print a color photo, or use the €4 photo booths in major Métro stations). For a weekly *(hebdomadaire)* version good for travel in central Paris (zones 1-2), you'll pay €19.15, which gives you free run of the bus, Métro, and non-suburban RER system from Monday to Sunday (expiring on Sunday, even if you buy it on, say, a Thursday). A monthly version is also available.

To use the Navigo, whether at a Métro turnstile or on the bus, touch the card to the purple pad, wait for the green validation light and the "ding," and you're on your way. The basic pass covers only central Paris, not regional destinations such as Versailles.

**Navigo or *Carnet*?** It's hard to beat the *carnet*. Two 10-packs of *carnets*—enough for most travelers staying a week—cost €25.40, are shareable, and don't expire. Though similar in price, the Passe Navigo is more of a hassle to buy, cannot be shared, and only becomes worthwhile for visitors who stay a full week (or more), start their trip early in the week (like on a Monday or Tuesday), and use the system a lot.

**Other Passes:** A handy one-day bus/Métro pass (called **Mobilis**) is available for €6.40. The overpriced **Paris Visite** passes are

# Métro Basics

- The same tickets are good on the Métro, RER (within the city), and city buses (but not to transfer between Métro/RER and bus).
- Save money by buying a *carnet* of tickets or a Passe Navigo.
- Beware of pickpockets, and don't buy tickets from men roaming the stations.
- Find your train by its end-of-the-line stops.
- Insert your ticket into the turnstile, retrieve it, and keep it until the end of your journey.
- Transfers *(correspondances)* within the Métro and RER system are free.

## Key Words for the Métro and RER

| French | Pronounced | English |
|---|---|---|
| *direction* | dee-rek-see-ohn | direction |
| *ligne* | leen-yuh | line |
| *correspondance* | kor-res-pohn- dahns | connection transfer |
| *sortie* | sor-tee | exit |
| *carnet* | kar-nay | discounted set of 10 tickets |
| *Pardon, madame/ monsieur.* | par-dohn, mah-dahm/ mes-yur | Excuse me, ma'am/ sir. |
| *Je descends.* | juh day-sahn | I'm getting off. |
| *Donnez-moi mon porte-monnaie!* | duh-nay-mwah mohn port-moh-nay | Give me back my wallet! |

poorly designed for tourists and offer minor reductions at minor sights (1 day/€9.75, 2 days/€15.85, 3 days/€21.60, 5 days/€31.15).

## By Métro

In Paris, you're never more than a 10-minute walk from a Métro station. Europe's best subway system allows you to hop from sight to sight quickly and cheaply (runs daily 5:30-24:30, Fri-Sat until 2:00 in the morning, www.ratp.fr). Learn to use it. Begin by studying the color Métro map at the beginning of this book (also free at Métro stations and included on freebie Paris maps at your hotel).

**Using the Métro System:** To get to your destination, determine the closest "Mo" stop and which line or lines will get you there. The lines are color-coded and numbered, and you

### Etiquette

- When your train arrives, board only after everyone leaving the car has made it out the door.

- Avoid using the hinged seats near the doors of some trains when the car is crowded; they take up valuable standing space.
- Always offer your seat to the elderly, those with disabilities, and pregnant women.
- Talk softly in cars. Listen to how quietly Parisians communicate (if at all) and follow their lead.
- If you find yourself blocking the door at a stop, step out of the car to let others off, then get back on.
- When you're getting off at a stop, the door may open automatically. If it doesn't, open the door by either pushing a square button (green or black) or lifting a metal latch.
- Métro doors close automatically. Don't try to hold open the door for late-boarding passengers.
- Dispose of used tickets after you complete your ride and leave the station (not before) to avoid confusing them with fresh ones.
- On escalators, stand on the right and pass on the left.
- When leaving a station, hold the door for the person behind you.

can tell their direction by their end-of-the-line stops. For example, the La Défense/Château de Vincennes line, also known as line 1 (yellow), runs between La Défense, on its west end, and Vincennes on its east end. Once in the Métro station, you'll see the color-coded line numbers and/or blue-and-white signs directing you to the train going in your direction (e.g., *direction: La Défense*). Insert your ticket in the automatic turnstile, reclaim your ticket, pass through, and keep it until you exit the system (some stations require you to pass your ticket through a turnstile to exit). The smallest stations are unstaffed and have ticket machines (coins are essential). Be warned that fare inspectors regularly check for cheaters and accept absolutely no excuses—keep that ticket or pay a minimum fine of €25.

Be prepared to walk significant distances within Métro stations (especially when you transfer). Transfers are free and can be made wherever lines cross, provided you do so within 1.5 hours. When you transfer, follow the appropriately colored line number

# Connecting with the Culture

Paris hosts more visitors than any other city in the world, and with such a robust tourism industry, many travelers feel cut off from the "real life" in the City of Light. Fortunately, Paris offers *beaucoup* ways for you to connect with locals—and thereby make your trip more personal...and more memorable.

Staying with a family is a simple way to experience everyday Parisian life firsthand. Several agencies set up **bed-and-breakfast** stays in private homes (listed on page 384 of the Sleeping in Paris chapter). Other opportunities abound:

## Meeting the Locals

I'm amazed at the number of groups that help travelers meet locals. These get good reviews:

**Meeting the French** puts travelers in touch with Parisians by organizing dinners in private homes, workplace tours to match your interests/career, and more (tel. 01 42 51 19 80, www.meetingthefrench.com).

**Paris Greeter** is an all-volunteer organization that connects travelers with English-speaking Parisians who want to share their knowledge of Paris. These volunteer "guides" are not licensed to give historical tours; rather they act as informal companions who can show you "their Paris"—it's like seeing Paris through the eyes of a friend. The tours are free (though donations are welcome), and you must sign up five weeks before your visit (www.parisiendunjour.fr).

**Cooking Schools:** It's easy to hook up with small cooking schools that provide an unthreatening and personal experience, such as trips to markets (see page 658 for a list of several schools).

**Wine Tasting:** Young, enthusiastic Olivier Magny and his team of sommeliers teach fun wine-tasting classes at Ô Château wine school/bar near the Louvre, in the 17th-century residence of Madame de Pompadour, King Louis XV's favorite mistress. Olivier's goal is to "take the snob out of wine." At these informal classes, you'll learn the basics of French wine regions, the techniques of tasting, and how to read a French wine label. Classes include Introductory Tasting (€30, 1 hour), Tour de France of Wine (€50, 2 hours), Wine and Cheese

for your next train, or find orange *correspondance* (connection) signs that lead to your next line.

When you reach your destination, look for the blue-and-white *sortie* signs pointing you to the exit. Before leaving the station, check the helpful *plan du quartier* (map of the neighborhood) to get your bearings. At stops with several *sorties*, you can save time by choosing the best exit.

lunches (€75, 1.5 hours), Grands Crus tasting (€120, 2 hours), and a wine-tasting dinner (€100, about 2 hours). Register online using code "RS2013" for a 10 percent discount (68 Rue Jean-Jacques Rousseau, Mo: Louvre-Rivoli or Etienne Marcel, tel. 01 44 73 97 80, www.o-chateau.com).

**Language Classes:** You're at the *Kilometre Zero* of the French language—where better to take a class? You'll have no problem finding French-language classes for any level. Class size is usually small (see page 657 for a list).

**Conversation Swap: Parler Paris** is a free-form conversation group organized for native French and English speakers who want to practice in a relaxed environment. In a small group, you'll discuss interesting topics—for the first 45 minutes in French, then for 45 minutes in English. Your first visit is free; after that it's €12 a session (several meetings per week possible, tel. 01 48 42 26 10 or 01 40 27 97 59, www.parler parlor.com, info@parlerparlor.com).

## Meeting the Americans

Long-term American residents can give you surprisingly keen insight into life in Paris.

The **American Church and Franco-American Center** is the community center for Americans living in Paris (see page 29).

The **American Library,** in the Rue Cler neighborhood, offers free programs and events for adults and children (10 Rue du Général Camou, Mo: Ecole Militaire, tel. 01 53 59 12 60, www.americanlibraryinparis.org).

**WICE (Women in Continuing Education)** is a non-profit association that provides an impressive array of cultural and educational programs in English. Check their schedule at www.wice-paris.org, or call 01 45 66 75 50.

**Meetup** connects people in cities around the world, whether they are in town for a day or longer. Sponsored events include picnics, museum tours, cocktail evenings and more. This is a particularly good tool for the 20-something traveler (www.meetup.com, search "Paris" to find groups according to your interests).

After you exit the system, toss or tear your used ticket so you don't confuse it with unused tickets—they look almost identical.

**Beware of Pickpockets:** Thieves dig the Métro and RER. Be on guard. If your pocket is picked as you pass through a turnstile, you end up stuck on the wrong side (after the turnstile bar has closed behind you) while the thief gets away. Stand away from Métro doors to avoid being a target for a theft-and-run just before the doors close. Any jostling or commotion—especially when

## Hop on the Bus, Gus

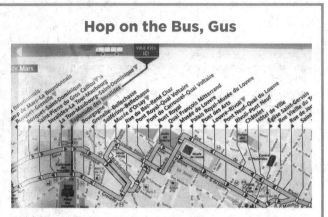

Just like the Métro, every bus stop has a name, and every bus is headed to one end-of-the-line stop or the other. The photo shows the route for bus #69. First, find your stop on the chart. It says *"vous êtes ICI"* ("you are HERE") at Esplanade des Invalides. Next, find your destination stop—let's say Bosquet-Grenelle, located a few stops to the west. Now, find out exactly where to catch the bus going in that direction. On the map showing the bus route, notice the triangle-shaped arrows pointing in the direction the bus is headed. You'll see that Esplanade des Invalides has two different bus stops—one for buses headed east, one for those going west. If you want to go west to Bosquet-Grenelle, head for that street corner to catch the bus. (With so many one-way streets in Paris, it's easy to get on the bus in the wrong direction.) When the bus pulls up, double-check that the sign on the front of the bus has the end-of-the-line stop going in your direction—to "Champ de Mars," in this case.

boarding or leaving trains—is likely the sign of a thief or a team of thieves in action. See page 30 for tips on keeping your bag close. Make any fare inspector show proof of identity (ask locals for help if you're not certain). Never show anyone your wallet.

### By RER

The RER (Réseau Express Régionale; air-ay-air) is the suburban arm of the Métro, serving outlying destinations such as Versailles, Disneyland Paris, and the airports. These routes are indicated by thick lines on your subway map and identified by the letters A, B, C, and so on.

Within the city center, the RER works like the Métro and can be speedier if it serves your destination directly, because it makes fewer stops. Métro tickets and the Passe Navigo card are good on the RER when traveling in the city center. You can transfer between the Métro and RER systems with the same ticket. But to travel outside the city (to Versailles or the airport, for example), you'll need a separate, more expensive ticket. Unlike the Métro, not every train stops at every station along the way; check the sign or screen over the platform to see if your destination is listed as a stop (*"toutes les gares"* means it makes all stops along the way), or confirm with a local before you board. For RER trains, you may need to insert your ticket in a turnstile to exit the system.

## By City Bus

Paris' excellent bus system is worth figuring out. Buses don't seem as romantic as the famous Métro and are subject to traffic jams, but savvy travelers know that buses can have you swinging through the city like Tarzan in an urban jungle.

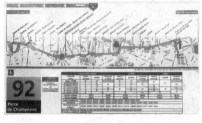

Buses require less walking and fewer stairways than the Métro, and you can see Paris unfold as you travel. Bus stops are everywhere, and every stop comes with all the information you need: a good city bus map, route maps showing exactly where each bus that uses this stop goes, a frequency chart and schedule, a *plan du quartier* map of the immediate neighborhood, and a *soirées* map explaining night service, if available (www.ratp.fr). Bus-system maps are also available in any Métro station (and in the €6.50 *Paris Pratique* map book sold at newsstands). For longer stays, consider buying the €6 *Le Bus* book of bus routes.

**Using the Bus System:** Buses use the same tickets and passes as the Métro and RER. One Zone 1 ticket buys you a bus ride anywhere in central Paris within the freeway ring road *(le périphérique)*. Use your Métro ticket or buy one on board for €0.20 more. (The ticket system has a few quirks—see "More Bus Tips," later.)

# Scenic Buses for Tourists

Of Paris' many bus routes, these are some of the most scenic. They provide a great, cheap, and convenient introduction to the city.

**Bus #69** runs east-west between the Eiffel Tower and Père Lachaise Cemetery by way of Rue Cler (recommended hotels), Quai d'Orsay, the Louvre, and the Marais (recommended hotels). For a self-guided tour, see the Bus #69 Sightseeing Tour chapter.

**Bus #87** also links the Marais and Rue Cler areas, but stays mostly on the Left Bank, connecting the Eiffel Tower, St. Sulpice Church, Luxembourg Garden (recommended hotels and restaurants), St. Germain-des-Prés, the Latin Quarter, the Bastille, and Gare de Lyon.

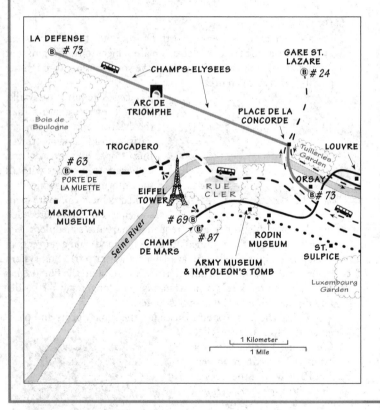

**Bus #24** runs east-west along the Seine riverbank from Gare St. Lazare to Madeleine, Place de la Concorde, Orsay Museum, the Louvre, St. Michel, Notre-Dame, and Jardin des Plantes, all the way to Bercy Village (cafés and shops).

**Bus #63** is another good east-west route, connecting the Marmottan Museum, Trocadéro (Eiffel Tower), Pont de l'Alma, Orsay Museum, St. Sulpice Church, Luxembourg Garden, Latin Quarter/Panthéon, and Gare de Lyon.

**Bus #73** is one of Paris' most scenic lines, starting at the Orsay Museum and running westbound around Place de la Concorde, then up the Champs-Elysées, around the Arc de Triomphe, and down Avenue Charles de Gaulle to La Défense.

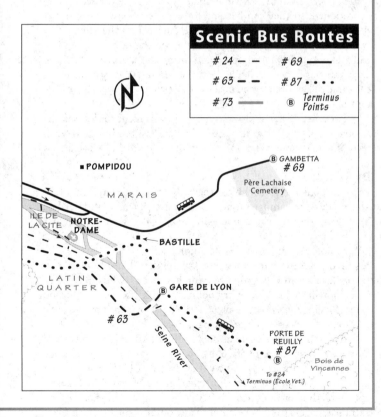

Board your bus through the front door. (Families with strollers can use any doors—the ones in the center are wider. To open the middle or back doors on long buses, push the green button located by those doors.) Validate your ticket in the machine and reclaim it. With a Passe Navigo, scan it on the purple touchpad. Keep track of what stop is coming up next by following the on-board diagram or listening to recorded announcements. When you're ready to get off, push the red button to signal you want a stop, then exit through the central or rear door. Even if you're not certain you've figured out the system, do some joyriding.

**More Bus Tips:** Avoid rush hour (Mon-Fri 8:00-9:30 & 17:30-19:30), when buses are jammed and traffic doesn't move. While the Métro shuts down at about 24:30, some buses continue much later (called *Noctilien* lines, www.noctilien.fr). Not all city buses are air-conditioned, so they can become rolling greenhouses on summer days. You can transfer from one bus to another on the same ticket (within 1.5 hours, revalidate your ticket on the next bus), but you can't do a round-trip or hop on and off on the same line. You also can't transfer between the bus and the Métro/RER systems using the same ticket, or between buses with a ticket bought on board (go figure).

For a list of Paris' most scenic and convenient routes, see the sidebar on page 40. I've also listed the handiest bus routes for each recommended hotel neighborhood in the Sleeping in Paris chapter.

## By Taxi

Parisian taxis are reasonable, especially for couples and families. The meters are tamper-proof. Fares and supplements (described in English on the rear windows) are straightforward and tightly regulated.

A taxi can fit three people comfortably. Cabbies are legally required to accept four passengers, though they don't always like it. If you have five in your group, you can book a larger taxi in advance (your hotelier can call), or try your luck at a taxi stand. Beyond three passengers, expect to pay €3 extra per person. For a sample taxi tour of the city at night, see page 502.

**Rates:** All Parisian taxis start with €2.40 on the meter and have a minimum charge of €6.40. A 20-minute ride (e.g., Bastille to the Eiffel Tower) costs about €20 (versus €1.27/person to get anywhere in town using a *carnet* ticket on the Métro or bus). Drivers charge higher rates at rush hour, at night, all day Sunday, for extra passengers (see above), and to any of the airports. Each piece of luggage you put in the trunk is €1 extra (though it won't appear on the meter, it is a legitimate charge). To tip, round up to the next euro (at least €0.50).

**How to Catch *un Taxi:*** You can try waving down a taxi, but it's often easier to ask someone for the nearest taxi stand (*"Où est une station de taxi?"*; oo ay ewn stah-see-ohn duh "taxi"). Taxi stands are indicated by a circled "T" on good city maps, and on many maps in this book. To order a taxi in English, call 01 41 27 66 99, or ask your hotelier for help. When you summon a taxi by phone, the meter starts running as soon as the call is received, often adding €6 or more to the bill.

Taxis are tough to find during rush hour, when it's raining, on weekend nights, or on any night after the Métro closes (Sun-Thu at 24:30, Fri-Sat at 2:00 in the morning). If you need to catch a train or flight early in the morning, book a taxi the day before (especially for weekday departures). Some taxi companies require a €5 reservation fee by credit card for weekday morning rush-hour departures (7:00-10:00) and only have a limited number of reservation spots.

## By Bike

Paris is surprisingly easy by bicycle. The city is flat, and riders have access to more than 370 miles of bike lanes and the many priority lanes for buses and taxis (though be careful on these). I biked along

the river from Notre-Dame to the Eiffel Tower in 15 wonderfully scenic minutes.

Urban bikers will find Paris a breeze. First-timers will get the hang of it quickly enough by following some simple rules. Always stay to the right in your lane, bike single-file, stay off sidewalks, watch out for opening doors on parked cars, signal with your arm before making turns, and use bike paths when available. Obey the traffic laws as if you were driving a car. Parisians use the same road rules as Americans, with two exceptions: When passing vehicles or other bikes, always pass on the left (it's illegal to pass on the right); and where there is no stoplight, always yield to traffic merging from the right, even if you're on a major road and the merging driver is on a side street. You'll find a bell on your bike; use it like a horn to warn pedestrians who don't see you.

Sundays are peaceful and best for pedaling, when the city's "Paris Respire" program opens up some streets to cyclists and rollerbladers (and bans cars) from 9:00 to 17:00. Participating neighborhoods include the Marais, Montmartre, the Rue Mouffetard area east of Luxembourg Garden, the Rue Daguerre area (near the Denfert-Rochereau Métro station), and sections of the small roads directly bordering the Seine—on the Left Bank from the Eiffel Tower to the Orsay and also outside of the Paris Plages (see page 60), on the Right Bank between the Louvre and Gare de Lyon. Neighborhood bike-path maps are available at www.paris.fr (search for "*Paris respire*" to get the exact link). The TIs have a helpful "Paris à Vélo" map, which shows all the dedicated bike paths. Many other versions are available for sale at newsstand kiosks, some bookstores, and department stores.

**Renting a Bike:** The following two rental companies offer organized bike tours as well (see "Tours by Bike," later). **Bike About Tours** is your best bet for bike rental. Some of their units are foldable, which allows you to collapse your bike and jump on the Métro if the weather turns bad or if you get tired (€15/day during office hours, €20/24 hours; includes locks, helmets, and comfy gel seats; daily mid-Feb-Dec 9:00-18:00, closed Dec-mid-Feb; shop located near Hôtel de Ville in Vinci parking garage—see map on page 398, Mo: Hôtel de Ville, www.bikeabouttours.com, info@bikeabouttours.com). **Fat Tire Bike Tours** has a limited supply of bikes for rent, so call ahead to check availability (€4/hour, €25/24 hours, includes helmets and locks, credit-card imprint required for deposit, €2 daily rental discount with this book; office open daily 9:00-18:30, May-Aug bike rental only after 11:30 as priority is given to those taking a tour, 24 Rue Edgar Faure—see map on page 67, Mo: Dupleix, tel. 01 56 58 10 54, www.fattirebiketours paris.com).

You'll see many bike-rack stations throughout Paris. The city's **Vélib'** program (from *vélo* + *liberté* or *libre* = "bike freedom" or "free bike") gives residents access to more than 20,000 bikes, which they can unlock from the nearly 1,500 stations scattered around the city. You can use the Vélib system, too, but only if you have a certain kind of credit card (American Express or a chip-and-PIN card—see page 14) or if you buy a subscription online (€1.70/1 day, €8/7 days, http://en.velib.paris.fr—click on "Subscriptions and Fees," tel. 01 30 79 79 30). The first 30 minutes of any trip are included with your subscription; after that there's a fee for each additional 30 minutes.

## By Rollerblade

Inline skaters take to the streets Sunday afternoons and Friday evenings. It's serious skaters only on Fridays (they meet at 21:30 and are ready to roll at 22:00), but anyone can join in on Sundays (at 14:30). Police close off different routes each week to keep locals engaged, but the starting points are always the same. On Sunday, skaters leave from the south side of Place de la Bastille (for the route, see www.rollers-coquillages.org); on Fridays it's from Place Raoul Dautry (Mo: Montparnasse; see route at www.pari-roller.com). You can rent skates near Sunday's starting point at Nomades (€5/half-day, €9/day, Tue-Fri 11:00-13:30 & 14:30-19:30, Sat

10:00-19:00, Sun 12:00-18:00, closed Mon, 37 Boulevard Bour-
don, near Place de la Bastille, Mo: Bastille, tel. 01 44 54 07 44,
www.nomadeshop.com).

## By Scooter

**Left Bank Scooters** will deliver and pick-up rental scooters to daring travelers over 20 years old with a valid driver's license (€80-100/
day, price depends on size of the scooter and how long you keep it,
mobile 06 78 12 04 24, www.leftbankscooters.com).

# Tours

To sightsee on your own, download my series of free audio tours
that illuminate some of Paris' top sights and neighborhoods, including the Historic Paris Walk, Louvre, Orsay, and Versailles
Palace (see sidebar on page 24 for details).

## Tours by Bus

**Bus Tours**—**Paris Vision** (also called Cityrama) offers bus tours
of Paris, day and night (advertised in hotel lobbies). I'd consider
a Paris Vision tour only for their nighttime tour (see page 501) or
for tricky-to-reach day trips (such as Vaux-le-Vicomte). During the
day, you'll get a better value and more versatility by taking a hop-
on, hop-off tour by bus (described next) or Batobus boat (see "By
Boat," later), which provide transportation between sights.

**Hop-on, Hop-off Bus Tours**—Double-decker buses connect
Paris' main sights, allowing you to hop on and off along the way.
You get a disposable set of earplugs to listen to a basic running
commentary (dial English for the so-so narration). You can get
off at any stop, tour a sight, then catch a later bus. These are best
in good weather, when you can sit up top. There are two companies: L'Open Tours and Les Cars Rouges (pick up their brochures
showing routes and stops from any TI or on their buses). You can
start either tour at just about any of the major sights, such as the
Eiffel Tower.

    **L'Open Tours** uses bright yellow buses and provides more
extensive coverage (and slightly better commentary) on four different routes, rolling by most of the important sights in Paris. Their
Paris Grand Tour (the green route) offers the best introduction.
The same ticket gets you on any of their routes within the validity
period. Buy your tickets from the driver (1 day-€31, 2 days-€34,
kids 4-11 pay €15 for 1 or 2 days, allow 2 hours per tour). Two
to four buses depart hourly from about 10:00 to 18:00; expect to
wait 10-15 minutes at each stop (stops can be tricky to find—look
for yellow signs; tel. 01 42 66 56 56, www.parislopentour.com). A

combo-ticket includes the Batobus boats, too (2 days-€43, 3 days-€46, kids 4-11 pay €20 for 2 or 3 days; see "By Boat," below).

**Les Cars Rouges'** bright red buses offer one route with just nine stops and recorded narration, but for a little less (adult-€29, kids 4-12 pay €15, good for 2 days, 10 percent cheaper if you book online, tel. 01 53 95 39 53, www.carsrouges .com).

**Do-It-Yourself Bus Tour—**Paris' cheapest "bus tour" is simply to hop on city bus #69 and follow my commentary (see the Bus #69 Sightseeing Tour chapter).

## Tours by Boat

**Seine Cruises—**Several companies run one-hour boat cruises on the Seine. For the best experience, cruise at twilight or after dark. (To dine while you cruise, see "Dinner Cruises" on page 457.) Two of the companies—Bateaux-Mouches and Bateaux Parisiens—are convenient to the Rue Cler hotels, and both run daily year-round (April-Oct 10:00-22:30, 2-3/hour; Nov-March shorter hours, runs

hourly). Some offer discounts for early online bookings.

**Bateaux-Mouches,** the oldest boat company in Paris, departs from Pont de l'Alma's right bank and has the biggest open-top, double-decker boats (higher up means better views). But this company caters to tour groups, making their boats jammed and noisy (€11.50, kids 4-12 pay €5.50, tel. 01 42 25 96 10, www.bateaux-mouches.fr).

**Bateaux Parisiens** has smaller covered boats with handheld audioguides, fewer crowds, and only one deck. It leaves from right in front of the Eiffel Tower. From April to October, they usually have a second departure point on the Quai de Montebello near Notre-Dame (€12, kids 3-12 pay €5, half-price if you have a valid France or France-Switzerland railpass—does not use up a day of a flexipass, tel. 01 76 64 14 45, www.bateauxparisiens.com).

**Vedettes du Pont Neuf** offers essentially the same one-hour tour as the other companies, but starts and ends at Pont Neuf, closer to recommended hotels in the Marais and Luxembourg Garden neighborhoods. The boats feature a live guide whose delivery (in English and French) is as stiff as a recorded narration—

and as hard to understand, given the quality of their sound system (€13, €11 if you book direct with this book in 2013, online booking costs just €9, kids 4-12 pay €7, tip requested, nearly 2/hour, daily 10:30-22:30, tel. 01 46 33 98 38, www.vedettesdupontneuf. com).

**Hop-on, Hop-off Boat Tour**—**Batobus** allows you to get on and off as often as you like at any of eight popular stops along the Seine. The boats, which make a continuous circuit, stop in this order: Eiffel Tower, Orsay Museum, St. Germain-des-Prés, Notre-Dame, Jardin des Plantes, Hôtel de Ville, the Louvre, and Pont Alexandre III, near the Champs-Elysées (1 day-€15, 2 days-€18, 5 days-€21, April-Aug boats run every 20 minutes 10:00-21:30, Sept-March every 25 minutes 10:00-19:00, 45 minutes one-way, 1.5-hour round-trip, worthless narration, www.batobus.com). If you use this for getting around—sort of a scenic, floating alternative to the Métro—it can be worthwhile, especially with a five-day pass. But if you just want a guided boat tour, the Seine cruises are a better choice (described above).

**Low-Key Cruise on a Tranquil Canal**—**Canauxrama** runs a lazy 2.5-hour cruise on a peaceful canal out of sight of the Seine. Tours start from Place de la Bastille and end at Bassin de la Villette (near Mo: Stalingrad). During the first segment of your trip, you'll pass through a long tunnel (built by order of Napoleon in the early 19th century, when canal boats were vital for industrial transport). Once outside, you glide—not much faster than you can walk—through sleepy Parisian neighborhoods and slowly climb through four double locks as a guide narrates the trip in French and English (adults-€16, kids 12 and under-€8.50, check online for discounts for advance booking, departs at 9:45 and 14:30 across from Opéra Bastille, just below Boulevard de la Bastille, opposite #50—where the canal meets Place de la Bastille, tel. 01 42 39 15 00, www. canauxrama.com). The same tour also goes in the opposite direction, from Bassin de la Villette to Place de la Bastille (departs at 9:45 and 14:45). It's OK to bring a picnic on board.

## Tours on Foot

**Paris Walks**—This company offers a variety of two-hour walks, led by British and American guides. Tours are thoughtfully prepared and entertaining. Don't hesitate to stand close to the guide to hear (€12-15, generally 2/day—morning and afternoon, private tours available, family guides and Louvre tours a specialty, call 01 48 09 21 40 for schedule in English or check printable online schedule at www.paris-walks.com). Tours focus on the Marais (4/week), Montmartre (3/week), medieval Latin Quarter (Mon), Ile de la Cité/Notre-Dame (Mon), the "Two Islands" (Ile de la Cité and Ile St. Louis, Wed), the Revolution (Tue), and Hemingway's

Paris (Fri). They also run less-regular tours of Paris' **Puces St. Ouen** flea market and of the Catacombs, plus a themed walk on the Occupation and Resistance in Paris during the 1940s. Call a day or two ahead to hear the current schedule and starting point. Most tours don't require reservations, but specialty tours—such as the Louvre, fashion, or chocolate tours—require advance reservations and prepayment with credit card (deposits aren't refundable).

**Context Paris**—These "intellectual by design" walking tours, geared for serious learners, are led by docents (historians, architects, and academics). They cover both museums and specific neighborhoods, and range from traditional topics such as French art history in the Louvre and the Gothic architecture of Notre-Dame to more thematic explorations like immigration and the changing face of Paris, jazz in the Latin Quarter, and the history of the baguette. It's best to book in advance—groups are limited to six participants and can fill up fast (€40-90/person, admission to sights extra, generally 3 hours, tel. 01 72 81 36 35, US tel. 800-691-6036, www.contextparis.com). They also offer private tours and excursions outside Paris.

**Classic Walks**—The antithesis of Context Paris' walks, these low-brow, lighter-on-information but high-fun walking tours are run by Fat Tire Bike Tours. Their 3.5-hour Classic Walk covers most major sights (€20, departs May-Sept daily at 10:00; Mon, Wed, Fri and Sun only March-April and Oct; meet at their office at 24 Rue Edgar Faure, Mo: Dupleix, tel. 01 56 58 10 54, www.classic walksparis.com). They also offer neighborhood walks of Montmartre, the Marais, and Latin Quarter, as well as themed walks on the French Revolution and World War II (€20, tours leave several times a week—see website for details). Their Easy Pass tours are designed to allow you to skip the lines at major sights. They run tours of the Louvre, Catacombs, Eiffel Tower, Pompidou, Orsay, and Versailles (€45-85/person, includes entry and guided tour, www. easypasstours.com). Ask also about their skip-the-line tickets to key sights. The company promises a €2 discount on all walks with this book.

**Local Guides**—For many, Paris merits hiring a Parisian as a personal guide. **Arnaud Servignat** is an excellent licensed guide (€190/half-day, also does car tours of the countryside around Paris for a little more, mobile 06 68 80 29 05, www.french-guide.com, arnotour@me.com). **Thierry Gauduchon** is a terrific guide well worth his fee (€200/half-day, €400/day, tel. 01 56 98 10 82, mobile 06 19 07 30 77, tgauduchon@aol.com). **Elisabeth Van Hest** is another likable and capable guide (€190/half-day, tel. 01 43 41 47 31, elisa.guide@gmail.com).

**Food Tours**—Friendly Canadian **Rosa Jackson** designs personalized "Edible Paris" itineraries based on your interests and three-hour "food-guru" tours of Paris led by her or one of her two colleagues (unguided itineraries from €125, €300 guided tours for up to 3, mobile 06 81 67 41 22, www.edible-paris.com, rosa@rosa jackson.com).

## Tours by Bike, Segway, or Pedicab

A bike tour is a fun way to see Paris. Two companies—Bike About Tours and Fat Tire Bike Tours—offer tours, sell bottled water and bike maps of Paris, and give advice on cycling routes in the city. Their tour routes cover different areas of the city, so avid cyclists could do both without much repetition.

**Bike About Tours**—Run by Christian (American) and Paul (New Zealander), this company offers easygoing tours with a focus on the eastern half of the city. Their four-hour tours run daily year-round at 10:00 (also at 15:00 June-Sept). You'll meet at the statue of Charlemagne in front of Notre-Dame, then walk to the nearby rental office to get bikes. The tour includes a good back-street visit of the Marais, Rive Gauche outdoor sculpture park, Ile de la Cité, heart of the Latin Quarter (with a lunch break), Louvre, Les Halles, and Pompidou Center. Group tours have a 12-person maximum—reserve online to guarantee a spot, or show up and take your chances (€30, €5 discount with this book, maximum 2 discounts per book, 15 percent discount for families, includes helmets upon request, private tours available, see listing on page 44 for contact info).

**Fat Tire Bike Tours**—A hardworking gang of young anglophone expats runs an extensive program of bike, Segway, and walking tours (see Classic Walks listing, earlier). Their high-energy guides run four-hour bike tours of Paris, by day and by night (adults-€30, kids-€28, show this book to get a €4 discount per person, maximum 2 discounts per book, reservations not necessary—just show up). Kid-sized bikes are available, as are nifty tandem attachments that hook on to a parent's bike.

On the day tour, you'll pedal with a pack of 10-20 riders, mostly in parks and along bike lanes, with a lunch stop in the Tuileries Garden (tours leave daily rain or shine at 11:00, April-Oct at 15:00 as well, no minimum number of participants required). Livelier night tours follow a route past floodlit monuments and include a boat cruise on the Seine (April-Oct daily at 19:00, March daily at 18:00, end of Feb and all of Nov Tue, Thu, and Sat-Sun at 18:00, no night tours Dec-mid-Feb). Both tours meet at the south pillar of the Eiffel Tower, where you'll get a short history lesson, then walk six minutes to the Fat Tire office to pick up bikes (helmets available upon request at no extra charge, for contact info see listing on page 44). They also run bike tours to Versailles and Giverny (reservations required, see website for details). Their office has Internet access with English keyboards.

Fat Tire's pricey four-hour **City Segway Tours**—on stand-up motorized scooters—are novel in that you learn to ride a Segway while exploring Paris (you'll get the hang of it after about half an hour). These tours take no more than eight people at a time, so reservations are

required (€85, daily at 9:30, April-Oct also at 14:00 and 18:30, March and Nov also at 14:00, tel. 01 56 58 10 54, www.citysegwaytours.com).

**TripUp Pedicab Tours**—You'll see these space-age pedicabs *(cyclopolitains)* everywhere in central Paris. The hard-pedaling, free-spirited drivers (who get some electrical assistance) are happy to either transport you from point A to B or give you a tour at a snail's pace—which is a lovely way to experience Paris (€40-50/hour, www.tripup.fr).

## Weekend Tour Packages for Students in Paris

Andy Steves (Rick's son) runs **Weekend Student Adventures**, offering experiential three-day weekend tours for €250 designed for American students studying abroad (see www.wsaeurope.com for details on tours of Paris and other great European cities).

## Excursions from Paris

Most of the local guides listed earlier will do excursion tours from Paris using your rental car. Or consider these companies, which provide transportation:

**Paris Webservices,** a reliable outfit, offers many services, including day trips with English-speaking chauffeur-guides in cushy minivans for private groups to all the destinations covered in this book (figure €90-120/person for groups of 4 or more, use promo code "RSteves 77" and show current edition of this book for a 10 percent discount on tours and airport transfers—discount not valid on services they book for you through other companies; see contact info in listing on page 655).

Many companies offer bus tours to regional sights, including all of the day trips described in this book. **Paris Vision** runs uninspired minivan and bus tours to several popular regional destinations, including the Loire Valley, Champagne region, D-Day beaches, and Mont St-Michel (tel. 01 42 60 30 01, www.parisvision.com). Their minivan tours are pricier, but more personal and given in English, and most offer convenient pickup at your hotel (half-day tour about €80/person, day tour about €190/person). Their full-size bus tours (operated by their Cityrama subsidiary, www.pariscityrama.fr) are multilingual, mass-marketed, and mediocre at best, but cheaper than the minivan tours—worthwhile for some travelers simply for the ease of transportation to the sights (about €70-150, destinations include Versailles, Giverny, and more).

For recommendations on guided tours to places farther afield, see page 658 in the appendix.

# SIGHTS IN PARIS

The sights listed in this chapter are arranged by neighborhood for handy sightseeing. When you see a ✪ in a listing, it means the sight is covered in much more depth in one of my walks or self-guided tours. This is why Paris' most important attractions get the least coverage in this chapter.

For tips on sightseeing, see page 17 in the Introduction. For advice on saving money, see "Affording Paris' Sights" on page 64. Also, be sure to check www.ricksteves.com/update for any significant changes that may have occurred since this book was printed.

## Paris Museum Pass

In Paris there are two classes of sightseers—those with a Paris Museum Pass, and those who stand in line. The pass admits you to many of Paris' most popular sights, allowing you to skip ticket-buying lines. You'll save time and money by getting this pass.

### Buying the Pass

The pass pays for itself with four key admissions in two days (for example, the Louvre, Orsay, Sainte-Chapelle, and Versailles), and it lets you skip the ticket line at most sights (2 days/€39, 4 days/€54, 6 days/€69, no youth or senior discount). It's sold at participating museums, monuments, FNAC department stores, and TIs (even at airports; see the Paris Connections chapter). Try to avoid buying the pass at a major museum (such as the Louvre), where the supply can be spotty and lines long. For more info, visit www.paris museumpass.com or call 01 44 61 96 60.

To see if the pass is a good value for your trip, tally up what you want to see from the list in the next section. And remember, an advantage of the pass is that you skip to the front of most (but not all) lines, which can save hours of waiting, especially in summer. Another benefit of the pass is that you can pop into lesser sights that otherwise might not be worth the expense.

**Families:** The pass isn't worth buying for children and teens, as most museums are free or discounted for those under 18 (teenagers may need to show ID as proof of age). If parents have a Museum Pass, kids can usually skip the ticket lines as well. A few places, such as the Arc de Triomphe and Army Museum, require everyone—even passholders—to stand in line to collect your child's free ticket.

## What the Paris Museum Pass Covers

Most of the sights listed in this chapter are covered by the pass. It even covers Versailles' two major sights—worth €25 alone. Notable exceptions that are *not* covered by the pass include: the Eiffel Tower, Montparnasse Tower, Marmottan Museum, Opéra Garnier, Notre-Dame Treasury, Jacquemart-André Museum, Grand Palais, Catacombs, Montmartre Museum, Sacré-Cœur's dome, Dalí Museum, Museum of Erotic Art, and the ladies of Pigalle. The pass also does not cover these recommended sights outside Paris: Vaux-le-Vicomte, Château d'Auvers in Auvers-sur-Oise, and Giverny (though it does include Fontainebleau and Chantilly).

Here's a list of key included sights and their admission prices without the pass:

### In Paris

| | |
|---|---|
| Louvre (€11) | Notre-Dame Tower (€8.50) |
| Orsay Museum (€9) | Paris Archaeological Crypt (€4) |
| Orangerie Museum (€7.50) | Paris Sewer Tour (€4.30) |
| Sainte-Chapelle (€8.50) | Cluny Museum (€8) |
| Arc de Triomphe (€9.50) | Pompidou Center (€11-13) |
| Rodin Museum (€6) | Jewish Art and History Museum (€7) |
| Army Museum (€9) | National Maritime Museum (€7) |
| Conciergerie (€8.50) | Delacroix Museum (€5) |
| Panthéon (€8.50) | Quai Branly Museum (€8.50) |
| Architecture and Monuments Museum (€8) | |

### Outside Paris

Versailles (€25 total—€15 for Château, €10 for Trianon Palaces and Domaine de Marie-Antoinette)
Château of Chantilly (€14)
Château of Fontainebleau (€10)

## Activating and Using the Pass

The pass is activated the first time you use it—you must write the starting date on the pass. Validate it only when you're ready to

SIGHTS IN PARIS

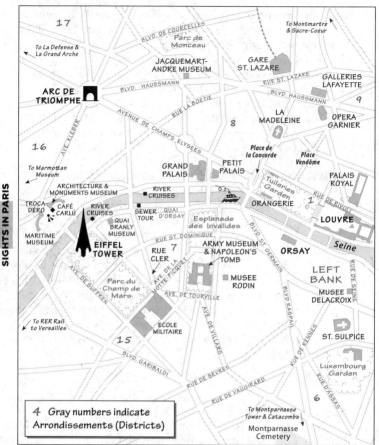

17

To La Defense &
La Grand Arche

BLVD. DE COURCELLES

Parc de
Monceau

To Montmartre
& Sacre-Coeur

JACQUEMART-
ANDRE MUSEUM

GARE
ST. LAZARE

RUE ST. LAZARE

GALLERIES
LAFAYETTE

ARC DE
TRIOMPHE

BLVD. HAUSSMANN

RUE LA BOETIE

BLVD. HAUSSMANN

9

AVENUE DE CHAMPS ELYSEES

8

LA
MADELEINE

OPERA
GARNIER

16

AVE. KLEBER

Place de
la Concorde

Place
Vendôme

PALAIS
ROYAL

To Marmottan
Museum

GRAND
PALAIS

PETIT
PALAIS

Tuileries
Garden

RUE DE RIVOLI

ARCHITECTURE &
MONUMENTS MUSEUM

RIVER
CRUISES

ORANGERIE

1

LOUVRE

TROCA-
DERO

CAFÉ
CARLÚ

RIVER
CRUISES

SEWER
TOUR

QUAI
D'ORSAY

ORSAY

Seine

MARITIME
MUSEUM

QUAI
BRANLY
MUSEUM

Esplanade
des Invalides

RUE DE SEINE

EIFFEL
TOWER

RUE
CLER

7

RUE ST. DOMINIQUE

ARMY MUSEUM
& NAPOLEON'S
TOMB

BLVD. ST. GERMAIN

LEFT
BANK

AVE. DE SUFFREN

AVE. DE LA
MOTTE-PICQUET

MUSEE
RODIN

MUSEE
DELACROIX

Parc du
Champ de
Mars

AVE. DE TOURVILLE

AVE. DE VILLARS

BLVD. RASPAIL

ST. SULPICE

15

ECOLE
MILITAIRE

RUE DE RENNES

Luxembourg
Garden

RUE D'ASSAS

To RER Rail
to Versailles

BLVD. GARIBALDI

RUE DE SEVRES

RUE DE VAUGIRARD

6

4  Gray numbers indicate
Arrondissements (Districts)

To Montparnasse
Tower & Catacombs

Montparnasse
Cemetery

tackle the covered sights on consecutive days. Plan carefully to
make the most of your pass. First, make sure the sights you want
to visit will be open (many museums are closed Mondays or Tuesdays). The pass provides the best value on days when sights close
later, letting you extend your sightseeing day. Take advantage of
these late hours. For instance, the Arc de Triomphe and Pompidou Center are always open later, while the Notre-Dame Tower,
Sainte-Chapelle, Louvre, Orsay, and Army Museum and Napoleon's Tomb have late hours on selected evenings (or at certain
times of year). On days that you don't have pass coverage, plan to
visit free sights and those not covered by the pass (see page 64 for
a list of free sights).

To use your pass at sights, boldly walk to the front of the ticket
line (after going through security if necessary), hold up your pass,
and ask the ticket-taker: *"Entrez, pass?"* (ahn-tray pahs). You'll ei-

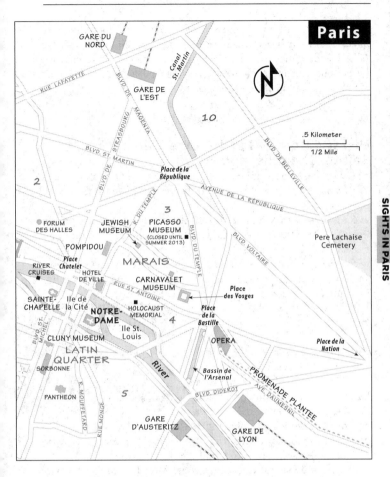

ther be allowed to enter at that point, or you'll be directed to a special entrance. For major sights, such as the Louvre and Orsay museums, I've identified passholder entrances on the maps in this book. Don't be shy—some places (Sainte-Chapelle and the Arc de Triomphe, in particular) have long lines in which passholders wait needlessly. At a few sights (including the Louvre, Sainte-Chapelle, Notre-Dame Tower, and Château de Versailles), everyone has to shuffle through the slow-moving baggage-check lines for security—but you still save time by avoiding the ticket line.

## Without a Pass

If a pass does not fit your needs, you do have other line-skipping options. TIs and FNAC department stores sell individual fast-track *"coupe-file"* tickets for some sights, which allow you to use the Museum Pass entrance. Several sights, such as the Eiffel Tower and Monet's gardens at Giverny, sell advance tickets online (see page 31 for more on both of these options). Certain key sights have ticket-vending machines that save time in line but only accept cash (usually no bills larger than €20) or chip-and-PIN cards (so most American credit cards won't work).

# Sights

## Historic Core of Paris: Notre-Dame, Sainte-Chapelle, and More

Many of these sights are covered in detail in the ✪ Historic Paris Walk chapter. If a sight is covered in the walk, I've listed only its essentials here.

▲▲▲**Notre-Dame Cathedral (Cathédrale Notre-Dame de Paris)**—This 700-year-old cathedral is packed with history and tourists. With a pair of 200-foot-tall bell towers, a facade studded with ornate statuary, beautiful stained-glass rose windows, famous gargoyles, a picture-perfect Seine-side location, and textbook flying buttresses, there's a good reason that this cathedral of "Our Lady" *(Notre-Dame)* is France's most famous church.

Check out the facade: Mary with the baby Jesus (in rose window) above the 28 Kings of Judah (statues that were beheaded during the Revolution). Stroll the interior, which echoes with history. Then wander around the exterior, through a forest of frilly buttresses, watched over by a fleet of whimsical gargoyles. The long line to the left is to climb the famous tower.

**Cost and Hours:** Cathedral—free, Mon-Fri 8:00-18:45, Sat-Sun 8:00-19:15; Treasury—€4, not covered by Museum Pass, Mon-Fri 9:30-17:40, Sat-Sun 9:30-18:10; audioguide—€5, free English tours—normally Wed-Thu at 14:15, Sat-Sun at 14:30; Mo: Cité, Hôtel de Ville, or St. Michel; tel. 01 42 34 56 10, www.notre damedeparis.fr.

For more on Notre-Dame (including information on weekday and Sun Mass, as well as organ performances and viewings of the Crown of Thorns), ✪ see page 96 in the Historic Paris Walk chapter.

**Tower:** You can climb to the top of the facade between the towers, and then to the top of the south tower, 400 steps total, for a grand view (€8.50, covered by Museum Pass but no bypass line for passholders; daily April-Sept 10:00-18:30, Sat-Sun until 23:00 in July-Aug, Oct-March 10:00-17:30, last entry 45 minutes before closing; to avoid long lines, arrive before 10:00 or after 17:00 April-

Sept—16:00 Oct-March—tel. 01 53 10 07 00, http://notre-dame-de-paris.monuments-nationaux.fr).

**Paris Archaeological Crypt**—This is a worthwhile 15-minute stop with your Museum Pass. You'll visit Roman ruins, trace the street plan of the medieval village, and see diagrams of how early Paris grew, all thoughtfully explained in English.

The first few displays put the ruins in historical context. Three models show the growth of Paris—from an uninhabited riverside plot to the Roman town of Lutèce, then to an early-medieval city with a church that preceded Notre-Dame. A fourth model shows the current Notre-Dame surrounded by buildings, along with the old, straight road—Rue Neuve de Notre-Dame—that led up to the church and ran right down what is now the center of the museum. The ruins in the middle of the museum are a confusing mix of foundations from all these time periods, including parts of the old Rue Neuve de Notre-Dame.

Press the buttons on the display cases to light up a particular section, such as the oldest (Gallo-Roman) rampart. Along the far side of the museum, you'll see a medieval Foundling's Hospital, a well-preserved Gallo-Roman-paved room, and a Roman building with "hypocaustal" heating (narrow passages pumped full of hot air to heat the room).

**Cost and Hours:** €4, covered by Museum Pass, Tue-Sun 10:00-18:00, closed Mon, last entry 30 minutes before closing, enter 100 yards in front of cathedral, tel. 01 55 42 50 10.

**▲Deportation Memorial (Mémorial de la Déportation)**—Climb down the steps into this memorial dedicated to the 200,000 French victims of the Nazi concentration camps. As Paris disappears above you, this monument draws you into the victims' experience. Once underground you enter a one-way hallway studded with tiny lights commemorating the dead, leading you to an eternal flame.

**Cost and Hours:** Free, April-Sept Tue-Sun 10:00-19:00, Oct-March Tue-Sun 10:00-18:00, closed Mon year-round, may randomly close at other times; at the east tip of the island named Ile de la Cité, behind Notre-Dame and near Ile St. Louis (Mo: Cité); tel. 06 14 67 54 98.

**Ile St. Louis**—The residential island behind Notre-Dame is known for its restaurants (see the Eating in Paris chapter), great ice cream, and shops (along Rue St. Louis-en-l'Ile).

○ Also see page 105 in the Historic Paris Walk chapter.

**Cité Métropolitain Stop and Flower Market**—On Place Louis Lépine, between the Notre-Dame and Sainte-Chapelle cathedrals, is an early-19th-century subway entrance and a flower market (which chirps with a bird market on Sun).

# Paris at a Glance

▲▲▲**Notre-Dame Cathedral** Paris' most beloved church, with towers and gargoyles. **Hours:** Cathedral Mon-Fri 8:00-18:45, Sat-Sun 8:00-19:15; tower daily April-Sept 10:00-18:30, Sat-Sun until 23:00 in July-Aug, Oct-March 10:00-17:30; Treasury Mon-Fri 9:30-17:40, Sat-Sun 9:30-18:10. See page 56.

▲▲▲**Sainte-Chapelle** Gothic cathedral with peerless stained glass. **Hours:** Daily March-Oct 9:30-18:00, Wed until 21:30 mid-May-mid-Sept, Nov-Feb 9:00-17:00. See page 60.

▲▲▲**Louvre** Europe's oldest and greatest museum, starring *Mona Lisa* and *Venus de Milo*. **Hours:** Wed-Mon 9:00-18:00, Wed and Fri until 21:45, closed Tue. See page 61.

▲▲▲**Orsay Museum** Nineteenth-century art, including Europe's greatest Impressionist collection. **Hours:** Tue-Sun 9:30-18:00, Thu until 21:45, closed Mon. See page 64.

▲▲▲**Eiffel Tower** Paris' soaring exclamation point. **Hours:** Daily mid-June-Aug 9:00-24:00, Sept-mid-June 9:30-23:00. See page 66.

▲▲▲**Champs-Elysées** Paris' grand boulevard. **Hours:** Always open. See page 77.

▲▲▲**Versailles** The ultimate royal palace (Château), with a Hall of Mirrors, vast gardens, a grand canal, plus a queen's playground (Trianon Palaces and Domaine de Marie-Antoinette). **Hours:** Château April-Oct Tue-Sun 9:00-18:30, Nov-March Tue-Sun 9:00-17:30, closed Mon year-round. Trianon/Domaine April-Oct Tue-Sun 12:00-18:30, Nov-March Tue-Sun 12:00-17:30, closed Mon year-round; in winter only the two Trianon Palaces are open. Gardens generally open April-Oct daily 9:00-20:30, Nov-March Tue-Sun 8:00-18:00, closed Mon. See the Versailles chapter.

▲▲**Orangerie Museum** Monet's water lilies, plus works by Utrillo, Cézanne, Renoir, Matisse, and Picasso, in a lovely setting. **Hours:** Wed-Mon 9:00-18:00, closed Tue. See page 63.

▲▲**Army Museum and Napoleon's Tomb** The emperor's imposing tomb, flanked by museums of France's wars. **Hours:** Museum—daily April-Sept 10:00-18:00, may be open Tue until 21:00, Oct-March 10:00-17:00, closed first Mon of month year-round. Tomb—daily April-June and Sept 10:00-18:00, may be open Tue until 21:00; July-Aug 10:00-19:00, may be open Tue until 21:00; Oct-March 10:00-17:00, closed first Mon of month Sept-May. See page 69.

▲▲**Rodin Museum** Works by the greatest sculptor since Michelangelo, with many statues in a peaceful garden. **Hours:** Tue-Sun 10:00-17:45, Wed until 20:45, closed Mon. See page 70.

▲▲**Marmottan Museum** Untouristy art museum focusing on Monet. **Hours:** Tue-Sun 10:00-18:00, Thu until 20:00, closed Mon. See page 70.

▲▲**Cluny Museum** Medieval art with unicorn tapestries. **Hours:** Wed-Mon 9:15-17:45, closed Tue. See page 71.

▲▲**Arc de Triomphe** Triumphal arch with viewpoint, marking start of Champs-Elysées. **Hours:** Interior—daily April-Sept 10:00-23:00, Oct-March 10:00-22:30. See page 77.

▲▲**Jacquemart-André Museum** Art-strewn mansion. **Hours:** Daily 10:00-18:00, Mon and Sat until 21:00 during special exhibits. See page 80.

▲▲**Pompidou Center** Modern art in colorful building with city views. **Hours:** Wed-Mon 11:00-21:00, closed Tue. See page 86.

▲▲**Sacré-Cœur and Montmartre** White basilica atop Montmartre with spectacular views. **Hours:** Daily 6:00-22:30; dome climb daily May-Sept 9:00-19:00, Oct-April 9:00-17:00. See page 90.

▲**Panthéon** Neoclassical monument celebrating the struggles of the French. **Hours:** Daily 10:00-18:30 in summer, until 18:00 in winter. See page 74.

▲**Opéra Garnier** Grand belle époque theater with a modern ceiling by Chagall. **Hours:** Generally daily 10:00-17:00, mid-July-Aug until 18:00. See page 78.

▲**La Défense and La Grande Arche** The city's own "little Manhattan" business district and its colossal modern arch. **Hours:** Always open. See page 84.

▲**Jewish Art and History Museum** Displays history of Judaism in Europe. **Hours:** Sun-Fri 11:00-18:00, closed Sat. See page 86.

▲**Carnavalet Museum** Paris' history wrapped up in a 16th-century mansion. **Hours:** Tue-Sun 10:00-18:00, closed Mon. See page 87.

▲**Père Lachaise Cemetery** Final home of Paris' illustrious dead. **Hours:** Mon-Fri 8:00-18:00, Sat 8:30-18:00, Sun 9:00-18:00, closes at 17:30 in winter. See page 90.

▲▲▲**Sainte-Chapelle**—The interior of this 13th-century chapel is a triumph of Gothic church architecture. Built to house Jesus' Crown of Thorns, Sainte-Chapelle is jam-packed with stained-glass windows, bathed in colorful light, and slippery with the drool of awestruck tourists. Ignore the humdrum exterior and climb the stairs into the sanctuary, where more than 1,100 Bible scenes—from the Creation to the Passion to Judgment Day—are illustrated by light and glass. There are tentative plans for Sainte-Chapelle to have a shared entrance with the Conciergerie at some point in the future.

**Cost and Hours:** €8.50, €12.50 combo-ticket with Conciergerie, free under age 18, covered by Museum Pass, audioguide-€4.50; daily March-Oct 9:30-18:00, Wed until 21:30 mid-May-mid-Sept, Nov-Feb 9:00-17:00; last entry 30 minutes before closing, be prepared for long lines, evening concerts—see page 496, 4 Boulevard du Palais, Mo: Cité, tel. 01 53 40 60 80, http://sainte-chapelle.monuments-nationaux.fr.

For a detailed tour of the cathedral's interior, ✪ see page 112 in the Historic Paris Walk chapter.

▲**Conciergerie**—Marie-Antoinette was imprisoned here, as were Louis XVI, Robespierre, Danton, and many others on their way to the guillotine. Exhibits with good English descriptions trace the history of the building and give some insight into prison life. You can also relive the drama in Marie-Antoinette's cell

on the day of her execution—complete with dummies and period furniture.

**Cost and Hours:** €8.50, €12.50 combo-ticket with Sainte-Chapelle, covered by Museum Pass, daily March-Oct 9:30-18:00, Nov-Feb 9:00-17:00, last entry 30 minutes before closing, 2 Boulevard du Palais, Mo: Cité, tel. 01 53 40 60 80, http://conciergerie.monuments-nationaux.fr.

✪ Also see page 118 in the Historic Paris Walk chapter.

▲**Paris Plages (Paris Beaches)**—The Riviera it's not, but this string of fanciful faux beaches—assembled in summer along a one-mile stretch of the Right Bank of the Seine—is a fun place to stroll, play, and people-watch on a sunny day. Each summer, the Paris city government closes the embankment's highway and trucks in potted palm trees, hammocks, lounge chairs, and 2,000 tons of sand to create colorful urban beaches. You'll also find "beach cafés," climbing walls, prefab pools, trampolines, *boules*, a library, beach volleyball, badminton, and Frisbee areas in three zones: sandy, grassy, and wood-tiled. (Other less-central areas of town, such as Bassin de la Vilette, have their own *plages*.)

**Cost and Hours:** Free, mid-July-mid-Aug daily 8:00-24:00, no beach off-season; on Right Bank of Seine, just north of Ile de la Cité, between Pont des Arts and Pont de Sully; for information, go to www.paris.fr, click on "English," then "Visit," then "Highlights."

## Major Museums Neighborhood

Paris' grandest park, the Tuileries Garden, was once the private property of kings and queens. Today it links the Louvre, Orangerie, Jeu de Paume, and Orsay museums. And across from the Louvre are the tranquil, historic courtyards of the Palais Royal. Shoppers like the boutique stroll (see map on page 63 and description on page 482).

▲▲▲**Louvre (Musée du Louvre)**—This is Europe's oldest, biggest, greatest, and second-most-crowded museum (after the Vatican). Housed in a U-shaped, 16th-century palace (accentuated by a 20th-century glass pyramid), the Louvre is Paris' top museum and one of its key landmarks. It's home to *Mona Lisa*, *Venus de Milo,* and hall after hall of Greek and Roman masterpieces, medieval jewels, Michelangelo statues, and paintings by the greatest artists from the Renaissance to the Romantics (mid-1800s).

Touring the Louvre can be overwhelming, so be selective. Focus

on the Denon wing (south, along the river), with Greek sculptures, Italian paintings (by Raphael and da Vinci), and—of course—French paintings (Neoclassical and Romantic), and the adjoining Sully wing, with Egyptian artifacts and more French paintings. For extra credit, tackle the Richelieu wing (north, away from the river), displaying works from ancient Mesopotamia (today's Iraq), as well as French, Dutch, and Northern art.

**Cost and Hours:** €11, free on first Sun of month, covered by Museum Pass, tickets good all day, reentry allowed; Wed-Mon 9:00-18:00, Wed and Fri until 21:45 (except on holidays), closed

Tue, galleries start shutting 30 minutes before closing; last entry 45 minutes before closing; crowds worst in the morning (arrive 30 minutes before opening) and all day Sun, Mon, and Wed; videoguides and guided tours available—see page 124, several cafés, tel. 01 40 20 53 17, recorded info tel. 01 40 20 51 51, www.louvre.fr.

**Getting There:** It's at the Palais Royal-Musée du Louvre Métro stop. (The old Louvre Métro stop, called Louvre-Rivoli, is farther from the entrance.) Bus #69 also runs past the Louvre.

○ See the Louvre Tour chapter.

**Palais Royal Courtyards**—Across from the Louvre are the lovely courtyards of the stately Palais Royal. Although the palace is closed to the public, the courtyards are open. Enter through a whimsical (locals say tacky) courtyard filled with stubby, striped columns and playful fountains (with fun, reflective metal balls). Next, you'll pass into another, perfectly Parisian garden. This is where in-the-know Parisians come to take a quiet break, walk their poodles and kids, or enjoy a rendezvous—amid flowers and surrounded by a serene arcade and a handful of historic restaurants. Bring a picnic and create your own quiet break, or have a drink at one of the outdoor cafés at the courtyard's northern end. This is Paris.

Though tranquil today, this was once a hotbed of political activism. The palace was built in the 17th century by Louis XIII and eventually became the head-quarters of the powerful Dukes of Orléans. Because the Dukes' digs were off-limits to the police, some shocking free-thinking took root here. This was the meeting place for the debating clubs—the precursors to modern political parties. During the Revolution, palace resident Duke Phillip (nicknamed Phillip Egalité for his progressive ideas) advocated a constitutional monarchy, and he voted in favor of beheading Louis XVI—his own cousin. Phillip hoped his liberal attitudes would spare him from the Revolutionaries, but he, too, was guillotined. His son, Louis-Philippe, became France's first constitutional monarch (r. 1830-1848). The palace's courtyards were backdrops for a riotous social and political scene, filled with lively café culture, revolutionaries, rabble-rousers, scoundrels, and...Madame Tussaud's first wax shop (she used the severed heads of guillotine victims to model her sculptures).

Exiting the courtyard at the side facing away from the Seine brings you to the Galeries Colbert and Vivienne, attractive examples of shopping arcades from the early 1900s (see page 492).

# Major Museums Neighborhood

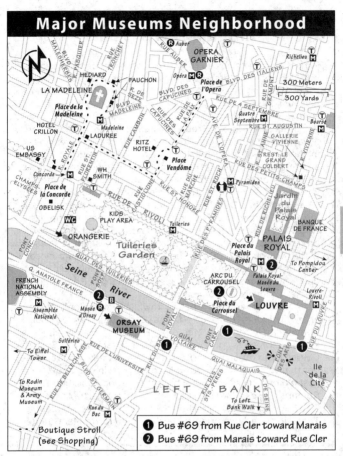

**①** Bus #69 from Rue Cler toward Marais
**②** Bus #69 from Marais toward Rue Cler

**Cost and Hours:** Courtyards are free and always open. The Palais Royal is directly north of the Louvre on Rue de Rivoli (Mo: Palais Royal-Musée du Louvre).

▲▲**Orangerie Museum (Musée de l'Orangerie)**—Located in the Tuileries Garden and drenched by natural light from

skylights, the Orangerie (oh-rahn-zhuh-ree) is the closest you'll ever come to stepping right into an Impressionist painting. Start with the museum's claim to fame: Monet's *Water Lilies*. Then head downstairs to enjoy the manageable collection of select works by Utrillo, Cézanne, Renoir, Matisse, and Picasso.

## Affording Paris' Sights

Paris is an expensive city for tourists, with lots of pricey sights, but—fortunately—lots of freebies, too. Smart, budget-minded travelers begin by buying and getting the most out of a **Paris Museum Pass** (see page 52), then considering these frugal sightseeing options.

**Free (or Almost Free) Museums:** Some museums are always free (with the possible exception of special exhibits), including the Carnavalet, Petit Palais, Victor Hugo's House, and Fragonard Perfume Museum. Many of Paris' most famous museums offer free entry on the first Sunday of the month, including the Louvre, Orsay, Rodin, Cluny, Pompidou Center, Quai Branly, and Delacroix museums. These sights are free on the first Sunday of off-season months: the Arc de Triomphe (Oct-March) and Versailles (Nov-March). Expect big crowds on free days. You can also visit the Orsay Museum for free at 17:00 (or Thu at 21:00), an hour before the museum closes. One of the best everyday values is the Rodin Museum's garden, where it costs just €1 to experience many of Rodin's finest works in a lovely outdoor setting.

**Other Freebies:** Many worthwhile sights don't charge entry, including the Notre-Dame Cathedral, Père Lachaise Cemetery, Deportation Memorial, Holocaust Memorial, Paris Plages (summers only), Sacré-Cœur Basilica, St. Sulpice Church (with organ recital), and La Défense mall. And remember that the neighborhood walks described in this book don't cost a dime unless you enter a sight (Historic Paris, Left Bank, Champs-Elysées, Marais, Rue Cler, and Montmartre).

Paris' glorious, entertaining parks are free, of course. These include Luxembourg Garden, Champ de Mars (under

**Cost and Hours:** €7.50, €5 after 17:00, under 18 free, €14 combo-ticket with Orsay Museum (valid for four days, one visit per sight), covered by Museum Pass; Wed-Mon 9:00-18:00, closed Tue, galleries shut down 15 minutes before closing time; audioguide-€5, €6 English tours usually offered Mon and Thu at 14:30; located in Tuileries Garden near Place de la Concorde (Mo: Concorde), 15-minute stroll from the Orsay, tel. 01 44 77 80 07, www.musee-orangerie.fr.

 See the Orangerie Museum Tour chapter.

▲▲▲**Orsay Museum (Musée d'Orsay)**—The Orsay boasts Europe's greatest collection of Impressionist works. It might be less important than the Louvre—but it's more purely enjoyable.

The Orsay, housed in an atmospheric old train station, picks up where the Louvre leaves off: the second half of the 19th century. This is art from the tumultuous time that began when revolutions swept across Europe in 1848 and ended when World War I broke the Eiffel Tower), Tuileries Garden (between the Louvre and Place de la Concorde), Palais Royal Courtyards, Jardin des Plantes, Parc Monceau, the Promenade Plantée walk, and Versailles' gardens (except when the fountains perform on Tue late May-late June and weekends April-Oct).

**Reduced Prices:** Several sights offer a discount if you enter later in the day, including the Orsay (Fri-Wed after 16:15 and Thu after 18:00), the Orangerie (after 17:00), the Army Museum and Napoleon's Tomb (after 17:00), and the Château of Fontainebleau (after 17:00 April-Sept or 16:00 Oct-March). The Eiffel Tower costs less if you're willing to restrict your visit to the two lower levels—and even less if you're willing to use the stairs.

**Free Concerts:** Venues offering free or cheap (€6-8) concerts include the American Church, Hôtel des Invalides, St. Sulpice Church, La Madeleine Church, and Notre-Dame Cathedral. For a listing of free concerts, check *Pariscope* magazine (under the "Musique" section) and look for events marked *entrée libre*.

**Good-Value Tours:** At €12-15, Paris Walks' tours are a good value. The €11-13 Seine River cruises, best after dark, are also worthwhile. The Bus #69 Sightseeing Tour, which costs only the price of a transit ticket, could be the best deal of all.

**Pricey...but worth it?** Certain big-ticket items—primarily the top of the Eiffel Tower, the Louvre, and Versailles—are expensive and crowded, but offer once-in-a-lifetime experiences. All together they amount to less than a ticket to Disneyland—only these are real.

out in 1914. Begin with the conservative art of the mid-1800s—careful, idealized Neoclassicism (with a few rebels mixed in). Then tour the late 1800s, when the likes of Manet, Monet, Degas, and Renoir jolted the art world with their colorful, lively new invention, Impressionism. (Somewhere in there, *Whistler's Mother* sits quietly.) The Orsay also displays the works of their artistic descendants, the post-Impressionists: Cézanne, Van Gogh, Gauguin, Seurat, and  Toulouse-Lautrec. On the mezzanine level, waltz through Rodin sculptures and Art Nouveau exhibits, and finish in the Grand Ballroom, which shows the chandeliered elegance of this former train station.

**Cost and Hours:** €9, €6.50 Fri-Wed after 16:15 and Thu after 18:00, free on first Sun of month and when ticket booth stops selling tickets at 17:00 (Thu at 21:00), covered by Museum Pass, €14 combo-ticket with Orangerie Museum (valid for four days, one visit per sight); Tue-Sun 9:30-18:00, Thu until 21:45, closed Mon, Impressionist galleries start shutting 45 minutes before closing, last entry one hour before closing (45 minutes before on Thu); crowded on Tue, when Louvre is closed; guided tours and audioguides available—see page 153, cafés and a restaurant, tel. 01 40 49 48 14, www.musee-orsay.fr.

**Getting There:** The museum, at 1 Rue de la Légion d'Honneur, sits above the RER-C stop called Musée d'Orsay; the nearest Métro stop is Solférino, three blocks southeast of the Orsay. Bus #69 also stops at the Orsay. From the Louvre, it's a lovely 15-minute walk through the Tuileries Garden and across the pedestrian bridge to the Orsay.

✪ See the Orsay Museum Tour chapter.

## Eiffel Tower and Nearby

▲▲▲**Eiffel Tower (La Tour Eiffel)**—Built on the 100th anniversary of the French Revolution (and in the spirit of the Industrial Revolution), the tower was the center-piece of a World Expo designed simply to show off what people could build in 1889. For decades it was the tallest structure the world had ever known, and though it's since been eclipsed, it's still the most visited monument. Ride the elevators to the top of its 1,063 feet for expansive views that stretch 40 miles. Then descend to the two lower levels, where the views are arguably even better, since the monuments are more recognizable.

**Cost and Hours:** €14 all the way to the top, €8.50 for just the two lower levels, €5 to skip the elevator line and climb the stairs to the first or second level (€3.50 if you're under 25), not covered by Museum Pass; daily mid-June-Aug 9:00-24:00, last ascent to top at 23:00 and to lower levels at 23:30; Sept-mid-June 9:30-23:00, last ascent to top at 22:00 and to lower levels at 22:30 (elevator), access to the stairs closes at 18:00 in off-season; cafés and great view restaurants, Mo: Bir-Hakeim and Trocadéro or Champ de Mars-Tour Eiffel RER stop (each about a 10-minute walk away).

**Reservations:** Since one- to two-hour waits are common, it's wise to make a reservation well in advance of your visit. An online reservation system allows you to book a half-hour time slot

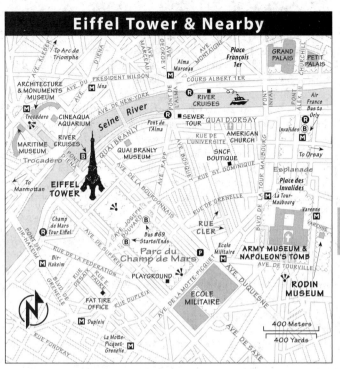

# Eiffel Tower & Nearby

to begin your ascent (and skip the initial entry line)—check www.
tour-eiffel.fr (tel. 01 44 11 23 23).

○ See the Eiffel Tower Tour chapter (which includes more tips
on making reservations online and avoiding lines).

▲**Architecture and Monuments Museum (Cité de
l'Architecture et du Patrimoine)**—This museum, on the east
side of Place du Trocadéro, takes you through 1,000 years of
French architecture, brilliantly displaying casts and models of
some of France's most cherished monuments from the 11th to 21st
centuries. Gaze into the eyes of medieval statues and wander under
doorways, tympanums, and arches from the abbey of Cluny, Chartres Cathedral, Château de Chambord, and much more. You'll see
how colorfully painted the chapels were in Romanesque churches
and discover a vast array of models from modern projects, along
with thought-provoking designs for low-income housing. The
views from the upper rooms to the Eiffel Tower are sensational, as
are those from the terrace of the on-site café, Café Carlu.

**Cost and Hours:** €8, covered by Museum Pass, audiogu-
ide-€3; Wed-Mon 11:00-19:00, Thu until 21:00, closed Tue; excellent English explanations, great view café (reasonable prices,
open same hours as museum and does not require entry into the

museum), 1 Place du Trocadéro, Mo: Trocadéro, RER: Champ de Mars-Tour Eiffel, tel. 01 58 51 52 00, www.citechaillot.fr.

**Quai Branly Museum (Museé du Quai Branly)**—This is the best collection I've seen anywhere of so-called Primitive Art from Africa, Polynesia, Asia, and America. It's presented in a wild, organic, and strikingly modern building that caused a stir in Paris when it opened in 2006. Masks, statuettes, musical instruments, clothes, voodoo dolls, and a variety of temporary exhibitions and activities are artfully presented and exquisitely lit. It's not, however, accompanied by much printed English information—to really appreciate the exhibit, you need to rent the audioguide. Even if you skip the museum, drop by its peaceful garden café for fine Eiffel Tower views (closes 30 minutes before museum) and enjoy the intriguing gardens. The pedestrian bridge that crosses the river and runs up to the museum has terrific views of the Eiffel Tower.

**Cost and Hours:** €8.50, free on first Sun of the month, covered by Museum Pass, audioguide-€5; museum—Tue-Sun 11:00-19:00, Thu-Sat until 21:00, closed Mon, ticket office closes one hour before closing; gardens—Tue-Sun 9:15-19:30, Thu-Sat until 21:15, closed Mon; 37 Quai Branly, 10-minute walk east (upriver) of Eiffel Tower, along the river (RER: Champ de Mars-Tour Eiffel or Pont de l'Alma), tel. 01 56 61 70 00, www.quaibranly.fr.

**National Maritime Museum (Musée National de la Marine)**—This extensive museum houses an amazing collection of ship models, submarines, torpedoes, cannonballs, *beaucoup* bowsprits, and naval you-name-it, including a small boat made for Napoleon. Don't miss the model and story of how the obelisk on Place de la Concorde was delivered from Egypt to Paris entirely by waterways (behind stairs leading down to special exhibits space). Take advantage of the audioguide that explains key exhibits and adds important context to your visit. Kids love it, too.

**Cost and Hours:** €7, 26 and under free, includes audioguide, covered by Museum Pass; Mon and Wed-Fri 11:00-18:00, Sat-Sun 11:00-19:00, closed Tue; on left side of Place du Trocadéro with your back to Eiffel Tower, tel. 01 53 65 69 69, www.musee-marine.fr.

**▲Paris Sewer Tour (Les Egouts de Paris)**—Discover what happens after you flush. This quick, interesting, and slightly stinky visit (a perfumed hanky helps) takes you along a few hundred yards of water tunnels in the world's first underground sewer system. Pick up the helpful English self-guided tour, then drop down into Jean Valjean's world of tunnels, rats, and manhole covers. (Victor Hugo was friends with the sewer inspector

when he wrote *Les Misérables*.) You'll pass well-organized displays with helpful English information explaining the history of water distribution in Paris, from Roman times to the present. The evolution of this amazing network of sewers is surprisingly fascinating. More than 1,500 miles of tunnels carry 317 million gallons of water daily through this underworld. It's the world's longest sewer system—so long, they say, that if it was laid out straight, it would stretch from Paris all the way to Istanbul.

It's enlightening to see how much work goes into something we take for granted. Sewage didn't always disappear so readily. In the Middle Ages, wastewater was tossed from windows to a center street gutter, then washed into the river. In castles, sewage ended up in the moat (enhancing the moat's defensive role). In the 1500s, French Renaissance King François I moved from château to château (he had several) when the moat-muck became too much.

Ask about the slideshow in the gift shop and occasional tours in English. The WCs are just beyond the gift shop.

**Cost and Hours:** €4.30, covered by Museum Pass, May-Sept Sat-Wed 11:00-17:00, Oct-April Sat-Wed 11:00-16:00, closed Thu-Fri, located where Pont de l'Alma greets the Left Bank—on the right side of the bridge as you face the river, Mo: Alma-Marceau, RER: Pont de l'Alma, tel. 01 53 68 27 81.

▲▲**Army Museum and Napoleon's Tomb (Musée de l'Armée)**—Europe's greatest military museum, in the Hôtel des Invalides, provides interesting coverage of several wars, particularly World Wars I and II. At the center of the complex, Napoleon lies majestically dead inside several coffins under a grand dome—a goose-bumping pilgrimage for historians. The dome overhead glitters with 26 pounds of thinly pounded gold leaf.

**Cost and Hours:** €9, €7 after 17:00, free for military personnel in uniform, free for kids but they must wait in line for ticket, covered by Museum Pass, audioguide-€6; museum—daily April-Sept 10:00-18:00, may be open Tue until 21:00, Oct-March 10:00-17:00, closed first Mon of month year-round; tomb—daily April-June and Sept 10:00-18:00, may be open Tue until 21:00; July-Aug 10:00-19:00, may be open Tue until 21:00; Oct-March 10:00-17:00, closed first Mon of month Sept-May, last tickets sold 30 minutes before closing, cafeteria, tel. 01 44 42 38 77 or 08 10 11 33 99, www.invalides.org.

**Getting There:** The Hôtel des Invalides is at 129 Rue de Grenelle; Mo: La Tour Maubourg, Varenne, or Invalides. Bus #69 from the Marais and Rue Cler area also takes you there, or it's a 10-minute walk from Rue Cler.

☼ See the Army Museum and Napoleon's Tomb Tour chapter.

▲▲**Rodin Museum (Musée Rodin)**—This user-friendly museum is filled with passionate works by the greatest sculptor since Michelangelo. You'll see *The Kiss, The Thinker, The Gates of Hell,* and many more, though due to ongoing renovations, some rooms may be closed.

Well-displayed in the mansion where the sculptor lived and worked, exhibits trace Rodin's artistic development, explain how

his bronze statues were cast, and show some of the studies he created to work up to his masterpiece (the unfinished *Gates of Hell*). Learn about Rodin's tumultuous relationship with his apprentice and lover, Camille Claudel. Mull over what makes his sculptures some of the most evocative since the Renaissance. And stroll the gardens, packed with many of his greatest works (including *The Thinker*). The beautiful gardens are ideal for artistic reflection.

**Cost and Hours:** €6, under 18 free, free on first Sun of the month, €1 for garden only (possibly Paris' best deal, as many works are on display there), both museum and garden covered by Museum Pass, audioguide-€4; Tue-Sun 10:00-17:45, Wed until 20:45, closed Mon, gardens close at 18:00, Oct-March at 17:00, last entry 30 minutes before closing; mandatory baggage check, self-service café in garden, near the Army Museum and Napoleon's Tomb at 79 Rue de Varenne, Mo: Varenne, tel. 01 44 18 61 10, www.musee-rodin.fr.

☼ See the Rodin Museum Tour chapter.

▲▲**Marmottan Museum (Musée Marmottan Monet)**—In this private, intimate, and untouristy museum, you'll find the best collection anywhere of works by Impressionist headliner Claude Monet. Follow Monet's life through more than a hundred works, from simple sketches to the *Impression: Sunrise* painting that gave his artistic movement its start—and a name. The museum also displays some of the enjoyable large-scale canvases featuring the water lilies from his garden at Giverny.

**Cost and Hours:** €10, not covered by Museum Pass, audioguide-€3, Tue-Sun 10:00-18:00, Thu until 20:00, closed Mon, last entry 30 minutes before closing, 2 Rue Louis-Boilly, Mo: La Muette, tel. 01 44 96 50 33, www.marmottan.com.

☼ See the Marmottan Museum Tour chapter.

## Left Bank

For more information on these sights, ✪ see the Left Bank Walk, the Historic Paris Walk (which dips into the Latin Quarter), and the "Sèvres-Babylone to St. Sulpice" stroll in the Shopping in Paris chapter.

**▲Latin Quarter (Quartier Latin)**—This Left Bank neighborhood, just opposite Notre-Dame, was the center of Roman Paris.

But the Latin Quarter's touristy fame relates to its intriguing, artsy, bohemian character. This was perhaps Europe's leading university district in the Middle Ages, when Latin was the language of higher education. The neighborhood's main boulevards (St. Michel and St. Germain) are lined with cafés—once the haunts of great poets and philosophers, now the hangouts of tired tourists. Though still youthful and artsy, much of this area has become a tourist ghetto filled with cheap North African eateries. Exploring a few blocks up or downriver from here gives you a better chance of feeling the pulse of what survives of Paris' classic Left Bank.

✪ See the Left Bank Walk chapter.

**▲▲Cluny Museum (Musée National du Moyen Age)**—This treasure trove of Middle Ages (Moyen Age) art fills old Roman baths, offering close-up looks at stained glass, Notre-Dame carvings, fine goldsmithing and jewelry, and rooms of tapestries. The star here is the exquisite Lady and the Unicorn series of six tapestries: A delicate, as-medieval-as-can-be noble lady introduces a delighted unicorn to the senses of taste, hearing, sight, smell, and touch.

**Cost and Hours:** €8, free on first Sun of month, covered by Museum Pass, ticket includes audioguide though passholders must pay €1; Wed-Mon 9:15-17:45, closed Tue, ticket office closes at 17:15; near corner of Boulevards St. Michel and St. Germain at 6 Place Paul Painlevé; Mo: Cluny-La Sorbonne, St. Michel, or Odéon; tel. 01 53 73 78 16, www.musee-moyenage.fr.

✪ See the Cluny Museum Tour chapter.

**St. Germain-des-Prés**—A church was first built on this site in A.D. 558. The church you see today was constructed in 1163 and is all that's left of a once sprawling and influential monastery. The colorful interior reminds us that medieval churches were originally

**Left Bank**

To Louvre

PONT DES ARTS

RIGHT BANK

Seine

LEFT BANK

To Orsay Museum

Rue du Bac

CAFES DEUX MAGOTS & LA FLORE

DELACROIX MUSEUM

SAINTE-CHAPELLE

Cité

Ile de la Cité

To Rodin Museum

RUE DE VARENNE

St. Germain-des-Prés

ST. GERMAIN-DES-PRES

St. Michel

NOTRE-DAME

R. DE BABYLONE

SEVRES

COLOMBIER ST. SULPICE

R. DU FOUR

Mabillion

Odéon

ST. GERMAIN

Cluny La Sorbonne

LATIN QUARTER

BON MARCHE

Sevres-Babylone

St. Sulpice

SHOPPING AREA

ST. SULPICE

THEATRE ODEON

CLUNY MUSEUM

Maubert-Mutualité

R. DES ECOLES

Vaneau

Rennes

RUE DE RENNES

RUE DE VAUGIRARD

LUXEMBOURG PALACE

SORBONNE

ST. ETIENNE DU MONT

St. Placide

Notre Dame des Champs

POND

Luxembourg Garden

R. SOUFFLOT

PANTHEON

Cardinal Lemoine

MONTPARNASSE TOWER

Montparnasse-Bienvenue

LE SELECT CAFE

KIDS' PLAY AREA

R. AUGUSTE COMTE

Luxembourg

Place Monge

LA COUPOLE CAFE

Vavin

RUE D'ASSAS

BLVD. SAINT MICHEL

RUE ST. JACQUES

RUE D'ULM

RUE MOUFFETARD

GARE MONTPARNASSE

Edgar Quinet

BLVD. DU MONTPARNASSE

Port-Royal

RUE CLAUDE BERNARD

Censier Daubenton

Gaité

Montparnasse Cemetery

Raspail

RUE FROIDEVAUX

N

400 Meters

RUE DAGUERRE

AVE. DU MAINE

Place Denfert-Rochereau

Denfert-Rochereau

CATACOMBS

400 Yards

To Pernety

To Catacomb exit

AVE. GENERAL LECLERC

AVE. RENE COTY

BLVD. ST. JACQUES

St. Jacques

Mounton-Duvernet

- - - Sevres-Babylone to St. Sulpice Boutique Stroll

painted in bright colors. The surrounding area hops at night with venerable cafés, fire-eaters, mimes, and scads of artists.

**Cost and Hours:** Free, daily 8:00-20:00, Mo: St. Germain-des-Prés.

▲**St. Sulpice Church**—Since it was featured in *The Da Vinci Code*, this grand church has become a trendy stop for the book's many fans. But the real reason to visit is to see and hear its intimately accessible organ. For pipe-organ enthusiasts, this is one of Europe's great musical treats. The Grand Orgue at St. Sulpice Church has a rich history, with a succession of 12 world-class organists—including Charles-Marie Widor and Marcel Dupré—that goes back 300 years. Widor started the tradition of opening the loft to visitors after the Sunday morning service. Daniel Roth (or his understudy) continues to welcome guests in three languages while playing five keyboards.

**Cost and Hours:** Free, church open daily 7:30-19:30, Mo: St. Sulpice or Mabillon. See www.stsulpice.com for special concerts.

**Sunday Organ Visits:** The 10:30-11:30 Sunday Mass (come appropriately dressed) is followed by a high-powered 25-minute recital. Then, at noon, the small, unmarked door is opened (left of entry as you face the rear). Visitors scamper like 16th notes up spiral stairs, past the 19th-century StairMasters that five men once pumped to fill the bellows, into a world of 7,000 pipes. You can see the

organ and visit with Daniel (or his substitute, who might not speak English). Space is tight—only 15 people are allowed in at a time, and only a few can gather around the organist at once—you need to be quick to allow others a chance to meet him. You'll likely have about 20 minutes to kill before watching the master play during the next Mass (church views are great, and there's a small lounge to wait in); you can leave at any time. If you're late or rushed, show up around 12:30 and wait at the little door (last entry is at 13:00). As someone leaves, you can slip in, climb up, and catch the rest of the performance.

For more on St. Sulpice, ✪ see page 275 in the Left Bank Walk chapter.

**Nearby:** Tempting boutiques surround the church (see the Shopping in Paris chapter), and Luxembourg Garden is nearby.

**Delacroix Museum (Musée National Eugène Delacroix)**—This museum for Eugène Delacroix (1798-1863) was once his home and studio. A friend of bohemian artistic greats—including George Sand and Frédéric Chopin—Delacroix is most famous for the flag-waving painting *Liberty Leading the People*, which is displayed at the Louvre, not here.

**Cost and Hours:** €5, free on first Sun of the month, covered by Museum Pass, Wed-Mon 9:30-17:00, Sat-Sun until 17:30 in summer, closed Tue, last entry 30 minutes before closing, 6 Rue de Furstenberg, Mo: St. Germain-des-Prés, tel. 01 44 41 86 50, www. musee-delacroix.fr.

For more on the Delacroix Museum, ✪ see page 272 in the Left Bank Walk chapter.

**▲Luxembourg Garden (Jardin du Luxembourg)**—This lovely 60-acre garden is an Impressionist painting brought to life. Slip into a green chair pondside, enjoy the radiant flower beds, go jogging, play tennis, sail a toy sailboat, or take in a chess game or puppet show. Some of the park's prettiest (and quietest) sections lie around its perimeter. Notice any pigeons? The story goes that a very poor Ernest Hemingway used to hand-hunt (read: strangle) them here.

**Cost and Hours:** Free, daily dawn until dusk, Mo: Odéon, RER: Luxembourg.

❂ For more on the garden and nearby sights, see page 277 in the Left Bank Walk chapter. Also see the kid-friendly activities in the garden (Paris with Children chapter), cafés listed in "Les Grands Cafés de Paris" (Eating in Paris chapter), and the description of the Panthéon mausoleum (below).

**Other Parks:** If you enjoy Luxembourg Garden and want to see more green spaces, you could visit the more elegant **Parc Monceau** (Mo: Monceau), the colorful **Jardin des Plantes** (Mo: Jussieu or Gare d'Austerlitz, RER: Gare d'Austerlitz), or the hilly and bigger **Parc des Buttes-Chaumont** (Mo: Buttes-Chaumont).

▲**Panthéon**—This state-capitol-style Neoclassical monument celebrates France's illustrious history and people, balances Foucault's pendulum, and is the final home of many French VIPs. In 1744, an ailing King Louis XV was miraculously healed by St. Geneviève, the city's patron saint, and he thanked her by replacing her ruined

church with a more fitting tribute. By the time the church was completed (1791), however, the secular-minded Revolution was in full swing, and the church was converted into a nonreligious mausoleum honoring the "Champions of French liberty": Voltaire, Rousseau, Descartes, and others. The Revolutionaries covered up the church's windows (as you can see from outside) to display grand, patriotic murals. On the entrance pediment (inspired by the ancient Pantheon in Rome), they carved the inscription, "To the great men of the Fatherland."

**Cost and Hours:** €8.50, under 18 free, covered by Museum Pass, daily 10:00-18:30 in summer, until 18:00 in winter, last entry 45 minutes before closing, Mo: Cardinal Lemoine. Ask about occasional English tours or call ahead for schedule; tel. 01 44 32 18 00, http://pantheon.monuments-nationaux.fr.

**Visiting the Panthéon:** Inside the vast building (360' by 280' by 270') are monuments tracing the celebrated struggles of the French people: a beheaded St. Denis (painting on left wall of nave),

St. Geneviève saving the fledgling city from Attila the Hun, and scenes of Joan of Arc (left transept).

Under the dome are four statue groups dedicated to more great Frenchmen: Jean-Jacques Rousseau (1712-1778), the philosopher who championed the idea of an equal Social Contract between government and the people; Diderot (1713-1784), whose Encyclopédie championed secular knowledge; orators and publicists (men in business suits) who served the state; and generals, including Napoleon on horseback.

Foucault's pendulum swings gracefully at the end of a 220-foot cable suspended from the towering dome. It was here in 1851 that the scientist Léon Foucault first demonstrated the rotation of the earth. Stand a few minutes and watch the pendulum's arc (appear to) shift as you and the earth rotate beneath it.

At the far end of the nave stands an inspirational altar dedicated to the political body that opposed the monarchy during the Revolution, inscribed with the familiar motto "Live free or die."

Stairs in the back lead down to the crypt, where a pantheon of greats is buried. Rousseau is along the right wall as you enter, Voltaire faces him across the hall. Also buried here are scientist Marie Curie, Victor Hugo *(Les Misérables, The Hunchback of Notre-Dame)*, Alexandre Dumas *(The Three Musketeers, The Count of Monte Cristo)*, and Louis Braille, who invented the script for the blind.

**Dome Climb:** For fine views, climb 206 steps to the dome gallery. Visits are by escort only and leave every hour until 17:30 from the bookshop near the entry—see schedule as you go in. Note that in 2013, dome access may be closed for renovation.

**Montparnasse Tower (La Tour Montparnasse)**—This sadly out-of-place 59-story superscraper has one virtue: Its sensational views are cheaper and far easier to access than the Eiffel Tower's. Come early in the day for clearest skies and be treated to views from a comfortable interior and from up on the rooftop. (Some say it's the very best view in Paris, as you can see the Eiffel Tower

clearly...and you can't see the Montparnasse Tower at all.)

Exit the elevator at the 56th floor, passing the eager photographer (they'll superimpose your group's image with the view) to views of *tout Paris*. Here you can have a drink or a light lunch (OK prices) with a view, peruse the gift shop, or use the good WCs. Take time to explore every corner of the floor. Dioramas identify highlights of the star-studded vista. From here it's easy to admire Haussmann's grand-boulevard scheme (see sidebar on page 82). Notice the lush courtyards hiding behind grand street fronts. The exhibits change often, but you'll likely see historic photos and enjoy a plush little theater playing a continuous video.

For more views, climb to the open terrace on the 59th floor to enjoy the surreal scene of a lonely man in a box and a helipad surrounded by the window-cleaner track. Here, 690 feet above Paris, you can scan the city with the wind in your hair.

**Cost and Hours:** €13, not covered by Museum Pass, April-Sept daily 9:30-23:30, Oct-March Sun-Thu 9:30-22:30, Fri-Sat 9:30-23:00, last entry 30 minutes before closing, sunset is great, but views are disappointing after dark, entrance on Rue de l'Arrivée, Mo: Montparnasse-Bienvenüe—from the Métro stay inside the station and follow the signs for *La Tour*; tel. 01 45 38 52 56, www.tourmontparnasse56.com.

**Sightseeing Tip:** The tower is an efficient stop when combined with a day trip to Chartres, which begins at the Montparnasse train station (see the Chartres chapter for details).

▲**Catacombs**—Descend 60 feet below the street and walk a one-mile (one-hour) route through tunnels containing the anonymous bones of six million permanent Parisians.

In 1786, health-conscious Parisians looking to relieve congestion and improve the city's sanitary conditions emptied the church cemeteries and moved the bones here, to former limestone quarries. For decades, priests led ceremonial processions of black-veiled, bone-laden carts into the quarries, where the bones were stacked in piles five feet high and as much as 80 feet deep. Ignore the sign announcing, "Halt, this is the empire of the dead," and walk through passageways of skull-studded tibiae, past more cheery signs: "Happy is he who is forever faced with the hour of his death and prepares himself for the end every day." You emerge far from where you entered, with white-limestone-covered toes, telling everyone you've been underground gawking at bones. Note to wannabe Hamlets: An attendant checks your bag at the exit for stolen souvenirs.

**Cost and Hours:** €8, not covered by Museum Pass, Tue-Sun 10:00-17:00, closed Mon, ticket booth closes at 16:00; tel. 01 43 22 47 63, www.catacombes-de-paris.fr.

**Warning:** Lines are long (figure an hour wait) and hard to avoid. Arrive no later than 14:30 or risk not getting in.

**Photography:** Photos are allowed, but flashes are not—bring a tripod, or forget it.

**Getting There:** 1 Place Denfert-Rochereau. Take the Métro to Denfert-Rochereau, then find the lion in the big traffic circle; if he looked left rather than right, he'd stare right at the green entrance to the Catacombs.

**Nearby:** Rue Daguerre, a pleasing pedestrian street (see the Shopping in Paris chapter) is a block from the Catacombs entrance (cross Avenue du Général Leclerc and turn left).

**After Your Visit:** You'll exit at 36 Rue Rémy Dumoncel, far from where you started. Turn right out of the exit and walk to Avenue du Général Leclerc, where you'll be equidistant from Métro stops Alésia (walk left) and Mouton Duvernet (walk right).

## Champs-Elysées and Nearby

▲▲▲**Champs-Elysées**—This famous boulevard is Paris' backbone, with its greatest concentration of traffic. From the Arc de Triomphe down Avenue des Champs-Elysées, all of France seems to converge on Place de la Concorde, the city's largest square. And though the Champs-Elysées has become as international as it is Parisian, a walk here is still a must.

To reach the top of the Champs-Elysées, take the Métro to the Arc de Triomphe (Mo: Charles de Gaulle-Etoile), then saunter down the grand boulevard (Métro stops every few blocks, including George V and Franklin D. Roosevelt).

○ See the Champs-Elysées Walk chapter.

▲▲**Arc de Triomphe**—Napoleon had the magnificent Arc de Triomphe commissioned to commemorate his victory at the battle of Austerlitz. The foot of the arch is a stage on which the last two centuries of Parisian history have played out—from the funeral of Napoleon to the goose-stepping arrival of the Nazis to the triumphant return of Charles de Gaulle after the Allied liberation. Examine the carvings on the pillars, featuring a mighty Napoleon and excitable Lady Liberty. Pay your respects at the Tomb of the Unknown Soldier. Then climb the 284 steps to the observation deck up top, with sweeping skyline panoramas and a mesmerizing view down onto the traffic that swirls around the arch.

**Cost and Hours:** Outside and at the base—free, always viewable; steps to rooftop—€9.50, under 18 free, free on first Sun of

month Oct-March, covered by
Museum Pass; daily April-Sept
10:00-23:00, Oct-March 10:00-
22:30, last entry 30 minutes
before closing; lines are slow—
see page 287 for advice; Place
Charles de Gaulle, use underpass to reach arch, Mo: Charles
de Gaulle-Etoile, tel. 01 55 37
73 77, http://arc-de-triomphe.
monuments-nationaux.fr.

   ✪ See the Champs-Elysées
Walk chapter.

**▲Opéra Garnier**—This gleaming grand theater of the belle
époque was built for Napoleon III and finished in 1875. (For the
best view, stand in front of the Opéra Métro stop.) From Avenue de
l'Opéra, once lined with Paris' most fashionable haunts, the facade
suggests "all power to the wealthy." And a shimmering Apollo,
holding his lyre high above the building, seems to declare, "This is
a temple of the highest arts."

   **Cost and Hours:** €9, not covered by Museum Pass, errat-
ic hours due to performances and rehearsals, but generally daily
10:00-17:00, mid-July-Aug until 18:00, last entry 30 minutes before closing, 8 Rue Scribe, Mo: Opéra, RER: Auber.

   **Tours:** English tours of the building run during summer and
off-season on weekends and Wed, usually at 11:30 and 14:30—call
to confirm schedule (€13.50, includes entry, 1.5 hours, tel. 01 40 01
17 89 or 08 25 05 44 05, press 2 for tours).

   **Visiting the Theater:** You'll enter around the left side of the
building—as you face the front, find the red carpet across from
American Express on Rue Scribe. As you pass the bust of the architect, Monsieur Garnier, pay your respects and check out the
bronze floor plan of the complex etched below. Notice how little
space is given to seating.

   The building is huge—though the auditorium itself seats only
2,000. The real show was before and after the performance, when
the elite of Paris—out to see and be seen—strutted their elegant
stuff in the extravagant lobbies. Think of the grand marble stairway as a theater. As you wander the halls and gawk at the decor,
imagine this place in its heyday, filled with beautiful people. The
massive foundations straddle an underground lake (inspiring the
mysterious world of the *Phantom of the Opera*). Visitors can peek
from two boxes into the actual red-velvet performance hall to view
Marc Chagall's colorful ceiling (1964) playfully dancing around
the eight-ton chandelier (guided tours take you into the performance hall; you can't enter when they're changing out the stage).

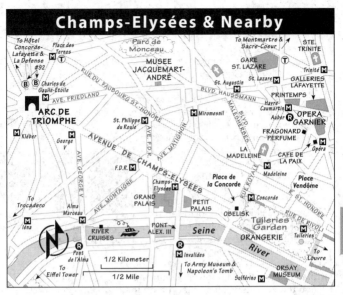

SIGHTS IN PARIS

Note the box seats next to the stage—the most expensive in the house, with an obstructed view of the stage...but just right if you're here only to be seen.

The elitism of this place prompted President François Mitterrand to have an opera house built for the people in the 1980s, situated symbolically on Place de la Bastille, where the French Revolution started in 1789. This left the Opéra Garnier home only to ballet and occasional concerts. The library/museum will interest opera buffs, but anyone will enjoy the second-floor grand foyer and Salon du Glacier, iced with decor typical of 1900.

For a novel souvenir, stop at the boutique as you leave and pick up a jar of honey cultivated from beehives on the Opéra's roof (not always available). The hives are tended by staff and can be seen from the seventh floor of Galleries Lafayette (behind the Opéra).

**Ballet and Concert Tickets:** To find out about upcoming performances, ask for a schedule at the information booth, consult *Pariscope* magazine (see page 493), or look on the website (www.operadeparis.fr). To buy tickets by phone, call 08 92 89 90 90 (toll call) or from the US dial 011 33 1 71 25 24 23 (office closed Sun). There are usually no performances mid-July-mid-Sept. You can also go directly to the ticket office (open daily 11:00-18:00).

**Nearby:** The Fragonard Perfume Museum (described next) is on the left side of the Opéra, and the venerable Galeries Lafayette department store (marvelous views from roof terrace, see page 477) is just behind. Across the street, the illustrious Café de la Paix has

# Best Views over the City of Light

Your trip to Paris is played out in the streets, but the brilliance of the City of Light can only be fully appreciated by rising above it all. Invest time to marvel at all the man-made beauty, seen best in the early morning or around sunset. Many of the viewpoints I've listed are free or covered by the Museum Pass; otherwise, expect to pay €8-14. Here are some prime locations for soaking in the views:

**Eiffel Tower:** It's hard to find a grander view of Paris than from the tower's second level. Go around sunset and stay after dark to see the tower illuminated; or go in the early morning to avoid the midday haze and crowds (not covered by Museum Pass, see page 66).

**Arc de Triomphe:** Without a doubt, this is the perfect place to see the glamorous Champs-Elysées (if you can manage the 284 steps). It's great during the day, but even greater at night, when the boulevard positively glitters (covered by Museum Pass, see page 77).

**Notre-Dame's Tower:** This viewpoint is brilliant—it couldn't be more central—but it requires climbing 400 steps and is usually crowded with long lines (try to arrive early or late). Up high on the tower, you'll get an unobstructed view of gargoyles, the river, the Latin Quarter, and the Ile de la Cité (covered by Museum Pass, see page 56).

**Steps of Sacré-Cœur:** Join the party on Paris' only hilltop. Walk uphill or take the funicular (if it's running), then hunker down on Sacré-Cœur's steps to enjoy the sunset and territorial views over Paris. Stay in Montmartre for dinner, then see the view again after dark (free, see page 90).

been a meeting spot for the local glitterati for generations. If you can afford the coffee, this spot offers a delightful break.

**Fragonard Perfume Museum**—Near Opéra Garnier, this perfume shop masquerades as a museum. Housed in a beautiful 19th-century mansion, it's the best-smelling museum in Paris—and you'll learn a little about how perfume is made, too (ask for the English handout).

   **Cost and Hours:** Free, Mon-Sat 9:00-18:00, Sun 9:00-17:00, 9 Rue Scribe, Mo: Opéra, RER: Auber, tel. 01 47 42 04 56, www.fragonard.com.

▲▲**Jacquemart-André Museum (Musée Jacquemart-André)**—This thoroughly enjoyable museum (with an elegant café) showcases the lavish home of a wealthy, art-loving, 19th-century

**Galeries Lafayette or Printemps:** Take the elevator or escalator to the top floor of either department store (they sit side by side) for a stunning overlook of the old Opéra district (free, see page 477).

**Montparnasse Tower:** The top of this solitary skyscraper has some of the best views in Paris, though they're disappointing after dark. Zip up 56 floors on the elevator, then walk to the rooftop (not covered by Museum Pass, see page 75.

**Pompidou Center:** Take the escalator up and admire the beautiful cityscape along with the exciting modern art. There may be better views over Paris, but this is the best one from a museum (covered by Museum Pass, see page 86).

**Place du Trocadéro and Café Carlu:** This is *the* place to see the Eiffel Tower. Come for a look at Monsieur Eiffel's festive creation day or night (when the tower is lit up). Consider starting or ending your Eiffel Tower visit here (free, see page 498) and having a drink or snack at Café Carlu. With its privileged spot on Place du Trocadéro, this café offers dramatic views of the Eiffel Tower from its terrace (Wed-Mon 11:00-19:00, closed Tue, in Architecture and Monuments Museum but open to public).

**Arab World Institute (Institut du Monde Arabe):** This building near Ile St. Louis has free views from its terrific roof terrace (Tue-Sun 10:00-18:00, closed Mon, 1 Rue des Fossés Saint-Bernard, Place Mohammed V, Mo: Jussieu, www.imarabe .org).

**Panthéon:** Climb to the top for great Paris views (must be escorted by guide, covered by Museum Pass, may be closed for renovation in 2013, see page 74).

**Bar at Hôtel Concorde-Lafayette:** This otherwise unappealing hotel is noteworthy for its 33rd-floor bar, where you can sip wine and enjoy a stunning Parisian panorama (free elevator but pricey drinks, see page 84).

Parisian couple. After wandering the grand boulevards, get inside for an intimate look at the lifestyles of the Parisian rich and fabulous. Edouard André and his wife Nélie Jacquemart—who had no children—spent their lives and fortunes designing, building, and then decorating this sumptuous mansion. What makes the visit so rewarding is the excellent audioguide tour (in English, included with admission, plan on spending an hour with the audioguide). The place is strewn with paintings by Rembrandt, Botticelli, Uccello, Mantegna, Bellini, Boucher, and Fragonard—enough to make a painting gallery famous.

**Cost and Hours:** €11, includes audioguide, not covered by Museum Pass; daily 10:00-18:00, Mon and Sat until 21:00 during special exhibits; can avoid lines by purchasing tickets online

# Baron Georges-Eugène Haussmann
## (1809-1891)

The elegantly uniform streets that make Paris so Parisian are the work of Baron Haussmann, who oversaw the modernization of the city in the mid-19th century. He cleared out the cramped, higgledy-piggledy, unhygienic medieval cityscape and replaced it with broad, straight boulevards lined with stately buildings and linked by modern train stations.

The quintessential view of Haussmann's work is from the pedestrian island immediately in front of the Opéra Garnier. You're surrounded by Paris, circa 1870, when it was the capital of the world. Spin slowly and find the Louvre in one direction, Place Vendôme in another, and all the cohesiveness of the uniform buildings. Haussmann's buildings are all five stories tall, with angled, black slate roofs and formal facades. The balconies on the second and fifth floors match with neighboring buildings to give strong lines of perspective, as the buildings stretch down the boulevard. Haussmann was so intent on putting the architecture at center stage that he ordered no trees be planted along these streets.

But there was more than aesthetics to the plan. In pre-Haussmann Paris, angry rioters would take to the narrow streets, setting up barricades (as made famous in Hugo's *Les Misérables*) to hold back government forces. With Haussmann's new design government troops could circulate easily and fire cannons down the long, straight boulevards. A whiff of "grapeshot"—chains, nails, and other buckshot-type shrapnel—could clear out any revolutionaries in a hurry.

The 19th century was a great time to be wealthy, thanks to the city's fancy covered market halls, civilized sidewalks, and even elevators. With the coming of elevators, the wealthy took the higher floors and enjoyed the view.

(€2 fee) and printing receipt, 158 Boulevard Haussmann, Mo: Miromesnil or St. Philippe-du-Roule, bus #80 makes a convenient connection to Ecole Militaire; tel. 01 45 62 11 59, www.musee-jacquemart-andre.com.

**After Your Visit:** Consider a break in the sumptuous museum tearoom, with delicious cakes and tea (daily 11:45-17:30). From here walk north on Rue de Courcelles to see Paris' most beautiful park, Parc Monceau.

▲**Petit Palais (and its Musée des Beaux-Arts)**—This free museum displays a broad collection of paintings and sculpture from the 1600s to the 1900s. It's a museum of second-choice art, but the building itself is impressive, and there are a few 19th-century diamonds in the rough, including pieces by Courbet and Monet.

**Cost and Hours:** Free, Tue-Sun 10:00-18:00, Thu until 20:00 for temporary exhibitions, closed Mon; across from Grand Palais on Avenue Winston Churchill, a looooong block west of Place de la Concorde; tel. 01 53 43 40 00, www.petitpalais.paris.fr.

**Visiting the Museum:** Enter the museum, ask for a ticket to the permanent collection (free but required), and head toward the left wing. Soak up turn-of-the-century ambience, with Art Nouveau vases and portraits of well-dressed, belle époque-era Parisians. The main hall features Romantics and Realists from the late 19th century. Midway down the main hall, Courbet's soft-porn *The Sleepers* (*Le Sommeil*, 1866) captures two women nestled in post-climactic bliss. His large, dark *Firefighters (Pompiers courant à un incendie)* is a Realist's take on an everyday scene—firefighters rushing to put out a blaze.

Turning the corner, you'll find artwork by Gustave Doré (1832-1883), the 19th century's greatest book illustrator. In the enormous *La Vallée de larmes* (1883), Christ and the cross are the only salvation from this "vale of tears."

At the end of the main hall, enter the smaller room to find Claude Monet's *Sunset on the Seine at Lavacourt* (*Soleil couchant sur la Seine a Lavacourt*, 1880). Painted the winter after his wife died, it looks across the river from Monet's home to two lonely boats in the distance, with the hazy town on the far bank. The sun's reflection is a vertical smudge down the water. Nearby are works by the American painter Mary Cassatt and other Impressionists.

The Palais also has a pleasant garden courtyard and café.

**Grand Palais**—This grand exhibition hall, built for the 1900 World's Fair, is used for temporary exhibits. The building's Industrial Age, erector-set, iron-and-glass exterior is striking, but the steep entry price is only worthwhile if you're interested in any of the several different exhibitions (each with different hours and

costs, located in various parts of the building). Many areas are undergoing renovations, which may still be under way during your visit. Get details on the current schedule from a TI, in *Pariscope*, or from the website.

**Cost and Hours:** Admission prices and hours vary with each exhibition; major exhibitions usually €11, not covered by Museum Pass; generally open daily 10:00-20:00, Wed until 22:00, some parts of building closed

Mon, other parts closed Tue, closed between exhibitions; Avenue Winston Churchill, Mo: Rond Point or Champs-Elysées, tel. 01 44 13 17 17, www.grandpalais.fr.

**View from Hôtel Concorde-Lafayette**—For a remarkable Parisian panorama and a suitable location for your next affair, head to the bar of Hôtel Concorde-Lafayette. Ride the free elevators (when entering, head to the rear of the lobby and take the elevators on the right) to the 33rd floor, and walk up one flight to the Panoramic Bar. You'll enter a sky-high world of semicircular vinyl make-out booths, glass walls, expensive drinks, and jaw-dropping views that are best before dark and not worthwhile in poor weather (bar open daily 17:00-1:30 in the morning, tel. 01 40 68 50 68, www.concorde-lafayette.com).

**Getting There:** It's at 3 Place du Général Koenig. Take the Métro to the pedestrian-unfriendly Porte Maillot stop. Follow signs to *Palais des Congrès*, and keep walking until you see *Hôtel* signs—plan on a long walk, expect to get lost, and ask if you're on the right track (if you're coming from the Rue Cler area, take RER-C from Invalides or Pont de l'Alma toward Pontoise to Porte Maillot). If you're pooped or strapped for time, the skies are clear, and the sun's about to set, spring for a taxi.

▲**La Défense and La Grande Arche**—Though Paris keeps its historic center classic and skyscraper-free, this district, nicknamed "le petit Manhattan," offers an impressive excursion into a side of Paris few tourists see: that of a modern-day economic superpower.

La Défense was first conceived more than 60 years ago as a US-style forest of skyscrapers that would accommodate the business needs of the modern world. Today La Défense is a thriving commercial and shopping center, home to 150,000 employees and 55,000 residents.

For an interesting visit, take the Métro to the La Défense Grande Arche stop, follow *Sortie Grande Arche* signs, and climb the steps of La Grande Arche for distant city views. Then stroll gradually downhill among the glass buildings to the Esplanade de la Défense Métro station, and return home from there.

**La Grande Arche de la Fraternité:** This is the centerpiece of this ambitious complex. Inaugurated in 1989 on the 200th anniversary of the French Revolution, it was, like the Revolution, dedicated to human rights and brotherhood. The place is big—Notre-Dame Cathedral could fit under its arch. The four-sided structure sits on enormous underground pillars and is covered with a veneer of beautiful white Carrara marble. The arch is a 38-story office

building for 30,000 people on more than 200 acres. The left side is government ministries, the right side is corporate offices, and the top is dedicated to human rights. The "cloud"—a huge canvas canopy under the arch—is an attempt to cut down on the wind-tunnel effect this gigantic building creates.

Wander behind the arch to see an unusual mix of glassy skyscrapers and a cemetery (in the orchard), and peek at the Le Corbusier-style planning, separating motor traffic (the freeway and trains that tunnel underneath) from pedestrian traffic (the sky-bridges).

***Lunch on the Steps:*** Join the locals and picnic on the arch steps; good to-go places are plentiful (and cafés are nearby).

**The Esplanade:** La Défense is much more than its eye-catching arch. Survey the skyscraping scene from the top of the steps. GDF is France's national gas company; SFR is the Verizon of France; and Areva is a global energy company that is big into nuclear power. Wander from the arch back toward the city center (and to the next Métro stop) along the Esplanade (a.k.a. "le Parvis"), the open area surrounded by skyscrapers. Take in the monumental structures around you: Les Quatre Temps is a giant shopping mall of 250 stores, and like malls at home, it's a teenage wasteland when school is out and eerily quiet at night.

Across the Esplanade, the Center of New Industries and Technologies (better known as CNIT—see white letters on plaza), built in 1958 and now a congress center, is a feat of modern architecture: It's the largest concrete vault anywhere that rests on only three points. Enter the vault to see a semicircle of dazzling offices and shops that recede as they rise, like the seating in an opera house.

In France, getting a building permit often comes with a requirement to dedicate 2 percent of the construction cost to art. Hence the Esplanade is a virtual open-air modern art gallery, sporting pieces by Joan Miró (blue, red, and yellow), Alexander Calder (red), and Yaacov Agam (the fountain with colorful stripes and rhythmically dancing spouts), among others. *La Défense de Paris*, the statue that gave the area its name, recalls the 1871 Franco-Prussian war—it's a rare bit of old Paris out here in the 'burbs.

As you descend the Esplanade, notice how the small gardens and *boules* courts (reddish dirt areas) are designed to integrate tradition into this celebration of modern commerce. Note also how the buildings decrease in height and increase in age—the Nexity Tower (closest to central Paris) looks old compared to the other skyscrapers. Dating from the 1960s, it was one of the first buildings at La Défense. Your walk ends at the amusing fountain of Bassin Takis, where you'll find the Esplanade de la Défense Métro station that zips you out of all this modernity and directly back into town.

## Marais Neighborhood and Nearby

To connect these sights with a fun, fact-filled stroll leading from Place de la Bastille to the Pompidou Center, ✪ see the Marais Walk chapter.

Don't waste time looking for the **Bastille,** the prison of Revolution fame. It's Paris' most famous nonsight. The building is long gone, and just the square remains, good only for its nightlife and as a jumping-off point for the Marais Walk or a stroll through Promenade Plantée Park (see page 89).

**▲▲Pompidou Center (Centre Pompidou)**—One of Europe's greatest collections of far-out modern art is housed in the Musée National d'Art Moderne, on the fourth and fifth floors of this colorful exoskeletal building. Created ahead of its time, the 20th-century art in this collection is still waiting for the world to catch up. After so many Madonnas-and-children, a piano smashed to bits and glued to the wall is refreshing.

The Pompidou Center and the square that fronts it are lively, with lots of people, street theater, and activity inside and out—a perpetual street fair. Kids of any age enjoy the fun, colorful fountain (called *Homage to Stravinsky*) next to the Pompidou Center. Ride the escalator for a great city view from the top (ticket or Museum Pass required), and consider eating at the good café.

**Cost and Hours:** €11-13 depending on current exhibits, free on first Sun of month, Museum Pass covers permanent collection and view escalators, €3 Panorama Ticket lets you ride to the top for the view (doesn't include museum entry); Wed-Mon 11:00-21:00, closed Tue, ticket counters close at 20:00, arrive after 17:00 to avoid crowds (mainly for special exhibits); café on mezzanine, pricey view restaurant on Level 6, Mo: Rambuteau or farther-away Hôtel de Ville, tel. 01 44 78 12 33, www.centrepompidou.fr.

✪ See the Pompidou Center Tour chapter.

**▲Jewish Art and History Museum (Musée d'Art et Histoire du Judaïsme)**—This fine museum, located in a beautifully restored Marais mansion, tells the story of Judaism in France and throughout Europe, from the Roman destruction of Jerusalem to the theft of famous artworks during World War II. Displays il-

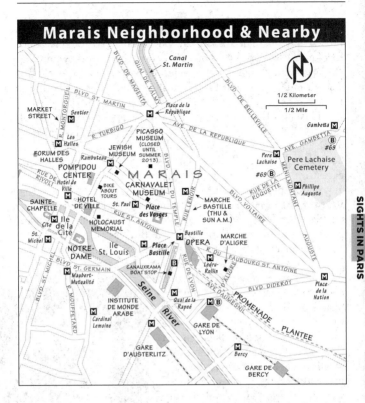

# Marais Neighborhood & Nearby

lustrate the cultural unity maintained by this continually dispersed population. You'll learn about the history of Jewish traditions, from bar mitzvahs to menorahs, and see the exquisite traditional costumes and objects central to daily life. The museum also displays paintings by famous Jewish artists, including Marc Chagall, Amedeo Modigliani, and Chaim Soutine. The English explanations posted in many rooms provide sufficient explanation for most; the included audioguide provides greater detail.

**Cost and Hours:** €7, includes audioguide, covered by Museum Pass, Sun-Fri 11:00-18:00, closed Sat, last entry 45 minutes before closing, 71 Rue du Temple; Mo: Rambuteau or Hôtel de Ville a few blocks farther away, RER: Châtelet-Les Halles; tel. 01 53 01 86 60, www.mahj.org.

▲▲**Picasso Museum (Musée Picasso)**—This museum, currently closed for a major renovation until summer 2013, contains the world's largest collection of Picasso's paintings, sculptures, sketches, and ceramics, along with his small collection of Impressionist art.

▲**Carnavalet Museum (Musée Carnavalet)**—The tumultuous history of Paris—starring the Revolutionary years—is well portrayed in this converted Marais mansion. Explanations are in French only, but many displays are self-explanatory. You'll see models of medieval Paris, maps of the city over the centuries, paintings of Parisian scenes, French Revolution paraphernalia—including a small guillotine—and fully furnished rooms re-creating life in Paris in different eras.

**Cost and Hours:** Free, fee for some temporary (but optional) exhibits, audioguide-€5, Tue-Sun 10:00-18:00, closed Mon; avoid lunchtime (12:30-14:30), when many rooms may be closed; 23 Rue de Sévigné, Mo: St. Paul, tel. 01 44 59 58 58, www.carnavalet. paris.fr.

○ See the Carnavalet Museum Tour chapter.

**Victor Hugo's House**—France's literary giant lived in this house on Place des Vosges from 1832 to 1848. (Hugo stayed in many places during his life, but he was here the longest.) He moved to this apartment after the phenomenal success of *The Hunchback of Notre-Dame,* and it was while living here that he wrote much of *Les Misérables* (when he wasn't entertaining Paris' elite). You'll see well-

decorated rooms re-creating different phases of his life, from his celebrity years, to his 19-year exile during the repressive reign of Napoleon III (Hugo said "When freedom returns, I will return"), to his final years as a national treasure. Rooms are littered with paintings of Hugo and his family and of some of his most famous character creations. The display cases show personal objects. Posted explanations in English provide sufficient context to grasp the importance of Hugo to France. The €5 audioguide adds greater depth.

**Cost and Hours:** Free, fee for optional exhibits (usually about €7, and usually not worth paying for), audioguide-€5, Tue-Sun 10:00-18:00, closed Mon, last entry at 17:40, 6 Place des Vosges; Mo: Bastille, St. Paul, or Chemin Vert; tel. 01 42 72 10 16, www. musee-hugo.paris.fr.

**Holocaust Memorial (Mémorial de la Shoah)**—This sight, commemorating the lives of the more than 76,000 Jews deported from France in World War II, has several facets: a WWII deportation memorial, a museum on the Holocaust, and a Jewish resource center. Displaying original deportation records, the museum takes you through the history of Jews in Europe and France, from medieval pogroms to the Nazi era. But its focal point is underground, where victims' ashes are buried.

**Cost and Hours:** Free, Sun-Fri 10:00-18:00, Thu until 22:00, closed Sat and certain Jewish holidays, 17 Rue Geoffroy l'Asnier, tel. 01 42 77 44 72, www.memorialdelashoah.org.

**Visiting the Memorial:** Before entering, visitors must pass through airport-like security. The entry courtyard contains a cylinder evoking concentration camp smokestacks. Large stone walls are engraved with the names of all of the French Jews deported during the war.

Enter the building (with an information desk, bookstore, café, and exhibits), and pick up a brochure. Go downstairs one floor to the crypt, which has a large Star of David in black marble. Ashes from some of the six million victims of Nazi brutality are buried underneath the star, in soil brought from Israel. Behind you is a small corridor containing the original French police files from the arrest, internment, and deportation of Paris' Jews. (Since 1995, the French—thanks to former President Jacques Chirac's leadership—have acknowledged the Vichy government's complicity in the Nazis' local ethnic cleansing.)

Go downstairs another floor to the permanent exhibition. Photos and videos (most with English explanations) present an introduction to Judaism and the history of Jews in Europe (including pogroms) and in France (including the notorious Dreyfus affair, concerning a Jewish officer unjustly imprisoned for treason). The displays trace the rise of Nazism, the deportations (12,884 Parisians were once rounded up in a single day), the death camps, and the liberation at the end of the war. The moving finale is a brightly lit collage of children lost to the Holocaust.

**Promenade Plantée Park (Viaduc des Arts)**—This two-mile-long, narrow garden walk on an elevated viaduct was once used for train tracks and is now a fine place for a refreshing stroll or run. Botanists appreciate the well-maintained and varying vegetation. From west (near Opéra) to east, the first half of the path is elevated until the midway point, the pleasant Jardin de Reuilly (a good stopping point for most, near Mo: Dugommier), then it continues on street level—with separate paths for pedestrians and cyclists—out to Paris' ring road, the *périphérique*.

**Cost and Hours:** Free, opens Mon-Fri at 8:00, Sat-Sun at 9:00, closes at sunset (17:30 in winter, 20:30 in summer). It runs from Place de la Bastille (Mo: Bastille) along Avenue Daumesnil to St. Mandé (Mo: Michel Bizot) or Porte Dorée, passing within a block of Gare de Lyon.

**Getting There:** To get to the park from Place de la Bastille (exit the Métro following *Sortie Rue de Lyon* signs), walk a looooong block down Rue de Lyon hugging the Opéra on your left. Find the low-key entry and steps up the red-brick wall a block after the Opéra.

▲**Père Lachaise Cemetery (Cimetière du Père Lachaise)** — Littered with the tombstones of many of the city's most illustrious dead, this is your best one-stop look at Paris' fascinating, romantic past residents. More like a small city,

the cemetery is big and confusing, but my self-guided tour directs you to the graves of Frédéric Chopin, Molière, Edith Piaf, Oscar Wilde, Gertrude Stein, Jim Morrison, Héloïse and Abélard, and many more.

**Cost and Hours:** Free, Mon-Fri 8:00-18:00, Sat 8:30-18:00, Sun 9:00-18:00, closes at 17:30 in winter, last entry 15 minutes before closing; two blocks from Mo: Gambetta (not Mo: Père Lachaise) and two blocks from bus #69's last stop (see the Bus #69 Sightseeing Tour chapter); tel. 01 55 25 82 10, searchable map available at non-official website: www.pere-lachaise.com.

⊙ See the Père Lachaise Cemetery Tour chapter.

## Montmartre

Connect these sights with the ⊙ Montmartre Walk chapter.

▲▲**Sacré-Cœur**—You'll spot Sacré-Cœur, the Byzantine-looking white basilica atop Montmartre, from most viewpoints in Paris. Though only 130 years old, it's impressive and iconic, with a climbable dome.

**Cost and Hours:** Church—free, daily 6:00-22:30, last entry at 22:15; dome—€6, not covered by Museum Pass, daily May-Sept 9:00-19:00, Oct-April 9:00-17:00; tel. 01 53 41 89 00, www.sacre-coeur-montmartre.com.

**Getting There:** You have several options. You can take the Métro to the Anvers stop (to avoid the stairs up to Sacré-Cœur, buy one more Métro ticket and ride the funicular, though it's sometimes closed for maintenance). The Abbesses stop is closer but less scenic. Or you can go to Place Pigalle, then take the tiny electric Montmartrobus, which drops you right by Place du Tertre, near Sacré-Cœur (costs one Métro ticket, 4/hour). A taxi to the top of the hill saves time and avoids sweat (about €13, €20 at night).

**Nearby:** Montmartre's main square (Place du Tertre), one block from the church, was once the haunt of Henri de Toulouse-Lautrec and the original bohemians. Today, it's mobbed with tourists and unoriginal bohemians, but it's still fun (to beat the crowds, go on a weekday or early on weekend mornings).

**Dalí Museum (L'Espace Dalí)**—This museum offers an entertaining look at some of Dalí's creations.

**Cost and Hours:** €11, not covered by Museum Pass, audioguide-€3, daily 10:00-18:00, July-Aug until 20:00, 11 Rue Poulbot, tel. 01 42 64 40 10, www.daliparis.com.

**Montmartre Museum (Musée de Montmartre)**—This 17th-century home re-creates the traditional cancan and cabaret Montmartre scene, with paintings, posters, photos, music, and memorabilia.

**Cost and Hours:** €8, includes good audioguide, not covered by Museum Pass, daily 10:00-18:00, 12 Rue Cortot, tel. 01 49 25 89 39, www.museedemontmartre.fr.

**Pigalle**—Paris' red light district, the infamous "Pig Alley," is at the foot of Butte Montmartre. *Ooh la la.* It's more racy than dangerous. Walk from Place Pigalle to Place Blanche, teasing desperate barkers and fast-talking temptresses. In bars, a €150 bottle of (what would otherwise be) cheap champagne comes with a friend. Stick to the bigger streets, hang on to your wallet, and exercise good judgment. Cancan can cost a fortune, as can con artists in topless bars. After dark, countless tour buses line the streets, reminding us that tour guides make big bucks by bringing their groups to touristy nightclubs like the famous Moulin Rouge (Mo: Pigalle or Abbesses).

**Museum of Erotic Art (Musée de l'Erotisme)**—Paris' sexy museum has five floors of risqué displays—mostly paintings and drawings—ranging from artistic to erotic to disgusting, with a few circa-1920 porn videos and a fascinating history of local brothels tossed in. It's in the center of the Pigalle red light district.

**Cost and Hours:** €10, €7 online, no...it's not covered by the Museum Pass, daily 10:00-2:00 in the morning, 72 Boulevard de Clichy, Mo: Blanche, tel. 01 42 58 28 73, www.musee-erotisme.com.

# HISTORIC
# PARIS WALK

*Ile de la Cité and the Latin Quarter*

Paris has been the cultural capital of Europe for centuries. We'll start where it did, on Ile de la Cité, with a foray onto the Left Bank, on a walk that laces together 80 generations of history—from Celtic fishing village to Roman city, bustling medieval capital, birthplace of the Revolution, bohemian haunt of the 1920s café scene, and the working world of modern Paris. Along the way, we'll step into two of Paris' greatest sights—Notre-Dame and Sainte-Chapelle.

## Orientation

**Length of This Walk:** Allow four hours to do justice to this three-mile walk.

**Paris Museum Pass:** Many sights on this walk that charge admission are covered by the Museum Pass. This pass can be a great money- and time-saver, as it often lets you skip ticket lines (sold at participating sights, see page 52 for details). On Ile de la Cité, you can buy a pass at the *tabac*/souvenir store (5 Boulevard du Palais), across the street from the entrance of Sainte-Chapelle.

**Notre-Dame Cathedral:** Cathedral—free, Mon-Fri 8:00-18:45, Sat-Sun 8:00-19:15; Treasury—€4, not covered by Museum Pass, Mon-Fri 9:30-17:40, Sat-Sun 9:30-18:10; audioguide -€5, free English tours—normally Wed-Thu at 14:15, Sat-Sun at 14:30. The cathedral hosts several Masses every morning, plus Vespers at 17:45. The international Mass is held Sun at 11:30, with an organ concert at 16:30. Call or check the website for a full schedule. On Good Friday and the first Friday of the month at 15:00, the (physically underwhelming) relic known as Jesus' Crown of Thorns goes on display (Mo: Cité,

**Historic Paris Walk**

① Point Zero – Notre-Dame
② Deportation Memorial
③ Ile St. Louis
④ Left Bank Booksellers
⑤ Medieval Paris –
   St. Julien-le-Pauvre
⑥ Shakespeare & Co. Bookstore
⑦ St. Séverin
⑧ Place St. André-des-Arts
⑨ Place St. Michel
⑩ Sainte-Chapelle
⑪ Cité Métro Stop
⑫ Conciergerie
⑬ Place Dauphine
⑭ Statue of Henry IV
⑮ Pont Neuf

Hôtel de Ville, or St. Michel; tel. 01 42 34 56 10, www.notre-damedeparis.fr).

**Summer Night Spectacles:** In summer, sound-and-light displays about the history of the church generally run twice a week (free, in French with English subtitles, usually Thu and Sat at 21:00, but schedule varies—check cathedral website or call).

**Tower Climb:** The entrance for Notre-Dame's towers is outside the cathedral, along the left side. It's 400 steps up, but it's worth it for the gargoyle's-eye view of the cathedral, Seine, and city (€8.50, covered by Museum Pass but no bypass line for pass-holders; daily April-Sept 10:00-18:30, Sat-Sun until 23:00

# Paris Through History

| | |
|---|---|
| **250 B.C.** | Small fishing village of the Parisii, a Celtic tribe. |
| **52 B.C.** | Julius Caesar conquers the Parisii capital of Lutetia (near Paris), and the Romans replace it with a new capital on the Left Bank. |
| **A.D. 497** | Roman Paris falls to the Germanic Franks. King Clovis (482-511) converts to Christianity and makes Paris his capital. |
| **885-886** | Paris gets wasted in a siege by Viking Norsemen = Normans. |
| **1163** | Notre-Dame cornerstone laid. |
| **c. 1250** | Paris is a bustling commercial city with a university and new construction, such as Sainte-Chapelle and Notre-Dame. |
| **c. 1600** | King Henry IV beautifies Paris with buildings, roads, bridges, and squares. |
| **c. 1700** | Louis XIV makes Versailles his capital. Parisians grumble. |
| **1789** | Paris is the heart of France's Revolution, which condemns thousands to the guillotine. |
| **1804** | Napoleon Bonaparte crowns himself emperor in a ceremony at Notre-Dame. |
| **1830 & 1848** | Parisians take to the streets again in revolutions, fighting the return of royalty. |
| **c. 1860** | Napoleon's nephew, Napoleon III, builds Paris' wide boulevards. |
| **1889** | The centennial of the Revolution is celebrated with the Eiffel Tower. Paris enjoys wealth |

in July-Aug, Oct-March 10:00-17:30, last entry 45 minutes before closing; to avoid long lines arrive before 10:00 or after 17:00—after 16:00 in winter; tel. 01 53 10 07 00, http://notre-dame-de-paris.monuments-nationaux.fr).

**Paris Archaeological Crypt:** €4, covered by Museum Pass, Tue-Sun 10:00-18:00, closed Mon, last entry 30 minutes before closing, enter 100 yards in front of the cathedral, tel. 01 55 42 50 10.

**Deportation Memorial:** Free, April-Sept Tue-Sun 10:00-19:00, Oct-March Tue-Sun 10:00-18:00, closed Mon year-round, may randomly close at other times, Mo: Cité, mobile 06 14 67 54 98.

**Shakespeare and Company Bookstore:** Mon-Fri 10:00-23:00,

| | |
|---|---|
| | and middle-class prosperity in the belle époque (beautiful age). |
| **1920s** | After the draining Great War, Paris is a cheap place to live, attracting expatriates such as Ernest Hemingway. |
| **1940-1944** | Occupied Paris spends the war years under gray skies and gray Nazi uniforms. |
| **1968** | In May, student protests and a general strike bring Paris to a halt. |
| **1981** | High-speed rail service (TGV) is inaugurated from Paris to Lyon, starting a trend that would change travel patterns in France (and make it easier for tourists to see more of the country). |
| **1981-1995** | Under President François Mitterand, Paris' cityscape is enriched by the new Louvre Pyramid, Musée d'Orsay, La Grande Arche de la Défense, and Opéra Bastille. |
| **1998** | Playing at its home stadium, France wins the World Cup in soccer. Ecstatic fans bring Paris to a halt. |
| **2008** | All bars, cafés, and restaurants in France become smoke-free, officially ending the era of the smoky Parisian café. |
| **2011** | Paris eliminates car traffic from the Left Bank riverfront, creating even more pedestrian space. |
| **2012** | New French President François Hollande moves into Paris' Elysées Palace. |

Sat-Sun 11:00-23:00, 37 Rue de la Bûcherie, across the river from Notre-Dame, Mo: St. Michel, tel. 01 43 25 40 93.

**Sainte-Chapelle:** €8.50, €12.50 combo-ticket with Conciergerie, free if you're under 18, covered by Museum Pass, audioguide -€4.50; daily March-Oct 9:30-18:00, Wed until 21:30 in mid-May-mid-Sept, Nov-Feb 9:00-17:00; last entry 30 minutes before closing, frequent evening concerts—see page 496, 4 Boulevard du Palais, Mo: Cité, tel. 01 53 40 60 80, http://sainte-chapelle.monuments-nationaux.fr.

There are often long lines to get in. First comes the security line (all sharp objects are confiscated). No one can skip this line. Security lines are shortest on weekday mornings and on weekends (when the courts are closed). Once past security, there's another line to buy tickets to go into the church. Those with combo-tickets or Museum Passes *can* skip the ticket-buying line. (The Annexe Café, across the street from the main entry, sells €1 coffee to-go—perfect for sipping while you wait in line.)

If you visit Sainte-Chapelle near the end of the day, being the last person in the chapel as it closes is an experience you'll never forget.

**Conciergerie:** €8.50, €12.50 combo-ticket with Sainte-Chapelle, covered by Museum Pass, daily March-Oct 9:30-18:00, Nov-Feb 9:00-17:00, last entry 30 minutes before closing, 2 Boulevard du Palais, Mo: Cité, tel. 01 53 40 60 80, http://conciergerie.monuments-nationaux.fr.

**Audio Tour:** You can download this chapter as a free Rick Steves audio tour (see page 24).

**Services:** There's a free (often crowded) public WC in front of Notre-Dame near the statue of Charlemagne. Find others at museums (Sainte-Chapelle and Conciergerie) and cafés.

## The Walk Begins

• *Start at Notre-Dame Cathedral on the island in the Seine River, the physical and historic bull's-eye of your Paris map. The closest Métro stops are Cité, Hôtel de Ville, and St. Michel, each a short walk away.*

## Notre-Dame and Nearby

• *On the square in front of the cathedral, stand far enough back to take in the whole facade. Find the circular window in the center.*

For centuries, the main figure in the Christian pantheon has been Mary, the mother of Jesus. Catholics petition her in times of trouble to gain comfort, and to ask her to convince God to be compassionate with them. The church is dedicated to "Our Lady" *(Notre Dame),* and there she is, cradling God, right in the heart of the facade, surrounded by the halo of the rose window. Though the church is massive and imposing, it has always stood for the grace and compassion of Mary, the "mother of God."

Imagine the faith of the people who built this cathedral. They broke ground in 1163 with the hope that someday their great-great-great-great-great-great grandchildren might attend the dedication

Mass, which finally took place two centuries later, in 1345. Look up the 200-foot-tall bell towers and imagine a tiny medieval community mustering the money and energy for construction. Master masons supervised, but the people did much of the grunt work themselves for free—hauling the huge stones from distant quarries, digging a 30-foot-deep trench to lay the foundation, and treading like rats on a wheel designed to lift the stones up, one by one. This kind of backbreaking, arduous manual labor created the real hunchbacks of Notre-Dame.

• *"Walk this way" toward the cathedral, and view it from the bronze plaque on the ground (30 yards from the central doorway) marked...*

## ❶ Point Zero: Notre-Dame

You're standing at the center of France, the point from which all

distances are measured. It was also the center of Paris 2,300 years ago, when the Parisii tribe fished where the east-west river crossed a north-south road. The Romans conquered the Parisii and built their Temple of Jupiter where Notre-Dame stands today (52 B.C.). Then as now, the center of religious power faced the center of political power (once the Roman military, today the police station, at the far end of the square). When Rome fell, the Germanic Franks sealed their victory by replacing the temple with the Christian church of St. Etienne in the sixth century. See the outlines of the former church in the pavement (in smaller gray stones), showing what were once walls and columns, angling out from Notre-Dame to Point Zero.

The grand equestrian statue (to your right, as you face the church) is of Charlemagne ("Charles the Great," 742-814), King of the Franks, whose reign marked the birth of France as a nation. He briefly united Europe and was crowned the first Holy Roman Emperor in 800, but after his death, the kingdom was divided into what would become modern France and Germany.

Before its renovation 150 years ago, this square was much smaller, a characteristic medieval shambles facing a run-down church, surrounded by winding streets and higgledy-piggledy buildings. (Yellowed bricks in the pavement show the medieval street plan and even identify some of the buildings.) The church's huge bell towers rose above this tangle of smaller buildings, inspiring Victor Hugo's story of a deformed bell-ringer who could look down on all of Paris.

Looking two-thirds of the way up Notre-Dame's left tower, those with binoculars or good eyes can find Paris' most photographed gargoyle. Propped on his elbows on the balcony rail, he watches all the tourists in line.

• *Much of Paris' history is right under your feet. Some may consider visiting it in the...*

## Archaeological Crypt

Two thousand years of dirt and debris have raised the city's altitude. In the crypt (entrance 100 yards in front of Notre-Dame's entrance) you can see remains of the many structures that have stood on this spot in the center of Paris: Roman buildings that surrounded a temple of Jupiter; a wall that didn't keep the Franks out; the main medieval road that once led grandly up the square to Notre-Dame; and even (wow) a 19th-century sewer. (For more info, see page 57.)

• *Now turn your attention to the...*

## Notre-Dame Facade

• *Look at the left doorway, and to the left of the door, find the statue with his head in his hands.*

### St. Denis

When Christianity began making converts in Roman Paris, the bishop of Paris, Denis, was beheaded as a warning to those forsaking the Roman gods. But those early Christians were hard to keep down. The man who would become St. Denis simply got up, tucked his head under his arm, "headed" north, paused at a fountain to wash it off, and continued until he found just the right place to meet his maker. The Parisians

were convinced by this miracle, Christianity gained ground, and a church soon replaced the pagan temple.

• *Above the central doorway, you'll find scenes from the **Last Judgment**.*

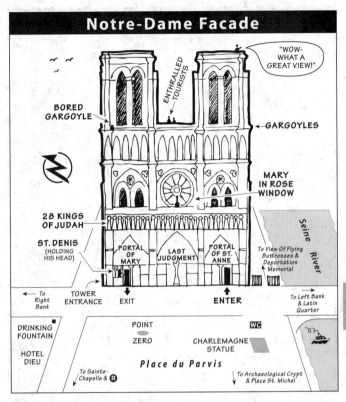

## Notre-Dame Facade

"WOW—WHAT A GREAT VIEW!"

ENTHRALLED TOURISTS

BORED GARGOYLE

GARGOYLES

MARY IN ROSE WINDOW

28 KINGS OF JUDAH

ST. DENIS (HOLDING HIS HEAD)

PORTAL OF MARY

LAST JUDGMENT

PORTAL OF ST. ANNE

To View Of Flying Buttresses & Deportation Memorial

Seine River

← To Right Bank

TOWER ENTRANCE

EXIT

ENTER

To Left Bank & Latin Quarter →

DRINKING FOUNTAIN

HOTEL DIEU

POINT ZERO

CHARLEMAGNE STATUE

WC

To Sainte-Chapelle & Ⓜ

*Place du Parvis*

To Archaeological Crypt & Place St. Michel

**HISTORIC PARIS WALK**

## Central Portal

It's the end of the world, and Christ sits on the throne of judgment (just under the arches, holding both hands up). Beneath him

an angel and a demon weigh souls in the balance; the demon cheats by pressing down. It's a sculptural depiction of the good, the bad, and the ugly. The good souls stand to the left, gazing up to heaven. The bad souls to the right are chained up and led off to a six-hour tour of the Louvre on a hot summer day. The ugly souls must be the crazy, sculpted demons to the right, at the base of the arch. Find the flaming cauldron with the sinner diving into it head-first. The lower panel shows Judgment Day, as angels with trumpets remind worshippers that all social classes will be judged—clergy, nobility, army, and peasants. Below that, Jesus stands between the 12 apostles—each barefoot and with his ID symbol (such as Peter with his keys).

• *Take 10 paces back. Above the arches is a row of 28 statues, known as...*

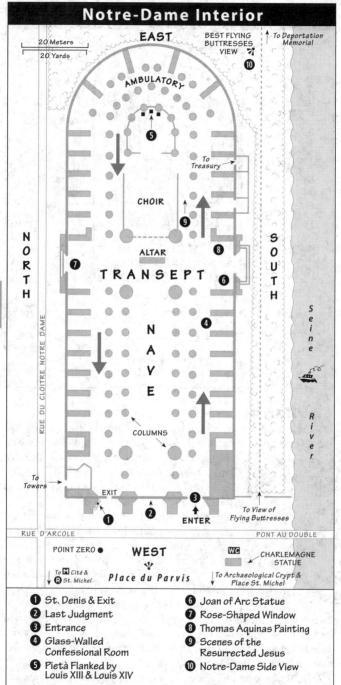

# Notre-Dame Interior

EAST

BEST FLYING
BUTTRESSES
VIEW ✈

🔟 To Deportation
Memorial

20 Meters
20 Yards

AMBULATORY

5️⃣

To
Treasury

CHOIR

9️⃣

8️⃣

To Towers

N
O
R
T
H

ALTAR

7️⃣

T R A N S E P T

6️⃣

S
O
U
T
H

RUE DU CLOITRE NOTRE DAME

N
A
V
E

4️⃣

Seine River

COLUMNS

To
Towers

EXIT

1️⃣  2️⃣  3️⃣

ENTER

To View of
Flying Buttresses

RUE D'ARCOLE

PONT AU DOUBLE

POINT ZERO ●

WEST
↓↓

WC

CHARLEMAGNE
STATUE

To Ⓜ Cité &
Ⓡ St. Michel

Place du Parvis

To Archaeological Crypt &
Place St. Michel

1️⃣ St. Denis & Exit
2️⃣ Last Judgment
3️⃣ Entrance
4️⃣ Glass-Walled
   Confessional Room
5️⃣ Pietà Flanked by
   Louis XIII & Louis XIV

6️⃣ Joan of Arc Statue
7️⃣ Rose-Shaped Window
8️⃣ Thomas Aquinas Painting
9️⃣ Scenes of the
   Resurrected Jesus
🔟 Notre-Dame Side View

## The Kings of Judah

In the days of the French Revolution (1789-1799), these biblical kings were mistaken for the hated French kings, and Notre-Dame represented the oppressive Catholic hierarchy. The citizens stormed the church, crying, "Off with their heads!" Plop—they lopped off the crowned heads of these kings with glee, creating a row of St. Denises that wasn't repaired for decades.

But the story doesn't end there. A schoolteacher who lived nearby collected the heads and buried them in his backyard for safekeeping. There they slept until 1977, when they were accidentally unearthed. Today, you can stare into the eyes of the original kings in the Cluny Museum, a few blocks away (see page 279).

• *Now let's head into the...*

# Notre-Dame Interior

• *Enter the church at the right doorway (the line moves quickly) and find a spot where you can view the long, high central aisle. (Be careful: Pickpockets attend church here religiously.)*

## Nave

Remove your metaphorical hat and become a simple bareheaded peasant, entering the dim medieval light of the church. Take a minute to let your pupils dilate, then take in the subtle, mysterious light show that God beams through the stained-glass windows. Follow the slender columns up 10 stories to the praying-hands arches of the ceiling, and contemplate the heavens. Let's say it's dedication day for this great stone wonder. The priest intones the words of the Mass that echo through the hall: *Terribilis est locus iste...*"This place is *terribilis*," meaning awe-inspiring or even terrifying. It's a huge, dark, earthly cavern lit with an unearthly light.

This is Gothic. Taller and filled with light, Notre-Dame was a major improvement over the earlier Romanesque style. Gothic

architects needed only a few structural columns, topped by crisscrossing pointed arches, to support the weight of the roof. This let them build higher than ever, freeing up the walls for windows.

Notre-Dame has the typical basilica floor plan shared by so many Catholic churches: a long central nave lined with columns and flanked by side aisles. It's designed in the shape of a cross, with the altar placed where the crossbeam intersects. The church can hold up to 10,000 faithful, and it's probably buzzing with visitors now, just as it was 600 years ago. The quiet, deserted churches we see elsewhere are in stark contrast to the busy, center-of-life places they were in the Middle Ages.

• *Walk up to the main altar.*

## Altar

This marks the place where Mass is said and the bread and wine of Communion are blessed and distributed. In olden days, there were no chairs. This was the holy spot for Romans, Christians...and even atheists. When the Revolutionaries stormed the church, they gutted it and turned it into a "Temple of Reason." A woman dressed like the Statue of Liberty held court at the altar as a symbol of the divinity of Man. France today, though nominally Catholic, remains

aloof from Vatican dogmatism. Instead of traditional wooden confessional booths, there's an inviting **glass-walled room** (right aisle), where modern sinners seek counseling as much as forgiveness.

Just past the altar is the so-called choir, the area enclosed with carved-wood walls, where more intimate services can be held in this spacious building. Looking past the altar to the far end of the choir (under the cross), you'll see a fine **17th-century** *pietà*, flanked by two kneeling kings: Louis XIII (1601-1643, not so famous) and his son Louis XIV (1638-1715, very famous, also known as the Sun King, who ruled gloriously and flamboyantly from Versailles).

## Right Transept (and Beyond)

A statue of **Joan of Arc** (Jeanne d'Arc, 1412-1431), dressed in armor and praying, honors the French teenager who rallied her country's soldiers to try to drive English invaders from Paris. The English and their allies burned her at the stake for claiming to hear heavenly voices. Almost immediately, Parisians rallied to condemn Joan's execution, and finally, in 1909, here in Notre-Dame, the former "witch" was beatified.

Join the statue in gazing up to the blue-and-purple, **rose-shaped window** in the opposite transept—with teeny green Mary and baby Jesus in the center—the only one of the three rose windows still with its original medieval glass. (See photo on next page.)

A large painting back down to your right shows portly **Thomas Aquinas** (1225-1274) teaching, while his students drink from the fountain of knowledge. This Italian monk did undergrad and master's work at the multicultural University of Paris, then taught

HISTORIC PARIS WALK

there for several years while writing his theological works. His "scholasticism" used Aristotle's logic to examine the Christian universe, aiming to fuse faith and reason.

• *Continue a few paces toward the far end of the church, pausing at the top of the three stair steps.*

## Circling the Choir

The back side of the choir walls feature **scenes of the resurrected Jesus** (c. 1350) appearing to his followers, starting with Mary Magdalene. Their starry robes still gleam, thanks to a 19th-century renovation. The niches below these carvings mark the tombs of centuries of archbishops. Just ahead on the right is the **Treasury**. It contains lavish robes, golden reliquaries, and the humble tunic of

King (and St.) Louis IX, but it probably isn't worth the entry fee. Surrounding the choir are chapels, each dedicated to a particular saint and funded by a certain guild. One chapel displays models of the church and an exhibit on medieval construction techniques—pulleys, wagons, hamster-wheel cranes, and lots of elbow grease. The faithful can pause at any of the other chapels to light a candle as an offering and meditate in the cool light of the stained glass.

• *Amble around the ambulatory, spill back outside, and make a slow U-turn left. Enter the park (named "Square Jean XXIII") through the iron gates along the riverside.*

## Notre-Dame Side View

Alongside the church you'll notice the flying buttresses. These 50-foot stone "beams" that stick out of the church were the key to the complex Gothic architecture. The pointed arches we saw inside cause the weight of the roof to push outward rather than downward. The "flying" buttresses support the roof by pushing back inward. Gothic architects were masters at playing architectural forces against

*It takes 13 tourists to build a Gothic church: six columns, six buttresses, and one steeple.*

each other to build loftier and loftier churches, opening the walls for stained-glass windows.

Picture Quasimodo (the fictional hunchback) limping around along the railed balcony at the base of the roof among the "gargoyles." These grotesque beasts sticking out from pillars and buttresses represent souls caught between heaven and earth. They also function as rainspouts (from the same French root word as "gargle") when there are no evil spirits to battle.

The Neo-Gothic 300-foot spire is a product of the 1860 reconstruction of the dilapidated old church. Victor Hugo's book *The Hunchback of Notre-Dame* (1831) inspired a young architecture student named Eugène-Emmanuel Viollet-le-Duc to dedicate his career to a major renovation in Gothic style. Find Viollet-le-Duc at the base of the spire among the green apostles and evangelists (visible as you approach the back end of the church). The apostles look outward, blessing the city, while the architect (at top) looks up the spire, marveling at his fine work.

• *Behind Notre-Dame, cross the street and enter through the iron gate into the park at the tip of the island. Look for the stairs and head down to reach the...*

## ❷ Deportation Memorial (Mémorial de la Déportation)

This memorial to the 200,000 French victims of the Nazi concentration camps (1940-1945) draws you into their experience. France was quickly overrun by Nazi Germany, and Paris spent the war years under Nazi occupation. Jews and dissidents were rounded up and deported—many never returned.

As you descend the steps, the city around you disappears. Surrounded by walls, you have become a prisoner. Your only

freedom is your view of the sky and the
tiny glimpse of the river below. Enter
the dark, single-file chamber up ahead.
Inside, the circular plaque in the floor
reads, "They went to the end of the earth
and did not return."

The hallway stretching in front of
you is lined with 200,000 lighted crys-
tals, one for each French citizen who
died. Flickering at the far end is the
eternal flame of hope. The tomb of the
unknown deportee lies at your feet.
Above, the inscription reads, "Dedicated to the living memory of
the 200,000 French deportees shrouded by the night and the fog,
exterminated in the Nazi concentration camps." The side rooms are
filled with triangles—reminiscent of the identification patches in-
mates were forced to wear—each bearing the name of a concentration camp. Above the exit as you leave is the message you'll find at
many other Holocaust sites: "Forgive, but never forget."

• *Back on street level, look across the river (north) to the island called...*

## ❸ Ile St. Louis

If Ile de la Cité is a tugboat laden with the history of Paris, it's tow-
ing this classy little residential dinghy, laden only with high-rent
apartments, boutiques, characteristic restaurants, and famous ice
cream shops.

Ile St. Louis wasn't developed until much later than Ile de la
Cité (17th century). What was a swampy mess is now harmonious
Parisian architecture and one of Paris' most exclusive neighborhoods. If you won't have time to return here for an evening stroll
(see page 499), consider taking a brief detour across the pedestrian
bridge, Pont St. Louis. It connects the two islands, leading right to
Rue St. Louis-en-l'Ile. This spine of the island is lined with appealing shops and reasonably priced restaurants. A short stroll takes
you to the famous Berthillon ice cream parlor at #31. Gelato-lovers
head instead to Amorino Gelati at 47 Rue St. Louis-en-l'Ile. This
walk is about as peaceful and romantic as Paris gets. When you're
finished exploring, loop back to the pedestrian bridge along the
parklike quays (walk north to the river and turn left). Cross the
bridge to return to Ile de la Cité, and stand near the Deportation
Memorial.

Look upstream (east) to the bridge (Pont Tournelle) that links
Ile St. Louis with the Left Bank (which is now on your right).
Where the bridge meets the Left Bank, you'll find one of Paris'
most exclusive restaurants, La Tour d'Argent (with a flag flying
from the rooftop). This restaurant was the inspiration for the movie

**Ile St. Louis**

- Berthillon Ice Cream
- Amorino Gelati
- Rest. La Tour d'Argent
- Good Picnic Spot
- Grocery Store

*Ratatouille.* Because the top floor has floor-to-ceiling windows, your evening meal comes with glittering views—and a golden price (allow €200 minimum, though you get a free photo of yourself dining elegantly with Notre-Dame floodlit in the background).

• *From the Deportation Memorial, cross the bridge to the Left Bank. All those* **padlocks** *adorning the railing are akin to lighting candles in a church. Locals and tourists alike honor loved ones by writing a brief message on the lock and attaching it to the railing. You can buy a lock (called* cadenas, €5) *at a nearby bookseller's stall along the river.*

*Turn right after crossing the bridge and walk along the river, toward the front end of Notre-Dame. Stairs detour down to the riverbank if you need a place to picnic. This side view of the church from across the river is one of Europe's great sights and is best from river level. For the best view and the sweetest crêpes you've ever had, look for the old river barge Daphné and see if Valeria is open (€2.50-3.50). If the sun is out, he should be there.*

# Left Bank

## ❹ Left Bank Booksellers

The Rive Gauche, or the Left Bank of the Seine—"left" if you were floating downstream—still has many of the twisting lanes and narrow buildings of medieval times. The Right Bank is more modern and business-oriented, with wide boulevards and stressed Parisians in suits. Here along the riverbank, the "big business" is secondhand

books, displayed in the green metal stalls on the parapet. These literary entrepreneurs pride themselves on their easygoing style. With flexible hours and virtually no overhead, they run their businesses as they have since medieval times. For more information, see the "*Les Bouquinistes* (Riverside Vendors)" sidebar on page 481.

• *When you reach the bridge (Pont au Double) that crosses over in front of Notre-Dame, veer to the left across the street to a small park called Square Viviani (fill your water bottle from fountain on left).*

*Angle across the square and pass by Paris' oldest inhabitant— an acacia tree nicknamed Robinier, after the guy who planted it in 1602. Imagine that this same tree might once have shaded the Sun King, Louis XIV. Just beyond the tree you'll find the small rough-stone church of St. Julien-le-Pauvre.*

## ❺ Medieval Paris (1000-1400)

Picture Paris in 1250, when the church of St. Julien-le-Pauvre was still new. Notre-Dame was nearly done (so they thought), Sainte-Chapelle had just opened, the university was expanding human

knowledge, and Paris was fast becoming a prosperous industrial and commercial center. The area around the church (and along nearby Rue Galande) gives you some of the medieval feel of ramshackle architecture and old houses leaning every which way. In medieval days, people were piled on top of each other, building at all angles, as they scrambled for this prime real estate near the main commercial artery of the day—the Seine. The smell of fish competed with the smell of neighbors in this knot of humanity.

Narrow dirt (or mud) streets sloped from here down into the mucky Seine until the 19th century, when modern quays and embankments cleaned everything up.

• *Return to the river and turn left on Rue de la Bûcherie. At #37, drop into the...*

## ❻ Shakespeare and Company Bookstore

In addition to hosting butchers and fishmongers, the Left Bank has been home to scholars, philosophers, and poets since medieval times. This funky bookstore—a reincarnation of the original shop from the 1920s on Rue de l'Odéon—has picked up the literary torch. Sylvia Beach, an American with a passion for free thinking, opened Shakespeare and Company for the post-WWI Lost Generation, who came to Paris to find themselves. American writers flocked to her shop for the cheap rent, fleeing the uptight, Prohibition-era United States. Beach's bookstore was famous as a meeting place for Paris' expatriate literary elite. Ernest Hemingway borrowed books from it regularly. James Joyce struggled

to find a publisher for his now-classic novel *Ulysses*—until Sylvia Beach published it. George Bernard Shaw, Gertrude Stein, and Ezra Pound also got their English fix at her shop.

Today, the bookstore carries on that literary tradition—the owner, Sylvia, is named after the original store's founder. Struggling writers are given free accommodations upstairs in tiny rooms with views of Notre-Dame. Downstairs, travelers enjoy a great selection of used English books.

Notice the green water fountain (1900) in front of the bookstore, one of the many in Paris donated by the English philanthropist Sir Richard Wallace. The hooks below the caryatids once held metal mugs for drinking the water.

• *Continue to Rue du Petit-Pont (which becomes Rue St. Jacques), and turn left. This bustling north-south boulevard was the Romans' busiest street 2,000 years ago, with chariots racing in and out of the city. (Roman-iacs can view remains from the third-century baths, along with a fine medieval collection, at the nearby Cluny Museum;* ✪ *see the Cluny Museum Tour chapter.)*

*A block south of the Seine, turn right at the Gothic church of St. Séverin and walk into the Latin Quarter.*

## ❼ St. Séverin

Don't ask me why, but building this church took a century longer than building Notre-Dame. This is Flamboyant, or "flame-like," Gothic, and you can see how the short, prickly spires are meant to make this building flicker in the eyes of the faithful. The church

gives us a close-up look at gargoyles, the decorative drain
spouts that also functioned to
keep evil spirits away.

Inside you can see the final
stage of Gothic, on the cusp of
the Renaissance. The stained-
glass windows favor the greens
and reds popular in St. Séverin's heyday. In the apse, admire
the lone twisted Flamboyant

Gothic column and the fan vaulting. The apse's stained-glass windows (by Jean Bazaine, c. 1960) echo the fan-vaulting effect in a
modern, abstract way. Each colorful window represents one of the
seven sacraments—blue for baptism, yellow for marriage, etc. The
impressive organ filling the entrance wall is a reminder that this
church is still a popular venue for evening concerts (see gate for
information posters, buy tickets at door).

• *At #22 Rue St. Séverin, you'll find the skinniest house in Paris, two
windows wide. Rue St. Séverin leads right through...*

## The Latin Quarter

Although it may look more like the Greek Quarter today (cheap
gyros abound), this area is the Latin Quarter, named for the language you'd have heard on these streets if you walked them in the
Middle Ages. The University of Paris (founded 1215), one of the
leading educational institutions of medieval Europe, was (and still
is) nearby.

A thousand years ago, the "crude" or vernacular local languages were sophisticated enough to communicate basic human
needs, but if you wanted to get philosophical, the language of
choice was Latin. Medieval Europe's class of educated elite tran-
scended nations and borders. From Sicily to Sweden, they spoke
and corresponded in Latin. Now the most "Latin" thing about this
area is the beat you may hear coming from some of the subterranean jazz clubs.

Walking along Rue St. Séverin, you can still see the shadow of
the medieval sewer system. The street slopes into a central channel
of bricks. In the days before plumbing and toilets, when people still
went to the river or neighborhood wells for their water, flushing
meant throwing it out the window. At certain times of day, maids
on the fourth floor would holler, *"Garde de l'eau!"* ("Watch out for
the water!") and heave it into the streets, where it would eventually
wash down into the Seine.

As you wander, remember that before Napoleon III commissioned Baron Haussmann to modernize the city with grand

boulevards (19th century), Paris was just like this—a medieval tangle. The ethnic feel of this area is nothing new—it's been a melting pot and university district for almost 800 years.

• *Keep wandering straight, and you'll come to...*

## Boulevard St. Michel

Busy Boulevard St. Michel (or "boul' Miche") is famous as the

main artery for Paris' café and arts scene, culminating a block away (to the left) at the intersection with Boulevard St. Germain. Although nowadays you're more likely to find pantyhose at 30 percent off, there are still many cafés, boutiques, and bohemian haunts nearby.

The Sorbonne—the University of Paris' humanities department—is also nearby, if you want to make a detour, though visitors are not allowed to enter. (Turn left on Boulevard St. Michel and walk two blocks south. Gaze at the dome from the Place de la Sorbonne courtyard.) Originally founded as a theological school, the Sorbonne began attracting more students and famous professors—such as St. Thomas Aquinas and Peter Abélard—as its prestige grew. By the time the school expanded to include other subjects, it had a reputation for bold new ideas. Nonconformity is a tradition here, and Paris remains a world center for new intellectual trends.

• *Cross Boulevard St. Michel. Just ahead is...*

## ❽ Place St. André-des-Arts

This tree-filled square is lined with cafés. In Paris, most serious thinking goes on in cafés. For centuries these have been social watering holes, where you can get a warm place to sit and stimulating conversation for the price of a cup of coffee. Every great French writer—from Voltaire and Jean-Jacques Rousseau to Jean-Paul Sartre and Jacques Derrida—had a favorite haunt.

Paris honors its writers. If you visit the Panthéon (described on page 74)—a few blocks up Boulevard St. Michel and to the left—you'll find French writers (Voltaire, Victor Hugo, Emile Zola, and Rousseau), inventors (Louis Braille), and scientists (including Marie and Pierre Curie) buried in a setting usually reserved for warriors and politicians.

• *Adjoining this square toward the river is the triangular Place St. Michel, with a Métro stop and a statue of St. Michael killing a devil. Note:*

*If you were to continue west along Rue St. André-des-Arts, you'd find more Left Bank action.*

## ❾ Place St. Michel

You're standing at the traditional core of the Left Bank's artsy, liberal, hippie, bohemian district of poets, philosophers, and winos. Nearby, you'll find international eateries, far-out bookshops, street singers, pale girls in black berets, jazz clubs, and—these days—tourists. Small cinemas show avant-garde films, almost always in the *version originale* (v.o.). For colorful wandering and café-sitting, afternoons and evenings are best. In the morning, it feels sleepy. The Latin Quarter stays up late and sleeps in.

In less commercial times, Place St. Michel was a gathering point for the city's malcontents and misfits. In 1830, 1848, and again in 1871, the citizens took the streets from the government troops, set up barricades *Les Miz*-style, and fought against royalist oppression. During World War II, the locals rose up against their Nazi oppressors (read the plaques under the dragons at the foot of the St. Michel fountain).

In the spring of 1968, a time of social upheaval all over the world, young students battled riot batons and tear gas by digging up the cobblestones on the street and hurling them at police. They took over the square and declared it an independent state. Factory workers followed their call to arms and went on strike, challenging the de Gaulle government and forcing change. Eventually, the students were pacified, the university was reformed, and the Latin Quarter's original cobblestones were replaced with pavement, so future scholars could never again use the streets as weapons. Even today, whenever there's a student demonstration, it starts here.

• *From Place St. Michel, look across the river and find the prickly steeple of the Sainte-Chapelle church. Head toward it. Cross the river on Pont St. Michel and continue north along the Boulevard du Palais. On your left, you'll see the doorway to Sainte-Chapelle.*

## Sainte-Chapelle and Nearby

Security is strict at the Sainte-Chapelle complex because this is more than a tourist attraction: France's Supreme Court meets to the right of Sainte-Chapelle. Expect a long wait unless you arrive before it opens. Once past security, you'll enter the courtyard outside Sainte-Chapelle, where you'll find WCs and information about upcoming church concerts.

The ticket office is near the church entry, which is often hidden

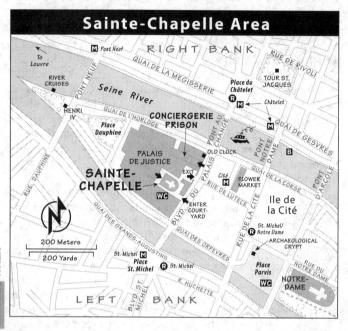

# Sainte-Chapelle Area

behind a long line of ticket buyers. Don't be shy—if you already have a Museum Pass or Conciergerie combo-ticket in hand, march up to the front, and you'll be allowed right in.

• *Enter the humble ground floor.*

## ❿ Sainte-Chapelle

This triumph of Gothic church architecture is a cathedral of glass like no other. It was speedily built between 1242 and 1248 for King Louis IX—the only French king who is now a saint—to house the supposed Crown of Thorns (now kept at Notre-Dame and shown only on Good Friday and on the first Friday of the month at 15:00). Its architectural harmony is due to the fact that it was completed under the direction of one architect and in only six years—unheard of in Gothic times. Recall that Notre-Dame took over 200 years.

Though the inside is beautiful, the exterior is basically functional. The muscular buttresses hold up the stone roof, so the walls are essentially there to display stained glass. The lacy spire is Neo-Gothic—added in the 19th century. Inside, the layout clearly shows an *ancien régime* approach to worship. The low-ceilinged basement was for staff and other common folks—worshipping under a sky filled with painted fleurs-de-lis, a symbol of the king. Royal Christians worshipped upstairs. The paint job, a 19th-century restoration, helps you imagine how grand this small, painted, jeweled chapel was. (Imagine Notre-Dame painted like this…) Each capital is playfully carved with a different plant's leaves.

• *Climb the spiral staircase to the Chapelle Haute. Leave the rough stone of the earth and step into the light.*

### The Stained Glass

*Fiat lux.* "Let there be light." From the first page of the Bible, it's clear: Light is divine. Light shines through stained glass like God's grace shining down to earth. Gothic architects used their new technology to turn dark stone buildings into lanterns of light. The glory of Gothic shines brighter here than in any other church.

There are 15 separate panels of stained glass (6,500 square feet—two thirds of it 13th-century original), with more than 1,100 different scenes, mostly from the Bible. These cover the entire Christian history of the world, from the Creation in Genesis (first window on the left, as you face the altar), to the coming of Christ (over the altar), to the end of the world (the round "rose"-shaped window at the rear of the church). Each individual scene is interesting, and the whole effect is overwhelming. Allow yourself a few minutes to bask in the glow of the colored light before tackling the window descriptions below, then remember to keep referring to the map to find the windows.

• *Working clockwise from the entrance, look for these notable scenes. (The sun lights up different windows at various times of day. Overcast days give the most even light. On bright, sunny days, some sections are glorious, while others look like sheets of lead.)*

**Genesis—Cain Clubbing Abel** (first window on the left, always dark because of a building butted up against it): On the bottom level in the third circle from the left, we see God create the round earth and hold it up. On the next level up, we catch glimpses of naked Adam and Eve. On the third level (far right circle), Cain, in red, clubs his brother Abel, committing the first murder.

**Life of Moses** (second window, the dark bottom row of diamond panels): The first panel shows baby Moses in a basket, placed by his sister in the squiggly brown river. Next he's found by the pharaoh's daughter. Then he grows up. And finally, he's a man, a prince of Egypt on his royal throne.

**More Moses** (third window, in middle and upper sections):

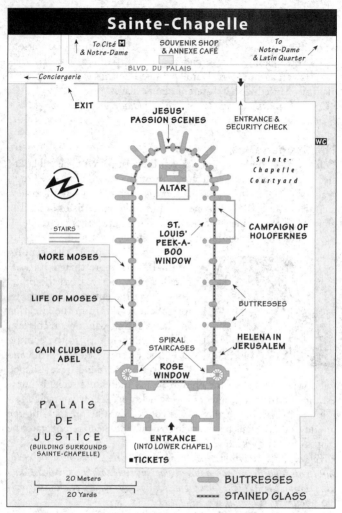

Sainte-Chapelle

To Cité M
& Notre-Dame

SOUVENIR SHOP
& ANNEXE CAFÉ

To
Notre-Dame
& Latin Quarter

To
Conciergerie

BLVD. DU PALAIS

EXIT

JESUS'
PASSION SCENES

ENTRANCE &
SECURITY CHECK

WC

Sainte-
Chapelle
Courtyard

ALTAR

STAIRS

ST.
LOUIS'
PEEK-A-
BOO
WINDOW

CAMPAIGN OF
HOLOFERNES

MORE MOSES

LIFE OF MOSES

BUTTRESSES

CAIN CLUBBING
ABEL

SPIRAL
STAIRCASES

HELENA IN
JERUSALEM

ROSE
WINDOW

PALAIS
DE
JUSTICE
(BUILDING SURROUNDS
SAINTE-CHAPELLE)

ENTRANCE
(INTO LOWER CHAPEL)
■TICKETS

20 Meters

20 Yards

BUTTRESSES

STAINED GLASS

See how many guys with bright yellow horns you can spy. Moses is shown with horns as the result of a medieval mistranslation of the Hebrew word for "rays of light," or halo.

**Jesus' Passion Scenes** (directly over the altar and behind the canopy): These scenes from Jesus' arrest and Crucifixion were the backdrop for the Crown of Thorns (originally displayed on the altar), which was placed on Jesus' head when the Romans were torturing and humiliating him before his execution. Stand close to the steps of the altar, look through the canopy just below its top, and find Jesus in yellow shorts, carrying his cross (fifth frame up from right bottom). Now, step back five paces and look just above

## Stained Glass Supreme

Craftsmen made glass—which is, essentially, melted sand—using this recipe:

- Melt one part sand with two parts wood ash.
- Mix in rusty metals to get different colors—iron makes red; cobalt makes blue; copper, green; manganese, purple; cadmium, yellow.
- Blow glass into a cylinder shape, cut lengthwise, and lay flat.
- Cut into pieces with an iron tool, or by heating and cooling a select spot to make it crack.
- Fit pieces together to form a figure, using strips of lead to hold them in place.
- Place masterpiece so high on a wall that no one can read it.

the altar table to see Jesus being whipped (left, arms around a green column) and—the key scene in this relic chapel—Jesus in purple, being fitted with the painful Crown of Thorns (right). Finally (as high as you can see), Jesus on the cross is speared by a soldier.

**Campaign of Holofernes** (window to the right of the altar wall): On the bottom row are four scenes of colorful knights (refer to map to get oriented). The second circle from the left is a battle scene (the campaign of Holofernes), showing three soldiers with swords slaughtering three men. The background is blue. The men have different-colored clothes—red, blue, green, mauve, and white. Examine some of the details. You can see the folds in the robes, the hair, and facial features. Look at the victim in the center—his head is splotched with blood. Details like the folds in the robes (see the victim in white, lower left) came about either by scratching on

the glass or by baking on paint. It was a painstaking process of finding just the right colors, fitting them together to make a scene...and then multiplying by 1,100.

**Helena in Jerusalem** (first window on the right wall by entrance): This window tells the story of how Christ's Crown of Thorns found its way from Jerusalem to Constantinople to this chapel. Start in the lower-left corner, where the Roman emperor Constantine (in blue, on his throne) waves goodbye to his Christian mom, Helena. She arrives at the gate of Jerusalem (next panel to the right). Her men (in the two-part medallion above Jerusalem) dig through ruins and find Christ's (tiny) cross and other relics. She returns to Constantinople with a stash of holy relics, including the Crown of Thorns. Nine hundred years later, French Crusader knights (the next double medallion above) invade the Holy Land and visit Constantinople. Finally, King Louis IX, dressed in blue (in the panel up one and to the right of the last one), returns to France with the sacred relic.

**Rose Window** (above entrance): It's Judgment Day, with a tiny Christ in the center of the chaos and miracles. This window, from the Flamboyant period, is 200 years newer than the rest. Facing west and the sunset, it's best late in the day.

If you can't read much into the individual windows, you're not alone. (For some tutoring, a little book with color photos is on sale downstairs with the postcards.)

## Altar

The altar was raised up high to better display the Crown of Thorns, the relic around which this chapel was built. Notice the staircase: Access was limited to the priest and the king, who wore the keys

to the shrine around his neck. Also note that there is no high-profile image of Jesus anywhere—this chapel was all about the Crown.

King Louis IX, convinced he'd found the real McCoy, spent roughly the equivalent of €500 million for the Crown, €370 million for the gem-studded shrine to display it in (later destroyed in the French Revolution), and a mere €150 million to build Sainte-Chapelle to house it. Today, the supposed Crown of Thorns is kept by the Notre-Dame Treasury (though it's occasionally brought out for display).

Lay your camera on the ground and shoot the ceiling. Those pure and simple ribs growing out of the slender columns are the essence of Gothic structure.

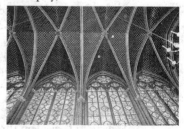

• *Exit Sainte-Chapelle. Back outside, as you walk around the church exterior, look down to see the foundation and take note of how much Paris has risen in the 750 years since Sainte-Chapelle was built.*

*Next door to Sainte-Chapelle is the...*

## Palais de Justice

Sainte-Chapelle sits within a huge complex of buildings that has housed the local government since ancient Roman times. It was

the site of the original Gothic palace of the early kings of France. The only surviving medieval parts are Sainte-Chapelle and the Conciergerie prison.

Most of the site is now covered by the giant Palais de Justice, built in 1776, home of the French Supreme Court. The motto *Liberté, Egalité, Fraternité* over the doors is a reminder that this was also the headquarters of the Revolutionary government. Here they doled out justice, condemning many to imprisonment in the Conciergerie downstairs or to the guillotine.

• *Now pass through the big iron gate to the noisy Boulevard du Palais. Cross the street to the wide, pedestrian-only Rue de Lutèce and walk about halfway down.*

## ⓫ Cité "Metropolitain" Métro Stop

Of the 141 original early-20th-century subway entrances, this is one of only a few survivors—now preserved as a national art treasure. (New York's Museum of Modern Art even exhibits one.) It marks Paris at its peak in 1900—on the cutting edge of Modernism, but with an eye for beauty. The curvy, plantlike ironwork is a textbook example of Art Nouveau, the style that rebelled against the erector-set squareness of the Industrial Age. Other similar

Métro stations in Paris are Abbesses and Porte Dauphine.

The flower and plant market on Place Louis Lépine is a pleasant detour. On Sundays this square flutters with a busy bird market. And across the way is the Préfecture de Police, where Inspector Clouseau of *Pink Panther* fame used to work, and where the local resistance fighters took the first building from the Nazis in August of 1944, leading to the Allied liberation of Paris a week later.

• *Pause here to admire the view. Sainte-Chapelle is a pearl in an ugly architectural oyster. Double back to the Palais de Justice, turn right onto Boulevard du Palais, and enter the...*

## ⑫ Conciergerie

Though pretty barren inside, this former prison echoes with history (and is free with the Museum Pass—remember that passholders can skip the ticket-buying line). Positioned next to the courthouse, the Conciergerie was the gloomy prison famous as the last stop for 2,780 victims of the guillotine, including France's last *ancien régime* queen, Marie-Antoinette. Before then, kings had used the

building to torture and execute failed assassins. (One of its towers along the river was called "The Babbler," named for the pain-induced sounds that leaked from it.) When the Revolution (1789) toppled the king, the building kept its same function, but without torture. The progressive Revolutionaries proudly unveiled a modern and more humane way to execute people—the guillotine.

Inside, pick up a free map and breeze through the one-way circuit. It's well-described in English. See the spacious, low-ceilinged Hall of Men-at-Arms (Room 1), used as the guards' dining room, with four large fireplaces (look up the chimneys). This big room gives a feel for the grandeur of the Great Hall (upstairs, not open to visitors), where the Revolutionary tribunals grilled scared prisoners on their political correctness. The raised area at the far end of the room (Room 4, today's bookstore) was notorious as the walkway of the executioner, who was known affectionately as "Monsieur de Paris."

Pass through the bookstore to find the Office of the Keeper, or "Concierge" of the place (who monitored torture...and recommended nearby restaurants). Next door is the *Toilette*, where condemned prisoners combed their hair or touched up their lipstick before their final public appearance—waiting for the open-air cart (tumbrel) to pull up outside. The tumbrel would carry them to the guillotine, which was on Place de la Concorde.

Upstairs is a memorial room with the names of the 2,780 citizens condemned to death by the guillotine. Here are some of the people you'll find, in alphabetical order. Anne Elisabeth Capet (a.k.a. Princess Elisabeth) was decapitated for the crime of being a "sister of the tyrant." Charlotte Corday *("dite d'Armais"),* a noblewoman, snuck into the bathroom of the revolutionary writer Jean-Paul Marat and stabbed him while he bathed. Georges Danton was a prominent revolutionary who was later condemned for being insufficiently liberal—a nasty crime. Louis XVI (called "Capet: last king of France") deserves only a modest mention, as does his wife, Marie-Antoinette (*veuve* means she's widowed). And finally—oh, the irony—there's Maximilien de Robespierre, the head of the

Revolution, the man who sent so many to the guillotine. He was eventually toppled, humiliated, imprisoned here, and beheaded.

Head down the hallway. Along the way, you'll see some reconstructed cells with mannequins that show how the poor slept on straw, whereas the wealthy got a cot.

After passing through a small museum (with explanations in English on small boards), go back downstairs to a tiny chapel built on the site where Marie-Antoinette's prison cell originally stood.

The chapel was made in Marie's honor by Louis XVIII, the brother of beheaded Louis XVI and the first king to reclaim the throne after the Revolution. The chapel's paintings show an idealized Marie-Antoinette in her cell, receiving the Last Sacrament on the night before her beheading. The walls drip with silver-embroidered tears.

The tour continues outside in the courtyard, where female prisoners were allowed a little fresh air (notice the spikes still guarding from above). Return indoors through the door at the opposite end of the courtyard, on your left. The next room (immediately on the left) is a re-creation of Marie-Antoinette's cell. Imagine the queen spending her last days—separated from her 10-year-old son and now widowed because the king had already been executed. Mannequins, period furniture, and the real cell wallpaper set the scene.

The guard stands modestly behind a screen, while the queen psyches herself up with a crucifix. In the glass display case, see her actual crucifix, rug, and small water pitcher. On October 16, 1793, the queen walked the corridor, stepped onto the cart, and was slowly carried to Place de la Concorde, where she had a date with "Monsieur de Paris." The video (just after the bookstore) gives a taste of prison life during the Reign of Terror.

• *Back outside, turn left on Boulevard du Palais and head north. On the corner is the city's oldest public clock. The mechanism of the present clock is from 1334, and even though the case is Baroque, it keeps on ticking.*

*Turn left onto Quai de l'Horloge and walk west along the river, past "The Babbler" tower. The bridge up ahead is the Pont Neuf, where we'll end this walk. At the first corner, veer left into a sleepy triangular square called...*

### ⓭ Place Dauphine

It's amazing to find such coziness in the heart of Paris. This city
of two million is still a city of neigh-
borhoods, a collection of villages.
The French Supreme Court building looms behind like a giant marble
gavel. Enjoy the village-Paris feeling
in the park. The **Caveau du Palais**
restaurant is a nice spot for a drink
or light meal (€22-26 *plats*, 17 Place
Dauphine, tel. 01 43 26 04 28). You
may see lawyers on their lunch break
playing *boules* (see sidebar on page 386).

• *Continue through Place Dauphine. As you pop out the other end, you're
face-to-face with a...*

### ⓮ Statue of Henry IV

Henry IV (1553-1610) is not as famous as his grandson, Louis XIV,
but Henry helped make Paris what it is today—a European capital
of elegant buildings and quiet squares. He built the Place Dauphine
(behind you), the Pont Neuf (to the right), residences (to the left,
down Rue Dauphine), the Louvre's long Grand Gallery (downriver
on the right), and the tree-filled Square du Vert-Galant (directly
behind the statue, on the tip of the island). The square is one of
Paris' make-out spots; its name comes from Henry's nickname, the
Green Knight, as Henry was a notorious ladies' man. The park is
a great place to relax, dangling your legs over the concrete prow of
this boat-shaped island.

• *From the statue, turn right onto the old bridge. Pause at the little nook
halfway across.*

### ⓯ Pont Neuf

This "new bridge" is now Paris' oldest. Built during Henry IV's
reign (about 1600), its arches span the widest part of the river.

Unlike other bridges, this one never
had houses or buildings growing on
it. The turrets were originally for
vendors and street entertainers. In
the days of Henry IV, who promised
his peasants "a chicken in every pot
every Sunday," this would have been
a lively scene. From the bridge, look
downstream (west) to see the next
bridge, the pedestrian-only Pont

des Arts. Ahead on the Right Bank is the long Louvre Museum.

Beyond that, on the Left Bank, is the Orsay. And what's that tall black tower in the distance?

## The Seine

Our walk ends where Paris began—on the Seine River. From Dijon to the English Channel, the Seine meanders 500 miles, cut-

ting through the center of Paris. The river is shallow and slow within the city, but still dangerous enough to require steep stone embankments (built 1910) to prevent occasional floods.

In summer, the roads that run along the river are replaced with acres of sand, as well as beach chairs and tanned locals, creating the Paris Plages (see page 60). The success of the Paris Plages event has motivated the city to take the next step: to permanently banish vehicles from those fast lanes, turning them into riverside parks instead.

Any time of year, you'll see tourist boats and the commercial barges that carry 20 percent of Paris' transported goods. And on the banks, sportsmen today cast into the waters once fished by Paris' original Celtic inhabitants.

• *We're done. You can take a boat tour that leaves from near the base of Pont Neuf on the island side (Vedettes du Pont Neuf; see page 46).*

*Or you could take my walking tour of the Left Bank, which begins one bridge downriver (see the Left Bank Walk chapter). You can also catch the Métro to your next destination in Paris (the nearest stop is Pont Neuf, across the bridge on the Right Bank). Bus #69 heads east along Quai du Louvre (at the north end of the bridge) and west along Rue de Rivoli (a block farther north; see the Bus #69 Sightseeing Tour chapter). In fact, you can go anywhere—you're standing in the heart of Paris.*

# LOUVRE TOUR

*Musée du Louvre*

Paris walks you through world history in three world-class museums—the Louvre (ancient world to 1850), the Orsay (1848-1914, including Impressionism), and the Pompidou (20th century to today). Start your "art-yssey" at the Louvre. With more than 30,000 works of art, the Louvre is a full inventory of Western civilization. To cover it all in one visit is impossible. Let's focus on the Louvre's specialties—Greek sculpture, Italian painting, and French painting.

We'll see "Venuses" through history, from the curvy *Venus de Milo* to the wind-blown *Winged Victory of Samothrace,* from placid medieval Madonnas to the *Mona Lisa* to the symbol of modern democracy. We'll see how each generation defined beauty differently, and gain insight into long-ago civilizations by admiring what they found beautiful.

In addition, those with a little more time can visit some impressive chunks of stone from the "Cradle of Civilization," modern-day Iraq.

## Orientation

**Cost:** €10, free on first Sun of month, covered by Museum Pass. Tickets good all day; re-entry allowed.

**Hours:** Wed-Mon 9:00-18:00, open Wed and Fri nights until 21:45 (except on holidays), closed Tue. Galleries start shutting down 30 minutes early. The last entry is 45 minutes before closing.

**When to Go:** Crowds can be miserably bad on Sun, Mon (the worst day), Wed, and in the morning (arrive 30 minutes before opening to secure a good place in line). Evening visits are quieter, and the glass pyramid glows after dark.

**Getting There:** You have a variety of options.

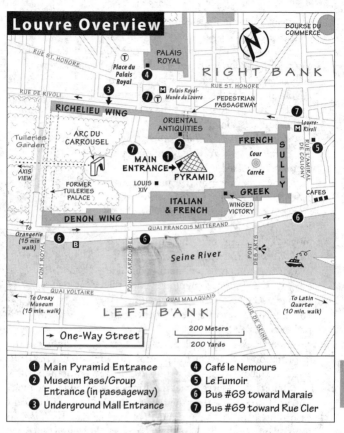

**Louvre Overview**

BOURSE DU COMMERCE

RUE ST. HONORE

PALAIS ROYAL

Place du Palais Royal ④

RIGHT BANK

RUE DE RIVOLI

RUE ST. HONORE

③ Ⓜ Palais Royal- Musée du Louvre ⑦ Ⓣ

PEDESTRIAN PASSAGEWAY

RICHELIEU WING

Louvre- Ⓜ Rivoli ⑦

Tuileries Garden

ARC DU CARROUSEL

ORIENTAL ANTIQUITIES

FRENCH

S U L L Y

RUE L'AMIRAL DE COLIGNY

⑤

⑦

② ①

Cour Carrée

AXIS VIEW

MAIN ENTRANCE➡

PYRAMID

FORMER TUILERIES PALACE

LOUIS XIV ■

GREEK

CAFES ■■■

To Orangerie (15 min walk)

ITALIAN & FRENCH

WINGED VICTORY

DENON WING

⑥ B

PONT ROYAL

QUAI FRANCOIS MITTERAND

⑥

PONT CARROUSEL

Seine River

PONT DES ARTS

⑥

QUAI VOLTAIRE

QUAI MALAQUAIS

RUE DE SEINE

To Orsay Museum (15 min. walk)

LEFT BANK

To Latin Quarter (10 min. walk)

➡ One-Way Street

200 Meters
200 Yards

① Main Pyramid Entrance
② Museum Pass/Group Entrance (in passageway)
③ Underground Mall Entrance
④ Café le Nemours
⑤ Le Fumoir
⑥ Bus #69 toward Marais
⑦ Bus #69 toward Rue Cler

LOUVRE

*By Métro:* The Métro stop Palais Royal-Musée du Louvre is closer to the entrance than the stop called Louvre-Rivoli. From the Palais Royal-Musée du Louvre stop, you can stay underground to enter the museum, or exit above ground if you want to go in through the pyramid (more details below).

*By Bus:* Handy bus #69 runs by the Louvre every 10-15 minutes. Buses coming from the Marais and going to the Rue Cler area stop next to the Palais Royal-Musée du Louvre Métro stop on Rue de Rivoli. Buses coming from Rue Cler and going to the Marais area stop along the Seine River (at Quai François Mitterand).

*By Taxi:* You'll find a taxi stand on Rue de Rivoli, next to the Palais Royal-Musée du Louvre Métro station.

**Getting In:** Enter through the pyramid, or opt for shorter lines elsewhere.

*Main Pyramid Entrance:* There is no grander entry than through the main entrance at the pyramid in the central courtyard, but metal detectors (not ticket-buyers) can create a long line.

**Museum Pass/Group Entrance:** Museum Pass-holders can use the group entrance in the pedestrian passageway (labeled *Pavilion Richelieu*) between the pyramid and Rue de Rivoli. It's under the arches, a few steps north of the pyramid; find the uniformed guard at the security checkpoint entrance, at the down escalator.

**Underground Mall Entrance:** Anyone can enter the Lou-

vre from its less crowded underground entrance, accessed through the Carrousel du Louvre shopping mall. Enter the mall at 99 Rue de Rivoli (the door with the red awning) or directly from the Métro stop Palais Royal-Musée du Louvre (stepping off the train, take the exit to *Musée du Louvre-Le Carrousel du Louvre*). Once inside the underground mall, continue toward the inverted pyramid and the Louvre's security entrance. Museum Pass holders can skip to the head of the security line.

**Information:** Pick up the free *Plan/Information* in English at the information desk under the pyramid as you enter. Tel. 01 40 20 53 17, recorded info tel. 01 40 20 51 51, www.louvre.fr.

**Buying Tickets:** Self-serve ticket machines located under the pyramid are faster to use than the ticket windows (machines accept euro bills, coins, and chip-and-PIN Visa cards). The *tabac* in the underground mall (near the Carrousel du Louvre entrance off Rue de Rivoli) sells tickets to the Louvre, Orsay, and Versailles, plus Museum Passes, for no extra charge (cash only).

**Tours:** Ninety-minute English-language **guided tours** leave twice daily (except the first Sunday of the month) from the *Accueil des Groupes* area, under the pyramid between the Sully and Denon wings (normally at 11:00 and 14:00, sometimes more often in summer; €9 plus your entry ticket, tour tel. 01 40 20 52 63). **Videoguides** on Nintendo 3DS portable game consoles provide tech-savvy visitors with commentary on about 700 masterpieces (€5, available at entries to the three wings, at the top of the escalators). A free Louvre **smartphone app** is also available through iTunes. Or you can download a free **audio version** of this chapter's tour to your mobile device; see page 24. You'll also find English explanations throughout the museum.

**Length of This Tour:** Allow at least two hours.

**With Limited Time:** String together the *Venus de Milo, Winged*

LOUVRE

*Victory, Mona Lisa,* and *Coronation of Napoleon*...and sightsee whatever else you can along the way.

**Baggage Check:** The free *bagagerie* is under the pyramid, to the right of the Denon wing entrance (it is signed *visiteurs individuels*). Large bags must be checked, and you can also check small bags to lighten your load. Coats cannot be left at the *bagagerie* unless they're stuffed into bags. (The coat check, or *Vestiaire,* is near the Richelieu wing.) The baggage-claim clerk might ask you in French, "Does your bag contain anything of value?" You can't check cameras, money, passports, or other valuables.

**Services:** WCs are located under the pyramid, behind the escalators to the Denon and Richelieu wings. Once you're in the galleries, WCs are scarce.

**Photography:** Photography without a flash is allowed. (Flash photography damages paintings and distracts viewers.)

**Cuisine Art:** The Louvre has several cafés, including **Café Mollien,** located near the end of our tour (€12 for sandwich or salad and drink on terrace overlooking pyramid, closes at 18:00). A reasonably priced self-service lunch **cafeteria** is up the escalator from the pyramid in the Richelieu wing. **Le Grand Louvre Café** under the pyramid is a pricier option. Your best bet is in the underground shopping mall, the **Carrousel du Louvre** (daily 8:30-23:00), which has an assortment of decent-value, multiethnic fast-food eateries, including—*quelle horreur*—a McDonald's (near the inverted pyramid). The mall also has glittering boutiques, a post office, two Starbucks, a huge Apple store (*vive* globalization), and a Métro entrance (Mo: Palais Royal-Musée du Louvre). Stairs at the far end take you right into the Tuileries Garden, a perfect antidote to the stuffy, crowded rooms of the Louvre.

For a fine, elegant lunch near the Louvre, head to the venerable **Café le Nemours** (good €10-12 *croque monsieur* and salads, open daily; leaving the Louvre, cross Rue de Rivoli and veer left to 2 Place Colette, adjacent to Comédie Française) or the classy **Le Fumoir** (€19 lunch *menu*, open daily, 6 Rue de l'Amiral de Coligny, near Louvre-Rivoli Métro stop). For listings, see page 460.

**Starring:** *Venus de Milo, Winged Victory, Mona Lisa,* Leonardo da Vinci, Raphael, Michelangelo, the French painters, and many of the most iconic images of Western civilization.

## Surviving the Louvre

Start by picking up a free map at the information desk and orienting yourself while standing underneath the glass pyramid.

The Louvre, the largest museum in the Western world, fills

three wings of this immense, U-shaped palace. The **Richelieu wing** (north side) houses Near Eastern antiquities (covered in the second part of this tour), decorative arts, and French, German, and Northern European art. The **Sully wing** (east side) has extensive French painting and collections of ancient Egyptian and Greek art. The **Denon wing** (south side) houses Greek and Roman antiquities as well as Italian, French, and Spanish paintings—plus a new Islamic art exhibit.

We'll concentrate on the **Denon and Sully wings,** which hold many of the superstars, including ancient Greek sculpture, Italian Renaissance painting, and French Neoclassical and Romantic painting.

**Expect changes**—the sprawling Louvre is constantly shuffling its collection. Rooms are periodically closed for renovation, and pieces are removed from display if they're being restored or loaned to other museums. A new addition is the Islamic art space—with its glass roof modeled on a head scarf—visible in the Cour de Visconti courtyard of the Denon wing.

Various galleries devoted to decorative arts are in flux until at least the spring of 2013. If you don't find the artwork you're looking for, ask the nearest guard for its new location. Point to the photo in your book and ask, *"Où est, s'il vous plaît?"* (oo ay, see voo play).

The bottom line: You could spend a lifetime here. Zero in on the biggies, and try to finish the tour with enough energy left to browse.

# The Tour Begins

• *Start at the famous* Venus de Milo *statue (pictured on next page). You'll find her not far from another famous sculpture, the* Winged Victory of Samothrace *(pictured on page 131).*

To reach the Venus de Milo *from inside the big glass pyramid, head for the Denon wing.*

*Escalate up one floor. After showing your ticket, continue up the stairs until you reach the top. Glance at the pyramid out the window, and then turn right, heading down a long sculpture hall. When you reach the base of a grand staircase, look up at the* Winged Victory of Samothrace. *We'll return to her later.*

*To find the* Venus de Milo, *walk to the left around the big staircase (and into the Sully wing). After about 50 yards, you'll reach Salle 16 (room 16), where you'll see* Venus *floating above a sea of worshipping tourists. It's been said that, among the warlike Greeks, this was the first statue to unilaterally disarm.*

# Ancient Greece (3,000 B.C.-A.D. 1)

The great Greek cultural explosion that changed the course of history unfolded over 50 years (starting around 450 B.C.) in Athens, a Greek town smaller than Muncie, Indiana. Having united Greece to repel a Persian invasion, Athens rebuilt, with the Parthenon as the centerpiece of the city. The Greeks dominated the ancient world through brain, not brawn, and their art shows their love of rationality, order, and balance. The ideal Greek was well-rounded—an athlete and a bookworm, a lover and a philosopher, a carpenter who played the lyre, a warrior and a poet. In art, the balance between timeless stability and fleeting movement made beauty.

In a sense, we're all Greek: Democracy, mathematics, theater, philosophy, literature, and science were practically invented in ancient Greece. Most of the art that we'll see in the Louvre either came from or was inspired by Greece.

### Venus de Milo (*Aphrodite,* late 2nd century B.C.)

This goddess of love created a sensation when it was discovered in 1820 on the Greek island of Melos. Europe was already in the grip of a classical fad, and this statue seemed to sum up all that ancient Greece stood for. The Greeks pictured their gods in human form (meaning humans are godlike), telling us they had an optimistic view of the human race. Venus' well-proportioned body captures the balance and orderliness of the Greek universe.

Split *Venus* down the middle from nose to toes and see how the two halves balance each other. Venus rests on her right foot (called *contrapposto,* or "counterpoise"), then lifts her left leg, setting her whole body in motion. As the left leg rises, her right shoulder droops down. And as her knee points one way, her head turns the other. *Venus* is a harmonious balance of opposites, orbiting slowly around a vertical axis. The twisting pose gives a balanced S-curve to her body (especially noticeable from the back view) that Golden Age Greeks and succeeding generations found beautiful.

Other opposites balance as well, like the smooth skin of her upper half that sets off the rough-cut texture of her dress (size 14). She's actually made from two different pieces of stone plugged together at the hips (the seam is visible). The face is realistic and

**Greek Statues**

SALLE 12

SALLE 16

TOUR BEGINS

❶ Venus de Milo
❷ Gallery of Statues
❸ Parthenon Friezes
❹ Roman Detour
❺ Winged Victory (upstairs)

SALLE 6 (SALLE DE DIANE)

SALLE 22

SALLE 5

SALLE 23   SALLE 24

SALLE 18

DOWN   UP

SALLE 30

Seine River

SULLY WING

PYRAMID

STAIRS UP FROM PYRAMID

LOUVRE

anatomically accurate, but it's also idealized, a goddess, too generic and too perfect. This isn't any particular woman, but Everywoman—all the idealized features that appealed to the Greeks.

Most "Greek" statues are actually later Roman copies. This is a rare Greek original. This "epitome of the Golden Age" was sculpted three centuries after the Golden Age, though in a retro style.

What were her missing arms doing? Some say her right arm held her dress, while her left arm was raised. Others say she was hugging a male statue or leaning on a column. I say she was picking her navel.

• *Orbit* Venus. *This statue is interesting and different from every angle. Remember the view from the back—we'll see it again later. Now make your re-entry to earth. Follow* Venus' *gaze and browse around the adjoining rooms (15, 14, and 13) of this long hall.*

## Gallery of Statues

Greek statues feature the human body in all its splendor. The anatomy is accurate, and the poses are relaxed and natural. Around the fifth century B.C., Greek sculptors learned to capture people in motion and to show them from different angles, not just face-forward. The undoubted master was Praxiteles, whose lifelike statues set the tone for later sculptors. He pioneered the classic *contrapposto* pose—with the weight resting on one leg—capturing a balance between timeless stability and fleeting motion. The stance is not only more lifelike, but also intrinsically beautiful. If the statue has clothes, the robes drape down naturally, following the body's curves. The intricate folds become part of the art.

In this gallery, you'll see statues of gods, satyrs, soldiers, athletes, and everyday people engaged in ordinary activities. For Athenians, the most popular goddess was their patron, Athena. She's usually shown as a warrior, wearing a helmet and carrying a (missing) spear, ready to fight for her city. Whatever the statue, Golden Age artists sought the perfect balance between down-to-earth humans (with human flaws and quirks) and the idealized perfection of a Greek god.

• *Head for Salle 6 (also known as Salle de Diane), located behind the* Venus de Milo. *(Facing* Venus, *make a counterclockwise loop to the right, of about 20 paces.) You'll find two carved panels on opposite walls.*

### Parthenon Friezes (mid-5th century B.C.)

These stone fragments once decorated the exterior of the greatest Athenian temple, the Parthenon. Built at the peak of the Greek Golden Age, the temple glorified the city's divine protector, Athena, and the superiority of the Athenians, who were feeling especially cocky, having just crushed their archrivals, the Persians. A model of the Parthenon shows where the panels might have hung. The centaur panel would have gone above the entrance. The panel of young women was placed under the covered colonnade, but above the doorway (to see it in the model, you'll have to crouch way down and look up).

The panel on the right side of the room shows a centaur (half-human/half-horse) sexually harassing a woman, telling the story of how these rude creatures crashed a party of regular people. But the humans fought back and threw the brutes out, just as Athens had defeated its Persian invaders.

The other relief shows the sacred procession of young women who marched up the temple hill every four years with an embroidered shawl for the 40-foot-high statue of Athena, the goddess of

LOUVRE

wisdom. Though headless, the maidens speak volumes about Greek craftsmanship. Carved in only a couple of inches of stone, they're amazingly realistic—more so than anything seen in the pre-Classical period. They glide along horizontally (their belts and shoulders all in a line), while the folds of their dresses drape down vertically. The man in the center is relaxed, realistic, and *contrapposto*. Notice the veins in his arm. The maid-

ens' pleated dresses make them look as stable as fluted columns, but their arms and legs step out naturally—their human forms emerging gracefully from the stone.

• *Make another 20-step loop into the nearby Salle 5 and turn left into Salle 22, the Roman Antiquities room (Antiquités Romaines), for a...*

## Roman Detour (Salles 22-30)

Stroll among the Caesars and try to see the person behind the public persona. Besides the many faces of the ubiquitous Emperor *Inconnu* ("unknown"), you might spot Augustus (Auguste), the first emperor, and his wily wife, Livia (Livie). Their son Tiberius (Tibère) was the Caesar that Jesus Christ "rendered unto." Caligula was notoriously depraved, curly-haired Domitia murdered her husband, Hadrian popularized the beard, Trajan ruled the Empire at its peak, and Marcus Aurelius

(Marc Aurèle) presided stoically over Rome's slow fall.

The pragmatic Romans (500 B.C.-A.D. 500) were great conquerors but bad artists. One area in which they excelled was realistic portrait busts, especially of their emperors, who were worshipped as gods on earth. Fortunately for us, the Romans also had a huge appetite for Greek statues and made countless copies. They took the Greek style and wrote it in capital letters, adding a veneer of sophistication to their homes, temples, baths, and government buildings.

The Roman rooms take you past several sarcophagi, an impressive mosaic floor that fills a massive courtyard, and beautiful wall-mounted mosaics from the ancient city of Antioch. Weary? Kick back and relax with the statues in the Etruscan Lounge (in Salle 18).

• *To reach the* Winged Victory, *get out your map, or simply continue clockwise through the Roman collection, which eventually spills out at the base of the stairs leading up to the first floor and the dramatic...*

LOUVRE

### Winged Victory of Samothrace
### (*Victoire de Samothrace, c. 190 B.C.*)

This woman with wings, poised on the prow of a ship, once stood on an island hilltop to commemorate a naval victory. Her clothes are windblown and sea-sprayed, clinging close enough to her body to win a wet T-shirt contest. (Look at the detail in the folds of her dress around the navel, curving down to her hips.) Originally, her right arm was stretched high, celebrating the victory like a Super Bowl champion, waving a "we're number one" finger.

This is the *Venus de Milo* gone Hellenistic, from the time after the culture of Athens was spread around the Mediterranean by Alexander the Great (c. 325 B.C.). As *Victory* strides forward, the wind blows her and her wings back. Her feet are firmly on the ground, but her wings (and missing arms) stretch upward. She is a pillar of vertical strength, while the clothes curve and whip around her. These opposing forces create a feeling of great energy, making her the lightest two-ton piece of rock in captivity.

The earlier Golden Age Greeks might have considered this statue ugly. Her rippling excitement is a far cry from the dainty Parthenon maidens and the soft-focus beauty of *Venus*. And the statue's off-balance pose, like an unfinished melody, leaves you hanging. But Hellenistic Greeks loved these cliff-hanging scenes of real-life humans struggling to make their mark.

In the glass case nearby is *Victory*'s open right hand with an outstretched finger, found in 1950, a century after the statue itself was unearthed. When the French learned the hand was in Turkey, they negotiated with the Turkish government for the rights to it. Considering all the other ancient treasures that France had looted from Turkey in the past, the Turks thought it only appropriate to give the French the finger.

• *Enter the octagonal room to the left as you face the* Winged Victory, *with Icarus bungee-jumping from the ceiling. Find a friendly window and look out toward the pyramid.*

## The Louvre as a Palace

Formerly a royal palace, the Louvre was built in stages over eight centuries. On your right (the Sully wing) was the original medieval fortress. About 500 yards to the west, in the now-open area past the pyramid and the triumphal arch, is where the Tuileries Palace used to stand. Succeeding kings tried to connect these two palaces, each monarch adding another section onto the long, skinny north and south wings. Finally, in 1852, after three centuries of building, the two palaces were connected, creating a rectangular Louvre. Nineteen years later, the Tuileries Palace burned down during a riot, leaving the U-shaped Louvre we see today.

The glass pyramid was designed by the Chinese-born American architect I. M. Pei (1989). Many Parisians hated the pyramid, just as they hated another new and controversial structure 100 years earlier—the Eiffel Tower.

In the octagonal room, a plaque at the base of the dome explains that France's Revolutionary National Assembly (the same people who brought you the guillotine) founded this museum in 1793. What could be more logical? You behead the king, inherit his palace and art collection, open the doors to the masses, and *voilà!* You have Europe's first public museum.

• *From the octagonal room, enter the Apollo Gallery (Galerie d'Apollon).*

## Apollo Gallery

This gallery gives us a feel for the Louvre as the glorious home of French kings (before Versailles). Imagine a chandelier-lit party in this room, drenched in stucco and gold leaf, with tapestries of leading Frenchmen and paintings featuring mythological and symbolic themes. The inlaid tables made from marble and semiprecious stones, and many other art objects, show the wealth of France, Europe's number-one power for two centuries.

Stroll past glass cases of royal dinnerware to the far end of the room. In a glass case are the crown jewels. The display varies, but you may see the jewel-studded crown of Louis XV and the 140-carat Regent Diamond, which once graced crowns worn by Louis XV, Louis XVI, and Napoleon.

• *A rare WC is not far away, near Salle 38 in the Sully wing. The Italian collection (Peintures Italiennes) is on the other side of* Winged Victory. *Cross back in front of* Winged Victory *and enter the Denon wing and Salle 1, where you'll find...*

### Two Botticelli Frescoes

Look at the paintings on the wall to the left. These pure maidens, like colorized versions of the Parthenon frieze, give us a preview of how ancient Greece would be "reborn" in the Renaissance.

• *But first, the Medieval World. Continue into the large Salle 3.*

# The Medieval World (1200-1500)

**Cimabue—*The Madonna and Child in Majesty Surrounded by Angels (La Vierge et l'Enfant en Majesté Entourés* de *Six Anges,* c. 1280)**

During the Age of Faith (1200s), almost every church in Europe had a painting like this one. Mary was a cult figure—even bigger than the late-20th-century Madonna—adored and prayed to by the faithful for bringing Baby Jesus into the world. After the collapse of the Roman Empire (c. A.D. 500), medieval Europe was a poor and violent place, with the Christian Church as the only constant in troubled times.

Altarpieces tended to follow the same formula: somber iconic faces, stiff poses, elegant folds in the robes, and generic angels. Violating the laws of perspective, the angels at the "back" of Mary's throne are the same size as those holding the front. These holy figures are laid flat on a gold background like cardboard cutouts, existing in a golden never-never land, as though the faithful couldn't imagine them as flesh-and-blood humans inhabiting our dark and sinful earth.

**Giotto—*St. Francis of Assisi Receiving the Stigmata (Saint François d'Assise Recevant les Stigmates,* c. 1295-1300)**

Francis of Assisi (c. 1181-1226), a wandering Italian monk of renowned goodness, kneels on a rocky Italian hillside, pondering the pain of Christ's torture and execution. Suddenly, he looks up, startled, to see Christ himself, with six wings, hovering above. Christ shoots lasers from his wounds to the hands, feet, and side of the empathetic monk, marking him with the stigmata. Francis went on to breathe the spirit of the Renaissance into medieval Europe. His humble love of man and nature inspired artists like Giotto to portray real human beings with real emotions, living in a physical world of beauty.

Like a good filmmaker, Giotto (c. 1266-1337) doesn't just *tell* us what happened, he *shows* us in the present tense, freezing the scene at its most dramatic moment. Though the perspective is crude—Francis' hut is smaller than he is, and Christ is somehow shooting at Francis while facing us—Giotto creates the illusion of three dimensions, with a foreground (Francis), middle ground (his hut), and background (the hillside). Painting a 3-D world on a 2-D surface is tough, and after a millennium of Dark Ages, artists were rusty.

In the predella (the panel of paintings below the altarpiece), birds gather at Francis' feet to hear him talk about God. Giotto

catches the late arrivals in mid-flight, an astonishing technical feat for an artist working more than a century before the Renaissance. The simple gesture of Francis' companion speaks volumes about his amazement. Breaking the stiff, iconic mold for saints, Francis bends forward at the waist to talk to his fellow creatures. The diversity of the birds—"red and yellow, black and white"—symbolizes how all humankind is equally precious in God's sight. Meanwhile, the tree bends down symmetrically to catch a few words from the beloved hippie of Assisi.

• *The long Grand Gallery displays Italian Renaissance painting—some masterpieces, some not.*

# Italian Renaissance (1400-1600)

## The Grand Gallery

Built in the late 1500s to connect the old palace with the Tuileries Palace, the Grand Gallery displays much of the Louvre's Italian Renaissance art. From the doorway, look to the far end and consider this challenge: I hold the world's record for the Grand Gallery Heel-Toe-Fun-Walk-Tourist-Slalom, going end to end in 1 minute, 58 seconds (only two injured). Time yourself. Along the way, notice some of the **features of Italian Renaissance painting**:

• **Religious:** Lots of Madonnas, children, martyrs, and saints.
• **Symmetrical:** The Madonnas are flanked by saints—two to the left, two to the right, and so on.
• **Realistic:** Real-life human features are especially obvious in the occasional portrait.

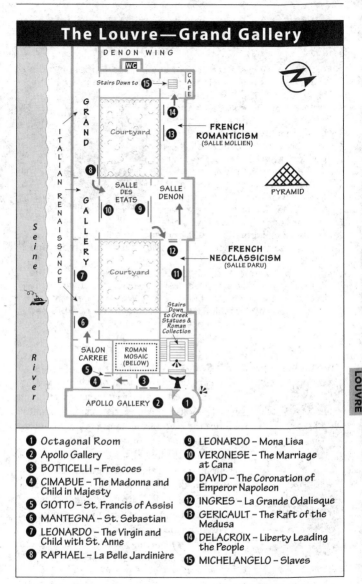

# The Louvre—Grand Gallery

DENON WING

WC

Stairs Down to ⑮

C A F E

G R A N D

Courtyard

❽

ITALIAN RENAISSANCE

⑭

⑬

**FRENCH ROMANTICISM** (SALLE MOLLIEN)

PYRAMID

SALLE DES ETATS

SALLE DENON

G A L L E R Y

⑩ ⑨

Seine

⑫

**FRENCH NEOCLASSICISM** (SALLE DARU)

❼

Courtyard

⑪

Stairs Down to Greek Statues & Roman Collection

❻

River

SALON CARREE

ROMAN MOSAIC (BELOW)

❺

❹ ❸

APOLLO GALLERY ❷ ❶

LOUVRE

❶ Octagonal Room
❷ Apollo Gallery
❸ BOTTICELLI – Frescoes
❹ CIMABUE – The Madonna and Child in Majesty
❺ GIOTTO – St. Francis of Assisi
❻ MANTEGNA – St. Sebastian
❼ LEONARDO – The Virgin and Child with St. Anne
❽ RAPHAEL – La Belle Jardinière

⑨ LEONARDO – Mona Lisa
⑩ VERONESE – The Marriage at Cana
⑪ DAVID – The Coronation of Emperor Napoleon
⑫ INGRES – La Grande Odalisque
⑬ GERICAULT – The Raft of the Medusa
⑭ DELACROIX – Liberty Leading the People
⑮ MICHELANGELO – Slaves

- **Three-Dimensional:** Every scene gets a spacious setting with a distant horizon.
- **Classical:** You'll see some Greek gods and classical nudes, but even Christian saints pose like Greek statues, and Mary is a *Venus* whose face and gestures embody all that was good in the Christian world.

## Italian Renaissance

A thousand years after Rome fell, plunging Europe into the Dark Ages, the Greek ideal of beauty was reborn in 15th-century Italy. The Renaissance—or "rebirth" of the culture of ancient Greece and Rome—was a cultural boom that changed people's thinking about every aspect of life. In politics, it meant democracy. In religion, it meant a move away from Church dominance and toward the assertion of man (humanism) and a more personal faith. Science and secular learning were revived after centuries of superstition and ignorance. In architecture, it was a return to the balanced columns and domes of Greece and Rome.

In painting, the Renaissance meant realism, and for the Italians, realism was spelled "3-D." Artists rediscovered the beauty of nature and the human body. With pictures of beautiful people in harmonious 3-D surroundings, they expressed the optimism and confidence of this new age.

### Andrea Mantegna—*St. Sebastian* (c. 1480)

This isn't the patron saint of acupuncture. St. Sebastian was a Christian martyr, although here he looks more like a classical Greek statue. Notice the *contrapposto* stance (all of his weight resting on one leg) and the Greek ruins scattered around him. His executioners look like ignorant medieval brutes bewildered by this enlightened Renaissance man. Italian artists were beginning to learn how to create human realism and earthly beauty on the canvas. Let the Renaissance begin.

• *Look for the following masterpieces by Leonardo 50 yards down the Grand Gallery, on the left.*

### Leonardo da Vinci—*The Virgin and Child with St. Anne* (*La Vierge à l'Enfant Jésus avec Sainte-Anne*, c. 1510)

Three generations—grandmother, mother, and child—are arranged in a pyramid, with Anne's face as the peak and the lamb as the lower right corner. Within this balanced structure, Leonardo sets the figures in motion. Anne's legs are pointed to our left. (Is Anne *Mona?* Hmm.) Her daughter Mary, sitting on her lap, reaches to the right. Jesus looks at her playfully while turning away. The lamb pulls away from him. But even with all the twisting and turning, this is still a placid scene. It's as orderly as the geometrically perfect universe created by the Renaissance god.

There's a psychological kidney punch in this happy painting. Jesus, the picture of childish joy, is innocently playing with a lamb—the symbol of his inevitable sacrificial death.

The Louvre has the greatest collection of Leonardos in the world—five of them. Look for the neighboring *Virgin of the Rocks* and *John the Baptist*. Leonardo was the consummate Renaissance Man, a musician, sculptor, engineer, scientist, and sometime painter, he combined knowledge from all these areas to create beauty. If he were alive today, he'd create a Unified Field Theory in physics—and set it to music.

• *You'll likely find Raphael's art on the right side of the Grand Gallery, just past the statue of* Diana the Huntress.

### Raphael—*La Belle Jardinière* (c. 1507)

Raphael perfected the style Leonardo pioneered. This configuration of Madonna, Child, and John the Baptist is also a balanced pyramid with hazy grace and beauty. Mary is a mountain of maternal tenderness (the title translates as "The Beautiful Gardener") as she eyes her son with a knowing look and holds his hand in a gesture of union. Jesus looks up innocently, standing *contrapposto* like a chubby Greek statue. Baby John the Baptist kneels lovingly at Jesus' feet, holding a cross that hints at his playmate's sacrificial death. The interplay of gestures and gazes gives the masterpiece both intimacy and cohesiveness, while Raphael's blended brushstrokes varnish the work with an iridescent smoothness.

With Raphael, the Greek ideal of beauty—reborn in the Renaissance—reached its peak. His work spawned so many imitators who cranked out sickly sweet, generic Madonnas that we often take him for granted. Don't. This is the real thing.

• *The* Mona Lisa (La Joconde) *is near the statue of* Diana, *in Salle 6—the Salle des Etats—midway down the Grand Gallery on the right. After several years and a €5 million renovation,* Mona *is alone behind glass on her own false wall. Six million heavy-breathing people crowd in each year to glimpse the most ogled painting in the world. (You can't miss her. Just follow the signs and the people...it's the only painting you can hear. With all the groveling crowds, you can even smell it.)*

LOUVRE

## Leonardo da Vinci—*Mona Lisa* (*La Joconde,* 1503-1506)

Leonardo was already an old man when François I invited him to France. Determined to pack light, he took only a few paintings with him. One was a portrait of Lisa del Giocondo, the wife of a wealthy Florentine merchant. When Leonardo arrived, François immediately fell in love with the painting, making it the centerpiece of the small collection of Italian masterpieces that would, in three centuries, become the Louvre museum. He called it *La Gioconda* (*La Joconde* in French)—a play on both her last name and the Italian word for "happiness." We know it as the *Mona Lisa*—a contraction of the Italian for "my lady Lisa."

*Mona* may disappoint you. She's smaller than you'd expect, darker, engulfed in a huge room, and hidden behind a glaring pane of glass. So, you ask, "Why all the hubbub?" Let's take a closer look. As you would with any lover, you've got to take her for what she is, not what you'd like her to be.

The famous smile attracts you first. Leonardo used a hazy technique called *sfumato,* blurring the edges of her mysterious smile. Try as you might, you can never quite see the corners of her mouth. Is she happy? Sad? Tender? Or is it a cynical supermodel's smirk? All visitors read it differently, projecting their own moods onto her enigmatic face. *Mona* is a Rorschach inkblot...so, how are you feeling?

Now look past the smile and the eyes that really do follow you (most eyes in portraits do) to some of the subtle Renaissance elements that make this painting work. The body is surprisingly massive and statue-like, a perfectly balanced pyramid turned at an angle, so we can see its mass. Her arm rests lightly on the armrest of a chair, almost on the level of the frame itself, as if she's sitting in a window looking out at us. The folds of her sleeves and her gently folded hands are remarkably realistic and relaxed. The typical Leonardo landscape shows distance by getting hazier and hazier.

Though the portrait is generally accepted as a likeness of Lisa del Giocondo, other hypotheses about the sitter's identity have been suggested, including the idea that it's Leonardo himself. Or she might be the Mama Lisa. A recent infrared scan revealed that she has a barely visible veil over her dress, which may mean (in the custom of the day) that she had just had a baby.

The overall mood is one of balance and serenity, but there's also an element of mystery. *Mona's* smile and long-distance beauty are subtle and elusive, tempting but always just out of reach, like

LOUVRE

strands of a street singer's melody drifting through the Métro tunnel. *Mona* doesn't knock your socks off, but she winks at the patient viewer.

• *Before leaving* Mona, *step back and just observe the paparazzi scene. The huge canvas opposite* Mona *is...*

### Paolo Veronese—*The Marriage at Cana* (*Les Noces de Cana,* 1562-1563)

Stand 10 steps away from this enormous canvas to where it just fills your field of vision, and suddenly...you're in a party! Help yourself to a glass of wine. This is the Renaissance love of beautiful things gone hog-wild. Venetian artists like Veronese painted the good life of rich, happy-go-lucky Venetian merchants.

In a spacious setting of Renaissance architecture, colorful lords and ladies, decked out in their fanciest duds, feast on a great spread of food and drink, while the musicians fuel the fires of good fun. Servants prepare and serve the food, jesters play, and animals roam. In the upper left, a dog and his master look on. A sturdy linebacker in yellow pours wine out of a jug (right foreground). The man in white samples some wine and thinks, "Hmm, not bad," while nearby a ferocious cat battles a lion. The wedding couple at the far left is almost forgotten.

Believe it or not, this is a religious work showing the wedding celebration in which Jesus turned water into wine. And there's Jesus in the dead center of 130 frolicking figures, wondering if maybe wine coolers might not have been a better choice. With true Renaissance optimism, Venetians pictured Christ as a party animal, someone who loved the created world as much as they did.

Now, let's hear it for the band! On bass—the bad cat with the funny hat—Titian the Venetian! And joining him on viola—Crazy Veronese!

• *Exit behind* Mona *into the Salle Denon. The dramatic Romantic room is to your left, and the grand Neoclassical room is to your right. These two rooms feature the most exciting French canvases in the Louvre. In the Neoclassical room (Salle Daru), kneel before the largest canvas in the Louvre.*

# French Neoclassicism (1780-1850)

### Jacques-Louis David—*The Coronation of Emperor Napoleon* (*Sacre de l'Empereur Napoléon,* 1806-1807)

Napoleon holds aloft an imperial crown. This common-born son of immigrants is about to be crowned emperor of a "New Rome." He has just made his wife, Josephine, the empress, and she kneels at his feet. Seated behind Napoleon is the pope, who journeyed from Rome to place the imperial crown on his head. But Napoleon feels that no one is worthy of the task. At the last moment, he shrugs the pope aside, grabs the crown, holds it up for all to see...and crowns himself. The pope looks p.o.'d.

After the French people decapitated their king during the Revolution (1793), their fledgling democracy floundered in chaos. France was united by a charismatic, brilliant, temperamental, upstart general who kept his feet on the ground, his eyes on the horizon, and his hand in his coat—Napoleon Bonaparte. Napoleon quickly conquered most of Europe and insisted on being made emperor (not merely king). The painter David (dah-VEED) recorded the coronation for posterity.

The radiant woman in the gallery in the background center wasn't actually there. Napoleon's mother couldn't make it to see her boy become the most powerful man in Europe, but he had David paint her in anyway. (There's a key on the frame telling who's who in the picture.)

The traditional setting for French coronations was the ultra-Gothic Notre-Dame cathedral. But Napoleon wanted a location that would reflect the glories of Greece and the grandeur of Rome. So, interior decorators erected stage sets of Greek columns and Roman arches to give the cathedral the architectural political correctness you see in this painting. (The *pietà* statue on the right edge of the painting is still in Notre-Dame today.)

David was the new emperor's official painter and propagan-dist, in charge of color-coordinating the costumes and flags for public ceremonies and spectacles. (Find his self-portrait with curly gray hair in the *Coronation*, way up in the second balcony, peeking around the tassel directly above Napoleon's crown.) His "Neoclas-sical" style influenced French fashion. Take a look at his *Madame Juliet Récamier* portrait on the opposite wall, showing a modern Parisian woman in ancient garb and Pompeii hairstyle reclining on a Roman couch. Nearby paintings, such as *The Oath of the Horatii (Le Serment des Horaces),* are fine examples of Neoclassicism, with Greek subjects, patriotic sentiment, and a clean, simple style.

• *As you double back toward the Romantic room, stop at...*

### Jean-Auguste-Dominique Ingres— *La Grande Odalisque* (1814)

Take *Venus de Milo,* turn her around, lay her down, and stick a hash pipe next to her, and you have the *Grande Odalisque.* OK, maybe you'd have to add a vertebra or two.

Using clean, polished, sculptur-al lines, Ingres (ang-gruh, with a soft "gruh") exaggerates the S-curve of a standing Greek nude. As in the *Venus de Milo,* rough folds of cloth set off her smooth skin. Ingres gave the face, too, a touch of *Venus'* idealized features, taking nature and improving on it. Contrast the cool colors of this statue-like nude with Titian's golden girls. Ingres preserves *Venus'* backside for posterior—I mean, posterity.

• *Cross back through the Salle Denon and into a room gushing with...*

# French Romanticism (1800-1850)

### Théodore Géricault—*The Raft of the Medusa* (*Le Radeau de la Méduse,* 1819)

In the artistic war between hearts and minds, the heart style was known as Romanticism. Stressing motion and emotion, it was the flip side of cool, balanced Neoclassicism, though they both flourished in the early 1800s.

What better setting for an emotional work than a shipwreck? Clinging to a raft is a tangle of bodies and lunatics sprawled over each other. The scene writhes with agitated, ominous motion—the ripple of muscles, churning clouds, and choppy seas. On the right is a deathly green corpse dangling overboard. The face of the man at left, cradling a dead body, says it all—the despair of spending weeks stranded in the middle of nowhere.

This painting was based on the actual sinking of the ship *Medusa* off the coast of Africa in 1816. About 150 people packed onto the raft. After floating in the open seas for 12 days—suffering hardship and hunger, even resorting to cannibalism—only 15 survived. The story was made to order for a painter determined to shock the public and arouse its emotions. That painter was young Géricault (ZHAIR-ee-ko). He interviewed survivors and honed his craft, sketching dead bodies in the morgue and the twisted faces of lunatics in asylums, capturing the moment when all hope is lost.

But wait. There's a stir in the crowd. Someone has spotted something. The bodies rise up in a pyramid of hope, culminating in a flag wave. They signal frantically, trying to catch the attention of the tiny ship on the horizon, their last desperate hope...which did finally save them. Géricault uses rippling movement and powerful colors to catch us up in the excitement. If art controls your heartbeat, this is a masterpiece.

### Eugène Delacroix—*Liberty Leading the People* (*La Liberté Guidant le Peuple,* 1831)

The year is 1830. King Charles has just issued the 19th-century equivalent of the Patriot Act, and his subjects are angry. Parisians take to the streets once again, *Les Miz*-style, to fight royalist oppressors. The people triumph—replacing the king with Louis-Philippe, who is happy to rule within the constraints of a modern constitution. There's a hard-bitten proletarian with a sword (far left), an intellectual with a top hat and a sawed-off shotgun, and even a little boy brandishing pistols.

Leading them on through the smoke and over the dead and dying is the figure of Liberty, a strong woman waving the French flag. Does this symbol of victory look familiar? It's the *Winged Victory*, wingless and topless.

To stir our emotions, Delacroix (del-ah-kwah) uses only three major colors—the red, white, and blue of the French flag. France is the symbol of modern democracy, and this painting has long stirred its citizens' passion for liberty. The French weren't the first to adopt democracy in its modern form (Americans were), nor are they the best working example of it, but they've had to try harder to achieve it than any other country. No sooner would they throw one king or dictator out than they'd get another. They're now working on their fifth republic.

This symbol of freedom is a fitting tribute to the Louvre, the first museum ever opened to the common rabble of humanity. The good things in life don't belong only to a small, wealthy part of society, but to everyone. The motto of France is *Liberté, Egalité, Fraternité*—liberty, equality, and brotherhood for all.

• *Exit the room at the far end (past the Café Mollien) and go downstairs, where you'll bump into the bum of a large, twisting male nude looking like he's just waking up after a thousand-year nap.*

# More Italian Renaissance

### Michelangelo—*Slaves* (*Esclaves,* 1513-1515)

These two statues by earth's greatest sculptor are a fitting end to this museum—works that bridge the ancient and modern worlds.

Michelangelo, like his fellow Renaissance artists, learned from the Greeks. The perfect anatomy, twisting poses, and idealized faces appear as if they could have been created 2,000 years earlier.

The so-called *Dying Slave* (also called the *Sleeping Slave,* looking like he should be stretched out on a sofa) twists listlessly against his T-shirt-like bonds, revealing his smooth skin. Compare the polished detail of the rippling, bulging left arm with the sketchy details of the face and neck.

With Michelangelo, the body does the talking. This is probably the most sensual nude that Michelangelo, the master of the male body, ever created.

The *Rebellious Slave* fights against his bondage. His shoulders rotate one way, his head and leg turn the other. He looks upward, straining to get free. He even seems to be trying to release himself from the rock he's made of. Michelangelo said that his purpose was to carve away the marble to reveal the figures God put inside. This slave shows the agony of that process and the ecstasy of the result.

• *Tour over! These two may be slaves of the museum, but you are free to go. You've seen the essential Louvre. To leave the museum, head for the end of the hall, turn right, and follow signs down the escalators to the* Sortie.

*But, of course, there's so much more. After a break (or on a second visit), consider a stroll through a few rooms of the Richelieu wing, which contain some of the Louvre's most ancient pieces. Bible students, amateur archaeologists, and Iraq War vets may find the collection especially interesting.*

LOUVRE

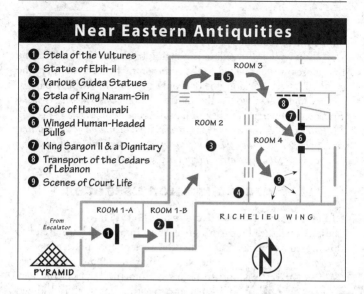

# Near Eastern Antiquities

**Near Eastern Antiquities**

1 Stela of the Vultures
2 Statue of Ebih-il
3 Various Gudea Statues
4 Stela of King Naram-Sin
5 Code of Hammurabi
6 Winged Human-Headed Bulls
7 King Sargon II & a Dignitary
8 Transport of the Cedars of Lebanon
9 Scenes of Court Life

ROOM 3
ROOM 2
ROOM 4
RICHELIEU WING
ROOM 1-A   ROOM 1-B
From Escalator
PYRAMID

## Near Eastern Antiquities

Saddam Hussein is only the latest iron-fisted, palace-building conqueror to fall in the long history of the region that roughly cor-
responds with modern Iraq. Its origins stretch back to the dawn of
time. Civilization began 6,000 years ago between the Tigris and
Euphrates rivers, in the area called the Fertile Crescent.

In the Richelieu wing, you can quickly sweep through 2,000
years of this area's ancient history, enjoying some of the Louvre's
biggest and oldest artifacts. See how each new civilization toppled
the previous one—pulling down its statues, destroying its palaces,
looting its cultural heritage, and replacing it with victory monuments of its own...only to be toppled again by the next wave of
history.

• *From under the pyramid, enter the Richelieu wing. Show your ticket,
then take the first right. Go up one flight of stairs and one escalator to
the ground floor (rez-de-chaussée), where you'll find the Near Eastern
antiquities. Walk straight off the escalator, enter Salle 1-a (Mesopotamie
Archaïque), and come face-to-face with fragments of the
broken...*

### Stela of the Vultures
### (Stèle des Vautours, 2600-2330 B.C.)

As old as the pyramids, this Sumerian stela (ceremonial stone pillar) is thought to be the world's
oldest surviving historical document. Its images
and words record the battle between the city of

Lagash (100 miles north of modern Basra) and its neighboring archrival, Umma.

"Read" the stela from top to bottom. Top level: Behind a wall of shields, a phalanx of helmeted soldiers advances, trampling the enemy underfoot. They pile the corpses (right), and vultures swoop down from above to pluck the remains. Middle level: Bearded King Eannatum waves to the crowd from his chariot in the victory parade. Bottom level: They dig a mass grave—one of 20 for the 36,000 enemy dead—while a priest (top of the fragment) gives thanks to the gods. A tethered ox (see his big head tied to a stake) is about to become a burnt sacrifice.

Circle around to the flip side of the stela to see the king waving the eagle flag of Lagash with one hand, while with the other he

clubs a puny enemy soldier trapped in a battle net, making his enemies pledge allegiance to Lagash's gods.

The inscription on the stela is in cuneiform, the world's first written language, invented by the Sumerians.
• *Continue into Salle 1-b, with the blissful statue of...*

**LOUVRE**

### Statue of Ebih-il, Superintendent of Mari (*Statue de l'Intendant Ebih-il,* c. 2400 B.C.)

Bald, bearded, blue-eyed Ebih-il (his name is inscribed on his shoulder) sits in his fleece skirt, folds his hands reverently across

his chest, and gazes rapturously into space, dreaming of...Ishtar. A high-ranking dignitary, Ebih-il placed this statue of himself in the goddess Ishtar's temple to declare his perpetual devotion to her.

Ishtar was the chief goddess of many Middle Eastern peoples. As goddess of both love and war, she was a favorite of horny soldiers. She was a giver of life (this statue is dedicated "to Ishtar the virile"), yet also miraculously a virgin. She was also a great hunter with bow and arrow, and a great lover ("Her lips are sweet... her figure is beautiful, her eyes are brilliant...women and men adore her," sang the *Hymn to Ishtar,* c. 1600 B.C.).

Ebih-il adores her eternally with his eyes made of seashells and lapis lazuli. The smile on his face reflects the pleasure the goddess has just given him, perhaps through one of the sacred prostitutes who resided in Ishtar's temple.

• *Go up the five steps behind* Ebih-il, *and turn left into Salle 2, containing a dozen statues, all of a man named...*

### Statue of Gudea, Prince of Lagash
### (Statue de Gudea, Prince de Lagash, c. 2120 B.C.)

Gudea (r. 2141-2122 B.C.), in his wool stocking cap (actually a royal turban), folds his hands and prays to the gods to save his people from invading barbarians. One of Sumeria's last great rulers, the peaceful and pious Gudea (his name means "the destined") rebuilt temples (where these statues once stood) to thank the gods for their help.

• *Behind you, find the rosy-colored...*

### Stela of King Naram-Sin
### (Stèle du Roi Narâm-Sîn, c. 2230 B.C.)

After a millennium of prosperity, Sumeria was plundered (c. 2250 B.C.), and the city-state of Akkad became the new top dog. On this victory stela, King Naram-Sin climbs up to the sunny heavens, crowned with the horned helmet of a god. His soldiers look up to admire him as he tramples his enemies. Next to him, a victim tries to remove a spear from his neck, while another pleads to the conqueror for mercy.

• *Exit Salle 2 at the far end and enter Salle 3, with the large black stela of Hammurabi.*

### Code of Hammurabi, King of Babylon
### (Code de Hammurabi, Roi de Babylone, 1792-1750 B.C.)

King Hammurabi (r. c. 1792-1750 B.C.) extended the reach of the great Babylonian empire, which joined Sumer and Akkad (stretching from modern-day Baghdad to the Persian Gulf). He proclaimed 282 laws, all inscribed on this eight-foot black basalt stela—one of the first formal legal documents, four centuries before the Ten Commandments. Stelas such as this likely dotted Hammurabi's empire, and this one may have stood in Babylon before being moved to Susa, Iran.

At the top of the stela, Hammurabi (standing and wearing Gudea's hat of kingship) receives the scepter of judgment from the god of justice and the sun, who radiates flames from his shoulders.

# Just Enough Geography and History for This Tour

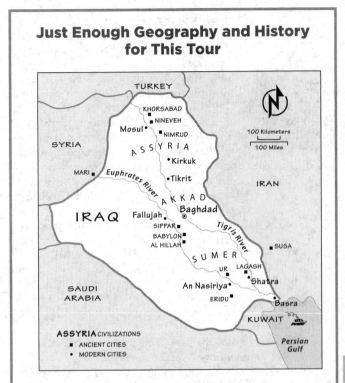

The ancient region of Mesopotamia generally matches the contours of present-day Iraq. The northern half is mountainous, and the southern half is the fertile delta of the Tigris and Euphrates rivers. Modern Baghdad sits roughly in the middle, along the Tigris. The Sumerians inhabited the south, the Assyrians the north, and the Akkadians and Babylonians the center, around Baghdad.

Here's a brief timeline:

**3500-2400 B.C.** Sumerian city-states flourish between the Tigris and Euphrates rivers. Sumerians invent cuneiform writing.

**2300 B.C.** Akkadians invade Sumer.

**1750 B.C.** Hammurabi establishes first Babylonian empire.

**710 B.C.** Sargon II rules over a vast Assyrian-controlled empire, encompassing modern Iraq, Israel, Syria, and Egypt.

**612 B.C.** Babylonians revolt against the Assyrians and destroy their capital of Nineveh, then build their own—Babylon.

The inscription begins, "When Anu the Sublime...called me, Hammurabi, by name...I did right, and brought about the well-being of the oppressed."

Next come the laws, scratched in cuneiform down the length of the stela, some 3,500 lines reading right to left. The laws cover very specific situations, everything from lying, theft, and trade to marriage and medical malpractice. The legal innovation was the immediate retribution for wrongdoing, often with poetic justice. Here's a sample:

#1:    If any man ensnares another falsely, he shall be put to death.

#57:   If your sheep graze another man's land, you must repay 20 gur of grain.

#129:  If a couple is caught in adultery, they shall both be tied up and thrown in the water.

#137:  If you divorce your wife, you must pay alimony and child support.

#218:  A surgeon who bungles an operation shall have his hands cut off.

#282:  If a slave shall say, "You are not my master," the master can cut off the slave's ear.

The most quoted laws—summing up the spirit of ancient Near Eastern justice—are #196 ("If a man put out the eye of another man, his eye shall be put out") and #200 ("a tooth for a tooth").

• *Make a U-turn to the right, entering the large Salle 4, dominated by colossal winged bulls with human heads. These sculptures—including five winged bulls and many relief panels along the walls—are from the...*

## Palace of Sargon II

Sargon II, the Assyrian king (r. 721-705 B.C.), spared no expense on his palace (see various reconstructions of the palace on plaques around the room). In Assyrian society, the palace of the king—not the temple of the gods—was the focus of life, and each ruler demonstrated his authority with large residences.

Sargon II actually built a whole new city for his palace, just north of the traditional capital of Nineveh (modern-day Mosul). He called it Dur Sharrukin ("Sargonburg"), and the city's vast dimensions were 4,000 cubits by—oh, excuse me—it covered about 150 football fields pieced together. The whole city was built on a raised, artificial mound, and the 25-acre palace itself sat even higher, surrounded by walls, with courtyards, temples, the king's residence, and a wedding cake-shaped temple (called a ziggurat) dedicated to the god Sin.

LOUVRE

## The Assyrians

This Semitic people from the agriculturally challenged hills of northern Mesopotamia became traders and conquerors, not farmers. They conquered their southern neighbors and dominated the Near East for 300 years (c. 900-600 B.C.).

Their strength came from a superb army (chariots, mounted cavalry, and siege engines), a policy of terrorism against enemies ("I tied their heads to tree trunks all around the city," reads a royal inscription), ethnic cleansing and mass deportations of the vanquished, and efficient administration (roads and express postal service). They have been called "The Romans of the East."

• *Start with the two big bulls supporting a (reconstructed) arch.*

### Winged Human-Headed Bulls
### (*Taureau Androcéphale Ailé,* c. 721-704 B.C.)

These 30-ton, 14-foot alabaster bulls with human faces once guarded the entrance to the throne room of Sargon II. A visitor to the palace back then could have looked over the bulls' heads and seen a 15-story ziggurat (stepped-pyramid temple) towering overhead. The winged bulls were guardian spirits, warding off demons and intimidating liberals.

Between their legs are cuneiform inscriptions such as: "I, Sargon, King of the Universe, built palaces for my royal residence...I had winged bulls with human heads carved from great blocks of mountain stone, and I placed them at the doors facing the four winds as powerful divine guardians...My creation amazed all who gazed upon it."

• *We'll see a few relief panels from the palace, working counterclockwise around the room. Start with the panel just to the left of the two big bulls (as you face them). Find the bearded, earringed man in whose image the bulls were made.*

### King Sargon II and a Dignitary
### (*Le Roi Sargon II et un Haut Dignitaire,* c. 710 B.C.)

Sargon II, wearing a fez-like crown with a cone on the top and straps down the back, cradles his scepter and raises his staff to receive a foreign ambassador who has come to pay tribute. Sargon II controlled a vast empire, consisting of modern-day Iraq

and extending westward to the Mediterranean and Egypt.

Before becoming emperor, Sargon II was a conquering general who invaded Israel (2 Kings 17:1-6). After a three-year siege, he took Jerusalem and deported much of the population, inspiring the legends of the "Lost" Ten Tribes. The prophet Isaiah saw him as God's tool to punish the sinful Israelites, "to seize loot and snatch plunder, and to trample them down like mud in the streets" (Isaiah 10:6).

• *On the wall to the left of Sargon are four panels depicting the...*

### Transport of the Cedars of Lebanon
### (Transport du Bois de Cèdre du Liban, c. 713-706 B.C.)

Boats carry the finest quality logs for Sargon II's palace, crossing a wavy sea populated with fish, turtles, crabs, and mermen. The transport process is described in the Bible (1 Kings 5:9): "My men will haul them down from Lebanon to the sea, and I will float them in rafts to the place you specify."

• *Continue counterclockwise around the room—past more big, winged animals, past the huge hero, Gilgamesh, crushing a lion—until you reach more relief panels. These depict...*

### Scenes of Court Life

The brown, eroded gypsum panels we see here were originally painted and varnished. Placed side by side, they would have stretched over a mile. The panels read like a comic strip, showing the king's men parading in to serve him.

First, soldiers *(guerriers en armée)* sheathe their swords and fold

their hands reverently. A winged spirit prepares them to enter the king's presence by shaking a pinecone to anoint them with holy perfume. Next, servants hurry to the throne room with the king's dinner, carrying his table, chair, and bowl. Other servants ready the king's horses and chariots.

## From Sargon to Saddam

Sargon II's palace remained unfinished and was later burned and buried. Sargon's great Assyrian empire dissolved over the next few generations. When the Babylonians revolted and conquered their northern neighbors (612 B.C.), the whole Middle East applauded. As the Bible put it: "Nineveh is in ruins—who will mourn for her?... Everyone who hears the news claps his hands at your fall, for who has not felt your endless cruelty?" (Nahum 3:7, 19).

The new capital was Babylon (50 miles south of modern Baghdad), ruled by King Nebuchadnezzar, who conquered Judea (586 B.C., the Bible's "Babylonian Captivity") and built a palace with the Hanging Gardens, one of the Seven Wonders of the World.

Over the succeeding centuries, Babylon/Baghdad fell to Persians (539 B.C.), Greeks (Alexander the Great, 331 B.C.), Persians again (second century B.C.), Arab Muslims (A.D. 634), Mongol hordes (Genghis Khan's grandson, 1258), Iranians (1502), Ottoman Turks (1535), British-controlled kings (1921), and military regimes (1958), the most recent headed by Saddam Hussein (1979).

After toppling Saddam Hussein in 2003, George W. Bush declared, "Mission accomplished!" Five thousand years of invasions, violence, and regime change, as well as current events, suggest otherwise.

LOUVRE

# ORSAY
# MUSEUM TOUR

*Musée d'Orsay*

The Musée d'Orsay (mew-zay dor-say) houses French art of the 1800s and early 1900s (specifically, 1848-1914), picking up where the Louvre's art collection leaves off. For us, that means Impressionism, the art of sun-dappled fields, bright colors, and crowded Parisian cafés. The Orsay houses the best general collection anywhere of Manet, Monet, Renoir, Degas, Van Gogh, Cézanne, and Gauguin. If you like Impressionism, visit this museum. If you don't like Impressionism, visit this museum. I personally find it a more enjoyable and rewarding place than the Louvre. Sure, ya gotta see the *Mona Lisa* and *Venus de Milo*, but after you get your gottas out of the way, enjoy the Orsay.

Keep in mind that the collection is always on the move—paintings on loan, in restoration, or displayed in different rooms. But with a little flexibility, you should be able to see most of the Orsay's masterpieces. The museum updates its website daily with the latest layout (www.musee-orsay.fr).

## Orientation

**Cost:** €9, €6.50 Fri-Wed after 16:15 and Thu after 18:00, free on first Sun of month, covered by Museum Pass. Tickets are good all day. Combo-tickets are available with the Orangerie Museum (€14); valid four days, with one visit per sight. Advance tickets can be purchased online and printed at home (for a small surcharge), or you can buy them in person at FNAC department stores and TIs; see www.musee-orsay.fr.

**Hours:** Tue-Sun 9:30-18:00, Thu until 21:45, closed Mon, last entry one hour before closing (45 minutes before on Thu). The top-floor Impressionist galleries begin closing 45 minutes early, frustrating unwary visitors. Tuesdays are particularly crowded, because the Louvre is closed.

**Free Entry near Closing Time:** Right when the ticket booth stops selling tickets, you're welcome to scoot in free of charge (Tue-Wed and Fri-Sun at 17:00, Thu at 21:00; they won't let you in much after that, however). Make a beeline for the Impressionist galleries, which start shutting down first.

**Getting There:** The museum sits above the RER-C stop called Musée d'Orsay. The Solférino Métro stop is three blocks southeast of the Orsay. Bus #69 from the Marais neighborhood stops at the museum on the river side (Quai Anatole France); from the Rue Cler area, it stops behind the museum on the Rue du Bac. From the Louvre, catch bus #69 along Rue de Rivoli. Or it's a lovely 15-minute walk through the Tuileries Garden and across the river on the pedestrian bridge from the Louvre or Orangerie museums. The museum is at 1 Rue de la Légion d'Honneur. A taxi stand is in front of the entrance on Quai Anatole France. The Batobus boat also makes a stop here (see page 47).

**Getting In:** The ticket-buying line can be long, but you can skip it with a Museum Pass or advance ticket, or by going on Thursday evening when the museum is open late. As you face the museum from Rue de la Légion d'Honneur (with the river on your left), passholders and ticket-holders enter on the right (Entrance C). Ticket purchasers enter closer to the river (Entrance A). A security check slows up all entrances.

**Information:** The booth inside the entrance provides free floor plans in English that can help you navigate the ever-changing museum. Tel. 01 40 49 48 14, www.musee-orsay.fr.

**Tours: Audioguides** cost €5. English guided tours usually run daily at 11:30 (€7.50/1.5 hours, none on Sun, may run at other times—inquire when you arrive). Or you can download this chapter as a free Rick Steves **audio tour** (see page 24).

**Length of This Tour:** Allow two hours.

**With Limited Time:** Focus on the Impressionists on the top floor, and Van Gogh and company on level 2.

**Cloakroom (Vestiaire):** Checking bags or coats is free. Day bags (but nothing bigger) are allowed in the museum. No valuables can be stored in checked bags. The cloakroom clerk might ask you in French not to check cameras, passports, or anything particularly precious.

**Photography:** Photography is forbidden.

**Cuisine Art:** The snazzy Le Restaurant is on the second floor, with affordable tea and coffee served 15:00-17:30 (daily except Thu). Cafés with fair prices are on the main floor near the entry and on the fifth-floor beyond the Impressionist galleries.

ORSAY MUSEUM

## The Orsay's "19th Century" (1848-1914)

Einstein and Geronimo. Abraham Lincoln and Karl Marx. The train, the bicycle, the horse and buggy, the automobile, and the balloon. Freud and Dickens. Darwin's *Origin of Species* and the Church's Immaculate Conception. Louis Pasteur and Billy the Kid. Ty Cobb and V. I. Lenin.

The 19th century was a mix of old and new, side by side. Europe was entering the modern Industrial Age, with cities, factories, rapid transit, instant communication, and global networks. At the same time, it clung to the past with traditional, rural—almost medieval—attitudes and morals.

According to the Orsay, the "19th century" began in 1848 with the socialist and democratic revolutions (Marx's *Communist Manifesto*). It ended in 1914 with the pull of an assassin's trigger, which ignited World War I and ushered in the modern world. The museum shows art that is also both old and new, conservative and revolutionary.

Outside, behind the museum, a number of classy eateries line Rue du Bac.

**Starring:** Manet, Monet, Renoir, Degas, Van Gogh, Cézanne, and Gauguin.

## The Tour Begins

### Gare d'Orsay: The Old Train Station

• *Pick up a free English map, and belly up to the stone balustrade overlooking the main floor.*

Trains used to run right under our feet down the center of the gallery. This former train station, or *gare*, barely escaped the wrecking ball in the 1970s, when the French realized it'd be a great place to house the enormous collections of 19th-century art scattered throughout the city.

The ground floor (level 0) houses early 19th-century art, mainly conservative art of the Academy and Salon, plus Realism. On the top floor (not visible from here) is the core of the collection—the Impressionist rooms. If you're pressed for time, go directly there (see directions following "Opéra Exhibit" on page 160). We'll start with conservatives and early rebels on the ground floor, then head upstairs to see how a few visionary young artists

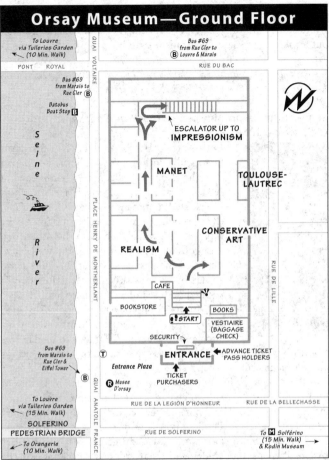

## Orsay Museum—Ground Floor

To Louvre
via Tuileries Garden
(10 Min. Walk)

QUAI VOLTAIRE

PONT ROYAL

Bus #69
from Rue Cler to
Ⓑ Louvre & Marais

RUE DU BAC

Bus #69
from Marais to
Rue Cler Ⓑ

Batobus
Boat Stop Ⓑ

Seine River

ESCALATOR UP TO
**IMPRESSIONISM**

PLACE HENRY DE MONTHERLANT

**MANET**

**TOULOUSE-
LAUTREC**

**CONSERVATIVE
ART**

**REALISM**

RUE DE LILLE

CAFÉ

BOOKSTORE

BOOKS

START

VESTIAIRE
(BAGGAGE
CHECK)

SECURITY

Bus #69
from Marais to
Rue Cler &
Eiffel Tower

Ⓑ

Ⓣ

Entrance Plaza

Ⓡ Musee
D'orsay

**ENTRANCE** ← ADVANCE TICKET
PASS HOLDERS

TICKET
PURCHASERS

QUAI ANATOLE FRANCE

RUE DE LA LÉGION D'HONNEUR

RUE DE LA BELLECHASSE

To Louvre
via Tuileries Garden
(15 Min. Walk)

SOLFERINO
PEDESTRIAN BRIDGE

← To Orangerie
(10 Min. Walk)

RUE DE SOLFERINO

To Ⓜ Solférino
(15 Min. Walk) →
& Rodin Museum

**ORSAY MUSEUM**

bucked the system and revolutionized the art world, paving the way for the 20th century. Clear as Seine water? *Bien.*

Remember that the museum rotates its large collection often, so find the latest arrangement on your current Orsay map, and be ready to go with the flow.

• *Walk down the steps to the main floor, a gallery filled with statues.*

## Conservative Art

### Main Gallery Statues

No, this isn't ancient Greece. These statues are from the same era as the Theory of Relativity. It's the conservative art of the French schools, and it was very popular throughout the 19th century. It was well-liked for its beauty and refined emotion. The balanced poses, perfect anatomy, sweet faces, curving lines, and gleaming white stone—all of this is very appealing. (I'll bad-mouth it later, but for now appreciate the exquisite craftsmanship of this "perfect" art.)

• *Take your first right into the small room 1, marked* Ingres, Delacroix. *Look for a nude woman with a pitcher of water.*

### Jean-Auguste-Dominique Ingres—*The Source* (*La Source,* 1856)

Let's start where the Louvre left off. Ingres (ang-gruh, with a soft "gruh"), who helped cap the Louvre collection, championed a Neoclassical style. *The Source* is virtually a Greek statue on canvas. Like *Venus de Milo,* she's a balance of opposite motions—her hips tilt one way, her breasts the other; one arm goes up, the other down; the water falling from the pitcher matches the fluid curve of her body. Her skin is porcelain-smooth, painted with seamless brushstrokes.

Ingres worked on this painting over the course of 35 years and considered it his "image of perfection." Famous in its day, *The Source* influenced many artists whose classical statues and paintings are in this museum.

In the Orsay's first few rooms, you're surrounded by visions of idealized beauty—nude women in languid poses, Greek mythological figures, and anatomically perfect statues. This was the art adored by French academics and the middle-class *(bourgeois)* public. The 19th-century art world was dominated by two conservative institutions: the Academy (the state-funded art school) and the Salon, where works were exhibited to the buying public. The art they produced was technically perfect, refined, uplifting, and heroic. Some might even say...boring.

• *Exit room 1 the way you came in, cross the main gallery of statues, and enter room 4 (directly across from Ingres), marked* Daumier.

## Realism and Early Rebels

### Honoré Daumier—*Celebrities of the Happy Medium* (*Célébrités du Juste Milieu,* 1832-1835)
This is a liberal's look at the stuffy bourgeois establishment that controlled the Academy and the Salon. In these 36 bustlets, Daumier, trained as a political cartoonist, exaggerates each subject's most distinct characteristic to capture with vicious precision the pomposity and self-righteousness of these self-appointed

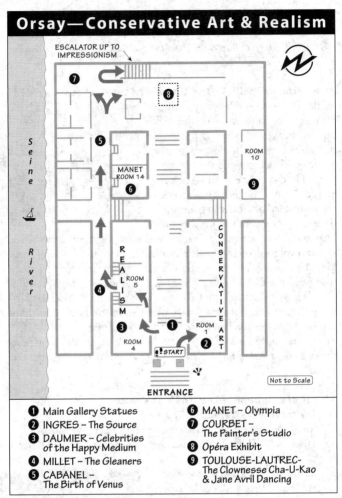

# Orsay—Conservative Art & Realism

ESCALATOR UP TO
IMPRESSIONISM

❼

⑧

❺

MANET
ROOM 14

❻

ROOM
10

❾

*Seine* ⚓ *River*

R
E
A
L
I
S
M

ROOM
5

❹

C
O
N
S
E
R
V
A
T
I
V
E
A
R
T

❸

ROOM
1

❶

ROOM
4

❷

🚻 START

Not to Scale

**ENTRANCE**

❶ Main Gallery Statues
❷ INGRES – The Source
❸ DAUMIER – Celebrities of the Happy Medium
❹ MILLET – The Gleaners
❺ CABANEL – The Birth of Venus

❻ MANET – Olympia
❼ COURBET – The Painter's Studio
❽ Opéra Exhibit
❾ TOULOUSE-LAUTREC- The Clownesse Cha-U-Kao & Jane Avril Dancing

**ORSAY MUSEUM**

arbiters of taste. The labels next to the busts give the name of the person being caricatured, his title or job (most were members of the French parliament), and an insulting nickname (like "gross, fat, and satisfied" or Monsieur "Plate-head"). Give a few nicknames yourself. Can you find Reagan, Clinton, Kerry, Sarkozy, Al Sharpton, and Gingrich?

These people hated the art you're about to see. Their prudish faces tightened as their fantasy world was shattered by the Realists.
• *Go uphill four steps into room 5 and turn left. Climb more steps leading to a hallway labeled* Barbizon, *where you'll find…*

### Jean-François Millet—*The Gleaners* (*Les Glaneuses,* 1867)

Millet (mee-yay) shows us three gleaners, the poor women who pick up the meager leftovers after a field has already been harvested for the wealthy. Millet grew up on a humble farm. He didn't attend the Academy and despised the uppity Paris art scene. Instead of idealized gods, goddesses, nymphs, and winged babies, he painted simple rural scenes. He was strongly affected by the socialist revolution of 1848, with its affirmation of the working class. Here he captures the innate dignity of these stocky, tanned women who bend their backs quietly in a large field for their small reward.

This is "Realism" in two senses. It's painted "realistically," not prettified. And it's the "real" world—not the fantasy world of Greek myth, but the harsh life of the working poor.
• *Continue up the hallway to the section called* Peintures de Salon *(near rooms 14 and 15). Find a pastel blue-green painting of a swooning Venus.*

### Alexandre Cabanel—*The Birth of Venus* (*La Naissance de Vénus,* 1863)

This painting and others nearby were popular items at the art market called the Salon. The public loved Cabanel's *Venus.* Emperor Napoleon III purchased it.

Cabanel lays Ingres' *The Source* on her back. This goddess is a perfect fantasy, an orgasm of beauty. The Love Goddess stretches back seductively, recently birthed from the ephemeral foam of the waves. This is art of a pre-Freudian society, when sex was dirty and mysterious and had to be exalted into a more pure and divine form. The sex drive was channeled into an acute sense of beauty. French folk would literally swoon in ecstasy before these works of art. Like it? Go ahead, swoon. If it feels good, enjoy it. (If you feel guilty, get over it.) Now, take a mental cold shower, and experience a Realist's take on the traditional Venus.
• *Find room 14 (Manet), which is down a few stair steps.*

ORSAY MUSEUM

### Edouard Manet—*Olympia* (1863)

"This brunette is thoroughly ugly. Her face is stupid, her skin cadaverous. All this clash of colors is stupefying." So wrote a critic when Edouard Manet's nude hung in the Salon. The public hated it, attacking Manet (man-ay) in print and literally attacking the canvas.

Compare this uncompromising nude with Cabanel's idealized, pastel, Vaseline-on-the-lens beauty in *The Birth of Venus*. Cabanel's depiction was basically soft-core pornography, the kind you see today selling lingerie and perfume.

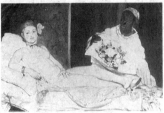

Manet's nude doesn't gloss over anything. The pose is classic, used by Titian, Goya, and countless others. But this is a Realist's take on the classics. The sharp outlines and harsh, contrasting colors are new and shocking. Her hand is a clamp, and her stare is shockingly defiant, with not a hint of the seductive, hey-sailor look of most nudes. This prostitute, ignoring the flowers sent by her last customer, looks out as if to say, "Next." Manet replaced soft-core porn with hard-core art.

• *Make your way to the far left corner of level 0, to a room called the Pavillon Amont, labeled* Courbet, grand formats, *dominated by a huge dark canvas…*

### Gustave Courbet—*The Painter's Studio* (*L'Atelier du Peintre,* 1855)

The Salon of 1855 rejected this dark-colored, sprawling, monumental painting that perplexed casual viewers. In an age when "Realist painter" was equated with "bomb-throwing Socialist," it took courage to buck the system. Dismissed by the so-called experts, Courbet (coor-bay) held his own one-man exhibit. He built a shed in the middle of Paris, defiantly hung his art out, and basically mooned the shocked public.

Courbet's painting takes us backstage, showing us the gritty reality behind the creation of pretty pictures. We see Courbet himself in his studio, working diligently on a Realistic landscape, oblivious to the confusion around him. Milling around are ordinary citizens, not Greek heroes. The woman who looks on is not a nude Venus but a naked artist's model. And the little boy with an adoring look on his face? Perhaps it's Courbet's inner child, admiring the artist who sticks to his guns, whether it's popular or not.

• *At the far end of the gallery, you'll walk on a glass floor over a model of Paris.*

## Opéra Exhibit

Expand to 100 times your size and hover over this scale-model section of the city. In the center sits the 19th-century Opéra Garnier, with its green-domed roof.

Nearby, you'll also see a cross-section model of the Opéra. You'd enter from the right end, buy your ticket in the foyer, then move into the entrance hall with its grand staircase, where you could see and be seen by *tout* Paris. At curtain time, you'd find your seat in the red-and-gold auditorium, topped by a glorious painted ceiling. (The current ceiling, painted by Marc Chagall, is even more wonderful than the one in the model.) Notice that the stage, with elaborate riggings to raise and lower scenery, is as big as the seating area. Nearby are models of set designs from some famous productions. These days, Parisians enjoy their Verdi and Gounod at the modern opera house at Place de la Bastille.

• *Before leaving the ground floor, consider seeing the Toulouse-Lautrec paintings tucked away in room 10, to the right of the* Opéra *exhibit. They rightly belong with the Post-Impressionist works on level 2, but since you're already here, enjoy these paintings incarnating the artist's love of nightlife and show business...*

## Henri de Toulouse-Lautrec—*The Clownesse Cha-U-Kao* (1895)

Henri de Toulouse-Lautrec (1864-1901) was the black sheep of a noble family. At age 15 he broke both legs, which left him disabled. Shunned by his family, a freak to society, he felt more at home in the underworld of other outcasts—prostitutes, drunks, thieves, dancers, and actors. He painted the lowlife in the bars, cafés, dance halls, and brothels he frequented. Toulouse-Lautrec died young of alcoholism.

*The Clownesse Cha-U-Kao* is one of his fellow freaks, a fat lady clown who made her living by being laughed at. She slumps wearily after a performance, indifferent to the applause, and adjusts her dress to prepare for the curtain call.

Toulouse-Lautrec was a true impression-ist, catching his models in candid poses. He worked spontaneously, never correct-ing his mistakes, as you can see from the blotches on her dark skirt and the unintentional yellow sash that hangs down. Can you see a bit of Degas here, in the subject matter, snapshot pose, and colors?

### Henri de Toulouse-Lautrec—*Jane Avril Dancing* (*Jane Avril Dansant,* 1891)

Toulouse-Lautrec hung out at the Mou-lin Rouge dance hall in Montmartre. One of the most popular performers was this slim, graceful, elegant, and melan-choly woman, who stood out above the rabble of the Moulin Rouge. Her legs keep dancing while her mind is far away. Toulouse-Lautrec, the "artistocrat," might have identified with her noble face—sad and weary of the nightlife, but immersed in it.

• *Next up—the Orsay's Impressionist collec-tion. Consider reading ahead on Impression-ism while you're still on the ground floor, as the Impressionist rooms can be very crowded. Then take the escalator up to the top floor. Pause to take in a commanding view of the*

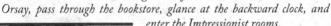

*Orsay, pass through the bookstore, glance at the backward clock, and enter the Impressionist rooms.*

*The Impressionist collection is scattered somewhat randomly through rooms 29-36. You'll see Monet hanging next to Renoir, Manet sprinkled among Pissarro, and a few Degas here and a few Degas there. Shadows dance and the displays mingle. Where they're hung is a lot like their brushwork...delight-fully sloppy. If you don't see a described painting, ask a guard or just move on. It's likely hanging farther down.*

# Impressionism

Light! Color! Vibrations! You don't hang an Impressionist canvas—you tether it. Impressionism features bright colors, easygoing open-air scenes, spontaneity, broad brush-strokes, and the play of light.

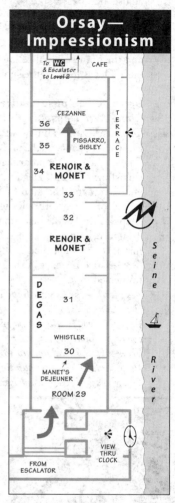

The Impressionists made their canvases shimmer by using a simple but revolutionary technique. Let's say you mix red, yellow, and green together—you'll get brown, right? But Impressionists didn't bother to mix them. They'd slap a thick brush-stroke of yellow down, then a stroke of green next to it, then red next to that. Up close, all you see are the three messy strokes, but as you back up...*voilà!* Brown! The colors blend in the eye, at a distance. But while your eye is saying "bland old brown," your subconscious is shouting, "Red! Yellow! Green! Yes!"

There are no lines in nature, yet someone in the classical tradition (Ingres, for example) would draw an outline of his subject, then fill it in with color. Instead the Impressionists built a figure with dabs of paint...a snowman of color.

Remember, the following tour is less a room-by-room itinerary than an introduction to the Orsay's ever-changing collection. Have fun exploring: Think of it as a sun-dappled treasure hunt.

### Edouard Manet—*Luncheon on the Grass* (*Le Déjeuner sur l'Herbe,* 1863)

A shocked public looked at this and wondered: What are these scantily clad women doing with these men? Or rather, what will they be doing after the last baguette is eaten? It isn't the nudity, but the presence of the men in ordinary clothes, that suddenly makes the nudes look naked. The public judged the painting on moral rather than artistic terms.

## Painting "in the Open Air"

The camera threatened to make artists obsolete. Now a machine could capture a better likeness faster than you could say "Etch-a-Sketch."

But true art is more than just painting reality. It gives us reality from the artist's point of view, with the artist's personal impressions of the scene. Impressions are often fleeting, so working quickly is essential.

The Impressionist painters rejected camera-like detail for a quick style more suited to capturing the passing moment. Feeling stifled by the rigid rules and stuffy atmosphere of the Academy, the Impressionists took as their motto, "Out of the studio, into the open air." They grabbed their berets and scarves and went on excursions to the country, where they set up their easels (and newly invented tubes of premixed paint) on riverbanks and hillsides, or they sketched in cafés and dance halls. Gods, goddesses, nymphs, and fantasy scenes were out; common people and rural landscapes were in.

The quick style and everyday subjects were ridiculed and called childish by the "experts." Rejected by the Salon, the Impressionists staged their own exhibition in 1874. They brashly took their name from an insult thrown at them by a critic who laughed at one of Monet's "impressions" of a sunrise. During the next decade, they exhibited their own work independently. The public, opposed at first, was slowly won over by the simplicity, the color, and the vibrancy of Impressionist art.

You can see that a new revolutionary movement was starting to bud—Impressionism. Notice the background: the messy brushwork of trees and leaves, the play of light on the pond, and the light that filters through the trees onto the woman who stoops in the haze. Also note the strong contrast of colors (white skin, black clothes, green grass). This is a true out-of-doors painting, not a studio production.

Edouard Manet (1832-1883) had an upper-class upbringing and some formal art training, and he had been accepted by the Salon. He could have cranked out pretty nudes and been a successful painter. Instead, he surrounded himself with a group of young artists experimenting with new techniques. Because of his reputation and strong personality, he was their master, though he learned equally from them.

Let the Impressionist revolution begin!

ORSAY MUSEUM

• *Among the colorful Impressionist works, find the non-Impressionist but equally famous...*

## James Abbott McNeill Whistler—*Portrait of the Artist's Mother (Portrait de la Mère de l'Auteur, 1871)*

Why's it so famous? I don't know either. Perhaps because it's by an American, and we see in his mother some of the monumental solidity of our own ancestral moms, who were made tough by pioneering the American wilderness.

Or perhaps because it was so starkly different for its day. In a roomful of golden goddesses, it'd stand out like a fish in a tree. The alternate title is *Arrangement in Gray and Black, No. 1,* and the whole point is the subtle variations of dark shades softened by the rosy tint of her cheeks. Nevertheless, the critics kept waiting for it to come out in Colorization.

## Edgar Degas—*The Dance Class (La Classe de Danse,* c. 1873-1875)

Clearly, Degas loved dance and the theater. (See several other dance-themed works nearby.) The play of stage lights off his dancers, especially the halos of ballet skirts, is made to order for an Impressionist. In *The Dance Class*, bored, tired dancers scratch their backs restlessly at the end of a long rehearsal. And look at

the bright green bow on the girl with her back to us. In the Impressionist style, Degas slopped green paint onto her dress and didn't even say, *"Excusez-moi."*

Edgar Degas (1834-1917, day-gah) was a rich kid from a family of bankers, and he got the best classical-style art training. Adoring Ingres' pure lines and cool colors, Degas painted in the Academic style. His work was exhibited in the Salon. He gained success and a good reputation, and then...he met the Impressionists.

Degas blends classical lines with Impressionist color, spontaneity, and everyday subjects from urban Paris. Degas loved the unposed "snapshot" effect, catching his models off guard. Dance students, women at work, and café scenes are approached from odd angles that aren't always ideal, but make the scenes seem more real.

### Edgar Degas—*In a Café,* or *Absinthe* (*Au Café, dit L'Absinthe,* 1876)

Degas hung out with low-life Impressionists, discussing art, love, and life in the cheap cafés and bars in Montmartre. Here, a weary lady of the evening meets morning with a last, lonely, nail-in-the-coffin drink in the glaring light of a four-in-the-morning café. The pale green drink at the center of the composition is the toxic substance absinthe, which fueled many artists and burned out many more.

• *Scattered all around you are works by two Impressionist masters at their peak, Monet and Renoir. You're looking at the quintessence of Impressionism. The two were good friends, often working side by side, and their canvases sometimes hang side by side in these rooms.*

### Pierre-Auguste Renoir—*Dance at the Moulin de la Galette* (*Bal du Moulin de la Galette,* 1876)

On Sunday afternoons, working-class folk would dress up and head for the fields on Butte Montmartre (near Sacré-Cœur basilica) to dance, drink, and eat little crêpes (galettes) till dark. Pierre-Auguste Renoir (1841-1919, ren-wah) liked to go there to paint the common Parisians living and loving in the afternoon sun. The sunlight filtering through the trees creates a kaleidoscope of colors, like the 19th-century equivalent of a mirror ball throwing darts of light onto the dancers.

He captures the dappled light with quick blobs of yellow staining the ground, the men's jackets, and the sun-dappled straw hat (right of center). Smell the powder on the ladies' faces. The painting glows with bright colors. Even the shadows on the ground, which should be gray or black, are colored a warm blue. Like a photographer who uses a slow shutter speed to show motion, Renoir paints a waltzing blur.

Renoir's work is lighthearted, with light colors, almost pastels. He seems to be searching for an ideal, the pure beauty we saw in paintings on the ground floor. In later years, he used more and more red tones, as if trying for even more warmth.

### Claude Monet—*The Cathedral of Rouen* (*La Cathédrale de Rouen,* 1893)

Claude Monet (1840-1926, mo-nay) is the father of Impressionism. He fully explored the possibilities of open-air painting and tried to faithfully reproduce nature's colors with bright blobs of paint.

Monet went to Rouen, rented a room across from the cathedral, set up his easel...and waited. He wanted to catch "a series of differing impressions" of the cathedral facade at various times of day and year. He often had several canvases going at once. In all, he did 30 paintings of the cathedral, and each is unique. The time-lapse series shows the sun passing slowly across the sky, creating different-colored light and shadows. The labels next to the art describe the conditions: in gray weather, in the morning, morning sun, full sunlight, and so on.

As Monet zeroes in on the play of colors and light, the physical subject—the cathedral—is dissolving. It's only a rack upon which to hang the light and color. Later artists would boldly throw away the rack, leaving purely abstract modern art in its place.

### Claude Monet—Paintings from the Garden at Giverny

One of Monet's favorite places to paint was the garden he landscaped at his home in Giverny, west of Paris (and worth a visit, provided you like Monet more than you hate crowds—see the Giverny and Auvers-sur-Oise chapter). The Japanese bridge and the water lilies floating in the pond were his two favorite subjects. As Monet aged and his eyesight failed, he made bigger canvases of smaller subjects. The final water lilies are monumental smudges of thick paint surrounded by paint-splotched clouds that are reflected on the surface of the pond.

Monet's most famous water lilies are in full bloom at the Orangerie Museum, across the river in the Tuileries Garden (see the Orangerie Museum Tour chapter). You can see more Monet at the Marmottan Museum (see the Marmottan Museum Tour chapter).

ORSAY MUSEUM

**Camille Pissarro, Alfred Sisley, and Others**

The Orsay features some of the "lesser" pioneers of the Impressionist style. Browse around and discover your own favorites. Pissarro is one of mine. His grainy landscapes are more subtle and subdued than those of the flashy Monet and Renoir—but, as someone said, "He did for the earth what Monet did for the water."

• *Break time. Continue to the jazzy café, with good prices and wild decor. In good weather, venture out on the terrace for fresh air and great views. Browse the upper floor's other exhibits (including interesting temporary exhibits), and then move on.*

# Post-Impressionism

Post-Impressionism—the style that employs Impressionism's bright colors while branching out in new directions—is scattered all around the museum. Surf on your own, or follow my route.

• *From the top-floor café, backtrack to room 36.*

## Paul Cézanne

Paul Cézanne (1839-1906, say-zahn) brought Impressionism into the 20th century. Compared with the color of Monet, the warmth of Renoir, and Van Gogh's passion, Cézanne's rather impersonal canvases can be difficult to appreciate. Bowls of fruit, landscapes, and a few portraits were Cézanne's passion. Because of his style (not his content), he is often called the first modern painter.

### Cézanne—*Self-Portrait* (*Portrait de l'Artiste,* c. 1873-1876)

Cézanne was virtually unknown and unappreciated in his lifetime. He worked alone, lived alone, and died alone, ignored by all but a few revolutionary young artists who understood his efforts. Cézanne's brush was a blunt instrument. With it, he'd bludgeon reality into submission, drag it across a canvas, and leave it there to dry. But Cézanne, the mediocre painter, was a great innovator. His work spoke for itself—which is good because, as you can see here, he had no mouth.

### Cézanne—*Landscape* (*Rochers près des Grottes au-dessus de Château-Noir,* 1904)

Cézanne used chunks of green, tan, and blue paint as building blocks to construct this rocky brown cliff. Whereas the Impressionists built a figure out of a mosaic of individual brushstrokes,

ORSAY MUSEUM

Cézanne used blocks of paint to give his composition a more solid, geometrical shape. A block of paint forming part of a rock in the foreground is the same size as one in the background, flattening the scene into a wall of brushstrokes.

These chunks are like little "cubes." It's no coincidence that Cézanne's experiments in reducing forms to their geometric basics influenced the...Cubists.

### Cézanne—*The Card Players* (*Les Joueurs de Cartes*, c. 1890-1895)

These aren't people. They're studies in color and pattern. The subject matter—two guys playing cards—is less important than the pleasingly balanced pattern they make on the canvas, two sloping forms framing a cylinder (a bottle) in the center. Later, abstract

artists would focus solely on the shapes and colors.

The jacket of the player to the right is a patchwork of tans, greens, and browns. Even the "empty" space between the men—painted with fragmented chunks of color—is almost as tangible as they are. As one art scholar puts it: "Cézanne confused intermingled forms and colors, achieving an extraordinarily luminous density in which lyricism is controlled by a rigorously constructed rhythm." Just what I said—chunks of color.

• *You'll find more Post-Impressionists on level 2. To get there, return to the café, find the escalators, and descend to level 2. Start down the right side of the open-air mezzanine, where you'll find the entrance to the darkened room 72, the first of several rooms with works by Van Gogh and Gauguin.*

## Vincent van Gogh

Impressionists have been accused of being "light"-weights. The colorful style lends itself to bright country scenes, gardens, sunlight on the water, and happy crowds of simple people. It took a remarkable genius to add profound emotion to the Impressionist style.

Like Michelangelo, Beethoven, Rembrandt, Wayne Newton, and a select handful of others, Vincent van Gogh (1853-1890, van-go, or van-HOCK by the Dutch and the snooty) put so much of himself into his work that art and life became one. In the Orsay's collection of paintings, you'll see both Van Gogh's painting style and his life unfold.

### Van Gogh—*Peasant Woman near the Hearth* (*Paysanne près de l'Atre,* 1885)

As the son of a Dutch minister, Van Gogh felt drawn to a religious vocation, and he spread the gospel among the poorest of the poor—peasants and miners in overcast Holland and Belgium. He painted these hardworking, dignified folks in a crude, dark style that reflects the oppressiveness of their lives...and the loneliness of his own as he roamed northern Europe in search of a calling.

### Van Gogh—*Self-Portrait, Paris* (*Portrait de l'Artiste,* 1887)

Encouraged by his art-dealer brother, Van Gogh moved to Paris, and *voilà!* The color! He met Monet, drank with Paul Gauguin and Henri de Toulouse-Lautrec, and soaked up the Impressionist style. (See how he built a bristling brown beard with thick, side-by-side strokes of red, yellow, and green.)

At first, Vincent painted like the others, but soon he developed his own style. His thick, swirling brushstrokes infused life into even inanimate objects. Van Gogh's brushstrokes curve and thrash like a garden hose pumped full of wine.

### Van Gogh—*Midday,* or *The Siesta, after Millet* (*La Méridienne, dit La Sieste, d'après Millet,* 1889-1890)

The social life of Paris became too much for the solitary Van Gogh, and he moved to southern France. At first, in the glow of the bright spring sunshine, he had a period of incredible creativity and happiness, as he was overwhelmed by the bright colors, landscape vistas, and common people—an Impressionist's dream.

### Van Gogh—*Van Gogh's Room at Arles* (*La Chambre de van Gogh à Arles,* 1889)

But being alone in a strange country began to wear on him. An ugly man, he found it hard to get a date. The close-up perspective of this painting makes his tiny rented room look even more cramped. He invited his friend Gauguin to join him, but after two months together arguing passionately about art, nerves frayed. Van Gogh threatened Gauguin with a knife, driving his friend back to Paris. In crazed despair, Van Gogh mutilated his own ear.

The people of Arles realized they had a madman on their hands and convinced Van Gogh to seek help. He entered a mental hospital.

### Van Gogh—*The Church at Auvers-sur-Oise* (*L'Eglise d'Auvers-sur-Oise,* 1890)

Van Gogh's later paintings are more meditative—fewer bright landscapes, more closed-in scenes with deeper and almost surreal colors. The sky is cobalt blue and the church's windows are also blue, as if we're looking right through the building to an infinite sky. There's a road that leads from us to the church, then splits to go behind it. A choice must be made: Which way?

Van Gogh, the preacher's son, saw painting as a calling, and he approached it with a spiritual intensity. You can visit this church as an easy day trip from Paris (see Auvers-sur-Oise on page 616).

### Van Gogh—*Self-Portrait, St. Rémy* (1889)

Van Gogh wavered between happiness and madness. He despaired of ever being sane enough to continue painting.

This self-portrait shows a man engulfed in a confused background of brushstrokes that swirl and rave, setting in motion the waves of the jacket. But in the midst of this rippling sea of mystery floats a still, detached island of a face with probing, questioning, yet wise eyes.

Do his troubled eyes know that only a few months on, he will take a pistol and put a bullet through his chest? Vincent van Gone.

• *Also in rooms 70-72, look for...*

## Paul Gauguin

Paul Gauguin (1848-1903, go-gan) got the travel bug early in childhood and grew up wanting to be a sailor. Instead, he became a stockbroker. In his spare time, he painted, and he was introduced to the Impressionist circle. He learned their bright clashing colors but diverged from their path about the time Van Gogh waved a knife in his face. At the age of 35, he got fed up with it all, quit his job, abandoned his wife (her stern portrait bust may be nearby) and family, and took refuge in his art.

### Gauguin—*Arearea*, or *Joyousness* (*Joyeusetés*, 1892)

Gauguin traveled to the South Seas in search of the exotic, finally settling on Tahiti. There he found his Garden of Eden. He simplified his life into a routine of eating, sleeping, and painting. He simplified his paintings still more, to flat images with heavy black outlines filled with bright, pure colors. He painted the native girls in their naked innocence (so different from Cabanel's seductive *Venus*). But this simple style had a deep undercurrent of symbolic meaning.

*Arearea* shows native women and a dog. In the "distance" (there's no attempt at traditional 3-D here), a procession goes by with a large pagan idol. What's the connection between the idol and the foreground figures, who are apparently unaware of it? In primitive societies, religion permeates life. Idols, dogs, and women are holy.

• *Next, in room 69, find...*

### Pointillist Paintings (Lots of Dots)

Pointillism, as illustrated by many paintings in the next rooms, brings Impressionism to its logical conclusion. Little dabs of pure colors are placed side by side to blend in the viewer's eye. In works such as *The Circus* (*Le Cirque*, 1891), Georges Seurat (1859-1891) used only red, yellow, blue, and green points of paint to create a mosaic of colors that shimmers at a distance, capturing the wonder of the dawn of electric light.

• *The open-air mezzanine of level 2 is lined with statues. Stroll the mezzanine from the near end (near room 72) to the far end, enjoying the work of Rodin, Claudel, and other greats of...*

# French Sculpture

### Auguste Rodin—*The Walking Man*
### (*L'Homme Qui Marche,* c. 1900)

Like this statue, Auguste Rodin (1840-1917) had one foot in the past, while the other was stepping into the future. Rodin combined classical solidity with Impressionist surfaces to become the greatest sculptor since Michelangelo.

This muscular, forcefully striding man could be a symbol of Renaissance Man with his classical power. With no mouth or hands, he speaks with his body. Get close and look at the statue's surface. This rough, "unfinished" look reflects light in the same way the rough Impressionist brushwork does, making the statue come alive, never quite at rest in the viewer's eye.

### Auguste Rodin—*Honoré de Balzac* (1897)

The great French novelist is given a heroic, monumental ugliness. Wrapped in a long cloak, he thrusts his head out at a defiant angle, showing the strong individualism and egoism of the 19th-century Romantic movement. Balzac is proud and snooty—but his body forms a question mark, and underneath the twisted features we can see a touch of personal pain and self-doubt. This is hardly camera-eye realism—Balzac wasn't that grotesque —but it captures a personality that strikes us even if we don't know the man.

### Camille Claudel—*Maturity*
### (*L'Age Mûr,* 1899-1903)

Camille Claudel, Rodin's student and mistress, may have portrayed their doomed love affair here. A young girl desperately reaches out to an older man, who is led away reluctantly by an older woman. The center of the composition is the empty space left when their hands separate. In real life, Rodin refused to leave his wife, and Claudel ended up in an insane asylum.

• *Continue along the mezzanine to the far end, where you'll find...*

**Auguste Rodin—*The Gates of Hell***
**(*La Porte de l'Enfer*, 1880-1917)**

Rodin worked for decades on these doors depicting Dante's hell, and they contain some of his greatest hits—small statues that he later executed in full size. Find *The Thinker* squatting above the doorway, contemplating Man's fate. And in the lower left is the same kneeling man eating his children *(Ugolin)* that you'll see in full size nearby. Rodin paid models to run, squat, leap, and spin around his studio however they wanted. When he saw an interesting pose, he'd yell, "freeze" (or "statue maker") and get out his sketch pad. (For more on *The Gates of Hell* and Rodin, see the Rodin Museum Tour.)

From this perch, look down to the main floor at all the classical statues between you and the big clock, and realize how far we've come—not in years, but in stylistic changes. Many of the statues below—beautiful, smooth, balanced, and idealized—were created at the same time as Rodin's powerful, haunting works. Rodin's sculptures capture the groundbreaking spirit of much of the art in the Orsay Museum. With a stable base of 19th-century stone, he launched art into the 20th century.

• *You've seen the essential Orsay and are permitted to cut out. But there's an "other" Orsay I think you'll find entertaining. It's on Level 2, starting in rooms 61-66.*

# The "Other" Orsay

The beauty of the Orsay is that it combines all the art from 1848 to 1914, both modern and classical, in one building. The classical art, so popular in its day, was maligned and largely forgotten in the later 20th century. It's time for a reassessment. Is it as gaudy and gawd-awful as we've been led to believe? From our 21st-century perspective, let's take a look at the opulent *fin de siècle* French high society and its luxurious art.

• *From the far end of level 2's open-air mezzanine (near Rodin's* Gates of Hell*), find the entrance to rooms 61-66. Browse through several galleries of curvaceous furniture as you make your way to room 66, in the corner.*

### Art Nouveau

The Industrial Age brought factories, row houses, machines, train stations, geometrical precision—and ugliness. At the turn of the 20th century, some artists reacted against the unrelieved geometry of harsh, pragmatic, iron-and-steel Eiffel Tower art with a "new art"—Art Nouveau. (Hmm. I think I had a driver's ed teacher by that name.)

Enter room 66 to stand amid a reconstructed wood-paneled

ORSAY MUSEUM

# Level 2—Post-Impressionism & Beyond

1. Van Gogh
2. Gauguin
3. Pointillism
4. RODIN – Balzac & Walking Man
5. CLAUDEL – Maturity
6. RODIN – Gates of Hell
7. Art Nouveau – Charpentier's Dining Room
8. Art Worth a Second Look
9. Art NOT Worth a Second Look
10. Grand Ballroom

Not to Scale

**ORSAY MUSEUM**

dining room designed by Alexandre Charpentier *(Boiserie de la Salle à Mangér)*. With its carved vines, leafy garlands, and tree-branch arches, it's one of the finest examples of Art Nouveau.

Like nature, which also abhors a straight line, Art Nouveau artists used the curves of flowers and vines as their pattern. They were convinced that "practical" didn't have to mean "ugly" as well. They turned everyday household objects into art. Another well-known example of Art Nouveau is the sinuous wrought-ironwork of some of Paris' early Métro entrances—which were commissioned by banker Adrien Bénard, the same man who ordered this dining room for his home.

• *Return to the open-air mezzanine and turn right. Enter room 59.*

## Art Worth a Second Look

We've seen some great art. Now let's see some not-so-great art—at least, that's what modern critics tell us. This is realistic art with a subconscious kick.

### Henri Martin—*Serenity* (*Sérénité,* 1899)

An idyll in the woods. Three nymphs with harps waft off to the right. These people are stoned on something.

### Jean Delville—*The School of Plato* (*L'Ecole de Platon,* 1898)

This painting could be subtitled "The Athens YMCA." A Christ-like Plato surrounded by adoring, half-naked nubile youths gives new meaning to the term "platonic relationship." Will the pendulum shift so that one day art like *The School of Plato* becomes the new, radical avant-garde style?

• *Continue down the mezzanine until you reach room 55, labeled* Naturalism.

## Art Not Worth a Second Look

A director of the Orsay once said, "Certainly, we have bad paintings. But we have only the greatest bad paintings." And here they are.

### Fernand Cormon—*Cain* (1880)

The world's first murderer, with the murder weapon still in his belt, is exiled with his family. Archaeologists had recently discovered a Neanderthal skull, so the artist makes the family part of a prehistoric hunter/gatherer tribe.

### Edouard Detaille—*The Dream* (*Le Rêve,* 1888)

Soldiers lie still, asleep without beds, while visions of Gatling guns dance in their heads.

### Léon Lhermitte—*Paying the Harvesters* (*La Paye des Moissonneurs,* 1882)

Called "the grandson of Courbet and Millet," Lhermitte depicts peasants getting paid. The subtitle of the work could be, "Is this all there is to life?" (Or, "The Paycheck...After Deductions.")

• *Continue along the mezzanine. Near the escalators, turn right and find the palatial room 51, with mirrors and chandeliers, marked* Salle des Fêtes *(Grand Ballroom).*

## The Grand Ballroom (Salle des Fêtes)

This room was part of the hotel that once adjoined the Orsay train station. One of France's poshest nightspots, it was built in 1900, abandoned after 1939, condemned, and then restored to the elegance you see today. You can easily imagine gowned debutantes and white-gloved dandies waltzing the night away

to the music of a chamber orchestra. Take in the interior decoration: raspberry marble-ripple ice-cream columns, pastel-colored ceiling painting, gold work, mirrors, and leafy garlands of chandeliers. Find the statue *(L'Aurore)* of the nymph with a canopy of hair, hide-and-seek face, and silver-dollar nipples, looking like a shampoo ad.

Is this stuff beautiful or merely gaudy? Divine or decadent? Whatever you decide, it was all part of the marvelous world of the Orsay's century of art.

• *A good place to ponder it all is Le Restaurant, located near the escalators on level 2. It's pricey, but there's an affordable coffee-and-tea happy hour (daily 15:00-17:30 except Thu). After all this art, you deserve it.*

ORSAY MUSEUM

# ORANGERIE MUSEUM TOUR

*Musée de l'Orangerie*

This Impressionist museum is as lovely as a water lily. Step out of the tree-lined, sun-dappled Impressionist painting that is the Tuileries Garden and into the Orangerie (oh-rahn-zhuh-ree), a little bijou of select works by Monet, Renoir, Matisse, Picasso, and others.

On the main floor you'll find the main attraction, Monet's *Water Lilies (Nymphéas)*, floating dreamily in oval rooms. The rooms were designed in the 1920s to display this art, following the artist's exacting specifications. But in the 1960s the museum added a floor above the *Water Lilies,* cutting them off from the daylight that was, after all, their inspiration and subject matter. In 2006, after a renovation that took six years and $36 million, the upstairs collection was moved underground, and the upper floor was transformed into a tall skylight—drenching the *Water Lilies* in natural light.

In the underground gallery are select works from the personal collection of Paris' trend-spotting art dealer of the 1920s, Paul Guillaume. The museum is small enough to enjoy in a short visit, but complete enough to show the bridge from Impressionism to Modernism. And it's all beautiful.

# Orientation

**Cost:** €7.50, €5 after 17:00 (they start kicking you out at 17:45—but you'll have ample time to saturate yourself in lilies), under 18 free, €14 combo-ticket with Orsay Museum (valid for four days, one visit per sight), covered by Museum Pass.

**Hours:** Wed-Mon 9:00-18:00, closed Tue, galleries shut down 15 minutes before closing time; tel. 01 44 77 80 07, www.musee-orangerie.fr.

**Getting There:** It's in the Tuileries Garden near Place de la Concorde (Mo: Concorde) and a lovely 15-minute stroll from the Orsay Museum.

**Tours:** €6 **guided tours** in English are usually offered Mon and Thu at 14:30. The €5 **audioguide** adds nothing beyond what's in this book on the *Water Lilies,* but provides good detail about individual canvases in the Walter-Guillaume collection.

**Length of This Tour:** Allow one hour. Temporary exhibitions often merit extra time.

**With Limited Time:** The museum is small, and you could see (if not "experience") the two rooms of *Water Lilies* in a glance.

**Starring:** Claude Monet's *Water Lilies* and select works by the pioneers of Modern painting.

# The Tour Begins

• *Monet's* Water Lilies *float serenely in two pond-shaped rooms straight ahead after passing the ticket takers. Examine them up close to see Monet's technique; stand back to take in the whole picture.*

## Main Floor

### Salle I

Like Beethoven going deaf, a nearly blind Claude Monet (1840-1926) wrote his final symphonies on a monumental scale. Even as he struggled with cataracts, he planned a series of huge six-foot-tall canvases of water lilies to hang in special rooms at the Orangerie.

These eight mammoth, curved panels immerse you in Monet's garden. We're looking at the pond in his garden at Giverny—dotted with water lilies, surrounded by foliage, and dappled by the reflections of the sky, clouds, and trees on the surface. The water lilies (*nymphéas* in French) range from plain green lily pads to flowers of red, white, yellow, lavender, and various combos.

The effect is intentionally disorienting; the different canvases feature different parts of the pond from different angles, at different times of day, with no obvious chronological order. Monet mingles the pond's many elements and lets us sort it out.

• *Start with the long wall on your right (as you enter) and work counterclockwise.*

It's *Morning* on the pond at Giverny. The blue pond is the center of the composition, framed by the green, foliage-covered banks at either end. Lilies float in the foreground, and the pond stretches into the distance.

The sheer scale of the Orangerie project was daunting for an artist in his twilight years. This vast painting is made from four separate canvases stitched together, and spans 6 feet 6 inches by 55 feet. Altogether, Monet painted 1,950 square feet of canvas to complete the *Water Lilies* series. Working at his home in Giverny, Monet built a special studio with skylights and wheeled easels to accommodate the canvases.

The panel at the far end, called *Green Reflections*, looks deep into the dark water. Green willow branches are reflected on the water in a vertical pattern; lily pads stretch horizontally.

Along the other long wall *(Clouds)*, green lilies float among lavender clouds reflected in blue water. Staring into Monet's pond, we see the intermingling of the four classical elements—earth (foliage), air (the sky), fire (sunlight), and water—the primordial soup of life.

The true subject of these works is the play of reflected light off the surface of the pond. Monet would work on several canvases at once, each dedicated to a different time of day. He'd move with the sun from one canvas to the next. Pan slowly around this hall. Watch the pond turn from pre-dawn darkness (far end) to clear morning light *(Morning)* to lavender late afternoon *(Clouds)* to glorious sunset—in the west, where the sun actually does set.

In *Sunset* (near end), the surface of the pond is stained a bright yellow. Get close and see how Monet worked. Starting from the gray of the blank canvas (lower right), he'd lay down big, thick brushstrokes of a single color, weaving them in a (mostly) horizontal and vertical pattern to create a dense mesh of foliage. Over this, he'd add more color for the dramatic highlights, until (in the center of the yellow) he got a dense paste of piled-up paint. Up close, it's a mess—but back up, and the colors begin to resolve into a luminous scene. There are no clearly identifiable objects in this canvas—no lilies, no trees, no clouds, no actual sun—just pure reflected color.

• *Continue into Salle II, starting with the long wall on your right and working counterclockwise.*

## Salle II

In this room, Monet frames the pond with pillar-like tree trunks and overhanging foliage. The compositions are a bit more symmetrical and the color schemes more muted, with blue and lavender and green-brown. Monet's paintings almost always deal with the foundation of life and unspoiled nature. This room begs you to stroll its banks, slowly ambling with the artist in a complete loop—perhaps while listening to Debussy.

In *Willows on a Clear Morning* (on the long wall to the right), we seem to be standing on the bank of the pond, looking out through overhanging trees at the water. The swirling branches and horizontal ripples on the pond suggest a gentle breeze.

*The Two Willows* (far end) frame a wide expanse of water dotted with lilies and the reflection of gray-pink clouds.

Stand close in front of *Morning Willows* (long left wall). Notice how a "brown" tree is a tangled Impressionist beard of purple, green, blue, and red. Each leaf is a long brushstroke, each lily pad a dozen smudges.

At the near end, *Reflections of Trees* is a mess of blue-purple paint brightened only by the lone rose lilies in the center. Each lily is made of many Impressionist brushstrokes—each brushstroke is itself a mix of red, white, and pink paints. Put a mental frame around a single lily, and it looks like an abstract canvas. Monet demonstrates both his mastery of color and his ability to render it with paint, applied generously and deftly. He wanted the vibrant colors to keep firing your synapses.

With this last canvas, darkness descends on the pond. The room's large, moody canvases, painted by an 80-year-old man in the twilight of his life, invite meditation.

For 12 years (1914-1926), Monet worked on these paintings obsessively. A successful eye operation in 1923 gave him new energy. Monet completed all the planned canvases, but didn't live to see

# Paul Guillaume (1891-1934)

For the first three decades of the 20th century, Paris was the center of the art world, and the center of Paris' art scene was  Paul Guillaume. An art dealer, promoter of "modern" art, and friend of out-there artists, Guillaume rose from humble beginnings to become wealthy and famous.

In his early days, this self-made businessman struggled alongside struggling painters in Montmartre—Picasso, Modigliani, Derain, Laurencin, and many others. When the art market boomed in the 1920s (along with the stock market), he and his fellow bohemians became the toasts of high society. With his flamboyant wife, Domenica (also called Juliette), Guillaume hosted exotic parties featuring what we would now call "performance art" to shock and titillate the buying public.

Many of their artist friends honored Paul and Domenica by painting their portraits. In Modigliani's *Novo Pilota* (pictured above), young Paul strikes a pose as the dapper man-of-the-world he was soon to become. The title of the painting is Italian for "new helmsman," reflecting Paul's growing status as a champion of Modernism. Marie Laurencin's portrait captures the winsome beauty of Domenica, whose charm helped establish the nouveau riche couple in social circles. Andre Derain's and Kees Van Dongen's portraits feature Paul and Domenica when they are older, more confident, and sophisticated.

The Orangerie displays Guillaume's personal collection of favorite paintings. After Paul's death, Domenica married Jean Walter and took her new husband's last name, which is why it's officially called the "Walter-Guillaume" collection.

them installed here. In 1927, the year after his death, these rooms were completed and the canvases put in place. Some call this the first "art installation"—art displayed in a space specially designed for it in order to enhance the viewer's experience.

Monet's final work was more "modern" than Impressionist. Each canvas is fully saturated with color, the distant objects as bright as the close ones. Monet's mosaic of brushstrokes forms a colorful design that's beautiful even if you just look "at" the canvas, like wallpaper. He wanted his paintings to be realistic and three-dimensional, but with a pleasant, two-dimensional pattern. As the subjects become fuzzier, the colors and patterns predominate. Monet builds a bridge between Impressionism and modern, abstract art.

To see more of Monet's work, take the Marmottan Museum Tour and day-trip to Giverny, both covered in this book.

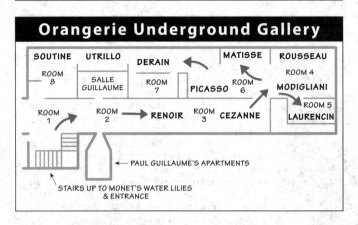

**Orangerie Underground Gallery**

| SOUTINE | UTRILLO | | DERAIN | | MATISSE | ROUSSEAU |
|---------|---------|--|--------|--|---------|----------|

ROOM 8 — SALLE GUILLAUME — ROOM 7 — PICASSO — ROOM 6 — ROOM 4

MODIGLIANI

ROOM 1 — ROOM 2 → RENOIR — ROOM 3 — CEZANNE — ROOM 5 — LAURENCIN

← PAUL GUILLAUME'S APARTMENTS

STAIRS UP TO MONET'S WATER LILIES & ENTRANCE

# Underground Gallery

## Walter-Guillaume Collection

These paintings—Impressionist, Fauvist, and Cubist—were amassed by the art dealer Paul Guillaume (and inherited by his wife, Domenica Guillaume Walter). They're a snapshot of what was hot in the world of art, circa 1920. The once-revolutionary Impressionists had become completely old-school, though their paintings—now classics—commanded a fortune. The bohemian Fauvists and Cubists, who invented Modern art atop Butte Montmartre (c. 1900-1915), had suddenly become the darlings of the art world. But they refused to be categorized, and their work in the 1920s branched out in dozens of new directions. Browse through the gallery and watch the various "isms" unfold.

• *Descend the stairs to the lower floor. Turn right and find several Renoir canvases midway down the gallery.*

### Pierre-Auguste Renoir (1841-1919)

Renoir loved to paint *les femmes*—women and girls—nude and innocent, taking a bath or practicing the piano, all with rosy red cheeks and a relaxed grace. We get a feel for the happy family life of middle-class Parisians (including Renoir's own family) during the belle époque— the beautiful age of the late 19th century. Renoir's warm, sunny colors (mostly red) are Impressionist, but he adds a classical touch with his clearer lines and, in the later nudes, the voluptuousness of classical statues and paintings. He seems to enjoy capturing the bourgeoisie, soft and elegant, enjoying their leisure pursuits.

### Paul Cézanne (1839-1906)

These small canvases of simple subjects pushed modern artists to reinvent the rules of painting.

The fruit of Cézanne's still lifes are "built" with an underlying geometry from patches of color. In the shapes of nature, Cézanne saw spheres, cylinders, and cones. He was fond of saying, "First you must learn to paint these simple shapes. Then you will be able to do whatever you want."

There's no traditional shading to create the illusion of three dimensions, but these fruit bulge out like cameos from the can-

vas. The fruit is clearly at eye level, yet it's also clearly placed on a table seen from above. Cézanne broke the rules, showing multiple perspectives at once. Picasso was fascinated with Cézanne's strange new world—which seems to give us a peek into the secret lives of fruits.

In his landscapes, Cézanne the Impressionist creates "brown" rocks out of red, orange, and purple; and "green" trees out of green, lime, and purple. Cézanne the proto-Cubist builds the rocks and trees with blocks of thick brushstrokes.

### Henri Rousseau (1844-1910)

Rousseau, a simple government worker, never traveled outside France. But in his artwork he created an exotic, dreamlike, completely unique world. Here, a Parisian wedding is set amid tropical trees. Figures are placed in a 3-D world, but the lines of

perspective recede so steeply into the distance that everyone is in danger of sliding down the canvas. Without any feet, the subjects seem barely tethered to the earth. The way Rousseau put familiar images in bizarre settings influenced the Surrealists. Enjoy France's biggest collection of Rousseaus.

### Amedeo Modigliani (1884-1920)

In his short, poverty-stricken, drug-addled life, Modigliani produced timeless-looking portraits of modern people. Born in Italy, Modigliani moved to Paris, where he hung around the fringes of the avant-garde crowd in Montmartre. He gained a reputation for his alcoholic excesses and outrageous behavior.

Turning his back on the prevailing Fauvist/Cubist ambience of the times, Modigliani developed a unique style, influenced by primitive tribal masks. His canvases feature stylized heads, almond eyes, long necks, and puckered mouths. *Novo Pilota* (1915, pictured on page 181) portrays Paul Guillaume as a cool dandy, suavely cradling a cigarette. Modigliani died young, just as his work was gaining recognition.

### Marie Laurencin (1883-1956)

As the girlfriend of the poet and art critic Guillaume Apollinaire, Laurencin was right at the heart of the Montmartre circle when Modern art was born. Her work, featuring women and cuddly animals intertwined in pink, blue, and gray tones, spreads a pastel sheen over this tumultuous time.

### Henri Matisse (1869-1954)

After World War I, Matisse moved to the south of France. He abandoned his fierce Fauvist style, and painted languid women in angular rooms with arabesque wallpaper. These paler tones evoke the sunny luxury of the Riviera. Traditional perspective is thrown

out the occasional hotel window as the women and furnishings in the "foreground" blend with the wallpaper "background" to become part of the decor.

### Pablo Picasso (1881-1973)

Picasso is a shopping mall of 20th-century artistic styles. In this room alone, he passes through his various periods: "Blue" (sad and tragic), "Rose" (red-toned nudes with timeless, masklike faces),

ORANGERIE MUSEUM

Cubist (flat planes of interwoven perspectives), and Classical (massive, sculptural nudes—warm blow-up dolls with substance). If all roads lead to Paris, all art styles flowed through Picasso.

### André Derain (1880-1954)

This former wild beast *(fauve)* tamed his colors in the 1920s. He and Picasso rode the rising wave of Classicism that surfaced after the chaos of the war years. With sharp outlines and studied realism, Derain's still lifes portrayed nudes, harlequins, portraits, and landscapes—all in odd, angular poses.

### Maurice Utrillo (1883-1955)

The hard-drinking, streetwise, bohemian artist is known for his postcard views of Montmartre—whitewashed buildings under perennially cloudy skies. For more on Utrillo, see page 366.

### Chaim Soutine (1893-1943)

When his friend Modigliani died (and Modigliani's widow committed suicide), Soutine went into a tailspin of depression that drove him to paint. The sub-

jects are ordinary—landscapes, portraits, and a fine selection of your favorite cuts of meat—but the style is deformed and Expressionistic. It shows a warped world in a funhouse mirror, smeared onto the canvas with thick, lurid colors. The never-cheerful Soutine was known to destroy work that did not satisfy him. Stand and ponder why these made the cut.

Did I say that the Orangerie's collection was as beautiful as an Impressionist painting? Well, Soutine's misery is so complete, it's almost a thing of beauty.

# RUE CLER WALK

*The Art of Parisian Living*

Paris is changing quickly, but a stroll down this street introduces you to a thriving, traditional Parisian neighborhood and offers insights into the local culture. Although this is a wealthy district, Rue Cler retains a workaday charm still found in most neighborhoods throughout Paris.

Shopping for groceries is the backbone of everyday life here. Parisians shop almost daily for three good reasons: refrigerators are small (tiny kitchens), produce must be fresh, and it's an important social event. Shopping is a chance to hear about the butcher's vacation plans, see photos of the florist's new grandchild, relax over *un café,* and kiss the cheeks of friends (the French standard is twice for regular acquaintances, four times for friends you haven't seen in a while; see "Le French Kiss" sidebar, page 194).

Rue Cler—traffic-free since 1984—offers plenty of space for slender stores and their patrons to spill out onto the street. It's an ideal environment for this ritual to survive and for you to explore. The street is lined with the essential shops—wine, cheese, chocolate, bread—as well as a bank and a post office. And the shops of this community are run by people who've found their niche: boys who grew up on quiche, girls who know a good wine.

For those learning the fine art of living Parisian-style, Rue Cler provides an excellent classroom. And if you want to assemble the ultimate French picnic, there's no better place. The Rue Cler Walk is the only tour in this guidebook you should start while hungry.

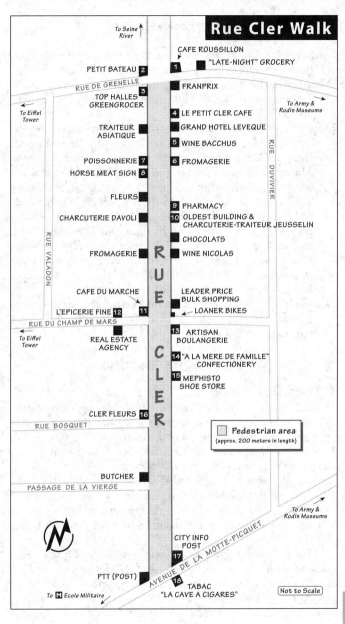

# Rue Cler Walk

1  CAFE ROUSSILLON
   "LATE-NIGHT" GROCERY

PETIT BATEAU 2

RUE DE GRENELLE

FRANPRIX

3  TOP HALLES
   GREENGROCER

To Eiffel
Tower

To Army &
Rodin Museums

4  LE PETIT CLER CAFE

TRAITEUR
ASIATIQUE

GRAND HOTEL LEVEQUE

5  WINE BACCHUS

RUE DUVIVIER

POISSONNERIE 7    6  FROMAGERIE

HORSE MEAT SIGN 8

FLEURS

9  PHARMACY

CHARCUTERIE DAVOLI    10  OLDEST BUILDING &
                          CHARCUTERIE-TRAITEUR JEUSSELIN

CHOCOLATS

FROMAGERIE    WINE NICOLAS

RUE VALADON

CAFE DU MARCHE    LEADER PRICE
                  BULK SHOPPING

L'EPICERIE FINE 12  11    LOANER BIKES

RUE DU CHAMP DE MARS

To Eiffel
Tower

REAL ESTATE
AGENCY

13  ARTISAN
    BOULANGERIE

14  "A LA MERE DE FAMILLE"
    CONFECTIONERY

15  MEPHISTO
    SHOE STORE

CLER FLEURS 16

RUE BOSQUET

Pedestrian area
(approx. 200 meters in length)

BUTCHER

PASSAGE DE LA VIERGE

R
U
E

C
L
E
R

To Army &
Rodin Museums

CITY INFO
POST

17

AVENUE DE LA MOTTE-PICQUET

PTT (POST)

18  TABAC
    "LA CAVE A CIGARES"

To Ⓜ Ecole Militaire

Not to Scale

**RUE CLER WALK**

# Orientation

**Length of This Walk:** Allow an hour to browse and café-hop along this short walk of two or three blocks.

**When to Go:** Visit Rue Cler when its markets are open and lively (Tue-Sat 8:30-13:00 & 15:00-19:30, Sun 8:30-12:00, dead on Mon).

**Etiquette:** Remember that these shops are busy serving regular customers; be careful not to get in the way. Be polite—say *"Bonjour, Madame* or *Monsieur"* as you enter and *"Au revoir, Madame* or *Monsieur"* when you leave. Get involved and buy something. Before making a purchase, watch the locals to see if self-service is allowed. Many shopkeepers prefer to serve you and don't want you to touch the goods. If you aren't sure of the protocol, ask, *"Je peux?"* (Can I?; zhuh puh). If you know what you want, say, *"S'il vous plaît"* (Please; see voo play) and point to your choice. For extra credit, add, *"Je voudrais"* (I would like; zhuh voo-dray). And don't forget *"Merci beaucoup"* (Thank you very much; mehr-see boh-koo).

**Getting There:** Start your walk at the northern end of the pedestrian section of Rue Cler, at Rue de Grenelle (Mo: Ecole Militaire or bus #69 stop).

# The Walk Begins

## ❶ Café Roussillon

This neighborhood fixture dumped its old-fashioned, characteristic look for the latest café style—warm, natural wood tones, easy lighting, and music. To the left of the door, you'll see the *Tarif des Consommations* sign required by French law, making the pricing clear: Drinks served at the bar *(comptoir)* are cheaper than drinks served at the tables *(salles)*. Notice that there is no café au lait listed. Parisians ask for *café crème* when they want coffee with steamed milk. Inside, the bar is always busy. The blackboard lists wines sold by the little, 7-centiliter glass (about 2.5 ounces), along with other drinks.

The little **late-night grocery** next door is one of many neighborhood shops nicknamed *dépanneurs* ("to help you out of difficulty"). Open nightly until midnight, these Parisian 7-Elevens are usually run by hardworking North Africans willing to keep long hours. Such shops are handy—not cheap. Locals happily pay the higher prices for the convenience *dépanneurs* provide.

• *If you're shopping for designer baby clothes, you'll find them across the street at...*

## ❷ Petit Bateau

The French spend at least as much on their babies as they do on their dogs—dolling them up with designer jammies. This store is one in a popular chain. Little children around here are really sophisticated. They speak French. And they just aren't comfortable unless they're making a fashion statement (such as underwear with sailor stripes). In the last generation, an aging and shrinking population has been a serious problem for Europe's wealthier nations. But France now has one of Europe's biggest baby populations—the fertile French average two children per family, compared to 1.6 for the rest of Europe. Babies are trendy today, and the government rewards parents with substantial tax incentives for their first two children—and then doubles the incentives after that. Making babies is good business—and revered. Notice how locals give pregnant women the royal treatment: They get priority seating on subways and buses, and they go straight to the front of any line—no waiting on those swollen feet. And the French love to ogle babies. The community celebrates every new addition.

• *Cross Rue de Grenelle to find...*

## ❸ Top Halles Fruits and Vegetables

Each morning, fresh produce is trucked in from farmers' fields to Paris' huge Rungis market—Europe's largest, near Orly Airport—and then dispatched to merchants with FedEx-like speed and precision. Good luck finding a shopping bag—locals bring their own two-wheeled carts or reusable bags. Also, notice how the earth-friendly French resist excessive packaging.

Parisians—who know they eat best by being tuned in to the seasons—shop with their noses. Try it. Smell the cheap foreign strawberries. One sniff of the torpedo-shaped French ones *(gariguettes)*, and you know which is better. Locals call those from Belgium "plastic strawberries"—red on the outside, white on the inside. Find the herbs in the back. Is today's delivery in? Look at the price of those melons. What's the country of origin? (It must be posted.) If they're out of season, they come from Guadeloupe. Many people buy only local products.

The **Franprix** across the street is a small outpost of a nationwide supermarket chain. Opposite Grand Hôtel Lévêque is a *traiteur asiatique.* Fast Asian food-to-go is popular in Paris. These

shops—about as common as bakeries—have had an impact on traditional Parisian eating habits.

## ❹ Le Petit Cler

This small café, a fine choice for lunch or dinner, was a *tabac* (tobacco shop) until a few years ago. It's a good example of how life
is changing on Rue Cler. It used to be that only the Brasserie aux
PTT, at the opposite end of the *rue,* had outdoor tables. Then Café
du Marché (described on page 433) joined in. Many locals regret
that shops are being lost to trendy café crowds.

• *Just past Grand Hôtel Lévêque is...*

## ❺ Wine Bacchus

Shoppers often visit the neighborhood wine shop last, after they've
assembled their meal and are able to pick the appropriate wine.
Wines are classified by region. Most "Parisians" (born elsewhere)
have an affinity for the wines of their home region. Check out the
great prices. Wines of the month—in the center—sell for as little
as €8. You can get a fine bottle for €12. The clerk is a counselor who
works with your menu and budget to help you select just the right
wine. He can put a bottle of white in the fridge for you to pick up
later (open until 20:00, except Sun).

• *Next door, smell the...*

## ❻ Fromagerie

A long, narrow, canopied cheese table brings the *fromagerie* into the
street. Wedges, cylinders, balls, and miniature hockey pucks are
all powdered white, gray, and burnt marshmallow—it's a festival
of mold. The street cart and front window feature both cow *(vache)*
and goat *(chèvre)* cheeses. Locals know the shape indicates the
region of origin (for example, a pyramid shape indicates a cheese
from the Loire). And this is important. Regions create the *terroir*
(physical and magical union of sun, soil, and generations of farmer
love) that gives the production—whether wine or cheese—its personality. *Ooh la la* means you're impressed. If you like cheese, show
greater excitement with more *la*s. *Ooh la la la la.* A Parisian friend
once held the stinkiest glob
close to her nose, took an orgas-
mic breath, and exhaled, "Yes,
it smells like zee feet of angels."
Go ahead...inhale.

Step inside and browse
through more than 200 types
of French cheese. A *fromagerie*
is lab-coat-serious but friendly.
Also known as a *crémerie* or a

"BOF" (for *beurre, oeuf,* and *fromage*), this is where people shop for butter, eggs, and cheese. Just like wines, quality cheeses need to be aged in the cool, humid environment of a *cave* (cellar). Under the careful watch of an *affineur* (the "finisher"), some cheeses will rest a few weeks, others for months. Like produce, cheeses are seasonal, as the milk produced by cows or goats changes flavor according to the animal's varied diet. Ask what's in season.

In the back room, the shop keeps *les meules*—big, 170-pound wheels of cheese, made from 250 gallons of milk. The "hard" cheeses are cut from these. Don't eat the skin of these big ones... they're rolled on the floor. But the skin on most smaller cheeses—the Brie, the Camembert—is part of the taste. "It completes the package," says my local friend.

If buying soft cheese, tell the shop when you're planning to eat it—they'll squeeze the cheese to make sure it'll reach *la maturité parfaite* on the day you want to consume it. One of your author's favorites is Epoisses, from Burgundy.

At dinner tonight you can take the cheese course just before or instead of dessert. On a good cheese plate you have a hard cheese (perhaps a Comté, similar to a white cheddar), a softer cheese (maybe Brie or Camembert), a bleu cheese, and a goat cheese—ideally from different regions. Because it's strongest, the goat cheese is usually eaten last.

• *Across the street, find the fish shop, known as the...*

## ❼ Poissonnerie

Fresh fish is brought into Paris daily from ports on the English Channel, 110 miles away. In fact, fish here is likely fresher than in many towns closer to the sea, because Paris is a commercial hub (from here, it's shipped to outlying towns). Anything wiggling? This *poissonnerie*, like all such shops, was upgraded to meet Europe-wide hygiene standards.

• *Next door at Crêperie Ulysée en Gaule (under the awning—get close to see) is a particularly tempting Rue Cler storefront.*

## ❽ No More Horse Meat

The stones and glass set over the doorway advertise horse meat: *Boucherie Chevaline.* While today this store serves souvlaki (the family is Greek) and crêpes, the classy old storefront survives from the previous occupant. Created in the 1930s and signed by the artist, it's a work of art fit for a museum—but it belongs right here, and that's where it will stay. Notice that the door is decorated with lunch coupon decals (like *chèque déjeuner* or *ticket restaurant*) for local workers. In France, an employee lunch-subsidy program is an expected perk. Employers—responding to strong tax incentives designed to keep the café culture vital—issue voucher checks (worth about €8 each) for each day an employee works in a month. The lunchtime *plat du jour* is often €8 or under at local cafés. Sack lunches are rare, since a good lunch is sacred...and subsidized.

• *Across the street is the...*

## ❾ Pharmacy

In France, as in much of Europe, pharmacists are the first point of contact for people who are ill. They make the first diagnosis and have the authority to prescribe certain drugs. If it's out of their league, they'll recommend a doctor. Pharmacies are also the only place to get many basic medical items, such as aspirin and simple reading glasses.

Inside, you'll notice locals handing over a green ID, the size of a credit card, with an embedded chip and a photo. This is the all-essential *Carte Vitale*, the French health insurance card. The national health-care system, *Sécurité Sociale*, pays about 75 percent of pharmacy, doctor, and hospital bills. Private employer-related insurance, a *Mutuelle*, covers a varying amount of the rest. Filling a prescription is often completely covered. The last time the World Health Organization ranked health-care systems by country, France came out on top. The French are deservedly proud of their nationalized health care.

## ❿ Oldest Building and Charcuterie-Traiteur Jeusselin

Next to the pharmacy is Rue Cler's oldest building (with the two garret windows on the roof). It's from the early 1800s, when this street was part of a village near Paris and lined with structures like this. Over the years, Paris engulfed these surrounding villages— and now the street is a mishmash of architectural styles.

Occupying the ground floor of this house is Charcuterie-Traiteur Jeusselin. *Traiteurs* (one who "treats" food) sell mouthwatering deli food to go. Because Parisian kitchens are so small, these gourmet delis are handy, even for those who cook. It lets the hosts concentrate on creating the main course, and then buy beautifully prepared side dishes to complete a fine dinner.

*Charcuteries* by definition are pork butchers, specializing in sausage, paté, and ham. The charcuterie business is fiercely competitive in France, with countless cooking contests allowing owners to test their products and show off their skills. Jeusselin proudly displays its hard-won awards by the entrance. One reads: *Medaille d'Or du Fromage de Tête du Jambon blanc 2009* (gold medal for head cheese with white ham). Head cheese is a meat jelly made from the head of a pig or cow. Who would brag about that? The French.

The other award—*Meilleur Traiteur de Paris, Gault & Millau 2008*—is for the "best deli," determined by the prestigious food-rating organization Gault Millau. Notice also, on the back wall inside, the prominently posted *Diplôme de Cordon Bleu*—a diploma awarded from the most famous cooking school in France, Cordon Bleu, which used to be in the neighborhood. Even with such credentials, many charcuteries have had to add *traiteur* services to survive. They're now selling prepared dishes, pastries, and wines-to-go, and often have a few tables where customers can sit and eat.

The photogenic Italian *charcuterie-traiteur* **Davoli** sits right across Rue Cler. Each day these two places go *tête-à-tête*, cooking up *plats du jour* (specials of the day), advertised on boards outside and inside, and sometimes on their websites. Note the system: Order, take your ticket to the cashier to pay, and return with the receipt to pick up your food.

• *A few doors down is...*

## ⓫ Café du Marché and More

Café du Marché, on the corner, is *the* place to sit and enjoy the action (described on page 433). It's Rue Cler's living room, where locals gather before heading home, many staying for a relaxed and affordable dinner. The owner has priced his menu so that residents can afford  to dine out on a regular basis, and it works—many patrons eat here five days a week. For a reasonable meal, grab a chair and check the chalk menu listing the *plat du jour.* Notice how the no-smoking-indoors laws have made outdoor seating and propane heaters a huge hit.

The shiny, sterile **Leader Price grocery store** (across the street) is a Parisian mini-Costco, selling bulk items. Because storage space is so limited in most Parisian apartments, bulk purchases are unlikely to become a big deal here. The latest trend is to stock up on nonperishables by shopping online, pick up produce three times a week, and buy fresh bread daily. Compare this storefront with the elegance of the other shops on this street. The awful exterior of this store suggests a sneaky bending of the rules. Normally, any proposed building modification on Rue Cler must undergo a rigorous design review in order for the owner to obtain the required permit.

## Le French Kiss (*Faire la Bise*)

You can't miss the cheek pecking in Paris. It's contagious—and it's how Parisians greet each other. Here's the skinny.

You won't see any American-style hugging in Paris; that's far too aggressive for the French. What you will see between acquaintances is a public display of proffered cheeks and puckered lips when saying hello and goodbye. The lips don't actually touch the cheek—only the cheeks touch, and a gentle kiss noise is made (except when parents kiss children). You usually start on the right side, then alternate to the left. The number of times varies with the region or circumstances—two, three, or four kisses. Different regions kiss a different number of times (two in Paris, three in the south, four in parts of Brittany, five after too much wine...). Parisians *faire la bise* in social settings but never in the workplace. When being introduced for the first time (at a dinner party, for example), women kiss women, men kiss women, but men shake hands. If you haven't seen someone in a long while, Parisians often double the standard two kisses into four.

How many kisses are appropriate for an American? If it happens to you, my recommendation is to go for two with confidence, and then—hover and wait.

The Paris city government has become enthusiastic about making the town bike-friendly. Notice the loaner bikes parked in the Vélib' rack. There are hundreds of these self-service stands around town for use by Vélib' subscribers. The system is intended to let people take short one-way rides by bike rather than car.

• From Café du Marché, hook right and side-trip a couple of doors down Rue du Champ de Mars to visit...

## ⓬ L'Epicerie Fine

A fine-foods boutique like this stands out because of its gentle owners, Pascal and Nathalie. Their mission in life is to explain to travelers, in fluent English, what the French fuss over food is all about. Say *bonjour* to Pascal and company. Let them help you assemble a picnic and tempt you with fine gourmet treats, Berthillon ice cream, and generous tastes of caramel, balsamic vinegar, and French and Italian olive oil. Their salted caramels from Normandy and small jars of mustards and jams make good souvenirs.

Across the street is a **real estate agency** advertising condos and apartments for rent or sale. The touch screen in the window gives the details: the arrondissement (neighborhood), if it's an apartment or condo, how many rooms ("*pieces*"—includes living and family rooms), square meters (25 square meters would be about 5 by 6 yards—the size of a spacious hotel room), and the monthly rent or sales price.

• *Return to Rue Cler. The neighborhood bakery on the corner is often marked by a line of people waiting to pick up their daily baguette.*

## ⓭ Artisan Boulangerie

Since the French Revolution, the government has regulated the cost of a basic baguette (meaning "wand" or "stick" of bread). By law, it must weigh 250 grams and consist of only four ingredients: flour, yeast, salt, and water. Parisians specify their preferences when they place a *boulangerie* order—some like their baguette well done, and others prefer it more doughy. More than one trip a day to the bakery is *normale* in Paris, as a good baguette can become stale in a matter of hours. To keep it fresh, wrap it in a cloth, never a plastic bag.

Locals debate the merits of Paris' many *boulangeries*, often remaining loyal to their local bread-baker. I know of hotels that won't serve breakfast until the corner bakery opens, to avoid having to set out yesterday's bread and croissants for their guests. Each spring, the city hosts a competition for the Best Baguette of Paris. The top prize? A cash award of €4,000 and the honor of providing the French president with baguettes for the coming year. This annual contest is the equivalent of Michelin's star system for bakeries.

It's said that a baker cannot be both good at bread and good at pastry—at cooking school they major in one or the other. So a baker either bakes bread or makes pastries and has the other done elsewhere. But here, the baker bucks the trend. Rue Cler regulars agree that this man makes both good bread and delicious pastries.

• *A bit farther along is...*

## ⓮ A la Mère de Famille Confectionery

This shop has been in the neighborhood for 30 years. The owner sells modern treats, but has always kept the traditional candies, too. "The old ladies, they want the same sweets that made them so happy 80 years ago," she says. You can buy "naked bonbons" right out of the jar and chocolate by the piece (about €0.75 each). You're welcome to assemble a small assortment.

Until a few years ago, the chocolate was dipped and decorated right on the premises. As was the tradition in Rue Cler shops, the merchants resided and produced in the back and sold in the front.

• *Next door, you'll find a...*

## ⓯ Mephisto Shoe Store

Shoe stores are almost as popular as bakeries in this city of footwear-loving fashionistas. (French-made Mephistos are cheaper here than in the US.) You may see the locals checking out your "foreign" shoes.

In a city where many people don't have cars, good shoes matter. The average Parisian's daily life is active: walking to the Métro, to lunch, to the shops after work, and then home. No need for the gym with this routine (gyms here are rare, expensive, and not well-maintained).

• *Across the street is...*

## ⑯ Cler Fleurs

Almost all Parisians who reside in the city center live in apartments or condos. Even the biggest, most luxury-laden city home shares walls with neighbors and has no yard. A lucky few may have access to a courtyard, but almost no one has a private garden. Parisians spend small fortunes bringing nature into their homes with plants and fresh flower arrangements. Notice the flower boxes on balconies—you work with what you have. When visiting friends in Paris, it's de rigueur to give a gift of flowers, and it's good form to have them delivered before you show up. Avoid chrysanthemums, as they are reserved for funerals.

Pop into the **butcher shop** a few doors down for a graphic peek at how far Parisians like to venture from beef when it comes to meat. You'll find everything here that'll be listed on your menu tonight (rabbit, lamb, duck, veal, and pigeon) and maybe even more (pig's ears, liver, and tripe).

• *Walk on to the end of Rue Cler, where it hits a busy street (the post office is on the corner).*

## ⑰ City Info Post

An electronic signpost directs residents to websites for local information—transportation changes, surveys, employment opportunities, community events, and so on. Notice the big, green glass recycling bin and the see-through green garbage sacks. In the 1990s, Paris suffered a rash of trash-can bombings. Bad guys hid rigged camp-stove canisters in metal garbage cans, which shredded into deadly "shrapnel" when they exploded. City authorities solved this by replacing metal cans with translucent bags.

• *Across the busy street is a* tabac.

## ⑱ Tabac La Cave à Cigares

Just as the US has liquor stores licensed to sell booze, the only place for people over 16 to buy tobacco legally in France is at a *tabac* (tah-bah) counter. Tobacco counters like this one are a much-appreciated fixture of each neighborhood, offering lots of services (and an insight into the local culture).

Even nonsmokers enjoy perusing the wares at a *tabac*. Notice how European laws require a bold warning sign on cigarettes—about half the size of the package—that says, bluntly, *fumer tue* (smoking kills). Even so, you may not be able to resist the temptation to pick up a *petit Corona*—your chance to buy a fine Cuban cigar (look for "Habano") for €6 without breaking US law.

*Tabacs* also serve their neighborhoods as a kind of government cash desk. All sell stamps and some sell public-transit tickets. This *tabac* also sells the Paris Museum Pass at no added charge—*très* handy. Locals pay for parking meters in *tabacs* by buying a card... or pay fines if they don't. Like back home, the LOTO is a big deal—and a lucrative way for the government to tax poor and less-educated people.

• *The Ecole Militaire Métro stop is just down the street to the right. If you bought a picnic along this walk, head for the nearby benches and gardens: From the post office, Avenue de la Motte-Picquet leads to two fine parks. Facing Rue Cler, turn right for the Army Museum or left for the Eiffel Tower. Or go straight ahead to dive back into neighborhood Paris.*

# EIFFEL TOWER TOUR

*La Tour Eiffel*

It's crowded, expensive, and there are probably better views in Paris, but visiting this 1,000-foot-tall ornament is worth the trouble. Visitors to Paris may find *Mona Lisa* to be less than expected, but the Eiffel Tower rarely disappoints, even in an era of skyscrapers. This is a once-in-a-lifetime, I've-been-there experience. Making the trip gives you membership in the exclusive society of the quarter of a billion other humans who have made the Eiffel Tower the most visited monument in the modern world.

## Orientation

**Cost:** €14 for an elevator ride all the way to the top, €8.50 if you're only going up to the two lower levels, not covered by Museum Pass.

You can save some time in line by climbing the stairs to the first and second levels for €5, or €3.50 if you're under 25. (Elevators and stairs are both free going down.)

Once inside the tower, you can buy your way to the top with no penalty—ticket booths and machines on the first and second levels sell supplements for €5.50 (walkers need to climb to second level to catch an elevator to the top).

**Hours:** Daily mid-June-Aug 9:00-24:00, last ascent to top at 23:00 and to lower levels at 23:30; Sept-mid-June 9:30-23:00, last ascent to top at 22:00 and to lower levels at 22:30 (elevator). Access to the stairs

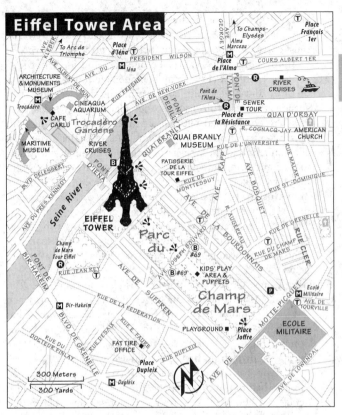

**Eiffel Tower Area**

closes at 18:00 in off-season. During windy weather, the top level may close to tourists.

**Reservations:** Frankly, you'd be crazy to show up without a reservation. At www.tour-eiffel.fr, you can book an entry time (for example, June 12 at 16:30) and skip the initial entry line (the longest)—at no extra cost. Book well in advance, as soon as you know when you'll be in Paris. Just pay online with a credit card and print your own ticket. Arrive at the tower 10 minutes before your entry time and look for either of the two entrances marked *Visiteurs avec Reservation* (Visitors with Reservation), where attendants scan your ticket and put you on the first available elevator. Even with a reservation, when you want to get from the second level to the summit, you'll still have to wait in line like everybody else (and show your ticket again).

The website is easy, but here are a few tips: First, when you "Choose a ticket," make sure you select "Lift entrance ticket with access to the summit" in order to go all the way to the top. For "Type of ticket," it doesn't really matter whether you pick "Group" or "Individual"; a "Group" ticket just gives you one piece of paper covering everyone in your party. You must enter a mobile phone number for identification purposes, so if you don't have one, make one up—and jot it down so you won't forget it (French mobile phone numbers begin with 06 or 07 and have 10 digits). To print the ticket, follow their specifications carefully (white paper, blank on both sides, etc.). If you're on the road without a printer, try forwarding your email confirmation notice to your hotel reception. They can click on a link to the website, where you can enter your information and print out your ticket. Alternatively, Classic Walks may have tickets with reservations (see page 48).

**When to Go:** For the best of all worlds, arrive with enough light to see the views, then stay as it gets dark to see the lights. The views are grand whether you ascend or not. At the top of the hour, a five-minute display features thousands of sparkling lights (best viewed from Place du Trocadéro or the grassy park below).

**Avoiding Lines:** Crowds overwhelm this place much of the year, with one- to two-hour waits to get in (unless it's rainy, when lines can evaporate). Weekends and holidays are worst, but prepare for ridiculous crowds almost any time. The best solution is to make an online reservation up (see above) and to take the stairs down (from first or second levels).

If you don't have a reservation, go early; get in line 30 minutes before the tower opens. Going later is the next-best bet (after 19:00 May-Aug, after 17:00 off-season—a bit earlier in winter as it gets dark by 17:00—see "Hours," earlier, for last-ascent times). If you're in line to buy tickets, estimate about 20 minutes for every 100 yards, plus 30 minutes more after you reach the security check near the ticket booths. When you buy tickets, all members of your party must be with you; you can't buy tickets in advance for people not present. To get reduced fares for kids, bring proof of ID.

You can bypass some (but not all) lines if you have a reservation at either of the tower's view restaurants (see "Eating," later) or hike the stairs (shorter lines).

**Getting There:** The tower is about a 10-minute walk from the Métro (Bir-Hakeim or Trocadéro stops) or train (Champ de Mars-Tour Eiffel RER stop). The Ecole Militaire Métro stop in the Rue Cler area is 20 minutes away. Buses #69 and #87 stop nearby on Avenue Joseph Bouvard in the Champ de Mars park.

**Information:** Eiffel Tower information offices are between the north and east pillars and at the west pillar, next to the Group Desk. Each level on the tower has displays pointing out the landmarks and monuments visible below. Tel. 01 44 11 23 23, www.tour-eiffel.fr.

**Length of This Tour:** Budget three to four hours to wait in line, get to the top, and sightsee your way back down. With online reservations and/or no crowds, figure two hours to the top and back (with time for sightseeing).

**With Limited Time:** Do the first level only (the views are fine), and avoid lines by taking the stairs or reserving an entry time.

**Pickpockets:** Beware. Street thieves plunder awestruck visitors gawking below the tower. And tourists in crowded elevators are like fish in a barrel for predatory pickpockets. *En garde.* There's a police station at the Jules Verne pillar.

**Security Check:** Bags larger than 19 × 8 × 12 inches are not allowed, but there is no baggage check. All bags are subject to a security search. No knives, glass bottles, or cans are permitted.

**Services:** Free WCs are at the base of the tower, behind the east pillar. Inside the tower itself, WCs are on all levels, but they're small, with long lines.

**Photography:** All photos and videos are allowed.

**Eating:** The first and second levels have small sandwich-and-pizza-type cafés (€6.50 for a sandwich). The tower's two classy restaurants offer great views. Making a reservation at either restaurant lets you skip the initial elevator line (though you still must pay for the elevator), but you can't skip every line and you can't ascend more than 30 minutes prior to your reservation time. Get details online when you book. Last-minute reservations for both restaurants may be available from their information kiosk at the tower's base, between the north and east pillars.

On the first level is 58 Tour Eiffel (€20 for two-course lunches, €70-85 dinner *menus*, daily 11:30-23:00, dinner seatings at 18:30 and 21:00). While you can order à la carte at lunch, at dinner, patrons are required to go with a complete *menu* (fixed-price meal). Dinner patrons should also reserve at least a month in advance for a view table, or a few days in advance for a nonview table. No reservations are available for lunch; it's first come, first served (tel. 01 72 76 18 46, toll tel. 08 25 56 66 62, www.restaurants-toureiffel.com).

The expensive, Michelin one-star Jules Verne Restaurant is on the second level (€90 weekday lunch *menu*, €170-220 weekend lunch *menus*, €220 dinner *menu*, daily 12:15-13:30 & 19:00-21:30). Reserve two to three months in advance, though tables sometimes open up sooner (tel. 01 45 55 61 44, www.lejulesverne-paris.com).

At the tower's base, there's not much besides sandwich stands. Rue Cler, with many options, is a 20-minute walk away (see page 186). Avenue de la Bourdonnais, a mere block east of the tower, has a few eateries and sandwich shops, including Boulangerie-Pâtisserie de la Tour Eiffel, with inexpensive salads, quiches, and sandwiches, as well as cool views of the tower (daily, outdoor and indoor seating, 21 Avenue de la Bourdonnais, tel. 01 47 05 59 81). The garden café at the Quai Branly Museum is nearby and an equally good choice (see page 68).

Your tastiest option may be to assemble a picnic beforehand from any of several handy shops near Métro stop Ecole Militaire and picnic in the Champ de Mars park (on the side grassy areas or on benches along the central grass; the middle stretch is off-limits).

**Best Views:** The best place to view the tower is from Place du Trocadéro to the north. It's a 10-minute walk across the river, a happening scene at night, and especially fun for kids. Consider arriving at the Trocadéro Métro stop for the view, then walking toward the tower. Another delightful viewpoint is from the Champ de Mars park to the south.

**Starring:** All of Paris...and beyond.

## Overview

There are three observation platforms, at roughly 200, 400, and 900 feet. Although being on the windy top of the Eiffel Tower is a thrill you'll never forget, the view is better from the second level, where you can actually see Paris' monuments. The first level also has nice views and more tourist-oriented sights. All three levels have some displays, WCs (usually with long lines), souvenir stores, and a few other services.

To get to the top, you need to change elevators at the second level. A separate elevator—with another line—shuttles between the second level and the top. (Note: Whether you have a ticket for the top or just for the second level, elevators going up do not stop at the first level. You can see the first level on the way back down.)

For the hardy, stairs lead from the ground level up to the first and second levels—and rarely have a long line. It's 360 stairs to the first level and another 360 to the second. The staircase is enclosed

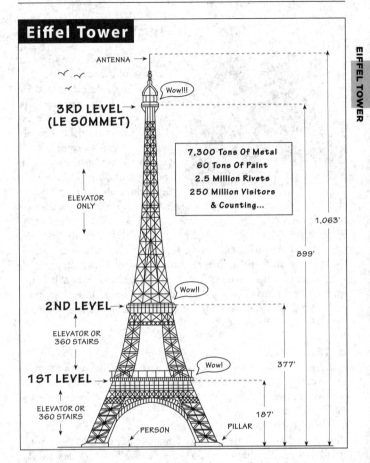

with a wire cage, so you can't fall, but those with vertigo issues may still find them dizzying.

If you want to see the entire tower, from top to bottom, then see it...from top to bottom. Ride the elevator to the second level, then immediately line up for the elevator to the top. Enjoy the views on top, then ride back down to the second level. Frolic there for a while and take in some more views. When you're ready, head to the first level by taking the stairs (no line and can take as little as 5 minutes) or lining up for the elevator (before boarding, ask if the elevator will stop on the first level—some don't). Explore the shops and exhibits on the first level and have a snack. Once you're ready to leave, you can line up for the elevator, but it's quickest and most memorable to take the stairs back down to earth.

# The Tour Begins

Find the various entrances at the base of the tower's four *piliers* (pillars), named for their compass points: *nord* (north), *sud* (south), *est* (east), and *ouest* (west). The various ticket offices move around from time to time, so make sure you get in the right line. Avoid lines selling tickets only for *Groupes*. If you have a reservation, look for signs saying *Visiteurs avec Reservations*. If you don't have a reservation, follow signs for *Individuels* or *Visiteurs sans Tickets*, or climb the stairs (pay the fee at the ticket office at the south pillar, next to the Jules Verne Restaurant entrance).

To pass the time in line, read the following background information, or pick up whatever free reading material is available at the ground-level tourist stands. Look up at the tower towering above you, and don't even think about what would happen if someone dropped a coin from the top.

## Exterior

Delicate and graceful when seen from afar, the Eiffel Tower is massive—even a bit scary—close up. You don't appreciate its size until you walk toward it; like a mountain, it seems so close but takes forever to reach.

The tower, including its antenna, stands 1,063 feet tall, or slightly higher than the 77-story Chrysler Building in New York. Its four support pillars straddle an area of 3.5 acres. Despite the tower's 7,300 tons of metal and 60 tons of paint, it is so well-engineered that it weighs no more per square inch at its base than a linebacker on tiptoes.

Once the world's tallest structure, it's now eclipsed by a number of towers (CN Tower, Toronto, 1,815 feet), radio antennae (KVLY-TV mast, North Dakota, 2,063 feet), and skyscrapers (Burj Khalifa in Dubai, UAE, 2,717 feet). France's sleek Le Viaduc de Millau, a 1.5-mile-long suspension bridge completed in late 2004, also has a taller tower (1,125 feet). The bridge was built by a consortium which included the same company that erected the Eiffel Tower.

The long green lawn stretching south of the tower is the Champ de Mars, originally the training ground for troops and students of the nearby military school (Ecole Militaire) and now a park. On the north side, across the Seine, is the curved palace colonnade framing a square called the Trocadéro, site of the 1878 world's fair.

## History

In 1889, the first visitor to Paris' Universal Exposition walked beneath the "arch" formed by the newly built Eiffel Tower and entered the fairgrounds. This world's fair celebrated both the centennial of the French Revolution and France's position as a global superpower. Bridge-builder Gustave Eiffel (1832-1923) won the contest to build the fair's centerpiece by beating out rival proposals such as a giant guillotine.

Eiffel deserved to have the tower named for him. He did much more than design it. He oversaw its entire construction, personally financed it, and was legally on the hook if the project floundered. His factory produced the iron beams, and his workers built it, using cranes and apparatus designed by Eiffel. Facing a deadline for the exposition, he brought in the project on time and under budget.

The tower was nothing but a showpiece, with no functional purpose except to demonstrate to the world that France had the wealth, knowledge, and can-do spirit to erect a structure far taller

than anything the world had ever seen. The original plan was to dismantle the tower as quickly as it was built after the celebration ended, but it was kept by popular demand.

To a generation hooked on technology, the tower was the marvel of the age, a symbol of progress and human ingenuity. Not all were so impressed, however; many found it a monstrosity. The writer Guy de Maupassant (1850-1893) routinely ate lunch in the tower just so he wouldn't have to look at it.

In subsequent years, the tower has come to serve many functions: as a radio transmitter (1909-present), a cosmic-ray observatory (1910), a billboard (spelling "Citroën" in lights, 1925-1934), a broadcaster of Nazi TV programs (1940-1944), a fireworks launch pad (numerous times), and as a framework for dazzling lighting displays, including the current arrangement, designed in 2000 for the celebration of the millennium.

• *To reach the top, ride the elevator or walk (720 stairs) to the second level. From there, get in line for the next elevator and continue to the top. Pop out 900 feet above the ground.*

## Building the Tower

As you ascend through the metal beams, imagine being a worker, perched high above nothing, riveting this thing together. It was a massive project, and it took all the ingenuity of the Industrial Age—including mass production, cutting-edge technology, and capitalist funding.

The foundation was the biggest obstacle. The soil, especially along the river, was too muddy to support big pillars. Gustave Eiffel drew on his bridge-building experience, where support piers needed to be constructed underwater. He sank heavy, bottomless compartments (caissons) into the wet soil. These were watertight and injected with breathable air, so workers could dig out the mud beneath them, allowing the caisson to sink further. When the workers were done, the hole was filled in with cement 20 feet thick and capped with stone. The massive iron pillars were sunk into the ground at an angle, anchored in the subterranean stone.

The tower went up like an 18,000-piece erector set, made of 15-foot iron beams held together with 2.5 million rivets. The pieces were mass-produced in factories in the suburbs and brought in on wagons. For two years, 300 workers assembled the pieces, the tower rising as they went. First, they used wooden scaffolding to support the lower (angled) sections,

## Third Level (Le Sommet)

The top level, called *le sommet*, is tiny. (It can close temporarily without warning when it reaches capacity.) All you'll find here are wind and grand, sweeping views. The city lies before you (pick out sights with the help of the panoramic maps). On a good day, you can see for 40 miles. Do a 360-degree tour of Paris. (Note that the following compass points are only approximate; in fact, what the tower's displays call "west" is more like southwest, etc.) Feeling proud you made it this high? You can celebrate your accomplishment with a €10 glass of champagne.

**Looking west** *(ouest):* The Seine runs east to west (though at this point it's flowing more southwest). At the far end of the skinny "island" in the river, find the tiny copy of the Statue of Liberty, looking 3,633 miles away to her big sister in New York. Gustave Eiffel, a man of many talents, also designed the internal supports of New York's Statue of Liberty, which was cast in copper by fellow Frenchman Frederic Bartholdi (1886).

**Looking north** *(nord):* At your feet is the curved arcade of the Trocadéro. Beyond that is the vast, forested expanse of the Bois de Boulogne, the three-square-mile park that hosts joggers and *boules*

until the pillars came together and the tower could support itself. Then the iron beams were lifted up with steam-powered cranes, including some on tracks (creeper cranes) that inched up the pillars as the tower progressed. There, daring work-

ers dangled from rope ladders, balanced on beams, and tightrope-walked their way across them as they put the pieces in place. The workers then hammered in red-hot rivets made on-site by blacksmiths. As the rivets cooled, they solidified the structure.

After a mere year and a half, the tower sur-passed what had been the tallest structure in the world—the Washington Monument (555 feet)—which had taken 36 years to build.

The tower was painted a rusty red. Since then, it's sported several colors, including mustard and the current brown-gray. It is re-painted every seven years, and will likely be receiving a new coat during your visit (it takes 25 full-time painters 18 months to apply 60 tons of paint by hand—no spraying allowed).

Two years, two months, and five days after construction began, the tower was done. On May 15, 1889, a red, white, and blue beacon was lit on the top, the Universal Exposition began, and the tower carried its first astounded visitor to the top.

players by day and prostitutes by night. The track with bleachers is Paris' horseracing track, the Hippodrome de Longchamp. In the far distance are the skyscrap-ers of La Défense. Find the Arc de Triomphe to the right of the Trocadéro. The lone skyscraper between the Arc and the Troca-déro is the Palais des Congrès, a complex that hosts international conferences, trade shows, and major concerts.

**Looking east** *(est):* At your feet are the Seine and its many bridges, in-cluding the Pont Alexan-dre, with its four golden statues. Looking farther upstream, find the Orsay

**EIFFEL TOWER**

Museum, the Louvre, Pont Neuf, and the twin towers of Notre-Dame.

On the Right Bank (which is to your left), find the Grand Palais, next to the Pont Alexandre. Beyond the glass-roofed Grand Palais is the bullet-shaped dome of Sacré-Cœur, atop Butte Montmartre.

**Looking south** *(sud):* In a line, find the Champ de Mars, the Ecole Militaire, the Y-shaped UNESCO building, and the 689-foot Montparnasse Tower skyscraper. To the left is the golden dome of Les Invalides, and beyond that, the state capitol-shaped dome of the Panthéon.

**The tippy top:** Ascend another short staircase to the open-air top. Look up at all the satellite dishes and communications equipment (and around to find the tiny WC). You'll see the tiny apartment given to the builder of the tower, Gustave Eiffel, now represented by a mannequin (he's the one with the beard).

The mannequins re-create the moment during the 1889 exposition when the American Thomas Edison paid a visit to his fellow techie, Gustave (and Gustave's daughter Claire), presenting them with his new invention, a phonograph. (Then they cranked it up and blasted The Who's "I Can See for Miles.")

• *Catch the elevator down to the...*

## Second Level

The second level (400 feet) has the best views because you're closer to the sights, and the monuments are more recognizable. (While the best views are up the short stairway, on the platform without the wire-cage barriers, at busy times much of that zone is taken up by people waiting for the elevator to the top.) As you survey the vistas from this middle level, refer to the descriptions given

earlier, under "Third Level." The second level has souvenir shops, public telephones to call home, and a small stand-up café.

The world-class Jules Verne Restaurant is on this level, but you won't see it; access is by a private elevator. The head chef is currently Alain Ducasse, who operates restaurants around the world. One would hope his brand of haute cuisine matches the 400-foot haute of the restaurant.

EIFFEL TOWER

## Up and Down

The tower—which was designed from the start to accommodate hordes of visitors—has always had elevators. Today's elevators are modern replacements. Back in the late 19th century, elevator technology was so new that this was the one job that Gustave Eiffel subcontracted to other experts (including an American company). They needed a special design to accommodate the angle of the tower's pillars. Today's elevators make about 100 round-trip journeys a day.

There are 1,665 stairs to the top level, though tourists can only climb 720 of them, up as far as the second level. During a race in 1905, a gentleman climbed from the ground to the second level—elevation gain nearly 400 feet—in 3 minutes, 12 seconds.

• *Catch the elevator (after confirming it'll stop at the first level) or take the 360 stairs down to the...*

## First Level

The first level (200 feet) has more great views, all well-described by the tower's panoramic displays. There are a number of photo exhibits on the tower's history, WCs, a conference hall (closed to tourists), an ATM, and souvenirs. A small café sells pizza and sandwiches (outdoor tables in summer). The 58 Tour Eiffel restaurant has more accessible prices than the Jules Verne Restaurant described above and is also run by Alain Ducasse. In winter, part of the first level is set up for winter activities (most recently as an ice-skating rink).

Climb the stairs to Cineiffel for a small gallery and theater. A tired eight-minute video that shows continuously features clips of the tower's construction, its paint job, its place in pop culture, and the millennium fireworks. If that whets your appetite for Eiffel history and trivia, there are more fun exhibits all around the first level.

In the northeast corner, a display on the impact of weather on the tower shows how the sun warms the metal, causing the top to expand and lean about five inches away from the sun. Nearby, a small model of the tower oscillates slightly, simulating the tower's real-time movement in the wind and sun. Because of its lacy design, even the strongest of winds could never blow the tower down, but only cause it to sway back and forth a few inches. In fact, Eiffel designed the tower primarily with wind resistance in mind, wanting a structure seemingly "molded by the action of the wind itself."

Many modern skyscrapers follow the mathematics pioneered by Eiffel.

Watch the original hydraulic pump (1889) at work. It once pumped water from this level to the second level to feed the machinery powering the upper elevator. Then look at the big wheels that wind and unwind heavy cables to lift the elevators.

• *Consider a drink or a sandwich while overlooking all of Paris, then take the elevator or stairs (5 minutes, 360 steps, free) to the ground.*

## The Tour Ends

Welcome back to earth. Nearby, you can catch the Bateaux Parisiens boat for a Seine cruise (see page 46 for details). Also nearby

are the Quai Branly Museum (page 68), Rue Cler area (page 186), Army Museum and Napoleon's Tomb (page 223), and Rodin Museum (next page).

After you've climbed the tower, you come to appreciate it even more from a distance. For a final look, stroll across the river to Place du Trocadéro or to the end of the Champ de Mars and look back for great views. However impressive it may be by day, the tower is an awesome thing to see at twilight, when it becomes engorged with light, and virile Paris lies back and lets night be on top. When darkness fully envelops the city, the tower seems to climax with a spectacular light show at the top of each hour...for five minutes.

# RODIN
# MUSEUM TOUR

*Musée Rodin*

Auguste Rodin (1840-1917) was a modern Michelangelo, sculpting human figures on an epic scale, revealing through their bodies his deepest thoughts and feelings. Like many of Michelangelo's unfinished works, Rodin's statues rise from the raw stone around them, driven by the life force. With missing limbs and scarred skin, these are prefab classics, making ugliness noble. Rodin's people are always moving restlessly. Even the famous *Thinker* is moving. While he's plopped down solidly, his mind is a million miles away. The museum presents a full range of Rodin's work, housed in a historic mansion where the artist once lived and worked.

**Ongoing Renovation:** The museum is undergoing a major renovation until 2014. Expect some statues to be moved around and some rooms to be closed altogether. The gardens remain open. To compensate for the closures, the museum has added a few rarely displayed Rodin pieces to its exhibits.

## Orientation

**Cost:** €6, under 18 free, free on the first Sun of the month, €1 for garden only, both museum and garden covered by Museum Pass. Optional temporary exhibits in the entrance hall cost extra and are not covered by the Museum Pass.

You can bypass the ticket-buyer line if you have a Museum Pass or a ticket you purchased online (www.musee-rodin.fr, €1.30 booking fee).

**Hours:** Tue-Sun 10:00-17:45, Wed until 20:45, closed Mon; gardens close at 18:00, Oct-March at 17:00; last entry 30 minutes before closing.

**Getting There:** It's at 79 Rue de Varenne, near the Army Museum and Napoleon's Tomb (Mo: Varenne). Bus #69 stops two

RODIN MUSEUM

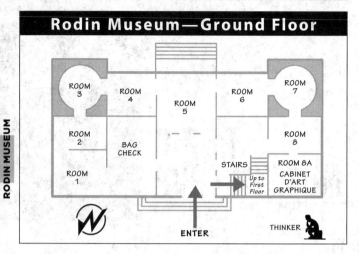

blocks away at the intersection of Rue Grenelle and Rue Bellechasse.

**Information:** Pick up the museum map. Tel. 01 44 18 61 10, www.musee-rodin.fr.

**Audioguide Tours:** €4, covering the museum and gardens.

**Length of This Tour:** Allow one hour.

**Baggage Check:** Even a fairly small bag must be checked, unless you tuck it under your arm like a purse.

**Photography:** You can take photos without a flash.

**Cuisine Art:** A peaceful self-service café is in the gardens behind the museum (€5 sandwiches, €10 salads). Picnics not allowed in the gardens. For better options, leave the museum, cross the Esplanade des Invalides, and find many recommended cafés and restaurants in the Rue Cler area (a 10-minute walk, see page 433). Coffee connoisseurs could seek out Le Coutume Café, two blocks southeast at 47 Rue de Babylone (Tue-Sun 10:00-19:00, closed Mon, coffee and pastry only except weekend brunch).

## The Tour Begins

Enter and buy tickets in the modern entrance hall. There's a bookstore, a gallery for temporary exhibits, and WCs. Pick up the museum map for the most current info on what's showing. The permanent collection is located outside this hall, in the mansion and the gardens.

• *Exit the entrance hall, walk across the courtyard, and enter the mansion. Turn left (baggage check here) and walk to the first room to start a circular tour of the ground floor.*

# Ground Floor

## Salle 1

Rodin's early works match the belle époque style of the time—noble busts of bourgeois citizens, pretty portraits of their daughters, and classical themes. Born of working-class roots, Rodin taught himself art by sketching statues at the Louvre and then sculpting copies.

*The Man with the Broken Nose* (*L'Homme au Nez Cassé*, 1865)—a deliberately ugly work—was 23-year-old Rodin's first break from

the norm. He meticulously sculpted this deformed man (one of the few models the struggling sculptor could afford), but then the clay statue froze in his unheated studio, and the back of the head fell off. Rodin loved it! Art critics hated it. Rodin persevered. (Note: The museum rotates the display of two different versions—the broken-headed one and another, repaired version Rodin made later that critics accepted.)

See the painting of Rodin's future wife, Rose Beuret *(Portrait de Madame Rodin)*, who suffered with him through obscurity and celebrity.

## Salle 2

To feed his family, Rodin cranked out small-scale works—portraits, ornamental vases, nymphs, and knickknacks to decorate buildings—with his boss's name on them (the more established sculptor Albert Carrier-Belleuse). Still, the series of mother-and-childs (Rose and baby Auguste?) al-

lowed him to experiment on a small scale with the intertwined twosomes he'd do later.

Rodin's work brought in enough money for him to visit Italy, where he was inspired by the boldness, monumental scale, restless figures, and "unfinished" look of Michelangelo's sculptures. Rapidly approaching middle age, Rodin was ready to rock.

## Salle 3

Rodin moved to Brussels, where his first major work, *The Age of Bronze* (*L'Âge d'Airain*, 1877), brought controversy and the fame that surrounds it. This nude youth, perhaps inspired by Michelangelo's *Dying Slave* (in the Louvre—see page 143), awakens to a new world. It was so lifelike that Rodin was accused of not sculpting it himself, but simply casting it directly from a live body. The boy's raised left arm looks like it should be leaning on a spear, but it's just that missing element that makes the pose more tenuous and interesting.

The art establishment still snubbed Rodin as an outsider, and no wonder. Look at his ultra-intense take on the winged symbol of France *(La Défense)*—this Marseillaise screams, "Off with their heads!" at the top of her lungs. Rodin was a slave to his muses, and some of them inspired monsters.

## Salle 4

Like the hand of a sculptor, *The Hand of God* (*La Main de Dieu*, 1896) shapes Adam and Eve from the mud of the earth to which they will return. Rodin himself worked in "mud," using his hands to model clay figures, which were then reproduced in marble or bronze, usually by his assistants. Inspect this masterpiece from every angle. Rodin first worked on the front view, then checked the back and side profiles, then filled in the in-between.

In *The Kiss* (*Le Baiser*, 1888-1889), a passionate woman twines around a solid man for their first, spontaneous kiss. Looking at their bodies, we can almost read the thoughts, words, and movements that led up to this meeting of lips. *The Kiss* was the first Rodin work the public loved. Rodin came to despise it, thinking it simple and sentimental.

Other works in this room show embracing couples who seem to emerge from the stone just long enough to love. Rodin left many works "unfinished," reminding us that all creation is a difficult process of dragging a form out of chaos.

## Salle 5

The two hands that form the arch of *The Ca-thedral* (*La Cathédrale*, 1908) are actually two right hands (a man's and a woman's?).

In the room's center, a bronze man strides forward, as boldly as the often controversial Rodin. Armless and headless, *The Walking Man* (*L'Homme Qui Marche*, 1900-1907) plants his back foot forcefully, as though he's about to stride, while his front foot already has stepped.

Rodin—who had one foot in the classical past, one in the modernist future—captures two poses at once.

Rodin worked with many materials—he chiseled marble (though not often), modeled clay, cast bronze, worked plaster, painted on canvas, and sketched on paper. He often created different versions of the same subject in different media.

## Salle 6

This room displays works by Camille Claudel, mostly in the style of her master. The 44-year-old Rodin took 18-year-old Claudel as his pupil, muse, colleague, and lover. We can follow the arc of their relationship in the exhibits.

Rodin was inspired by young Camille's beauty and spirit, and he often used her as a model. (See several versions of her head.)

As his student, "Mademoiselle C" learned from Rodin, doing portrait busts in his lumpy, molded-clay style. Her bronze bust of Rodin shows the steely-eyed sculptor with strong frontal and side profiles, barely emerging from the materials they both worked with.

Soon they were lovers. *The Waltz* (*La Valse*, 1892) captures the spinning exuberance the two must have felt as they embarked together on a new life. The couple twirls—hands so close but not touching—in a delicate balance.

But Rodin was devoted as well to his lifelong companion, Rose (see her face emerging from a block of marble). Claudel's *Maturity* (*L'Age Mûr*, 1895-1907, also in Orsay Museum) shows the breakup. A young woman on her knees begs the man not to leave her, as he's reluctantly led away by an older woman. The statue may literally depict a scene from real life, in which a naked, fragile Claudel begged Rodin not to return to his wife. In the larger sense, it may also be a metaphor for the cruel passage of time, as Youth tries to save Maturity from the clutches of Old Age.

Rodin did leave Claudel. Talented in her own right but tormented by grief and jealousy, she became increasingly unstable and spent her final years in an institution. Claudel's *The Wave* (*La Vague*, 1900), carved in green onyx in a very un-Rodin style, shows tiny, helpless women huddling together as a tsunami is about to engulf them.

## Salles 7 and 8

What did Rodin think of women? Here are many different images from which you can draw your own conclusions.

*Eve* (1881) buries her head in shame, hiding her nakedness. But she can't hide the consequences—she's pregnant.

Rodin became famous, wealthy, and respected, and society ladies all wanted him to do their portraits. In Salle 8, you may see a sculpture of his last mistress *(La Duchesse de Choiseul)*, an American who lived with him here in this mansion. Rodin purposely left in the metal base points (used in the sculpting process), placing them suggestively.

## Salle 8A

This room houses temporary exhibits, often displaying Rodin's works-in-progress—preparatory sketches or plaster casts. The first flash of inspiration for a huge statue might be a single line sketched on notepaper. Rodin wanted nude models in his studio at all times—walking, dancing, and squatting—in case they struck some new and interesting pose. Rodin thought of sculpture as simply "drawing in all dimensions."

# First Floor

• *Upstairs, you'll find a glass display case on the mezzanine that tries hard to explain...*

## The Bronze Casting Process

Rodin made his bronze statues not by hammering sheets of metal, but by using the classic "lost wax" technique. He'd start by shaping the figure from wet plaster. This sculptural model was covered with a form-fitting mold. By pouring molten bronze into the narrow space between the model and the mold around it, letting it cool, and removing the mold—*voilà!*—Rodin had a hollow bronze stat-

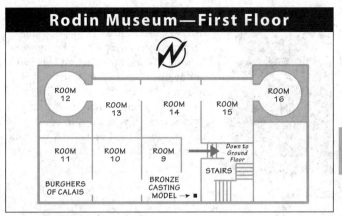

## Rodin Museum—First Floor

ROOM 12
ROOM 13
ROOM 14
ROOM 15
ROOM 16
ROOM 11
ROOM 10
ROOM 9
Down to Ground Floor
STAIRS
BURGHERS OF CALAIS
BRONZE CASTING MODEL →

ue ready to be polished and varnished. With a mold, he could produce other copies, which is why there are many authorized bronze versions of Rodin's masterpieces all over the world.

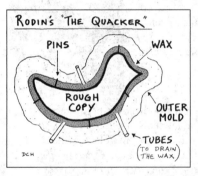

RODIN'S "THE QUACKER"

PINS
WAX
ROUGH COPY
OUTER MOLD
TUBES (TO DRAIN THE WAX)
DCH

As the display case teaches, there are actually a number of additional steps involving two models and two molds. From the original plaster model, Rodin made a first mold, which was used to make a heat-resistant clay copy of the original plaster model. He sanded down the clay copy, coated it with a wax skin, and then touched up the wax to add surface details. He used this touched-up copy to make the more detailed final mold. He fitted the mold with ventilation tubes and started pouring in the molten bronze. The wax melted away—the "lost wax" technique—and the bronze cooled and hardened in its place, thus forming the final bronze statue.

### Salle 9

*The Thinker* was to have been the centerpiece of a massive project that Rodin wrestled with for decades—a doorway encrusted with characters from Dante's *Inferno*. These *Gates of Hell* were never completed (we'll later see the partly finished piece in the garden), but the studies for it (scattered throughout this room and in a display cabinet) are some of Rodin's masterpieces.

These figures struggle to come into existence. Rodin was fascinated by the theory of evolution—not Darwin's version of the

survival of the fittest, but the Frenchman Jean-Baptiste Lamarck's ideas. Rodin's figures survive not by the good fortune of random mutation (Darwin), but by virtue of their own striving (Lamarck). They are driven by the life force, a restless energy that animates and shapes dead matter. Rodin must have felt that force even as a child, when he first squeezed soft clay and saw a worm emerge.

## Salle 10

Rodin's feverish attempts to capture a portrait of the novelist Balzac ranged from a pot-bellied Bacchus to a headless nude cradling an erection (the display changes, showing various versions). In a moment of inspiration, Rodin threw a plaster-soaked robe (borrowed from Balzac's tailor) over a nude form and watched it dry. This became the inspiration for the proud, definitive version of his *Monument to Balzac* (*Monument à Balzac*, 1898).

## Salle 11

A virtual unknown until his mid-30s, Rodin slowly began receiving major commissions for public monuments. *The Burghers of Calais* (in the center of the room, described later in "The Gardens") depicts the actual event in 1347, when, in order to save their people, the city fathers surrendered the keys of the city—and their lives—to the king of England. Rodin portrays them not in some glorious pose drenched in pomp and allegory, but as a simple example of men sacrificing their lives together. As the men head to the gallows, with ropes already around their necks, each body shows a distinct emotion, ranging from courage to despair. Compare the small plaster model in this room with the final, life-size bronze group outside the window in the garden (near the street).

• *Double back past the bronze-casting display, to the rooms overlooking the gardens in the back.*

## Salle 14

Here you'll see studies of the female body in its different forms—crouching, soaring, dying, open, closed, wrinkled, intertwined. Newsreel footage of Rodin is often on display in this room or nearby.

## Salle 15

In a display case, dancers stretch, pose, and leap. Nearby, legendary lovers kiss, embrace, and intertwine in yin-yang bliss.

## Salle 16

For the 1900 World's Fair, Paris considered building a huge monument honoring common workers, who were powering the Industrial Revolution (and demanding bathroom breaks and overtime pay). Rodin submitted this model of a Tower of Labor *(La Tour du Travail)*. A column wrapped in a corkscrew symbolizes the march of progress. At the base, statues of Day and Night remind everyone that factories operated 24/7. Reliefs spiraling up the column honored workers: workers at the base doing manual labor, then climbing the career ladder to desk jobs and the arts. Crowning the monument are the fruits of man's labor—the spinning angels of Love and Joy. Rodin's model was much admired but never built.
• *Backtrack through Salle 14 to reach...*

## Salle 13

See Rodin's portrait busts of celebrities and some paintings by (yawn, are we through yet?) Vincent van Gogh, Claude Monet, and Pierre-Auguste Renoir. Rodin enjoyed discussions with Monet and other artists and incorporated their ideas into his work. Rodin is often considered an Impressionist because he captured spontaneous "impressions" of figures and created rough surfaces that catch reflected light.

## Salle 12

Get a sense of Rodin's working process by comparing the small plaster "sketches" (in the glass case) with the final large-scale marble versions that line the walls. Rodin employed and mentored many artists who executed these designs. By the end of his long, productive life, Rodin was more famous than his works.

# The Gardens

Rodin lived and worked in this mansion, renting rooms alongside Henri Matisse, the poet Rainer Maria Rilke (Rodin's secretary), and the dancer Isadora Duncan. He loved placing his creations in the overgrown gardens. These, his greatest works, show Rodin at his most expansive. The epic human figures are enhanced, not dwarfed, by the nature surrounding them.
• *Leaving the house, you've got five more stops: two on the left and three on the right. Beyond these stops is a big, breezy garden ornamented with statues, a cafeteria, and a WC.*

### The Thinker (Le Penseur, 1906)

Leaning slightly forward, tense and compact, every muscle working toward producing that one great thought, Man contemplates his fate. No constipation jokes, please.

This is not an intellectual, but a linebacker who's realizing there's more to life than frat parties. It's the first man evolving beyond his animal nature to think the first thought. It's anyone who's ever worked hard to reinvent himself or to make something new or better. Said Rodin: "It is a statue of myself."

There are 29 other authorized copies of this statue, one of the most famous in the world.

• *To the left of* The Thinker, *you'll find...*

### Balzac (1898)

The iconoclastic novelist turns his nose up at the notion he should be honored with a statue. Other casts of this final version also stand in the Orsay Museum and on a street median in Montparnasse. When the statue was unveiled, the crowd booed, a fitting tribute to both the defiant novelist and the bold man who sculpted him.

• *Along the street opposite the ticket booth are...*

### The Burghers of Calais (Bourgeois de Calais, 1889)

The six city fathers trudge to their execution, and we can read in their faces and poses what their last thoughts are. They mill about, dazed, as each one deals with the decision he's made to sacrifice himself for his city.

• *Circling counterclockwise...*

The man carrying the key to the city tightens his lips in determination. The bearded man is weighed down with grief. Another buries his head in his hands. One turns, seeking reassurance from his friend, who turns away and gestures helplessly. The final key-bearer (in back) raises his hand to his head.

Each is alone in his thoughts, but they're united by their mutual sacrifice, by the base they stand on, and by their weighty robes—gravity is already dragging them down to their graves.

Pity the poor souls; view the statue from various angles (you

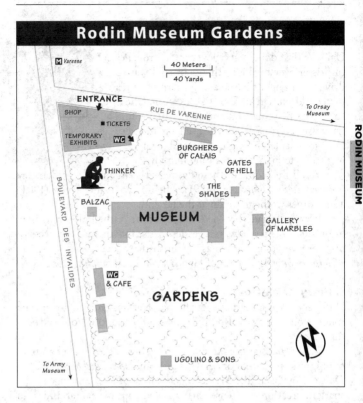

## Rodin Museum Gardens

M Varenne

40 Meters
40 Yards

**ENTRANCE**

SHOP

RUE DE VARENNE

To Orsay
Museum →

TICKETS

TEMPORARY
EXHIBITS   WC

BURGHERS
OF CALAIS

THINKER

GATES
OF HELL

THE
SHADES

BALZAC

MUSEUM

GALLERY
OF MARBLES

BOULEVARD DES INVALIDES

WC
& CAFE

GARDENS

UGOLINO & SONS

To Army
Museum ↓

N

RODIN MUSEUM

can't ever see all the faces at once); then thank King Edward III, who, at the last second, pardoned them.

• *Follow* The Thinker's *gaze across the gardens. Standing before a tall, white backdrop is a big, dark door...*

### The Gates of Hell (*La Porte de l'Enfer,* 1880-1917)

These doors (never meant to actually open) were never finished for a museum that was never built. But the vision of Dante's trip into hell gave Rodin a chance to explore the dark side of human experience. "Abandon all hope ye who enter here," was hell's motto. The three Shades at the top of the door point down—that's where we're going. Beneath the Shades, pondering the whole scene from above, is Dante as the Thinker. Below him, the figures emerge from the darkness just long enough to tell their sad tale of depravity. There are Paolo and Francesca (in the

center of the right door), who were driven into the illicit love affair that brought them here. Ugolino (left door, just below center) crouches in prison over his kids. This poor soul was so driven by hunger that he ate the corpses of his own children. On all fours like an animal, he is the dark side of natural selection. Finally, find what some say is Rodin himself (at the very bottom, inside the right doorjamb, where it just starts to jut out), crouching humbly.

You'll find some of these figures writ large in the garden. *The Thinker* and *The Shades* (c. 1889) are behind you, and *Ugolino* (1901-1904) dines in the fountain at the far end.

It's appropriate that the *Gates*—Rodin's "cathedral"—remained unfinished. He was always a restless artist for whom the process of discovery was as important as the finished product.

• *To the right of* The Gates of Hell *is a glassed-in building, the...*

## Gallery of Marbles

Unfinished, these statues show human features emerging from the rough stone. Imagine Rodin in his studio, working to give them life.

*Victor Hugo* (at the far end of the gallery), the great champion of progress and author of *Les Misérables* and *The Hunchback of Notre-Dame*, leans back like Michelangelo's nude *Adam,* waiting for the spark of creation. He tenses his face and cups his ear, straining to hear the call from the blurry Muse above him. Once inspired, he can bring the idea to life (just as Rodin did) with the strength of his powerful arms. It's been said that all of Rodin's work shows the struggle of mind over matter, of brute creatures emerging from the mud and evolving into a species of thinkers.

# ARMY MUSEUM AND NAPOLEON'S TOMB TOUR

*Musée de l'Armée*

If you're ever considering trying to conquer Europe to become its absolute dictator, come here before gathering your army. Hitler did, but still went out and made the same mistakes as his role model. (Hint: Don't invade Russia.) Napoleon's tomb rests beneath the golden dome of Les Invalides church.

In addition to the tomb, the complex of Les Invalides—a former veterans' hospital built by Louis XIV—has various military collections, collectively called the Army Museum. See medieval armor, Napoleon's horse stuffed and mounted, Louis XIV-era uniforms and weapons, and much more. The best part is the section dedicated to the two world wars, especially World War II. Visiting the different sections, you can watch the art of war unfold from stone axes to Axis powers.

## Orientation

**Cost:** €9, €7 after 17:00, covered by Museum Pass, admission includes Napoleon's Tomb and all the museum collections within the Invalides complex. Children are free, but you must line up to get them a free ticket. The sight is also free for military personnel in uniform.

**Hours: Museum**—daily April-Sept 10:00-18:00, may be open Tue until 21:00, Oct-March 10:00-17:00, closed first Mon of month year-round; **tomb**—daily April-June and Sept 10:00-18:00, may be open Tue until 21:00; July-Aug 10:00-19:00, may be open Tue until 21:00; Oct-March 10:00-17:00, closed first Mon of month Sept-May; last tickets sold 30 minutes before closing.

**Getting There:** The museum and tomb are at Hôtel des Invalides, with its hard-to-miss golden dome (129 Rue de Grenelle,

ARMY MUSEUM

# Overview of the Army Museum and Napoleon's Tomb

The Army Museum and Napoleon's Tomb are in the Invalides complex (or should I say "Napoleon complex"?). The buildings house several noteworthy sights, each with different entrances. All are included in your ticket price. The tomb is on the back (south) side, and the various collections of the Army Museum surround the main courtyard on the north side. For exact locations, see the map in this chapter and the free English map/guide available at the ticket office.

Pick your favorite war. With limited time, visit only Napoleon's Tomb and the excellent World War I and World War II wings. Most other displays consist of dummies in uniforms and endless glass cases full of muskets without historical context.

Of the various sights, I've rated the best in order of importance (the first four are described more fully in self-guided tours in this chapter):

▲▲▲**Napoleon's Tomb**—The emperor's final resting place, under the golden dome of Les Invalides church (at the back of the complex, farthest from the river).

near Rodin Museum; Mo: La Tour Maubourg, Varenne, or Invalides). Bus #69 from the Marais and Rue Cler area is also handy. The museum is a 10-minute walk from Rue Cler. There are two entrances: one from the Grand Esplanade des Invalides (river side), the other from behind the gold dome on Avenue de Tourville.

**Information:** A helpful, free English map/guide is available at the ticket office. The excellent €6 audioguide covers the whole complex (except the Charles de Gaulle Exhibit, which provides a separate audioguide). Tel. 01 44 42 38 77 or 08 10 11 33 99, www.invalides.org.

**Length of This Tour:** Women—two hours, men—three hours.

**With Limited Time:** Conquer Napoleon's Tomb and the World War II wing.

**Photography:** Allowed without flash.

**Eating:** A reasonable cafeteria is next to the ticket office, the rear gardens are picnic-perfect, and Rue Cler is a 10-minute walk away (see page 433).

▲▲▲**World War II Wing**—Interesting coverage of this critical war (entrance at southwest corner of courtyard).

▲▲**World War I Wing**—A manageable series of rooms setting the stage for World War II (same entrance as World War II wing, at southwest corner of courtyard).

▲**From Louis XIV to Napoleon I** (east wing)—French military history from 1643 to 1814, with a focus on Napoleon (entrance on east side of courtyard).

▲**Charles de Gaulle Exhibit** (in the basement of the east wing)—A 25-minute film plus high-tech displays of photos and videos trace the life of France's towering 20th-century figure.

**Arms and Armor** (west wing)—Weapons from the 13th to 17th century (entrance on west side of courtyard). Connoisseurs of suits of armor, cannons, swords, crossbows, and early guns will love it; others can browse a few rooms and move on.

**The Rest**—Your ticket is good for all the exhibits in the complex (consult your free museum map), including the St. Louis Church (a pristine-white place to remember fallen soldiers), the Museum of the Order of Liberation (honoring heroes of the WWII Resistance), and the Musée des Plans Reliefs (on the top floor of the east wing), which exhibits the 18th-century models (1:1,600 scale) of France's cities that strategists used to thwart enemy attacks. Survey Antibes and ponder which hillside you'd use to launch an attack.

**ARMY MUSEUM**

**Nearby:** You'll likely see the French playing *boules* on the esplanade (as you face Les Invalides from the riverside, look for the dirt area to the upper right; for the rules of *boules*, see page 386).

## The Tour Begins

• *Start at Napoleon's Tomb, underneath the golden dome. The entrance to this vast complex of churches and museum exhibits is at the back end (farthest from the Seine).*

## Napoleon's Tomb

Enter the church, gaze up at the dome, then lean over the railing and bow to the emperor lying inside the scrolled, red porphyry tomb (see photo at the beginning of chapter). If the lid were opened, you'd find an oak coffin inside, holding another ebony coffin, housing two lead ones, then mahogany, then tinplate...until finally, you'd find Napoleon himself, staring up, with his head closest to the door. When his body was exhumed from the original grave and transported here (1840), it was still perfectly preserved, even after 19 years in the ground.

Born of humble Italian heritage on the French-owned isle of Corsica, Napoleon Bonaparte (1769-1821) went to school at Paris' Ecole Militaire, quickly rising through the ranks amid the chaos of the Revolution. The charismatic "Little Corporal" won fans by fighting for democracy at home and abroad. In 1799, he assumed power and, within five short years, conquered most of Europe. The great champion of the Revolution had become a dictator, declaring himself emperor of a new Rome.

Napoleon's red tomb on its green base stands 15 feet high in the center of a marble floor, circled by a mosaic crown of laurels and exalted by a glorious dome above.

Napoleon is surrounded by family. After conquering Europe, he installed his big brother, Joseph, as king of Spain (turn around to see Joseph's black-and-white marble tomb in the alcove to the left of the door); his little brother, Jerome, became king of the German kingdom of Westphalia (tucked into the chapel to the right of the door); and his baby boy, Napoleon II (downstairs), sat in diapers on the throne of Rome.

In other alcoves, you'll find more dead war heroes, including Marshal Ferdinand Foch, the commander in chief of the multinational Allied forces in World War I, his tomb lit with otherworldly blue light. To the right of Foch lies Maréchal Vauban, Louis XIV's great military engineer, who designed the fortifications of more than 100 French cities. Vauban's sarcophagus shows him reflecting on his work with his engineer's tools, flanked by figures of war and science. These heroes, plus many painted saints, make this the French Valhalla in the Versailles of churches.

Before moving on, consider the design of the church itself. It's actually a double church—one for the king and one for his soldiers—built under Louis XIV in the 17th century. You're standing in the "dome chapel," decorated to the glory of Louis XIV and intended for royalty before it became the tomb of Napoleon. The original altar was destroyed in the Revolution. What you see today dates from the mid-1800s, and was inspired by the altar and canopy at St. Peter's Basilica in Rome.

Behind the altar is the Church of St. Louis, where the veterans hospitalized here attended (mandatory) daily Mass. You can

ARMY MUSEUM

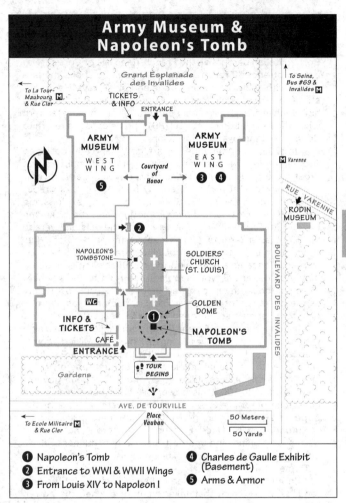

# Army Museum & Napoleon's Tomb

Grand Esplanade des Invalides

← To La Tour-Maubourg M, & Rue Cler

TICKETS & INFO

ENTRANCE ↓

↑ To Seine, Bus #69 & Invalides M

**ARMY MUSEUM**
WEST WING
**❺**

Courtyard of Honor
←→

**ARMY MUSEUM**
EAST WING
**❸ ❹**

M Varenne

RUE VARENNE

RODIN MUSEUM

NAPOLEON'S TOMBSTONE

SOLDIERS' CHURCH (ST. LOUIS)

GOLDEN DOME

WC

INFO & TICKETS

CAFÉ

ENTRANCE ↑

**❶** NAPOLEON'S TOMB

**❷**

BOULEVARD DES INVALIDES

Gardens

🔊 TOUR BEGINS
↓

AVE. DE TOURVILLE

← To Ecole Militaire M & Rue Cler

Place Vauban

50 Meters

50 Yards

**❶** Napoleon's Tomb
**❷** Entrance to WWI & WWII Wings
**❸** From Louis XIV to Napoleon I

**❹** Charles de Gaulle Exhibit (Basement)
**❺** Arms & Armor

peek into this church as you descend to the floor level of Napoleon's tomb. (You can't enter the Church of St. Louis from here, but you can from the main courtyard.)

• *The stairs behind the altar (with the corkscrew columns) take you down to crypt level for a closer look at the tomb.*

## The Crypt

As you descend the stairs from the altar, notice how Napoleon's tomb is a kind of grand room within this church. At the bottom of the steps, face its entrance, which is flanked by two bronze giants representing civic and military strength. The writing above the door is Napoleon's wish for his remains to be with the French

# Napoleon Bonaparte (1769-1821)

Born to Italian parents on the French-ruled isle of Corsica, Napoleon attended French schools, although he spoke the language with an Italian accent to the end of his days. He graduated from Paris' Ecole Militaire, where he trained in the latest high-tech artillery. His military career took an unexpected turn when the Revolution erupted (1789), and he chose to return to Corsica to fight royalist oppression.

In 1793, as commander of artillery, Napoleon besieged Toulon, forcing the royalists to surrender and earning his first great victory. He later defended the Revolutionary government from royalist mobs in Paris by firing a "whiff of grapeshot" into the crowd (1795). Such daring military exploits and personal charisma earned him promotions and the nickname the "Little Corporal"—not for his height (he was an average 5'7") but as a term of endearment from the rank and file. When he married the classy socialite Josephine Beauharnais, Napoleon became a true celebrity. In 1798, having conquered Italy, Austria, and Egypt, Napoleon returned to Paris, where the weak government declared him First Consul—ostensibly as the champion of democracy, but, in fact, he was a virtual dictator over much of Europe. He was 29 years old.

During the next 15 years, Napoleon solidified his reign with military victories over Europe's kings—now allied against France. Under his rule, France sealed the Louisiana Purchase with America, and legal scholars drew up the Code of Napoleon, a system of laws still used by many European governments today. In 1804, his power peaked when he crowned himself emperor in a ceremony in Notre-Dame blessed by the pope. The Revolutionary general was now, paradoxically, part of Europe's royalty. Needing an heir to the throne, he divorced barren Josephine and married an Austrian duchess, Marie Louise, who bore him the boy known to historians as the "King of Rome."

In 1812, Napoleon decided to invade Russia, and the horrendous losses from that failed venture drained his power. Many of Europe's conquered nations saw their chance to pig-pile on France, toppling Napoleon and sending him to exile on the isle of Elba (1814). Napoleon escaped long enough to raise an army for a final hundred-day campaign before finally being defeated by British and Prussian forces at the Battle of Waterloo (1815). Guilty of war crimes, he was sentenced to exile on the remote South Atlantic island of St. Helena, where he talked to his dog, studied a little English, penned his memoirs, spoke his final word—"Josephine"—and died.

people. And, like a welcome mat, a big inlaid N welcomes you into the tomb of perhaps the greatest military and political leader in French history.

Wandering clockwise, read the names of Napoleon's battles on the floor around the base of the tomb. Rivoli marks the battle where the rookie 26-year-old general took a ragtag band of "citizens" and thrashed the professional Austrian troops in Italy, returning to Paris a celebrity. In Egypt *(Pyramides),* he fought Turks and tribesmen to a standstill. The exotic expedition caught the public eye, and he returned home a legend.

Napoleon's huge victory over Austria at Austerlitz on the first anniversary of his coronation made him Europe's top dog. At the head of the million-man Great Army *(La Grande Armée),* he made a three-month blitz attack through Germany and Austria. As a military commander, he was daring, relying on top-notch generals and a mobile force of independent armies. His personal magnetism on the battlefield was said to be worth 10,000 additional men.

Pause halfway around to gaze at the grand statue of Napoleon the emperor in the alcove at the head of the tomb—royal scepter and orb of earth in his hands. By 1804, all of Europe was at his feet. He held an elaborate ceremony in Notre-Dame, where he proclaimed his wife, Josephine, empress, and himself—the 35-year-old son of humble immigrants—emperor. The laurel wreath, the robes, and the Roman eagles proclaim him the equal of the Caesars. The floor at the statue's feet marks the grave of his son, Napoleon II *(Roi de Rome,* 1811-1832).

Around the crypt are relief panels showing Napoleon's constructive side. Dressed in toga and laurel leaves, he dispenses justice, charity, and pork-barrel projects to an awed populace.
• *In the first panel to the right of the statue...*

He establishes an Imperial University to educate naked boys throughout *"tout l'empire."* The roll of great scholars links modern France with those of the past: Plutarch, Homer, Plato, and Aristotle. Three panels later, his various building projects (canals, roads, and so on) are celebrated with a list and his quotation, "Everywhere he passed, he left durable benefits" *("Partout où mon regne à passé...").*

Hail Napoleon. Then, at his peak, came his fatal mistake.
• *Turn around and look down to* Moscowa *(the Battle of Moscow—marked beneath his tomb).*

Napoleon invaded Russia with 600,000 men and returned to Paris with 60,000 frostbitten survivors. Two years later, the Russians marched into Paris, and Napoleon's days were numbered. After a brief exile on the isle of Elba, he skipped parole, sailed to France, bared his breast, and said, "Strike me down or follow me!" For 100 days, they followed him, finally into Belgium, where the British hammered the French at the Battle of Waterloo (conspicuously absent on the floor's decor). Exiled again by a war tribunal, he spent his last years in a crude shack on the small South Atlantic island of St. Helena.

• *To get to the Courtyard of Honor and the various military collections, exit the same way you entered, make a U-turn right, and march past the cafeteria and ticket hall. Pause halfway down the long hallway. On the right, through the glass, you'll see...*

## Napoleon's Tombstone

This bare stone slab, surrounded by shrubs and weeping willows, once rested atop Napoleon's grave on the island of St. Helena. The epitaph was never finished because the French and British wrangled over what to call the hero/tyrant. The stone simply reads, "Here lies..."

• *Continuing to the end of the hallway, you'll find the entrance to the World War I and World War II wings (in the southwest corner of the main courtyard). Go upstairs, following blue banners reading* Les Deux Guerres Mondiales, *1871-1945. The museum is laid out so you first see the coverage of World War I, though some may choose to skip ahead to the more substantial WWII section.*

# World War I Wing

World War I (1914-1918) introduced modern technology to the age-old business of war. Tanks, chemical weapons, monstrous cannons, rapid communication, and airplanes made their debut, conspiring to kill nearly 10 million people. In addition, the war ultimately seemed senseless: It started with little provocation, raged on with few decisive battles, and ended with nothing resolved, a situation that sowed the seeds of World War II.

This 20-room exhibit leads you chronologically through the background, causes, battles, and outcome. There's good English information, but the displays themselves are lackluster and low-tech; move quickly and don't burn out before World War II. Even a quick walk-through gives you the essential background for the next world war. (For a better understanding of World War I, take the fast TGV train from Paris' Gare de l'Est station to Verdun and spend a day touring the battlefields, where 700,000 soldiers died.)

### Room 1: "Honoured Be the Unfortunate Bravery"

**Paintings** of dead and wounded soldiers from the Franco-Prussian War make it clear that World War I actually "began" in 1871, when Germany thrashed France. Suddenly, a recently united Germany was the new bully in Europe.

### Rooms 2-3: France Rebounds

Snapping back from its loss, France began re-arming itself, with spiffy new **uniforms** and weapons like the American-invented **Gatling gun** (early machine gun).

The French replaced the humiliation of defeat with a proud and extreme nationalism. An English-language **video** shows how fanatical patriots hounded a (Jewish) officer named Alfred Dreyfus on trumped-up treason charges (1890s). They convicted and imprisoned him (after ceremonially breaking his sword in the Invalides courtyard), before he was finally acquitted.

### Rooms 4-6: Tensions Rise

France, Germany, and the rest of Europe were in a race for wealth and power, jostling to acquire lucrative colonies in Africa and Asia **(map, video, exotic uniforms)**. In a climate of mutual distrust, nations allied with their neighbors, vowing to protect each other if war ever erupted. In room 6, a **map of Europe** in 1914 shows France, Britain, and Russia (the Allies) teaming up against Germany, Austria-Hungary, and Italy (the Central Powers). Meanwhile, the Ottoman Empire (Turkey and the Balkans) was breaking apart, creating a tense and unstable Western world. Europe was ready to explode, but the spark that would set it off had nothing to do with Germany or France.

### Room 7: Assassination: War Begins

Bang. On June 28, 1914, an Austrian archduke was shot to death (see **video** of the political mood, assassination, and mobilization). It happened in modern-day Bosnia—a region not very central, but very politically charged. One by one, Europe's nations were dragged into the regional dispute by their webs of alliances. All of Europe mobilized its troops. The **1914 stone** on the floor is the first of the museum's year-stones. The Great War had begun.

## Room 8: The Battle of the Marne

In September, German forces swarmed into France, hoping for a quick knockout blow. Germany brought its big guns (photo and miniature model of **Big Bertha**). The **projection map** shows how the armies tried to outflank each other along a 200-mile battlefront. As the Germans (brown arrows) zeroed in on Paris, the French

(blue arrows) scrambled to send 6,000 crucial reinforcements, shuttled to the front lines in 670 Parisian **taxis.** The German tide was stemmed, and the two sides faced off, expecting to duke it out and get this war over quickly. It didn't work out that way.

• *The war continues upstairs.*

## Rooms 9-10: The War in the Trenches

La guerre des tranchées

By 1915, the two sides reached a stalemate, and they settled in to a long war of attrition—French and Britons on one side, Germans on the other. The battle line, known as the Western Front, snaked 450 miles across Europe from the North Sea to the Alps. For protection against flying bullets, the soldiers dug **trenches**, which soon became home—24 hours a day, 7 days a week—for millions of men.

Life in the trenches was awful—cold, rainy, muddy, disease-ridden—and, most of all, boring. Every so often, generals waved their swords and ordered their men "over the top" and into "no man's land." Armed with rifles and bayonets, they advanced into a hail of machine gun fire. In a number of battles, France lost 70,000 men in a single day. The "victorious" side often won only a few hundred yards of meaningless territory that was lost the next day after still more deaths.

The war pitted 19th-century values of honor, bravery, and chivalry against **20th-century weapons**: grenades, machine guns,

tanks, and gas masks. To shoot over the tops of trenches while staying hidden, they even invented crooked and periscope-style guns.

### Rooms 11-13: "World" War
Besides the Western Front, the war extended elsewhere, including
the colonies, where many natives joined the armies of their mother
countries. On the Eastern Front, Russia and Germany wore each
other down. (Finally, the Russian people had enough; they killed
their czar, brought the troops home, and fomented a revolution that
put Communists in power.)
• *Down a short hallway, enter...*

### Room 14: The Allies
By 1917, the Allied forces were
beginning to outstrip the Central
Powers, thanks to help from around
the world. Britain drew heavily
from its Commonwealth nations,
such as Canada and Australia.

And when Uncle Sam said, **"I
Want You,"** five million Americans
answered the call to go "Over There"
(in the words of a popular song) and
fight the Germans. Though the US
didn't enter the War until April
1917 (and was never an enormous
military factor), its very presence
was one more indication that the Allies seemed destined to prevail.

### Room 15: Armistice
Under the command of French Marshal Ferdinand Foch, the Allies undertook a series of offensives that, by 1918, would prove decisive. At the 11th hour of the 11th day of the 11th month (November 11, 1918), the guns fell silent. Europeans celebrated with
**victory parades.**

### Room 16: A Costly Victory
Weary soldiers returned home to be honored (painting of **Arc de
Triomphe** parade). After four years of battle, the war had left 9.5
million dead and 21 million wounded (see **plaster casts** of disfigured faces). Three out of every four French soldiers had been either
killed or wounded. A generation was lost.

### Rooms 17-19: From 1918 to 1938
The Treaty of Versailles (1919), signed in the Hall of Mirrors,
officially ended the war. A map shows how it radically redrew

**Europe's borders**. Germany was punished severely, leaving it crushed, humiliated, stripped of crucial land, and saddled with demoralizing war debts. Marshal Foch prophetically said of the Treaty: "This is not a peace. It is an armistice for 20 years."

France, one of the "victors," was drained, trying to hang on to its prosperity and its colonial empire.

But by the 1930s—swamped by the Great Depression and a stagnant military **(dummy on horseback)**—France was reeling, unprepared for the onslaught of a retooled Germany seeking revenge.

• *World War II is covered directly across the hall, in the rooms marked 1939-1942.*

# World War II Wing

World War II was the most destructive of earth's struggles. In this exhibit, the war unfolds in photos, displays, and newsreels, with special emphasis on the French contribution. (You may not have realized that it was Charles de Gaulle who won the war for us.)

The free museum map is helpful for locating the displays. Climb to the top floor and work back down, from Germany's quick domination (third floor), to the Allies turning the tide (second floor), to the final surrender (first floor).

There are fine English descriptions throughout. Be ready—rooms come in rapid succession—and treat the following text simply as an overview.

## Third Floor—Axis Aggression (1939-1941)
### Room 1: The Phony War

On September 1, 1939, Germany, under Adolf Hitler, invaded Poland, starting World War II. But in a sense the war had really begun in 1918, when the "war to end all wars" ground to a halt, leaving 9.5 million dead, Germany defeated, and France devastated (if victorious). For the next two decades, Hitler fed off German resentment over the Treaty of Versailles, which humiliated and ruined Germany.

After Hitler's move into Poland, France and Britain mobilized.

For the next six months, the two sides faced off, with neither actually doing battle—a tense time known to historians as the "phony" war *(Drôle de Guerre).*

## Room 2: The Defeat of 1940
Then, in spring 1940, came the Blitzkrieg ("lightning war"), and Germany's better-trained and better-equipped soldiers and tanks (see **turret**) swept west through Belgium. France was immediately overwhelmed, and British troops barely escaped across the English Channel from Dunkirk. Within a month, Nazis were goose-stepping down the Champs-Elysées, and Hitler was on his way to Napoleon's tomb. Hitler made a three-hour blitz tour of the city, after which he said, "It was the dream of my life to be permitted to see Paris. I cannot say how happy I am to have that dream fulfilled today."

## Room 3: De Gaulle's Appeals
Just like that, virtually all of Europe was dominated by Fascists. During those darkest days, as France fell and Nazism spread across the Continent, one Frenchman—an obscure military man named **Charles de Gaulle**—refused to admit defeat. He escaped to London, made inspiring speeches over the radio, beginning with a famous address broadcast on June 18, 1940. He slowly convinced a small audience of French expatriates that victory was still possible.
• *Through the small door to your right is...*

## Room 4: Charles de Gaulle
This 20th-century John of Arc had an unshakable belief in his mission to save France. De Gaulle (1890-1970) was born into a literate, upper-class family, raised in military academies, and became a WWI hero and POW. (After the war, he helped administer the occupied Rhineland.) When World War II broke out, he was only a minor officer (the title of

Our War Album.—44.   France's Voice in London

"Brigadier General" was hastily acquired during the invasion). He had limited political experience and was virtually unknown to the French public. But he rallied France, became the focus of French patriotism, and later guided the country in the postwar years.

## Rooms 5-6: France After the Armistice
After France's surrender, Germany ruled northern France, including

Paris—see the **photo** of Hitler as a tourist at the Eiffel Tower. The Nazis allowed the French to administer the south and the colonies (North Africa). This puppet government, centered in the city of Vichy, was right-wing and traditional, bowing to Hitler's demands as he looted France's raw materials and manpower for the war machine. (The movie *Casablanca*, set in Vichy-controlled Morocco, shows French officials following Nazi orders while French citizens defiantly sing "The Marseillaise.")

### Room 7: The Battle of Britain

Facing a "New Dark Age" in Europe, British Prime Minister Winston Churchill pledged, "We will fight on the beaches....We will fight in the hills. We will never surrender."

In June 1940, Germany mobilized to invade Britain across the Channel. From June to September, they paved the way, sending bombers—up to 1,500 planes a day—to destroy military and industrial sites. When Britain wouldn't budge, Hitler concentrated on London and civilian targets. This was "The Blitz" of the winter of 1940, which killed 30,000 and left London in ruins. But Britain hung on, armed with newfangled radar, speedy Spitfires, and an iron will.

They also had the Germans' secret "Enigma" code. The **Enigma machine** (in display case), with its set of revolving drums, allowed German commanders to scramble orders in a complex code that could be broadcast safely to their troops. The British (with crucial help from Poland) captured a machine, broke the code (in a project called "Ultra"), then monitored German airwaves. For the rest of the war, they had advance knowledge of many top-secret plans. (Occasionally, Britain even let Germany's plans succeed—sacrificing its own people—to avoid suspicion.)

By spring 1941, Hitler had given up any hope of invading the Isle of Britain. Churchill said of his people: "This was their finest hour."

### Room 10: Germany Invades the Soviet Union

Perhaps hoping to one-up Napoleon, Hitler sent his state-of-the-art tanks speeding toward Moscow in June 1941 (betraying his former ally Joseph Stalin). By winter, the advance had stalled at the gates of Moscow and was bogged down by bad weather and Soviet stubbornness. The Third Reich had reached its peak. From now on, Hitler would have to fight a two-front war. The French Renault

**tank** (displayed) was downright puny compared to the big, fast, high-caliber German Panzers. This war was often a battle of factories, to see who could produce the latest technology fastest and in the greatest numbers. And what nation might have those factories...?

### Room 12: The United States Joins the War

On December 7, 1941, "a date which will live in infamy" (as US President Franklin D. Roosevelt put it), Japanese planes made a sneak attack on the US base at **Pearl Harbor**, Hawaii, and destroyed the pride of the Pacific fleet in two hours.

The US quickly entered the fray against Japan and her ally, Germany. In two short years, America had gone from isolationist observer to supplier of Britain's arms to full-blown war ally against fascism. The US now faced a two-front war—in Europe against Hitler, and in Asia against Japan's imperialist conquest of China, Southeast Asia, and the South Pacific.

America's first victory came when Japan tried a sneak attack on the US base at Midway Island (June 3, 1942). This time—thanks to the Allies who had cracked the Enigma code—America had the aircraft carrier **USS *Enterprise*** (see model) and two of her buddies lying in wait. In five minutes, three of Japan's carriers (with valuable planes) were fatally wounded, their major attack force was sunk, and Japan and the US were dead even, settling in for a long war of attrition.

Though slow to start, America eventually had an army of 16 million strong, 80,000 planes, the latest technology, $250 million a day, unlimited raw materials, and a population of Rosie the Riveters fighting for freedom to a boogie-woogie beat.

• *Continue downstairs to the second floor.*

## Second Floor—The Tide Turns (1942-1944)

In 1942, the Continent was black with fascism, and Japan was secure on a distant island. The Allies had to chip away on the fringes.

### Room 13: Battle of the Atlantic

**German U-boats** (short for *Unterseeboot*) and battleships such as the *Bismarck* patrolled Europe's perimeter, where they laid spiky mines and kept America from aiding Britain. (Until long-range transport planes were invented near war's end, virtually all military transport was by ship.) The Allies traveled in convoys with air cover, used sonar and radar, and dropped depth charges, but for years they endured the loss of up to 60 ships per month.

• *Don't bypass room 14, tucked in the corner.*

## Room 14: Pivotal Battles

Three crucial battles in the autumn of 1942 put the first chink in the Fascist armor. Off the east coast of Australia, 10,000 US Marines (see kneeling soldier in glass case 14D) took an airstrip on Guadalcanal, while 30,000 Japanese held the rest of the tiny, isolated island. For the next six months, the two armies were marooned together, duking it out in thick jungles and malaria-infested swamps while their countries struggled to reinforce or rescue them. By February 1943, America had won and gained a crucial launch pad for bombing raids.

A world away, German tanks under General Erwin Rommel rolled across the vast deserts of North Africa. In October 1942, a well-equipped, well-planned offensive by British General Bernard ("Monty") Montgomery attacked at El-Alamein, Egypt, with 300 tanks. (See **British tank soldier** with headphones.) Monty drove "the Desert Fox" west into Tunisia for the first real Allied victory against the Nazi *Wehrmacht* war machine.

Then came Stalingrad. (See kneeling **Soviet soldier** in heavy coat.) In August 1942, Germany attacked the Soviet city, an in-dustrial center and gateway to the Caucasus oil fields. By October, the Germans had battled their way into the city center and were fighting house-to-house, but their supplies were running low, the Soviets wouldn't give up, and winter was coming. The snow fell, their tanks had no fuel, and relief efforts failed. Hitler ordered them to fight on through the bitter cold. On the worst days, 50,000 men died. (America lost a total of 58,000 in Vietnam.) Finally, on January 31, 1943, the Germans surrendered, against Hitler's orders. The six-month totals? Eight hundred thousand German and other Axis soldiers dead, 1.1 million Soviets dead. The Russian campaign put hard miles on the German war machine.

Also in 1942, the Allies began long-range bombing of German-held territory, including saturation bombing of civilians. It was global war and total war.

## Room 15: The Allies Land in North Africa

**Winston Churchill** and US President **Franklin D. Roosevelt** (see photo with de Gaulle), two of the 20th century's most dynamic and strong-willed statesmen, decided to attack Hitler indirectly by invading Vichy-controlled Morocco and Algeria. On November 8,

1942, 100,000 Americans and British—under the joint command of an unknown, low-key problem-solver named General Dwight ("Ike") Eisenhower—landed on  three separate beaches (including Casablanca). More than 120,000 Vichy French soldiers, ordered by their superiors to defend the Fascist cause, confronted the Allies and...gave up. (See display of some standard-issue **weapons:** Springfield rifle, Colt 45, Thompson machine gun, hand grenade.)

The Allies moved east, but bad weather, inexperience, and the powerful Afrika Korps under Rommel stopped them in Tunisia. But with flamboyant General George S. ("Old Blood-and-Guts") Patton punching from the west, and Monty pushing from the south, they captured the port town of Tunis on May 7, 1943. The Allies now had a base from which to retake Europe.

### Room 17: The French Resistance

Inside occupied France, other ordinary heroes fought the Nazis—the "underground," or Resistance. Bakers hid radios within loaves of bread to secretly contact London. Barmaids passed along tips from tipsy Nazis. Communists in black berets cut telephone lines. Farmers hid downed airmen in haystacks. Housewives spread news from the front with their gossip. Printers countered Nazi propaganda with pamphlets.

**Jean Moulin** (see photo in exhibit), de Gaulle's assistant, secretly parachuted into France and organized these scattered heroes into a unified effort. In May 1943, Moulin was elected chairman of the National Council of the Resistance. A month later, he was arrested by the Gestapo (Nazi secret police), imprisoned, tortured, and sent to Germany, where he died in transit. Still, Free France now had a (secret) government again, rallied around de Gaulle, and was ready to take over when liberation came. (See additional Resistance exhibits in room 20.)

### Room 18: The Red Army

Monty, Patton, and Ike certainly were heroes, but the war was won on the Eastern Front by Soviet grunts, who slowly bled Germany dry. Maps show the shifting border of the Eastern Front.

### Rooms 21-22: The Italian Campaign

On July 10, 1943, the assault on Hitler's European fortress began. More than 150,000 Americans and British sailed from Tunis and landed on the south shore of Sicily. (See **maps** and **video clips** of the campaigns.) Speedy Patton and methodical Monty began a "horse race" to take the city of Messina (the US won the friendly competition by a few hours). They met little resistance from 300,000 Italian soldiers, and were actually cheered as liberators by the Sicilian people. Their real enemies were the 50,000 German troops sent by Hitler to bolster his ally Benito Mussolini. By September, the island was captured. On the mainland, Mussolini was arrested by his own people, and Italy surrendered to the Allies. Hitler quickly poured troops into Italy (and reinstalled Mussolini) to hold off the Allied onslaught.

In early September, the Allies launched a two-pronged landing onto the beaches of southern Italy. Finally, after four long years of war, free men set foot on the European continent. Lieutenant General Mark Clark, leading the slow, bloody push north to liberate Rome, must have been reminded of the French trenches he'd fought in during World War I. As in that bloody war, the fighting in Italy was a war of attrition, fought on the ground by foot soldiers and costing many lives for just a few miles.

In January 1944, the Germans dug in between Rome and Naples at Monte Cassino, a rocky hill topped by the monastery of St. Benedict. Thousands died as the Allies tried inching up the hillside. In frustration, the Allies air-bombed the historic **monastery** to smithereens, killing many noncombatants...but no Germans, who dug in deeper. Finally, after four months of vicious, sometimes hand-to-hand combat by the Allies (Americans, Brits, Free French, Poles, Italian partisans, Indians, etc.), a band of Poles stormed the monastery, and the German back was broken.

Meanwhile, 50,000 Allies had landed near Rome at Anzio and held the narrow beachhead for months against massive German attacks. When reinforcements arrived, Allied troops broke out and joined the two-pronged assault on the capital. Without a single bomb threatening its historic treasures, Rome fell on June 4, 1944.

• Room 23 (with chairs) shows a film on...

## Room 23: D-Day

Three million Allies and six million tons of material were massed in England in preparation for the biggest fleet-led invasion in history—across the Channel to France, then eastward to Berlin. The Germans, hunkered down in northern France, knew an invasion was imminent, but the Allies kept the details top secret. On the night of June 5, 150,000 soldiers boarded ships and planes without knowing where they were headed until they were under way. Each one carried a note from General Eisenhower: "The tide has turned. The free men of the world are marching together to victory."

At 6:30 a.m. on June 6, 1944, Americans spilled out of troop transports into the cold waters off a beach in Normandy, code-named Omaha. The weather was bad, seas were rough, and the prep bombing had failed. The soldiers, many seeing their first action, were dazed and confused. Nazi machine guns pinned them against the sea. Slowly, they crawled up the beach on their stomachs. A thousand died. The survivors held on until the next wave of transports arrived.

All day long, Allied confusion did battle with German indecision; the Nazis never really counterattacked, thinking D-Day was just a ruse, instead of the main invasion. By day's end, the Allies had taken several beaches along the Normandy coast and began building artificial harbors, providing a tiny port-of-entry for the reconquest of Europe. The stage was set for a quick and easy end to the war. Right.

• *Go downstairs to the…*

## First Floor—The War Slowly Ends (1944-1945)

### Rooms 24-25: Battle of Normandy and Landing in Provence

Through June, the Allies (mostly Americans) secured Normandy by taking bigger ports (Cherbourg and Caen) and amassing troops and supplies for the assault on Germany. In July they broke out and sped eastward across France, with Patton's tanks covering up to 40 miles a day. They had "Jerry" on the run.

On France's Mediterranean coast, American troops under General Alexander Patch landed near Cannes (see **parachute** photo), took Marseilles, and headed north to meet with Patton.

### Room 26: "Les Maquis"

French Resistance guerrilla fighters helped reconquer France from behind the lines. (Don't miss the **folding motorcycle** in its parachute case.) The liberation of Paris was started by a Resistance attack on a German garrison.

### Room 27: Liberation of Paris

As the Allies marched on Paris, Hitler ordered his officers to torch the city—but they sanely disobeyed and prepared to surrender. On August 26, 1944, General Charles de Gaulle walked ramrod-straight down the Champs-Elysées, followed by Free French troops and US GIs passing out chocolate and Camels. Two million Parisians went crazy.

### Room 28: Toward Berlin

The quick advance from the west through France, Belgium, and Luxembourg bogged down at the German border in autumn of 1944. Patton outstripped his supply lines, a parachute invasion of

Holland (the Battle of Arnhem) was disastrous, and bad weather grounded planes and slowed tanks.

On December 16, the Allies met a deadly surprise. An enormous, well-equipped, energetic German army appeared from nowhere, punched a "bulge" deep into Allied lines, and demanded surrender. General Anthony McAuliffe sent a one-word response—"Nuts!"—and the momentum shifted. The Battle of the Bulge was Germany's last great offensive.

The Germans retreated across the Rhine River, blowing up bridges behind them. The last bridge, at Remagen, was captured by the Allies just long enough for them to cross and establish themselves on German soil. Soon US tanks were speeding down the autobahns and Patton could wire the good news back to Ike: "General, I have just pissed in the Rhine."

Soviet soldiers did the dirty work of taking fortified Berlin by launching a final offensive in January 1945, and surrounding the city in April. German citizens fled west to surrender to the more-benevolent Americans and Brits. Hitler, defiant to the end, hunkered in his underground bunker. (See photo of **ruined Berlin.**)

On April 28, 1945, Mussolini and his girlfriend were killed and hung by their heels in Milan. Two days later, Adolf Hitler and his new bride, Eva Braun, avoided similar humiliation by committing suicide (pistol in mouth), and having their bodies burned beyond recognition. Germany formally surrendered on May 8, 1945.

## Corridor Left of Room 28: Concentration Camps

Lest anyone mourn Hitler or doubt this war's purpose, gaze at photos from Germany's concentration camps. Some camps held political enemies and prisoners of war, including two million French. Others were expressly built to exterminate peoples considered "genetically inferior" to the "Aryan master race"—particularly Jews, Gypsies, homosexuals, and the mentally ill. The criminals who perpetrated these acts were tried and sentenced in an international court—the first of its kind—held in Nuremburg, Germany.

## Room 29: War of the Pacific

Often treated as an afterthought, the final campaign against Japan was a massive American effort, costing many lives, but saving millions of others from Japanese domination.

Japan was an island bunker surrounded by a vast ring of fortified Pacific islands. America's strategy was to take one island at a time, "island-hopping" until close enough for B-29 Superfortress bombers to attack Japan itself. The war spread across thousands of miles. In a new form of warfare, ships carrying planes led the attack and prepared tiny islands for troops to land and build an airbase. While General Douglas MacArthur island-hopped south to retake the Philippines ("I have returned!"), others pushed north toward Japan.

In February 1945, marines landed on Iwo Jima, a city-size island-volcano close enough to Japan (800 miles) to launch air raids. Twenty thousand Japanese had dug in on the volcano's top and were picking off the advancing Americans. On February 23, several US soldiers raised the Stars and Stripes on the mountain (that famous photo), which inspired their mates to victory, at a cost of nearly 7,000 men.

## Japan Surrenders

On March 9, Tokyo was firebombed, and 90,000 were killed. Japan was losing, but a land invasion would cost hundreds of thousands of

lives. The Japanese had a rep-utation for choosing death over the shame of surren-der—they even sent bomb-laden "kamikaze" planes on suicide missions.

America unleashed its secret weapon, an atomic bomb (originally suggested by German-turned-American Albert Einstein). On August 6, a B-29 dropped one (named **"Little Boy,"** see the replica dan-gling overhead) on the city of Hiroshima and instantly vaporized 100,000 people and four square miles. Three days later, a second bomb fell on Nagasaki. The next day, Emperor Hirohito unoffi-cially surrendered. The long war was over, and US sailors returned home to kiss their girlfriends in public places.

## The Closing Chapter

The death toll for World War II (September 1939-August 1945) totaled 80 million soldiers and civilians. The Soviet Union lost 26 million, China 13 million, France 580,000, and the US 340,000.

World War II changed the world, with America emerging as the dominant political, military, and economic superpower. Eu-rope was split in two. The western half recovered, with American aid. The eastern half remained under Soviet occupation. For 45 years, the US and the Soviet Union would compete—without ever actually doing battle—in a "Cold War" of espionage, propaganda, and weapons production that stretched from Korea to Cuba, from Vietnam to the moon.

• *Return to the large Courtyard of Honor, where Napoleon honored his troops, Dreyfus had his sword broken, and de Gaulle once kissed*

*Churchill. Two exhibits—one in the east wing and one in the west wing—flank the courtyard. The west wing contains arms and armor from the 13th to 17th century (see page 225 for a short description). The east wing houses an exhibit that takes you...*

# From Louis XIV to Napoleon I (1643-1814)

• *The exhibit is located in the east wing off the courtyard. The main collection is upstairs on the second floor.*

This display traces the evolution of uniforms and weapons through France's glory days, with the emphasis on Napoleon Bonaparte. As you circle the second floor, the exhibit unfolds chronologically in four parts: the Ancien Régime (Louis XIV, XV, and XVI), the Revolution, the First Empire (Napoleon), and the post-Waterloo world. Many (but not all) exhibits have some English information.

The following is not a room-by-room tour—this is more a museum for browsing. Instead, I've simply highlighted a handful of the (many) exhibits you might see. Explore, and let the museum surprise you.

### Hall 1: Ancien Régime (Louis XIV, XV, and XVI)

Louis XIV unified the army as he unified the country, creating the first modern nation-state with a military force. You'll see how gunpowder was quickly turning swords, pikes, and lances to pistols, muskets, and bayonets. Uniforms became more uniform, and everyone got a standard-issue flintlock.

At the end of the hall, a display case has some amazingly big and odd-shaped rifles. Nearby, a projection screen (with English commentary) shows a re-enactment of the Battle of Fontenoy (in present-day Belgium) in 1745. Watch how, at the turning point in the battle, the British troops (in red) cluster into a dense column and penetrate the French line of defenses. But the French swarm around them on three sides, then drive them back, affirming French superiority on the Continent.

• *Turn the corner and enter...*

### Hall 2: Révolution

Room 13 features the American War of Independence. You'll see the sword *(épée)* of the French aristocrat Marquis de La Fayette, who—full of revolutionary fervor—sailed to America, where he took a bullet in the leg and fought alongside George Washington.

After France underwent its own Revolution, the king's Royal Army became the people's National Guard, protecting their fledgling democracy from Europe's monarchies while spreading revolutionary ideas by conquest. A young, relatively obscure officer distinguished himself on the battlefield and quickly rose through the ranks—Napoleon Bonaparte.

Midway down the hall, find the large model of the Battle of Lodi in 1796. The French and Austrians faced off on opposite sides of a northern Italian river, each trying to capture a crucial bridge. The model shows the dramatic moment when the French cavalry charged across the bridge, overpowering the exhausted Austrians. Stories spread that it was the brash General Bonaparte himself who personally sighted the French cannons on the enemy—normally the job of a lesser officer. It turned the tide of battle and earned him a reputation and a nickname, "The Little Corporal."

Room 23 chronicles Napoleon as emperor. While pledging allegiance to Revolutionary ideals of democracy, Napoleon staged a coup and soon ruled France as a virtual dictator. The museum displays General Bonaparte's hat, sword, and medals. In 1804, Napoleon donned royal robes and was crowned Emperor. The famous portrait by J. A. D. Ingres shows him at the peak of his power,

stretching his right arm to supernatural lengths. The ceremonial collar and medal he wears in the painting are displayed nearby, as are an eagle standard and Napoleon's elaborate saddle.

And speaking of horses, continue to the end of Hall 2 to find Napoleon's beloved Arabian horse. Le Vizir weathered many a campaign with Napoleon, grew old with him in exile, and now stands stuffed and proud.

## Hall 3: The Reign of Napoleon

Ambitious Napoleon plunged France into draining wars against all of Europe. In **room 29** (midway down the hall), you'll see Napoleon's tent and bivouac equipment: a bed with mosquito netting, a director's chair, his overcoat and pistols, and a table that you can imagine his generals hunched over as they made battle plans.

Napoleon's plans to dominate Europe ended with disastrous losses when he attempted to invade Russia. The rest of Europe

ganged up on France, and in 1814 Napoleon was forced to abdicate. **Room 35** shows a portrait of a crestfallen Napoleon, now replaced by King Louis XVIII (whose bust stands opposite). Napoleon spent a year in exile on the isle of Elba. In March of 1815, he escaped, returned to France, rallied the army, and prepared for one last hurrah.

• *Turning the corner into Hall 4, you run right into what Napoleon did—Waterloo.*

## Hall 4: Waterloo and the First Restoration

A projection screen maps the course of the history-changing Battle of Waterloo, fought on the outskirts of Brussels, June 15-19, 1815.

On June 15, 72,000 French (the blue squares) faced off against the allied armies of 68,000 British-Dutch under Wellington (red and yellow) and 45,000 Prussians under Blücher (purple). Napoleon's only hope was to split the two armies and defeat them individually.

First, Napoleon's Marshal Ney advances on the British-Dutch, commanded by the Prince of Orange. Then the French attack the Prussians on the right. They rout the Prussians, driving them north. Napoleon's strategy is working. Now he prepares to finish Wellington off.

On the morning of June 18, Wellington hunkers down atop a ridge at Waterloo. Napoleon waits two hours to attack, to let the field dry—some say it was his fatal mistake. At 11:30, Napoleon fakes to the left, then punches hard at the center. Wellington holds firm. Meanwhile, the Prussians have regrouped and begun advancing from the right. Napoleon must now fight both armies, on two flanks—Wellington on the ridge, the Prussians to the right.

Caught in a pincer, Napoleon has no choice but to send in his elite troops, the Imperial Guard, who have never been defeated. The British surprise the Guard in a cornfield, and Wellington swoops down from the ridge, routing the French. By nightfall, the British and Prussian armies have come together, and Napoleon's reign of glory is over.

Napoleon was sent into exile on St. Helena. His reconstructed room lets you imagine a lonely man suffering from ulcers, passing his days in his nightcap and slippers, and playing chess, not war.

• *From here head downstairs, following the signs to the...*

## Charles de Gaulle Exhibit

Finish at this engaging memorial, the "Historial Charles de Gaulle," which brings France's history of war into the modern age. With the help of a free infrared-activated audioguide, the exhibit leads you through the life of the greatest figure in 20th-century French history—from de Gaulle's youth, through two world wars, to the rebuilding of France during his presidency and the social unrest of the 1960s that toppled him. The excellent 25-minute biographical video plays at :15 and :45 after the hour.

# BUS #69 SIGHTSEEING TOUR

*From the Eiffel Tower to Père Lachaise Cemetery*

Why pay €25 for a tour company to give you an overview of Paris, when city bus #69 can do it for the cost of a Métro ticket? Get on the bus and settle in for a ride through some of the city's most interesting neighborhoods. Or use this tour as a handy way to lace together many of Paris' most important sightseeing districts (you'll need a new ticket each time you board the bus). On this ride from the Eiffel Tower to Père Lachaise Cemetery, you'll learn how great the city's bus system is—and you'll wonder why you've been tunneling by Métro under this gorgeous city. And if you're staying in the Marais or Rue Cler neighborhoods, line #69 is a useful route for just getting around town.

At times the bus goes faster than you can read. It's best to look through this chapter ahead of time, then ride with an eye out for the various sights described here. Ask your hotelier to print the route map for you or do it yourself before leaving (go to www.ratp.fr—only the French version works—click on *"plan des lignes)."*

## Orientation

**Length of This Tour:** Allow one hour.

**With Limited Time:** End early at Bastille, with good Métro connections.

**Cost:** One Métro ticket per one-way ride.

**When to Go:** You can board daily until 22:30 (last departure from Eiffel Tour stop). It's best to avoid weekday rush hours (8:00-9:30 & 17:30-19:30) and hot days (no air-conditioning). Sundays are quietest, and it's easy to get a window seat. Evening bus rides are magical from fall through spring (roughly Sept-April), when it gets dark early enough to see the floodlit monuments before the bus stops running.

**Getting There:** Eastbound line #69 leaves from the Eiffel Tower on Avenue Joseph Bouvard (the street that becomes Rue St. Dominique as it crosses the Champ de Mars, two blocks away from the tower through the park). Board at one of the first stops to secure a view seat (see map on page 250). The first stop is at the southwestern end of the avenue; the second stop is at the eastern end (just before Avenue de la Bourdonnais). Stops are located about every three blocks along the route. At whatever stop you plan to catch the bus, check if "69" is posted at the stop to make sure you're on the right route. (The map on page 38 shows most stops for Bus #69.)

**Bus Tips:** Use a ticket from your *carnet*. If you hop off to see a sight, you'll need a new ticket to hop back on. Métro tickets work on buses, but you can't use the same ticket to transfer between the bus and Métro—you'll need to buy a new one. Board through the front door, then validate your ticket in the machine behind the driver. If it's hot, you can usually open the upper part of the window. To let the driver know you'd like to get off at the next stop, push a red button. Exit through the rear door. Buses run every 10-15 minutes except in the late evening.

## Overview

Handy line #69 crosses the city east-west, running between the Eiffel Tower and Père Lachaise Cemetery, and passing these great monuments and neighborhoods: Eiffel Tower, Ecole Militaire, Rue Cler, Les Invalides (Army Museum and Napoleon's Tomb), Louvre Museum, Ile de la Cité, Ile St. Louis, Hôtel de Ville, Pompidou Center, Marais, Bastille, and Père Lachaise.

This tour is best done in the direction it's written (east from the Eiffel Tower to Père Lachaise Cemetery), because in the other direction one-way streets change the route. Grab a window seat—right side toward the back is best (rear seats are higher). If you get on at one of the

**BUS #69 TOUR**

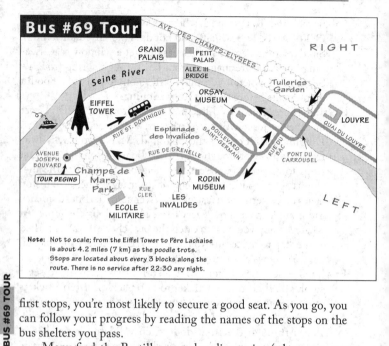

**Bus #69 Tour**

GRAND PALAIS
PETIT PALAIS
ALEX. III BRIDGE
AVE. DES CHAMPS-ELYSEES
RIGHT
Seine River
Tuileries Garden
ORSAY MUSEUM
EIFFEL TOWER
LOUVRE
RUE ST. DOMINIQUE
QUAI DU LOUVRE
Esplanade des Invalides
BOULEVARD SAINT-GERMAIN
RUE DE GRENELLE
RUE DU BAC
PONT DU CARROUSEL
AVENUE JOSEPH BOUVARD
TOUR BEGINS
Champs de Mars Park
RUE CLER
RODIN MUSEUM
LEFT
ECOLE MILITAIRE
LES INVALIDES

Note: Not to scale; from the Eiffel Tower to Père Lachaise is about 4.2 miles (7 km) as the poodle trots. Stops are located about every 3 blocks along the route. There is no service after 22:30 any night.

BUS #69 TOUR

first stops, you're most likely to secure a good seat. As you go, you can follow your progress by reading the names of the stops on the bus shelters you pass.

Many find the Bastille a good ending point (where you can begin my walking tour of the Marais; ○ see the Marais Walk chapter). This ride also ties in well after a visit to the Eiffel Tower or on your way to visiting Père Lachaise Cemetery. Think of this as an overview. The sights you'll survey are written up in more depth elsewhere in the book. OK—let's roll.

# The Tour Begins

## Champ de Mars and the Eiffel Tower

Your tour begins below this 1,000-foot, reddish-brown hood ornament. While you're waiting for the bus, you could read up on the Eiffel Tower (○ see the Eiffel Tower Tour chapter). The park surrounding you is called Champ de Mars (named for the god of war). It served as a parade ground for the military school, Ecole Militaire, which seals the park at the right end. Napoleon Bonaparte is the school's most famous graduate.

In 1889, the Champ de Mars was covered with a massive temporary structure to house exhibitions of all sorts; it was a celebration of the Centennial World's Fair (the 100th anniversary of the French Revolution), the same event for which the Eiffel Tower was built. The apartments surrounding the park are among the most exclusive in Paris.

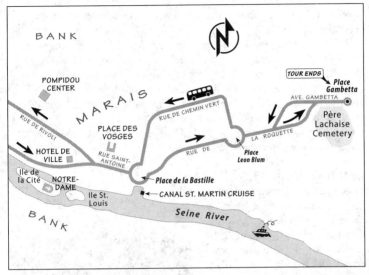

The grass that runs down the center of the park is strictly off-limits—so you can't walk on the grass, except on the side sections. Evening picnics are a delight (where allowed), and warm evenings are grand social affairs. Dogs romp as soccer balls fly past, all within the glow of the Eiffel Tower.

• *Leaving the Champ de Mars, the bus slices through the 7th arrondissement along its primary shopping street. As you head onto Rue St. Dominique, notice how well your driver navigates past delivery trucks and illegally parked cars.*

## Rue St. Dominique

Paris functions as a city of hundreds of small neighborhoods. This area, which was once the village of Grenelle (before it was consumed by Paris), is a good example. Shops and cafés line the streets, topped by several floors of apartments, giving the district a liveliness not found in less-vibrant commercial districts. You can shop for anything you need on Rue St. Dominique (but not at any hour). Many locals feel no need to leave the area, and neighbors trust each other. The dry cleaner knows that if his customer forgets to bring her wallet, she'll return to pay him another time. If the plumber can only come during work hours, locals can leave their apartment keys with the nearest shop owner, who will make sure the plumber gets them.

This neighborhood has long been an attraction for Americans—it's where you'll find the American Church (two blocks to the left), the American Library, the American University of Paris, and lots of my readers (in recommended hotels). As you cross Avenue Bosquet, you'll see a church spire to the far left; it's the American Cathedral, on the Right Bank.

• *After crossing Boulevard de la Tour Maubourg, you'll enter the open world of Esplanade des Invalides.*

## Esplanade des Invalides

This sprawling green esplanade links the **river** (to the left) and Europe's first veteran's hospital, **Les Invalides** (right), built by Louis XIV. Napoleon lies powerfully dead under the brilliant golden dome.

Afternoon ***boules*** (lawn bowling), near the Invalides building under the trees on the far right, is an engaging spectator sport. I spend more time watching the players' mannerisms than the game itself (see "The Rules of *Boules*" sidebar on page 386). In summer, American football games are played on the grassy esplanade, with teams composed of Franco-American friends. They even have a league and drink beer after the games. The Rodin Museum lies just beyond the esplanade, left of Les Invalides.

Look left and see the **Pont Alexandre III (Alexander III Bridge)** crossing the Seine. Spiked with golden statues and ironwork lamps, the bridge was built to celebrate a turn-of-the-20th-century treaty between France and Russia. Just across the bridge are the glass-and-steel-domed **Grand** and **Petit Palais** exhibition halls, built for the 1900 World's Fair. Like the bridge, they are fine examples of belle époque architecture. Impressive temporary exhibits fill the huge Grand Palais, and the smaller Petit Palais houses a permanent collection of 19th-century paintings, starring works by Courbet and Monet (among others). The **Air France building** (just this side of the river) is an Orly airport shuttle stop (4/hour).

• *Leaving Les Invalides, you'll re-enter narrow streets lined with…*

## Government Buildings

Many of France's most important ministries occupy these golden-hued buildings (look for police guarding doorways, heavily barred windows, and people in suits speaking in hushed tones). Opposite the frilly **Gothic church** (on your right at the Bourgogne bus stop)

BUS #69 TOUR

sprawls the **Ministry of Defense,** originally the mansion of Napoleon's mother.
• *You'll emerge from the government ghetto onto the stylish and leafy...*

## Boulevard St. Germain

Along this stretch, colorful furniture stores tempt the neighborhood's upper-crust residents. Notice the fine Haussmann-era architecture. Several blocks farther down are the boulevard's famous cafés, once frequented by existentialists Albert Camus and Jean-Paul Sartre. But we turn left onto **Rue du Bac,** and cross streets (to the right) filled with antiques, art galleries, and smart hotels. The Orsay Museum is a few blocks to the left (if you need an art break, the best stop for this museum is at Pont Royal, just before the river; ✪ see the Orsay Museum Tour chapter).
• *Next, you'll cross the river (see the Orsay Museum behind on the left) and enter the Right Bank.*

## Tuileries Garden and Louvre Museum

The Tuileries Garden (Jardin des Tuileries) lies ahead and to the left as you cross the Seine. This was the royal garden of the Louvre palace and a wonderful place to clear your mind after touring the Louvre. Scattered among these pretty gardens are several cafés, ponds with toy boats for rent, and trampolines for jumping. After turning right along the river, you'll follow the immense Grand Gallery of the **Louvre,** dominating the left side of the street. Notice the bus lane you're in, separated from the traffic by a low curb. Bicyclists have the right to use these lanes, making vast parts of Paris bike-friendly.

The U-shaped Louvre, once the biggest building in the world, now houses 12 miles of galleries wallpapered with thousands of the world's greatest paintings. Various kings added new wings, marking their contributions with their initials and medallions carved into the decor. The statues put on a stony toga fashion show as you roll by.

Just before the end of the Louvre building, passing over the river on the right, is the view-perfect pedestrian bridge **Pont des Arts** (described at the beginning of the ✪ Left Bank Walk chapter). The bridge is adorned with countless padlocks—couples leave them here to promise lasting love. That curved **building with a dome** on the other side is where the Académie Française has met since the 1600s to defend the French language from corrupting influences (like English) and to compose the official French dictionary. Notice the inviting **café-boats** across the river. There are about 2,000 barges docked on the Seine in Paris.

• *Next on the right is the island where Paris was founded. As you roll past the end of the long Louvre building, get ready for quick right-left-right head movements.*

## Ile de la Cité

The river splits around this island where Paris began over 2,000 years ago. The first bridge you see dates from about 1600. While it's called **Pont Neuf,** meaning "new bridge," it's Paris' oldest. Pont Neuf leads to an equestrian statue of King Henry IV, who doesn't face a tiny and romantic tip-of-the-island park from which Seine tour boats depart (see listing for Vedettes du Pont Neuf on page 46). Those green boxes mounted on the wall to your right keep *bouquinistes'* books and souvenirs dry; see "*Les Bouquinistes* (Riverside Vendors)" sidebar on page 481.

On your left is Paris' primary **department-store shopping district.** Next along this street are sidewalk **pet stalls**—a hit with local children, who dream of taking home a turtle, canary, or rabbit. Back across the river, find the squat and round medieval towers (wearing pointy black cone hats) of the **Conciergerie,** named for the concierge (or caretaker) who ran these offices when the king moved to the Louvre. The towers guard Ile de la Cité's law courts, the Palais de Justice, the prison famous as the last stop for those about to be guillotined. That intricate needle—the **spire of Sainte-Chapelle**—marks the most beautiful Gothic interior in Paris. You'll see the substantial twin towers and thin spire of **Notre-Dame Cathedral** soon after the Conciergerie. Back to the left, the grand **Hôtel de Ville** (Paris' city hall) stands proudly behind playful fountains, energizing its generally lively big front yard. Each of the 20 arrondissements (governmental areas) in Paris has its own city hall, and this one is the big daddy of them all. In the summer, the square in front of Hôtel de Ville hosts sand volleyball courts and, at Christmastime, a big ice-skating rink. It's beautifully lit after dark all year.

In summer, the street out of sight below you, running along the riverbank, is "paved" with sand and turned into a one-mile-long beach party (see Paris Plages, page 60). Even though this is a major artery through the city, officials can close it because Parisians take their summer vacations en masse, leaving the city relatively free of traffic. As the bus curves away from the river, take a quick look through the trees back across the river to see the gray, steel **modern pedestrian bridge** that connects Paris' two islands.

• *The bus angles through the Marais neighborhood.*

## Le Marais

This is jumbled, medieval Paris at its finest. It's been a swamp, an aristocratic district, and a bohemian hangout. Today, classy stone mansions sit alongside trendy bars, keeping the antiques shops and fashion-conscious boutiques company. The Picasso Museum (closed for renovation until summer 2013), Carnavalet Museum, Victor Hugo's House, Jewish Art and History Museum, and Pompidou Center all have Marais addresses. On your left, two blocks past the Eglise St. Gervais bus stop, you'll see the **oldest houses** in Paris—tall, skinny, and half-timbered—clustered around #13.

The narrow street soon merges into **Rue St. Antoine,** the main street through the Marais and the main street of Paris in medieval times. The small-but-grand **Church of St. Paul and St. Louis** (on the right, with classical columns) is the only Jesuit church in Paris. It was the neighborhood church of Victor Hugo. You may want to return to this charming district to browse and window-shop later.

• *Rue St. Antoine leads straight into the Place de la Bastille, marked with a giant pillar in the center. If you want to cut this bus tour short, get off at the next stop after Biraque, just before Place de la Bastille. Options if you get off: my Marais Walk (❂ see the Marais Walk chapter), Canauxrama canal boat tour (page 47), Promenade Plantée Park (page 89), and Marais eateries (see the Eating in Paris chapter).*

## Place de la Bastille

The namesake of this square, a fortress-turned-prison that symbolized royal tyranny, is long gone. But for centuries, the fortress that stood here was used to defend the city, mostly from its own people. On July 14, 1789, angry Parisians swarmed the Bastille, released its prisoners, and kicked off the French Revolution. Since then, the French celebrate their Independence Day on July 14 (a.k.a. Bastille Day) as enthusiastically as Americans commemorate July 4.

In the middle of the square, you'll actually cross over **Canal St. Martin** (look to the right), which runs from the Seine underneath the tree-lined boulevard Richard Lenoir (on the left) to northern Paris. You'll curve in front of the reflecting-glass **Opéra Bastille.**

• *Leaving Place de la Bastille, you'll angle left up Rue de la Roquette all the way to Père Lachaise.*

## Rue de la Roquette

This street begins at the Bastille in a hip, less touristy neighborhood. Here you'll find a fun mix of galleries, wholesale clothing shops, seedy bars, and trendy, cheap eateries. The first street to the right is **Rue de Lappe,** one of the wildest nightspots in Paris; it's filled with a dizzying array of wacky bistros, bars, and dance halls.

• *The bus eventually turns left onto Boulevard de Ménilmontant (which locals happily associate with a famous Maurice Chevalier tune) and rumbles past the Père Lachaise Cemetery. Although the bus stops at the front gate of the vast cemetery, stay on to Place Gambetta (a better jumping-off point for visiting the cemetery), where bus #69 ends its trip through the heart of Paris. Place Gambetta's centerpiece is another grandiose city hall (this one for the 20th arrondissement). You'll also see some inviting cafés and Avenue du Père Lachaise (right after you pass McDonald's). Follow this street 100 yards, past flower shops selling cyclamen, heather, and chrysanthemums—the standard flowers for funerals and memorials—to the gate of the cemetery. Take a short stroll through the evocative home of so many permanent Parisians (Mo: Gambetta or Père Lachaise).*

## Père Lachaise Cemetery

Navigating the labyrinthine rows is a challenge, but maps and my walking tour (❂ see the Père Lachaise Cemetery Tour chapter) will help you find the graves of greats such as Frédéric Chopin, Oscar Wilde, Gertrude Stein, and Jim Morrison. The tour is over. What better place for your final stop?

# MARMOTTAN MUSEUM TOUR

*Musée Marmottan Monet*

The Marmottan has the best collection of works by the master Impressionist, Claude Monet. In this mansion on the fringe of urban Paris, you can walk through Monet's life, from black-and-white sketches to colorful open-air paintings to the canvas that gave Impressionism its name. The museum's highlights are scenes of his garden at Giverny, including larger-than-life water lilies. In addition, the Marmottan features a world-class collection of works by Berthe Morisot.

Paul Marmottan (1856-1932) lived here amid his collection of exquisite 19th-century furniture and paintings. He donated his home and possessions to a private trust (which is why your Museum Pass isn't valid here). After Marmottan's death, the more daring art of Monet and others were added.

Because the layout of the museum changes often, this chapter is not designed as a room-by-room tour of the museum, but, rather, as a general background on Monet and some of the paintings you're likely to encounter. Read it before you go, then let the museum surprise you.

## Orientation

**Cost:** €10, not covered by Museum Pass.

**Hours:** Tue-Sun 10:00-18:00, Thu until 20:00, closed Mon, last entry 30 minutes before closing.

**Getting There:** It's in southwest Paris at 2 Rue Louis-Boilly. The Métro, RER, and buses all will get you there:

Take the Métro to La Muette, cross the street to the brown *Marmottan* sign, and follow signs down Chaussée de la Muette (turns into Avenue Ranelagh) through the delightful park with its old-time kiddie carousel to the museum (six blocks, 10 minutes).

From the Rue Cler area, take the RER-C from Invalides or Pont de l'Alma (catch any train called NORA or GOTA), get off at the Boulainvilliers stop, and follow signs to *sortie Rue des Vignes*. Turn right up Rue Boulainvilliers, then turn left down Chaussée de la Muette to reach the museum. When returning to your hotel on the RER, make sure your stop is listed on the monitor: You don't want to end up in Versailles.

Bus #63 works from Rue Cler and St. Sulpice, but requires a long walk of about 600 yards. Get off at the Octave Feuillet stop on Avenue Henri Martin, cross Avenue Henri Martin, and follow the tree-lined street to the right that curves around to the museum.

**Information:** The audioguide is €3. Tel. 01 44 96 50 33, www. marmottan.com.

**Length of This Tour:** Allow one hour.

**Photography:** Not allowed.

**Family Tip:** The park in front of the museum is terrific for families with small kids. Parents can take turns: While one visits the museum, the other can stay outside with the children.

**Starring:** Claude Monet, including *Impression: Sunrise* (shown at the top of this chapter); paintings of Rouen Cathedral, Gare St. Lazare, and Houses of Parliament; scenes from Giverny; and water lilies.

**Post-Museum Stroll:** Wander one of Paris' most pleasant (and up-scale) shopping streets, Rue de Passy (two blocks up Chaussée de la Muette, opposite direction from La Muette Métro stop—follow that tower). After Rue de Passy ends, you can continue straight—on Boulevard Delessert—all the way to the Eiffel Tower. It takes one full hour of walking, without stops, to get from the Marmottan Museum to the Eiffel Tower.

## Overview

The museum traces Monet's life chronologically, but in a way that's as rough and fragmented as a Monet canvas. The collection is reorganized periodically and some paintings go on road shows, so have patience and hold on to the big picture.

The ground floor displays Paul Marmottan's eclectic collection of non-Monet objects—period furnishings, a beautifully displayed series of illuminated manuscript drawings, and non-Monet paintings created in the seamless-brushstroke style that Monet rebelled against.

The permanent collection (mainly Monet) is in the basement and on the first floor. The basement displays Monet's large-scale works from his gardens at Giverny, whereas the first floor hosts

## Monet's Family

You'll likely see portraits of Monet's wife and children. Monet's first wife, Camille, died in 1879, leaving Monet to raise 12-year-old Jean and babe-in-arms Michel. (Michel would grow up to inherit the family home and many of the paintings that ended up here.) But Monet was also involved with Alice Hoschede, who had recently been abandoned by her husband. Alice moved in with her six kids and took care of the dying Camille, and the two families made a Brady Bunch-style merger. Baby Michel became bosom buddies with Alice's baby, Jean-Pierre, while teenage Jean Monet and stepsister Blanche fell in love and later married.

special exhibits and paintings by Impressionist colleagues Pierre-Auguste Renoir, Camille Pissarro, Berthe Morisot, and more.

Now, explore.

# The Tour Begins

## Claude Monet (1840-1926)

Claude Monet was the leading light of the Impressionist movement that revolutionized painting in the 1870s. Fiercely independent and dedicated to his craft, Monet gave courage to Renoir and other like-minded artists, who were facing harsh criticism.

The museum often displays a timeline, where you can survey Monet's long life:

Born in Paris in 1840, Monet began his art career sketching **caricatures** of townspeople. Baby **Jean** was born to Monet and his partner **Camille** in 1867, the year his work was rejected by the Salon. They moved to the countryside of **Argenteuil,** where he developed his open-air, Impressionist style. *Impression: Sunrise* was his landmark work at the breakthrough 1874 Impressionist Exhibition. He went on to paint several series of scenes, such as *Gare Saint-Lazare,* at different times of day.

After the birth of **Michel,** Camille's health declined, and she later died. Monet traveled a lot, painting landscapes *(Bordighera),* people *(Portrait de Poly),* and more series, including the famous **Cathedral of Rouen.**  In 1890, he settled down at his farmhouse in **Giverny** and married **Alice Hoschede.** He traveled less, but visited

London to paint the **Halls of Parliament**. Mostly, he painted his own **water lilies** and **flowers** in an increasingly messy style. He died in 1926 a famous man.

Nearby, you may find some Monet memorabilia: letters, an actual palette, or portraits and photos of Monet and his family.

## Growing Up in Le Havre—Caricature Drawings (1840-1860)

Teenage Monet's first works—black and white, meticulously drawn, humorous sketches of small-town celebrities—are as different as can be from the colorful, messy oils that would make him famous. Still, they show his gift for quickly capturing an overall impression with a few simple strokes.

The son of a grocer, Monet defied his family, insisted he was an artist, and sketched the world around him—beaches, boats, and small-town life. Fellow artist Eugène Boudin encouraged Monet to don a scarf, set up his easel outdoors, and paint the scene exactly as he saw it. Today, we say, "Well, duh!" But "open-air" painting was unorthodox for artists of the day, who were trained to study their subjects thoroughly in the perfect lighting of a controlled studio setting.

At 19, Monet went to Paris but refused to enroll in the official art schools. Letters in the glass case (unless they're out on loan) from Monet asking for survival money from his friends show the price he paid for his early bohemian lifestyle.

## The 1870s: Pure Impressionism

Monet teamed up with Renoir and Alfred Sisley, leading them on open-air painting safaris to the countryside. Inspired by the realism of Edouard Manet, they painted everyday things—landscapes, seascapes, street scenes, ladies with parasols, family picnics—in bright, basic colors.

In 1870, Monet married his girlfriend, Camille (the dark-haired woman in many of his paintings), and moved just outside Paris to the resort town of Argenteuil. Playing host to Renoir, Manet, and others, he perfected the Impressionist style—painting nature as a mosaic of short brushstrokes of different colors placed side by side, suggesting shimmering light.

First, he simplified. In *On the Beach at Trouville* (*Sur la Plage à Trouville*, 1870-1871; pictured at top of next page), a lady's dress is a few thick strokes of paint. Monet gradually broke things down into smaller dots of different shades. If you back up from a Monet canvas, the pigments blend into one (for example, red plus green

plus yellow equals a brown boat). Still, they never fully resolve, creating the effect of shimmering light. Monet limited his palette to a few bright basics— cobalt blue, white, yellow, two shades of red, and emerald green abound. But no black—even shadows are a combination of bright colors.

Monet's constant quest was to faithfully reproduce nature in blobs of paint. His eye was a camera lens set at a very slow shutter speed to admit maximum light. Then he "developed" the impression made on his retina with an oil-based solution. Even as the heartbroken Monet watched Camille die of tuberculosis in 1879, he was (he admitted later) intrigued by the changing colors in her dying face.

### *Impression: Sunrise* (*Impression Soleil Levant,* 1873)

This is the painting that started the revolution—a simple, serene view of boats bobbing under an orange sun (see the photo that opens this chapter). At the first public showing by Monet, Renoir, Degas, and others in Paris in 1874, critics howled at this work and ridiculed the title. "Wallpaper," one called it. The sloppy brushstrokes and ordinary subject looked like a study, not a finished work. The style was dubbed "Impressionist"—an accurate name.

The misty harbor scene obviously made an "impression" on Monet, who faithfully rendered the fleeting moment in quick strokes of paint. The waves are simple horizontal brushstrokes. The sun's reflection on the water is a few thick, bold strokes of orange tipped with white. They zigzag down the canvas, the way a reflection shifts on moving water.

### Monet the Traveler

In search of new light and new scenes, Monet traveled throughout France and Europe. As you enjoy landscapes painted in all kinds of weather, picture Monet at work—hiking to a remote spot; carrying an easel, several canvases, brushes (large-size), a palette, tubes of paint (an invention that made open-air painting practical), food and drink, a folding chair, and an umbrella; and wearing his trademark hat, with a cigarette on his lip. He weathered the elements, occasionally putting himself in danger by clambering on cliffs to get the scenes he wanted.

The key was to work fast, before the weather changed and the light shifted, completely changing the colors. Monet worked "wet-in-wet," applying new paint before the first layer dried, mixing colors on the canvas, and piling them up into a thick paste.

## The 1890s: Series

Monet often painted the same subject several times under different light (such as one of Paris' train stations, Gare St. Lazare, 1870s). In the 1890s, he conceived of a series of paintings to be shown as a group, giving a time-lapse view of a single subject.

He rented several rooms offering different angles overlooking the Rouen Cathedral and worked on up to 14 different canvases at a time, shuffling the right one onto the easel as the sun moved across the sky. The cathedral is made of brown stone, but at sunset it becomes gold and pink with blue shadows, softened by thick smudges of paint. The true subject is not the cathedral, but the full spectrum of light that bounces off it.

These series—of the cathedral, haystacks, poplars, and mornings on the Seine—were very popular. Monet, poverty-stricken until his mid-40s, was slowly becoming famous, first in America, then London, and finally in France.

## The 1900s: London

Turning a hotel room into a studio, Monet—working on nearly a hundred different canvases simultaneously—painted the changing light on the River Thames. The *London Houses of Parliament, Reflected in the Thames* (*Londres, Le Parlement, Reflets sur la Tamise*, 1905) stretch and bend with the tide. *Charing Cross Bridge* is only a few smudgy lines enveloped in fog.

London's fog epitomized Monet's favorite subject—the atmosphere that distorts distant objects. That filtering haze gives even different-colored objects a similar tone, resulting in a more harmonious picture. When the light was just right and the atmosphere glowed, the moment of "instantaneity" had arrived, and Monet worked like a madman.

In truth, Monet started many of his canvases in the open air, and then painstakingly perfected them later in the studio. He composed his scenes with great care—clear horizon lines give a strong horizontal axis, while diagonal lines (of trees or shorelines)

## Berthe Morisot (1841-1895)

The Marmottan's large collection of Morisot's work cements her reputation as one of Impressionism's Founding Mothers. Born into a cultured, supportive family, she found early success painting landscapes (in the open air) in the proto-Impressionist style of her mentor, Camille Corot. Still in her 20s, Morisot exhibited to good reviews at the official Salon for seven straight years.

Meanwhile, she'd met Edouard Manet, married his brother, and experimented with the Impressionist style. She threw away her black paint and replaced it with a brighter palette. In 1874, she joined the Impressionist gang, exhibiting her work at the same "Salon des Refusés" where Monet's *Impression: Sunrise* caused a minor revolution.

Her paintings focus mainly on women, either in gardens or in peaceful, domestic situations. Her subjects were landscapes, friends (such as Manet), and family (her daughter, Julie). She had a keen eye for ladies' fashions (*At the Ball,* 1875). Like Manet, Morisot's brand of Impressionism was always naturalistic and understated. She avoided the gritty urban scenes of Degas and the pointillistic color theory of Monet and others. The tranquil Marmottan mansion is the perfect setting for the peaceful world of Morisot.

create solid triangles. And he wasn't above airbrushing out details that might spoil the composition—such as Cleopatra's Needle near Charing Cross.

## Paintings of Giverny (1883-1926)
### *Rose Trellises (L'Allée des Rosiers,* **several versions)** **and the** *Japanese Bridge (Le Pont Japonais)*

In 1883, Monet's brood settled into a farmhouse in Giverny (50 miles west of Paris, see page 610). Financially stable and domestically blissful, he turned Giverny into a garden paradise and painted nature without the long commute.

In 1890, Monet started work on his Japanese garden, inspired by tranquil scenes from the Japanese prints he collected. He diverted a river to form a pond, planted willows and bamboo on the shores, filled the pond with water lilies, then crossed it with this wooden footbridge. As years passed, the bridge became overgrown with wisteria. Compare several different versions. He painted the bridge at different times of day and year, exploring different color schemes.

Monet uses the bridge as the symmetrical center of simple, pleasing designs. The water is drawn with horizontal brushstrokes that get shorter as you move up the canvas (farther away), creating the illusion of distance. The horizontal water contrasts with the vertical willows, while the bridge "bridges" the sides of the square canvas and laces the scene together.

In 1912, Monet began to go blind. Cataracts distorted his perception of depth and color, and sent him into a tailspin of despair. The (angry?) red paintings date from this period.

### Early Water Lilies (*Nymphéas,* several versions)

As his vision slowly failed, Monet concentrated on painting close-ups of the surface of the pond and its water lilies—red, white, yellow, and lavender. Some lilies are just a few broad strokes on a bare canvas (a study); others are piles of paint formed with overlapping colors.

But more than the lilies, the paintings focus on the changing reflections on the surface of the pond. Pan slowly around the room and watch the pond go from predawn to bright sunlight to twilight.

Early lily paintings (c. 1900) show the shoreline as a reference point. But increasingly, Monet crops the scene ever closer, until there is no shoreline, no horizon, no sense of what's up or down. Stepping back from the canvas, you see the lilies just hang there on the museum wall, suspended in space. The surface of the pond and the surface of the canvas are one. Modern abstract art—a colored design on a flat surface—is just around the corner.

## *Nymphéas* and Large-Scale Canvases
### Big Weeping Willow (Le *Saule Pleureur,* 1918-1919)
Get close—Monet did—and analyze the trunk. Rough "brown" bark is made of thick strokes (an inch wide and four inches long) of pink, purple, orange, and green. Impressionism lives. But to get these colors to resolve in your eye, you'd have to back up all the way to Giverny.

### Later Water Lilies (*Nymphéas,* 1915-1926)

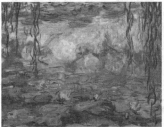

In the midst of the chaos of World War I, Monet began a series of large-scale paintings of water lilies. They were installed at the Orangerie (for information, see the Orangerie Museum Tour chapter). Here at the Marmottan are smaller-scale studies for that series.

Some lilies are patches of thick paint circled by a squiggly "caricature" of a lily pad. Monet simplifies in a way that Henri Matisse and Pablo Picasso would envy. But getting close, you can see that the simple smudge of paint that composes the flower is actually a complex mix of different colors. The sheer size of these studies (and his Orangerie canvases) is impressive.

When Monet died in 1926, he was a celebrity. Starting with meticulous line drawings, he had evolved into an open-air realist, then Impressionist color analyst, then serial painter, and finally master of reflections. In the latter half of his life, Monet's world shrank—from the broad vistas of the world traveler to the tranquility of his home, family, and garden. But his artistic vision expanded as he painted smaller details on bigger canvases and helped invent modern abstract art.

MARMOTTAN MUSEUM

# LEFT BANK WALK

*From the Seine to*
*Luxembourg Garden*

The Left Bank is as much an attitude as it is an actual neighborhood. But this walk, which is a little over a mile—from the Seine to St. Germain-des-Prés to Luxembourg Garden—captures some of the artistic, intellectual, and countercultural spirit long associated with the south side of the river. We'll pass through an upscale area of art galleries, home-furnishing boutiques, antiques dealers, bookstores, small restaurants, classic cafés, evening hot spots, and the former homes of writers, painters, and composers. Though trendy now, the area still has the offbeat funkiness that has always defined the Rive Gauche. (*Gauche,* or left-handed, has come to imply social incorrectness, like giving a handshake with the wrong—left—hand.)

Use this walk as a series of historical markers as you explore the Left Bank of today. The walk dovetails perfectly with a shopping stroll (see "Sèvres-Babylone to St. Sulpice" on page 478). It also works well after a visit to the Louvre or after the Historic Paris Walk, and it's ideal for connoisseurs of contemporary art galleries.

## Orientation

**Length of This Walk:** Allow two hours.

**With Limited Time:** End the walk at St. Germain-des-Prés, with good Métro connections.

**When to Go:** Evenings are pleasant, and many art galleries are open until 19:00 or 19:30.

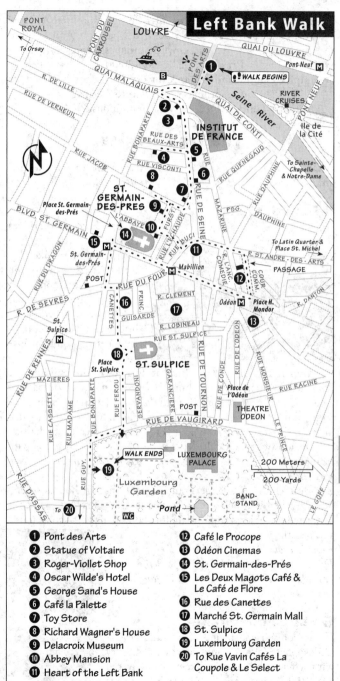

| | | | |
|---|---|---|---|
| ❶ | Pont des Arts | ⓬ | Café le Procope |
| ❷ | Statue of Voltaire | ⓭ | Odéon Cinemas |
| ❸ | Roger-Viollet Shop | ⓮ | St. Germain-des-Prés |
| ❹ | Oscar Wilde's Hotel | ⓯ | Les Deux Magots Café & |
| ❺ | George Sand's House | | Le Café de Flore |
| ❻ | Café la Palette | ⓰ | Rue des Canettes |
| ❼ | Toy Store | ⓱ | Marché St. Germain Mall |
| ❽ | Richard Wagner's House | ⓲ | St. Sulpice |
| ❾ | Delacroix Museum | ⓳ | Luxembourg Garden |
| ❿ | Abbey Mansion | ⓴ | To Rue Vavin Cafés La |
| ⓫ | Heart of the Left Bank | | Coupole & Le Select |

**Delacroix Museum:** €5, free on first Sun of month, covered by
    Museum Pass, Wed-Mon 9:30-17:00, Sat-Sun until 17:30 in
    summer, closed Tue, last entry 30 minutes before closing.
**St. Germain-des-Prés:** Free, daily 8:00-20:00.
**St. Sulpice Church and Organ Concert:** Free, church open daily
    7:30-19:30, Sun morning organ concerts (see page 73.
**Luxembourg Garden:** Free, daily dawn until dusk.

# The Walk Begins

• *Start on the pedestrian-only bridge across the Seine, the Pont des Arts*
*(next to Louvre, Mo: Pont Neuf or Louvre-Rivoli).*

## ❶ Pont des Arts

Before dozens of bridges
crossed the Seine, the two
riverbanks were like dif-
ferent cities—royalty on
the right, commoners on
the left. This bridge has
always been a pedestrian
bridge...and long a popu-
lar meeting point for lovers.

    Under the dome of the Institut de France (the building the
Pont des Arts leads to), 40 linguists meet periodically to decide
whether it's acceptable to call mail *"le mail"* (as the French commonly do), or whether it should be the French word *courriel* (which
linguists prefer). The Académie Française, dedicated to halting
the erosion of French culture, is wary of new French terms with
strangely foreign sounds—like *le week-end, le marketing, le fast-food,*
and *c'est cool.*
    Besides the Académie Française, the Institut houses several
other Académies, such as the Académie des Beaux-Arts, which is
dedicated to subjects appropriate for the Left Bank, such as music
and painting.
• *Circle around the right side of the Institut de*
*France building to the head of Rue de Seine. You're*
*immediately met by a statue in a street-corner gar-*
*den.*

## ❷ Statue of Voltaire

"Jesus committed suicide." The mischievous
philosopher Voltaire could scandalize a party
with a wicked comment like that, delivered
with an enigmatic smile and a twinkle in his

# Art Galleries

You'll see many galleries in this vibrant neighborhood. Paris' art scene thrives. In the 20th century, the city attracted many of the foreigners (Picasso, Chagall, Modigliani) who pioneered modern art. Artists here still get respect not always given to artists in the States ("So you're an artist, huh? And what's your real job?"). Paris remains a clearinghouse of creative ideas... and fine art is big business, too. Lots of money passes through this city. Oil-rich sultans come here looking for trendy new works to hang over their sofas back home. Museum curators from America troll these Left Bank streets, taking notes on what's hot. In general, people with money come to Paris on vacation to enjoy the finer things in life. If they come across something they love, they pull out their plastic and make it their own. An impulse buy can gladden the hearts of these gallery owners. Paris is one city in the world where art supply does not necessarily outstrip art demand.

You're welcome to window-shop or enter the galleries. Remember the niceties of shopping in Paris. Always say, *Bonjour, Madame* (or *Mademoiselle* or *Monsieur*) when entering, and *Au revoir, Madame* (or *Mademoiselle* or *Monsieur*) when leaving. *Je regarde* means "I'm just looking." "*Je voudrais acheter* means "I would like to buy." The reality is that most clerks speak English and are happy to help or to let you browse. If you stroll neighborhoods in the evening, you're likely to pass what looks like a cocktail party spilling out of an art gallery. These "art openings," called *vernissages,* are sometimes private, though usually open to the public (even Americans). Be bold and join the party if you come across one.

eye (meaning if Christ is truly God, he could have prevented his crucifixion). Voltaire—a commoner more sophisticated than the royalty who lived across the river—introduces us to the Left Bank.

Born François-Marie Arouet (1694-1778), he took up Voltaire as his one-word pen name. Although Voltaire mingled with aristocrats, he was constantly in trouble for questioning the ruling class and for fueling ideas that would soon spark a revolution. He did 11 months in the Bastille prison, then spent 40 years in virtual exile from his beloved Paris. Returning as an old man, he got a hero's welcome so surprising it killed him.

The Rue de Seine and adjoining streets are lined with art galleries and upscale shops selling lamps, sconces, vases, bowls, and statues for people who turn their living rooms into art.

• *From here we'll head south down Rue de Seine to Boulevard St. Germain, making a few detours along the way. The first stop is at 6 Rue de Seine...*

### ❸ Roger-Viollet

Look in the windows at black-and-white photos of Paris' storied past. The display changes often, but you might see a half-built Eiffel Tower, glitterati of yesteryear (Colette, Simone de Beauvoir, Jean Cocteau), Hitler in Paris, and so on. Many more photos are tucked away inside the binders lining the walls, labeled alphabetically. This humble shop is the funky origin of a worldwide press agency dealing in historic photographs. The family of photographer Henri Roger expanded his photographs into an archive of millions of photos, chronicling Paris' changes through the years.

• At the first intersection, a half-block detour to the right leads to 13 Rue des Beaux-Arts and...

### ❹ Oscar Wilde's Hotel

Oscar Wilde (1854-1900), the Irish playwright with the flamboyant clothes and outrageous wit, died in this hotel on November 30, 1900 (don't blame the current owners).

Just five years before, he'd been at his peak. He had several plays running simultaneously in London's West End and had returned to London triumphant from a lecture tour through America. Then, news of his love affair with a lord leaked out, causing a scandal, and he was sentenced to two years in prison for "gross indecency." Wilde's wife abandoned him, refusing to let him see their children again.

After his prison term, a poor and broken Wilde was exiled to Paris, where he succumbed to an ear infection and died here in a (then) shabby hotel room. Among his last words in the run-down place were: "Either this wallpaper goes, or I do."

Wilde is buried in Paris (see Père Lachaise Cemetery Tour).

• Return to Rue de Seine and continue south. A plaque at 31 Rue de Seine marks...

### ❺ George Sand's House

George Sand (1804-1876) divorced her abusive husband, left her children behind, and moved into this apartment, determined to become a writer. In the year she lived here (1831), she wrote articles for *Le Figaro* while turning her real-life experiences with men into a sensational novel, *Indiana*. It made her a celebrity and allowed her to afford a better apartment.

George Sand is known for her novels, her cross-dressing (men's suits, slicked-down hair, and cigars), and for her complex love affair with a sensitive pianist from Poland, Frédéric Chopin.

• At 43 Rue de Seine is...

## ❻ Café la Palette

Though less famous than more historic cafés, this is a "real" one, where a *café crème*, beer, or glass of wine at an outdoor table is still reasonable. Inside, the 100-year-old, tobacco-stained wood paneling and faded Art Nouveau decor exude Left Bank chic. Toulouse-Lautrec would have liked it here. Have something to drink at the bar, and examine your surroundings—notice the artist palettes above the bar. Nothing seems to have changed since it was built in 1903, except the modern espresso machine (open daily, tel. 01 43 26 68 15).

• *At the fork, you could follow Rue de Seine straight down to Boulevard St. Germain. But we'll branch off, veering right down small Rue de l'Echaudé. Four doors up, at 6 Rue de l'Echaudé, is a...*

## ❼ Toy Store

French and American kids share many of the same toys and storybook characters: Babar the Elephant, Maisy Mouse, Tintin, the Smurfs, Madeline, Asterix, and the Little Prince. This store features figurines of these and other whimsical folk.

In *The Little Prince* (1943), written by Antoine de Saint-Exupéry, a pilot crashes in the Sahara, where a mysterious little prince takes him to various planets, teaching him about life from a child's wise perspective.

"Saint-Ex" (1900-1944) was himself a daring aviator who had survived wrecks in the Sahara. After France fell to the Nazis, he fled to America, where he wrote and published *The Little Prince*. A year later, he returned to Europe, then disappeared while flying a spy mission for the Allies. Lost for six decades, his plane was finally found off the coast of Marseille. Then, in 2008, a former Luftwaffe pilot—a childhood fan of Saint-Ex—said he believed himself responsible for shooting down the plane. Archival sources dispute this, however, and the cause of the crash remains a mystery, part of a legend as enduring in France as Amelia Earhart's is in the US.

• *At the intersection with Rue Jacob, a half-block detour to the right leads to 14 Rue Jacob...*

## ❽ Richard Wagner's House

Having survived a storm at sea on the way here, the young German composer (1813-1883) spent the gray winter of 1841-1842 in Paris in this building writing *The Flying Dutchman*, an opera about a ghost ship. It was the restless young man's lowest point of poverty. Six months later, a German company staged his first opera *(Rienzi),* plucking him from obscurity and leading to a production of *The Flying Dutchman* that launched his career.

Now the premises are occupied by a hip-looking bar.

• *Backtrack a few steps along Rue Jacob, then turn right and continue south on Rue de Furstemberg to #6, the...*

## ❾ Delacroix Museum

The painter Eugène Delacroix (1798-1863) lived here on this tiny, quiet square. Today, his home is a museum with paintings and memorabilia. It's delightful for his fans, skippable for most, and free with the Museum Pass.

You start in an anteroom with a chronology of his life. An ambassador's son, Delacroix moved to Paris and studied at the Beaux-Arts. By his early 20s, he had exhibited at the Salon. His *Liberty Leading the People* (1831, see page 142) was an instant classic, a symbol of French democracy. Trips to North Africa added exotic Muslim elements to his palette. He hobnobbed with aristocrats and bohemians like George Sand and Frédéric Chopin (whom he painted). He painted large-scale murals for the Louvre, Hôtel de Ville, and Luxembourg Palace.

In 1857, his health failing, Delacroix moved here, seeking a quiet home/studio where he could concentrate on his final great works for the Church of St. Sulpice (which we'll see later).

Next comes the living room, decorated with a few pieces of original furniture, along with portraits and memorabilia. To the left is the bedroom (with fireplace) where Delacroix died in 1863, nursed by his long-time servant, Lucile-Virginie "Jenny" Le Guillou (her portrait is on display). You'll also see a haunting painting of Mary Magdalene, and Delacroix's work table (where he kept his paints). Backtracking, you pass through the library, then go outside and down some stairs to his studio *(atelier)* in the pleasant backyard.

Delacroix built the studio to his own specifications, with high ceilings, big windows, and a skylight, ideal for an artist working prior to electric lights. See his easel and some more paintings, including a small-scale study for *The Death of Sardanapalus,* which hangs in the Louvre. Some of Delacroix's most popular works were book illustrations (lithographs for Goethe's *Faust*, Revolutionary history, and Shakespeare). Admire Delacroix's artistic range—from messy, colorful oils to meticulously detailed lithographs. This room has frequent temporary exhibits.

Finally, in the peaceful backyard, soak up the meditative atmosphere that inspired Delacroix's religious paintings in St. Sulpice.

• *Rue de Furstemberg runs directly into the ❿ Abbey Mansion. This building (1586) was the administrative center for the vast complex of monks gathered around the nearby church of St. Germain-des-Prés.*

*Facing the mansion, turn left on Rue de l'Abbaye and work your way two blocks east to the intersection of Rue de Seine and Rue de Buci. This intersection is, arguably, the geographical (if not spiritual)...*

## ⓫ Heart of the Left Bank

Explore. The Rue de Buci hosts *pâtisseries* and a produce market by day, and bars by night. Mixing earthiness and elegance, your Left Bank is here. A right on Rue de Buci leads to Boulevard St. Germain. A left on Rue de Buci leads to Place St. Michel and the Latin Quarter.

• *Wherever you wander, we'll meet up a block south of here on Boulevard St. Germain. But first, I'm making a several-block detour to find Voltaire's favorite café. Head east (left) on Rue de Buci, which becomes Rue St. André-des-Arts. At #61 Rue St. André-des-Arts, turn right into the covered passageway called Cour du Commerce St. André. Stroll a half-block down this colorful alleyway, past shops and over cobblestones. On your right, you'll pass the back door of. . .*

## ⓬ Café le Procope

Le Procope is just one of many eating options in this pleasant restaurant mall. Founded in 1686, Le Procope is one of the world's oldest continuously operating restaurants, and was one of Europe's first places to sample an exotic new stimulant—coffee—recently imported from the Muslim culture.

In the 1700s, Le Procope caffeinated the Revolution. Voltaire reportedly drank 30 cups a day, fueling his intellectual passion (his favorite table bears his carved initials). Benjamin Franklin recounted old war stories about America's Revolution. Robespierre, Danton, and Marat plotted coups over cups of double-short-two-percent-mochaccinos. And a young lieutenant named Napoleon Bonaparte ran up a tab he never paid.

Located midway between university students, royalty, and the counterculture Comédie Française, Le Procope attracted literary types who loved the free newspapers, writing paper, and quill pens. Today, the one-time coffeehouse is an appealing full-service restaurant (affordable if mediocre *menus*, open daily). If you're interested in a meal surrounded by memorabilia-plastered walls, enter through the main entrance at 13 Rue de l'Ancienne Comédie.

• *Continue on the Cour du Commerce St. André until it spills out onto Boulevard St. Germain at an intersection (and Métro stop) called Odéon.*

## ⑬ Odéon Cinemas

When night falls, Paris' many lovers of film converge here for the latest releases at several multiplexes in the area. Looking south up Rue de l'Odéon, you can see the classical columns of the front of the Théâtre de l'Odéon, the descendant of the original Comédie Française (now housed in the Palais Royal).

• *Walk to the right (west) along busy Boulevard St. Germain for six blocks, passing Café Vagenande (famous for its plush Art Nouveau interior) and other fashionable, noisy cafés with outdoor terraces. You'll reach the large stone church and square of...*

## ⑭ St. Germain-des-Prés

Paris' oldest church, dating from the 11th century (the square bell tower is original), stands on a site where a Christian church has stood since the fall of Rome. (The first church was destroyed by Vikings in the 885-886 siege.)

The restored interior is still painted in the medieval manner, just like Notre-Dame (and others). The church is in the Romanesque style, with round—not pointed—arches over the aisles of the nave.

The square outside is one of Paris' great gathering spots on warm evenings. The church is often lit up and open late. This is where the rich come to see and be seen, and the poor come for a night of free spectacle.

• *Note that Métro stop St. Germain-des-Prés is here, and the Mabillon stop is just a couple of blocks east. On Place St. Germain-des-Prés, you'll find...*

## ⑮ Les Deux Magots Café and Le Café de Flore

Since opening in 1885, "The Two Chinamen Café" (wooden statues inside) has taken over from Le Procope as the café of ideas. From Oscar Wilde's Aestheticism (1900) to Picasso's Cubism (1910s) to Hemingway's spare prose ('20s) to Sartre's Existentialism (with Simone de Beauvoir and Albert Camus, 1930s and '40s) to rock singer Jim Morrison ('60s), worldwide movements have been born in the simple atmosphere of these two cafés. Le Café de Flore, once frequented by Picasso, is more hip, but Deux Magots, next door, is more inviting for just coffee. Across the street is Brasserie Lipp, a classic brasserie where Hemingway wrote much of *A Farewell to Arms* (see also "Les Grands Cafés de Paris," on page 458).

• *From Place St. Germain-des-Prés, cross Boulevard St. Germain and head south on Rue Bonaparte (not Rue de Rennes, from which you can see the Montparnasse Tower skyscraper in the distance). Turn left on busy Rue du Four, then right on...*

## ⑯ Rue des Canettes

Small, midpriced restaurants, boutique shops, and comfortable brewpubs make this neighborhood a pleasant nightspot. It's easy to find a *plat du jour* or a two-course *formule* for under €20 (see restaurant listings on page 450). The recommended Chez Georges (at #11) is the last outpost of funkiness (and how!) in an increasingly gentrified neighborhood.

• *A one-block detour left down Rue Guisarde leads to more restaurants, shops, and pubs, and the* ⑰ *Marché St. Germain shopping mall, a former farmers market where fish and produce have been replaced by the Gap and other chain stores.*

*Continue south on Rue des Canettes to the church of...*

## ⑱ St. Sulpice

The impressive Neoclassical arcaded facade, with two round, half-finished towers, is modeled on St. Paul's in London. It has a remarkable organ and offers Sunday-morning concerts. The lone café on the square in front (Café de la Mairie) is always lively and perfectly located for a break.

Inside, circle the church counterclockwise, making a few stops. In the first chapel on the right, find **Delacroix's three murals** (on the chapel's ceiling and walls) of fighting angels, completed during his final years, while fighting illness. They sum up his long career, from Renaissance/Baroque roots to furious Romanticism to proto-Impressionism.

The most famous is the agitated *Jacob Wrestling the Angel*. The two grapple (or are they dancing?) in a leafy wood that echoes the wrestlers' rippling energy. Jacob fights the angel to a standstill, bringing him a well-earned blessing for his ordeal. The shepherd Laban and his daughter Rachel (Jacob's future wife) hover in the background. Get close and notice the thick brushwork that influenced the next generation of Impressionists—each leaf is a single brushstroke, often smudging two different colors in a single stroke. The "black" pile of clothes in the foreground is built from rough strokes of purple, green, and white. (Too much glare? Take a couple of steps to the right to view it. Also, there are three light buttons nearby.)

On the opposite wall, *Heliodorus Chased from the Temple* has the smooth, seamless brushwork of Delacroix's prime. The Syrian Heliodorus has killed the king, launched a coup, and has now entered the sacred Jewish Temple in Jerusalem trying to steal the treasure. Angry angels launch themselves at him, sending him sprawling. The vibrant, clashing colors, swirling composition, and over-the-top subject are trademark Delacroix Romanticism. On the ceiling, *The Archangel Michael* drives demons from heaven.

Notice the **unmarked door** at the foot of the three steps leading to Delacroix's chapel. On Sundays, just after noon, this door opens, and you can go upstairs to the organ loft to hear music played for the Mass (see page 73 for details).

Walking up the right side of the church, pause at the **fourth chapel,** with a statue of Joan of Arc and wall plaques listing hundreds upon hundreds of names. These are France's WWI dead—from this congregation alone. In the chapel at the end of the church, ponder the cryptic symbolism of Mary and Child lit by a sunburst, standing on an orb, and trampling a snake, while a stone cloud tumbles down to a sacrificial lamb.

Continue around the church. On the wall of the north transept is an Egyptian-style obelisk used as a **gnomon,** or part of a sundial. At Christmas Mass, the sun shines into the church through a tiny hole—it's opposite the obelisk, high up on the south wall (in the upper-right window pane). The sunbeam strikes a mark on the obelisk that indicates the winter solstice. Then, week by week, the sunbeam moves down the obelisk and across the bronze rod in the floor, until, at midsummer, the sun lights up the area near the altar.

In the final chapel before the exit, you may see a display on the **Shroud of Turin.** This burial cloth (which is in Turin, Italy) is purported to have wrapped the body of Christ, who left it with a mysterious, holy stain in his image.

• *Back out on Place St. Sulpice, take note that several interesting shopping streets branch off from here. You could see them now, or backtrack here after the Left Bank Walk is done. (The "Sèvres–Babylone to St. Sulpice" boutique stroll is on page 478.)*

*To complete the Left Bank Walk, turn left out of the church and continue south on Rue Henry de Jouvenel (soon turning into Rue Férou), which leads directly to Luxembourg Garden. On Rue Férou, you'll pass a wall inscribed with a quotation from one of France's most famous poems, "Le Bateau Ivre," by Arthur Rimbaud (1854-1891). He describes the feeling of drifting along aimlessly, like a drunken boat:* "Comme je descendais...As I floated down calm rivers, I could no longer feel the control of my handlers..."

*Drift along to Luxembourg Garden. If the gate ahead of you is closed, circle to the right around the fence until you find an open entrance.*

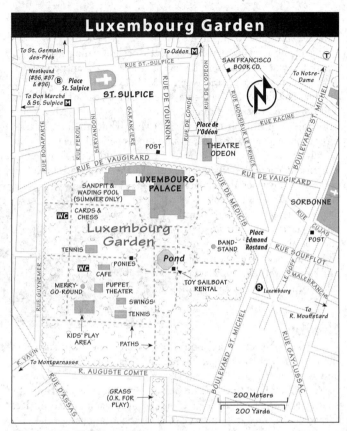

# Luxembourg Garden

To St. Germain-
des-Prés

To Odéon Ⓜ

RUE ST.-SULPICE

SAN FRANCISCO
BOOK CO.

Westbound
(#86, #87
& #96) Ⓑ Place
St. Sulpice

To Bon Marché
& St. Sulpice Ⓜ

**ST. SULPICE**

RUE DE TOURNON

RUE DE L'ODÉON

RUE DE CONDÉ

RUE MONSIEUR LE PRINCE

To Notre-
Dame

GARANCIÈRE

RUE FÉROU

RUE BONAPARTE

RUE SERVANDONI

RUE RACINE

BOULEVARD ST. MICHEL

Place de
l'Odéon

POST

THEATRE
ODEON

RUE DE VAUGIRARD

RUE DE VAUGIRARD

**LUXEMBOURG
PALACE**

SANDPIT &
WADING POOL
(SUMMER ONLY)

SORBONNE

WC CARDS &
CHESS

RUE DE MÉDICIS

RUE CUJAS

Luxembourg
Garden

BAND-
STAND

Place
Edmond
Rostand

POST

TENNIS

Pond

RUE SOUFFLOT

RUE GUYNEMER

WC

PONIES

CAFE

LE GOFF

RUE MALEBRANCHE

MERRY-
GO-ROUND

PUPPET
THEATER

TOY SAILBOAT
RENTAL

Ⓡ Luxembourg

SWINGS

To
R. Mouffetard

TENNIS

RUE GAY-LUSSAC

KIDS' PLAY
AREA

PATHS

R. YAVIN

To Montparnasse

BOULEVARD ST. MICHEL

RUE D'ASSAS

R. AUGUSTE COMTE

GRASS
(O.K. FOR
PLAY)

200 Meters

200 Yards

## ⑲ Luxembourg Garden

Paris' most beautiful, interesting, and enjoyable garden/park/recreational area, le Jardin du Luxembourg, is a great place to watch Parisians at rest and play. This 60-acre garden, dotted with fountains and statues, is the property of the French Senate, which meets here in the Luxembourg Palace. Although it seems like something out of *The Da Vinci Code*, it's a fact that France's secret service *(Générale de la Sécurité Extérieure)* is "secretly" headquartered beneath Luxembourg Garden.

The palace was created in 1615 by Marie de Médici. Recently widowed (by Henry IV) and homesick for Florence, she built the palace as a re-creation of her girlhood home, the Pitti Palace.

When her son grew to be Louis XIII, he drove his mother from the palace, exiling her to Germany.

Luxembourg Garden has special rules governing its use (for example, where cards can be played, where dogs can be walked, where joggers can run, and when and where music can be played). The brilliant flower beds are completely changed three times a year, and the boxed trees are brought out of the *orangerie* in May. Children enjoy the rentable toy sailboats. (Meanwhile, the French CIA plots espionage in their underground offices beneath the park.) The park hosts marionette shows several times weekly (*Les Guignols*, or Punch and Judy; described more fully in the Paris with Children chapter). Pony rides are available from April through October.

Challenge the card and chess players to a game (near the tennis courts), or find a free chair near the main pond and take a well-deserved break, here at the end of our Left Bank Walk.

## Nearby

The grand Neoclassical-domed Panthéon, now a mausoleum housing the tombs of great French notables, is three blocks away and worth touring (see page 74). The historic cafés of Montparnasse—**㉀ La Coupole** and **Le Select**—are a few blocks from the southwest-corner exit of the park (down Rue Vavin, listed in "Les Grands Cafés de Paris" on page 458; for the locations, see the map on page 452).

• *Getting home: The Luxembourg Garden is ringed with Métro stops (all a 10-minute walk away). North of the garden, the two closest Métro stops are St. Sulpice and Odéon. A convenient RER stop (Luxembourg) is at the park's east entry.*

LEFT BANK WALK

# CLUNY MUSEUM TOUR

*Musée National du Moyen Age*

The National Museum of the Middle Ages doesn't sound quite so boring as I sink deeper into middle age myself. Aside from the solemn religious art, there is some lively stuff here.

Paris emerged on the world stage in the Middle Ages, the time between ancient Rome and the Renaissance. Europe was awakening from a thousand-year slumber. Trade was booming, people actually owned chairs, and the Renaissance was moving in like a warm front from Italy.

## Orientation

**Cost:** €8, free on first Sun of the month, covered by Museum Pass.

**Hours:** Wed-Mon 9:15-17:45, closed Tue, ticket office closes at 17:15.

**Getting There:** The museum, a five-minute walk from Ile de la Cité, is a block above the intersection of Boulevard St. Germain and Boulevard St. Michel, at 6 Place Paul Painlevé (Mo: Cluny-La Sorbonne, St. Michel, or Odéon; bus #63 from Rue Cler or #86 from the Marais).

**Information:** The helpful audioguide is included with admission, though Museum Pass holders must pay €1. Pick up the free, handy museum map and look for the explanations in English in many rooms. Tel. 01 53 73 78 16, www.musee-moyenage.fr.

**Length of This Tour:** Allow one hour for my self-guided tour of the museum's highlights, but there's much more to the underrated Cluny. You'll find medieval altarpieces, weaponry, eighth-century Visigothic crowns, a wonderful chapel with an elaborate stone ceiling, and a medieval garden. The audioguide lets you key in more exhibits.

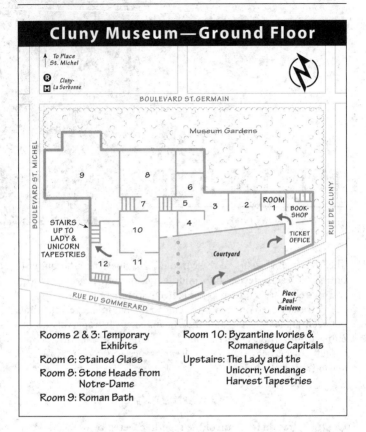

# Cluny Museum—Ground Floor

To Place St. Michel

ⓡ Cluny-
Ⓜ La Sorbonne

BOULEVARD ST. GERMAIN

Museum Gardens

BOULEVARD ST. MICHEL

9   8   6

7   5   3   2   ROOM 1   BOOK-SHOP

4   TICKET OFFICE

STAIRS UP TO LADY & UNICORN TAPESTRIES

10

12   11   Courtyard

RUE DE CLUNY

RUE DU SOMMERARD

Place Paul-Painleve

Rooms 2 & 3: Temporary Exhibits
Room 6: Stained Glass
Room 8: Stone Heads from Notre-Dame
Room 9: Roman Bath

Room 10: Byzantine Ivories & Romanesque Capitals
Upstairs: The Lady and the Unicorn; Vendange Harvest Tapestries

**With Limited Time:** The must-sees are the Roman Bath and the Lady and the Unicorn tapestries.

**Baggage Check:** Required for bags larger than a purse, and free.

**Photography:** OK without flash.

**Cuisine Art:** Just a few blocks away, the charming Place de la Sorbonne has several good cafés (see page 454; walk up Boulevard St. Michel toward the Panthéon).

# The Tour Begins

• *Our official tour begins in room 6, with medieval stained glass. But take a moment to enjoy the first few rooms, which are usually reserved for temporary exhibits related to the theme of medieval life.*

## Rooms 2 and 3: Temporary Exhibits

The museum may surprise you with its lack of grim, gray crucifixions and other symbols associated with medieval times. The Cluny feels more like a celebration of life in the Middle Ages. Among the

temporary displays (they change often), you may find joyfully elegant tapestries, golden altarpieces, and statues with a budding realism. Colorful woven fabrics were brought back to France by Crusaders, who went off to conquer barbarian infidels but returned with tales of enlightened peoples on the fringes of Europe.

Not every work of art in the later medieval period was centered on religious themes. Having survived their Y1K crisis, these people realized the world wasn't about to end, and they turned their attention to the beauty of their surroundings.

*• After the two rooms of temporary exhibits, you enter a small hall. Turn right into a little, dark room full of luminous stained glass.*

## Room 6: Stained Glass

Enter the Dark Ages, when life was harsh and brutal, angels and demons made regular appearances, and the Church was your only refuge. This room offers a rare close-up look at stained glass, which gave poor people a glimpse of the glories of heaven. These panels (many from the basilica of light, Sainte-Chapelle) give us a window into the magical, supernatural, miraculous—and often violent—medieval mind.

Read clockwise around the room, all at eye level (the bottom): 1) The angel Gabriel blasts his horn on Resurrection morning, rousting the grateful dead from their coffins. Notice that Gabriel's royal robe is made up of several different pieces of glass—purples, whites, blues—held together with lead. 2) Naked Christ is baptized in the squiggly River Jordan. 3) A red-faced, horned, horny demon, accompanied by an equally lascivious wolf and henchman, carries off a frightened girl in red on a date from hell. 4) Blond, pious Joseph is sold into slavery to camel merchants by his plotting brothers.

Next wall: 5) Samson is about to pull down the temple.... 6) Then he has his eyes gouged out by Philistines. 7) Slaughter on the battlefield. Men with bloodstained hands and faces hack at each

other with golden swords. 8) Aaron, disobeying God and Moses, worships a golden calf. 9) A king on a throne closes his eyes to all this wickedness.

Next wall (with some panels from the first Gothic church, St. Denis): 10) Two monks with prayer books gaze up, as one of their brothers disappears into heaven. The Latin inscription "*hec est via*" means "This is the way." 11) Seated Jesus, in a royal purple robe, is consoled by two angels. 12) Theophilus ("Lover of God") has struck a Faustian deal—shaking hands with the red-faced devil, yet feeling buyer's remorse. 13) Sleeping St. Martin is visited by a heavenly vision. 14) Angels in Rock-and-Roll Heaven.

Last wall: Four apostles—John (Ioannes), James (with his scallop shell), Paul, and Peter (Petrus, with key).

• *Before leaving, turn around and take in all the narrative medieval glass.*

## Room 8: Stone Heads from Notre-Dame

This room has occasional exhibits, as well as the permanent displays, so be prepared to search for the objects described.

The 21 stone heads (sculpted 1220-1230) of the Biblical kings of Judah once decorated the front of Notre-Dame. In 1793, an angry mob of Revolutionaries mistook the kings of Judah for the kings of France and abused and decapitated the statues. (Today's heads on the Notre-Dame statues are reconstructions.) Someone gathered up the heads and buried them in his backyard near the present-day Opéra Garnier. There they slept for two centuries, unknown and noseless, until 1977, when some diggers accidentally unearthed them and brought them to an astounded world. Their stoic expressions accept what fate, time, and liberals have done to them.

The statue of Adam (nearby) is also from Notre-Dame. He's scrawny and flaccid by Renaissance standards. And it will be another 200 years before naked Adam can step out from behind that bush.

## Room 9: Roman Bath

This echoing cavern was a Roman *frigidarium*. Pretty cool. The museum is located on the site of a Roman bathhouse, which was in the center of town during the Roman years. After hot baths and exercise in adjoining rooms, ordinary Romans would take a cold dip in the sunken pool (in the alcove), then relax cheek to cheek with such notables as Emperor Julian the Apostate (see his statue), who lived next door. As the empire decayed in the fourth century, Julian avoided the corrupt city of Rome and made Paris a northern power base.

The 40-foot-high ceiling is the largest Roman vault in France, and it took the French another 1,000 years to improve on that crisscross-arch technology. The sheer size of this room—constructed in A.D. 200, when Rome was at its peak—gives an idea of the epic scale on which the Romans built. It inspired Europeans to greatness during the less civilized Middle Ages.

The four square column fragments *(Le Pilier des Nautes)* are the oldest man-made objects you'll see from Paris. These pillars once fit together to support a 20-foot-high altar to the king of the gods in the Temple of Jupiter, where Notre-Dame now stands. The fragment labeled *Pierre de la dedicace* is inscribed "TIB. CAESARE," announcing that the altar was built in the time of the Emperor Tiberius (A.D. 14-37), and was paid for by the Parisian boatmen's union (see them holding their shields). On the column labeled *Pierre aux quatre divinites*, find the horned Celtic god Cernunnos, who is also known as the Stag Lord and god of the hunt. The eclectic Romans allowed this local "druid" god to support the shrine of Jupiter, in league with their own Vulcan, who hammers, and Castor and Pollux, who pet their horses.

### Room 10: Byzantine Ivories and Romanesque Capitals

Rome lived on after the fall of the empire. The finely carved Byzantine ivories (first glass case) show how pagan gods, emperors, and griffins became Christian saints, gargoyles, and icons. Constantinople—the eastern half of the empire that survived the fall—preserved Roman tastes and imagery. In painting, Byzantine gold-background icons inspired medieval altarpieces. Study the exquisite detail. (Adam and Eve, in the tiny double panel, are not really "sword fighting.")

Rome also lived on in the "Roman"-esque grandeur of Christian churches such as St. Germain-des-Prés (see the 12 column

capitals). In the central capital, Christ sits in robes on a throne, ruling the world like a Roman emperor. These capitals were originally painted, much like the painted wooden statues across the room.
• *Continue to room 12, which leads upstairs to...*

## Room 13: The Lady and the Unicorn Tapestries

As Europeans emerged from the Dark Ages, they rediscovered the beauty of the world around them.

These six mysterious tapestries were designed by an unknown (but probably French) artist before A.D. 1500 and were woven in Belgium out of wool and silk. Loaded with symbols—some serious, some playful—they have been interpreted many ways, but, in short, the series deals with each of the five senses (handheld English explanations that you can pick up from slots hanging on the wall add more detail).

In medieval lore, unicorns were enigmatic, solitary creatures that could only be tamed by a virgin. In secular society, they symbolized how a feral man was drawn to his lady love. Religiously, the unicorn was a symbol of Christ—radiant, pure, and somewhat remote—who is made accessible to humankind by the Virgin Mary. These tapestries likely draw inspiration from all these traditions.
• *Moving clockwise around the room...*

**Taste:** A blond lady takes candy from a servant's dish to feed it to her parakeet. A unicorn and a lion look on. At the lady's feet, a monkey also tastes something, while the little white dog behind her wishes he had some. This was the dawn of the Age of Discovery, when overseas explorers spiced up Europe's bland gruel with new fruits, herbs, and spices.

The lion (symbol of knighthood?) and unicorn (symbol of "bourgeois nobility," purity, or fertility?) wave flags with the coat of arms of the family that commissioned the tapestries—three silver crescents in a band of blue.

**Hearing:** Wearing a stunning dress, the lady plays sweet music on an organ, which soothes the savage beasts around her. The pattern and folds of the tablecloth are lovely. Humans and their fellow creatures live in harmony in an enchanted blue garden filled with flowers, all set in a red background.

**Sight:** The unicorn cuddles up and looks at himself in the lady's mirror, pleased with what he sees. The lion turns away and snickers. As the Renaissance dawns, vanity is a less-than-deadly sin.

Admire the great artistic skill in some of the detail work, such as the necklace and the patterns in her dress. This tapestry had quality control in all its stages: the drawing of the scene, its enlargement and transfer to a cartoon, and the weaving. Still, the design itself is crude by Renaissance 3-D standards. The fox and rabbits, supposedly in the distance, simply float overhead, as big as the animals at the lady's feet.

**Smell:** The lady picks flowers and weaves them into a sweet-smelling wreath. On a bench behind, the monkey apes her. The flowers, trees, and animals are exotic and varied. Each detail is exquisite alone, but if you step back they blend together into pleasing patterns.

**Touch:** This is the most basic and dangerous of the senses. The lady "strokes the unicorn's horn," if you know what I mean, and the lion gets the double entendre. Unicorns, a species extinct since the Age of Reason, were so wild that only virgins could entice and tame them. Medieval Europeans were exploring the wonders of love and the pleasures of sex.

**Tapestry #6:** The most talked-about tapestry gets its name from the words on our lady's tent: *A Mon Seul Désir* (To My Sole Desire). What *is* her only desire? Is it jewelry, as she grabs a necklace from the jewel box? Or is she putting the necklace away and renouncing material things in order to follow her only desire?

Our lady has tried all things sensual and is now prepared to follow the one true impulse. Is it God? Love? Her friends the unicorn and lion open the tent doors. Flickering flames cover the tent. Perhaps she's stepping out from the tent. Or is she going in to meet the object of her desire? Human sensuality is awakening, an old dark age is ending, and the Renaissance is emerging.

## The Rest of the Cluny

There's much more to this fine museum here on the upper floor. From the unicorn tapestries, continue on. In room 19, pay your respects to the **tusk of a narwhal** (in a tall glass case in the corner), which must have convinced superstitious folk to believe in unicorns. In room 22, the large **Vendange Harvest Tapestry** shows grape-stomping peasants during the *vendange,* the annual autumn harvest and wine celebration. A peasant man treads grapes in a vat, while his wife collects the juice. A wealthy man gives orders. Above that, a peasant with a big wart turns a newfangled mechanical press. On the right, you'll see the joy of picking—pawns, knights, and queens all working side by side.

• *Finally, you'll pass one more room displaying medieval shields and helmets before leaving the Middle Ages and returning to your modern, fast-paced lives....*

# CHAMPS-ELYSEES WALK

*From the Arc de Triomphe to
Place de la Concorde*

Don't leave Paris without a stroll along Avenue des Champs-Elysées (shahnz ay-lee-zay). This is Paris at its most Parisian: monumental sidewalks, stylish shops, elegant cafés, glimmering showrooms, and proud Parisians on parade. It's a great walk by day, and even better at night, allowing you to tap into the city's increasingly global scene.

## Orientation

**Length of This Walk:** This two-mile walk takes three hours, including a one-hour visit to the Arc de Triomphe. Métro stops are located every few blocks along the Champs-Elysées.

**With Limited Time:** End the walk at Rond-Point (Mo: FDR).

**Getting There:** To reach the Arc de Triomphe at Place Charles de Gaulle, take the Métro to Charles de Gaulle-Etoile. Then follow the *Sortie #1, Champs-Elysées/Arc de Triomphe* signs. From Rue Cler and the Montparnasse area, bus #92 works best.

**Arc de Triomphe:** Outside and at the base—free and always viewable; steps to rooftop—€9.50, under 18 free, free on first Sun of month Oct-March, covered by Museum Pass; daily April-Sept 10:00-23:00, Oct-March 10:00-22:30, last entry 30 minutes before closing. Bypass the slooow ticket line with your Museum Pass (though if you have kids, you'll need to line up to get the free tickets for children). There may be another line (that you can't skip) at the entrance to the stairway up the arch. The elevator, only for people with disabilities, runs to the museum level, but not to the top, which requires a 40-step climb. Lines disappear after 17:00—come for sunset.

**Grand Palais:** Major exhibitions usually €11, not covered by

# Champs-Elysées Walk

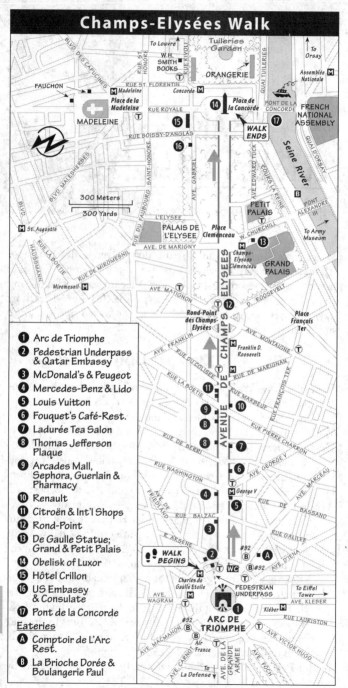

1 Arc de Triomphe
2 Pedestrian Underpass & Qatar Embassy
3 McDonald's & Peugeot
4 Mercedes-Benz & Lido
5 Louis Vuitton
6 Fouquet's Café-Rest.
7 Ladurée Tea Salon
8 Thomas Jefferson Plaque
9 Arcades Mall, Sephora, Guerlain & Pharmacy
10 Renault
11 Citroën & Int'l Shops
12 Rond-Point
13 De Gaulle Statue; Grand & Petit Palais
14 Obelisk of Luxor
15 Hôtel Crillon
16 US Embassy & Consulate
17 Pont de la Concorde

**Eateries**

A Comptoir de L'Arc Rest.
B La Brioche Dorée & Boulangerie Paul

CHAMPS-ELYSEES WALK

Museum Pass, generally open daily 10:00-20:00, Wed 10:00-22:00, closed between exhibitions.

**Petit Palais:** Free, Tue-Sun 10:00-18:00, Thu until 20:00 for temporary exhibitions, closed Mon.

**Services:** A small WC is inside the Arc de Triomphe, near the top, but it's often crowded. The Petit Palais has a nice WC with no lines, and the Tuileries Garden, at the end of the walk, also has a public WC. Most restaurants (McDonald's, etc.) and bigger stores along the route have WCs as well.

**Cuisine Art:** See "Eating near the Champs-Elysées" (page 290).

**Starring:** Grand boulevards, grander shops, and grandiose monuments.

## The Walk Begins

Start at the Arc de Triomphe at the top of the Champs-Elysées (on the right side as you look at the Arc). Take the underground pedestrian walkway in front of you to the arch. (Don't try to cross in the traffic—there are no crosswalks on the roundabout.) It's worthwhile to get to the base of the arch even if you don't climb it. There's no cost to wander around (and no lines).

• *Cross through the tunnel, take the first left up a few steps, where you'll find the ticket booth (with a Museum Pass, skip the line). Then walk up to the arch.*

## The Arc de Triomphe
### Exterior

Construction of the 165-foot-high arch began in 1809 to honor Napoleon's soldiers, who, despite being vastly outnumbered by the Austrians, scored a remarkable victory at the Battle of Austerlitz. Patterned after the ceremonial arches of ancient Roman conquerors (but more than twice the size), it celebrates Napoleon as emperor of a "New Rome." On the arch's massive left pillar, a relief sculpture shows a toga-clad Napoleon posing confidently, while an awestruck Paris—crowned by her city walls—kneels at his imperial feet. Napoleon died before the Arc's completion, but it was

## Eating near the Champs-Elysées

Good eating options on the Champs-Elysées are slim. Most sit-down restaurants have lazy service, mediocre food, and inflated prices. For a better value, try one of these places:

**Comptoir de L'Arc,** a block from the Arc toward the Eiffel Tower, is a bustling place dishing out good €10-12 and *plats du jour* to locals just beyond the tourist flow (Mon-Fri 7:00-24:00, closed Sat-Sun, 73 Avenue Marceau, tel. 01 47 20 72 04).

**La Brioche Dorée** and **Boulangerie Paul** sit side by side smack on the Champs-Elysées, each offering great Champsside tables and good sandwiches and salads for €5-9. Both are located halfway along this walk at #82. Dorée has WCs, air-conditioning, and extra seating upstairs (plus a second location closer to the Arc, at #144, near McDonald's)—Paul doesn't.

finished in time for his 1840 funeral procession to pass underneath, carrying his remains (19 years dead) from exile in St. Helena to Paris.

On the right pillar is the Arc's most famous relief, *La Marseillaise* (*Le Départ des Volontaires de 1792*, by François Rude, pictured on previous page). Lady Liberty—looking like an ugly reincarnation of Joan of Arc—screams, "Freedom is this way!" and points the direction with a sword. The soldiers below her are tired, naked, and stumbling, but she rallies them to carry on the fight against oppression.

Today, the Arc de Triomphe is dedicated to the glory of all French armies. Walk to its center and stand directly beneath it on the faded eagle. You're surrounded by the lists of French victories since the Revolution—19th century on the arch, 20th century in the pavement. On the columns you'll see lists of generals (with a line under the names of those who died in battle). Find the nearby Tomb of the Unknown Soldier (from World War I). Every day at 18:30 since just after World War I, the flame has been rekindled and new flowers set in place.

Like its Roman ancestors, this arch has served as a parade gateway for triumphal armies (French or foe) and important ceremonies. From 1940 to 1944, a large swastika flew from here as Nazis goose-stepped down the Champs-Elysées. In August 1944

General Charles de Gaulle led Allied troops under this arch as they celebrated liberation. Today, national parades start and end here with one minute of silence.

## Interior and View from the Top

Ascend the Arc de Triomphe via the 284 steps inside the north pillar. Catch your breath two-thirds of the way up in the small exhibition area (WC also on this mezzanine level). It generally hosts exhibits about the arch and its founder, Napoleon.

From the top you have an eye-popping view of *tout Paris*. You're gazing at the home of 11 million people, all crammed into an area the size of an average city in the US (the city center has 2,234,000 residents and covers 40 square miles). Paris has the highest density of any city in Europe, about 20 times greater than that of New York City.

**Looking East:** Look down the Champs-Elysées to the Tuileries Garden and the Louvre. Scan the cityscape of downtown Paris. That lonely hill to the left is Montmartre, topped by the white dome of Sacré-Cœur; until 1860, this hill town was a separate city. To the right, find the blue top of the modern Pompidou Center, then the distant twin towers of Notre-Dame, the dome of the Panthéon breaking the horizon, a block of small skyscrapers on a hill (the Quartier d'Italie), and the golden dome of Les Invalides. Now find the lonely-looking Montparnasse Tower, standing like the box the Eiffel Tower came in; in the early 1970s, it served as a wake-up call to city planners that they needed to preserve building height restrictions and strengthen urban design standards. Aside from the Montparnasse Tower, notice the symmetry. Each corner building surrounding the arch is part of an elegant grand scheme. The beauty of Paris—basically a flat basin with a river running through it—is man-made. There's a harmonious relationship between the width of its grand boulevards and the standard height and design of the buildings.

**Looking West:** Cross the arch and look to the west. In the distance, the huge, white, rectangular Grande Arche de la Défense, standing amid skyscrapers, is the final piece of a grand city axis—from the Louvre, up the Champs-Elysées to the Arc de Triomphe, continuing on to a forest of skyscrapers at La Défense, three miles away. Former French president François Mitterrand had the Grande Arche built as a centerpiece of this mini-Manhattan. Notice the contrast between the skyscrapers of La Défense and the more uniform heights of the buildings closer to the Arc de Triomphe. Below you, the wide boulevard lined with grass and trees angling to your left is Avenue Foch (named after the WWI hero), which ends at the huge Bois de Boulogne park. Avenue Foch is the best address to have in Paris. Nicknamed the "Avenue of Millionaires," it was home to the Shah of Iran and Aristotle Onassis. Today many fabulously rich Arabs call it home. And though Parisians pride themselves on being discreet, some not-so-discreet Homes-of-the-Stars-type tours are offered here.

The Etoile: Gaze down at what appears to be a chaotic traffic mess. The 12 boulevards that radiate from the Arc de Triomphe (forming an *étoile*, star) were part of Baron Haussmann's master plan for Paris: the creation of a series of major boulevards intersecting at diagonals, with monuments (such as the Arc de Triomphe) as centerpieces of those intersections (see sidebar on page 82). Haussmann's plan did not anticipate the automobile—obvious when you watch the traffic scene below. But see how smoothly it functions. Cars entering the circle have the right of way (the only roundabout in France with this rule); those in the circle must yield. Still, there are plenty of accidents, many caused by tourists oblivious to the rules. Tired of disputes, insurance companies split the fault and damages of any Arc de Triomphe accident 50/50. The trick is to make a parabola—get to the center ASAP, and then begin working your way out two avenues before you want to exit.

• *We'll start our stroll down the Champs-Elysées at the Charles de Gaulle-Etoile Métro stop, on the north (sunnier) side of the street where the tunnel deposits you. Look straight down the Champs-Elysées to the Tuileries Garden at the far end.*

## The Champs-Elysées

You're at the top of one of the world's grandest and most celebrated streets, home to big business, celebrity cafés, glitzy nightclubs, high-fashion shopping, and international people-watching. People gather here to celebrate Bastille Day (July 14), World Cup triumphs, the finale of the Tour de France (see sidebar later in the chapter), and the ends of wars.

In 1667, Louis XIV opened the first section of the street as a short extension of the Tuileries Garden. This year is considered the birth of Paris as a grand city. The Champs-Elysées soon became *the* place to cruise in your carriage. (It still is today; traffic can be gridlocked even at midnight.) One hundred years later, the café scene arrived. From the 1920s until the 1960s, this boulevard was pure elegance; Parisians actually dressed up to come here. It was mainly residences, rich hotels, and cafés. Then, in 1963, the government pumped up the neighborhood's commercial metabolism by bringing in the RER (commuter train). Suburbanites had easy access, and *pfft*—there went the neighborhood.

• *Start your descent, pausing at the first tiny street you cross, Rue de Tilsitt. This street is part of a shadow ring road—an option for drivers who'd like to avoid the chaos of the Arc—complete with stoplights.*

A few steps down Rue de Tilsitt is a building now housing the **Qatar Embassy.** It's one of the few survivors of a dozen uniformly U-shaped buildings from Haussmann's original 1853 grand design. Peek into the foyer for a glimpse of 19th-century Champs-Elysées classiness.

Back on the main drag, look across to the other side of the Champs-Elysées at the big, gray, concrete-and-glass "Publicis" building. Ugh. In the 1960s, venerable old buildings (similar to the Qatar Embassy building) were leveled to make way for new commercial operations like Publicis. Then, in 1985, a law prohibited the demolition of the old building fronts that gave the boulevard a uniform grace. Today, many modern businesses hide behind preserved facades. Consider dashing to the center of the Champs for a great Arc view (from a crosswalk, of course), then come back. Stroll another block while marveling at the people-watching scene.

The *nouveau* Champs-Elysées, revitalized in 1994, has new benches and lamps, broader sidewalks, all-underground parking, and a fleet of green-suited workers who drive motorized street cleaners. Blink away the modern elements, and it's not hard to imagine the boulevard pre-1963, with only the finest structures lining both sides all the way to the palace gardens.

## McDonald's

The arrival of McDonald's—a hundred yards farther down on the left at #140—was a shock to the boulevard. At first it was allowed to have only white arches painted on the window. Today, it spills out legally onto the sidewalk—provided it offers café-quality chairs and flower boxes—and dining at *chez MacDo* has become typically Parisian. France has a thousand McDonald's, and the Champs-Elysées branch is the most profitable one in the world.

A €4.50 Big Mac here buys an hour of people-watching. (The WC inside has quarter-pounder lines.) Notice how many of the happy clients are French. The popularity of *le fast-food* in Paris is a sign that life is changing, and that the era of two-hour lunches is over. The French must now compete in a global world, and if that means adopting a more American lifestyle, *c'est la vie.*

## Glitz

Fancy car dealerships include **Peugeot,**
at #136 (showing off its futuristic concept
cars, often alongside the classic models),
and **Mercedes-Benz,** a block down at
#118, where you can pick up a Mercedes
watch and cufflinks to go with your new
car. In the 19th century this was an area
for horse stables; today, it's the district of
garages, limo companies, and car dealerships. If you're serious about selling cars in
France, you must have a showroom on the
Champs-Elysées.

Next to Mercedes is the famous
**Lido,** Paris' largest cabaret (and a multiplex cinema). You can walk
all the way into the lobby. Paris still offers the kind of burlesque-
type spectacles that have been performed here since the 19th century, combining music, comedy, and scantily clad women. Movie-
going on the Champs-Elysées provides another kind of fun, with
theaters showing the very latest releases. Check to see if there are
films you recognize, then look for the showings *(séances).* A "v.o."
*(version originale)* next to the time indicates the film will be shown
in its original language; a "v.f." stands for *version française.*

• *Now cross the boulevard from in front of the Mercedes showroom. Look
up at the Arc de Triomphe, its rooftop bristling with tourists. Notice
the variety of architecture along this street—old and elegant, new, and
new-behind-old-facades. The white spire you see down Avenue Georges
V is the American Cathedral. Continue to #101.*

## Louis Vuitton

The flagship store of this famous producer of leather bags may be
the largest single-brand luxury store in the world. Step inside. The
store insists on providing enough salespeople to treat each customer
royally—if there's a line, it means shoppers have overwhelmed the
place. The vintage suitcase/trunks hanging all around (there are
101 of them, since the address is 101 Champs-Elysées) were Vuitton's claim to fame back in 1854. That's when he came up with
this flat, hard-sided, stackable alternative to the standard, rounded
trunks of an earlier age. If you need clothing and shoes to put in
your fancy new bag, head upstairs.

• *Across the street is a Paris institution.*

## Café Culture

**Fouquet's** café-restaurant (#99), under the red awning, is a popular spot among French celebrities, serving the most expensive shot
of espresso I've found in downtown Paris (€8). Opened in 1899

as a coachman's bistro, Fouquet's gained fame as the hangout of France's WWI biplane fighter pilots—those who weren't shot down by Germany's infamous "Red Baron." It also served as James Joyce's dining room.

Since the early 1900s, Fouquet's has been a favorite of French actors and actresses. The golden plaques at the entrance honor winners of France's Oscar-like film awards, the Césars (one is cut into the ground at the end of the carpet). There are plaques for Gérard Depardieu, Catherine Deneuve, Roman Polanski, Juliette Binoche, and several famous Americans (but not Jerry Lewis). More recent winners are shown on the floor just inside.

The hushed interior is at once classy and intimidating—and also a grand experience...if you dare (to say "I'm just looking" in French, say *"Je regarde"*—zhuh ruh-gard). The outdoor setting is more relaxed. Once threatened with foreign purchase and eventual destruction, Fouquet's was spared that fate when the government declared it a historic monument. For his election-night victory party in 2007, the flamboyant ex-President Sarkozy celebrated at Fouquet's, along with France's glitterati—including the "French Elvis," Johnny Hallyday.

**Ladurée** (two blocks downhill at #75) is a classic 19th-century tea salon/restaurant/*pâtisserie*. Non-patrons can discreetly wander around the place, though photos are not allowed. A coffee here is *très élégant* (only €3.50). The bakery sells traditional *macarons*, cute little cakes, and gift-wrapped finger sandwiches to go (your choice of four mini-*macarons* for €7.50).

• *Cross back to the lively (north) side of the street.*

At #92 (a bit uphill), a wall plaque marks the place **Thomas Jefferson** lived (with his 14-year-old slave, Sally Hemings) while serving as minister to France (1785-1789). He replaced the popular Benjamin Franklin but quickly made his own mark, extolling the virtues of America's Revolution to a country approaching its own.

You'll soon pass two good-value lunch options, **La Brioche Dorée** and **Boulangerie Paul** (see the sidebar near the beginning of this chapter).

## French Shopping

Stroll into the **Arcades des Champs-Elysées** mall at #76 (not the unappealing Galerie des Champs). With its fancy lamps, mosaic floors, glass skylight, and classical columns (try to ignore the Starbucks), it captures faint echoes of the *années folles*—the "crazy years," as the roaring '20s were called in France. Architecture buffs can observe how flowery Art Nouveau became simpler, more geometric Art Deco. Down the street at #74, the Galerie du Claridge building sports an old facade. Its ironwork awning, balconies, *putti*, and sculpted fantasy faces disguise an otherwise new building. One of the current tenants is FNAC, a large French chain that sells electronics, CDs, and concert tickets. They also sell tickets to key sights in and around Paris (including the Arc de Triomphe, Opéra Garnier, Versailles, and Monet's gardens in Giverny)—the time saved may be worth their surcharge (10-20 percent).

For a noisy and fragrant commercial carnival of perfumes, and a chance to sense the French passion for cosmetics, take your nose sightseeing at #72 and glide down the ramp of the largest **Sephora** in France. Grab a disposable white strip from a lovely clerk, spritz it with a sample, and sniff. The entry hall is lined with new products. In the main showroom, women's perfumes line the right wall and men's line the left—organized alphabetically by company, from Armani to Versace.

While Sephora seems to be going all out to attract the general public, two venerable **Guerlain** perfume shops sit side by side next door, showing off a dash of the Champs-Elysées' old gold-leaf elegance. Notice the 1914 details. Climb upstairs (in the second shop). It's *très* French. If Sephora is a mosh-pit for your nose, Guerlain is a harem.

At the intersection with Rue la Boëtie, the English-speaking **pharmacy** is open until midnight.

Car buffs should detour across the Champs and park themselves at the sleek bar in the **Renault** store (open until midnight). The car exhibits change regularly, but the great tables looking down onto the Champs-Elysées are permanent.

## International Shopping

Back on earth, a half block farther down on the north side, the **Virgin Megastore** (#52-60)—the biggest music store in Paris—sells a world of music. Nearby, the Disney, Gap, Quiksilver, Zara, and Adidas stores are reminders of global economics: The French may live in a world of their own, but they love these places as much as Americans do. For a classic French brand, check out the five floors of glassy glitz at the **Citroën** auto showroom at #42. This isn't your father's *deux chevaux*, though you'll see echoes of that simple-but-dependable "two-horsepower" car from the '50s and '60s.

## Rond-Point and Beyond

At the Rond-Point des Champs-Elysées, the shopping ends and the park begins. This round, leafy traffic circle is always colorful, lined with flowers or seasonal decorations (thousands of pumpkins at Halloween, hundreds of decorated trees at Christmas). Avenue Montaigne, jutting off to the right, is lined by the most exclusive shops in town—the kinds of places where you need to make an appointment to buy a dress.

A long block past the Rond-Point, at Avenue de Marigny, look to the other side of the Champs-Elysées to find a statue of **Charles de Gaulle**—ramrod-straight and striding purposefully, as he did the day Paris was liberated in 1944.

## Grand and Petit Palais

From the statue of de Gaulle, a grand boulevard (Avenue Winston Churchill) passes through the site of the 1900 World's Fair, leading between the glass-and-steel-domed Grand and Petit Palais exhibition halls, and across the river over the ornate bridge called Pont Alexandre III. Imagine pavilions like the two you see today lining this street all the way to the golden dome of Les Invalides—examples of the "can-do" spirit that ran rampant in Europe at the dawn of the 20th century.

Today, the huge Grand Palais (on the right side) houses impressive temporary exhibits. Classical columns and giant, colorful mosaics running the length of the Palais' facade wowed fairgoers. The Petit Palais (left side) has a permanent collection of lesser paintings by Courbet, Monet, Pissarro, and other 19th-century masters. It's a breathtaking building with a peaceful café (worth a quick detour) and just as important, fine WCs with no lines. For more on both museums, see page 82.

The exquisite Pont Alexandre III, spiked with golden statues and ironwork lamps, was built to celebrate a turn-of-the-20th-century treaty between France and Russia. Les Invalides was built by Louis XIV as a veterans' hospital for his battle-weary troops (covered in the Army Museum and Napoleon's Tomb Tour). The esplanade leading up to Les Invalides—possibly the largest patch of accessible grass in the city—gives soccer balls and Frisbees a rare-in-Paris welcome.

Return to the Champs-Elysées. A long block north up Avenue de Marigny, in the opposite direction from the Grand and Petit Palais, is the Elysée Palace, France's version of the White House. It's interesting how no one seems to pay much attention to it.

Now it's a straight shot down the rest of the Champs-Elysées to the finish line. The plane trees that you'll see—a kind of sycamore with peeling bark—do well in big-city pollution. They're a legacy of Napoleon III—president/emperor from 1849 to 1870—who had 600,000 trees planted to green up the city.

• *Finally, you reach the 21-acre Place de la Concorde. View it from the obelisk in the center.*

## La Tour de France

For three weeks every July, French sporting life comes to a standstill as the Tour de France whizzes across the nation's landscape and television screens, pushing the world's top cyclists to their physical extremes and fans to the edges of their seats. What began in 1903 as a six-day publicity stunt for a cycling newspaper—in the era of wood-framed bikes and wine-and-cigarette breaks—has since grown into the sport's most prestigious race: a grueling 21-day, 2,000-mile test of strength and stamina, fueled by cutting-edge equipment and training regimens. The route changes each year (and usually spills into a neighboring country or two), but always finishes here on the Champs-Elysées.

Professional cycling is hugely popular in France, and while the Tour's on, media coverage is inescapable (despite—or perhaps thanks to—recent doping scandals). If you're here in July, it's easy to get caught up in the excitement. Casual spectators can appreciate the Tour's athletic demands and visual appeal, as cyclists travel in high-speed, multicolored packs through some of Europe's most scenic landscapes. But serious fans also love the complex, overlapping tests of speed, endurance, and strategy.

The long race is divided into daily stages, during which riders compete both as individuals and as members of their nine-man team. While the Tour produces only one overall winner, cycling is very much a team sport, and each member is critical (the loss of any rider along the way generally dooms a team's chances).

Minimizing air resistance is key to strategy, and riders spend most of each stage "drafting" behind *domestiques* ("servants," usually young riders still paying their dues), who take turns pedaling in front. The team's constant internal maneuvering is a matter of choreographed precision, aimed at minimizing fatigue...and the chance of a collision. At the end of each stage, fans breathlessly watch for that critical moment when the lead riders break away for the final sprint. Meanwhile, the team must jockey its way as a whole to the best

## Place de la Concorde

During the Revolution, this was the Place de la Révolution. The guillotine sat on this square, and many of the 2,780 people who were beheaded during the Revolution lost their bodies here during the Reign of Terror. A bronze plaque in the ground in front of the obelisk memorializes the place where Louis XVI, Marie-Antoinette, Georges Danton, Charlotte Corday, and Maximilien de Robespierre, among about 1,200 others, were made "a foot shorter on top." Three people worked the guillotine: One managed position within the peloton (cluster of riders), all while plotting how best to tap its members' varied talents over the course of the race.

Specialists ride not just to bolster their team, but also compete for their own distinctions: Climbers, usually smaller racers, battle to wear the *maillot à pois rouges* (red-polka-dot jersey), awarded to the "King of the Mountains." Bigger riders are usually sprinters, who save their energy for short bursts of speed, while vying for the *maillot à vert* (green jersey). Time trialists help lower the team's aggregate time by excelling at individual races, where they must maintain high speeds over a long distance. The team's star is its captain, usually a solid "all-rounder." He's going for the famous *maillot jaune* (yellow jersey), worn by whoever holds the overall lead in the "general classification" standings at the end of each stage. (It may be called "the" yellow jersey, but each day's jersey is a new, un-sweaty one.) A complex points system helps determine who has the lowest cumulative time—and, ultimately, who gets the €1.5 million (about $2 million) prize, and recognition as the world's greatest cyclist.

Unlike most spectator sports, cycling is perhaps best en-joyed on TV, where the intricate maneuvering is easier to fol-low, and the action stays in the camera's frame. Each day's race climax occurs around 17:00. If you're in France, just turn on your set at that time, flip among the first few channels, and you'll find coverage.

If you do catch the Tour in person, you'll experience the excitement firsthand and hear the loud whoosh of passing cyclists—but they're gone in a blink (viewing is best—and most crowded—on uphill slopes; for dates and details, see www.letour.fr).

Any time of year, you can at least picture the Tour's final stretch here on the nation's grandest avenue, where cheering crowds cram the sidewalks, necks craned for a glimpse of the yellow jersey.

the blade, one held the blood bucket, and one caught the head, raising it high to the roaring crowd. (In 1981, France abolished the death penalty—one of many preconditions for membership in today's European Union.)

The 3,300-year-old, 72-foot, 220-ton, red granite, hieroglyph-inscribed **obelisk of Luxor** now forms the centerpiece of Place de la Concorde. Here—on the spot where Louis XVI was beheaded—his brother (Charles X) erected this obelisk to honor those who'd been executed. (Charles became king when the monarchy was re-stored after Napoleon.) The obelisk was carted here from Egypt in the 1830s. The gold pictures on the pedestal tell the story of the obelisk's incredible two-year journey: pulled down from the entrance to Ramses II's Temple of Amon in Luxor; encased in wood; loaded onto a boat built to navigate both shallow rivers and  open seas; floated down the Nile, across the Mediterranean, along the Atlantic coast, and up the Seine; and unloaded here, where it was re-erected in 1836. Its glittering gold-leaf cap is a recent addition (1998), replacing the original, which was stolen 2,500 years ago.

The obelisk also forms a center point along a line that locals call the "royal perspective." You can hang a lot of history along this straight line (Louvre-obelisk-Arc de Triomphe-Grande Arche de la Défense). The Louvre symbolizes the old regime (divine-right rule by kings and queens). The obelisk and Place de la Concorde symbolize the people's Revolution (cutting off the king's head). The Arc de Triomphe calls to mind the triumph of nationalism (victorious armies carrying national flags under the arch). And the huge modern arch in the distance, surrounded by the headquarters of multinational corporations, heralds a future in which business entities are more powerful than nations.

## Near Place de la Concorde

Your guided walk is over. From here the closest Métro stop is Concorde (entrance on the Tuileries Garden side of the square, away from the river). But, of course, Paris offers so much more.

The beautiful Tuileries Garden (with a public WC just inside on the right) is through the iron gates. Pull up a chair next to a pond or at one of the cafés in the garden. From the garden you can access the Orangerie Museum and, at the other end, the Louvre  (this book includes tours of both museums).

On the north side of Place de la Concorde is **Hôtel Crillon,** one of Paris' most exclusive hotels. Of the twin buildings that guard the entrance to Rue Royale (which leads to the Greek-style Church of the Madeleine), it's the one on the left. This hotel is so fancy that one of its belle époque rooms is displayed in New York's Metropolitan

Museum of Art. For a memorable splurge, consider high tea at the Crillon (see page 460).

Eleven years before Louis XVI lost his head on this square, he met with Benjamin Franklin in this hotel to sign a treaty recognizing the US as an independent country. (Today's low-profile, heavily fortified **US Embassy and Consulate** are located next door.)

North of Place de la Concorde, you can go to a fancy shopping area near Place de la Madeleine (see the Shopping in Paris chapter).

South of Place de la Concorde (across the river) stands the building where the **French National Assembly** (similar to the US

Congress) meets. If you walk toward it, you'll cross a bridge, the **Pont de la Concorde,** over a freeway underpass. This stretch of road is similar to the one at the Pont de l'Alma, three bridges downstream, where Princess Diana lost her life in a 1997 car accident. The Pont de la Concorde, built of stones from the Bastille prison (which was demolished by the Revolution in 1789), symbolizes the *concorde* (harmony) that can come from chaos—through good government.

Stand midbridge and gaze upriver (east). Using an imaginary clock as a compass, the Orangerie hides behind the trees at 10 o'clock, and the tall building with the skinny chimneys at 11 o'clock is the architectural caboose of the sprawling Louvre palace. The thin spire of Sainte-Chapelle is dead center at 12 o'clock, with the twin towers of Notre-Dame to its right. The Orsay Museum is closer on the right, connected with the Tuileries Garden by a sleek pedestrian bridge (the next bridge upriver). Paris awaits.

# MARAIS WALK

*From Place Bastille to the Pompidou Center*

This walk takes you through one of Paris' most characteristic quarters, the Marais, and finishes in the artsy Beaubourg district. Naturally, when in Paris you want to see the big sights—but to experience the city, you also need to visit a vital neighborhood. To better appreciate the zest and flair of this neighborhood, take a look at the Marais section of the Shopping in Paris chapter. If time allows, you may want to linger along the walk or even consider a return trip. The Marais is liveliest on a Sunday afternoon.

The Marais, containing more pre-Revolutionary lanes and buildings than anywhere else in town, is more atmospheric than touristy. It's medieval Paris, and the haunt of the old nobility. After the aristocrats left, the Marais became a dumpy bohemian quarter so sordid it was nearly slated for destruction. In the mid-1800s, the wrecking ball was poised over the Marais: Napoleon III had ordered Baron Georges-Eugène Haussmann to modernize Paris by blasting out narrow streets to construct broad boulevards (wide enough for the big guns of the army, too wide for revolutionary barricades). By 1910, the renovation was almost complete, and a big boulevard was planned to slice right through the Marais. But then the march of "progress" was halted by one tiny little event—World War I.

Today the Marais is a thriving, trendy, real community—home to fashion boutiques, quiet cafés, Jewish bakeries, nightlife, and real Parisians. Follow this walk for a start, then explore.

## Orientation

**Length of This Walk:** Allow about 2.5 hours for this 2.25-mile walk. Figure on an additional hour for each museum you visit along the way (listed below).

**Victor Hugo's House:** Free, Tue-Sun 10:00-18:00, closed Mon, 6 Place des Vosges.

**Carnavalet Museum:** Free, Tue-Sun 10:00-18:00, closed Mon, 23 Rue de Sévigné. ✪ See the Carnavalet Museum Tour chapter.

**Jewish Art and History Museum:** €7, covered by Museum Pass, Sun-Fri 11:00-18:00, closed Sat, 71 Rue du Temple (described on page 86).

**Pompidou Center:** €11-13 depending on current exhibits, Museum Pass covers permanent collection and view escalators, €3 Panorama Ticket just to ride to the top for the view, Wed-Mon 11:00-21:00, closed Tue. ✪ See the Pompidou Center Tour chapter.

**Tours:** Paris Walks offers guided tours of this area (4/week, see page 47).

**Starring:** The grand Place des Vosges, the Jewish Quarter, several museums, and the boutiques and trendy lifestyle of today's Marais.

# The Walk Begins

• *Start at the west end of Place de la Bastille. From the Bastille Métro, exit following signs to Rue St. Antoine (not the signs to Rue du Faubourg St. Antoine). Ascend onto a noisy traffic circle dominated by the bronze Colonne de Juillet (July Column). The bronze god on the top is, like you, headed west. Lean against the black railing in front of the Banque de France.*

## ❶ Place de la Bastille

There are more Revolutionary images in the Métro station murals than on the square. And though Place de la Bastille is famous for its part in the French Revolution of 1789, little from that time remains. The Bastille itself, a royal-fortress-turned-prison that once symbolized old-regime tyranny and now symbolizes the Parisian emancipation, is long gone. Only an outline of the fortress' round turrets survives on the road (under the traffic where Rue St. Antoine hits the square), though the story of the Bastille is indelibly etched into the city's psyche.

For centuries the Bastille was used to defend the city (mostly from its own people). On July 14, 1789, the people of Paris stormed the prison, releasing its seven prisoners and hoping to find arms. They demolished the stone fortress and decorated their pikes with the heads of a few bigwigs. By shedding blood, the leaders of the gang made sure it would be tough to turn back the tides of revolution. Ever since, the French have celebrated July 14 as their independence day—Bastille Day.

The monument on the square—with its gilded statue of

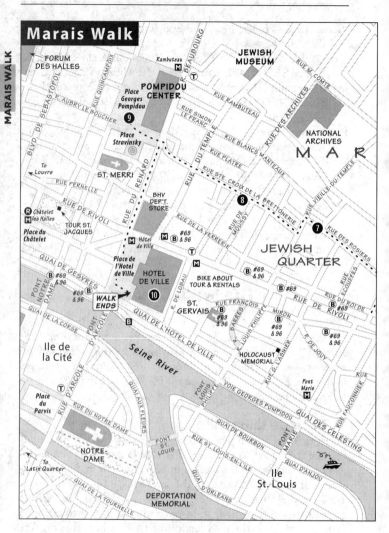

# Marais Walk

liberty—is a symbol of France's long struggle to establish democracy, commemorating the revolutions of 1830 and 1848. In 1830, the conservative King Charles X—who forgot all about the Revolution of the previous generation—needed to be tossed out. In 1848, a time of social unrest throughout Europe, the streets of Paris were barricaded by the working class, as dramatized in *Les Misérables*. Today, winged Mercury carries the torch of freedom into the future.

The southeast corner of the traffic circle is dominated (some say overwhelmed) by the flashy, curved, glassy gray facade of the controversial Opéra Bastille. In a symbolic attempt to bring high

1. Place de la Bastille
2. Hôtel de Sully
3. Place des Vosges
4. Rue des Francs Bourgeois
5. Carnavalet Museum
6. Rue Pavée
7. Rue des Rosiers – Jewish Quarter
8. Rue Ste. Croix de la Bretonnerie
9. Pompidou Center
10. Hôtel de Ville

culture to the masses, former French president François Mitterrand chose this location for the building that would become Paris' main opera venue, edging out Paris' earlier "palace of the rich," the Garnier-designed opera house (see page 78). Designed by the Canadian architect Carlos Ott, this grand Parisian project was opened with fanfare by Mitterrand on the 200th Bastille Day, July 14, 1989. Tickets are heavily subsidized to

## Bastille Day in France

Bastille Day—July 14, the symbolic kickoff date of the French Revolution—became the French national holiday in 1880. Traditionally, Parisians celebrate at Place de la Bastille starting at 20:00 on July 13, but the best parties are on the numerous smaller squares, where firefighter units sponsor dances. At 10:00 on the morning of the 14th, a grand military parade fills the Champs-Elysées. Then, at 22:30, there's a fireworks display at the Eiffel Tower (arrive at the Champs de Mars park by 20:00 to get a seat on the grass). *Vive la France!*

encourage the unwashed masses to attend, though how much high culture they have actually enjoyed here is a subject of debate. (For opera ticket information, see page 497.)

You'll now turn your back on this Haussmann-style grandeur and walk down what was—before the Revolution—one of the grandest streets in Paris: Rue St. Antoine. In 1350, there was a gate to the city here, Porte St. Antoine, defended by a drawbridge and fortress—a *bastille.*

• *Passing the Banque de France (BF), head west down Rue St. Antoine about four blocks into the Marais. Notice the minimalist curbside gas station and ponder how much space most gas stations take up in the US. This station is part of a full-service garage with precious in-city parking (€40/day!) and "lavage traditionnel à la main" (car wash by hand). At the intersection with Rue de Birague, old hippies may wish to make a 100-yard detour to the left, down Rue Beautrellis to #17, the nondescript apartment where rock star Jim Morrison died. (For more on Morrison, see page 350.) Otherwise, continue down Rue St. Antoine to #62 and enter the grand courtyard of Hôtel de Sully (daily 10:00-19:00, fine bookstore inside). If the building is closed, you'll need to backtrack one block to Rue de Birague to reach the next stop, Place des Vosges.*

## ❷ Hôtel de Sully

During the reign of Henry IV, this area—originally a swamp *(marais)*—became the hometown of the French aristocracy. In the 17th century, big shots built their private mansions *(hôtels),* like this one, close to Henry's stylish Place des Vosges. *Hôtels* that survived the Revolution now house museums, libraries, and national institutions.

The first of two courtyards is

carriage-friendly and elegant, separating the mansion from the noisy and very public street. Look up at statues of Autumn (carrying grapes from the harvest), Winter (a feeble old man), and the four elements.

Continue into a passageway to find a bookstore with skillfully carved and painted ceilings. Exit into the back courtyard, where noisy Paris takes a back seat. Use the bit of Gothic window tracery (on the right) for a fun framed photo of your travel partner as a Madonna. At the far end, the French doors are part of a former *orangerie*, or greenhouse, for homegrown fruits and vegetables throughout winter; these days it warms office workers.

• *Continue through the small door at the far-right corner of the second courtyard, and pop out into one of Paris' finest squares.*

## ❸ Place des Vosges

Walk to the center, where Louis XIII, on horseback, gestures, "Look at this wonderful square my dad built." He's surrounded by

locals enjoying their community park. You'll see children frolicking in the sandbox, lovers warming benches, and pigeons guarding their fountains while trees shade this escape from the glare of the big city (you can refill your water bottle in the center of the square).

Study the architecture: nine pavilions (houses) per side. The two highest—at the front and back—were for the king and queen (but were never used). Warm red brickwork—some real, some fake—is topped with sloped slate roofs, chimneys, and another quaint relic of a bygone era: TV antennas. Beneath the arcades are cafés, art galleries, and restaurants—it's a romantic place for dinner (for recommendations, see page 441).

Henry IV (r. 1589-1610) built this centerpiece of the Marais in 1605 and called it "Place Royal." As he'd hoped, it turned the

Marais into Paris' most exclusive neighborhood. Just like Versailles 80 years later, this was a magnet for the rich and powerful of France. With the Revolution, the aristocratic splendor of this quarter passed. To encourage the country to pay its taxes, Napoleon promised naming rights to the district that paid first—the Vosges region (near Germany).

In the 19th century the Marais became a working-class quarter, filled with gritty shops, artisans, immigrants, and a Jewish community.

The insightful writer **Victor Hugo** lived at #6—at the southeast corner of the square—from 1832 to 1848. This was when he wrote much of his most important work, including his biggest hit, *Les Misérables*. Inside you'll wander through eight plush rooms and enjoy a fine view of the square (marked by the French flag in the corner closest to the Bastille; see page 88).

• *Sample the upscale art galleries ringing the square (the best ones are behind Louis), then exit the square at the northwest (far left) corner. Head west on...*

## ❹ Rue des Francs Bourgeois

From the Marais of yesteryear, immediately enter the lively neighborhood of today. Stroll down a block full of cafés and clothing boutiques with the latest fashions. A few doorways (including #8 and #13) lead into courtyards with more shops.

• *Continue west one block along Rue des Francs Bourgeois, and turn right on Rue Sévigné to reach the entrance (at #23) of the...*

## ❺ Carnavalet Museum

Housed inside a Marais mansion, this museum features the history of Paris, particularly the Revolution years. Since this provides the best possible look at the elegance of the neighborhood back when Place des Vosges was Place Royal—and the museum is free—I'd interrupt this walk and splice in a trip to the Carnavalet. ❂ See the Carnavalet Museum Tour chapter.

• *From the Carnavalet continue west one block down Rue des Francs Bourgeois to the post office. (Modern-art fans: The nearby Picasso Museum, which has been under renovation for several years, is scheduled to reopen in summer 2013.) Turn left onto...*

## ❻ Rue Pavée

At #24 you'll pass the 16th-century Paris Historical Library (Bibliothèque Historique de la Ville de Paris). Step into the courtyard of this rare Renaissance mansion to see the clear windows and clean classical motifs. Because the neighborhood is built upon a swamp, many buildings in this area have foundation problems.

Farther down the street, on your right, a funky bookstore at #17 bis has more inside than meets the eye (it's called Mona Lisait, which means "Mona was reading").

Continue another half-block along Rue Pavée to #10 and

find the Agoudas Hakehilos synagogue with its fine (but filthy) Art
Nouveau facade (c. 1913, closed to
public). It was designed by Hector
Guimard, the same architect who
designed Paris' Art Nouveau Métro
stations.

• *Backtrack a few steps and turn left
onto Rue des Rosiers (named for the
roses that once lined the city wall),
which runs straight for three blocks
through Paris' Jewish Quarter—lively
every day except Saturday.*

## ❼ Rue des Rosiers—Jewish Quarter

Once the largest in Western Europe, Paris' Jewish Quarter is much
smaller today but is still colorful. Notice the sign above #4, which
says *Hamam* (Turkish bath). Although still bearing the sign of an
old public bath, it now showcases steamy women's clothing. Next
door, at #4 bis, the Ecole de Travail (trade school) has a plaque on
the wall remembering the headmaster, staff, and students who were
arrested here during World War II and killed at Auschwitz.

The size of the Jewish population here has fluctuated. It expanded
in the 19th century when Jews arrived from Eastern Europe, escaping
pogroms (surprise attacks on villages). The numbers swelled during the
1930s as Jews fled Nazi Germany.
Then, during World War II, 75 percent of the Jews here were taken to
concentration camps (for more information, visit the nearby Holocaust Memorial—see page 88). And, most recently, Algerian
exiles, both Jewish and Muslim, have settled in—living together
peacefully here in Paris. (Nevertheless, much of the street has
granite blocks on the sidewalk—an attempt to keep out any ter-
rorists' cars.) Currently the district's traditional population is being
squeezed out by the trendy boutiques of modern Paris.

The intersection of Rue des Rosiers and Rue des Ecouffes
marks the heart of the small neighborhood that Jews call the Pletzl
("little square"). Lively Rue des Ecouffes, named for a bird of prey,
is a derogatory nod to the moneychangers' shops that once lined
this lane. Rue des Rosiers features kosher *(cascher)* restaurants and
fast-food places selling falafel, *shawarma*, *kefta*, and other Mediterranean dishes. Bakeries specialize in braided challah, bagels,
and strudels. Delis offer gefilte fish, piroshkis, and blintzes. Art

galleries exhibit Jewish-themed works, and store windows post flyers for community events. Need a menorah? You'll find one here. You'll likely see Jewish men in yarmulkes, a few bearded Orthodox Jews, and Hasidic Jews with black coat and hat, beard, and earlocks.

**Lunch Break:** This is a good place to stop. You'll be tempted by kosher pizza and plenty of cheap fast-food joints selling falafel

"to go" *(emporter)*. The falafel at L'As du Falafel, with its bustling New York deli atmosphere, is terrific (at #34, sit-down or to go). The Sacha Finkelsztajn Yiddish bakery at #27 is also good (Polish and Russian cuisine, pop in for a tempting treat, sit for the same price as takeaway). Nearby, Chez Marianne cooks up traditional Jewish meals and serves excellent falafel to go (at corner of Rue des Rosiers and Rue des Hospitalières-St.-Gervais; see page 445).

• *Rue des Rosiers dead-ends at Rue Vieille du Temple. Turn left on Rue Vieille du Temple, then take your first right onto Rue Ste. Croix de la Bretonnerie (see next section).*

**Possible Detour to the Holocaust Memorial:** *Consider a (10-block round-trip) detour to visit the memorial (free, Sun-Fri 10:00-18:00, Thu until 22:00, closed Sat and certain Jewish holidays, 17 Rue Geoffroy l'Asnier). To get there, head south on Rue Vieille du Temple and cross Rue de Rivoli. Make your second left after Rue de Rivoli onto the cobbled passageway, Allée des Justes. Note the bronze plaque on the right, with the names of those who saved Jewish lives during World War II. Next is the entrance to the stark Holocaust Memorial. (For more on the memorial, see page 88.)*

## ❽ Rue Ste. Croix de la Bretonnerie

Gay Paree's openly gay main drag is lined with cafés, lively shops, and crowded bars at night. Check the posters at #7, Le Point Virgule theater (means "The Semicolon") to see what form of edgy musical comedy is showing tonight (most productions are in French). A block farther, at #38, peruse real estate prices in the area—€400,000 for a one-bedroom flat?!

At Rue du Temple, some may wish to detour half a block to the right to The Studio (41 Rue du Temple), a dance school wonderfully located in a 17th-century courtyard. At the restaurant in the courtyard, you can sip a *café crème*—or have a Tex-Mex meal—surrounded by ballet, tap dance, and tango.

A block beyond the dance school is the Jewish Art and History Museum (see page 86).

• *Continue west on Rue Ste. Croix (which turns into Rue St. Merri). Up ahead you'll see the colorful pipes of the Pompidou Center. Cross Rue du Renard and enter the Pompidou's colorful world of fountains, restaurants, and street performers.*

## ❾ Pompidou Center

Survey this popular spot from the top of the sloping square. Tubular escalators (free with Museum Pass) lead to the museum and a great view. ❷ See the Pompidou Center Tour chapter.

The Pompidou Center subscribes with gusto to the 20th-century architectural axiom "form follows function." To get a more spacious and functional interior, the guts of this exoskeletal building are draped on the outside and color-coded: vibrant red for people lifts, cool blue for air ducts, eco-green for plumbing, don't-touch-it yellow for electrical stuff, and white for the structure's bones. (Compare the Pompidou Center to another exoskeletal building, Notre-Dame.)

Enjoy the adjacent *Homage to Stravinsky* fountains. Jean Tinguely and Niki de Saint-Phalle designed these as a tribute to the composer: Every fountain represents one of his hard-to-hum scores. For low-stress meals or an atmospheric spot for a drink, try the lighthearted Dame Tartine, which overlooks the fountains and serves good, inexpensive food. (To learn about nearby sights, see "West of the Pompidou Center," later.)

• *Double back to Rue du Renard, turn right and stroll toward the river until you find...*

## ❿ Hôtel de Ville

Looking more like a grand château than a public building, Paris' city hall stands proudly. This spot has been the center of city government since 1357. Each of Paris' 20 arrondissements has its own city hall and mayor, but this one is the big daddy of them all.

The Renaissance-style building (built 1533-1628, and rebuilt after a 19th-century fire) displays hundreds of statues of famous Parisians on its facade. Peek through the doors to see elaborate spiral stairways, which are reminiscent of Château de Chambord in the Loire. Playful fountains energize the big, lively square in front.

This spacious stage has seen much of Paris' history. On July 14, 1789, Revolutionaries rallied here on their way to the Bastille. In 1870, it was home to the radical Paris Commune. During World War II, General Charles de Gaulle appeared at the windows to proclaim Paris' liberation from the Nazis. And in 1950, Robert Doisneau snapped a famous black-and-white photo of a kissing couple, with Hôtel de Ville as a romantic backdrop.

Today, this is the symbolic heart of the city of Paris. Demonstrators gather here to speak their minds. Crowds cheer during big soccer games shown on huge TV screens. In summer, the square hosts sand volleyball courts; in winter, a big ice-skating rink. Year-round, the place is always beautifully lit after dark.

The mayor of Paris, who has one of the most powerful positions in France, presides here. Current mayor Bertrand Delanoë—responsible for the *Vélib'* bicycle-sharing program, bike lanes, and the *Autolib'* car-sharing program—is single-handedly turning Paris into Europe's green capital.

## West of the Pompidou Center

If you have time to explore the neighborhood near the Pompidou Center, head west along the cobbled pedestrian mall, then cross the busy Boulevard de Sébastopol to reach the ivy-covered pavilions of **Les Halles.** The shopping center, which replaced Paris' down-and-dirty central produce market in the 1970s, is glitzy and soulless, but its grassy rooftop park is endearing. The Gothic **St. Eustache Church** overlooking this contemporary scene has a famous 8,000-pipe organ.

For a more soulful shopping experience, find your way behind St. Eustache Church and cross Rue Montmartre onto the delightfully traffic-free **Rue Montorgueil** (mohn-tor-goo-ee; for more information, see page 490). This happy pedestrian street is the site of pleasant cafés and colorful produce markets. If you've walked here all the way from Place de la Bastille, you deserve a break at one of the street's cafés.

# POMPIDOU CENTER TOUR

*Centre Pompidiou*

Some people hate Modern art. But the Pompidou Center contains what is possibly Europe's best collection of 20th-century art. After the super-serious Louvre and Orsay museums, finish things off with this artistic kick in the pants. You won't find classical beauty here—no dreamy Madonnas-and-children—just a stimulating, offbeat, and, if you like, instructive walk through nearly every art style of the wild-and-crazy last century.

The Pompidou's "permanent" collection...isn't. It changes so often that a painting-by-painting tour is impossible. So, this chapter is more a general overview of the major trends of 20th-century art, with emphasis on artists you're likely to find in the Pompidou. Read this chapter ahead of time for background, or take it with you to the museum to look up specific painters as you stumble across their work.

## Orientation

**Cost:** A combo-ticket is €11-13, depending on current exhibits. This gets you into all of the building's various exhibits—both the permanent collection (the *Musée National d'Art Moderne*) and the temporary exhibits that make this place so edgy. You can't buy a ticket for only the permanent collection or the exhibits.

The Museum Pass includes the permanent collection, but not the temporary exhibits. Buy tickets on the ground floor. If lines are long, use the red ticket machines (credit cards only). The museum is free on the first Sunday of the month.

**Hours:** Wed-Mon 11:00-21:00, closed Tue, ticket counters close at 20:00. To avoid crowds (mainly for the special exhibits), arrive after 17:00.

**Getting There:** The nearest Métro stop is Rambuteau; a few blocks farther away is Hôtel de Ville. Bus #69 from the Marais and Rue Cler also stops a few blocks away at Hôtel de Ville. The wild, color-coded exterior of the museum makes it about as hard to locate as the Eiffel Tower.

**Information:** Most rooms have informative English explanations. Audioguides can include temporary exhibits (depends on exhibit).

Note that Parisians call the complex the "Centre Beaubourg" (sahn-truh boh-boor), but official publications call it the "Centre Pompidou." Tel. 01 44 78 12 33, www.centrepompidou.fr.

**Length of This Tour:** Allow one hour.

**Baggage Check:** Ground floor, free, and required for bags bigger than a large purse.

**Shopping:** There's a terrific museum store with zany gift ideas on the main floor.

**Cuisine Art:** You'll find a sparse, sandwich-and-coffee café on the mezzanine and a pricey view restaurant on level 6. Outside the museum, the neighborhood abounds with cheap, hip bistros and crêpe stands. My favorite places are to the right of the museum, lining the playful fountain, *Homage to Stravinsky.* Dame Tartine and Crêperie Beaubourg both have reasonable prices.

**View Art:** The sixth floor (where the pricey restaurant is) has stunning views of the Paris cityscape. You can get there by riding the view escalators, for which you'll need a Museum Pass, combo-ticket, or €3 Panorama Ticket (good for sixth floor only).

**Starring:** Matisse, Picasso, Chagall, Dalí, Warhol, and contemporary art.

## The Tour Begins

That slight tremor you may feel comes from Italy, where Michelangelo has been spinning in his grave ever since 1977, when the Pompidou Center first disgusted Paris. Still, it's an appropriate modern temple for the controversial art it houses.

The building itself is "exoskeletal" (like Notre-Dame or a crab), with its functional parts—the pipes, heating ducts, and escalator—on the outside, and the meaty art inside. It's the epitome of Modern architecture, where "form follows function."

This chapter covers the *Musée National d'Art Moderne: Collection*

*Permanente,* which is on the fourth and fifth floors. But there's plenty more art scattered all over the building. Ask at the ground-floor information booth, or just wander.

• *Buy your ticket on the ground floor, then ride up the escalator (or run up the down escalator to get in the proper mood). When you see the view, your opinion of the Pompidou's exterior should improve a good 15 percent. Find the permanent collection—the entrance is either on the fourth or fifth floor (it varies).*

*Enter, show your ticket, and get the current floor plan* (plan du musée). *Generally, art from 1905 to 1960 is on the fifth floor, and the fourth floor contains more recent art. But 20th-century art resents being put in chronological order, and the Pompidou's collection is rarely in any neat-and-tidy arrangement. Use the museum's map to find select artists, and don't hesitate to ask,* "Où est Kandinsky?"

*Remember, the following text is not a "tour" of the museum—it's a chronological overview of Modern art.*

# Modern Art 1905-1960

A.D. 1900: A new century dawns. War is a thing of the past. Science will wipe out poverty and disease. Rational Man is poised at a new era of peace and prosperity...

Right. This cozy Victorian dream was soon shattered by two world wars and rapid technological change. Nietzsche murdered God. Freud washed ashore on the beach of a vast new continent inside each of us. Einstein made everything merely "relative." Even the fundamental building blocks of the universe, atoms, were behaving erratically.

The 20th century—accelerated by technology and fragmented by war—was exciting and chaotic, and the art reflects the turbulence of that century of change.

## Cubism: Reality Shattered (1907-1912)

I throw a rock at a glass statue, shatter it, pick up the pieces, and glue them onto a canvas. I'm a Cubist.

### Pablo Picasso (1881-1973) and
### Georges Braque (1882-1963)

Born in Spain, Picasso moved to Paris as a young man, settling into a studio (the Bateau-Lavoir) in Montmartre (see page 369). He worked with next-door neighbor Georges Braque in poverty so dire they often didn't know where their next bottle of wine was coming from. They corrected each other's paintings (it's hard to tell whose is whose without the titles), and they shared ideas, meals, and girlfriends while inventing a whole new way to look at the world.

They show the world through a kaleidoscope of brown and gray. The subjects are somewhat recognizable (with the help of the titles), but they are broken into geometric shards (let's call them "cubes," though there are many different shapes), then pieced back together.

Cubism gives us several different angles of the subject at once—say, a woman seen from the front and side angles simultaneously, resulting in two eyes on the same side of the nose. This involves showing three dimensions, plus Einstein's new fourth dimension, the time it takes to walk around the subject to see other angles. Newfangled motion pictures could capture this moving 4-D world, but how to do it on a 2-D canvas? The Cubist "solution" is a kind of Mercator projection, where the round world is sliced up like an orange peel and then laid as flat as possible.

Notice how the "cubes" often overlap. A single cube might contain both an arm (in the foreground) and the window behind (in the background), both painted the same color. The foreground and the background are woven together, so that the subject dissolves into a pattern.

## Picasso: Synthetic Cubism (1912-1915) and Beyond

If the Cubists were as smart as Einstein, why couldn't they draw a picture to save their lives? Picasso was one Modern artist who could draw exceptionally well (see his partly finished *Harlequin*). But he constantly explored and adapted his style to new trends, and so became the most famous painter of the century. Scattered throughout the museum are works from the many periods of Picasso's life.

Picasso soon began to use more colorful "cubes" (1912-1915). Eventually, he used curved shapes to build the subject, rather than the straight-line shards of early Cubism.

Picasso married and had children. Works from this period (the 1920s) are more realistic, with full-bodied (and big-nosed) women and children. He tries to capture the solidity, serenity, and volume of classical statues.

As his relationships with women deteriorated, he vented his sexual demons by twisting the female body into grotesque balloon-animal shapes (1925-1931).

All through his life, Picasso explored new materials. He made collages, tried his hand at making "statues" out of wood, wire, or whatever, and even made statues out of everyday household objects.

These multimedia works, so revolutionary at the time, have become stock-in-trade today.

## Marc Chagall (1887-1985)

At age 22, Marc Chagall arrived in Paris with the wide-eyed wonder of a country boy. Lovers are weightless with bliss. Animals smile and wink at us. Musicians, poets, peasants, and dreamers ignore gravity, tumbling in slow-motion circles high above the rooftops. The colors are deep, dark, and earthy—a pool of mystery with figures bleeding through below the surface. (Chagall claimed his early poverty forced him to paint over used canvases, inspiring the overlapping images.)

Chagall's very personal style fuses many influences. He was raised in a small Belarus village, which explains his "naive" outlook and fiddler-on-the-roof motifs. His simple figures are like Russian Orthodox icons, and his Jewish roots produced Old Testament themes. Stylistically, he's thoroughly Modern—Cubist shards, bright Fauve colors, and Primitive simplification. This otherworldly style was a natural for religious works, and so his murals and stained glass, which feature both Jewish and Christian motifs, decorate buildings around the world—including the ceiling of Paris' Opéra Garnier (see page 78).

## Georges Rouault (1871-1958)

Young Georges Rouault was apprenticed to a stained-glass-window-maker. Enough said?

The paintings have the same thick, glowing colors, heavy black outlines, simple subjects, and (mostly) religious themes. The style is Modern, but the mood is medieval, solemn, and melancholy. Rouault captures the tragic spirit of those people—clowns, prostitutes, and sons of God—who have been made outcasts by society.

## Henri Matisse (1869-1954)

Matisse's colorful "wallpaper" works are not realistic. A man is a few black lines and blocks of paint. The colors are unnaturally bright. There's no illusion of the distance and 3-D that were so important to Renaissance Italians. The "distant" landscape is as bright as any close-up, and the slanted lines meant to suggest depth are crudely done.

Traditionally, the canvas was like a window you looked "through" to see a slice of the real world stretching off into the distance. Now, a camera could do that better. With Matisse, you look "at" the canvas, like wallpaper. Voilà! What was a crudely drawn scene now becomes a sophisticated and decorative pattern of colors and shapes.

Though fully "Modern," Matisse built on 19th-century art—the bright colors of Vincent van Gogh, the primitive figures of Paul Gauguin, the colorful designs of Japanese prints, and the Impressionist patches of paint that blend together only at a distance.

## Primitive Masks and Statues

Matisse was one of the Fauves ("wild beasts") who, inspired by African and Oceanic masks and voodoo dolls, tried to inject a bit of the jungle into bored French society. The result? Modern art that looked primitive: long, masklike faces with almond eyes; bright, clashing colors; simple figures; and "flat," two-dimensional scenes.

## Abstract Art

Abstract art simplifies. A man becomes a stick figure. A squiggle is a wave. A streak of red expresses anger. Arches make you want a cheeseburger. These are universal symbols that everyone from a caveman to a banker understands. Abstract artists capture the essence of reality in a few lines and colors, and they capture things even a camera can't—emotions, abstract concepts, musical rhythms, and spiritual states of mind. Again, with abstract art, you don't look *through* the canvas to see the visual world, but *at* it to read the symbolism of lines, shapes, and colors.

### Wassily Kandinsky (1866-1944)

The bright colors, bent lines, and lack of symmetry tell us that Kandinsky's world was passionate and intense.

Notice titles like *Improvisation* and *Composition*. Kandinsky was inspired by music, an art form that's also "abstract," though it still packs a punch. Like a jazz musician improvising a new pattern of notes from a set scale, Kandinsky plays with new patterns of related colors as he looks for just the right combination. Using lines and color, Kandinsky translates the unseen reality into a new medium...like lightning crackling over the radio. Go, man, go.

### Piet Mondrian (1872-1944)

Like blueprints for Modernism, Mondrian's T-square style boils painting down to its basic building blocks (black lines, white canvas) and the three primary colors (red, yellow, and blue), all arranged in orderly patterns.

(When you come right down to it, that's all painting ever has been. A schematic drawing of, say, the *Mona Lisa* shows that it's less about a woman than about the triangles and rectangles of which she's composed.)

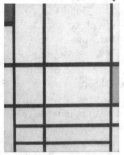

Mondrian started out painting realistic landscapes of the orderly fields in his native Netherlands. Increasingly, he simplified them into horizontal and vertical patterns. For Mondrian, who was heavy into Eastern mysticism, "up vs. down" and "left vs. right" were the perfect metaphors for life's dualities: "good vs. evil," "body vs. spirit," "man vs. woman." The canvas is a bird's-eye view of Mondrian's personal landscape.

### Constantin Brancusi (1876-1957)

Brancusi's curved, shiny statues reduce objects to their essence. A bird is a single stylized wing, the one feature that sets it apart from other animals. He rounds off to the closest geometrical form, so a woman's head becomes a perfect oval on a cubic pedestal.

Humans love symmetry (maybe because our own bodies are roughly symmetrical) and find geometric shapes restful, even worthy of meditation. Brancusi follows the instinct for order that has

driven art from earliest times, from circular Stonehenge and Egyptian pyramids, to Greek columns and Roman arches, to Renaissance symmetry and the Native American "medicine wheel."

### Paul Klee (1879-1940)

Paul Klee's small and playful canvases are deceptively simple, containing shapes so basic they can be read as universal symbols. Klee thought a wavy line, for example, would always suggest motion, whereas a stick figure would always mean a human—like the psychiatrist Carl Jung's universal dream symbols, part of our "collective unconscious."

Klee saw these universals in the art of children, who express themselves without censoring or cluttering things up with learning.

His art has a childlike playfulness and features simple figures painted in an uninhibited frame of mind.

Klee also turned to nature. The same forces that cause the wave to draw a line of foam on the beach can cause a meditative artist to draw a squiggly line of paint on a canvas. The result is a universal shape. The true artist doesn't just paint nature, he becomes Nature.

## Design: Chairs by Gerrit Rietveld and Alvar Aalto

If you can't handle Modern art, sit on it! (Actually, please don't.) The applied arts—chairs, tables, lamps, and vases—are as much a part of the art world as the fine arts. (Some say the first art object was the pot.) As machines became as talented as humans, artists embraced new technology and mass production to bring beauty to the masses.

## Fernand Léger (1881-1955)

Fernand Léger's style has been called "Tubism"—breaking the world down into cylinders, rather than cubes. (He supposedly got his inspiration during World War I from the gleaming barrel of a cannon.) Léger captures the feel of the encroaching Age of Machines, with all the world looking like an internal-combustion engine.

## Robert Delaunay (1885-1941) and Sonia Delaunay (1885-1979)

This married couple both painted colorful, fragmented canvases (including a psychedelic Eiffel Tower) that prove the Modern style doesn't have to be ugly or enigmatic.

## World War I: The Death of Values

Ankle-deep in mud, a soldier shivers in a trench, waiting to be ordered "over the top." He'll have to run through barbed wire, over fallen comrades, and into a hail of machine-gun fire, only to capture a few hundred yards of meaningless territory that will be lost the next day. This soldier was not thinking about art.

World War I left nine million dead. (During the war, France

sometimes lost more men in a single month than America lost in the entire Vietnam War.) The war also killed the optimism and faith in mankind that had guided Europe since the Renaissance. Now, rationality just meant schemes, technology meant machines of death, and morality meant giving your life for an empty cause.

## Expressionism: Ernst Ludwig Kirchner, Max Beckmann, George Grosz, Chaïm Soutine, Otto Dix, and Oskar Kokoschka

Cynicism and decadence settled over postwar Europe. Artists "expressed" their disgust by showing a distorted reality that emphasized the ugly. Using the lurid colors and simplified figures of the Fauves, they slapped paint on in thick brushstrokes and depicted a hypocritical, hard-edged, dog-eat-dog world that had lost its bearings. The people have a haunted look in their eyes—the fixed stare of corpses and those who have to bury them.

## Dada: Marcel Duchamp's Urinal (1917)

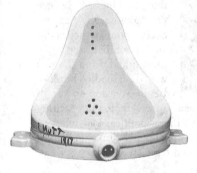

When people could grieve no longer, they turned to grief's giddy twin: laughter. The war made all old values, including art, a joke. The Dada movement, choosing a purposely childish name, made art that was intentionally outrageous: a moustache on the *Mona Lisa*, a shovel hung on a wall, or a modern version of a Renaissance "fountain"—a urinal (by either Marcel Duchamp, or I. P. Freeley, 1917). It was a dig at all the pompous prewar artistic theories based on the noble intellect of Rational Women and Men. While the experts ranted on, Dadaists sat in the back of the class and made cultural fart noises.

Hey, I love this stuff. My mind says it's sophomoric, but my heart belongs to Dada.

## Surrealism: Salvador Dalí, Max Ernst, and René Magritte (1920-1940)

Greek statues with sunglasses, a man as a spinning top, shoes becoming feet, and black ants as musical notes...Surrealism. The world was moving fast, and Surrealists caught the jumble of images. The artist scatters seemingly unrelated items on the canvas, which leaves us to trace the links in a kind of connect-the-dots without numbers. If it comes together, the synergy of unrelated things can be pretty startling. But even if the juxtaposed images don't ultimately connect, the artist has made you think, re-routing your thoughts through new neural paths. If you don't "get" it...you got it.

Complicating the modern world was Freud's discovery of the "unconscious" mind that thinks dirty thoughts while we sleep. Many a Surrealist canvas is an uncensored, stream-of-consciousness "landscape" of these deep urges, revealed in the bizarre images of dreams.

In dreams, sometimes one object can be two things at once: "I dreamt that you walked in with a cat...no, wait, maybe you *were* the cat...no...." Surrealists paint opposites like these and let them speak for themselves.

## Salvador Dalí (1904-1989)

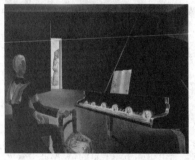

Salvador Dalí could draw exceptionally well. He painted "unreal" scenes with photographic realism, thus making us believe they could really happen. Seeing familiar objects in an unfamiliar setting—like a grand piano adorned with disembodied heads of Lenin—creates an air of mystery, the feeling that anything can happen. That's both exciting and unsettling. Dalí's images—crucifixes, political and religious figures, naked bodies—pack an emotional punch. Take one mixed bag of reality, jumble in a blender, and serve on a canvas...Surrealism.

## Abstract Surrealists: Joan Miró, Alexander Calder, and Jean Arp

Abstract artists described their subconscious urges using color and shapes alone, like Rorschach inkblots in reverse.

The thin-line scrawl of Joan Miró's work is like the doodling of a three-year-old. You'll recognize crudely drawn birds, stars, animals, and strange cell-like creatures with whiskers ("Biological Cubism"). Miró was try-ing to express the most basic of human emotions using the most basic of techniques.

Alexander Calder's mobiles hang like Mirós in the sky, wait-ing for a gust of wind to bring them to life.

And talk about a primal image! Jean Arp builds human beings out of amoeba-like shapes.

## Decorative Art: Pierre Bonnard, Balthus, and Later Picasso and Braque

Most 20th-century paintings are a mix of the real world ("repre-sentation") and the colorful patterns of "abstract" art. Artists pur-posely distort camera-eye reality to make the resulting canvas more decorative. So, Picasso flattens a woman into a pattern of colored shapes, Bonnard makes a man from a shimmer of golden paint, and Balthus turns a boudoir scene into colorful wallpaper.

## Patterns and Textures: Jean Dubuffet Lucio Fontana, and Karel Appel

Increasingly, you'll have to focus your eyes to look *at* the canvases, not *through* them.

Enjoy the lines and colors, but also a new element: texture. Some works have very thick paint piled on—you can see the brush-stroke clearly. Some have substances besides paint applied to the canvas, such as Dubuffet's brown, earthy rectangles of real dirt and organic waste. Fontana punctures the canvas so that the fabric it-self (and the hole) becomes the subject. Artists show their skill by mastering new materials. The canvas is a tray, serving up a delight-ful array of different substances with interesting colors, patterns, shapes, and textures.

## Alberto Giacometti (1901-1966)

Giacometti's skinny statues have the emaciated, haunted, and face-less look of concentration camp survivors. The simplicity of the figures may be "primitive," but these aren't stately, sturdy, Easter Island heads. Here, man is weak in the face of technology and the winds of history.

## Abstract Expressionism

America emerged from World War II as the globe's superpower. With Europe in ruins, New York replaced Paris as the art capital of the world. The trend was toward bigger canvases, abstract designs, and experimentation with new materials and techniques. It was called "Abstract Expressionism"—expressing emotions and ideas using color and form alone.

## Jackson Pollock (1912-1956)

"Jack the Dripper" attacks convention with a can of paint, dripping and splashing a dense web onto the canvas. Picture Pollock in his studio, as he jives to the hi-fi, bounces off the walls, and throws paint in a moment of enlightenment. Of course, the artist loses some control this way—control over the paint flying in midair and over himself, now in an ecstatic trance. Painting becomes a whole-body activity, a "dance" between the artist and his materials.

The act of creating is what's important, not the final product. The canvas is only a record of that moment of ecstasy.

## Big, Empty Canvases: Barnett Newman and Robert Rauschenberg

All those huge, sparse canvases with just a few lines or colors—what reality are they trying to show?

In the modern world, we find ourselves insignificant specks in a vast and indifferent universe. Every morning each of us must confront that big, blank, existentialist canvas and decide how we're going to make our mark on it. Like, wow.

Another influence was the simplicity of Japanese landscape painting. A Zen master studies and meditates for years to achieve the state of mind in which he can draw one pure line. These canvases, again, are only a record of that state of enlightenment. (What is the sound of one brush painting?)

On more familiar ground, postwar painters were following in the footsteps of artists such as Mondrian, Klee, and Kandinsky (whose work they must have considered "busy"). The geometrical forms here reflect the same search for order, but these artists painted to the 5/4 asymmetry of Dave Brubeck's jazz classic, "Take Five."

• If you're on the fifth floor, descend to the fourth floor, where you'll usually find "contemporary" art, from the last 50 years.

# The Contemporary Collection 1960-Present

## Pop Art: Andy Warhol (1928-1987)

America's postwar wealth made the consumer king. Pop art is created from the "pop"-ular objects of that throwaway society—a soup can, a car fender, mannequins, tacky plastic statues, movie icons, advertising posters. Take something out of

Sears and hang it in a museum, and you have to think about it in a wholly different way.

Is this art? Are all these mass-produced objects beautiful? Or crap? If they're not art, why do we work so hard to acquire them? Pop art, like Dada, questions our society's values.

Andy Warhol (who coined the idea of everyone having "15 minutes of fame" and became a pop star himself) concentrated on another mass-produced phenomenon: celebrities. He took publicity photos of famous people and repeated them. The repetition—like the constant bombardment we get from repeated images on television—cheapens even the most beautiful things.

## New Media for a New Century

The "modern" world is history. Picasso and his ilk are now gathering dust and boring art students everywhere. Minimalist painting and abstract sculpture are old-school. Enter the "postmodern" world, as seen through the eyes of current artists.

You'll see fewer traditional canvases or sculptures. Artists have traded paintbrushes for blowtorches (Miró said he was out to "murder" painting), and blowtorches for computer mice. Mixed-media work is the norm, combining painting, sculpture, welding, photography, video, computer programming, new resins, plastics, industrial techniques, and lighting and sound systems.

Here are some of the trends:

**Installations:** An entire room is given to an artist to prepare. Like entering an art funhouse, you walk in without quite knowing what to expect. (I'm always thinking, "Is this safe?") Using the latest technology, the artist engages all your senses by controlling the lights, sounds, and sometimes even smells.

**Assemblages:** Artists raid Dumpsters, recycling junk into the building blocks for larger "assemblages." Each piece is intended to be interesting and tell its own story, and so is the whole sculpture. Weird, useless, Rube Goldberg machines make fun of technology.

**Natural Objects:** A rock in an urban setting is inherently interesting.

**The Occasional Canvas:** This comes as a familiar relief. Artists of the New Realism labor over painstaking, hyper-realistic canvases to re-create the glossy look of a photo or video image.

**Interaction:** Some exhibits require your participation, whether you push a button to get the contraption going, touch something, or just walk around the room. In some cases the viewer "does" art, rather than just staring at it. If art is really meant to change, it has to move you, literally.

**Deconstruction:** Late-20th-century artists critiqued (or "deconstructed") society by examining our underlying assumptions. One way to do it is to take a familiar object (say, a crucifix) out of its normal context (a church), and place it in a new setting (a jar of urine). Video and film can deconstruct something by playing it over and over, ad nauseam. Ad copy painted on canvas deconstructs itself.

**Conceptual Art:** The *concept* of which object to pair with another to produce maximum effect is the key. (Crucifix + urine = million-dollar masterpiece.)

**Performance Art:** This is a kind of mixed media of live performance. Many artists—who in another day would have painted canvases—have turned to music, dance, theater, and performance art. This art form is often interactive, by dropping the illusion of a performance and encouraging audience participation. When you finish with the Pompidou Center, go outside for some of the street theater.

**Playful Art:** Children love the art being produced today. If it doesn't put a smile on your face, well, then you must be a jaded grump like me, who's seen the same repetitious s#%t passed off as "daring" since Warhol stole it from Duchamp. I mean, it's *so* 20th century.

# CARNAVALET
# MUSEUM TOUR

*Musée Carnavalet*

At the Carnavalet Museum, French history unfolds in a series of stills—like a Ken Burns documentary, except you have to walk. The Revolution is the highlight, but you get a good overview of everything—from Louis XIV-period rooms to Napoleon to the belle époque.

## Orientation

**Cost:** Free, fee for some temporary (but optional) exhibits.

**Hours:** Tue-Sun 10:00-18:00, closed Mon. Avoid lunchtime (12:30-14:30), when many rooms may be closed.

**Getting There:** It's in the heart of the Marais district at 23 Rue de Sévigné. The best Métro stop is St. Paul, or you can get there by following my Marais Walk (see page 302). Although there is a second, larger entrance on Rue des Francs Bourgeois, this tour begins from the courtyard on Rue de Sévigné.

**Information:** Pick up the free (necessary) map at the information desk *(accueil)*. The €5 audioguide is overkill for most. Tel. 01 44 59 58 58, www.carnavalet.paris.fr.

**Length of This Tour:** Allow two hours.

**With Limited Time:** You could do the Revolution in an hour.

**Starring:** François I, Louis XIV, Louis XV, Louis XVI, the Bastille, Robespierre, the guillotine, Napoleon, Napoleon III, the Paris Commune, and the belle époque.

## Overview

The museum is housed in two Marais mansions connected by a corridor. The first half of the museum (pre-Revolution) is difficult to follow—rooms are numbered out of order, there are no English descriptions, and sections can be closed if there's not enough staff. See this part quickly, so you can concentrate your energy on the Revolution and beyond (Revolution section located on second floor—access from room 45 on the first floor). If you get lost or frustrated, we'll meet up again in room 45, where the Revolution begins.

To do this whole tour is a major course in French history. Consider limiting your visit to just the Revolution (see page 331).

# The Tour Begins
# Main Building—1500-1789

• *Go in through the entrance on Rue de Sévigné (not the one on Rue des Francs Bourgeois). Begin outside in the...*

## Courtyard

You're surrounded by the in-your-face richness of the *ancien régime*—back when people generally accepted the notion that some were born to rule, and most were born to be ruled. And the embodiment of that age stands atop the statue in the center: Louis XIV, the ultimate divine monarch.

Notice the date: July 14, 1689, exactly 100 years before the French Revolution ended rule by divine right. This statue is a rare surviving pre-Revolutionary bronze. In 1792, nearly all bronzes were melted down to make weapons, as Revolutionary France took on the rest of Europe in an all-out war. Notice the right-side relief below—a great piece of counter-Reformation propaganda. France (the angel with the royal shield) and heaven (portrayed by the angel protecting the Communion Host) are literally stomping the snakes and reformers of Protestantism (Hus, Calvin, Wycliffe, and Luther). Subtle.

• *Now go inside, turn left, and find room 7 on the ground floor at the base of the wooden stairway. Remember, if you get lost or rooms are closed, we'll meet up again in room 45, located one floor up. (To go directly to the Revolution rooms, go inside, turn right, make a quick left and walk under the iron signs, then go up the steps at the end of the room. Walk through the red hall to the next room where you'll see the stairs leading up to* La Révolution.)

## 1500s—Renaissance and Reformation
### Room 7

A **model of Ile de la Cité** (made by a monk around 1900) shows the medieval city in about 1520 before France became a world power—crowded, narrow-laned, and steeple-dotted, with houses piled even on top of bridges. There's Notre-Dame on the east end, and Sainte-Chapelle, with its royal palace and gardens, on the west. The only straight road in town was the old Roman road that splits the island north-south and is still used today.

King **François I** (1494-1547, r. 1515-1547) brought Paris into the modern world. Handsome, athletic François—a writer of poems, leader of knights, and lover of women—embodied the optimism of the Italian Renaissance. *"Le grand roi François"* (it rhymes) centralized the government around his charismatic self and made a rebuilt Louvre his home. He affirmed his absolute right to rule every time he ordered something done: "For such is our pleasure!"

### Rooms 8 and 9

Renaissance open-mindedness brought religious debate, leading to open warfare between Catholics and Protestants (called Huguenots in France). You'll find a large painting of the Catholic **King Charles IX** (1550-1574, r. 1560-1574) and a small painting of his mother, **Catherine de Médicis,** who plotted to assassinate several prominent Protestants. Their plan quickly snowballed into the slaughter of thousands of Parisian Huguenots on St. Bartholomew's Day in 1572. Paintings in both of these rooms show events organized by the **Catholic League:** parades, Bible studies, and the occasional Protestant barbecue to keep the faithful in good spirits.

### Room 10

**King Henry IV** (1553-1610, r. 1589-1610, Louis XIV's grandfather) was perhaps France's most popular king. His **bust** depicts him with a faint smile and smile lines around the eyes, capturing his reputation as a witty conversationalist and friend of commoners. Henry helped reconcile Catholics and Protestants, and rebuilt Paris. Still, that didn't stop a Revolutionary mob from tearing his equestrian statue to pieces *(Fragment du monument).* The grotesque **stone faces** are 4 of the 300 that adorn Henry's greatest creation, the Pont Neuf.

• *Head upstairs to the first floor.*

# First Floor

## The Luxury of Louis XIV, XV, and XVI

Browse around the furnished rooms, getting a feel for the luxurious life of France's kings and nobles before the Revolution. In fact, several rooms are straight out of the mansions lining the nearby Place des Vosges. The best route around the first floor is to go clockwise from the top of the stairs, using the following material as background.

• *See you in room 45, located in the far-right corner (look for the round, green booth). If you get lost, ask a guard, "Où est la Révolution?" and they'll direct you to the right place.*

## Louis XIV (1638-1715, r. 1643-1715)

The flowery walls, Greek-myth ceiling paintings, and powdered-wig portraits offer a tiny glimpse of the opulence of Louis XIV and his greatest monument, the palace at Versailles. You'll see luxurious wallpaper, tables, chairs, parquet floors, clocks, gaming tables, statues, paintings, and even a doghouse that costs more than a peasant hut. Versailles was the physical symbol of Louis' absolute power over the largest, most populous, and richest nation in Europe.

**Louis XIV Style: Baroque.** In rooms from this period, ceilings are decorated with curved ornamental frames (cartouches) that hold paintings of Greek myths, and furnishings are gilded. The heavy tables and chairs have thick, curved legs, animal feet, and bronze corner protectors.

## Louis XV (1710-1774, r. 1715-1774)

Louis XV ascended the throne of Europe's most powerful nation when his great-grandfather, the Sun King, died after reigning for 72 years. Only five years old at the time, he was for many years a figurehead, while the government was run by his mentors: a regent during his childhood, his teacher during his youth, one of his many mistresses (Madame de Pompadour) during his middle age, and bureaucrats by the end. Louis was intelligent and educated, and he personally embraced the budding democratic ideals of the Enlightenment, but he spent his time at Versailles, where he gamed and consorted with Europe's most cultured and beautiful people. Meanwhile, France's money was spent on costly wars with Austria and England (including the "French and Indian War" in America). Louis, basking in the lap of luxury and the glow of the Enlightenment, looked to the horizon and uttered his prophetic phrase: *"Après moi—le déluge!"* ("After me—the flood!").

**Louis XV Style: Rococo.** The rooms are decorated in pastel colors, with lighter decoration and exotic landscapes. The chairs are made of highly polished, rare woods, with delicate curved legs and padded seats and backs. Note the Chinese decor and objects such as the Ming vase.

## Louis XVI (1754-1793, r. 1774-1792)

With a flood watch in effect, the next Louis stubbornly clung to the rules of the *ancien régime* (the traditional chessboard society with king on top, pawns on bottom, and bishops that walk diagonally).

While peasants groaned in the fields, the rich enjoyed their mansions: parties lit by chandeliers glimmering off mirrors, the sound of a string quartet, exotic foods from newly colonized lands, billiards in one room and high-stakes card games in another, a Molière comedy downstairs, dangerous ideas by radicals like Voltaire and Jean-Jacques Rousseau, and dangerous liaisons among social butterflies—male and female—dressed in high heels, makeup, wigs, and perfume.

**Louis XVI Style: Neoclassical.** Influenced by recently excavated Pompeii, the rooms are simpler—with classical motifs—and the furniture is straighter. The chairs' straight legs taper to a point.
• *From room 45, walk down three steps and go straight through the red hallway, following signs reading* La Révolution. *At the far end, turn left and climb the stairs to* La Révolution Française.

# Second Floor

## The Revolution: 1789-1799

No period of history is as charged with the full range of human emotions and actions as the French Revolution: bloodshed, martyrdom, daring speeches, murdered priests, emancipated women, backstabbing former friends—all in the name of government "by, for, and of the people." Common people with their everyday concerns were driving the engine of history. Or perhaps they were only foam bubbles, swept along in the shifting tides of vast socioeconomic trends.

### Room 101: The Estates-General

It's 1789, France is bankrupt from wars and corruption, and the people want change. The large allegorical painting *L'Espoir du Bonheur* shows King Louis XVI in the boat of France, navigating stormy seas. Lady Truth is trying to light the way, but the winged demon of tyranny keeps nagging at the king. Above shines the fleur-de-lis, whose petals are labeled with the three social groups that held all power in France: clergy, king, and nobles. Now they are laced together by the new power...the people.

In May, the king called each sector of society together at Versailles to solve the financial crisis. But in a bold and unheard-of move, the Third Estate (the people), tired of being outvoted by the clergy and nobility, split and formed their own National Assembly—see *The Oath* ("Serment") *of the Jeu-de-Paume* on the opposite wall, a preparatory painting by Jacques-Louis David for a huge canvas that was never undertaken. Amid the chaos of speeches, debate, and deal-making, the people raised their hands, bravely pledging to stick together until a new constitution was written. Vacillating between democratic change and royalist repression, **Louis XVI** (see his pink-faced portrait to the left) ordered the Assembly to dissolve (they refused), sent 25,000 Swiss mercenary soldiers to Paris, and fired his most popular, liberal minister.

### Room 102: The Bastille (July 14, 1789)

The Bastille (see the **model**) was a medieval fortress turned prison. With its eight towers and 100-foot-high walls, it dominated the Parisian skyline, a symbol of oppression. (Check out the series of **paintings** that illustrate some of the following events.)

On the hot, muggy morning of July 14, Paris' citizens waited, on edge, listening to reports of attacks on the populace by the king's Swiss guards. A crowd formed, marched on the Invalides armory, and seized 30,000 rifles...but no gunpowder. Word spread that it was stored across town at the Bastille. The mob grew bigger and angrier as it traveled. By noon they stood at the foot of the walls of the Bastille and demanded gunpowder. They captured the fort's governor, and then two citizens managed to scale the wall and cut the chains. The drawbridge crashed down, and the mob poured through. Terrified guards opened fire, killing dozens and wounding hundreds. At the battle's peak, French soldiers in red and blue appeared on the horizon...but whose side were they on?

A loud cheer went up as they pointed their cannons at the Bastille, and the fort surrendered. The mob trashed the Bastille, opened the dark dungeons, and brought seven prisoners into the light of day. They then stormed City Hall (Hôtel de Ville) and arrested the mayor, who was literally torn apart by the hysterical crowd. His head was stuck on a stick and carried through the city. The Revolution had begun.

Today, the events of July 14 are celebrated every Bastille Day with equally colorful festivities. The Bastille itself was soon dismantled, stone by stone. Nothing remains but the open space of Place de la Bastille, but the memory became a rallying cry throughout the Revolution: *"Vive le quatorze juillet!"* ("Long live July 14th!")

## Room 103: The Celebration
## (La Fête de la Fédération, 1790)

Imagine the jubilation! To be able to shout out things formerly whispered in fear—finally.

The large painting of *La Fête de la Fédération* shows the joy and exuberance of the people as they celebrate the first anniversary of Bastille Day (July 14, 1790). Liberty! Equality! Fraternity! Members of every social class (even including, it appears, three women) hugged, kissed, and mingled on the Champ de Mars, where the Eiffel Tower stands today. The crowd built an artificial mound for heroes of the Revolution to ascend while a choir sang. Women dressed to symbolize Truth, Freedom, Justice, and other capital-letter virtues were worshipped in a new kind of secular religion. Public demonstrations like these must have infuriated the king, queen, bishops, and nobles, who were now quarantined in their palaces, fuming impotently.

The *Declaration* ("Tables") *of the Rights of Man and the Citizen* (see two different versions) made freedom the law. The preamble makes it clear that *"Le Peuple Français"* (the French people)—not the king—were the ultimate authority. "Men are born free and equal," it states, possessing "freedom of the individual, freedom of conscience, freedom of speech."

## Room 104: Louis XVI Quietly Responds
## (De la Monarchie à la République, 1789-1792)

**Louis XVI** (see the bust)—studious, shy, aloof, and easily dominated—was stunned by the ferocious summer of 1789. The Bastille's violence spread to the countryside, where uppity peasants tenderized their masters with pitchforks. The Assembly was changing France with lightning speed: abolishing Church privileges, nationalizing nobles' land, and declaring the king irrelevant. Louis accepted his role as a

rubber-stamp monarch, hoping the furor would pass and trying to appear idealistic and optimistic.

But looming on the horizon was...*Le docteur Joseph-Ignace Guillotin* (see portrait, opposite the window). The progressive Assembly abolished brutal, medieval-style torture and executions. In their place, Dr. Guillotin proposed a kinder, gentler execution device that would make France a model of compassion. The guillotine—also known as "the national razor," or simply "The Machine"—could instantly make someone "a head shorter at the top." (It claimed its last victim in 1977; capital punishment is now abolished in France.)

## Room 105: Royalty Loses Its Head
## (La Famille Royale, 1793)

Louis' wife, **Queen Marie-Antoinette** (several portraits), became the focus of the citizens' disgust. Reports flew that she spent extravagantly and had plunged France into debt. More decisive than her husband, she steered him toward repressive measures meant to snuff out the Revolution. Worst of all, she was foreign-born, known simply as "The Austrian," and soon Austria was trying to preserve the monarchy by making war on the French. A rumor spread—one that had been common among the poor in France for more than a decade—that when Marie was informed that the Parisians had no bread to eat, she had sneered, "Let them eat cake!" ("Cake" was the term for the burnt crusts peeled off the oven and generally fed only to cattle.) Historians today find no evidence Marie ever said it.

Enraged and hungry, 6,000 Parisian women (backed by armed men) marched through the rain to Versailles to demand lower bread prices. On the night of October 5, 1789, a small band infiltrated the palace, burst into the queen's room, killed her bodyguards, and chased her down the hall. The royal family was kidnapped and taken to Paris, where—though still monarchs—they were placed under house arrest in the Tuileries Palace (which once stood where the Louvre now meets the Tuileries Garden).

Three years later, the royal family became actual prisoners (see the reconstructed and rather cushy **Prison du Temple** in room 106) after trying to escape to Austria to begin a counterrevolution. One of their servants pretended to be a German baroness, while Louis dressed up as her servant (the irony must have been killing him). When a citizen recognized Louis from his portrait on a franc note, the family was captured, thrown into prison, and soon put on trial as traitors to France. The National Convention (the Assembly's successor) declared the monarchy abolished.

The royal family—Louis, Marie-Antoinette, and their eight-year-old son—was tearfully split up (see the painting *Les Adieux de Louis XVI à Sa Famille* in room 105), and Marie-Antoinette was imprisoned in the Conciergerie.

On January 21, 1793 (see **execution painting**), King Louis

XVI (excuse me, that's "Citizen Capet") was led to Place de la Concorde and laid face down on a slab, and then—*shoop!*—a thousand years of monarchy that dated back to before Charlemagne was decapitated. On October 16, 1793 (see **painting**), Marie-Antoinette also met her fate on Place de la Concorde. Genteel to the end, she apologized to the executioner for stepping on his foot. The blade fell, the blood gushed, and her head was shown to the crowd on a stick—an exclamation point for the new rallying cry: *Vive la nation!*

Little **Louis XVII** (portrait in opposite corner) died in prison at age 10. Rumors spread that the boy-king had escaped, fueled by Elvis-type sightings and impersonators. But DNA evidence confirms that the *dauphin* (heir to the throne) did indeed die in prison in 1795.

## Room 108: The Reign of Terror
## (La Convention—La Terreur, 1793-1794)

Here are **portraits** of key players in the Revolutionary spectacle. Some were moderate reformers, some radical priest-killers. With Europe ganging up on the Revolution, they all lived in fear that any backward step could tip the delicate balance of power back to the *ancien régime.* Enemies of the Revolution were everywhere—even in their own ranks.

By the summer of 1793, the left-of-center Jacobin party took control of France's fledgling democracy. Pug-faced but silver-tongued **Georges Danton** (look for portrait of this Newt Gingrich look-alike) drove the Revolution with his personal charisma and bold speeches: "To conquer the enemies of the fatherland, we need daring, more daring, daring now, always daring." He led the Committee of Public Safety to root out and execute those enemies, even moderates opposed to the Jacobins.

More radical still was **Jean-Paul Marat,** the "Friend of the People" (his portrait is two down from Danton—after Robespierre, whom we'll get to in a moment). Marat dressed and burped like a man of the street, but he wrote eloquently against all forms of authority. Wildly popular with the commoners, he was seen by others as a loose cannon. A beautiful 25-year-old noblewoman named **Charlotte Corday** decided it was her mission in life to save France by silencing him. On July 11, 1793, she entered his home under the pretext of giving him names of counterrevolutionaries.

Marat, seated in a bathtub to nurse a skin condition, wrote down the names and said, "Good. I'll have them all guillotined." Corday stood up, whipped a knife out from under her dress, and stabbed him through the heart. Corday was guillotined, and Marat was hailed as a martyr to the cause.

Marat's death was further "proof" that counterrevolutionaries were everywhere. For the next year (summer of 1793 to summer of 1794, see fiery **paintings of guillotine scenes** and a small guillotine model nearby), the Jacobin government arrested, briefly tried, and then guillotined everyone suspected of being "enemies of the Revolution": nobles, priests, the rich, and many true Revolutionaries who simply belonged to the wrong political party. More than 2,500 Parisians were beheaded, 18,000 were executed by other means, and tens of thousands died in similar violence throughout the country. The violence that began at the **Bastille** in July of 1789 would climax in July of 1794.

Master of the Reign of Terror was **Maximilien de Robespierre** (the portrait next to Danton's), a 35-year-old lawyer who promoted the Revolution with a religious fervor. By July of 1794, the guillotine was slicing 30 necks a day. In Paris' main squares, grim executions alternated with politically correct public spectacles that honored "Liberty," "Truth," and the heroes of France. As the death toll rose, so did public cynicism. Finally, Robespierre even sentenced to death his old friend Danton, who had spoken out against the bloodshed. As Danton knelt under the blade, he joked, "My turn." The people had had enough.

## Room 109: Terror Ends (Thermidor—Le Directoire, July 1794)

**Engravings** show the chaos—riots, assassinations, food shortages, inflation—that fueled Robespierre's meteoric fall from power. Robespierre's own self-righteousness made him an easy target. On July 27, 1794, as Robespierre prepared to name the daily list of victims, his fellow committee members started yelling "Tyrant!" and shouted him down. Stunned by the sudden fall from grace, Robespierre unsuccessfully attempted suicide by shooting himself in the mouth.

The next day he walked the walk he'd ordered thousands to take. Hands tied behind his back, he was carried through the streets on a two-wheeled cart, while citizens jeered and spat on him. At the guillotine, the broken-down demagogue had no last words, thanks to his wounded jaw. When the executioner yanked off the bandage, Robespierre let out a horrible cry, the blade fell, and the Reign of Terror came to an end.

From 1795 to 1799, France caught its breath, ruled by the Directory, a government so intentionally weak and decentralized (two houses of parliament, five executives, and no funding) that it could never create another Robespierre.

### Room 110: France vs. Europe (La Guerre)

The blade that dropped on Louis XVI rattled royal teacups throughout Europe. Even as early as 1792, France had to defend its young democracy against Austria and Prussia. France's new army was composed of ordinary citizens from a universal draft and led by daring young citizen-officers, who sang a stirring, bloodthirsty new song, "La Marseillaise." Surprisingly, they quickly defeated the apathetic mercenaries they faced. France vowed to liberate all Europe from tyranny. Europe feared that, by "exporting Revolution," France would export democracy...plus senseless violence and chaos.

A young Corsican named **Napoleon Bonaparte** (see the bust) rose quickly through the ranks and proved himself by fighting royalists in Italy, Egypt, and on the streets of Paris. In 1799, the 29-year-old general returned to Paris as a conquering hero. Backed by an adoring public, he dissolved the Directory, established order, and gave himself the Roman-style title of "first consul."

### Room 111: The Revolution vs. Religion (Vandalisme et Conservation)

Three-fourths of France's churches were destroyed or vandalized during the Revolution, a backlash against the wealthy and politically repressive Catholic Church. In Notre-Dame, Christ was mothballed, and a woman dressed as "Dame Reason" was worshipped on the altar.

### Room 113: Souvenirs of Revolution

After the Reign of Terror, *Liberté, Egalité, Fraternité* was just a slogan, remembered fondly on commemorative **plates and knick-knacks.** The Revolution was history.

• *The visit continues down three flights of stairs—or down the elevator—on the ground floor.*

## French National Anthem: "La Marseillaise"

The genteel French have a gory past.

| | |
|---|---|
| *Allons enfants de la Patrie,* | Let's go, children of the motherland, |
| *Le jour de gloire est arrivé.* | The day of glory has arrived. |
| *Contre nous de la tyrannie* | The blood-covered flag of tyranny |
| *L'étendard sanglant est levé.* | Is raised against us. |
| *L'étendard sanglant est levé.* | Is raised against us. |
| *Entendez-vous dans les campagnes* | Do you hear these ferocious soldiers |
| *Mugir ces féroces soldats?* | Howling in the countryside? |
| *Qui viennent jusque dans nos bras* | They're coming nearly into our grasp |
| *Egorger vos fils et vos compagnes.* | To slit the throats of your sons and your women. |
| *Aux armes, citoyens,* | Grab your weapons, citizens, |
| *Formez vos bataillons,* | Form your battalions, |
| *Marchons, marchons,* | We march, we march, |
| *Qu'un sang impur* | So that their impure blood |
| *Abreuve nos sillons.* | Will fill our trenches. |

## Room 115: Napoleon Conquers Europe (Le Premier Empire, 1799-1815)

Here's **Napoleon I** at the peak of power, master of Western Europe (see **portrait, breastplate, pistols,** and **death mask** in glass case). Dressed in his general's uniform, he's checking the maps to see who's left to conquer. Behind him is a throne with his imperial seal. This Corsican-born commoner (1769-1821, ruled as emperor 1804-1815), educated in Paris' military schools, became a young Revolutionary and a daring general, rising to prominence as a champion of democracy. Once in power, he preached revolution, but in fact became a dictator and crowned himself emperor (1804).

During the Empire, all things classical became popular. Wealthy socialites such as **Juliette Récamier** (see painting) donned robes and lounged on couches, while Paris was rebuilt with Neoclassical monuments, such as the Arc de Triomphe, to make it the "New Rome."

In 1812, Napoleon foolishly invaded Russia, thus starting a downward spiral that ended in defeat by allied Europe at the Battle of Waterloo in Belgium (1815). Napoleon was exiled. He died in 1821 on the island of St. Helena, off the coast of Africa.

## Room 118: The Monarchy Restored
## (La Restauration, 1815-1830)

After almost 25 years in exile, royalty returned. First, Louis XVIII (the younger brother of headless Louis XVI) ruled as a constitutional monarch. The next king, **Charles X** (youngest brother of Louis XVI), dressed in glorious coronation robes, revived the fashion and oppression of the *ancien régime* as he plotted to dissolve the people's Assembly. But the French people were not about to turn back the clock.

## Room 119: Revolution of 1830 (Juillet 1830)

Parisians again blocked off the narrow streets with barricades to fight the king's red-coated soldiers (see various **street battle paintings**). After "Three Glorious Days" of fighting, order was restored by Louis-Philippe (see **model of Hôtel de Ville**), an unassuming nobleman who appeared on the balcony of the Hôtel de Ville and was cheered by royalists, the middle class, and peasants alike. They made him king.

## Room 120: Constitutional Monarchy
## (La Monarchie de Juillet, 1830-1848)

**King Louis-Philippe** (1773-1850, r. 1830-1848, see black bust with epaulettes)—a former lieutenant turned banker, with a few drops of royal blood—was a true constitutional monarch, harmlessly presiding over an era of middle-class progress fueled by the Industrial Revolution. Still, liberal reforms came too slowly. New factories brought division between wealthy employers and poor workers, and only 200,000 out of 30 million French citizens (1/150) could vote.

## Room 121: Revolution of 1848
## (La Deuxième République)

In February of 1848—a time of Europe-wide depression and socialist strikes—Parisians took to the streets again **(battle scenes)**. They battled at the Palais-Royal, Panthéon, and Place de la Concorde, and they toppled the king. After five decades of dictators (including Napoleon), retread Bourbons (the Restoration), and self-proclaimed monarchs (Louis-Philippe), France was back in the hands of the people—the Second Republic.

## Room 122: Romanticism (Le Romantisme)

Freedom of expression, the uniqueness of each person, the glories of the human spirit and the natural world—these values from the 1789 Revolution were extolled by artists of the 1800s known as Romantics.

You'll see **caricature busts** of many famous Frenchmen and visitors to Paris, the center of European culture. There's Victor Hugo (author of *Les Misérables* and *The Hunchback of Notre-Dame*), Frédéric Chopin (Polish pianist who charmed Parisian society), Giuseppe Verdi (composer of stirring operas, such as *Aida*), and Gioacchino Rossini *(William Tell Overture)*.

There are also **paintings** of the glamorous pianist Franz Liszt and his mistress, Marie d'Agoult—the ultimate Romantic. She left her husband and children to follow the dynamic Liszt on a journey of self-discovery in Italy and Switzerland—"the years of pilgrimage."

• *Journey upstairs and to the left toward...*

## Room 128: Napoleon III and the Second Empire (Le Second Empire, 1852-1870)

**Louis-Napoleon Bonaparte** (1808-1873, ruled as emperor 1852-1871; in the big painting, with red pants and sash, waxed moustache, and goatee) was the nephew of the famous Emperor Napoleon I. He used his well-known name to get elected president by a landslide in 1848, and then combined democracy with monarchy to be voted "Emperor Napoleon III." He suppressed opposition while promoting liberal reforms as well as economic and colonial expansion.

Here he hands an order to **Baron Georges Haussmann** (mutton-chop sideburns) to modernize Paris. Haussmann cut the wide, straight boulevards of today to move goods, open up the crowded city...and prevent barricades in future revolutions. Parks, railroad stations, and the Opéra Garnier made Paris the model for world capitals. (Room 129 shows building projects.)

The **boat-like cradle** (room 128) is a copy of the famous cradle of Napoleon II (1811-1832, known to history as the King of Rome), the only son of Napoleon I, who died at 21 of tuberculosis before ever ruling anything.

Napoleon III pursued popular wars (the **model** in room 129 celebrates Crimean War vets, 1855) and unpopular ones (backing Austrian Emperor Maximilian in Mexico). In the summer of 1870,

he personally led a jubilant French Army to crush upstart Prussia—
"On to Berlin!" Uh-oh.

## Room 130: The Franco-Prussian War
## (Le Siège de Paris, 1870-1871)

Within weeks the overconfident French were surrounded, Napoleon III himself was captured, and he surrendered. Paris was
stunned. (See the big **painting of a crowd** hearing the news on the
legislature steps.) The Germans quickly put a stranglehold on Paris,
and a long, especially cold winter settled in.

Some would not give up. Without an emperor, they proclaimed yet another democratic republic (France's third in a century) and sent minister Léon Gambetta in a newfangled balloon
**(painting)** over the Germans' heads to rally the countryside to
come save Paris. The Parisians themselves held out bravely (**painting of Tuileries** as army camp), but German efficiency and modern
technology simply overwhelmed the French.

## Room 131: The Paris Commune
## (La Commune, Spring 1871)

The Republic finally agreed to a humiliating surrender. Paris' liberals—enraged at the capitulation after such a brave winter and fearing a return of monarchy—rejected the surrender and proclaimed
their own government, the Paris Commune. **Portraits** honor the
proud idealists, who barricaded themselves inside Paris' neighborhoods, refusing to bow to the German emperor.

Then, in one "bloody week" in May **(battle scenes),** French
troops backing the Republic stormed through Paris, leaving 15,000
dead, 5,000 jailed, and 8,000 deported. The Commune was snuffed
out, but the memory was treasured by generations of liberals in
popular **souvenirs:** a jar of bread from the hungry winter, a carrier
pigeon's feather, a box reading *"Vive la Commune!"*

The church of Sacré-Cœur (see **painting** way up high) was
built after the war as a form of national penance for the sins of
liberalism.

## Rooms 132-142: The Beautiful Age
## (La Belle Epoque, 1871-1914)

The Third Republic restored peace to a prosperous middle-class
society. The **Eiffel Tower** (rooms 132-133) marked the 1889 centennial of the Revolution, and the **Statue of Liberty** honored
America's revolution.

Paris was a capital of world culture in the era known as the
belle époque (beautiful age). It was a city of **Impressionist painters**
(room 135) and of writers and actors, including the actress **Sarah
Bernhardt** (room 136), called the world's first international star ("a

force of nature, a fiery soul, a marvelous intelligence, a magnificent creature of the highest order," raved one of the smitten).

And it was the city of Art Nouveau (see two delightful **Art Nouveau** rooms, 141-142)—don't miss the facade as you leave room 142.

### Room 145: World War I (1914-1918)
Three costly wars with Germany—the Franco-Prussian War, World War I, and World War II—drained France's resources. Although **Marshal Foch** (big painting above the elevator) is hailed as the man who coordinated the Allied armies to defeat Germany in World War I, France was hardly a winner. More than 1.5 million Frenchmen died, a generation was lost, and the country would be a pushover when Hitler invaded in 1940. France's long history as a global superpower was over.

### Room 147: Remembrance of Things Past (La Vie Littéraire du XXe Siècle)
The last room is filled with portraits of Paris' 20th-century literary greats. By producing such figures as the writer **Marcel Proust** (see his reconstructed bedroom) and the dreamy writer/filmmaker **Jean Cocteau,** France has remained a cultural superpower.
• *To find the exit, walk back through that red hall, then down the stairs.*

CARNAVALET MUSEUM

# PERE LACHAISE CEMETERY TOUR

*Cimetière du Père Lachaise*

Enclosed by a massive wall and lined with 5,000 trees, the peaceful, car-free lanes and dirt paths of Père Lachaise cemetery encourage park-like meandering. Named for Father *(Père)* La Chaise, whose job was listening to Louis XIV's sins, the cemetery is relatively new, having opened in 1804 to accommodate Paris' expansion. Today, this city of the dead (pop. 70,000) still accepts new residents, but real estate prices are sky high (a 21-square-foot plot costs more than €11,000).

The 100-acre cemetery is big and confusing, with thousands of graves and tombs crammed every which way, and only a few pedestrian pathways to help you navigate. The maps available from any of the nearby florists help guide your way, but you're better off taking my tour as you play grave-hunt with the cemetery's other visitors. This walk takes you on a one-way tour between two convenient Métro/bus stops (Gambetta and Père Lachaise), connecting a handful of graves from some of this necropolis' best-known residents.

## Orientation

**Cost:** Free.

**Hours:** Mon-Fri 8:00-18:00, Sat 8:30-18:00, Sun 9:00-18:00, closes at 17:30 in winter, last entry 15 minutes before closing.

**Getting There:** Catch bus #69 to the end of the line (see the Bus #69 Sightseeing Tour chapter), or take the Métro to the Gambetta stop (not to the Père Lachaise stop). Bus #69 ends at Place Gambetta, two blocks from the cemetery. Walk past McDonald's, then follow signs to the cemetery. If you're taking the Métro, exit at Gambetta Métro, take *sortie* #3 (Père Lachaise exit), turn left, and follow signs to Père Lachaise.

PÈRE LACHAISE CEMETERY

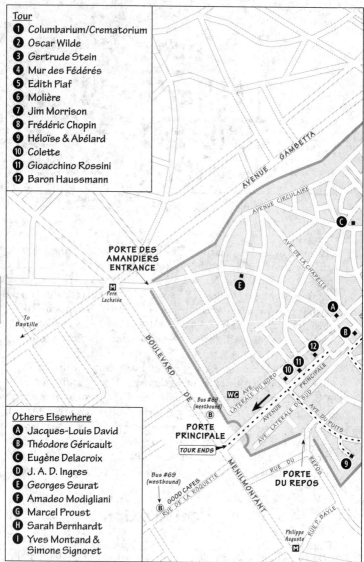

**Tour**
1. Columbarium/Crematorium
2. Oscar Wilde
3. Gertrude Stein
4. Mur des Fédérés
5. Edith Piaf
6. Molière
7. Jim Morrison
8. Frédéric Chopin
9. Héloïse & Abélard
10. Colette
11. Gioacchino Rossini
12. Baron Haussmann

**Others Elsewhere**
A. Jacques-Louis David
B. Théodore Géricault
C. Eugène Delacroix
D. J. A. D. Ingres
E. Georges Seurat
F. Amadeo Modigliani
G. Marcel Proust
H. Sarah Bernhardt
I. Yves Montand & Simone Signoret

Either way, it's two short blocks up Avenue du Père Lachaise, which ends at the cemetery.

**Information:** Maps are sold at nearby florists. This non-official website has a searchable map: www.pere-lachaise.com. Tel. 01 55 25 82 10.

**Length of This Tour:** Allow 1.5 hours for this walk, and another

Père Lachaise Cemetery Tour

Bus #69 B (Start & End Point)

M Gambetta

PORTE GAMBETTA ENTRANCE

WC

TOUR BEGINS

AVE. DE PÈRE LACHAISE

RUE DE RONDEAUX

AVENUE CIRCULAIRE

AVE. DES COMBATTANTES-ETRANGERS

AVENUE TRANSVERSALE NO. 2

G

1 COLUMBARIUM

I

H

AVE. ST. MORYS

AVENUE TRANSVERSALE MARRONIERS

D

CHAPEL

BASSIN MOLIERE

6

AVE. CANETTE

AVE. GREFFULHE

2

AVENUE TRANSVERSALE NO. 3

3

4

F

5

NO. 1

8

DENON

GRAND ROND

AVE. CAS PERIER

CHEM. BEDOYERE

LESSEPS

7

CHEMIN SERRE

TRANSVERSAL NO. 1

AVE. CIRCULAIRE

PORTE DE LA REUNION

100 Meters

100 Yards

PÈRE LACHAISE CEMETERY

30 minutes for your own detours. Bring good walking shoes for the rough, cobbled streets.

**Services:** There are WCs at the start of this tour, just inside the Porte Gambetta entrance, and at the end of this tour, at Porte Principale.

**Eating:** You'll pass several cafés and a small grocery shop between Place Gambetta and the cemetery. After the tour, you can walk downhill from the cemetery on Rue de la Roquette to a gaggle of lively, affordable cafés on the right side of the street, near the return stop for bus #69.

**Starring:** Oscar Wilde, Edith Piaf, Gertrude Stein, Molière, Jim Morrison, Frédéric Chopin, Héloïse and Abélard, Colette, and Rossini.

## Overview

From the Porte Gambetta entrance, we'll walk roughly southwest (mostly downhill) through the cemetery. At the end of the tour, we'll exit Porte Principale onto Boulevard de Ménilmontant, near the Père Lachaise Métro entrance and another bus #69 stop. (You can follow the tour heading the other direction, but it's not recommended—it's confusing, and almost completely uphill.)

Be sure to keep referring to the map on page 344, and follow street signs posted at intersections. The layout of the cemetery makes an easy-to-follow tour impossible. It's a little easier if you buy a more detailed map to use along with our rather general one. Be patient, make a few discoveries of your own, and ask passersby for graves you can't locate.

## The Tour Begins

• *Entering the cemetery at the Porte Gambetta entrance, walk straight up Avenue des Combattants past World War memorials, cross Avenue Transversale No. 3, pass the first building, and look left to the...*

## ❶ Columbarium/Crematorium

Marked by a dome with a gilded flame and working chimneys on top, the columbarium sits in a courtyard surrounded by about 1,300 niches, small cubicles for cremated remains, often decorated with real or artificial flowers.

Beneath the courtyard (steps leading underground) are about 12,000 smaller niches, including one for Maria Callas (1923-1977), an American-born opera diva known for her versatility, flair for drama, and affair with Aristotle Onassis (niche #16258, down aisle J).

• *Turn around and walk back to the intersection with Avenue Transversale No. 3. Turn right, heading southeast on the avenue, turn left on*

*Avenue Carette, and walk half a block to the block-of-stone tomb (on the left) with heavy-winged angels trying to fly.*

## ❷ Oscar Wilde (1854-1900)

The writer and martyr to homo-sexuality is mourned by "outcast men" (as the inscription says) and by wearers of heavy lipstick, who used to cover the tomb and the angels' emasculated privates with kisses. (Now the tomb is behind glass.) Despite Wilde's notoriety, an inscription says, "He died fortified by the Sacraments of the Church." There's a short résumé scratched (in English) into the back side of the tomb. For more on Wilde and his death in Paris, see page 270.

*"Alas, I am dying beyond my means."*

—Oscar Wilde

• *Continue along Avenue Carette and turn right (southeast) down Avenue Circulaire. A block and a half down, you'll reach Gertrude Stein's unadorned, easy-to-miss grave (on the right just before a yellow stone structure).*

## ❸ Gertrude Stein (1874-1946)

While traveling through Europe, the twentysomething American dropped out of med school and moved to Paris, her home for the rest of her life. She shared an apartment at 27 Rue de Fleurus (a couple of blocks west of Luxembourg Garden) with her brother Leo and, later, with her life partner, Alice B. Toklas (who's also buried here, see gravestone's flipside). Every Saturday night, Paris' brightest artistic lights converged *chez vingt-sept* (at 27) for dinner and intellectual stimulation. Picasso painted her portrait, Hemingway sought her approval, and Virgil Thompson set her words to music.

America discovered "Gerty" in 1933 when her memoirs, the slyly titled *Autobiography of Alice B. Toklas*, hit the best-seller list. After 30 years away, she returned to the United States for a triumphant lecture tour. Her writing is less well-known than her persona, except for the oft-quoted, "A rose is a rose is a rose."

Stein's last words: When asked, "What is the answer?" she replied, "What is the question?"

• *Ponder Stein's tomb again and again and again, and continue southeast on Avenue Circulaire to where it curves to the right. Emaciated statues remember victims of the concentration camps and Nazi resistance heroes. Pebbles on the tombstones represent Jewish prayers. At the corner of the cemetery, veer left off the road a few steps, to the wall marked* Aux Morts de la Commune.

## ❹ Mur des Fédérés

The "Communards' Wall" marks the place where the quixotic Paris Commune came to a violent end.

In 1870, Prussia invaded France, and the country quickly collapsed and surrendered—all except the city of Paris. For six months, through a bitter winter, the Prussians laid siege to the city. Defiant Paris held out, even opposing the French government, which had fled to Versailles and was collaborating with the Germans. Parisians formed an opposition government that was revolutionary and socialist, called the Paris Commune.

The Versailles government sent French soldiers to retake Paris. In May of 1871, they breached the west walls and swept eastward. French soldiers fought French citizens, and tens of thousands died during a bloody week of street fighting (La Semaine Sanglante). The remaining resisters holed up inside the walls of Père Lachaise and made an Alamo-type last stand before they were finally overcome.

At dawn on May 28, 1871, the 147 Communards were lined up against this wall and shot by French soldiers. They were buried in a mass grave where they fell. With them the Paris Commune died, and the city entered five years of martial law.

• *Return to the road, continue to the next (unmarked) street, Avenue Transversale No. 3, and turn right. A half-block uphill, Edith Piaf's grave is on the right. It's one grave off the street, behind a white tombstone with a small gray cross. Edith Gassion-Piaf rests among many graves. Hers is often adorned with photos, fresh flowers, and love notes.*

## ❺ Edith Piaf (1915-1963)

A child of the Parisian streets, Piaf was raised in her grandma's bordello and her father's traveling circus troupe. The teenager sang for spare change in Paris' streets, where a nightclub owner discovered her. Waif-like and dressed in black, she sang in a warbling voice under the name "La Môme Piaf" (The Little Sparrow). She became the toast of pre-WWII Paris society.

Her offstage love life was busy and often messy, including a teenage pregnancy (her daughter is buried along with her, in a grave marked *Marcelle Dupont, 1933-1935*), a murdered husband, and a heartbreaking affair with costar Yves Montand.

With her strong but trembling voice, she buoyed French spirits under the German occupation, and her most famous song, "La Vie en Rose" (The Rosy Life) captured the joy of postwar Paris. In her personal life she struggled with alcohol, painkillers, and poor health, while onstage she sang, *"Non, je ne regrette rien"* ("No, I don't regret anything").

• *From Edith Piaf's grave, continue up along Avenue Transversale No. 3, and turn left on Avenue Greffulhe. Follow Greffulhe straight (even when it narrows), until it dead-ends at Avenue Transversale No. 1. Continue ahead on a dirt path (veering slightly to the right) and walk 20 paces to where you reach Chemin Molière et La Fontaine. Turn right. Molière lies 30 yards down, on the right side of the street, just beyond the highest point of this lane.*

## ❻ Molière (1622-1675)

In 1804, the great comic playwright was the first to be reburied in Père Lachaise, a publicity stunt that gave instant prestige to the new cemetery.

Born in Paris, Molière was not of noble blood, but as the son of the king's furniture supervisor, he had connections. The 21-year-old Molière joined a troupe of strolling players, who ranked very low on the social scale, touring the provinces. Twelve long years later, they returned to Paris to perform before Louis XIV. Molière, by now an accomplished comic actor, cracked the king up. He was instantly famous—writing, directing, and often starring in his own works. He satirized rich nobles, hypocritical priests, and quack doctors, creating enemies in high places.

On February 17, 1675, an aging Molière went on stage in the title role of his latest comedy, *The Imaginary Invalid*. Though sick, he insisted he had to go on, concerned for all the little people. His role was of a hypochondriac who coughs to get sympathy. The deathly ill Molière effectively faked coughing fits...which soon turned to real convulsions. The unaware crowd roared with laughter while his fellow players fretted in the wings.

In the final scene, Molière's character becomes a doctor himself in a mock swearing-in ceremony. The ultimate trouper, Molière finished his final line—*"Juro"* ("I accept")—and collapsed while coughing blood. The audience laughed hysterically. He died shortly thereafter.

Irony upon irony for the master of satire: Molière—a sick man whose doctors thought he was a hypochondriac—dies playing a well man who is a hypochondriac, succumbing onstage while the audience cheers.

Molière lies next to his friend and fellow writer, La Fontaine (1621-1695), who wrote a popular version of Aesop's Fables.

> *"We die only once, and for such a long time."*
>
> —Molière

• *Continue downhill on Chemin Molière (which becomes the paved Chemin du Bassin), and turn left on Avenue de la Chapelle. It leads to the Rond Point roundabout intersection.*

*Cross Carrefour Rond Point and continue straight (opposite where you entered, on unmarked Chemin de la Bédoyère). Just a few steps along, veer to the right onto Chemin Lauriston. Keep to the left on Chemin de Lesseps, and look (immediately) for the temple on the right with three wreaths. Jim Morrison lies just behind, often with a personal security guard. You can't miss the commotion.*

## ❼ Jim Morrison (1943-1971)

An American rock star has perhaps the most visited tomb in the cemetery. An iconic, funky bust of the rocker, which was stolen by fans, was replaced with a more toned-down headstone. Even so, Morrison's faithful still gather here at all hours. The headstone's Greek inscription reads: "To the spirit (or demon) within." Graffiti-ing nearby tombs, fans write: "You still Light My Fire" (referring to Jim's biggest hit), "Ring my bell at the Dead Rock Star Hotel," and "Mister Mojo Risin'" (referring to the legend that Jim faked his death and still lives today).

Jim Morrison—singer for the popular rock band The Doors (named for the "Doors of Perception" they aimed to open)—arrived in Paris in the winter of 1971. He was famous, notorious for his erotic onstage antics, now a burned-out alcoholic. Paris was to be his chance to leave celebrity behind, get healthy, and get serious as a writer.

Living under an assumed name in a nondescript sublet apartment near Place de la Bastille (head west down Rue St. Antoine, and turn left to 17 Rue Beautrellis), he spent his days as a carefree artist. He scribbled in notebooks at Le Café de Flore and Les Deux Magots (☉ see the Left Bank Walk chapter), watched the sun set from the steps of Sacré-Cœur, visited Baudelaire's house, and jammed with street musicians. He drank a lot, took other drugs, gained weight, and his health declined.

In the wee hours of July 3, he died in his bathtub at age 27, officially of a heart attack, but likely from an overdose. (Any police investigation was thwarted by Morrison's social circle of heroin users, leading to wild rumors surrounding his death.)

Jim's friends approached Père Lachaise Cemetery about burying the famous rock star there, in accordance with his wishes. The director refused to admit him, until they mentioned that Jim was a writer. "A writer?" he said, and he found a spot.

> *"This is the end, my only friend, the end."*
>
> —Jim Morrison

• *Return to Rond Point, cross it, and retrace your steps—sorry, but there are no straight lines connecting these dead geniuses. Retrace your steps up Avenue de la Chapelle. At the intersection with the small park and chapels, turn left onto Avenue Laterale du Sud. Walk down two sets of stairs and turn left onto narrow Chemin Denon. "Fred" Chopin's grave— usually adorned with flowers, burning candles, and his fans—is about 80 yards down on the left.*

## ➑ Frédéric Chopin (1810-1849)

Fresh-cut flowers and geraniums on the gravestone speak of the emotional staying power of Chopin's music, which still connects souls across the centuries. A muse sorrows atop the tomb, and a carved relief of Chopin in profile captures the delicate features of this sensitive artist.

The 21-year-old Polish pianist arrived in Paris, fell in love with the city, and never returned to his homeland (which was occupied by an increasingly oppressive Russia). In Paris, he could finally shake off the "child prodigy" label and performance schedule he'd lived with since age seven. Cursed with stage fright ("I don't like concerts. The crowds scare me, their breath chokes me, I'm paralyzed by their stares...") and with too light a touch for big venues, Chopin preferred playing at private parties for Paris' elite. They were wowed by his technique; his ability to make a piano sing; and his melodic,

# Other Notable Residents

Though not along our walking tour, the following folks can be found on our map, as well as the maps for sale from the florists.

**A Jacques-Louis David (1748-1825)—Section 56**
The Neoclassical painter David chronicled the heroic Revolution and the Napoleonic Era. See his *Coronation of Napoleon* in the Louvre (page 140).

**B Théodore Géricault (1791-1824)—Section 12**
Géricault was the master of painting extreme situations (shipwrecks, battles) and extreme emotions (noble sacrifice, courage, agony, insanity) with Romantic realism. See his *Raft of the Medusa* in the Louvre (page 141).

**C Eugène Delacroix (1798-1863)—Section 49**
For more on this Romantic painter, see his *Liberty Leading the People* in the Louvre (page 142) or visit the Delacroix Museum (see the Left Bank Walk chapter).

**D Jean-August-Dominique Ingres (1780-1867)—Section 23**
Often considered the anti-Delacroix, Ingres was a painter of placid portraits and bathing nudes, using curved outlines and smooth-surfaced paint. Despite his deliberate distortions (see his beautifully deformed *La Grande Odalisque* in the Louvre, page 141), he was hailed as the champion of traditional Neoclassical balance against the furious Romantic style (see his *The Source* in the Orsay, page 156).

**E Georges Seurat (1859-1891)—Section 66**
Georges spent Sunday afternoons in the park with his easel, capturing shimmering light by using tiny dots of different-colored paint. See his Pointillist canvas *The Circus* in the Orsay (page 171).

**F Amadeo Modigliani (1884-1920)—Section 96, not far from Edith Piaf**
Poor, tubercular, and strung out on drugs and alcohol in Paris, this young Italian painter forged a distinctive style. His portraits and nudes have African mask-like faces and elongated necks and arms.

**G Marcel Proust (1871-1922)—Section 85**
Some who make it through the seven volumes and 3,000

soul-stirring compositions. Soon he was recognized as a pianist, composer, and teacher, and even idolized as a brooding genius. He ran in aristocratic circles with fellow artists, such as pianist Franz Liszt, painter Delacroix, novelists Victor Hugo and Balzac, and composer Rossini. (All but Liszt and Hugo lie in Père Lachaise—although Hugo has another memorial in the Panthéon, so he may actually be buried there.)

Chopin composed nearly 200 pieces, almost all for piano, in many different styles—from lively Polish dances to the Bach-like counterpoint of his *Preludes* to the moody, romantic *Nocturnes*.

pages of Proust's autobiographical novel, *Remembrance of Things Past*, close the book and cry, "Brilliant!" Others get lost in the meandering, stream-of-consciousness style, and forget that the whole "Remembrance" began with the taste of a *madeleine* (a type of cookie) that triggered a flashback to Proust's childhood, as relived over the last 10 years of his life, during which he labored alone in his apartment on Boulevard Haussmann—midway between the Arc de Triomphe and Gare de l'Est—penning his life story with reflections on Time (as we experience it, not as we measure it on the clock) and Memory... in long sentences.

### ⓗ Sarah Bernhardt (1844-1923)—Section 44

The greatest actress of her generation, she conquered Paris and the world. Charismatic Sarah made a triumphant tour of America and Europe (1880-1881), starring in *La Dame aux Camélias*. No one could die onstage like Sarah, and in the final scene—when her character succumbs to tuberculosis— she had cowboys and railroad workers sniffling in the audience. Of her hundred-plus stage roles and many silent films, her most memorable one may have been playing...Hamlet (1899). Offstage, her numerous affairs and passionate, capricious personality set a standard for future divas to aspire to.

### ⓘ Yves Montand (1921-1991) and
### Simone Signoret (1921-1985)—Section 44

Yves Montand was a film actor and nightclub singer with blue-collar roots, left-wing politics, and a social conscience. Montand's career was boosted by his lover, Edith Piaf, when they appeared together at the Moulin Rouge during World War II. Yves went on to stardom throughout the world (except in America, thanks partly to a 1960 flop film with Marilyn Monroe, *Let's Make Love*). In 1951, he married actress Simone Signoret, whose on-screen persona was the long-suffering lover. They remain together still, despite rumors of Yves' womanizing. After their deaths, their eternal love was tested in 1998, when Yves' body was exhumed to take a DNA sample for a paternity suit (it wasn't him).

In 1837, the quiet, refined, dreamy-eyed genius met the scandalous, assertive, stormy novelist George Sand (see the Left Bank Walk chapter). Sand was swept away by Chopin's music and artistic nature. She pursued him, and sparks flew. Though the romance faded quickly, they continued living together for nearly a decade in an increasingly bitter love-hate relationship. When Chopin developed tuberculosis, Sand nursed him for years (Chopin complained she was killing him). Sand finally left, Chopin was devastated, and he died two years later at age 39. At the funeral, they played perhaps Chopin's most famous piece, the *Funeral March* (it's that

11-note dirge that everyone knows). The grave contains Chopin's body, but his heart lies in Warsaw, embedded in a church column.

> *"The earth is suffocating. Swear to make them cut me open, so that I won't be buried alive."*
>
> —Chopin, on his deathbed

• *Continue walking down Chemin Denon, as it curves down and to the right. Stay left at the* Chemin du Coq *sign and walk down to Avenue Casimir Perier. Turn right and walk downhill 30 yards, looking to the left, over the tops of the graves, for a tall monument that looks like a church with a cross perched on top. Under this stone canopy lie...*

## ❾ Héloïse (c. 1101-1164) and Abélard (1079-1142)

Born nearly a millennium ago, these are the oldest residents in Père Lachaise, and their story is timeless.

In an age of faith and Church domination of all aspects of life, the independent scholar Peter Abélard dared to say, "By questioning, we learn truth." Brash, combative, and charismatic, Abélard shocked and titillated Paris with his secular knowledge and reasoned critique of Church doctrine. He set up a school on the Left Bank (near today's Sorbonne) that would become the University of Paris. Bright minds from all over Europe converged on Paris, including Héloïse, the brainy niece of the powerful canon of Notre-Dame.

Abélard was hired (c. 1118) to give private instruction to Héloïse. Their intense intellectual intercourse quickly flared into physical passion and a spiritual bond. They fled Paris and married in secret, fearing the damage to Abélard's career. After a year, Héloïse gave birth to a son (named Astrolabe), and the news got out, soon reaching Héloïse's uncle. The canon exploded, sending a volley of thugs in the middle of the night to Abélard's bedroom, where they castrated him.

Disgraced, Abélard retired to a monastery and Héloïse, to a convent, never again to live as man and wife. But for the next two decades, the two remained intimately connected by the postal service, exchanging letters of love, devotion, and intellectual discourse

that survive today. (The dog at Abélard's feet symbolizes their fidelity to each other.) Héloïse went on to become an influential abbess, and Abélard bounced back with some of his most critical writings. (He was forced to burn his *Theologia* in 1121 and was on trial for heresy when he died.) Abélard used logic to analyze Church pronouncements—a practice that would flower into the "scholasticism" accepted by the Church a century later.

When they died, the two were buried together in Héloïse's convent and were later laid to rest here in Père Lachaise. The canopy tomb we see today (1817) is made out of stones from both Héloïse's convent and Abélard's monastery.

> *"Thou, O Lord, brought us together, and when it pleased Thee, Thou hast parted us."*
> —From a prayer of Héloïse and Abélard

• *Continue walking downhill along Avenue Casimir Perier, keeping right as it merges into Avenue du Puits. Stay the course until you cross Avenue Principale, the street at the cemetery's main entrance. Cross Principale to find Colette's grave (third grave from corner on right side).*

## ❿ Colette (1873-1954)

France's most honored female writer led an unconventional life—thrice married and often linked romantically with other women—and wrote about it in semi-autobiographical novels. Her first fame came from a series of novels about naughty teenage Claudine's misadventures. In her 30s, Colette went on to a career as a music hall performer, scandalizing Paris by pulling a Janet Jackson onstage. Her late novel, *Gigi* (1945)—about a teenage girl groomed to be a professional mistress, who blossoms into independence—became a musical film starring Leslie Caron and Maurice Chevalier (1958). Thank heaven for little girls!

> *"The only misplaced curiosity is trying to find out here, on this side, what lies beyond the grave."*
> —Colette

• *Retrace your steps to Avenue Principale and go uphill a half-block. On the left, find Rossini, with Haussmann a few graves up.*

## ⓫ Gioacchino Rossini (1792-1868)

Dut. Dutta-dut. Dutta dut dut dut dut dut dut dut, dut dut dut dut dut dut dut....

The composer of the *William Tell Overture* (a.k.a. the *Lone Ranger* theme) was Italian, but he moved to Paris (1823) to bring his popular comic operas to France. Extremely prolific, he could crank out a three-hour opera in weeks, including the highly successful *Barber of Seville* (based on a play by Pierre Beaumarchais, who is also buried in Père Lachaise). When *Guillaume Tell* debuted (1829), Rossini, age 37, was at the peak of his career as an opera composer.

Then he stopped. For the next four decades, he never again wrote an opera and scarcely composed anything else. He moved to Italy, went through a stretch of bad health, and then returned to Paris, where his health and spirits revived. He even wrote a little music in his old age. Rossini's impressive little sepulchre is empty, as his remains were moved to Florence.

• *Four graves uphill, find...*

## ⑫ Baron Georges-Eugène Haussmann (1809-1891)

(Look through the green door long enough for your eyes to dilate.) Love him or hate him, Baron Haussmann made the Paris we see today. In the 1860s, Paris was a construction zone, with civil servant Haussmann overseeing the city's modernization. Narrow medieval lanes were widened and straightened into broad, traffic-carrying boulevards. Historic buildings were torn down. Sewers, bridges, and water systems were repaired. Haussmann rammed the Boulevard St. Michel through the formerly quaint Latin Quarter (as part of Emperor Napoleon III's plan to prevent revolutionaries from barricading narrow streets). The Opéra Garnier, Bois de Boulogne park, and avenues radiating from the Arc de Triomphe were all part of Haussmann's grand scheme, which touched 60 percent of the city. How did he finance it all? That's what the next government wanted to know when they canned him.

## Thank God You Can Leave

Have you seen enough dead people? To leave the cemetery, return downhill on Avenue Principale and exit onto Boulevard de Ménilmontant. The Père Lachaise Métro stop is one long block to the right. To find the bus #69 stop heading west to downtown, cross Boulevard de Ménilmontant and walk downhill on the right side of Rue de la Roquette; the stop is four blocks down, on the right-hand side.

# MONTMARTRE WALK

*From Sacré-Cœur to the
Moulin Rouge*

Stroll along the hilltop of Butte Montmartre amid traces of the many people who've lived here over the years—monks stomping grapes (1200s), farmers grinding grain in windmills (1600s), dust-coated gypsum miners (1700s), Parisian liberals (1800s), Modernist painters (1900s), and all the struggling artists, poets, dreamers, and drunkards who came here for cheap rent, untaxed booze, rustic landscapes, and cabaret nightlife.

Many tourists make the almost obligatory trek to the top of Paris' Butte Montmartre, eat an overpriced crêpe, and marvel at the view—but most miss out on the neighborhood's charm and history. Both are uncovered in this stroll.

We'll start at the radiant Sacré-Cœur Basilica, wander through the hilltop village, browse affordable art, ogle the Moulin Rouge nightclub, and catch echoes of those who once partied to a bohemian rhapsody during the belle époque. We'll end by going through part of a red light district (once adored by American GIs and expat African Americans) and finally down a lively neighborhood market street.

## Orientation

**Length of This Walk:** Allow more than two hours for this two-mile uphill/downhill walk.

**With Limited Time:** Skip the "Detour to Renoir's House" and end the walk at the Moulin Rouge (Mo: Blanche).

# Montmartre Walk

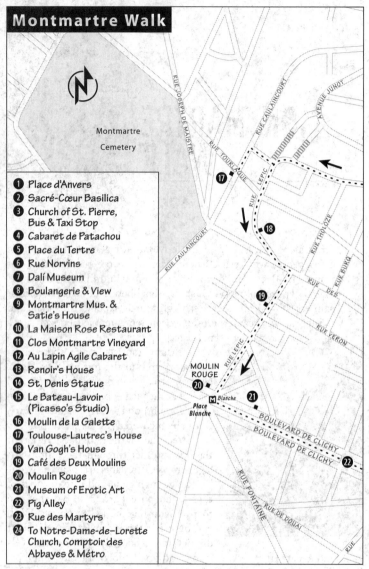

Montmartre
Cemetery

1 Place d'Anvers
2 Sacré-Cœur Basilica
3 Church of St. Pierre,
  Bus & Taxi Stop
4 Cabaret de Patachou
5 Place du Tertre
6 Rue Norvins
7 Dalí Museum
8 Boulangerie & View
9 Montmartre Mus. &
  Satie's House
10 La Maison Rose Restaurant
11 Clos Montmartre Vineyard
12 Au Lapin Agile Cabaret
13 Renoir's House
14 St. Denis Statue
15 Le Bateau-Lavoir
  (Picasso's Studio)
16 Moulin de la Galette
17 Toulouse-Lautrec's House
18 Van Gogh's House
19 Café des Deux Moulins
20 Moulin Rouge
21 Museum of Erotic Art
22 Pig Alley
23 Rue des Martyrs
24 To Notre-Dame-de-Lorette
  Church, Comptoir des
  Abbayes & Métro

MONTMARTRE WALK

**When to Go:** To avoid crowds at Sacré-Cœur, come on a weekday
  or by 9:30 on a weekend. Sunny weekends are the busiest—especially on Sunday, when Montmartre becomes a pedestrian-
  only zone and shops stay open. On Friday afternoon, Place
  d'Anvers hosts a small open-air food market (15:00-20:30, at
  far side of square). If crowds don't get you down, come for the
  sunset and stay for dinner. This walk is best under clear skies,

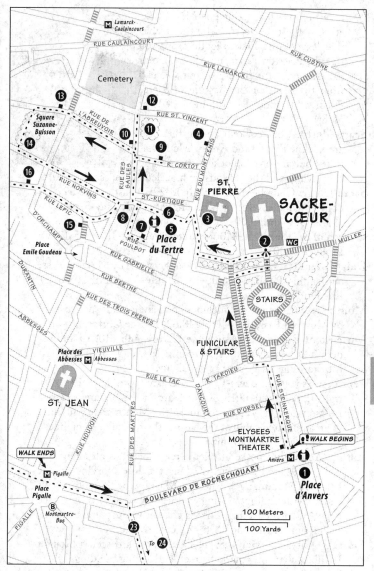

when views are sensational. Regardless of when you go, prepare for more seediness—particularly near Place Pigalle and Place d'Anvers—than you're accustomed to in Paris.

**Getting There:** This walk begins at Métro stop Anvers. Other stops nearby include Abbesses and Pigalle. (Avoid the seedy Métro station Barbès.) You have several options to avoid climbing the hill to Sacré-Cœur: The simplest approach is to

take the funicular (costs one Métro ticket). Or, the tiny electric Montmartrobus
that leaves from Place Pigalle drops you
right by Place du Tertre, near Sacré-Cœur
(costs one Métro ticket, 4/hour). A taxi
from the Seine or the Bastille to Sacré-
Cœur costs about €13 (figure on €20 at
night).

**Scam Alert:** At Sacré-Cœur and in the areas
around the Pigalle and Anvers Métro stations, beware of pickpockets, the "found
ring" scam, and the "friendship bracelet" scam; see page 30.

**Sacré-Cœur:** Church—free, daily 6:00-22:30, last entry at 22:15;
dome-€6, not covered by Museum Pass, daily May-Sept 9:00-
19:00, Oct-April 9:00-17:00.

**Church of St. Pierre-de-Montmartre:** Free, Sat-Thu 8:45-19:00,
Fri 8:45-17:00.

**Dalí Museum (L'Espace Dalí):** €11, not covered by Museum Pass,
audioguide-€3, daily 10:00-18:00, July-Aug until 20:00, 11
Rue Poulbot.

**Montmartre Museum:** €8, includes good audioguide, not covered
by Museum Pass, daily 10:00-18:00, 12 Rue Cortot.

**Museum of Erotic Art (Musée de l'Erotisme):** €10, €7 online,
definitely not covered by Museum Pass, daily 10:00-2:00 in
the morning, 72 Boulevard de Clichy.

**Services:** As you face Sacré-Cœur, WCs are down the stairs to the
right (free, 10:00-18:15). Others are in the Square Suzanne
Buisson park (at #13 on the tour), the Montmartre Museum,
in an automated cabin at the base of the funicular (long lines),
and any cafés you patronize.

**Eating:** You'll find peaceful, picnic-ready benches all along this
walk, and good sandwiches along the Rue Norvins (in the
heart of Montmartre). Rue des Martyrs, at the end of this
walk, has several interesting eateries (see page 373). Also, see
page 455 of the Eating in Paris chapter for restaurant recommendations, including L'Eté en Pente Douce.

**Starring:** Cityscape views, Sacré-Cœur, postcard scenes brought
to life, a charming market street, and boring buildings where
interesting people once lived.

# The Walk Begins

• *To reach Sacré-Cœur by Métro, get off at Métro stop Anvers.*

## ❶ Place d'Anvers

The **Elysées Montmartre** theater across the street is the oldest cancan dance hall in Paris. Today, it's a rowdy dance club and concert hall, signaling this area's transition. (The famous Chat Noir—or Black Cat—cabaret was a half-block down at #84.) Historically, people have moved to this neighborhood for cheap rents—and though it still feels neglected, urban gentrification is under way, as young professionals restore dilapidated apartments, hotels renovate for a more upscale clientele, and rents increase. A TI kiosk is a few steps to your left (daily 10:00-18:00). If you're here late Friday afternoon, check out the open-air food market (behind you on the far side of Place d'Anvers), then come back to this spot.

You're standing on Boulevard de Rochechouart, where a wall once separated Montmartre from Paris (*boulevard* literally means "road that replaced a wall"). Turn around and notice how better off the other side of the boulevard looks. Let's take a walk on the wild side.

Walk two blocks up Rue de Steinkerque (the street to the right of Elysées Montmartre), through an eclectic, low-rent urban bazaar, past bolts of fabric, cheap clothing, and souvenir shops (pick up inexpensive postcards and €3 blue jeans). You'll reach a grassy park way below the white Sacré-Cœur church. The terraced hillside was once dotted with openings to gypsum mines, the source of the white "plaster of Paris" that plastered Paris' buildings for centuries.

• *Hike up to the church, or ride the funicular (station to your left, costs one Métro ticket, closes periodically for maintenance). At the top, find a good viewing spot at the steps of the church.*

## ❷ Sacré-Cœur Basilica and View

From Paris' highest point (420 feet), the City of Light fans out at your feet. Pan from left to right. The long triangular roof on your left is the Gare du Nord train station. The blue-and-red Pompidou Center is straight ahead, and the skyscrapers in the distance define the southern limit of central Paris. Next is the domed Panthéon, atop Paris' other (and far smaller) butte. Then comes the modern Montparnasse Tower and, finally (if you're in position to see this far to the right), the golden dome of Les Invalides.

Now face the church. The Sacré-Cœur (Sacred Heart) Basilica's exterior, with its onion domes and bleached-bone pallor, looks ancient, but was finished only a century ago by Parisians humiliated by German invaders. Otto von Bismarck's Prussian army laid siege to Paris for more than

four months in 1870. Things got so bad for residents that urban hunting for dinner (to cook up dogs, cats, and finally rats) became accepted behavior. Convinced they were being punished for the country's liberal sins, France's Catholics raised money to build the church as a "praise the Lord anyway" gesture. Some say the church was also built as a kind of penitence by the French: Many were disgusted that in 1871 their government actually shot its own citizens, the Communards, who held out here on Montmartre after the French leadership surrendered to the Prussians.

The five-domed, Roman-Byzantine-looking basilica took 44 years to build (1875-1919). It stands on a foundation of 83 pillars sunk 130 feet deep, necessary because the ground beneath was honeycombed with gypsum mines. The exterior is laced with gypsum, which whitens with age.

**Interior:** In the impressive mosaic high above the altar, Christ exposes his sacred heart, burning with love and compassion for humanity. Christ is flanked by biblical figures on the left and French figures on the right. Among the French are Joan of Arc (in her trademark armor, at Jesus' feet), clergymen (who offer a model of this church to the Lord), government leaders (in business suits), and French saints (including St. Bernard, above, with his famous dog, and St. Louis, with the crown of thorns). The centerpiece of the mosaic is the Holy Trinity: Jesus; a dove representing the Holy Spirit; and God the father high above. Right now, in this church, at least one person is praying for Christ to be understanding of the world's sins—part of a tradition that's been carried out here, day and night, 24/7, since Sacré-Cœur's completion.

• *Find the first pillar to the left (as you face the altar), across from the statue of St. Thérèse.*

A plaque on the pillar *("L'an 1944...")* shows where the 13 WWII bombs fell—all in a line, all near the church—killing no one. This fueled local devotion to the Sacred Heart and to this church.

Shuffling clockwise around the ambulatory, find a scale model of the church. Because the church's original windows were broken by the concussion of WWII bombs, all the glass you see is post-1945. Turn around to see colorful mosaics of the Stations of the Cross. Move along and rub St. Peter's bronze foot and look up to the heavens.

Continue your circuit around the church. As you approach the entrance you'll walk straight toward three stained-glass windows dedicated to Joan of Arc (Jeanne d'Arc, 1412-1431). See the teenage girl as she hears the voice of the Archangel Michael (right panel, at bottom) and later (above, on right) as she takes up the Archangel's sword. Next, she kneels to take communion (central panel), then kneels before the bishop to tell him she's been sent by God to rally France's soldiers and save Orléans from English invaders. However, French forces allied with England arrest her, and she's burned at the stake as a heretic (above, on left), dying with her eyes fixed on a crucifix and chanting, "Jesus, Jesus, Jesus...."

• *Exit the church. A public WC is to your left, down 50 steps. To your right is the entrance to the church's...*

**Dome and Crypt:** For an unobstructed panoramic view of Paris, climb 260 feet (300 steps) up the tight and claustrophobic spiral stairs to the top of the dome (especially worthwhile if you have kids with excess energy). The crypt is just a big, empty basement.

• *Leaving the church, turn right and walk west along the ridge, following tree-lined Rue Azaïs. At Rue St. Eleuthère, turn right and walk uphill a block to the Church of St. Pierre-de-Montmartre (at top on right). The small square in front of the church has a convenient taxi stand and a bus stop for the Montmartrobus to and from Place Pigalle (bus costs one Métro ticket).*

You're in the heart of Montmartre, Place du Tertre. But first, check out the church.

## ❸ Church of St. Pierre-de-Montmartre

This church was the center of Montmartre's first claim to fame, a sprawling abbey of Benedictine monks and nuns. The church is one of Paris' oldest (1147), founded by King Louis VI and his wife, Adelaide. (Some say Dante prayed here.) Find Adelaide's tombstone *(pierre tombale)* midway down on the left wall. Older still are the four gray columns—two flank the entrance, and two others are behind the altar. These may have stood in a temple of Mercury or Mars in Roman times. The name "Montmartre" comes from the Roman "Mount of Mars," though later generations—thinking of their beheaded patron St. Denis—preferred a less pagan version, "Mount of Martyrs."

Along the right wall, rub St. Peter's toe (again), look up, and ask for *déliverance* from the tourist mobs outside. Now step back outside, where a sign for the *Cabaret de la Bohème* reminds visitors that in the late 19th and early 20th centuries, this was the world capital of bohemian life. The artist-filled Place du Tertre awaits.

• *Before entering the square, a short detour to the right leads to 13 Rue du Mont–Cenis, the former...*

## ❹ Cabaret de Patachou

This building, now a pleasant art gallery, is where singer Edith Piaf (1915-1963) once trilled "La Vie en Rose." Piaf—a destitute teenager who sang for pocket change in the streets of pre-WWII Paris—was discovered by a nightclub owner and became a star. Her singing inspired the people of Nazi-occupied Paris. In the heady days after the war, she sang about the joyous, rosy life in the city. For more on this warbling-voiced singer, see page 348.

• *Head back to the always-lively square, and stand on its cusp for the best perspective of...*

## ❺ Place du Tertre—Bohemian Montmartre

Lined with cafés, shaded by acacia trees, and filled with artists, hucksters, and tourists, the scene mixes charm and kitsch in ever-changing proportions. The Place du Tertre has been the town square of the small village of Montmartre since medieval times. (*Tertre* means "stepped lanes" in French.)

In 1800, a wall separated Paris from this hilltop village. To enter Paris you had to pass tollbooths that taxed anything for sale. Montmartre was a mining community where the wine flowed cheap (tax-free) and easy. Life here was a working-class festival of cafés, bistros, and dance halls. Painters came here for the ruddy charm, the light, and the low rents. In 1860, Montmartre was annexed into the growing city of Paris. The "bohemian" ambience survived, and it attracted sophisticated Parisians ready to get down and dirty in the belle époque of cancan. The Restaurant Mère Catherine is often called the first bistro—this is where Russian soldiers first coined the word by saying, "I'm thirsty, bring my drink *bistro!*" (meaning "right away").

The square's artists, who at times outnumber the tourists, are the great-great-grandkids of the Renoirs, Van Goghs, and Picassos who once roamed here—poor, carefree, seeking inspiration, and occasionally cursing a world too selfish to bankroll their dreams.

• *Plunge headfirst into the square. The Montmartre TI (Syndicat d'Initiative) across the square sells good maps (daily 10:00-19:00 except Sat-Sun closed 13:00-14:00, tel. 01 42 62 21 21). Just south of the square is the quiet, tiny Place du Calvaire, with the recommended café Chez Plumeau (closed Tue Oct-April and Wed year-round). But for now continue west along the main drag, called...*

## ❻ Rue Norvins

Montmartre's oldest and main street is still the primary commercial artery, serving the current trade—tourism.

• *If you're a devotee of Dalí, a detour left on Rue Poulbot will lead to the...*

## ❼ Dalí Museum (L'Espace Dalí)

This beautifully lit black gallery (well-described in English) offers a walk through statues, etchings, and paintings by the master of Surrealism. The Spaniard found fame in Paris in the 1920s and '30s. He lived in Montmartre for a while, hung with the Surrealist crowd in Montparnasse, and shocked the world with his dreamscape paintings and experimental films. Don't miss the printed interview on the exit stairs.

• *Continue west down Rue Norvins a dozen steps to the intersection with Rue des Saules, where you'll find a...*

## ❽ Boulangerie with a View

The venerable *boulangerie* (bakery) on the left, dating from 1900, is one of the last surviving bits of the old-time community, made famous in a painting by the artist Maurice Utrillo (see sidebar).

From the *boulangerie*, look back up Rue Norvins, then backpedal a few steps to catch the classic view of the dome of Sacré-Cœur rising above the rooftops.

• *Let's lose the tourists. Follow Rue des Saules downhill (north) onto the back side of Montmartre. A block downhill, turn right on Rue Cortot to reach the...*

**MONTMARTRE WALK**

## Maurice Utrillo (1883-1955)

Born to a free-spirited single mom and raised by his grand-mother, Utrillo had his first alcohol detox treatment at age 18. Encouraged by his mother and doctors, he started painting as occupational therapy. That, plus guidance from his mother (and, later, from his wife), allowed him to live productively into his 70s, becoming wealthy and famous, despite occasional relapses into drinking and mental problems.

Utrillo grew up on Montmartre's streets. He fought, broke street lamps, and haunted the cafés and bars, paying for drinks with masterpieces. A very free spirit, he's said to have exposed himself to strangers on the street, yelling, "I paint with this!"

His simple scenes of streets, squares, and cafés in a vaguely Impressionist style became popular with commoners and scholars alike. He honed his style during his "white period" (c. 1909-1914), painting a thick paste of predominantly white tints—perfect for capturing Sacré-Cœur. In later years, after he moved out of Montmartre, he still painted the world he knew in his youth, using postcards and photographs as models.

Utrillo's mom, Suzanne Valadon, was a former trapeze performer and artist's model who posed for Toulouse-Lautrec, slept with Renoir, studied under Degas, and went on to become a notable painter in her own right.

MONTMARTRE WALK

## ❾ Montmartre Museum and Satie's House

In what is now the museum (at 12 Rue Cortot), Pierre-Auguste Renoir once lived while painting his best-known work, *Bal du Moulin de la Galette* (pictured on page 165). Every day he'd lug the four-foot-by-six-foot canvas from here to the other side of the butte to paint in the open air *(en plein air)* the famous windmill ballroom, which we'll see later.

A few years later, Utrillo lived and painted here with his mom, Suzanne Valadon. In 1893, she carried on a torrid six-month relationship with the lonely, eccentric man who lived two doors up at #6—composer Erik Satie, who wrote *Trois Gymnopédies* and who was eking out a living playing piano in Montmartre nightclubs.

The Montmartre Museum fills several floors in this creaky 17th-century manor house with paintings, posters, old photos, music, and memorabilia. From bottom to top, it tells the Butte's history in roughly

chronological order. In the basement, see headless St. Denis and an abbey bell from the hill's religious origins. Next come photos of the gypsum quarries and flour-grinding windmills of the Industrial Age. Learn how Sacré-Cœur's construction was an act of national penitence resulting from the Prussian invasion of 1870 (see page 361).

Climbing to the ground floor, you reach Montmartre's Golden Age, the cabaret years. There's the original *Lapin Agile* sign, the famous Chat Noir poster, and Toulouse-Lautrec's dashing portrait of red-scarved Aristide Bruant, the earthy cabaret singer and club owner (pictured on previous page). A scale model of the hill lets you find the famous cabarets and homes of the bohemians who lived here—Renoir, Picasso, Edith Piaf, Toulouse-Lautrec, and more.

Upstairs, you learn about the artsy inhabitants of this former house—Renoir, alcoholic Utrillo and his mother Valadon, and paintings by her husband, André Utter. Finally, see more Toulouse-Lautrec posters and an exhibit on the biggest and most famous cabaret of all, the cancan-kickers of the Moulin Rouge.
• *Return to Rue des Saules and walk downhill to...*

## ❿ La Maison Rose Restaurant

The restaurant, made famous by a Utrillo painting, was once frequented by Utrillo, Pablo Picasso, and Gertrude Stein. Today it serves lousy food to nostalgic tourists.
• *Just downhill from the restaurant is Paris' last remaining vineyard.*

## ⓫ Clos Montmartre Vineyard

What originally drew artists to Montmartre was country charm like this. Ever since the 12th century, the monks and nuns of the large abbey have produced wine here. With vineyards, wheat fields, windmills, animals, and a village tempo of life, it was the perfect escape from grimy Paris. In 1576, puritanical laws taxed wine in Paris, bringing budget-minded drinkers to Montmartre. Today's vineyard is off-limits to tourists except during the annual grape-harvest fest (first Sat in Oct, www.fetedesvendangesde montmartre.com), when a thousand costumed locals bring back the boisterous old days. The vineyard's annual production of 300 liters is auctioned off at the fest to support local charities. Bottles average €45 apiece and are considered mediocre at best.
• *Continue downhill to the intersection with Rue St. Vincent.*

## ⓬ Au Lapin Agile Cabaret

The poster above the door gives the place its name. A rabbit *(lapin)* makes an agile leap out of the pot while balancing the bottle of wine that he can now drink—rather than be cooked in. This was the village's hot spot. Picasso and other artists and writers (Renoir, Utrillo, Paul Verlaine, Aristide Bruant, Amedeo Modigliani, etc.) would gather for "performances" of serious poetry, dirty limericks, sing-alongs, parodies of the famous, or anarchist manifestos. Once, to play a practical joke on the avant-garde art community, patrons tied a paintbrush to the tail of the owner's donkey and entered the resulting "abstract painting" in a show at the Salon. Called *Sunset over the Adriatic,* it won critical acclaim and sold for a nice price.

The old Parisian personality of this cabaret survives. Every night except Monday a series of performers takes a small, French-speaking audience on a wistful musical journey back to the good old days (for details, see the Entertainment chapter).

• *Before heading back uphill on Rue des Saules to the* boulangerie *(at the intersection with Rue Norvins), some may wish to make a detour (an extra 15 minutes) to see a more residential part of Montmartre. If you're pooped, we'll meet you back at the* boulangerie.

## Detour to ⓭ Renoir's House and ⓮ St. Denis Statue

• *Walk up Rue des Saules and turn right at La Maison Rose, heading west one block on Rue de l'Abreuvoir. At the busty bust of singer/actress Dalida (1933-1987, who popularized disco in France), continue straight (west) along the small walkway called Allée des Brouillards. You'll pass another of **Renoir's homes** (at #6). Walk down the steps at the walkway's end, then stroll up through the small, fenced, multilevel park called Square Suzanne Buisson.*

In the park, find the stone statue of headless **St. Denis.** This early Christian bishop was sentenced to death by the Romans for spreading Christianity. As they marched him up to the top of Montmartre to be executed, the Roman soldiers got tired and just beheaded him near here. But Denis popped right up, picked up his head, and carried on another three miles north before he finally died. The statue of Denis cradles his head in his hands, looks over a regulation-size *boules* court...and gets ready to play ball.

• *At the top of the park, turn left onto Avenue Junot, which becomes Rue Norvins. (Wish you could just walk right through these hills? You'll pass a statue that looks like it could do it.) The* boulangerie *is at the top of Rue Norvins.*

*Once reunited at the* boulangerie, *we all go downhill (south). Don't curve right on car-filled Rue Lepic; instead, go straight, down the pedestrian-only Place J. B. Clement, hugging the buildings on the left. Turn right on Rue Ravignan and follow it down to the leafy little square with the TIM Hôtel. Next to the hotel, at 13 Place Emile Goudeau, is...*

## ⑮ Le Bateau-Lavoir (Picasso's Studio)

A humble facade marks the place where Modern art was born. Here, in a lowly artists' abode (destroyed by fire in 1970, rebuilt a few years later), as many as 10 artists lived and worked. This former piano factory, converted to cheap housing, was nicknamed the "Laundry Boat" for its sprawling layout and crude facilities (sharing one water tap). It was "a weird, squalid place," wrote one resident, "filled with every kind of noise: arguing, singing, bedpans clattering, slamming doors, and suggestive moans coming from studio doors."

In 1904, a poor, unknown Spanish émigré named Pablo Picasso (1881-1973) moved in. He met dark-haired Fernande Olivier, his first real girlfriend, in the square outside. She soon moved in, lifting him out of his melancholy Blue Period into his rosy Rose Period. *La belle Fernande* posed nude for him, inspiring a freer treatment of the female form.

In 1907, Picasso started on a major canvas. For nine months he produced hundreds of preparatory sketches, working long into the night. When he unveiled the work, even his friends were shocked. *Les Demoiselles d'Avignon* showed five nude women in a brothel (Fernande claimed they were all her), with primitive mask-like faces and fragmented bodies. Picasso had invented Cubism.

For the next two years, he and his neighbors Georges Braque and Juan Gris revolutionized the art world. Sharing paints, ideas, and girlfriends, they made Montmartre "The Cubist Acropolis," attracting freethinking "Moderns" from all over the world to visit their studios—the artists Amedeo Modigliani, Marie Laurencin, and Henri Rousseau (see page 183); the poet Guillaume Apollinaire; and the American expatriate writer Gertrude Stein. By the time Picasso moved to better quarters (and dumped Fernande), he was famous. Still, Picasso would later say, "I know one day we'll return to Bateau-Lavoir. It was there that we were really happy— where they thought of us as painters, not strange animals."

• *Walk back half a block uphill and turn left on Rue d'Orchampt. (Notice the windows of another studio on your left.) Walk the length of this short street and into a tiny alley, which spits you out the other end at the intersection with Rue Lepic, where you're face-to-face with a wooden windmill.*

## ⑯ Moulin de la Galette

Only two windmills *(moulins)* remain on a hill that was once dotted with 30 of them. Originally, they pressed monks' grapes and farmers' grain, and crushed gypsum rocks into powdery plaster of Paris. When the gypsum mines closed (c. 1850) and the vineyards sprouted apartments, this windmill turned into the ceremonial centerpiece of a popular outdoor dance hall. Renoir's *Bal du Moulin de la Galette* (in the Orsay, see page 165) shows it in its heyday—a sunny Sunday afternoon in the acacia-shaded gardens with working-class people dancing, laughing, drinking, and eating the house crêpes, called galettes. Some call Renoir's version the quintessential Impressionist work and the painting that best captures—on a large canvas in bright colors—the joy of the Montmartre lifestyle. The Moulin de la Galette restaurant offers good meals and a few historic black-and-white photos of the windmill and old Montmartre (recommended in the Eating in Paris chapter).

• *Follow Rue Lepic as it winds down the hill. The green-latticed building on the right side was also part of the Moulin de la Galette (the second surviving windmill is just above, through the trees). Rounding the bend, look to the right when you reach Rue Tourlaque. The building one block down Rue Tourlaque was...*

## ⑰ Henri de Toulouse-Lautrec's House

Find the building on the southwest corner (across the intersection on the left) with the tall, brick-framed art-studio windows under the heavy mansard roof. Every night Toulouse-Lautrec (1864-1901, see page 160)—a nobleman turned painter, whose legs were deformed in a horse-riding accident during his teenage years—would dress up here and then journey down Rue Lepic to the Moulin Rouge. One of Henri's occasional drinking buddies and fellow artists lived nearby.

• *Continue down Rue Lepic and, at #54, find...*

## ⑱ Vincent van Gogh's House

Vincent van Gogh lived here with his brother from 1886 to 1888, enjoying a grand city view from his top-floor window. In those two short years, Van Gogh transformed from a gloomy Dutch painter of brown and gray peasant scenes into an inspired visionary with wild ideas and Impressionist colors.

• *Follow Rue Lepic downhill as it makes a hard right at #36 and becomes a lively market street. Enjoy the small shops and neighborhood ambience. Two blocks down, on the corner to your right (at #15), you'll find the pink...*

## ⑲ Café des Deux Moulins

This café has become a pilgrimage site for movie buffs worldwide, since it was featured in the quirky 2001 film *Amélie*. Today it's just another funky place with unassuming ambience and reasonably priced food and drinks, frequented by another generation of real-life Amélies who ignore the movie poster on the back wall (daily 7:00-24:00, 15 Rue Lepic, tel. 01 42 54 90 50).

• *Now continue downhill on Rue Lepic to Place Blanche. On busy Place Blanche is the...*

## ⑳ Moulin Rouge

*Ooh la la.* The new Eiffel Tower at the 1889 World's Fair was nothing compared to the sight of pretty cancan girls kicking their legs at the newly opened "Red Windmill." The nightclub seemed to sum up the belle époque—the age of elegance, opulence, sophistication, and worldliness. The big draw was amateur night, when working-class girls in risqué dresses danced "Le Quadrille" (dubbed "cancan" by a Brit). Wealthy Parisians slummed it by coming here.

On most nights you'd see a small man in a sleek black coat, checked pants, a green scarf, and a bowler hat peering through his pince-nez glasses at the dancers and making sketches of them—Henri de Toulouse-Lautrec. Perhaps he'd order an absinthe, the dense green liqueur (evil ancestor of today's *pastis*) that was the toxic muse for so many great (and so many forgotten) artists. Toulouse-Lautrec's sketches of dancer Jane Avril and comic La Goulue hang in the Orsay (see reproductions in the entryway).

After its initial splash, the Moulin Rouge survived as a venue for all kinds of entertainment. In 1906, the novelist Colette kissed her female lover onstage, and the authorities closed the "Dream of

Egypt" down. Yves Montand opened for Edith Piaf (1944), and the two fell in love offstage. It has hosted such diverse acts as Ginger Rogers, Dalida, and the Village People—together on one bill (1979). Mikhail Baryshnikov leaped across its stage (1986). And the club celebrated its centennial (1989) with Ray Charles, Tony Curtis, Ella Fitzgerald, and...a French favorite, Jerry Lewis.

Tonight they're showing...well, find out yourself: Walk into the open-air entryway or step into the lobby to mull over the photos, show options, and prices. Their souvenir shop is back up Rue Lepic a few steps at #9.

• *Turn left out of the Moulin Rouge. The Blanche Métro stop is here in Place Blanche, a good place to end if you are tired. (Plaster of Paris from the gypsum found on this mount was loaded sloppily at Place Blanche... the white square.) Others may want to sully themselves by continuing east along Boulevard de Clichy to the...*

## ㉑ Museum of Erotic Art (Musée de l'Erotisme)

Basically a sexy art gallery, this museum has five floors of displays—mostly paintings and drawings—ranging from artistic to erotic to disgusting. They also toss in a few circa-1920 porn videos and a fascinating history of local brothels (see page 91).

• *Walk to the median at the center of the boulevard, crossing a bike lane. Paris has fallen in love with bikes, and this separated bike path is part of a 275-mile network of lanes available to cyclists. Continue east down the boulevard and you'll find...*

## ㉒ Pig Alley

The stretch of the Boulevard de Clichy from Place Blanche eastward (toward Sacré-Cœur) to Place Pigalle is the den mother of all iniquities. Remember, this was once the border between Montmartre and Paris, where bistros had tax-free status, wine was cheap, and prostitutes roamed freely. Today, sex shops, peep shows, live sex shows, chatty pitchmen, and hot dog stands line the busy boulevard. Dildos abound.

In the Roaring Twenties, this neighborhood at the base of the hill became a new center of cabaret nightlife. It was settled by African American jazz musicians and WWI veterans who didn't want to return to a segregated America. Black-owned nightclubs sprang up. There was Zelli's (located at 16 bis Rue Fontaine, a block southeast of the Moulin Rouge), where clarinetist-saxophonist Sidney Bechet played. A block away was the tiny Le Grand Duc (at Rue Fontaine and Rue Pigalle), where poet Langston Hughes bused tables. Next door was the most famous of all, Bricktop's (at #73 and then at 66 Rue Pigalle), owned by the vivacious faux-redhead who hosted Cole Porter, Duke Ellington, Picasso, the Prince of Wales, F. Scott Fitzgerald, Josephine Baker, and many more. The area was

"Harlem East," where rich and poor, black and white, came for a good time.

By World War II, the good times were becoming increasingly raunchy, and GIs nicknamed the Pigalle neighborhood "Pig Alley." Today, though the government is cracking down on prostitution, and the ladies of the night are being driven deeper into their red-velvet bars as the area is being gentrified, very few think of the great French sculptor Pigalle when they hear the district's name. Bars lining the streets downhill from Place Pigalle (especially Rue Pigalle) are lively with working girls eager to share a drink with anyone passing by.

Escape home via the fine Art Nouveau Métro stop, Pigalle. After all that, the Métro system seems cleaner.

• *Although you can pop into the Métro from here, the next (optional) leg of this walk starts a block away and takes you downhill six blocks through a lively market street, ending at Métro station Notre-Dame-de-Lorette (which may be more convenient to your travel plans). Continue walking down Boulevard de Clichy to the next street, where you turn right on...*

## ❷ Rue des Martyrs

As they race from big museum to big museum, visitors often miss the market streets and village-like charm that give Paris a warm and human vibrancy. Rue Cler remains my favorite market street (❂ see the Rue Cler Walk chapter). But for an authentic, less-touristy market street serving village Paris, stroll down Rue des Martyrs (note that market streets are generally quiet on Sun from 12:00 on, all day Mon, and the rest of the week from 12:00 to 15:00, when shops close for a break).

Entering Rue des Martyrs, you pass into a finer neighborhood with broader streets, richer buildings...and signs of the reality of raising a family in an urban setting. Security can be a concern. The school immediately on your right has barriers to keep possible car bombs at a distance. (Since terrorist attacks rocked Paris decades ago, there's been no parking in front of schools or near buildings that serve a predominantly Jewish clientele.) Several side streets are "*voie privée*"—private lanes or high-rise, gated communities.

Slalom past people strolling with dogs and babies. Goods spill out onto the sidewalk. People know their butcher and baker as if they lived in a village. Locals willingly pay more in a shop that's not part of a chain.

**MONTMARTRE WALK**

At #62, hardworking Aussies steam up American-style lattes at Kooka Boora. Make a short detour down Rue Victor Massé to #3 and you'll find the hot bistro Le Pantruche, which is breathing new life into traditional dishes.

Back on Rue des Martyrs, the traditional charcuterie at #58 still sells various meats, but it has morphed with the times into an appealing *"traiteur"* with more variety, food to eat in as well as to go, and prepared dishes sold by weight.

Right next door you'll see one of Paris' countless late-night grocery stores. These are generally run by North African immigrants who are willing to work the night shift for the convenience of others. Pay attention: Produce with rip-off prices is often priced by the half-kilo.

Le Cul de Poule ("Chicken Butt"), at #53, serves creative French food to trendy locals. At #50, a favorite cheese monger has been serving the neighborhood ever since it actually had goats and cows grazing out back. Notice the marble shelves, old milk jugs, and small artisanal cheeses.

At #46, the English-owned Rose Bakery serves a young, affluent, and health-conscious crowd with top-quality organic and vegetarian breakfasts and lunches. At #42 sits Terra Corsa, a café/gourmet food shop selling fine foods from Corsica and tasty lunch plates served with wine, beer, or Corsican cola. Across the street, the baker Delmontel at #39 proudly displays his "best baguette in Paris" award from 2007.

If you turn right and walk a few steps up Rue Clauzel, at #3 you'll see the final site of the first African American restaurant in Paris—established by Leroy Haynes in this neighborhood in 1949. For 60 years it was a black-American-in-Paris hangout, but it closed in 2009.

Continuing your stroll on Rue des Martyrs, take a look at the traditional butcher at #21. You know he's good because the ceiling hooks—where butchers once hung sides of beef—now display a red medallion that certifies the slaughtered cow's quality.

The *pâtisserie* at #22 is worth popping in to see the typically French works of art. Bakers often make special treats in sync with the season: Easter, Christmas, First Communion, and so on.

Nearby, the tobacco shop/café at #20 is coping well with the smoking ban by putting out heaters (in cool weather) and as many tables as will fit on the sidewalk. Shops like this—once run by rural people from what was then France's poorest region, Auvergne—are now generally managed by Chinese immigrants.

At #10, Eat Sushi delivers its food like a pizzeria—notice the motorbikes parked outside. A step above fast food, places like these are trendy, serving modern professionals who don't want to cook after a long day of work. Sushi places are everywhere in Paris—the locals love it, and since the sushi vendors don't actually "cook" anything, it's easier to get a restaurant zoning permit.

Rue des Martyrs ends at the neighborhood church—the Neoclassical ㉔ **Notre-Dame-de-Lorette** (circa 1836). To the left of the church sits the inviting Comptoir des Abbayes at Rue Flechier 4. This fragrant two-story shop sells gift-worthy products—honey wine, herbal medicine, and traditional pottery—made by crafty French monks and nuns. With that, this walk comes to a heavenly end.

• *Our walk is over. The Métro station Notre-Dame-de-Lorette (line 12) awaits. Find the discreet entrance on the opposite (front) side of the church.*

# SLEEPING IN PARIS

Paris is a good hotel city. A comfortable hotel in Paris costs less than a comparable hotel in London, Amsterdam, or Rome. I've focused most of my recommendations in four safe, handy, and colorful neighborhoods: the village-like Rue Cler (near the Eiffel Tower), the artsy and trendy Marais (near Place de la Bastille), the historic island of Ile St. Louis (next door to Notre-Dame), and the lively and Latin yet classy Luxembourg Garden neighborhood (on the Left Bank). I recommend the best accommodations values in each, from €25 dorm beds to deluxe €500 doubles with all the comforts.

For each neighborhood I list good hotels, helpful hints, and a selection of restaurants (see Eating in Paris chapter). Before choosing a hotel, read the descriptions of the neighborhoods closely. Each offers different pros and cons: Your neighborhood is as important as your hotel for the success of your trip.

Near the end of this chapter, you'll find recommendations for good budget accommodations in Montmartre and along lively Rue Mouffetard—two more neighborhoods—a few bed-and-breakfast and apartment-rental agencies, and suggestions for sleeping near Paris' airports. Less expensive accommodations are listed in chapters on Versailles, Chartres, and Reims, plus other nearby destinations (Fontainebleau, Giverny, Auvers-sur-Oise, and Disneyland Paris).

A major feature of this book is its extensive listing of good-value rooms. I like places that are clean, central, relatively quiet at night, reasonably priced, friendly, small enough to have a hands-on owner and stable staff, run with a respect for French traditions, and not listed in other guidebooks. (In Paris, for me, six out of these eight criteria means it's a keeper.) I'm more impressed by a handy location and a fun-loving philosophy than flat-screen TVs and shoeshine machines.

Reserve ahead for Paris—the sooner, the better. In August and at other times when business is slower, some hotels offer lower rates to fill their rooms. Check hotel websites for the best deals. See page 664 for a list of major holidays and festivals in Paris; for tips on making reservations, see page 382.

## Rates and Deals

I've described my recommended accommodations using a Sleep Code (see sidebar). Prices listed are for one-night stays in peak season, do not include breakfast, and assume you're booking directly (not through a TI or online hotel-booking engine). Using an online booking service costs the hotel about 20 percent and logically closes the door on special deals. Book direct.

Prices at many Parisian hotels are impossible to pin down, and vary greatly based on demand. Email several hotels to ask for their best price and compare offers—you may be astonished at the range. You'll almost always find the lowest rates through a hotel's own website (rather than a booking agency). Reserve as early as you can. Paris is popular, and available rooms can be hard to find.

As you look over the listings, you'll notice that some accommodations promise special prices to my readers who book direct (without using a room-finding service or hotel-booking website, which take a commission). To get these rates, you must mention this book when you reserve, and then show the book upon arrival. Rick Steves discounts apply to readers with ebooks as well as printed books. Discounts may not apply toward promotional rates.

# Types of Accommodations

## Hotels

In this book, the price for a double room will normally range from €55 (very simple; toilet and shower down the hall) to €500 (grand lobbies, maximum plumbing, and the works), with most clustered around €100-150 (with private bathrooms).

The French have a simple hotel rating system based on amenities and indicated by stars (expressed in this book by asterisks, from * through *****). One star is modest, two has most of the comforts, and three is generally just a two-star with a fancier lobby and more elaborately designed rooms. Four and five stars offer more luxury than you have time to appreciate. Two- and three-star hotels are required to have an English-speaking staff, though virtually all hotels I recommend

# Sleep Code

**(€1 = about $1.30, country code: 33)**

## Price Rankings
To help you easily sort through my listings, I've divided the accommodations into three categories based on the price for a standard double room with bath during high season:

**$$$** **Higher Priced**—Most rooms €200 or more.
**$$** **Moderately Priced**—Most rooms between €150-200.
**$** **Lower Priced**—Most rooms €150 or less.

I always rate hostels as $, whether or not they have double rooms, because they have the cheapest beds in town. Prices can change without notice; verify the hotel's current rates online or by email.

## Abbreviations
To pack maximum information in minimum space, I use the following code to describe the accommodations in this book. Prices listed are per room, not per person. When a price range is given for a type of room (such as a double room listing for €140-180), it means the price fluctuates with the season, size of room, or length of stay; expect to pay the upper end for peak-season stays.

**S** = Single room (or price for one person in a double).
**D** = Double or Twin room.
**T** = Triple (generally a double bed with a single).
**Q** = Quad (usually two double beds); adding an extra child's bed to a T is usually cheaper.
**b** = Private bathroom with toilet and shower or tub.
**s** = Private shower or tub only (the toilet is down the hall).
**\*** = French hotel rating system, ranging from zero to five stars.

According to this code, a couple staying at a "Db-€140" hotel would pay a total of €140 (about $180) for a double room with a private bathroom. Unless otherwise noted, hotel staff speak basic English, credit cards are accepted, and breakfast is not included (but is usually optional).

All hotels in these listings have elevators, air-conditioning, Internet access (a public terminal in the lobby or occasionally a portable loaner), and Wi-Fi, unless otherwise noted. "Wi-Fi only" means there's no public computer available.

have someone who speaks English (unless I note otherwise in the listing).

The number of stars does not generally reflect room size or guarantee quality. Some two-star hotels are better than many three-star hotels. One- and two-star hotels are inexpensive, but some three-star (and even a few four-star hotels) offer good value, justifying the extra cost. Unclassified hotels (no stars) can be bargains or depressing dumps.

Old, characteristic, budget Parisian hotels have always been cramped. Retrofitted with toilets, private showers, and elevators (as most are today), they are even more cramped.

Most hotels have lots of doubles and a few singles, triples, and quads. Traveling alone can be expensive, as singles (except for the rare closet-type rooms that fit only one twin bed) are simply doubles used by one person—so they cost about the same as a double. Room prices vary within each hotel depending on size and whether the room has a bath or shower, and twin beds or a double bed (tubs and twins cost more than showers and double beds). A triple is often the same as a double room, with a double or queen-size bed plus a sliver-sized single. Quad rooms usually have two double beds. Hotels cannot legally allow more in the room than what's shown on their price list. Many hotels have a few family-friendly rooms that open up to each other *(chambres communiquantes)*.

Hotels in France must charge a daily room tax *(taxe du séjour)* of about €1-2 per person per day. Some hotels include it in the listed prices, but most add it to your bill.

You can save as much as €25 by finding the rare room without a private shower or toilet. A room with a bathtub costs €10-15 more than a room with a shower and is generally larger. Hotels often have more rooms with tubs than showers and are inclined to give you a room with a tub (which the French prefer). Always check the hotel's website for better rates.

A double bed is usually cheaper than twins, though rooms with twin beds tend to be larger, and French double beds are smaller than American double beds. Many hotels have queen-size beds (a bed that's 63 inches wide—most doubles are 55). To learn if a hotel has queen-size beds, ask, *"Avez-vous des lits de cent-soixante?"* (ah-vay-voo day lee duh sahn-swah-sahnt). Some hotels push two twins together under king-size sheets and blankets to make *le king size*.

If you prefer a double bed (instead of twins) and a shower (instead of a tub), you need to ask for it—and you'll save up to €30 at more expensive hotels. If you'll take either twins or a double, ask generically for *une chambre pour deux* (room for two) to avoid being needlessly turned away.

Hotel lobbies, halls, and breakfast rooms are off-limits to smokers, though they can light up in their rooms. Still, I seldom

## Types of Rooms

Study the price list on the hotel's website or posted at the desk, so you know your options. Receptionists often don't mention the cheaper rooms—they assume you want a private bathroom or a bigger room. Here are the types of rooms and beds:

| | |
|---|---|
| *une chambre sans douche et WC* | room without a private shower or toilet (uncommon these days) |
| *une chambre avec cabinet de toilette* | room with a toilet but no shower (some hotels charge for down-the-hall showers) |
| *une chambre avec bain et WC* | room with private bathtub and toilet |
| *une chambre avec douche et WC* | room with private shower and toilet |
| *chambres communiquantes* | connecting rooms (ideal for families) |
| *un grand lit* | double bed (55 inches wide) |
| *deux petits lits* | twin beds (30-36 inches wide) |
| *un lit single* | a true single room |
| *un lit de cent-soixante* | queen-size bed (literally 160 centimeters, or 63 inches, wide) |
| *le king size* | king-size bed (usually two twins pushed together) |
| *un lit pliant* | folding bed |
| *un berceau* | baby crib |
| *un lit d'enfant* | child's bed |

smell any smoke in my rooms. Some hotels have nonsmoking rooms or floors—ask about them if this is important to you. If your room smells of smoke, ask for another one.

Most hotels offer some kind of breakfast (see the Eating in Paris chapter for details), but it's rarely included in the room rates. Pay attention when comparing rates between hotels. This per-person charge can add up, particularly for families. While hotels hope you'll buy their breakfast, it's optional unless otherwise noted; to save money, head to a bakery or café instead.

Note that Parisian hoteliers uniformly detest it when people bring food into bedrooms. Dinner picnics are particularly frowned upon: Hoteliers worry about cleanliness, smells, and attracting insects. Please be tidy and considerate.

Most hotel rooms have a TV, phone, and Wi-Fi *(le wee-fee)*. To turn on your TV, press the channel-up or channel-down button on the remote. If it still doesn't work, see if there's a power button on the TV itself, then press the up or down button again.

Towels aren't routinely replaced every day. Hang up your towel to dry. Extra pillows and blankets are often in the closet or available on request. To get a pillow, ask for *"Un oreiller, s'il vous plaît"* (uhn oh-ray-yay, see voo play).

Get suggestions from your hotelier for safe parking. Consider long-term parking at either airport—Orly is closer and easier for drivers to navigate than Charles de Gaulle. Garages are plentiful (€28-40/day, with special rates through some hotels). Curb parking is free at night (19:00-9:00), all day Sunday, and throughout the month of August. (For more information, see "Parking in Paris" at the end of the Paris Connections chapter.)

If you're arriving early in the morning, your room probably won't be ready. You can drop your bag safely at the hotel and dive right into sightseeing.

Hoteliers can be a great help and source of advice. Most know their city well, and can assist you with everything from public transit and airport connections to calling an English-speaking doctor, or finding a good restaurant, the nearest Internet café (*café internet*, kah-fay an-ter-net), or a self-service launderette (*laverie automatique*, lah-vay-ree oh-to-mah-teek).

Even at the best places, mechanical breakdowns occur: Air-conditioning malfunctions, sinks leak, hot water turns cold, and toilets gurgle and smell. Report your concerns clearly and calmly at the front desk. For more complicated problems, don't expect instant results.

If you suspect night noise will be a problem (if, for instance, your room is over a café), ask for a quieter room in the back or on an upper floor. To guard against theft in your room, keep valuables out of sight. Some rooms come with a safe, and other hotels have safes at the front desk. Use them if you're concerned.

Checkout can pose problems if surprise charges pop up on your bill. If you settle your bill the afternoon before you leave, you'll have time to discuss and address any points of contention (before 19:00, when the night shift usually arrives).

Above all, keep a positive attitude. Remember, you're on vacation. If your hotel is a disappointment, spend more time out enjoying the city you came to see.

## Hostels

Parisian hostels charge about €23-35 per bed. Travelers of any age are welcome if they don't mind dorm-style accommodations and meeting other travelers. Most hostels offer kitchen facilities, Internet access, Wi-Fi, and a self-service laundry. Nowadays, concerned about bedbugs, hostels are likely to provide all bedding, including sheets. Family and private rooms are sometimes available on request.

# Making Reservations

Given the good value of the accommodations I've found for this book, reserve your rooms months in advance, or as soon as you've pinned down your travel dates, particularly if you'll be traveling during peak season. Note that some national holidays jam things up and merit your making reservations far in advance (see "Holidays and Festivals" on page 664).

**Requesting a Reservation:** It's usually easiest to book your room through the hotel's website; many have a reservation-request form built right in. (For the best rates, be sure to use the hotel's official site and not a booking agency's site.) Just type in your preferred dates and the website will automatically display a list of available rooms and prices. Simpler websites will generate an email to the hotelier with your request. If there's no reservation form, or for complicated requests, send an email from your personal address. Other options include calling (see "Phoning" below, and be mindful of time zones) or faxing.

The hotelier wants to know these key pieces of information (also included in the sample request form in the appendix):

- number and type of rooms
- number of nights
- date of arrival
- date of departure
- any special needs (e.g., bathroom in the room or down the hall, twin beds vs. double bed, air-conditioning, quiet, view, ground floor, etc.)

When you request a room, use the European style for writing dates: day/month/year. For example, for a two-night stay in July of 2013, I would request: "1 double room for 2 nights, arrive 16/07/13, depart 18/07/13." Consider carefully how long you'll stay; don't just assume you can tack on extra days once you arrive. Make sure you mention any discounts—for Rick Steves readers or otherwise—when you make the reservation.

If you don't get a response to your email, it usually means the hotel is already fully booked—but try sending the message again or call to follow up.

**Confirming a Reservation:** Most places will request your credit-card number to hold the room. To confirm a room using a hotel's secure online reservation form, enter your contact information and credit-card number; the hotel will email a confirmation.

If you sent an email to request a reservation, the hotel will reply with its room availability and rates. This is not a confirmation. You must email back to say that you want the room at the given rate. While you can email your credit-card information (I do), it's safer to share that confidential info via phone call, two emails (splitting your number between them), or the hotel's secure online reservation form.

**Canceling a Reservation:** If you must cancel your reservation, it's courteous to do so with as much notice as possible. Make a quick phone call or send an email. Family-run places lose money if they turn away customers while holding a room for someone who doesn't show up. Understandably, many hotels bill no-shows for one night.

Cancellation policies can be strict: For example, you might lose a deposit if you cancel within two weeks of your reserved stay, or you might be billed for the entire visit if you leave early. Internet deals may require prepayment, with no refunds for cancellations. Ask about cancellation policies before you book.

If canceling via email, request confirmation that your cancellation was received to avoid being accidentally billed.

**Reconfirm Your Reservation:** Always call to reconfirm your room reservation a few days in advance from the road. (Don't have a TI call for you; they may take a commission.) Smaller hotels and B&Bs appreciate knowing your time of arrival. If you'll be arriving late (after 17:00), alert your hotelier. On the small chance that a hotel loses track of your reservation, bring along a hard copy of their confirmation.

**Reserving Rooms as You Travel:** You can make reservations as you travel, calling hotels or B&Bs a few days to a week before your arrival. If everything's full, don't despair. Call a day or two in advance and fill in a cancellation. If you'd rather travel without any reservations at all, you'll have greater success snaring rooms if you arrive at your destination early in the day. When you anticipate crowds (weekends are worst), call hotels around 9:00 or 10:00 on the day you plan to arrive, when the receptionist knows who'll be checking out and just which rooms will be available. If you encounter a language barrier, ask the fluent receptionist at your current hotel to call for you.

**Phoning:** To call France from the US or Canada, dial 011-33 and then the local number—without the initial 0. (The 011 is our international access code, and 33 is France's country code.) If you're calling France from another European country, dial 00-33-local number—without the initial 0. (The 00 is Europe's international access code.) To make calls within France, simply dial the local number. For more tips on calling, see page 646.

**Independent hostels** tend to be easygoing, colorful, and informal (no membership required); see www.hostelz.com, www.hostelseurope.com, www.hostels.com, and www.hostelbookers.com. **Official hostels** are part of Hostelling International (HI) and share an online booking site (www.hihostels.com). HI hostels require that you either have a membership card or pay extra per night.

## Bed-and-Breakfasts

Several agencies can help you go local by staying in a private home in Paris. While prices and quality can range greatly, most rooms have a private bath and run from €80 to €120. Generally, agency websites allow you to select by neighborhood. Most owners won't take bookings for fewer than two nights. If you want to limit stair-climbing, ask whether the building has an elevator. The agencies listed below have a good selection, but there's no good way to check the quality of the rooms as I do with hotels (agencies work with an ever-changing list of owners—each with a few rooms at most). You are at the mercy of whatever information you get from the agency and its website. Buyer beware.

**Alcôve & Agapes** is the most used B&B resource in Paris, offering a broad selection of addresses throughout the city. Their useful website helps you sort through the options with prices, information about the owners, and helpful photos (tel. 01 44 85 06 05, www.bed-and-breakfast-in-paris.com).

**Good Morning Paris** is another source, listing more than 100 properties (tel. 01 47 07 28 29, www.goodmorningparis.fr).

## Apartments

It's easy, though not necessarily cheaper than a hotel room, to rent a furnished apartment in Paris. Consider this option if you're traveling as a family or with friends, staying a week or longer, and planning to cook most of your own meals. For more information on apartment rentals, and a list of rental agencies, see page 416.

# In the Rue Cler Neighborhood

**(7th arrondissement, Mo: Ecole Militaire, La Tour Maubourg, or Invalides)**

Rue Cler, lined with open-air produce stands six days a week, is a safe, tidy, village-like pedestrian street. It's so French that when I step out of my hotel in the morning, I feel like I must have been a poodle in a previous life. How such coziness lodged itself between the high-powered government district, the Eiffel Tower, and Les Invalides, I'll never know. This is a neighborhood of wide, tree-lined boulevards, stately apartment buildings, and lots of Americans. The American Church, American Library, American University, and many of my readers call this area home. Hotels here are a relatively good value, considering the elegance of the neighborhood and the higher prices of the more cramped hotels in other central areas. And for sightseeing, you're within walking distance of the Eiffel Tower, Army Museum, Quai Branly Museum, Seine River, Champs-Elysées, and Orsay and Rodin museums.

Become a local at a Rue Cler café for breakfast, or join the afternoon crowd for *une bière pression* (a draft beer). On Rue Cler you can eat and browse your way through a street full of cafés, pastry shops, delis, cheese shops, and colorful outdoor produce stalls. Afternoon *boules* (outdoor bowling) on the Esplanade des Invalides is a relaxing spectator sport (look for the dirt area to the upper right as you face the front of Les Invalides; see "The Rules of *Boules*" sidebar on the next page). The manicured gardens behind the golden dome of the Army Museum are free, peaceful, and filled with flowers (at southwest corner of grounds, closes at about 19:00).

Though hardly a happening nightlife spot, Rue Cler offers many low-impact after-dark activities. Take an evening stroll above the river through the parkway between Pont de l'Alma and Pont des Invalides. For an after-dinner cruise on the Seine, it's a 15-minute walk to the river and the Bateaux-Mouches (see page 46 in the Orientation to Paris chapter). For a post-dinner cruise on foot, saunter into the Champ de Mars park to admire the glowing Eiffel Tower. For more ideas on Paris after hours, see the Entertainment in Paris chapter.

The American Church and Franco-American Center is the community center for Americans living in Paris. It hosts interdenominational worship services every Sunday (traditional services at 9:00 and 11:00; contemporary service at 13:30) and free Sunday concerts (generally Sept-June at 17:00—but not every week and not in Dec), and distributes the useful *France-USA Contacts* (reception open Mon-Sat 9:00-12:00 & 13:00-22:00, Sun 14:30-19:00, 65 Quai d'Orsay, Mo: Invalides, tel. 01 40 62 05 00, www.acparis. org).

**Services:** There's a large **post office** at the end of Rue Cler on Avenue de la Motte-Picquet, and a handy **SNCF Boutique** at 80 Rue St. Dominique (Mon-Sat 8:30-19:30, closed Sun, get there when it opens to avoid a long wait). At both of these offices, take a number and wait your turn. A smaller post office is closer to the Eiffel Tower on Avenue Rapp, one block past Rue St. Dominique toward the river. You can buy your Paris Museum Pass at **Tabac La Cave à Cigares** on Avenue de la Motte-Picquet, across from where the Rue Cler ends (see page 196 of my Rue Cler walk).

## The Rules of *Boules*

Throughout Paris—and particularly on Les Invalides' big "front lawn" near the Rue Cler neighborhood—you'll see Parisians playing *boules*.

Each player starts with three iron balls, with the object of getting them close to the target, a small wooden ball called a *cochonnet* (piglet). The first player tosses the *cochonnet* about 30 feet, then throws the first of his iron balls near the target. The next player takes a turn. As soon as a player's ball is closest, it's the other guy's turn. Once all balls have been lobbed, the score is tallied—the player with the closest ball gets one point for each ball closer to the target than his opponent's. The loser gets zero. Games are generally to 15 points.

A regulation *boules* field is 10 feet by 43 feet, but the game is played everywhere—just scratch a throwing circle in the sand, toss the *cochonnet,* and you're off. Strategists can try to knock the opponent's balls out of position, knock the *cochonnet* itself out of position, or guard their best ball with the other two.

**Markets:** Cross the Champ de Mars park to mix it up with bargain-hunters at the twice-weekly open-air market, **Marché Boulevard de Grenelle,** under the Métro, a few blocks southwest of the Champ de Mars park (Wed and Sun 7:00-12:30, between Mo: Dupleix and Mo: La Motte-Picquet-Grenelle). Two miniscule grocery stores, both on Rue de Grenelle, are open until midnight: **Epicerie de la Tour** (at #197) and **Alimentation** (at corner with Rue Cler). **Rue St. Dominique** is the area's boutique-browsing street and well worth a visit if shopping for clothes.

**Internet Access: Com Avenue** is good (about €5/hour, shareable and multi-use accounts, Mon-Sat 10:00-20:00, closed Sun, 24 Rue du Champ de Mars, tel. 01 45 55 00 07).

**Laundry:** Launderettes are omnipresent; ask your hotel for the nearest. Here are three handy locations: on Rue Augereau, on Rue Amélie (both between Rue St. Dominique and Rue de Grenelle), and at the southeast corner of Rue Valadon and Rue de Grenelle.

**Booking Agency:** To book tickets for key sights, or for assistance with hotels, transportation, or excursions, contact the helpful staff at **Paris Webservices** (Mon-Fri 9:00-21:00, Sat-Sun 9:00-18:00, 12 Rue de l'Exposition, Mo: Ecole Militaire, RER: Pont de l'Alma, tel. 09 52 06 02 59, www.pariswebservices.com, contactpws@pariswebservices.com).

**Métro Connections:** Key Métro stops are Ecole Militaire, La Tour Maubourg, and Invalides. The useful RER-C line runs from the Pont de l'Alma and Invalides stations, serving Versailles to the southwest; the Marmottan Museum and Auvers-sur-Oise to the northwest; and the Orsay Museum, Latin Quarter (St. Michel stop), and Austerlitz train station to the east.

**Bus Routes:** Smart travelers take advantage of these bus routes (see map on page 388 for stop locations):

**Line #69** runs east-west along Rue St. Dominique and serves Les Invalides, Orsay, Louvre, Marais, and Père Lachaise Cemetery (see Bus #69 Sightseeing Tour chapter).

**Line #63** runs along the river (the Quai d'Orsay), serving the Latin Quarter along Boulevard St. Germain to the east (ending at Gare de Lyon), and Trocadéro and areas near the Marmottan Museum to the west.

**Line #92** runs along Avenue Bosquet, north to the Champs-Elysées and Arc de Triomphe (faster than the Métro) and south to the Montparnasse Tower and Gare Montparnasse.

**Line #87** runs from Avenue Joseph Bouvard in the Champ de Mars park up Avenue de la Bourdonnais and serves the Sèvres-Babylone shopping area, St. Sulpice Church, Luxembourg Garden, the Bastille, and Gare de Lyon (also more convenient than Métro for these destinations).

**Line #80** runs on Avenue Bosquet, crosses the Champs-Elysées, and serves Gare St. Lazare.

**Line #28** runs on Boulevard de la Tour Maubourg and serves Gare St. Lazare.

**Line #42** runs from Avenue Joseph Bouvard in the Champs de Mars park (same stop as #87), crosses the Champs-Elysées at the Rond-Point, then heads to Place de la Concorde, Place de la Madeleine, Opéra Garnier, and finally to Gare du Nord—a long ride to the train station but less tiring than the Métro if you're carrying suitcases.

## In the Heart of Rue Cler

Many of my readers stay in the Rue Cler neighborhood. If you want to disappear into Paris, choose a hotel elsewhere. The following hotels are within Camembert-smelling distance of Rue Cler.

**$$$ Hôtel Relais Bosquet***** is a fine hotel in an ideal location, with comfortable public spaces and well-configured rooms that are large by local standards and feature effective darkness blinds. The staff are politely formal and offer a 15 percent discount off the public rate to anyone booking direct with this book in 2013. But you'll often get far better rates by "liking" the hotel on Facebook. Book well in advance for the best rates, which vary enormously based on demand (standard Db-€150-235, bigger Db-€175-275, superior Db-€190-305, extra bed-€29, good €15 breakfast buffet with eggs and sausage, 19 Rue du Champ de Mars, tel. 01 47 05 25 45, www.hotel-paris-bosquet.com, hotel@relaisbosquet.com).

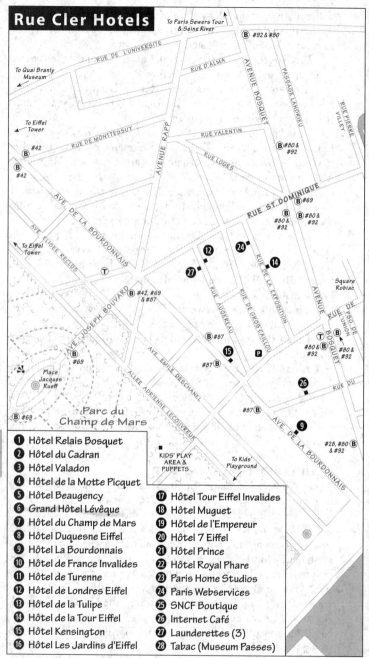

# Rue Cler Hotels

To Paris Sewers Tour & Seine River

#92 & #80

RUE DE L'UNIVERSITÉ

RUE D'ALMA

To Quai Branly Museum

To Eiffel Tower

RUE DE MONTTESSUY

AVENUE RAPP

RUE VALENTIN

AVENUE BOSQUET

PASSAGE LANDRIEU

RUE PIERRE VILLEY

#80 & #92

RUE LOGES

B #42

B #42

AVE. DE LA BOURDONNAIS

AVE. ÉLISÉE RECLUS

RUE ST. DOMINIQUE

B #69

B #80 & #92

B #80 & #92

To Eiffel Tower

12

24

14

Square Robiac

T

27

AVE. JOSEPH BOUVARD

B #42, #69 & #87

RUE AUGEREAU

RUE DE LA EXPOSITION

RUE DE GROS CAILLOU

AVENUE BOSQUET

RUE DE L'UNION

RUE DE PSG. DE

T

B #80 & #92

B #80 & #92

B #87

15

P

B #69

AVE. EMILE DESCHANEL

#87 B

Place Jacques Rueff

ALLÉE ADRIENNE LECOUVREUR

26

RUE DU

9

B #69

Parc du Champ de Mars

#87 B

AVE. DE LA BOURDONNAIS

#28, #80 B & #92

KIDS' PLAY AREA & PUPPETS

To Kids' Playground

1. Hôtel Relais Bosquet
2. Hôtel du Cadran
3. Hôtel Valadon
4. Hôtel de la Motte Picquet
5. Hôtel Beaugency
6. Grand Hôtel Lévêque
7. Hôtel du Champ de Mars
8. Hôtel Duquesne Eiffel
9. Hôtel La Bourdonnais
10. Hôtel de France Invalides
11. Hôtel de Turenne
12. Hôtel de Londres Eiffel
13. Hôtel de la Tulipe
14. Hôtel de la Tour Eiffel
15. Hôtel Kensington
16. Hôtel Les Jardins d'Eiffel
17. Hôtel Tour Eiffel Invalides
18. Hôtel Muguet
19. Hôtel de l'Empereur
20. Hôtel 7 Eiffel
21. Hôtel Prince
22. Hôtel Royal Phare
23. Paris Home Studios
24. Paris Webservices
25. SNCF Boutique
26. Internet Café
27. Launderettes (3)
28. Tabac (Museum Passes)

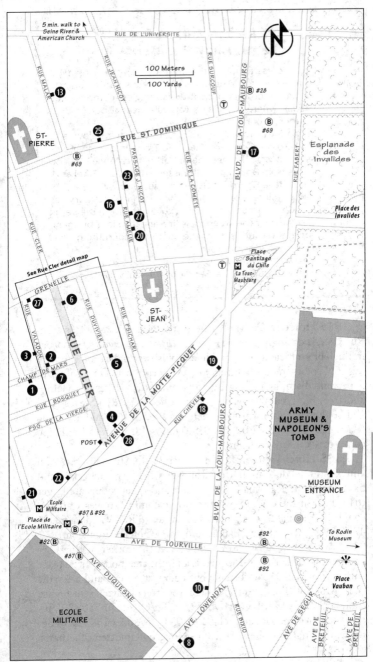

---

## Rue Cler Musts for Temporary Residents

- Watch *boules* action in the afternoon on the Esplanade des Invalides (see "The Rules of *Boules*" sidebar, earlier).
- Relax in the flowery park at the southwest corner of Les Invalides, where Avenue de Tourville meets Boulevard de la Tour Maubourg.
- See the Eiffel Tower at night, from the park below, and from across the river on Place du Trocadéro (dinner picnics are best). The best neighborhood café view of the tower is from Boulangerie-Pâtisserie de la Tour Eiffel at 21 Avenue de la Bourdonnais (see page 438).
- See the golden dome of Les Invalides in all its glory—at night. Choose from two good viewpoints: from the paths along the river (between the Alma and Invalides bridges), or from the south side of the complex, along the greenway in the middle of Avenue de Breteuil.
- Take a Bateaux-Mouches cruise after dark (see page 46).
- Linger at a Rue Cler café and observe daily life.

---

**$$$ Hôtel du Cadran\*\*\***, perfectly located a *boule* toss from Rue Cler, is daringly modern—with a *chocolat-et-macaron* shop/bar in the lobby, efficient staff, and über-stylish yet tight rooms featuring cool colors, mood lighting, and every comfort (Db-€250-290; 5 percent discount off lowest rates—including Internet deals—and free, big breakfast when you use the code "RickSteves rate" and book by email or through their website; 10 Rue du Champ de Mars, tel. 01 40 62 67 00, fax 01 40 62 67 13, www.cadranhotel.com, resa@cadranhotel.com).

**$$$ Hôtel Valadon\*\*\***, almost across the street, is really an annex of Hôtel du Cadran (listed above), where you'll check in and have breakfast. The Valadron's 12 cute-and-quiet rooms are larger than those at the Cadran, with the same comfort, prices, and discounts (Tb available, one good family suite, 16 Rue Valadon, tel. 01 47 53 89 85, www.hotelvaladon.com, info@hotelvaladon.com).

**$$ Hôtel de la Motte Picquet\*\*\***, at the corner of Rue Cler and Avenue de la Motte-Picquet, is an intimate, modest little place with narrow halls, comfortable but compact rooms, and a terrific staff (Moe and Tina). Get a room off the street to avoid street noise (standard Db-€150, bigger Db-€230, Tb/Qb-€270-350, 30 Avenue de la Motte-Picquet, tel. 01 47 05 09 57, fax 01 47 05 74 36, www.hotelmottepicquetparis.com, book@hotelmottepicquetparis.com).

**$$ Hôtel Beaugency\*\*\***, a good value on a quieter street a short block off Rue Cler, has 30 smallish rooms with standard furnishings and a lobby that you can stretch out in (Sb-€120, Db-€155, twin Db-€165, occasional discounts for Rick Steves readers—ask when you book, 21 Rue Duvivier, tel. 01 47 05 01 63, fax 01 45 51 04 96, www.hotel-beaugency.com, infos@hotel-beaugency.com).

*Warning:* The next two hotels are very busy with my readers (reserve long in advance).

**$$ Grand Hôtel Lévêque**\*\*, ideally located on Rue Cler, is all about location. It's a busy place with a sliver-size elevator, a sleek breakfast room that doubles as a lounge, impersonal service, and so-so accommodations (some rooms are fine, while others feel neglected). Rooms on Rue Cler come with fun views but morning noise as the market sets up (S-€75-120, Db-€140-170, Tb-€200, don't let them talk you into a pricier room than the one you booked, 29 Rue Cler, tel. 01 47 05 49 15, fax 01 45 50 49 36, www.hotel-leveque.com, info@hotel-leveque.com).

**$ Hôtel du Champ de Mars**\*\*, with adorable rooms and serious owners Françoise and Stephane, is a cozy Rue Cler option. This plush little hotel has a small-town feel from top to bottom. The rooms are snug but lovingly kept, and single rooms can work as tiny doubles. It's an excellent value despite the lack of air-conditioning (Sb-€100, Db-€120, 30 yards off Rue Cler at 7 Rue du Champ de Mars, tel. 01 45 51 52 30, fax 01 45 51 64 36, www.hotelduchamp demars.com, reservation@hotelduchampdemars.com).

## Near Rue Cler, Close to Ecole Militaire Métro Stop

The following listings are a five-minute walk from Rue Cler, near Métro stop École Militaire or RER: Pont de l'Alma.

**$$$ Hôtel Duquesne Eiffel**\*\*\*, a few blocks farther from the action, is calm, hospitable, and very comfortable. It features handsome rooms (some with terrific Eiffel Tower views for only €20 more), a welcoming lobby, and a big, hot breakfast for €13 (Db-€190-250, price grows with room size, Tb-€270, 10 percent less with this book in 2013, 23 Avenue Duquesne, tel. 01 44 42 09 09, fax 01 44 42 09 08, www.hotel-duquesne-eiffel-paris.com, contact@hde.fr).

**$$$ Hôtel La Bourdonnais**\*\*\* is *très* Parisian, mixing an Old World feel with creaky, comfortable rooms and generous public spaces. Its mostly spacious rooms are traditionally decorated, and its bathrooms are due for an upgrade (Db-€200-300, Tb-€240-320, Qb-€280-350, Sophie promises free breakfast with this book through 2013, 111-113 Avenue de la Bourdonnais, tel. 01 47 05 45 42, fax 01 45 55 75 54, www.hotellabourdonnais.fr, hlb@hotellabourdonnais.fr).

**$$ Hôtel de France Invalides**** is an okay mid-range option away from most other hotels I list. It's run by a brother-sister team (Alain and Marie-Hélène) with a small bar/lounge and 60 well-maintained rooms, some with knockout views of Invalides' golden dome. Rooms on the courtyard are very quiet, while those facing Les Invalides face a large street (Sb-€115, standard Db-€140-250, 5 percent discount with this book in 2013, connecting rooms possible for families, no air-con, 102 Boulevard de la Tour Maubourg, tel. 01 47 05 40 49, fax 01 45 56 96 78, www.hoteldefrance.com, contact@hoteldefrance.com).

**$ Hôtel de Turenne**** is modest, with the cheapest air-conditioned rooms I've found and a lobby with windows on the world. Rooms are simple but comfortable, and the price is right. There are five true singles and several connecting rooms good for families (Sb-€70, Db-€85-107, Tb-€150, Wi-Fi only, 20 Avenue de Tourville, tel. 01 47 05 99 92, fax 01 45 56 06 04, www.hotel-turenne-paris.com, info@hotel-turenne-paris.com).

## Near Rue Cler, Closer to Rue St. Dominique (and the Seine)

**$$$ Hôtel de Londres Eiffel**** is my closest listing to the Eiffel Tower and the Champ de Mars park. Here you get immaculate, warmly decorated rooms (several are connecting for families), snazzy public spaces, and a service-oriented staff. Some rooms are pretty small—request a bigger room. It's less convenient to the Métro (10-minute walk), but very handy to buses #69, #80, #87, and #92, and to RER-C: Pont de l'Alma (Sb-€175, small Db-€190, bigger Db-€205, Db with Eiffel Tower view-€230, Tb-€270, 1 Rue Augereau, tel. 01 45 51 63 02, fax 01 47 05 28 96, www.hotel-paris-londres-eiffel.com, info@londres-eiffel.com, helpful Cédric and Arnaud). The owners also run a good two-star hotel with similar comfort in the cheaper Montparnasse area, **$$ Hôtel Apollon Montparnasse** (Db-€140-170, look for Web deals, 91 Rue de l'Ouest, Mo: Pernety, tel. 01 43 95 62 00, fax 01 43 95 62 10, www.apollon-montparnasse.com, info@apollon-montparnasse.com).

**$$ Hôtel de la Tulipe****, three blocks from Rue Cler toward the river, feels pricey but unique. The 20 small and simple rooms surround a seductive, wood-beamed lounge and a peaceful, leafy courtyard. The owners promise a 10 percent discount when you book direct with this book in 2013 (Sb-€160, Db-€182, Tb-€224, 4-person apartment-€335, 2-room suite for up to 5 people-€365, no air-con, no elevator, 33 Rue Malar, tel. 01 45 51 67 21, fax 01 47

53 96 37, www.paris-hotel-tulipe.com, hoteldelatulipe@wanadoo. fr).

**$ Hôtel de la Tour Eiffel**\*\* is a good two-star value on a quiet street near several of my favorite restaurants. The rooms are well-designed and comfortable, but some have thin walls and none have air-conditioning (snug Db-€110, bigger Db-€120-140, no breakfast offered, Wi-Fi only, 17 Rue de l'Exposition, tel. 01 47 05 14 75, fax 01 47 53 99 46, www.hotel-toureiffel.com, hte7@ wanadoo.fr).

**$ Hôtel Kensington**\*\* is a good budget value close to the Eiffel Tower and run by elegant, though formal, Daniele. It's an unpretentious place with mostly small, basic, but well-kept rooms (Sb-€65-74, Db-€80-97, big Db on back side-€98-117, Eiffel Tower views for those who ask, no air-con, pay Internet access, 79 Avenue de la Bourdonnais, tel. 01 47 05 74 00, fax 01 47 05 25 81, www.hotel-kensington.com, hk@hotel-kensington.com).

## Near La Tour Maubourg Métro Stop

The next four listings are within three blocks of the intersection of Avenue de la Motte-Picquet and Boulevard de la Tour Maubourg.

**$$$ Hôtel Les Jardins d'Eiffel**\*\*\*, on a quiet street, feels like the modern motel it is, with professional service, its own parking garage (€24/day), and a spacious lobby. Most rooms are big and quiet by Parisian standards (standard Db-€180-210, renovated Db-€215-240, 15 percent Rick Steves discount when you book direct in 2013, check website for special discounts, 8 Rue Amélie, tel. 01 47 05 46 21, fax 01 45 55 28 08, www.hoteljardinseiffel.com, reservations@hoteljardinseiffel.com).

**$$$ Hôtel Tour Eiffel Invalides**\*\*\* advertises its Best Western status proudly and offers a generous-size lobby with a small courtyard and good, traditionally decorated rooms with big beds but no firm prices (the Internet decides). Allow about €220-280 for a double but look for better rates on their website. Ask for a non-smoking room (35 Boulevard de la Tour Maubourg, tel. 01 45 56 10 78, fax 01 47 05 65 08, www.timhotel.fr, invalides@timhotel.fr).

**$$$ Hôtel Muguet**\*\*\*, a peaceful, stylish, immaculate refuge, gives you three-star comfort for a two-star price. This delightful spot offers 43 tasteful rooms, a greenhouse lounge, and a small garden courtyard. The hands-on owner, Catherine, gives her guests a restful and secure home in Paris (Sb-€140-175, Db-€195-245— more with view, Tb-€195-245, strict cancellation policy: cancel 7 days before arrival or lose deposit, 11 Rue Chevert, tel. 01 47 05 05 93, fax 01 45 50 25 37, www.hotelparismuguet.com, muguet@ wanadoo.fr).

**$$$ Hôtel de l'Empereur**\*\* is well-run and offers good service. It delivers smashing views of Invalides from most of its very comfortable and tastefully designed rooms. Fifth-floor rooms have small balconies, and all rooms have queen-size beds (Sb-€140-175, Db-€195-245—more with view, Tb-€195-245, two-room Qb-€370, strict cancellation policy: cancel 7 days before arrival or lose deposit, 2 Rue Chevert, tel. 01 45 55 88 02, fax 01 45 51 88 54, www.hotelempereurparis.com, contact@hotelempereur.com).

## Lesser Values in the Rue Cler Area

Given how fine this area is, these are acceptable last choices.

**$$$ Hôtel 7 Eiffel****** is an ultra-modern, high-design, four-star splurge, complete with bar and fireplace lounge in lobby, colorful rooftop terrace, room service, and all the usual comforts of a business hotel (Db-€270-370, check Web for deals, 17 bis Rue Amélie, tel. 01 45 55 10 01, fax 01 47 05 28 68, www.7eiffel.com, reservation@7eiffel.com).

**$ Hôtel Prince**,** across from the Ecole Militaire Métro stop, has a spartan lobby, drab halls, and plain-but-acceptable rooms for the price (Sb-€109, Db-€130, Tb-€150, free breakfast with this book in 2013, Wi-Fi only, 66 Avenue Bosquet, tel. 01 47 05 40 90, fax 01 47 53 06 62, www.hotel-paris-prince.com, paris@hotel-prince.com).

**$ Hôtel Royal Phare**,** facing the busy Ecole Militaire Métro stop, is a humble place. The 34 basic, pastel rooms are unimaginative but sleepable. Rooms on the courtyard are quietest, with peek-a-boo views of the Eiffel Tower from the fifth floor up (Sb-€84, Db with shower-€98, Db with tub-€108, Tb-€120, fridges in rooms, no air-con but fans, no Wi-Fi, 40 Avenue de la Motte-Picquet, tel. 01 47 05 57 30, fax 01 45 51 64 41, www.hotel-royalphare-paris. com, hotel-royalphare@wanadoo.fr, friendly manager Hocin).

# In the Marais Neighborhood

**(4th arrondissement, Mo: Bastille, St. Paul, and Hôtel de Ville)**
Those interested in a more SoHo/Greenwich Village-type locale should make the Marais their Parisian home. Once a forgotten Parisian backwater, the Marais—which runs from the Pompidou Center east to the Bastille—is now one of Paris' most popular residential, tourist, and shopping areas. This is jumbled, medieval Paris at its finest, where classy stone mansions sit alongside trendy bars, antiques shops, and fashion-conscious boutiques. The streets are a fascinating parade of artists, students, tourists, immigrants, and baguette-munching babies in strollers. The Marais is also known as a hub of the Parisian gay and lesbian scene. This area is *sans* doubt livelier (and louder) than the Rue Cler area.

In the Marais you have these major sights close at hand: the Carnavalet Museum, Victor Hugo's House, the Jewish Art and

History Museum, the Pompidou Center, and the Picasso Museum (closed until summer of 2013). You're also a manageable walk from Paris' two islands (Ile St. Louis and Ile de la Cité), home to Notre-Dame and Sainte-Chapelle. The Opéra Bastille, Promenade Plantée park, Place des Vosges (Paris' oldest square), Jewish Quarter (Rue des Rosiers), the Latin Quarter, and nightlife-packed Rue de Lappe are also walkable. Strolling home (day or night) from Notre-Dame along Ile St. Louis is marvelous.

Most of my recommended hotels are located a few blocks north of the Marais' main east-west drag, Rue St. Antoine/Rue de Rivoli.

**Tourist Information:** The nearest TI is at the Pyramides Métro station (daily May-Oct 9:00-19:00, Nov-April 10:00-19:00).

**Services:** Most banks and other services are on the main street, Rue de Rivoli, which becomes Rue St. Antoine. Marais **post offices** are on Rue Castex and at the corner of Rue Pavée and Rue des Francs Bourgeois. There's a busy **SNCF Boutique** where you can take care of all train needs on Rue St. Antoine at Rue de Turenne (Mon-Fri 8:00-20:30, Sat 10:00-20:30, closed Sun). A quieter SNCF Boutique is nearer Gare de Lyon at 5 Rue de Lyon (Mon-Sat 8:30-18:00, closed Sun).

**Markets:** The Marais has two good open-air markets: the sprawling **Marché de la Bastille,** along Boulevard Richard Lenoir, on the north side of Place de la Bastille (Thu and Sun until 14:30); and the more intimate, untouristy **Marché d'Aligre** (Tue-Sat 9:00-14, closed Mon, cross Place de la Bastille and walk about 10 blocks down Rue du Faubourg St. Antoine, turn right at Rue de Cotte to Place d'Aligre; or, take Métro line 8 from Bastille in the direction of Créteil-Préfecture, get off at the Ledru-Rollin stop, and walk a few blocks southeast). A small **grocery** is open until 23:00 on Rue St. Antoine (near intersection with Rue Castex). To shop at a Parisian Sears, find the **BHV** department store next to Hôtel de Ville. Paris' oldest covered market, **Marché des Enfants Rouges,** lies a 10-minute walk north of Rue de Rivoli (see page 491).

**Bookstore:** The Marais is home to a fine English-language bookstore, **Red Wheelbarrow,** which unfortunately is up for sale and may not be open in 2013. They sell most of my guidebooks at good prices, and carry a great collection of other books about Paris and France for both adults and children (2012 hours: Mon 10:00-18:00, Tue-Sat 10:00-19:00, Sun 14:00-18:00, 22 Rue St. Paul, Mo: St. Paul, tel. 01 48 04 75 08).

**Internet Access:** Try **Paris CY** (Mon-Sat 10:00-20:00, Sun 13:00-20:00, 8 Rue de Jouy, Mo: St. Paul, tel. 01 42 71 37 37).

**Laundry:** There are many launderettes; ask your hotelier for the nearest. Here are three you can count on: on Impasse Guéménée

## Marais Musts for Temporary Residents

- Have dinner or a drink on Place du Marché Ste. Catherine.
- Dine or enjoy a drink on Place des Vosges.
- Take a late-night art gallery stroll around Place des Vosges.
- Have lunch at Paris' oldest covered market (Marché des Enfants Rouges—see page 491).
- Mix it up with local shoppers one morning at the Marché d'Aligre.
- Walk Ile St. Louis after dark and enjoy the floodlit view of Notre-Dame (see page 498).
- Have tea and a pastry at Le Loir dans la Théière (daily 12:00-19:00, 3 Rue des Rosiers) and/or a glass of wine at La Belle Hortense wine bar/bookstore (daily 17:00-late, 31 Rue Vieille du Temple).
- Follow my "Boutique Stroll" through the Marais (see page 485 of the Shopping in Paris chapter)—best on Sunday afternoon.

(north of Rue St. Antoine), on Rue Ste. Croix de la Bretonnerie (just east of Rue du Temple), and on Rue du Petit Musc (south of Rue St. Antoine).

**Métro Connections:** Key Métro stops in the Marais are, from east to west: Bastille, St. Paul, and Hôtel de Ville (Sully-Morland, Pont Marie, and Rambuteau stops are also handy). Métro connections are excellent, with direct service to the Louvre, Champs-Elysées, Arc de Triomphe, and La Défense (all on line 1); the Rue Cler area and Opéra Garnier (line 8 from Bastille stop); and four major train stations: Gare de Lyon, Gare du Nord, Gare de l'Est, and Gare d'Austerlitz (all accessible from Bastille stop).

**Bus Routes:** For stop locations, see the "Marais Hotels" map.

**Line #69** on Rue St. Antoine takes you eastbound to Père Lachaise Cemetery and westbound to the Louvre, Orsay, and Rodin museums, plus the Army Museum, ending at the Eiffel Tower (see Bus #69 Sightseeing Tour chapter).

**Line #87** runs down Boulevard Henri IV, crossing Ile St. Louis and serving the Latin Quarter along Boulevard St. Germain, before heading to St. Sulpice Church/Luxembourg Garden, the Eiffel Tower, and the Rue Cler neighborhood to the west. The same line, running in the opposite direction, brings you to Gare de Lyon.

**Line #96** runs on Rues Turenne and Rivoli, serves Ile de la Cité and St. Sulpice Church (near Luxembourg Garden), and ends at Gare Montparnasse.

**Line #65** runs from Gare de Lyon up Rue de Lyon, around

Place de la Bastille, and then up Boulevard Beaumarchais to Gare de l'Est and Gare du Nord.

**Line #67** runs from Place d'Italie to the Jardin des Plantes (just south of the Seine), across Ile St. Louis (on Boulevard Henri IV), along Rue de Rivoli past the Louvre, then up to Montmartre.

**Taxis:** You'll find taxi stands on Place de la Bastille (where Boulevard Richard Lenoir meets the square), on the south side of Rue St. Antoine (in front of St. Paul Church), behind the Hôtel de Ville on Rue du Lobau (where it meets Rue de Rivoli), and a quieter one on the north side of Rue St. Antoine (where it meets Rue Castex).

## Near Place des Vosges

**$$ Hôtel Castex***,** on a quiet street near Place de la Bastille, is a well-located place with tile-floored rooms (that amplify noise). Their clever system of connecting rooms allows families total privacy between two rooms, each with its own bathroom. The 30 rooms are narrow (Sb-€145, Db-€175, Tb-€220, free buffet breakfast with this book through 2013, just off Place de la Bastille and Rue St. Antoine at 5 Rue Castex, Mo: Bastille, tel. 01 42 72 31 52, fax 01 42 72 57 91, www.castexhotel.com, info@castexhotel.com).

**$$ Hôtel Bastille Spéria***,** a short block off Place de la Bastille, offers business-type service in a great location. The 42 well-configured rooms are modern and comfortable, with big beds (Sb-€135-150, Db-€165-185, good buffet breakfast-€13, 1 Rue de la Bastille, Mo: Bastille, tel. 01 42 72 04 01, fax 01 42 72 56 38, www.hotelsperia.com, info@hotelsperia.com).

**$$ Hôtel St. Louis Marais***,** an intimate little hotel, lies on a quiet street closer to the river. The well-maintained rooms come with character and reasonable rates (Db-€175-195, 1 Rue Charles V, tel. 01 48 87 87 04, www.saintlouismarais.com).

**$$ Hôtel Original Paris***,** on a busy street barely off Place de la Bastille, has artsy rooms and a good location (Db-€155-190, 8 Boulevard Beaumarchais, Mo: Bastille, tel. 01 47 00 91 50, fax 01 47 00 06 31, www.hoteloriginalparis.com, info@hoteloriginal paris.com).

**$ Hôtel du 7ème Art**,** two blocks south of Rue St. Antoine toward the river, is a young, carefree, Hollywood-nostalgia place with a full-service café-bar and Charlie Chaplin murals. Its 23 good-value rooms have brown 1970s decor, but are comfortable enough. Sadly, smoking is allowed in all rooms, so you might detect an odor. The large rooms are American-spacious (small Db-€100, standard Db-€115, large Db-€130-160, Tb-€150-180, extra bed-€20, no elevator, 20 Rue St. Paul, Mo: St. Paul, tel. 01 44 54 85 00, fax 01 42 77 69 10, www.paris-hotel-7art.com, hotel7art@ wanadoo.fr).

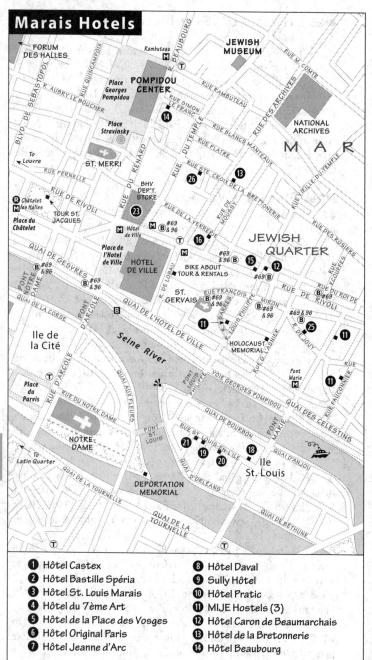

# Marais Hotels

Legend:
1. Hôtel Castex
2. Hôtel Bastille Spéria
3. Hôtel St. Louis Marais
4. Hôtel du 7ème Art
5. Hôtel de la Place des Vosges
6. Hôtel Original Paris
7. Hôtel Jeanne d'Arc
8. Hôtel Daval
9. Sully Hôtel
10. Hôtel Pratic
11. MIJE Hostels (3)
12. Hôtel Caron de Beaumarchais
13. Hôtel de la Bretonnerie
14. Hôtel Beaubourg

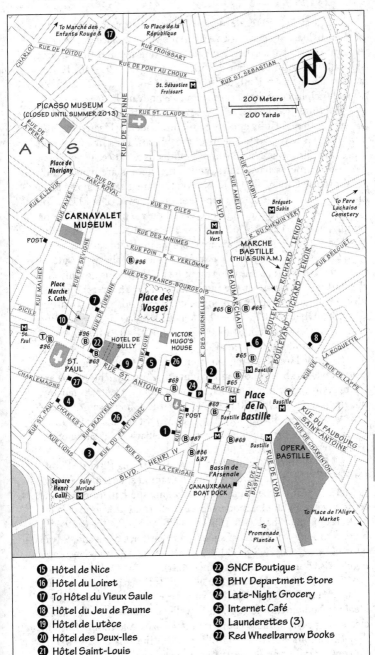

↑ To Marché des Enfants Rouge & ⑰

↑ To Place de la République

RUE DE POITOU

RUE FROISSART

CHARLOT

RUE DE PONT AU CHOUX

RUE ST. SEBASTIAN

St. Sébastien Froissart Ⓜ

200 Meters

200 Yards

Ⓝ

RUE DE TURENNE

RUE ST. CLAUDE

PICASSO MUSEUM
(CLOSED UNTIL SUMMER 2013)

RUE DE LA PERLE

A I S

Place de Thorigny

RUE DE PARC ROYAL

RUE EL'ZEVIR

RUE ST. GILES

BLVD.

RUE ST. SABIN

Bréguet-Sabin Ⓜ

To Pere Lachaise Cemetery →

RUE FAYEE

CARNAVALET MUSEUM

RUE DES MINIMES

Ⓜ Chemin Vert

R. DU CHEMIN VERT

RUE BRÉGUET

BOULEVARD RICHARD LENOIR

POST ◾

RUE DE SÉVIGNÉ

RUE FOIN — R.R. VERLOMME

MARCHE BASTILLE
(THU & SUN A.M.)

RUE MALHER

Ⓑ＃96

RUE DES FRANCS-BOURGEOIS

Place Marche S. Cath.

⑦

Place des Vosges

BEAUMARCHAIS

#65 ⒷＢ #65

SICILE

⑩

＃96

RUE DE TURENNE

HOTEL DE SULLY

VICTOR HUGO'S HOUSE

R. DES TOURNELLES

⑥

⑧

St. Paul Ⓜ

Ⓣ Ⓑ ＃96

㉒

RUE BIRAGUE

⑤ ㉖

#65 Ⓑ

Ⓜ Bastille

RUE DE LA ROQUETTE

＃69 Ⓑ

⑨

RUE ST. ANTOINE

②

RUE DE LAPPE

ST. PAUL

㉗

⑤

㉔

R. BASTILLE

#65 Ⓑ

Ⓣ Bastille Ⓜ

CHARLEMAGNE

④

RUE ST. PAUL

RUE BEAUTREILLIS

㉖

＃69 Ⓑ Ⓣ

POST ◾

Ⓟ

＃69 Ⓑ

Place de la Bastille

RUE DU FAUBOURG SAINT-ANTOINE

RUE CHARLES V

①

Ⓜ

Ⓜ Bastille Ⓜ

RUE DE CHARENTON

RUE LIONS

③

RUE DU PETIT MUSC

Ⓑ＃87

Ⓑ ＃69

OPERA BASTILLE

RUE DE HENRI IV

Ⓑ＃86 & 87

BLVD. LA CERISAIE

Bassin de l'Arsenale

BLVD. DE LA BASTILLE

RUE DE LYON

Square Henri Galli Ⓜ

Sully Morland Ⓜ

CANAUXRAMA BOAT DOCK

To Place de l'Aligre Market →

To Promenade Plantée ↓

**SLEEPING IN PARIS**

**$ Hôtel de la Place des Vosges**\*\* has simple, chic rooms and is brilliantly located between Rue St. Antoine and Place des Vosges. Amenities are sparse, there's no air-conditioning, and the elevator skips floors five and six, but the price is right (Db-€95-140, 12 Rue de Biraque, Mo: St. Paul, tel. 01 42 72 60 46, fax 01 42 72 02 64, www.hotelplacedesvosges.com, contact@hpdv.net).

**$ Hôtel Jeanne d'Arc**\*\*, a lovely little hotel with a stylish lobby and thoughtfully appointed rooms, is ideally located for (and very popular with) connoisseurs of the Marais. It's a fine value and worth booking way ahead (three months in advance, if possible). Sixth-floor rooms have views, and corner rooms are wonderfully bright in the City of Light. Rooms on the street can be noisy until the bars close (Sb-€65-96, Db-€96, larger twin Db-€119, Tb-€149, good Qb-€164, no air-con, Wi-Fi only—in lobby, 3 Rue de Jarente, Mo: St. Paul, tel. 01 48 87 62 11, fax 01 70 24 83 38, www.hoteljeannedarc.com, information@hoteljeannedarc.com).

**$ Hôtel Daval**\*\*, an unassuming place on the wild side of Place de la Bastille, is ideal for night owls. The rooms are tiny and the halls are narrow, but the rates are good for an air-conditioned place. Ask for a quieter room on the courtyard side if sleep matters (Sb-€86, Db-€92-101, Tb-€112, Qb-€131, Wi-Fi only, 21 Rue Daval, Mo: Bastille, tel. 01 47 00 51 23, fax 01 40 21 80 26, www.hoteldaval.com, info@hoteldaval.com).

**$ Sully Hôtel,** sitting right on Rue St. Antoine, is a basic, cheap dive run by no-nonsense Monsieur Zeroual. The rooms are frumpy, dimly lit, and can smell of smoke, and the entry is narrow, but the price fits (Db-€80, Tb-€90, Qb-€110, no elevator, no air-con, Wi-Fi only, 48 Rue St. Antoine, Mo: St. Paul, tel. 01 42 78 49 32, fax 01 44 61 76 50, www.sullyhotelparis.com, sullyhotel@orange.fr).

**$ Hôtel Pratic,** just off the quiet and charming Place du Sainte Catherine, works for travelers who don't mind squeezing sideways to make it past the bed into the bathroom. The half-timbered interior gives this hotel a modest level of charm, but also makes for dark rooms and hallways (Sb-€69, Db-€69-119, Tb-€119-159, more for rooms with view of square, no elevator, no air-con, 9 Rue d'Ormesson, tel. 01 48 87 80 47, fax 01 48 87 40 04, www.pratichotelparis.com, pratic.hotel@wanadoo.fr).

**$ MIJE Youth Hostels:** The Maison Internationale de la Jeunesse et des Etudiants (MIJE) runs three classy old residences, ideal for budget travelers. Each is well-maintained, with simple, clean, single-sex (unless your group takes a whole room), one- to four-bed rooms for travelers of any age. The hostels are **MIJE Fourcy** (biggest and loudest, €11 dinners available with a membership card, 6 Rue de Fourcy, just south of Rue de Rivoli), **MIJE Fauconnier** (no elevator, 11 Rue du Fauconnier), and **MIJE**

**Maubisson** (smallest and quietest, no outdoor terrace, 12 Rue des Barres). None have double beds or air-conditioning; all have private showers in every room (all prices per person: Sb-€51, Db-€38, Tb-€33, Qb-€31, credit cards accepted, includes breakfast but not towels, required membership card-€2.50 extra/person, 7-day maximum stay, rooms locked 12:00-15:00, curfew at 1:00 in the morning). They all share the same contact information (tel. 01 42 74 23 45, fax 01 40 27 81 64, www.mije.com, info@mije.com) and Métro stop (St. Paul). Reservations are accepted (six weeks ahead online, 10 days ahead by phone)—though you must show up by noon, or call the morning of arrival to confirm a later arrival time.

## Near the Pompidou Center

These hotels are farther west, closer to the Pompidou Center than to Place de la Bastille. The Hôtel de Ville Métro stop works well for all of these hotels, unless a closer stop is noted.

**$$ Hôtel Caron de Beaumarchais***,** on a busy corner, feels like a fluffy folk museum, with 20 pricey but cared-for and character-filled rooms. Its small lobby is cluttered with bits from an elegant 18th-century Marais house (small Db in back-€165, larger Db facing the front-€195, Wi-Fi only, 12 Rue Vieille du Temple, tel. 01 42 72 34 12, fax 01 42 72 34 63, www.carondebeaumarchais.com).

**$$ Hôtel de la Bretonnerie***,** three blocks from the Hôtel de Ville, makes a fine Marais home. It has a warm, welcoming lobby and 29 well-appointed, good-value rooms with an antique, open-beam warmth but no air-conditioning (standard "classic" Db-€145, bigger "charming" Db-€175, Db suite-€200, Tb/Qb-€225, between Rue Vieille du Temple and Rue des Archives at 22 Rue Ste. Croix de la Bretonnerie, tel. 01 48 87 77 63, fax 01 42 77 26 78, www.bretonnerie.com, hotel@bretonnerie.com).

**$$ Hôtel Beaubourg***** is a solid three-star value on a small street in the shadow of the Pompidou Center. The lounge is inviting, and the 28 rooms are comfy, well-appointed, and quiet (standard Db-€140, bigger twin or king-size Db-€160 and worth the extra cost, rates vary wildly with availability, 11 Rue Simon Le Franc, Mo: Rambuteau, tel. 01 42 74 34 24, fax 01 42 78 68 11, www.beaubourg-paris-hotel.com, reservation@hotelbeaubourg.com).

**$ Hôtel de Nice**,** on the Marais' busy main drag, features a turquoise-and-fuchsia "Marie-Antoinette-does-tie-dye" decor. Its narrow halls are littered with paintings and layered with carpets, and its 23 Old World rooms have thoughtful touches and tight bathrooms. Twin rooms, which cost the same as doubles, are larger and on the street side—but have effective double-paned windows (Sb-€80-130, Db-€110-160, Tb-€135-170, reception on second floor, 42 bis Rue de Rivoli, tel. 01 42 78 55 29, fax 01 42 78 36 07, www.hoteldenice.com, contact@hoteldenice.com, laissez-faire management).

**$ Hôtel du Loiret\*** is a centrally located and rare Marais budget hotel. It's basic, but the rooms are surprisingly sharp, considering the price and location (Db-€80-100, Tb-€130, no air-con, expect some noise, 8 Rue des Mauvais Garçons, tel. 01 48 87 77 00, fax 01 48 04 96 56, www.hotel-du-loiret.fr, hotelduloiret@hotmail.com).

## Near the Marché des Enfants Rouges
**$$ Hôtel du Vieux Saule\*\*\*** has 27 simple rooms with little character in a great location. Rooms are tight and modern. Avoid the smoking rooms on the first floor (Sb-€95-140, Db-€110-160, *supérieure* Db-€145-190, deluxe Db-€180-250, rates vary greatly with season, check online for best deals, small sauna free for guests, 6 Rue de Picardie, Mo: Filles du Calvaire or Temple, tel. 01 42 72 01 14, fax 01 40 27 88 21, www.hotelvieuxsaule.com, reserv@hotelvieuxsaule.com).

# On Ile St. Louis

**(4th arrondissement; Mo: Pont Marie and Sully-Morland)**
The peaceful, residential character of this river-wrapped island, with its brilliant location and homemade ice cream, has drawn Americans for decades. There are no budget values here—all of the hotels are three-star or more—though prices are reasonable for the level of comfort. The island's village ambience and proximity to the Marais, Notre-Dame, and the Latin Quarter make this area well worth considering. All of the following hotels are on the island's main drag, Rue St. Louis-en-l'Ile, where I list several restaurants (see page 448 in the Eating in Paris chapter). For nearby services, see the Marais neighborhood section; for locations, see the Marais Hotels map, earlier.

**$$$ Hôtel du Jeu de Paume\*\*\*\***, occupying a 17th-century tennis center, is the most expensive hotel I list in Paris. When you enter its magnificent lobby, you'll understand why. Greet Scoop, *le chien*, then take a spin in the glass elevator for a half-timbered-tree-house experience. The 30 rooms are carefully designed and tasteful, though not particularly spacious (you're paying for the location and public areas). Most rooms face a small garden; all are pin-drop peaceful (standard Db-€290-330, deluxe Db-€400-560, €18 breakfast, 54 Rue St. Louis-en-l'Ile, tel. 01 43 26 14 18, fax 01 40 46 02 76, www.jeudepaumehotel.com, info@jeudepaumehotel.com).

**$$$ Hôtel de Lutèce\*\*\*** comes with a sit-awhile wood-paneled lobby and a real fireplace. Rooms at this appealing hotel are handsome, and those on lower floors have high ceilings. Twin rooms are larger and the same price as double rooms. Rooms with bathtubs are on the louder street-side, while those with showers are on the courtyard (Db-€220, Tb-€255, 65 Rue St. Louis-en-l'Ile, tel. 01 43 26 23 52, fax 01 43 29 60 25, www.hoteldelutece.com, info@hoteldelutece.com).

**$$$ Hôtel des Deux-Iles\*\*\*** has the same owners and same prices as the Lutèce (listed above), with a tad less personality (59 Rue St. Louis-en-l'Ile, tel. 01 43 26 13 35, fax 01 43 29 60 25, www.hoteldesdeuxiles.com, info@hoteldesdeuxiles.com).

**$$ Hôtel Saint-Louis\*\*\*** blends character with modern comforts. The well-maintained rooms come with cool stone floors and exposed beams. Rates are reasonable...for the location (Db-€175-195, top-floor Db with micro-balcony-€245, Tb-€289, iPads available for guest in-room use, 75 Rue St. Louis-en-l'Ile, tel. 01 46 34 04 80, fax 01 46 34 02 13, www.hotelsaintlouis.com, slouis@noos.fr).

# Luxembourg Garden Area

**(5th and 6th arrondissements, Mo: St. Sulpice, Mabillon, Odéon, and Cluny-La Sorbonne; RER: Luxembourg)**
This neighborhood revolves around Paris' loveliest park and offers quick access to the city's best shopping streets and grandest café-hopping. Hotels in this central area are more expensive than those in the Rue Cler area or Marais neighborhood, but a better value than accommodations on Ile St. Louis. Sleeping in the Luxembourg area offers a true Left Bank experience without a hint of the low-end commotion of the nearby Latin Quarter tourist ghetto. The Luxembourg Garden, Boulevard St. Germain, Cluny Museum, and Latin Quarter are all at your doorstep. Here you get the best of both worlds: youthful Left Bank energy and the classic trappings that surround the monumental Panthéon and St. Sulpice Church.

Having the Luxembourg Garden as your backyard allows strolls through meticulously cared-for flowers, a great kids' play area (see the Paris with Children chapter), and a purifying escape from city traffic. Place St. Sulpice presents an elegant, pedestrian-friendly square and quick access to some of Paris' best boutiques (see Shopping in Paris chapter). Sleeping in the Luxembourg area also puts several movie theaters at your fingertips (at Métro stop:

Odéon), as well as lively cafés on Boulevard St. Germain, Rue de Buci, Rue des Canettes, Place de la Sorbonne, and Place de la Contrescarpe, all of which buzz with action until late.

While it takes only 15 minutes to walk from one end of this neighborhood to the other, I've located the hotels by the key monument they are close to (St. Sulpice Church, the Odéon Theater, and the Panthéon). Most hotels are within a five-minute walk of the Luxembourg Garden (and none is more than 15 minutes away).

**Services:** The nearest **TI** is across the river at the Pyramides Métro station (daily May-Oct 9:00-19:00, Nov-April 10:00-19:00). There are two useful **SNCF Boutiques** for easy train reservations and ticket purchase: at 79 Rue de Rennes (Mon-Sat 10:00-19:00, closed Sun) and at 54 Boulevard St. Michel (Tue-Sat 8:15-19:45, Mon 13:00-19:45, closed Sun).

**Markets:** The colorful street market at the south end of Rue Mouffetard is a worthwhile 10- to 15-minute walk from these hotels (Tue-Sat 10:00-13:00 & 16:00-19:00, Sun 10:00-13:00, closed Mon, five blocks south of Place de la Contrescarpe, Mo: Place Monge).

**Bookstore: San Francisco Book Company** is a welcoming bookstore with a full selection of English-language books, including mine (Mon-Sat 11:00-21:00, Sun 14:00-19:30, 17 Rue Monsieur le Prince, tel. 01 43 29 15 70).

**Internet Access:** Try **Cyber Cube** at 5 Rue Mignon (Mon-Sat 10:00-10:00, closed Sun).

**Métro Connections:** Métro lines 10 and 4 serve this area (10 connects to the Austerlitz train station, and 4 runs to the Montparnasse, Est, and Nord train stations). Neighborhood stops are Cluny-La Sorbonne, Mabillon, Odéon, and St. Sulpice. RER-B (Luxembourg station is handiest) provides direct service to Charles de Gaulle airport and Gare du Nord trains, and access to Orly airport via the Orlybus (transfer at Denfert-Rochereau).

**Bus Routes:** Buses #86 and #87 run eastbound through this area on or near Boulevard St. Germain, and westbound along Rue des Ecoles, stopping on Place St. Sulpice. Lines #63 and #87 provide a direct connection west to the Rue Cler area. Line #63 also serves the Orsay and Marmottan museums to the west and Gare de Lyon to the east. Lines #86 and #87 run east to the Marais, and #87 continues to Gare de Lyon. Line #96 stops at Place St. Sulpice southbound en route to Gare Montparnasse and runs north along Rue de Rennes and Boulevard St. Germain into the Marais.

## Near St. Sulpice Church

These hotels are all within a block of St. Sulpice Church and two blocks from famous Boulevard St. Germain. This is nirvana for boutique-minded shoppers—and you'll pay extra for the location. Métro stops St. Sulpice and Mabillon are equally close.

**$$$ Hôtel de l'Abbaye****** is a lovely refuge just west of Luxembourg Garden; it's a find for well-heeled connoisseurs of this area. The hotel's four-star luxury includes refined lounges inside and out, with 44 sumptuous rooms and every amenity (standard Db-€265-285, bigger Db-€385-415, suites and apartments available for €480-580, includes breakfast, 10 Rue Cassette, tel. 01 45 44 38 11, fax 01 45 48 07 86, www.hotelabbayeparis.com, hotel. abbaye@wanadoo.fr).

**$$$ Hôtel le Récamier**** , romantically tucked in the corner of Place St. Sulpice, is high-end defined, with designer public spaces, elaborately appointed rooms, a courtyard tea salon, and professional service (classic Db-€260, deluxe Db-€300, traditional Db-€330, deluxe rooms offer best value, 3 bis Place St. Sulpice, tel. 01 43 26 04 89, fax 01 43 26 35 76, www.hotelrecamier .com, contact@hotelrecamier.com).

**$$$ Hôtel Relais St. Sulpice*****, burrowed on the small street just behind St. Sulpice Church, is a high-priced boutique hotel with a cozy lounge and 26 dark, stylish rooms, most surrounding a leafy glass atrium. Top-floor rooms get more light and are worth requesting (Db-€222-270 depending on size, much less off-season, sauna free for guests, 3 Rue Garancière, tel. 01 46 33 99 00, fax 01 46 33 00 10, www.relais-saint-sulpice.com, relaisstsulpice @wanadoo.fr).

**$$$ Hôtel la Perle*****, is a spendy pearl in the thick of the lively Rue des Canettes, a block off Place St. Sulpice. This modern, business-class hotel is built around a central bar and atrium (standard Db-€210, bigger Db-€225, luxury Db-€250, check website or call for last-minute deals within 5 days of your stay, 14 Rue des Canettes, tel. 01 43 29 10 10, fax 01 46 34 51 04, www. hotellaperle.com, frontdesk@hotellaperle.com).

**$ Hôtel Bonaparte****, an unpretentious and welcoming place wedged between boutiques, is a few steps from Place St. Sulpice. Although the 29 Old World rooms don't live up to the handsome entry, they're plenty comfortable and spacious by Paris standards, with big bathrooms, traditional decor, and molded ceilings (Sb-€104-128, Db-€130-169, Tb-€171, 61 Rue Bonaparte, tel. 01 43 26 97 37, fax 01 46 33 57 67, www.hotelbonaparte.fr, reservation@ hotelbonaparte.fr; helpful Fréderic and owner Eric at reception).

## West of Luxembourg Garden

**$ Hôtel Jean Bart**** feels like it's from another era—prices included. Run by smiling Madame Lechopier, it's a rare budget hotel find in this neighborhood, one block from Luxembourg Garden. Beyond the dark, retirement home-like lobby, you'll find

# Hotels near Luxembourg Garden

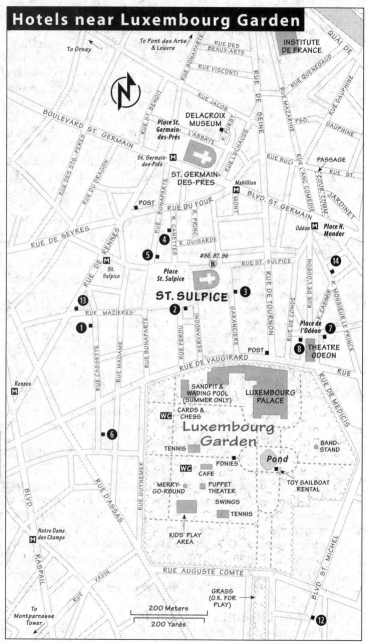

To Orsay

To Pont des Arts & Louvre

INSTITUTE DE FRANCE

QUAI DE

RUE DES BEAUX-ARTS

RUE VISCONTI

RUE JACOB

RUE DE SEINE

RUE MAZARINE

RUE QUENEGAUD

RUE DAUPHINE

PSG

DAUPHINE

BOULEVARD ST. GERMAIN

RUE ST.-BENOÎT

RUE BONAPARTE

L'ABBAYE

Place St. Germain-des-Prés

DELACROIX MUSEUM

R. FÜRST

R. CARDINALE

R. DE L'ÉCHAUDE

RUE BUCI

RUE ST. ANC COMEDIE

PASSAGE

RUE ST.

COUR DU COMM.

JARDINET

St. Germain-des-Prés Ⓜ

ST. GERMAIN-DES-PRÉS

Mabillion

BLVD. ST. GERMAIN

Ⓜ MABILLION

Odéon Ⓜ Place H. Mondor

RUE DES STS.-PÈRES

RUE DU DRAGON

POST

RUE DU FOUR

RUE BONAPARTE

R. CANETTES

R. PRINCE

R. GUISARDE

❹

❺

RUE DE RENNES

RUE DE SEVRES

St. Sulpice

Place St. Sulpice

#86, 87, 96 Ⓑ

RUE ST.-SULPICE

ST. SULPICE

❸

RUE DE TOURNON

RUE DE L'ODÉON

RUE DE CONDÉ

R. CASIMIR

MONSIEUR LE PRINCE

❶⁴

❶³

RUE MAZIERES

RUE FEROU

SERVANDONI

GARANCIÈRE

❷

RUE CASSETTE

RUE MADAME

RUE BONAPARTE

Place de l'Odéon

❼

❶

RUE DE VAUGIRARD

POST

❽ THÉÂTRE ODÉON

RUE

SANDPIT & WADING POOL (SUMMER ONLY)

LUXEMBOURG PALACE

CARDS & CHESS

WC

RUE DE MÉDICIS

Rennes Ⓜ

Luxembourg Garden

TENNIS

BAND-STAND

❻

WC

PONIES

CAFÉ

Pond

RUE GUYNEMER

MERRY-GO-ROUND

PUPPET THEATER

SWINGS

TENNIS

TOY SAILBOAT RENTAL

RUE D'ASSAS

Notre Dame des Champs Ⓜ

KIDS' PLAY AREA

BLVD

RASPAIL

RUE VAVIN

RUE AUGUSTE COMTE

BLVD. ST. MICHEL

To Montparnasse Tower

GRASS (O.K. FOR PLAY)

❶²

200 Meters

200 Yards

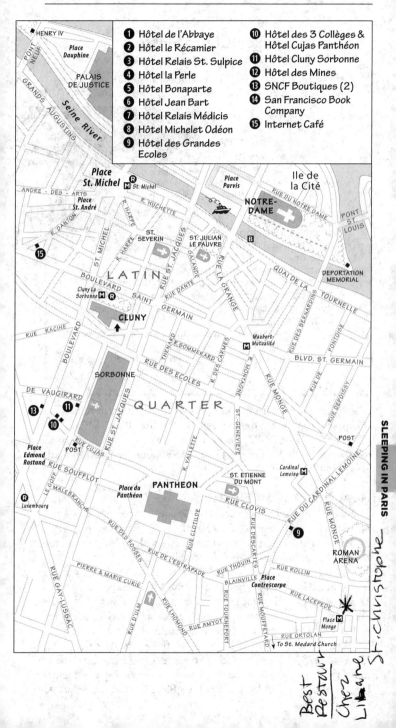

1. Hôtel de l'Abbaye
2. Hôtel le Récamier
3. Hôtel Relais St. Sulpice
4. Hôtel la Perle
5. Hôtel Bonaparte
6. Hôtel Jean Bart
7. Hôtel Relais Médicis
8. Hôtel Michelet Odéon
9. Hôtel des Grandes Ecoles
10. Hôtel des 3 Collèges & Hôtel Cujas Panthéon
11. Hôtel Cluny Sorbonne
12. Hôtel des Mines
13. SNCF Boutiques (2)
14. San Francisco Book Company
15. Internet Café

SLEEPING IN PARIS

Best Restury
Chez Liliane
St. Christophe

## Luxembourg Musts for Temporary Residents

- Pass oodles of time at Luxembourg Garden, sitting in a green chair with your feet propped up on the pond's edge.
- Observe Daniel Roth's Sunday organ mastery up close at St. Sulpice Church (see page 72).
- Join the locals at the only café on Place St. Sulpice for a morning coffee or afternoon drink.
- Stroll Rue Mouffetard day or night, and stop for a drink on Place de la Contrescarpe.

- Window-shop the boutiques between Sèvres-Babylone and St. Sulpice (described on page 478).
- Spend too much for a coffee at a grand café and watch the world go by (see "Les Grands Cafés de Paris," page 458).
- Wander the Rue de Buci and find Voltaire's favorite café (Café le Procope, now a restaurant—see page 273).
- Ponder the history of France in the Panthéon (see page 74).

33 spotless rooms with creaking floors and tight bathrooms. The cheapest rooms share one shower on the first floor (S-€57, Sb-€70, D-€57, Db-€78-82, cash only, no air-con, 9 Rue Jean-Bart, tel. 01 45 48 29 13, fax 01 45 48 10 79, hotel.jean.bart@gmail.com).

### Near the Odéon Theater

These two hotels are between the Odéon Métro stop and Luxembourg Garden (five blocks east of St. Sulpice) and may have rooms when others don't. In addition to the Odéon Métro stop, the RER-B Luxembourg stop is a short walk away.

**$$$ Hôtel Relais Médicis***** is ideal if you've always wanted to live in a Monet painting and can afford it. A glassy entry hides 17 rooms surrounding a fragrant little garden courtyard and fountain, giving you a countryside break fit for a Medici in the heart of Paris. This delightful refuge is tastefully decorated with floral Old World charm and permeated with thoughtfulness (Sb-€172, Db-€208-228, deluxe Db-€258, Tb-€298, Qb-€348, €30 cheaper mid-July-Aug and Nov-March, includes extravagant continental breakfast, faces the Odéon Theater at 5 Place de l'Odéon, tel. 01 43

26 00 60, fax 01 40 46 83 39, www.relaismedicis.com, reservation @relaismedicis.com, kind Marie at reception).

**$ Hôtel Michelet Odéon**\*\* sits in a corner of Place de l'Odéon with big windows on the square. Though it lacks personality, it's a fair value in this pricey area, with 24 simple rooms with modern decor and views of the square (Db-€120-140, Tb-€170, Qb-€190, no air-con, 6 Place de l'Odéon, tel. 01 53 10 05 60, fax 01 46 34 55 35, www.hotelmicheletodeon.com, hotel@micheletodeon.com).

## Near the Panthéon and Rue Mouffetard

**$ Hôtel des Grandes Ecoles**\*\*\* is idyllic. A private cobbled lane leads to three buildings that protect a flower-filled garden courtyard, preserving a sense of tranquility rare in this city. Its 51 rooms are French-countryside-pretty and reasonably spacious, but have no air-conditioning. This romantic spot is deservedly popular, so book ahead. Reservations are not accepted more than four months in advance; new openings become available on the 15th of each month (Db-€120-150 depending on size, extra bed-€20, no TVs in rooms, parking garage-€30/day, 75 Rue du Cardinal Lemoine, Mo: Cardinal Lemoine, tel. 01 43 26 79 23, fax 01 43 25 28 15, www.hotel-grandes-ecoles.com, hotel.grandes.ecoles@free.fr; mellow Marie speaks English, Mama does not).

**$ Hôtel des 3 Collèges**\*\* greets clients with a bright lobby, narrow hallways, and unimaginative rooms. Rates are fair and the smiling staff is eager to please (Sb-€89-114, Db-€111-160, Tb-€160-180, 16 Rue Cujas, tel. 01 43 54 67 30, fax 01 46 34 02 99, www.3colleges.com, hotel@3colleges.com).

**$ Hôtel Cujas Panthéon**\*\* gives boring, standard two-star comfort with air-conditioning at fair prices (Db-€130-145, Tb-€170-180, free Wi-Fi, 18 Rue Cujas, tel. 01 43 54 58 10, fax 01 43 25 88 02, www.cujas-pantheon-paris-hotel.com, hotel-cujas-pantheon@wanadoo.fr).

**$ Hôtel Cluny Sorbonne**\*\* is a modest place located in the thick of things across from the famous university and below the Panthéon. Rooms are well-worn with thin walls (small Db-€105-110, really big Db/Tb/Qb-€160, check website for deals, no air-con, Wi-Fi only, 8 Rue Victor Cousin, tel. 01 43 54 66 66, fax 01 43 29 68 07, www.hotel-cluny.fr, cluny@club-internet.fr).

## South of Luxembourg Garden

**$$ Hôtel des Mines**\*\* is less central, but its 50 well-maintained rooms are a fair value and come with updated bathrooms and an inviting lobby (Sb-€125, Db-€160, Tb-€190, Qb-€220, less for last-minute bookings and stays of 3 nights or more, frequent Web deals, between Luxembourg and Port-Royal stations on the RER-B line, a 10-minute walk from Panthéon, one block past Luxembourg

Garden at 125 Boulevard St. Michel, tel. 01 43 54 32 78, fax 01 46 33 72 52, www.hoteldesminesparis.com, hotel@hoteldesmines paris.com).

# Budget Accommodations
## Away from the Center

Acceptable budget accommodations in central neighborhoods are few and far between in Paris. I've listed the best I could find in the neighborhoods described previously, most at about €100 for a double room. These are great (moderate) budget options, but if you want even lower rates or greater selection, you need to look farther away from the river (prices drop proportionally with distance from the Seine). Below you'll find more budget listings in less-central, but still-appealing neighborhoods. You'll spend more time on the Métro or bus getting to sights but save money by sleeping in these areas.

To save even more, those staying two or more nights should consider a room at a B&B (see "Bed and Breakfasts," earlier). Those staying at least a week can save on meal costs (if not lodging) by renting an apartment (see "Apartment Rentals," later).

## Bottom of Rue Mouffetard

These accommodations, away from the Seine and other tourists in an appealing workaday area, offer more room for your euro. Rue Mouffetard is the bohemian soul of this area. Two thousand years ago, it was the principal Roman road south to Italy. Today, this small, meandering street has a split personality. The lower half thrives in the daytime as a pedestrian shopping street. The upper half sleeps during the day, but comes alive after dark. Use Métro stop Censier Daubenton or Les Gobelins. A terrific Saturday market sprawls along Boulevard Port Royal, just east of the Port Royal Métro stop.

**$ Port-Royal-Hôtel\*** has only one star, but don't let that fool you. Its 46 rooms are polished top to bottom and have been well-run by the same proud family for 81 years. You could eat off the floors of its spotless, comfy rooms...but you won't find air-conditioning, Internet access, or Wi-Fi. Ask for a room away from the street (S-€49-60, D-€60, Db-€86-96 depending on size, big shower down the hall-€3, cash only, nonrefundable cash deposit required, on busy Boulevard de Port-Royal at #8, Mo: Les Gobelins, tel. 01 43 31 70 06, fax 01 43 31 33 67, www.hotelportroyal.fr, portroyalhotel @wanadoo.fr).

**$ Hôtel de L'Espérance\*\*** is simply a terrific two-star value. It's quiet and cushy, with soft rooms, canopy beds, and nice public spaces (Sb-€85, Db-€85-100, Tb-€120, 15 Rue Pascal, Mo:

**Hotels & Restaurants near Rue Mouffetard**

① Port-Royal-Hôtel
② Hôtel de L'Espérance
③ Young & Happy Hostel
④ Café Delmas
⑤ Cave de Bourgogne
⑥ Café de la Mosquée

Censier Daubenton, tel. 01 47 07 10 99, fax 01 43 37 56 19, www.hoteldelesperance.fr, hotel.esperance@wanadoo.fr).

**$ Young & Happy Hostel** is easygoing, well-run, and English-speaking, with Internet access, kitchen facilities, and acceptable hostel conditions. It sits dead-center in the Rue Mouffetard action... which can be good or bad (all rates per person: bunk in 4- to 10-bed co-ed dorm-€24-32, in 3- to 5-bed female-only dorm-€28, in double room-€35, includes breakfast, sheet deposit-€5, towel-€1, credit cards accepted, no air-con, no lockers but safety box at reception, pay Wi-Fi, 11:00-16:00 lockout but reception stays open, no curfew, 80 Rue Mouffetard, Mo: Place Monge, tel. 01 47 07 47 07, fax 01 47 07 22 24, www.youngandhappy.fr, smile@youngandhappy.fr, friendly Alex at the helm).

## Montmartre

Montmartre is surprisingly quiet once you get away from the touristy top of the hill. Ditch the flow of visitors streaming from Place d'Anvers to Sacré-Cœur Basilica, and you'll find a charming neighborhood happily living in the shadow of the hulking monument. Montmartre is a mix of young families, artists, and spritely

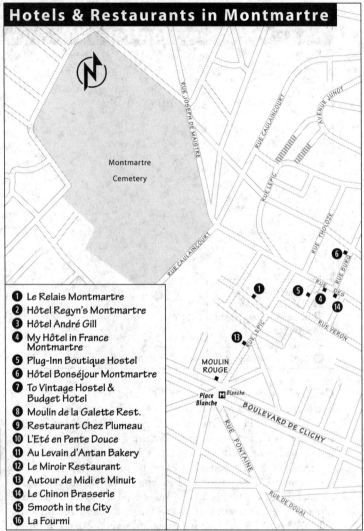

# Hotels & Restaurants in Montmartre

**Montmartre Cemetery**

**MOULIN ROUGE**

**Place Blanche** Ⓜ Blanche

BOULEVARD DE CLICHY

1 Le Relais Montmartre
2 Hôtel Regyn's Montmartre
3 Hôtel André Gill
4 My Hôtel in France Montmartre
5 Plug-Inn Boutique Hostel
6 Hôtel Bonséjour Montmartre
7 To Vintage Hostel & Budget Hotel
8 Moulin de la Galette Rest.
9 Restaurant Chez Plumeau
10 L'Eté en Pente Douce
11 Au Levain d'Antan Bakery
12 Le Miroir Restaurant
13 Autour de Midi et Minuit
14 Le Chinon Brasserie
15 Smooth in the City
16 La Fourmi

SLEEPING IN PARIS

senior citizens, and is becoming increasingly popular with the *bobo* crowd (*bourgeois bohemian*, French for "hipster"). Travelers will find good deals on hotel rooms and a lively atmosphere, especially in the evenings when the terraces are full and tiny bars spill crowds onto the narrow streets. There's a TI at the Anvers Métro stop (daily 10:00-18:00, 72 Boulevard Rochechouart).

Most of the action is centered around Rue des Abbesses, starting at Place des Abbesses, and stretching several blocks to Rue Lepic. Rue Lepic is also lively, but the lower you go the seedier

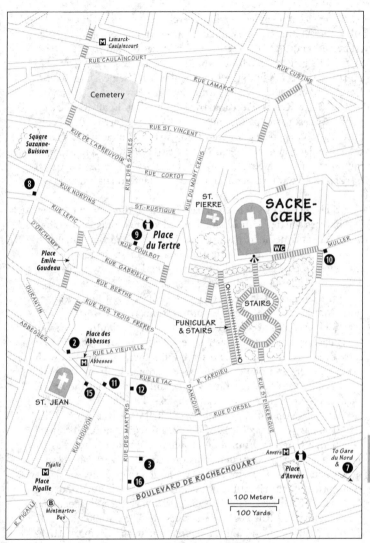

it gets: Scammers and shady characters swarm the base of the hill after hours (along Boulevard Clichy and Boulevard Rochechouart, where you'll find what's left of Paris' red light district). For fun nightlife, explore the narrow streets uphill from Rue des Abbesses around Rue Durantin and Rue des Trois Frères. For restaurant suggestions, see page 455.

**Métro and Bus Connections:** Métro line 12 is the handiest (use the Abbesses stop). Line 2 is also close, using the Blanche, Pigalle, or Anvers stops, but requires a four-block uphill walk to reach my recommended hotels. There's only one bus line on the hill—the Montmartrobus electric bus—which connects Pigalle, Abbesses, and Place du Tertre in 10 minutes (4/hour). At the base of the hill you can catch bus #67 (next to the Pigalle Métro station) and ride straight to the Louvre, along the Seine, across Ile St. Louis, and eventually to the Jardin des Plantes.

**$$$ Le Relais Montmartre** is a spotless hotel with cushy public spaces, pastel paint, and 26 cozy rooms sporting floral curtains. There are lots of guest-centered amenities, including a shared iPad, fireplace, and quiet central courtyard (Db-€185-240 depending on room size, 6 Rue Constance, tel. 01 70 64 25 25, fax 01 70 64 25 00, www.relaismontmartre.fr, contact@relaismontmartre.fr).

**$ Hôtel Regyn's Montmartre**** is located directly on the lively Abbesses square, with 22 small but adequate rooms, no air-conditioning, and mediocre bathrooms. Rooms in the front come with pleasant views and noise from the square. Guests in fourth- and fifth-floor rooms can see all the way to the Eiffel Tower (Sb-€91-110, Db-€122-142, check website for specials, 18 Place des Abbesses, tel. 01 42 54 45 21, fax 01 42 59 08 85, www.hotel-regyns-paris.com, info@hotel-regyns-montmartre.net.

**$ Hôtel André Gill** ** makes me smile. It's a family affair: The front desk is run by two lovely sisters, two lap dogs, and two fat cats. Breakfast is included and served in a living room filled with plastic flowers and photos of the sisters' grandchildren. The hallways and elevator are alarmingly dark and narrow, but the rooms themselves are bright and clean (Sb-€45, Db-€63-89, Tb-€105, large double with Eiffel Tower view-€120-150, 4 Rue André Gill, tel. 01 42 62 48 48, fax 01 42 62 77 92, andregill@hotmail.com).

**$ My Hôtel in France Montmartre,** a chain hotel, has 41 small, basic-but-good-value rooms on six floors, with no elevator or air-conditioning. Twin rooms are larger than doubles for the same price. Continental breakfast and a sandwich lunch-box are included (Sb-€80-89, Db-€90-99, prices vary greatly depending on occupancy, 57 Rue des Abbesses, tel. 01 42 51 50 00, fax 01 42 51 08 68, www.myhotelinfrance-montmartre.com, montmartre@my-hotel-in-france.com).

**$ Plug-Inn Boutique Hostel** is part hotel and part hostel, but with a hotel vibe. Half a block off Rue des Abbesses, it has a young clientele, bathrooms in all 30 rooms, free Wi-Fi, and several public computer terminals. Early arrivals can leave their luggage and take a shower. Not all rooms are available online, so book by phone or email (all prices per person: bunk in dorm-€29-36, private Db room-€49-52, female-only rooms available, includes breakfast, kitchen facilities, elevator, 24-hour front desk staff, no curfew, 7

Rue Aristide Bruant, tel. 01 42 58 42 58, fax 01 42 23 93 88, www.
plug-inn.fr, bonjour@plug-inn.fr).

**$ Hôtel Bonséjour Montmartre**, run by eager Michel and his
family, is an old, worn, hostelesque place with dirt-cheap prices.
All rooms have sinks, but share a hallway toilet. Some rooms share
one public shower on main floor, and others have small, oddly-
placed shower cabins right next to the bed (S-€35-50, D-€56-69,
Tb-€80, higher price for private shower, no elevator, no air-con,
11 Rue Burq, tel. 01 42 54 22 53, fax 01 42 54 25 92, www.hotel-
bonsejour-montmartre.fr, hotel-bonsejour-montmartre@wanadoo.
fr).

**$ The Vintage Hostel & Budget Hotel** sits halfway between
the hill of Montmartre and Gare du Nord (both destinations are a
10-minute walk away). This hostel/hotel hybrid appeals to young-
sters and oldsters alike. Private double rooms—an especially good
value—are on the top two floors, and most come with romantic
balconies just big enough for a table and two chairs (bunk in dorm
room with private toilet and shower-€35-45, Sb-€75-85, Db-
€90-120, includes breakfast, towel-€1, Wi-Fi only—in lobby, 73
Rue de Dunkerque, tel. 01 40 16 16 40, www.vintage-hostel.com,
contact@vintage-hostel.com).

# At or near Paris' Airports

## At Charles de Gaulle Airport
Both of these places are located outside the T-3 RER stop, and
both have restaurants. For locations, see the map on page 514.

**$$ Novotel*** is a step up from cookie-cutter airport hotels
(Db-€145-200, can rise to €290 for last-minute rooms, tel. 01 49 19
27 27, fax 01 49 19 27 99, www.novotel.com, h1014@accor.com).

**$ Hôtel Ibis CDG Airport*** is huge and offers standard air-
port accommodations (Db-€115-155, tel. 01 49 19 19 19, fax 01 49
19 19 21, www.ibishotel.com, h1404@accor.com).

## Near Charles de Gaulle Airport, in Roissy
The small village of **Roissy-en-France** (you'll see signs just be-
fore the airport as you come from Paris), which gave its name to
the airport (Roissy Charles de Gaulle), has better-value chain ho-
tels with free shuttle service to and from the airport (4/hour, 15
minutes, look for *navettes hôtels* signs to reach these hotels). Ho-
tels have reasonably priced restaurants with long hours, though it's
more pleasant to walk into the town, where you'll find a bakery,
pizzeria, cafés, and a few restaurants. Most Roissy hotels list spe-
cials on their websites. These hotels are within walking distance of
the town: **$ Hôtel Ibis CDG Paris Nord 2*** (Db-€90-110, usu-
ally cheaper than the Ibis right at the airport, 335 Rue de la Belle

Etoile, tel. 01 48 17 56 56, fax 01 48 17 56 51, www.ibishotel.com, h0815@accor.com), **$ Hôtel Campanile Roissy***** (Db-€90-120, allée des Vergers, tel. 01 34 29 80 40, fax 01 34 29 80 39, www. campanile-roissy.fr, roissy@campanile.fr), and **$$ Hôtel Golden Tulip Paris CDG***** (Db-€130-200, 11 Allée des Vergers, tel. 01 34 29 00 00, fax 01 34 29 00 11, www.goldentulipcdgvillepinte. com, info@goldentulipcdgvillepinte.com). The cheapest option is **$ B&B Hôtel Roissy CDG*,** where many flight attendants stay (Db-€55, 17 Allée des Vergers, tel. 01 34 38 55 55, fax 01 34 38 55 00, www.hotelbb.com).

To avoid rush-hour traffic, drivers can consider sleeping north of Paris in either **Auvers-sur-Oise** (30 minutes west of airport; see recommendations on page 621) or in the pleasant medieval town of **Senlis** (15 minutes north of airport). **$ Hôtel Ibis Senlis**** is a few minutes from town (Db-€80-110, Route Nationale A1, tel. 03 44 53 70 50, fax 03 44 53 51 93, www.ibishotel.com, h0709@accor. com). If you don't have a car, sleep elsewhere.

### Near Orly Airport

Two chain hotels, owned by the same company and very close to the Sud terminal, are your best options near Orly. Both have free shuttles *(navettes)* to the terminal.

**$$$ Hôtel Mercure Paris Orly***** provides high comfort for a high price; check their website for discounts (Db-€140-220, book early for better rate, tel. 01 49 75 15 51, fax 01 49 75 15 51, www. accorhotel.com, h1246@accor.com).

**$ Hôtel Ibis Orly Aéroport**** is reasonable and basic (Db-€85-110, tel. 01 56 70 50 60, fax 01 56 70 50 70, www.ibishotel. com, h1413@accor.com).

# Apartment Rentals

Most rental apartments in Paris come with a living room, washing machine, and a small, equipped kitchen. Some apartments also provide a computer with Internet access and free telephone calls to the US (ask ahead). If you make good use of the kitchen (and Paris' great food markets), you'll save on your meal budget. And you'll have more privacy and a behind-the-scenes peek into how Parisians live.

The trade-off is service. You won't have hotel staff to serve your breakfast, answer your questions, telephone ahead to reserve restaurants, or make your bed daily. Air-conditioning is not as common as at hotels (something you'll probably want in summer months), and cleaning happens usually only once a week for an extra fee, and just like at home, you'll use the same towels and linens all week. Remember that Paris apartments, like hotel rooms, are small by US standards.

## Rental Agencies

Among the many English-speaking organizations renting apartments, the following have proven most reliable. Their websites are good and essential to understanding your options. Read the rental conditions very carefully.

Most of the agencies listed below are middlemen, offering an ever-changing selection of private apartments for rent on a weekly basis (or longer). If staying a month or longer, you may save money by renting directly from the apartment owners. Check the housing section in the ad-filled paper *France-USA Contacts* (available at the American Church and elsewhere in Paris), or check out www. fusac.fr. Readers give Craigslist mixed reviews (www.craigslist. org).

Paris Perfect has offices in Paris with English-speaking staff who seek the "perfect apartment" for their clients and are selective about what they offer. Their service gets rave reviews. Many units have Eiffel Tower views, and most include free Internet, free local and international phone calls, satellite TV, air-conditioning, and washers and dryers (studio-€125/night, one-bedroom apartment-€199/night, two-bedroom apartment-€285/night, 5 percent discount off regular rates for Rick Steves readers, US toll-free tel. 888-520-2087, www.parisperfect.com).

**Cobblestone Paris Rentals** is a small, American-run outfit offering furnished rentals with a focus on the Marais and central Paris. All apartments offer free Wi-Fi, free international phone calls, and free cable TV. Apartments come stocked with English-language DVDs, coffee, tea, cooking spices, and basic bathroom amenities (two free river cruises for Rick Steves readers who book a stay of five nights or more, www.cobblestoneparis.com, reservations @cobblestoneparis.com).

**Paris Appartements Services** rents studios (€100-170/night) and one-bedroom apartments (€150-230/night) in central neighborhoods (20 Rue Bachaumont, tel. 01 40 28 01 28, fax 01 40 28 92 01, www.paris-appartements-services.com, info@paris-apts.com).

**France Homestyle** is run by Claudette, a service-oriented French woman who now lives in Seattle and has hand-picked every apartment she lists (US tel. 206/325-0132, www.francehomestyle. com, info@francehomestyle.com).

**Home Rental Service** has been in business for 18 years and offers a big selection of apartments throughout Paris with no agency fees (120 Champs-Elysées, tel. 01 42 25 65 40, fax 01 42 25 65 45, www.homerental.fr, info@homerental.fr).

**Locaflat** offers accommodations ranging from studios to

five-room apartments, with occasional specials online (63 Avenue de la Motte-Picquet, tel. 01 43 06 78 79, fax 01 40 56 99 69, www. locaflat.com, locaflat@gmail.com).

**Immo Marais** has over 100 apartments in all sizes in the Marais (60 Rue Roi de Sicile, tel. 01 42 74 06 17, fax 01 42 74 68 82, www.parislocationsmeublees.com, contact@palocme.com).

**Paris Home** is a small outfit with only two little studios, but both are located on Rue Amélie in the heart of the Rue Cler area (see map on page 388). Each has modern furnishings and laundry facilities. Friendly Slim, the owner, is the best part (€590/week, no minimum stay, special rates for longer stays, credit cards accepted, free Internet access and US or France telephone calls, free maid service, airport/train station transfers possible, mobile 06 19 03 17 55, www.parishome2000.com, parishome2000@yahoo.fr).

**Paris for Rent,** a San Francisco-based group, has been renting top-end apartments in Paris for more than a decade (US tel. 866-4-FRANCE, www.parisforrent.com).

**VRBO** is an international network of apartment rentals (houses, apartments, *gîtes*, etc.) that cuts out the middleman by putting you directly in touch with the owners. Paris has several hundred rentals available, organized by arrondissement, complete with online calendars to check availability and reviews from previous renters (www.vrbo.com).

**Tournights,** run by Frederick and Mayra, rents several apartments around Paris (www.tournights.com).

**Cross-Pollinate** is a reputable online booking agency representing B&Bs and apartments in a handful of European cities. Paris listings range from a Bastille B&B room for two for €90 per night to a two-bedroom Montmartre apartment sleeping six for €160 per night. Minimum stays vary from one to five nights (US tel. 800-270-1190, France tel. 09-75-18-11-10, www.cross-pollinate.com, info@cross-pollinate.com).

**SLEEPING IN PARIS**

# EATING IN PARIS

The Parisian eating scene is kept at a rolling boil. Entire books (and lives) are dedicated to the subject. Paris is France's wine-and-cuisine melting pot. Though it lacks a style of its own (only French onion soup is truly Parisian; otherwise, there is no "Parisian cuisine" to speak of), it draws from the best of France. Paris could hold a gourmet Olympics and import nothing.

Parisians eat long and well. Relaxed lunches, three-hour dinners, and endless hours of sitting in outdoor cafés are the norm. Cafés, cuisine, and wines become a highlight of any Parisian adventure—sightseeing for your palate. Even if the rest of you is sleeping in a cheap hotel, let your taste buds travel first-class in Paris. (They can go coach in London.)

You can eat well without going broke, but choose carefully—you're just as likely to blow a small fortune on a mediocre meal as you are to dine wonderfully for €20. Follow the suggestions offered in this chapter, and you'll have a better dining experience.

All café and restaurant interiors are smoke-free. Today the only smokers you'll find are at outside tables.

Waiters probably won't overwhelm you with friendliness. As their tip is already included in the bill (see the next page), there's less schmoozing than we're used to at home. Notice how hard they work. They almost never stop. Cozying up to clients (French or foreign) is probably the last thing on their minds. They're often stuck with client overload, too, because the French rarely hire part-time employees, even to help with peak times. To get a waiter's attention, try to make meaningful eye contact, which is a signal that you need something. If this doesn't work, raise your hand and simply say, *"S'il vous plaît"* (see voo play)—"please." To get the most out of a Parisian restaurant—slow down. Allow enough time for the meal, engage the waiter, show you care about food, and enjoy the experience as much as the food itself.

**Tipping:** Prices at cafés and restaurants include a service charge (12-15 percent, referred to as *service compris* or *prix net* but generally not broken out on your bill). It's polite, though not expected, to round up for a drink or meal well-served. This bonus tip should be no more than 5 percent of the bill (e.g., if your bill is €19, you can leave €20). If you want the waiter to keep the change when you pay, say, *"C'est bon"* (say bohn), meaning, "It's good." Most of my Parisian friends don't tip, even for good service.

# Types of Meals

## Breakfast

For about €8-15, most hotels offer an optional breakfast, which is usually pleasant and convenient. A few hotels serve a classic continental breakfast, called *petit déjeuner* (puh-tee day-zhuh-nay). Traditionally, this consisted of a café au lait, hot chocolate, or tea; a roll with butter and marmalade; and a croissant. But these days most hotels put out a buffet breakfast (cereal, yogurt, fruit, cheese, croissants, juice, and the occasional hard-boiled egg).

If all you want is coffee or tea and a croissant, the corner café offers more atmosphere and is cheaper (though you get more coffee at your hotel). Go local at the café and ask for *une tartine* (oon tart-een; baguette slathered with butter or jam) with your café au lait. To keep it really cheap, pick up some fruit at a grocery store and pastries at your favorite *boulangerie* and have a picnic breakfast, then savor your coffee at the bar *(comptoir)* while standing (like locals do). Some cafés and bakeries offer cheap breakfast deals (a few are listed later).

## Picnics and Snacks

Great for lunch or dinner, Parisian picnics can be first-class affairs and adventures in high cuisine. Be daring. Try the smelly cheeses, ugly pâtés, sissy quiches, and minuscule yogurts. Shopkeepers are accustomed to selling small quantities of produce. Try the succulent salads-to-go, and ask for a plastic fork *(une fourchette en plastique)*. A small container is *une barquette*. A slice is *une tranche*. If you need a knife *(couteau)* or corkscrew *(tire-bouchon)*, borrow one from your hotelier.

## Picnic Vocabulary

| English | French | Pronounced |
|---|---|---|
| please | *s'il vous plaît* | see voo play |
| a plastic fork | *une fourchette en plastique* | oon foor-sheht ahn plah-steek |
| a box | *une barquette* | oon bar-keht |
| a knife | *un couteau* | uhn koo-toh |
| corkscrew | *tire-bouchon* | teer-boo-shohn |
| sliced | *tranché* | trahn-shay |
| a slice | *une tranche* | oon trahnsh |
| a small slice | *une petite tranche* | oon puh-teet trahnsh |
| more | *plus* | ploo |
| less | *moins* | mwan (rhymes with fan) |
| It's just right. | *C'est bon.* | say bohn |
| That'll be all. | *C'est tout.* | say too |
| Thank you. | *Merci.* | mehr-see |

## Assembling a Picnic

Visit several small stores to put together a complete meal. Shop early, as many shops close from 13:00 to 15:00 for their lunch break. Say *"Bonjour"* as you enter, then point to what you want and say, *"S'il vous plaît."*

At the *boulangerie* (bakery), buy some bread. A baguette does the trick, or choose from the many square loaves of bread on display: *pain aux céréales* (whole grain with seeds), *pain de campagne* (country bread, unbleached bread flour), *pain complet* (wheat bread) or *pain de seigle* (rye bread). To ask for it sliced, say, *"Tranché s'il vous plaît."* The sales clerk will invariably ask if you would like anything else. If you've ordered all the treats you want, you can reply, *"C'est tout, merci"* (say too, mehr-see), meaning, "That'll be all, thanks."

At the *pâtisserie* (pastry shop, which is often the same place you bought the bread), choose a dessert that's easy to eat with your hands. My favorites are *éclairs* (*chocolat* or *café* flavored), individual fruit tarts (*framboise* is raspberry, *fraise* is strawberry, *citron* is lemon), and *macarons* (made of flavored cream sandwiched between two meringues, not coconut cookies like in the US).

At the *crémerie* or *fromagerie* (cheese shop), choose a sampling of cheeses. I usually get one hard cheese (like Comté, Cantal, or Beaufort), one soft cow's milk cheese (like Brie or Camembert), one goat's milk cheese (anything that says chèvre), and one blue cheese (Roquefort or Bleu d'Auvergne). Goat cheese usually comes in individual portions. For all other large cheeses, point to the cheese you want and ask for *une petite tranche* (a small slice). The shopkeeper will place a knife on the cheese indicating the size of the slice they are about to cut, then look at you for approval. If you'd like more, say, "*Plus.*" If you'd like less, say, "*Moins.*" If it's just right, say, "*C'est bon!*"

At the **charcuterie** or *trait-eur* (for deli items, prepared salads, meats, and pâtés), I like a slice of *pâté de campagne* (country pâté made of pork) and *saucissons sec* (dried sausages, some with pepper crust or garlic—you can ask to have it sliced thin like salami). I also get a fresh vegetable salad. Typical options are *carottes râpées* (shredded carrots

in a tangy vinaigrette), *salade de betteraves* (beets in vinaigrette), and *céleri rémoulade* (celery root with a mayonnaise sauce). The food comes in easy-to-carry takeout boxes, and they may supply a plastic fork *(fourchette)*.

At a *cave à vin* you can buy chilled wines that the merchant is usually happy to open and re-cork for you. Note: Bottles of champagne don't require a corkscrew to open!

At a *supermarché, épicerie* or *magasin d'alimentation* (small grocery store or minimart), you'll find plastic cutlery and glasses, paper plates, napkins, drinks, chips, and sometimes a meek display of produce.

## Good Picnic Spots
Paris is picnic-friendly. Almost any park will do. Many have benches or grassy areas, though some lawns are off-limits—obey the signs. Parks generally close at dusk, so plan your sunset picnics carefully. Hoteliers frown on in-room picnics. Here are some especially scenic areas located near major sights:

**Palais Royal**: Escape to a peaceful courtyard full of relaxing locals across from the Louvre (Mo: Palais Royale). The nearby Louvre courtyard surrounding the pyramid is less tranquil, but very handy.

**Place des Vosges**: Relax in an exquisite grassy courtyard in the Marais, surrounded by royal buildings (Mo: Bastille).

**Square du Vert-Galant**: For great river views, try this little triangular park on the west tip of Ile de la Cité. It's next to the statue of King Henry IV (Mo: Pont Neuf).

**Pont des Arts:** Munch from a perch on this pedestrian bridge over the Seine (near the Louvre)—it's equipped with benches (Mo: Pont Neuf).

**Along the Seine:** A grassy parkway runs along the left bank of the Seine between Les Invalides and Pont de l'Alma (Mo: Invalides, near Rue Cler).

**Tuileries Garden:** Have an Impressionist "Luncheon on the Grass" nestled between the Orsay and Orangerie museums (Mo: Tuileries).

**Luxembourg Garden:** The classic Paris picnic spot is this expansive Left Bank park (Mo: Odéon).

**Les Invalides:** Take a break from the Army Museum and Napoleon's Tomb in the gardens behind the complex (Mo: Varenne).

**Champ de Mars:** The long grassy strip below the Eiffel Tower has breathtaking views of this Paris icon. However, you must eat along the sides of the park, as the central lawn is off-limits (Mo: Ecole Militaire).

**Pompidou Center:** There's no grass, but the people-watching is unbeatable; try the area by the *Homage to Stravinsky* fountains (Mo: Rambuteau or Hôtel de Ville).

## Sandwiches and Other Quick Bites

Across Paris you'll find bakeries and small stands selling baguette sandwiches, quiches, and pizza-like items to go for €4-6. Usually filling and tasty, they also streamline the picnic process. Here are some sandwiches you'll see:

*Fromage* (froh-mahzh): Cheese (white on beige).

*Jambon beurre* (zhahn-bohn bur): Ham and butter (boring for most).

*Jambon crudités* (zhahn-bohn krew-dee-tay): Ham with tomatoes, lettuce, cucumbers, and mayonnaise.

*Pain salé* (pan sa-lay) or *fougasse* (foo-gas): Bread rolled up with salty bits of bacon, cheese, or olives.

*Poulet crudités* (poo-lay krew-dee-tay): Chicken with tomatoes, lettuce, maybe cucumbers, and always mayonnaise.

*Saucisson beurre* (saw-see-sohn bur): Thinly sliced sausage and butter.

*Thon crudités* (tohn krew-dee-tay): Tuna with tomatoes, lettuce, and maybe cucumbers, but definitely mayonnaise.

Search for anything *à la provençale*—made with marinated peppers, tomatoes, and eggplant—and grilled *panini* sandwiches *à la italienne*.

Typical **quiches** you'll see at shops and bakeries are *lorraine* (ham and cheese), *fromage* (cheese only), *aux oignons* (with onions), *aux poireaux* (with leeks—my favorite), *aux champignons* (with mushrooms), *au saumon* (salmon), or *au thon* (tuna).

## Café Culture

French cafés and brasseries provide user-friendly meals and a relief from museum and church overload. At either, feel free to order only a bowl of soup and a salad or *plat* (main course) for lunch or dinner. Cafés and brasseries generally open by 7:00, but closing hours vary.

Unlike restaurants, which open only for lunch and dinner, some cafés and all brasseries serve food throughout the day (though with a more limited menu than at restaurants)—making them the best option for a late lunch or an early dinner. Cafés are not necessarily less expensive than many restaurants and bistros. Their key advantage is flexibility: They offer longer serving hours, and you're welcome to order just a salad, a sandwich, or a bowl of soup, even for dinner. It's also fine to split starters and desserts, though not main courses.

If you're a novice, it's easier to sit and feel comfortable when you know the system. Check the price list first, which by law must be posted prominently (if you don't see one, go elsewhere). You'll see two sets of prices: You'll pay more for the same drink if you're seated at a table *(salle)* than if you're seated at the bar or counter *(comptoir)*. At large cafés, outdoor tables are most expensive, and prices can rise after 22:00. For a cheap mini-café au lait, hang out at the counter and order *une noisette* (oon nwah-zeht; espresso with a little milk)—for some unknown reason an espresso or *une noisette* costs half as much as a café au lait (for more tips on beverages, see the next page).

**Standard Menu Items:** *Croque monsieur* (grilled ham and cheese sandwich) and *croque madame* (*monsieur* with a fried egg on top) are generally served day and night. Sandwiches are least expensive, but very plain (*boulangeries* serve better ones). To get more than a piece of ham (*jambon*) on a baguette, order a sandwich *jambon crudité*, which means garnished with veggies. Omelets come lonely on a plate with a basket of bread. The daily special—*plat du jour* (plah dew zhoor), or just *plat*—is your fast, hearty, and garnished hot plate for €12-18. At most cafés, feel free to order only *entrées* (which in French means the starter course); many find these lighter and more interesting than a main course. A vegetarian can enjoy a tasty, filling meal by ordering two entrées. Regardless of what you order, bread is free but al-

# Coffee and Tea Lingo

By law, the waiter must give you a glass of tap water with your coffee or tea if you request it; ask for *"un verre d'eau, s'il vous plaît"* (uhn vayr doh, see voo play).

## Coffee

| French | Pronounced | English |
|---|---|---|
| *un café* | uhn kah-fay | shot of espresso |
| *une noisette* | oon nwah-zeht | espresso with a shot of milk |
| *café au lait* | kah-fay oh lay | coffee with lots of steamed milk |
| *un grand crème* | uhn grahn krehm | big coffee with steamed milk |
| (Parisians commonly say *un grand crème* instead of *café au lait;* it's the same thing) | | |
| *un petit crème* | uhn puh-tee krehm | small coffee with steamed milk |
| *un café allongé* (a.k.a. *café longue*) | uhn kah-fay ah-lohn-zhay (kah-fay lohn) | closest to an American cup of coffee |
| *un décaffiné* | uhn day-kah-fee-nay | decaf—available for any of the above drinks |

## Tea

| French | Pronounced | English |
|---|---|---|
| *un thé nature* | uhn tay nah-tour | plain tea |
| *un thé au lait* | uhn tay oh lay | tea with milk |
| *un thé citron* | uhn tay see-trohn | tea with lemon |
| *une infusion* | oon an-few-see-yohn | herbal tea |

most never comes with butter; to get more, just hold up your bread basket and ask, *"Encore, s'il vous plaît?"*

**Salads:** They're typically large and often can be ordered with warm ingredients mixed in, such as melted goat cheese, fried gizzards, or roasted potatoes. One salad is perfect for lunch or a light dinner. The classic salads include:

*Salade niçoise* (nee-swahz), a specialty from Nice, usually features green salad topped with green beans, boiled potatoes, tomatoes, anchovies, olives, hard-boiled eggs, and lots of tuna. It makes for a good, fast, reliable, and filling budget lunch.

**Salade au chèvre chaud** is a mixed green salad topped with warm goat cheese on small pieces of toast.

**Salade composée** is "composed" of any number of ingredients, such as *lardons* (bacon), Comté (a Swiss-style cheese), Roquefort (blue cheese), *œuf* (egg), *noix* (walnuts), and *jambon* (ham, generally thinly sliced).

**Salade paysanne** usually comes with potatoes *(pommes de terre)*, walnuts *(noix)*, tomatoes, ham, and egg.

**Salade aux gesiers** has chicken gizzards (and often slices of duck).

**Wine and Beer:** House wine at the bar is cheap (about €3-5 per glass) and cheapest by the pitcher, or *pichet* (pee-shay; only available if you're seated and also ordering food). The local beer is cheaper on tap (*une pression;* oon pres-yohn) than in the bottle (*bouteille;* boo-teh-ee). France's best beer is Alsatian; try Kronenbourg or the heavier Pelfort (even heavier is the Belgian beer Leffe). *Une panaché* (oon pan-a-shay) is a refreshing French shandy (7-Up and beer).

**Soft Drinks:** For a fun, bright, nonalcoholic drink of 7-Up with mint syrup, order *un diabolo menthe* (uhn dee-ah-boh-loh mahnt). For 7-Up with fruit syrup, order *un diabolo grenadine* (think Shirley Temple). Kids love Orangina, a carbonated orange juice with pulp and without caffeine. They also like flavored syrups mixed with bottled water (*sirops à l'eau;* wsee-roh ah loh). In France *limonade* (lee-moan-ahd) is Sprite or 7-Up.

Be very clear when ordering drinks, as you can easily pay €8 for an oversized Coke and €12 for a huge beer. When you order a drink, state the size in centiliters (don't say "small," "medium," or "large," because the waiter might bring a bigger drink than you want). For something small, ask for 25 cl (about 8 ounces); for a medium drink, order 33 cl (about 12 ounces—a normal can of soda); a large is 50 cl (about 16 ounces); and a super-size is one liter (about a quart—which is more than I would ever order in France). The ice cubes melted after the last Yankee tour group left.

## Restaurants

Choose restaurants filled with locals. Consider my suggestions and your hotelier's opinion, but trust your instincts. If a restaurant doesn't post its prices outside, move along. Refer to my restaurant recommendations to get a sense of what a reasonable meal should cost.

Restaurants open for dinner around 19:00, and small local favorites get crowded after 21:00. To minimize crowds, go early (around 19:30). Many restaurants close Sunday and Monday.

If a restaurant serves lunch, it generally begins at 12:00 and goes until 14:30, with last orders taken at about 14:00. If you're hungry when restaurants are closed (late afternoon), go to a brasserie; for more information, see "Café Culture," earlier.

If you ask for the *menu* (muh-noo) at a restaurant, you won't get a list of dishes; you'll get a fixed-price meal. *Menus*, which usually include two or three courses, are a good value if you're hungry. With a three-course *menu*, you'll select a starter *(entrée)*, a main course with vegetables *(plat principal)*, plus a cheese course or a dessert. Two-course *menus* (often referred to as *formules*) always include the *plat principal* and usually a choice between a starter or a dessert *(entrée et plat* or *plat et dessert)*. These fixed-price *menus* are a great way to pace your meal: Make your selection, then sit back and enjoy as the waves of food land on your table.

To save money and not overeat, couples can order two courses per person and share a starter and a dessert. Restaurants and cafés usually offer great-value lunch *menus*, and many restaurants have a reasonable *menu-enfant* (kid's meal). If all you want is a salad or soup, go to a café.

Ask for *la carte* (lah kart) if you want to see an actual menu and order à la carte rather than get a fixed-price meal. Consider the waiter's recommendations and anything *de la maison* (of the house), as long as it's not an organ meat (tripes, *rognons*, or andouillette).

Galloping gourmets should bring a menu translator. The most complete (and priciest) menu reader around is *A to Z of French Food* by G. de Temmerman. The *Marling Menu-Master* is also good. The *Rick Steves' French Phrase Book & Dictionary*, with a menu decoder, works well for most travelers.

Parisians are willing to pay for bottled water with their meal *(eau minérale;* oh mee-nay-rahl) because they prefer the taste over tap water. To get a free pitcher of tap water, ask for *une carafe d'eau* (oon kah-rahf doh). Otherwise, you may unwittingly buy bottled water. Wines are often listed in a separate *carte des vins*. To order inexpensive wine at a restaurant, ask for table wine in a pitcher *(un pichet;* uhn pee-shay), rather than a bottle (though finer restaurants usually offer only bottles of wine). If all you want is a glass of wine, ask for *un verre de vin* (uhn vehr duh van). A half carafe of wine is *un demi-pichet* (uhn duh-mee pee-shay), a quarter carafe (ideal for one) is *un quart* (uhn kar).

Tune into the relaxed pace of French dining. The French don't do dinner and a movie on date nights; they just do dinner. Evening meals last a long time in restaurants, and once you've been seated, that table is yours for the night.

At the end of your meal, your waiter might ask, *"Ça vous a plû?"* ("Did you enjoy your meal?"). If you did, say, *"Oui, c'était délicieux!"* (wee, say-tay day-lee-see-uh), meaning, "Yes, it was delicious!"

In restaurants, a waiter will never bring you the check unless you request it. For a French person, having the bill dropped off before asking for it is akin to being kicked out—*très* rude. But busy travelers are often ready for the check sooner rather than later. Here's a tip: When your server comes to clear your plates, he or she will often ask if you would like a post-meal coffee. It's the waiter's way of asking, "Are we all done here folks? Can I get you anything else?" Here's your chance. First, say *"oui"* or *"non"* to the coffee, and then ask for the bill, by saying, *"L'addition, s'il vous plaît."* If you don't ask now, the wait staff may become scarce as they leave you to digest in peace.

# Types of Cuisine

The fun part of dining in Paris is that you can sample fine cuisine from throughout France. Most restaurants serve dishes from several regions, though some focus on a particular region's cuisine. (I list restaurants specializing in food from Provence, Burgundy, Alsace, Normandy, Brittany, Dordogne, Languedoc, and the Basque region.) You can be a galloping gourmet and try several types of French cuisine without ever leaving the confines of Paris.

## French Specialties by Region

**Alsace:** The German influence is obvious—sausages, potatoes, onions, and sauerkraut. Look for *choucroute garnie* (sauerkraut and sausage—although it seems a shame to eat it in a fancy restaurant), the more traditionally Alsatian *Baeckeoffe* (potato, meat, and onion stew), *Rösti* (an oven-baked potato-and-cheese dish), fresh trout, foie gras, and *flammekueche* (a paper-thin pizza topped with bacon, onions, and sour cream).

**Burgundy:** Considered by many to be France's best, Burgundian cuisine is peasant cooking elevated to an art. This wine region excels in coq au vin (chicken with wine sauce), *bœuf bourguignon* (beef stew cooked with wine, bacon, onions, and mushrooms), *œufs en meurette* (eggs poached in red wine), escargots (snails), and *jambon persillé* (ham with garlic and parsley).

**Basque:** Mixing influences from the mountains, sea, Spain, and France, it's dominated by seafood, tomatoes, and red peppers. Look for anything *basquaise* (cooked with tomatoes, eggplant, red peppers, and garlic), such as *thon* (tuna) or *poulet* (chicken). Try *piperade*, a dish combining peppers, tomatoes, garlic, and eggs (ham optional), and *ttoro,* a seafood stew that is the Basque answer to bouillabaisse.

**Languedoc and Périgord:** The cuisine of these regions is referred to in Paris as "Southwest cuisine" *(cuisine du sudouest).* This hearty peasant cooking uses full-bodied red wines and lots of duck. Try the hearty *cassoulet* (white bean, duck, and sausage stew), *canard* (duck), pâté de foie gras (goose-liver pâté), *pommes sarladaise* (potatoes fried in duck fat), *truffes* (truffles, earthy mushrooms), and anything with *noix* (walnuts).

**Normandy and Brittany:** Normandy specializes in cream sauces, sea salt, organ meats (sweetbreads, tripe, and kidneys—the "gizzard salads" are great), and seafood *(fruits de mer).* Dairy products are big here. Try the *moules* (mussels) and *escalope normande* (veal in cream sauce). Brittany is famous for its oysters and crêpes. Both regions use lots of *cidre* (hard apple cider) in their cuisine.

**Provence:** The extravagant use of garlic, olive oil, herbs, and tomatoes makes Provence's cuisine France's liveliest. To sample it, order anything *à la provençale.* Among the area's spicy specialties are ratatouille (a thick mixture of vegetables in an herb-flavored tomato sauce), *brandade* (a salt cod, garlic, and cream mousse), aioli (a garlicky mayonnaise often served atop fresh vegetables), tapenade (a paste of puréed olives, capers, anchovies, herbs, and sometimes tuna), *soupe au pistou* (vegetable soup with basil, garlic, and cheese), and *soupe à l'ail* (garlic soup).

**Riviera:** The Côte d'Azur gives Provence's cuisine a Mediterranean flair. Local specialties are bouillabaisse (the spicy seafood stew/soup that seems worth the cost only for those with a seafood fetish), *bourride* (a creamy fish soup thickened with aioli garlic sauce), and *salade niçoise* (nee-swahz; a tasty tomato, potato, olive, anchovy, and tuna salad).

## Common French Dishes

The French eat dinner in courses, rather than all on one plate. For general, classic, anywhere-in-France dishes, consider these suggestions:

### First Course (*Entrée*)

*Crudités:* A mix of raw and lightly cooked fresh vegetables, usually including grated carrots, celery root, tomatoes, and beets, often with a hefty dose of vinaigrette dressing. If you want the dressing on the side, say, *"La sauce à côté, s'il vous plaît"* (lah sohs ah koh-tay, see voo play).

*Escargots:* Snails cooked in parsley-garlic butter. You don't even have to like the snail itself. Just dipping your bread in garlic butter is more than satisfying. Prepared a variety of ways, the classic is *à la bourguignon* (served in their shells).

*Foie gras:* Rich and buttery in consistency—and hefty in price—this pâté is made from the swollen livers of force-fed geese (or ducks, in *foie de canard*). Spread it on bread with your knife, and never add mustard. For a real French experience, try this dish with some sweet white wine (often offered by the glass for an additional cost).

*Huîtres:* Oysters served raw any month and delivered fresh from nearby Brittany. This food is particularly popular at Christmas and New Year's, when every café seems to have overflowing baskets lining the storefront.

*Œuf mayo:* A simple hard-boiled egg topped with a dollop of flavorful mayonnaise.

*Pâtés and Terrines:* Slowly cooked ground meat (usually pork, though game, poultry liver, and rabbit are also common) that is highly seasoned and served in slices with mustard and *cornichons* (little pickles). Pâtés are smoother than the similarly prepared but chunkier *terrines*.

*Salades:* With the exception of a *salade mixte* (simple green salad, often difficult to find), the French get creative with their *salades*. (See "Café Culture," earlier, for good salad suggestions.)

*Soupe à l'oignon:* Hot, salty, and filling, French onion soup is a beef broth served with a baked cheese-and-bread crust over the top. This is not easy to find in Paris, as locals prefer other types of soup.

## Main Course *(Plat Principal)*

*Bœuf bourguignon:* A Burgundian specialty, this classy beef stew is cooked slowly in red wine, then served with onions, potatoes, and mushrooms.

*Confit de canard:* This Southwest favorite is duck that has been preserved and then cooked in its own fat, and often served with potatoes cooked in the same fat. Not for dieters. (*Magret de canard*, sliced duck breast, is very different in taste.)

*Coq au vin:* This Burgundian dish is rooster marinated ever so slowly in red wine, then cooked until it melts in your mouth. It's served (often family-style) with vegetables.

*Escalope normande:* A specialty of Normandy, this is turkey or veal in a cream sauce.

*Gigot d'agneau:* Leg of lamb served in many styles, often with white beans. The best lamb is *pré salé*, which means the lamb has been raised in salt-marsh lands (like at Mont St-Michel).

*Poulet roti:* Roasted chicken on the bone—French comfort food.

*Saumon:* You'll see salmon dishes served in various styles. The salmon usually comes from the North Sea and is always served with sauce, most commonly a sorrel *(oseille)* sauce. *Saumon tartare* is raw salmon. Some love it, while others are careful to avoid it.

***Steak:*** Referred to as *pavé* (thick hunk of prime steak), *bavette* (skirt steak), *faux filet* (sirloin), or *entrecôte* (rib steak), French steak is usually thinner and tougher than American steak and is always served with sauces (*au poivre* is a pepper sauce, *une sauce roquefort* is a blue-cheese sauce). French cows get more exercise, so their beef is somewhat stringy and chewy. Because steak is usually better (fattier) in North America, I avoid it in France (unless the sauce sounds good). You will also see *steak haché*, which is a lean, gourmet hamburger patty served *sans* bun. When it's served as *steak haché à cheval*, it comes with a fried egg on top, but still no bun.

By American standards, the French undercook meats: Their version of rare, *saignant* (seh-nyahn), means "bloody" and is close to raw. What they consider medium, or *à point* (ah pwan), is what an American would call rare. Their term for well-done, or *bien cuit* (bee-yehn kwee), would translate as medium for Americans.

***Steak tartare:*** This wonderfully French dish is for adventurous types only. It's very lean, raw hamburger served with savory seasonings (usually Tabasco, capers, raw onions, salt, and pepper on the side) and topped with an uncooked egg yolk. This is not hamburger as we know it, but freshly ground beef. While it can be extremely tasty, it's very rich, and portions are bigger than what most Americans need. Splitting a plate can be a great idea.

## Cheese Course *(Le Fromage)*

In France the cheese course is served just before (or instead of) dessert. It not only helps with digestion, it gives you a great opportunity to sample the tasty regional cheeses—and time to finish up your wine. There are more than 400 different French cheeses to try. Some restaurants will offer a cheese platter, from which you select a few different cheeses. A good cheese plate has at least four types: hard cheese (like Emmentaler—a.k.a. Swiss cheese), a flowery cheese (like Brie or Camembert), a blue or Roquefort cheese, and a goat cheese.

Cheeses most commonly served in Paris are Brie de Meaux (mild and creamy, from just outside Paris), Camembert (semi-creamy and pungent, from Normandy), chèvre (goat cheese with a sharp taste, usually from the Loire), and Roquefort (strong and blue-veined, from south-central France).

If you'd like to sample several types of cheese from the cheese plate, say, *"Un assortiment, s'il vous plaît"* (uhn ah-sor-tee-mahn, see voo play). If you serve yourself from the cheese plate, observe French etiquette and keep the shape of the cheese. It's best to politely shave off a slice from the side or cut small wedges.

If you've run out of wine, consider ordering more. A glass of good red wine complements your cheese course in a heavenly way.

## Dessert *(Le Dessert)*

If you order espresso, it will always come after dessert. To have coffee with dessert, ask for *"café avec le dessert"* (kah-fay ah-vehk luh day-sayr). See the list of coffee terms earlier in this chapter.

Here are the types of treats you'll see:

*Baba au rhum:* Brioche-like cake, drenched in rum and served with whipped cream.

*Café gourmand:* An assortment of small desserts selected by the restaurant—a great way to sample several desserts and learn your favorite.

*Crème brulée:* A rich, creamy, dense, caramelized custard.

*Crème caramel:* Flan in a caramel sauce.

*Fondant au chocolat* or *Moelleux au chocolat:* A molten chocolate cake with a runny (not totally cooked) center.

*Fromage blanc:* A light dessert similar to plain yogurt (yet different), served with sugar or herbs.

*Glace:* Ice cream—typically vanilla, chocolate, or strawberry *(fraise).*

*Ile flottante:* A light dessert consisting of islands of meringue floating on a pond of custard sauce.

*Mousse au chocolat:* Chocolate mousse.

*Profiteroles:* Cream puffs filled with vanilla ice cream, smothered in warm chocolate sauce.

*Riz au lait:* Rice pudding.

*Sorbets:* Light, flavorful, and fruity ices, sometimes laced with brandy.

*Tartes:* Narrow strips of fresh fruit, baked in a crust and served in thin slices (without ice cream).

*Tarte tatin:* Apple pie like grandma never made, with caramelized apples, cooked upside down, but served upright.

# Restaurants

My recommendations are centered on the same great neighborhoods listed in the Sleeping in Paris chapter; you can come home exhausted after a busy day of sightseeing and find a good selection of restaurants right around the corner. And evening is a fine time to explore any of these delightful neighborhoods, even if you're sleeping elsewhere.

To save piles of euros, go to a bakery for takeout, or stop at a café for lunch. Cafés and brasseries are happy to serve a *plat du jour* (garnished plate of the day, about €12-18) or a chef-like salad

---

## Restaurant Price Code

To help you choose among these listings, I've divided the restaurants into three categories, based on the price for a typical main course.

**$$$** **Higher Priced**—Most main courses €25 or more.
**$$** **Moderately Priced**—Most main courses between €15-25.
**$** **Lower Priced**—Most main courses €15 or less.

---

(about €10-13) day or night. To save even more, consider picnics (tasty take-out dishes available at charcuteries).

Linger longer over dinner—restaurants expect you to enjoy a full meal. Most restaurants I've listed have set-price *menus* between €20 and €35. In most cases, the few extra euros you pay are well-spent, and open up a variety of better choices. Remember that a service charge is included in the prices (so little or no tipping is expected). Eat early with tourists or late with locals. Before choosing a seat outside, remember that smokers love outdoor tables.

## In the Rue Cler Neighborhood

The Rue Cler neighborhood caters to its residents. Its eateries, while not destination places, have an intimate charm. I've provided a full range of choices—from cozy ma-and-pa diners to small and trendy boutique restaurants to classic, big, boisterous bistros. For all restaurants listed in this area, use the Ecole Militaire Métro stop (unless another station is listed).

### On Rue Cler

**$ Café du Marché** boasts the best seats, coffee, and prices on Rue Cler. The owner's philosophy: Brasserie on speed—crank out good food at great prices to chic locals and savvy tourists. It's high-energy, with young waiters who barely have time to smile...*très* Parisian. This place is ideal if you don't mind a limited selection and want to eat an inexpensive one-course meal among a commotion of people. The chalkboard lists your choices: good, hearty €10 salads or more filling €10-12 *plats du jour*. If coming for dinner, arrive before 19:30; it's packed at 21:00, and service can be slow (Mon-Sat 11:00-23:00, Sun 11:00-17:00, at the corner of Rue Cler and Rue du Champ de Mars, 38 Rue Cler, tel. 01 47 05 51 27).

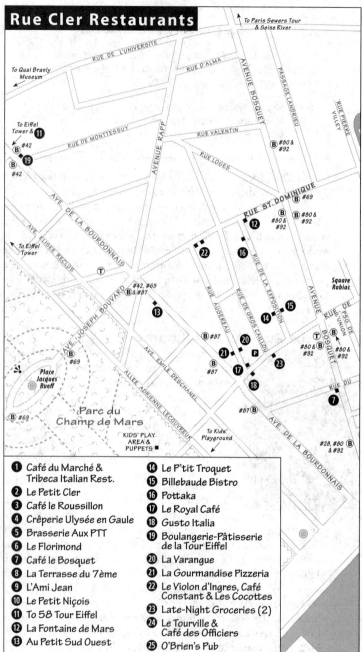

# Rue Cler Restaurants

To Paris Sewers Tour & Seine River

To Quai Branly Museum

RUE DE L'UNIVERSITE

RUE D'ALMA

AVENUE BOSQUET

PASSAGE LANDRIEU

RUE PIERRE VILLEY

To Eiffel Tower & ⑪ ⑲
Ⓑ #42
Ⓑ #42

RUE DE MONTTESSUY

RUE VALENTIN

AVENUE RAPP

RUE LOGES

Ⓑ #80 & #92

RUE ST. DOMINIQUE

Ⓑ #69
Ⓑ #80 & #92
⑫ Ⓑ #80 & #92

AVE. DE LA BOURDONNAIS

AVE. ELISEE RECLUS

To Eiffel Tower

Ⓣ

⑬
Ⓑ #42, #69 & #87

AVE. JOSEPH BOUVARD

Square Robiac

RUE DE LA EXPOSITION

⑮

RUE AUGEREAU

RUE DE GROS CAILLOU

⑭

AVENUE BOSQUET

RUE DE L'UNION

Ⓣ
Ⓑ #80 & #92
Ⓑ #80 & #92

⑳ Ⓑ #87
㉑ ⑰
P
㉓

Ⓑ #69

Place Jacques Rueff

AVE. EMILE DESCHANEL

ALLEE ADRIENNE LECOUVREUR

⑱

⑦

RUE DU

Ⓑ #69

Parc du Champ de Mars

KIDS' PLAY AREA & PUPPETS ▪

To Kids' Playground

#87 Ⓑ

AVE. DE LA BOURDONNAIS

#28, #80 & #92 Ⓑ

❶ Café du Marché & Tribeca Italian Rest.
❷ Le Petit Cler
❸ Café le Roussillon
❹ Crêperie Ulysée en Gaule
❺ Brasserie Aux PTT
❻ Le Florimond
❼ Café le Bosquet
❽ La Terrasse du 7ème
❾ L'Ami Jean
❿ Le Petit Niçois
⓫ To 58 Tour Eiffel
⓬ La Fontaine de Mars
⓭ Au Petit Sud Ouest

⓮ Le P'tit Troquet
⓯ Billebaude Bistro
⓰ Pottaka
⓱ Le Royal Café
⓲ Gusto Italia
⓳ Boulangerie-Pâtisserie de la Tour Eiffel
⓴ La Varangue
㉑ La Gourmandise Pizzeria
㉒ Le Violon d'Ingres, Café Constant & Les Cocottes
㉓ Late-Night Groceries (2)
㉔ Le Tourville & Café des Officiers
㉕ O'Brien's Pub

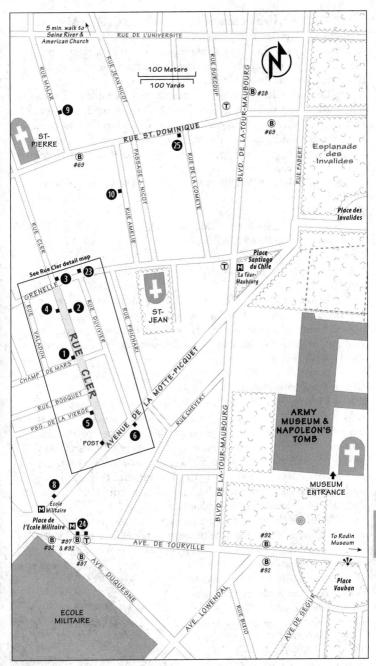

5 min. walk to Seine River & American Church

RUE DE L'UNIVERSITE

RUE MALAR

RUE JEAN NICOT

RUE SURCOUF

RUE GURCOUF

**(T)**

**(N)**

100 Meters

100 Yards

**9**

ST-PIERRE

RUE ST. DOMINIQUE

**25**

PASSAGE J. NICOT

RUE DE LA COMETE

BLVD. DE LA-TOUR-MAUBOURG

**#28**

**(B) #69**

RUE FABERT

Esplanade des Invalides

**(B) #69**

**10**

RUE AMELIE

RUE CLER

Place des Invalides

See Rue Cler detail map

GRENELLE

**3** **23**

**4** **2**

RUE VALADON

RUE DUVIVIER

RUE PSICHARI

CHAMP DE MARS

**1**

RUE CLER

RUE BOSQUET

**5**

PSG. DE LA VIERGE

POST

**6**

AVENUE DE LA MOTTE-PICQUET

RUE CHEVERT

ST-JEAN

Place Santiago du Chile

**(T)**

**M** La Tour-Maubourg

**ARMY MUSEUM & NAPOLEON'S TOMB**

BLVD. DE LA-TOUR-MAUBOURG

MUSEUM ENTRANCE

**8**

**M** Ecole Militaire

Place de l'Ecole Militaire

**M** **24**

**(B) #87** **(B)**

**#92 & #92** **(T)**

**(B) #87**

AVE. DE TOURVILLE

**(B)** **#92**

To Rodin Museum →

AVE. DUQUESNE

**(B) #92**

Place Vauban

**ECOLE MILITAIRE**

AVE. LOWENDAL

RUE BIXIO

AVE. DE SEGUR

**$ Tribeca Italian Restaurant,** next door to Café du Marché, is run by the same people with essentially the same formula *à la it-alienne*. They offer similar value and more space with a calmer ambience. Choose from family-pleasing €13 pizzas and Italian *plats* (open daily, tel. 01 45 55 12 01).

**$ Le Petit Cler** is a small, authentic, and adorable café with long leather booths, a vintage interior, a handful of outdoor tables, and simple, delicious, inexpensive dishes (€9 omelets, €7 soup of the moment, €12 salads, €13 *plats,* mouthwatering *petit pots* of chocolate or vanilla pudding, closed Mon, next to Grand Hôtel Lévêque at 29 Rue Cler, tel. 01 45 50 17 50).

**$ Café le Roussillon** offers good-value café food at fair prices (daily, indoor seating only, at the corner of Rue de Grenelle and Rue Cler, tel. 01 45 51 47 53).

**$ Crêperie Ulysée en Gaule** offers cheap seats on Rue Cler with crêpes to go. Readers of this book don't have to pay an extra charge to sit if they buy a drink. The family adores its Greek dishes, but their crêpes are your least expensive hot meal on this street (28 Rue Cler, tel. 01 47 05 61 82).

**$ Brasserie Aux PTT,** a simple traditional café delivering fair-value fare, reminds Parisians of the old days on Rue Cler. Rick Steves diners are promised a free *kir* with their dinner (closed Sun, 2-minute walk from most area hotels, opposite 53 Rue Cler, tel. 01 45 51 94 96).

## Close to Ecole Militaire

**$$ Le Florimond** is fun for a special occasion. The setting is intimate and welcoming. Locals come for classic French cuisine at fair prices. Friendly English-speaking Laurent, whose playful ties change daily, gracefully serves one small room of tables and loves to give suggestions. The stuffed cabbage and the *confit de canard* are particularly tasty, and the house wine is wonderful (€36 *menu*, affordable wine selection, closed Sun, reservations smart, 19 Avenue de la Motte-Picquet, tel. 01 45 55 40 38).

**$$ Café le Bosquet** is a modern Parisian brasserie with dressy waiters. Dine in their snappy interior or at tables on a broad sidewalk. Come here for standard café fare—salad, French onion soup, steak, or a *plat du jour* for about €14-19. The escargots are tasty, and the house red wine is plenty good (continental breakfast for €6, free Wi-Fi, closed Sun, reservations smart Fri-Sat, corner of Rue du Champ de Mars and Avenue Bosquet, 46 Avenue Bosquet, tel. 01 45 51 38 13).

**$$ La Terrasse du 7ème** is a

sprawling, happening café with grand outdoor seating and a living room-like interior with comfy love seats. Located on a corner,
it overlooks a busy intersection with a constant parade of people.
Chairs are set up facing the street, as a meal here is like dinner
theater—and the show is slice-of-life Paris (€16-22 *plats*, good €13
*salade niçoise*, no fixed-price *menu*, daily until at least 24:00 and
sometimes until 2:00 in the morning, at Ecole Militaire Métro
stop, tel. 01 45 55 00 02).

### Between Rue de Grenelle and the River, East of Avenue Bosquet

**$$$ L'Ami Jean** offers top Basque specialties. You'll get hearty
portions at palatable prices (considering the quality), while sitting
in snug-but-fun, get-to-know-your-neighbor spaces. Parisians de-
tour long distances to savor the gregarious chef's special cuisine
and convivial atmosphere. Arrive by 19:30 or call ahead (€43 *menu*,
closed Sun-Mon, 27 Rue Malar, Mo: La Tour-Maubourg, tel. 01
47 05 86 89).

$$ **Le Petit Niçois** celebrates fish from southern France.
Come here for everything from bouillabaisse to bass to paella to
mussels, and enjoy the area's top seafood at decent prices (a few
meat dishes are available). Start with the delectable *escargot à la
provençale*, dive into the *marmite du pêcheur*—a delicious version of
bouillabaisse, sample the sinful puréed potatoes, and finish yourself off with the lemon twist finale *(citron confit givré aux frais)* or
*café gourmand* desserts. The atmosphere is contemporary—warm
though formal—and the welcome is genuine (€22 two-course
*menu*, €32 three-course *menu*; better yet, ask the owner, caring
Carlos, to give you the royal treatment—matching three courses
with wine and apéritifs for €50; daily, 10 Rue Amélie, Mo: La Tour
Maubourg, tel. 01 45 51 83 65).

### Between Rue de Grenelle and the River, West of Avenue Bosquet

Some of these places line peaceful Rue de l'Exposition (a few blocks
west of Rue Cler), allowing you to comparison shop *sans* stress.

**$$$ 58 Tour Eiffel,** on the tower's first level (about 300 feet
up), is popular both for its incredible views and the cuisine of its
famed French chef, Alain Ducasse. Dinner here is pricey (you must
order a complete *menu*—€70-85) and requires a reservation (two
seatings: 18:30 and 21:00; reserve long in advance, especially if you
want a view, either by calling or going online; within France, dial
toll tel. 08 25 56 66 62; from outside France, dial 01 76 64 14 64;
www.restaurants-toureiffel.com). Lunch is easier (€20 *menu*, daily
11:30-16:00, no reservations possible, Mo: Bir-Hakeim or Troca-
déro, RER: Champ de Mars-Tour Eiffel).

**$$$ La Fontaine de Mars,** a longtime favorite and neighborhood institution, draws Parisians who want to be seen. It's charmingly situated on a tiny, jumbled square with tables jammed together for the serious business of eating. Reserve in advance for a table on the ground floor or on the square, and enjoy the same meal Barack Obama did. Street-level seats come with the best ambience (€20-30 *plats du jour,* superb foie gras, superb-er desserts, 129 Rue St. Dominique, tel. 01 47 05 46 44).

**$$ Au Petit Sud Ouest** has stone walls and wood beams, making it a cozy place to sample fine cuisine from southwestern France. Duck, goose, foie gras, *cassoulet,* and truffles are among its specialties. Tables come with toasters to heat your bread—it enhances the flavors of the foie gras (closed Sun-Mon, 46 Avenue de la Bourdonnais, tel. 01 45 55 59 59).

**$$ Le P'tit Troquet** is a petite eatery taking you back to the Paris of the 1920s. Marie welcomes you warmly, and chef José cooks a delicious three-course €33 *menu* with a range of traditional choices prepared creatively. The homey charm and gourmet quality make this restaurant a favorite of connoisseurs (opens at 18:30, closed Sun, reservations smart, 28 Rue de l'Exposition, tel. 01 47 05 80 39).

**$$ Billebaude,** run by patient Pascal, is a small, authentic Parisian bistro popular with locals. The focus is on what's fresh, including catch-of-the-day fish and meats from the hunt (available in the fall and winter). Chef Sylvain, an avid hunter (as the decor will remind you), is determined to deliver quality at a fair price—and he succeeds. Try *filet de bar* (sea bass) for your main course and *œufs à la neige* for dessert (€33 *menu,* closed Sun-Mon, 29 Rue de l'Exposition, tel. 01 45 55 20 96).

**$$ Pottaka** is a snug eatery where in-the-know locals go for delicious Basque cuisine at reasonable prices (€34 *menu,* €19 *plats,* reservations smart for Wed-Sat nights, 4 Rue de l'Exposition, tel. 01 45 51 88 38).

**$ Le Royal** is a tiny neighborhood fixture. This humble time-warp place, with prices and decor from another era, comes from an age when cafés sold firewood and served food as an afterthought. Parisians dine here because "it's like eating at home." Gentle Michele runs the counter while hustling Giles tends to the tables (€5 omelets, €9 *plats,* filling three-course *menu*-€13, closed Sat-Sun, 212 Rue de Grenelle, tel. 01 47 53 92 90).

**$ Gusto Italia** serves up tasty, good-value Italian cuisine in a shoebox-size place with a few tables outside. Arrive early or plan to wait (€12 salads, €14 pasta, daily, 199 Rue de Grenelle, tel. 01 45 55 00 43).

**$ Boulangerie-Pâtisserie de la Tour Eiffel** delivers inexpensive salads, quiches, and sandwiches. Enjoy the views of the Eiffel

Tower (daily, outdoor and indoor seating, one block southeast of the tower at 21 Avenue de la Bourdonnais, tel. 01 47 05 59 81).

**$ La Varangue** is an entertaining one-man show featuring English-speaking Philippe, who once ran a catering business in Pennsylvania. He now lives upstairs and has found his niche serving a mostly American clientele. The food is cheap and basic, the tables are few, and he opens at 17:30. Norman Rockwell would dig his miniscule dining room—with the traditional kitchen sizzling just over the counter. Try his snails and chocolate cake—but not together (€12 *plats*, €18 *menu*, always a vegetarian option, closed Sun, 27 Rue Augereau, tel. 01 47 05 51 22).

**$ La Gourmandise** is a kid-friendly, cheap pizzeria across from La Varangue (closed Sun, eat in or take out, 28 Rue Augereau, tel. 01 45 55 45 16).

*The Constant Lineup:* Ever since leaving the venerable Hôtel Crillon, famed chef Christian Constant has made a career of taking the "snoot" out of French cuisine—and making it accessible to people like us. Today you'll find three of his restaurants strung along one block of Rue St. Dominique between Rue Augereau and Rue de l'Exposition. Each is distinct, and each offers a different experience and price range. None of these places is cheap, but they all deliver top-quality cuisine.

**$$$ Le Violon d'Ingres,** where Christian won his first Michelin star, makes for a good excuse to dress up and really dine finely in Paris. Glass doors open onto a lively and chic eating scene, service is formal yet helpful, and the cuisine is what made this restaurateur's reputation (€60-80 *menus*, daily, reservations essential, 135 Rue St. Dominique, tel. 01 45 55 15 05).

**$$ Les Cocottes** is a trendy, bar-stool-only place serving simple dishes in small iron pots to yuppie Parisians (daily, no reservations taken, 135 Rue St. Dominique).

**$$ Café Constant** is a cool, two-level place that feels more like a small bistro-wine bar than a café. Delicious and fairly priced dishes are served in a fun setting to a dedicated clientele. Arrive early to get a table (downstairs seating is better); the friendly staff speak English (€11 entrées, €16 *plats*, €7 desserts, closed Sun-Mon, no reservations taken, corner of Rue Augereau and Rue St. Dominique, next to recommended Hôtel Londres Eiffel, tel. 01 47 53 73 34).

## Picnicking near Rue Cler

Rue Cler is a festival of food. The street is lined with businesses run by people whose lives seem to be devoted to their specialty: polished produce, rotisserie chicken, crêpes, or cheese. For a self-guided tour of all the temptations, see the Rue Cler Walk chapter.

For a magical picnic dinner at the Eiffel Tower, assemble it in no fewer than five shops on Rue Cler. Then lounge on the best grass in Paris, with the dogs, Frisbees, a floodlit tower, and a cool breeze in the Champ de Mars park (picnics are allowed off to the sides, but not in the central area, which is off-limits).

**Asian delis** (generically called *traiteurs asiatique*) provide low-stress, low-price take-out treats (€8 dinner plates; the one on Rue Cler near Rue du Champ de Mars has tables). **Crêperie Ulysée en Gaule,** the Greek restaurant on Rue Cler across from Grand Hôtel Lévêque, sells take-away crêpes (see page 436). For the cheapest, easiest meals, consider getting sandwiches or kebabs, just beyond the cute zone a few steps past the Ecole Militaire Métro stop on Avenue de Tourville.

Small, **late-night groceries** are at 197 Rue de Grenelle (open daily until midnight), as well as where Rues Cler and Grenelle cross.

### Breakfast on Rue Cler

Hotel breakfasts, though convenient, are generally not a good value. For a great Rue Cler start to your day, drop by **Brasserie Aux PTT,** where Rick Steves readers are promised a *deux pour douze* breakfast special (two "American" breakfasts—juice, a big coffee, croissant, bread, ham, and eggs—for €12; closed Sun, 53 Rue Cler). For a continental breakfast for about €6, try nearby **Café le Bosquet** (closed Sun, 46 Avenue Bosquet).

### Nightlife in Rue Cler

This sleepy neighborhood was not made for night owls, but there are a few notable exceptions. The focal point of before- and after-dinner posing occurs along the broad sidewalk at the intersection of Avenues de la Motte-Picquet and Tourville (Mo: Ecole Militaire). **Le Tourville** and **Café des Officiers** gather a sea of outward-facing seats for the important business of people-watching—and fashion-model recruiting.

**La Terrasse du 7ème,** across the avenue, has a less-pretentious clientele (see listing, earlier). Nearby, **Café du Marché** (listed earlier) attracts a Franco-American crowd until at least midnight, as does the younger **Café Roussillon** (good French pub atmosphere, corner of Rue de Grenelle and Rue Cler). **O'Brien's Pub** is a relaxed Parisian rendition of an Irish pub, full of Anglophones (77 Rue St. Dominique, Mo: La Tour Maubourg).

## In the Marais Neighborhood

The trendy Marais is filled with diners enjoying good food in colorful and atmospheric eateries. The scene is competitive and changes all the time. I've listed an assortment of eateries—all handy to recommended hotels—that offer good food at decent prices, plus a memorable experience.

## On Romantic Place des Vosges

This square offers Old World Marais elegance, a handful of eateries, and an ideal picnic site until dusk, when the park closes (use Bastille or St. Paul Métro stops). Strolling around the arcade after dark is more important than dining here—fanciful art galleries alternate with restaurants and cafés. Choose a restaurant that best fits your mood and budget; most have arcade seating and provide big space heaters to make outdoor dining during colder months an option. Also consider a drink or dessert on the square at Café Hugo or Carette after eating elsewhere.

**$$$ Ma Bourgogne** is a vintage eatery where you'll sit under warm arcades in a whirlpool of Frenchness, as bow-tied and black-aproned waiters serve you traditional French specialties: blood-red steak (try the *brochette de bœuf*), piles of fries, escargot, and good red wine. Monsieur Cougoureux (koo-goo-ruh) has commanded this ship since de Gaulle was sniveling at Americans. He offers anyone with this book a free *amuse-bouche* ("amusement for your mouth") of his homemade steak tartare—but you may need to remind him (show him my picture in this book). This is your chance to try this "raw spiced hamburger" delicacy without dedicating an entire meal to it (€40 *menu*, daily, cash only, at northwest corner at #19, tel. 01 42 78 44 64).

**$$ La Place Royale** offers a fine location on the square; there's comfortable seating inside or you can sit outside under the arches. The cuisine is traditional, well-priced, and served nonstop all day (€23-39 *menus*, daily, 2 bis Place des Vosges, tel. 01 42 78 58 16).

**$$ Café Hugo,** named for the square's most famous resident, is best for drinks only, as the cuisine does not live up to its setting (daily, 22 Place des Vosges, tel. 01 42 72 64 04).

## Near Place des Vosges

**$$ Les Bonnes Soeurs,** a block from the square, blends modern and traditional fare with simple, contemporary ambience. Portions are big and inventive. The delicious and filling *pressé de chèvre* starter (a hunk of goat cheese topped with tapenade and tomatoes) begs to be shared. Their hearty French hamburger comes with a

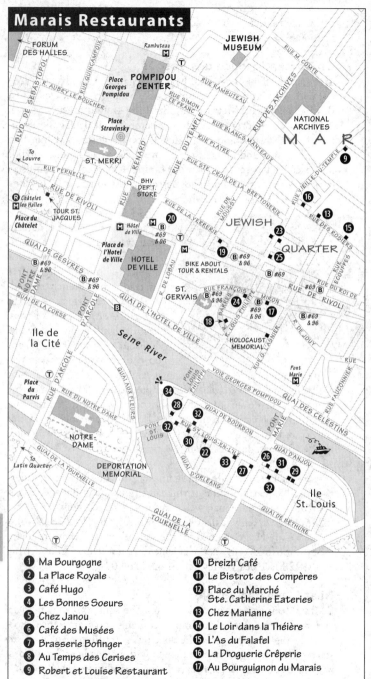

# Marais Restaurants

FORUM
DES HALLES

Rambuteau

JEWISH
MUSEUM

Place
Georges
Pompidou

POMPIDOU
CENTER

Place
Stravinsky

ST. MERRI

NATIONAL
ARCHIVES

M A R

RUE DE RIVOLI

BHV
DEP'T.
STORE

JEWISH

QUARTER

Place du
Châtelet

TOUR ST.
JACQUES

Hôtel
de Ville

Place de
l'Hôtel de
Ville

HOTEL
DE VILLE

BIKE ABOUT
TOUR & RENTALS

ST.
GERVAIS

HOLOCAUST
MEMORIAL

Ile de
la Cité

Seine River

Place
du
Parvis

NOTRE-
DAME

Pont
Marie

To
Latin Quarter

DEPORTATION
MEMORIAL

Ile
St. Louis

1  Ma Bourgogne
2  La Place Royale
3  Café Hugo
4  Les Bonnes Soeurs
5  Chez Janou
6  Café des Musées
7  Brasserie Bofinger
8  Au Temps des Cerises
9  Robert et Louise Restaurant
10 Breizh Café
11 Le Bistrot des Compères
12 Place du Marché
   Ste. Catherine Eateries
13 Chez Marianne
14 Le Loir dans la Théière
15 L'As du Falafel
16 La Droguerie Crêperie
17 Au Bourguignon du Marais

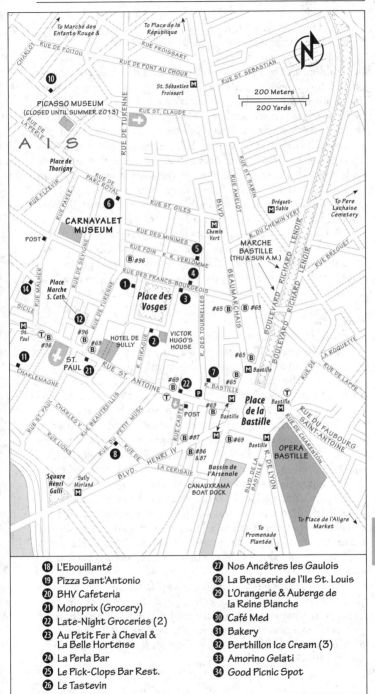

⑱ L'Ebouillanté
⑲ Pizza Sant'Antonio
⑳ BHV Cafeteria
㉑ Monoprix (Grocery)
㉒ Late-Night Groceries (2)
㉓ Au Petit Fer à Cheval & La Belle Hortense
㉔ La Perla Bar
㉕ Le Pick-Clops Bar Rest.
㉖ Le Tastevin

㉗ Nos Ancêtres les Gaulois
㉘ La Brasserie de l'Ile St. Louis
㉙ L'Orangerie & Auberge de la Reine Blanche
㉚ Café Med
㉛ Bakery
㉜ Berthillon Ice Cream (3)
㉝ Amorino Gelati
㉞ Good Picnic Spot

salad and the best fries I've tasted in Paris (*plats* from €16, no *menu*, daily, 8 Rue du Pas de la Mule, tel. 01 42 74 55 80).

**$$ Chez Janou,** a Provençal bistro, tumbles out of its corner building and fills its broad sidewalk with happy eaters. At first glance, you know this place has a following. Don't let the trendy and youthful crowd intimidate you: It's relaxed and charming, with helpful and patient service. The curbside tables are inviting, but I'd sit inside (with very tight seating) to immerse myself in the happy commotion. The style is French Mediterranean, with an emphasis on vegetables (€16-20 *plats du jour* that change with the season, daily from 19:45—book ahead or arrive when it opens, 2 blocks beyond Place des Vosges at 2 Rue Roger Verlomme, tel. 01 42 72 28 41). They're proud of their 81 varieties of *pastis* (licorice-flavored liqueur, €3.50 each, browse the list above the bar).

**$ Café des Musées** is an unspoiled, zinc-countered bistro serving traditional dishes with little fanfare and a €22 daily *menu* special that's hard to beat. The place is just far enough away to be overlooked by tourists but packed with locals, so arrive early or book ahead (daily, 49 Rue de Turenne, tel. 01 42 72 96 17).

### Near the Bastille
To reach these restaurants, use the Bastille Métro stop.

**$$$ Brasserie Bofinger,** an institution for over a century, is famous for fish and traditional cuisine with Alsatian flair. You'll eat in a sprawling interior, surrounded by brisk, black-and-white-attired waiters. It's a high-energy feast for all the senses. Downstairs rooms are elaborately decorated and reminiscent of the Roaring Twenties, while upstairs rooms have traditional Alsatian decor. Eating under the grand 1919 *coupole* is a memorable treat (as is using the "historic" 1919 WC downstairs). Check out the boys shucking and stacking seafood platters out front before you enter. Their €29 two-course and €34 three-course *menus,* while not top cuisine, are a good value. If you've always wanted one of those picturesque seafood platters, this is a good place—you can take the standard platter or create one à la carte (open daily for lunch and for dinner, fun kids' menu, reasonably priced wines, 5 Rue de la Bastille, don't be confused by the lesser "Petite" Bofinger across the street, tel. 01 42 72 87 82).

**$$ Au Temps des Cerises** is a cozy place serving wines by the glass and simple meals with a smile. The woody 1950s atmosphere has tight seating and wads of character. Come for a glass of wine and move on, or better yet, stay for a tasty dinner (€9 starters, €18 *plats*, cheap wine, daily, at Rue du Petit Musc and Rue de la Cerisaie, tel. 01 42 72 08 63).

## In the Heart of the Marais

These are closest to the St. Paul Métro stop.

**$$ Robert et Louise** (now run by Pascal *et* François) crams tables into a tiny, rustic-as-it-gets interior, warmed by a fireplace grill. The food is red-meat good, well-priced, and popular with tourists (€7 starters, €18 *plats*, €6 desserts, closed Mon, 64 Rue du Vieille du Temple, tel. 01 42 78 55 89).

**$ Breizh (Brittany) Café** is worth the walk. It's a simple Breton joint serving organic crêpes and small rolls made for dipping in rich sauces and salted butter. The crêpes are the best in Paris and run the gamut from traditional andouille (pork sausage) to Asian fusion (buckwheat crêpe topped with seaweed butter). They also serve oysters, have a fantastic list of sweet crêpes, and talk about cider like a sommelier would talk about wine. Try a sparkling cider, a Breton cola, or my favorite—*lait ribot*, a buttermilk-like drink (€7-12 dinner crêpes and *plats*, serves nonstop from 12:00 to late, closed Mon-Tue, 109 Rue du Vieille du Temple, tel. 01 42 72 13 77).

**$ Le Bistrot des Compères** has a privileged location on a quiet corner in the thick of the Marais; there's a warm and welcoming feel whether you sit inside or out. The cuisine is traditional with creative twists, the staff is relaxed, and the prices are very fair (€7 starters, €15 *plats*, €7 desserts, closed Sun-Mon, 16 Rue Charlemagne, tel. 01 42 72 14 16).

**$ *On Place du Marché Ste. Catherine:*** This small, romantic square, just off Rue St. Antoine, is an international food festival cloaked in extremely Parisian, leafy-square ambience. On a balmy evening, this is clearly a neighborhood favorite, with a handful of restaurants offering €20-30 three-course meals. Study the square, and you'll find three popular French bistros with similar features: **La Terrasse Ste. Catherine**, **Le Marché,** and **Au Bistrot de la Place** (all open daily with €24 three-course *menus* on weekdays, must order à la carte on weekends, tight seating on flimsy chairs indoors and out). Other inviting eateries nearby serve a variety of international food. You'll eat under the trees, surrounded by a futuristic-in-1800 planned residential quarter.

**$** Several hardworking **Asian fast-food eateries,** great for an €8 meal, line Rue St. Antoine.

***On Rue des Rosiers in the Jewish Quarter:*** These places line up along the same street in the heart of the Jewish Quarter.

**$ Chez Marianne** is a neighborhood fixture that blends delicious Jewish cuisine with Parisian *élan* and wonderful atmosphere. Choose from several indoor zones with a cluttered wine shop/deli feeling, or sit outside. You'll select from two dozen *Zakouski* elements to assemble your €12-16 *plat*. Vegetarians will find great options (€8 falafel sandwich—only €6 if you order it to go, long hours daily, corner of Rue des Rosiers and Rue des Hospitalières-St.-Gervais, tel. 01 42 72 18 86). For takeout, pay inside first and get a ticket before you order outside.

**$ Le Loir dans la Théière** ("The Dormouse in the Teapot") is a cozy, mellow teahouse offering a welcoming ambience for tired travelers. It's ideal for lunch and popular for weekend brunch. They offer a daily assortment of creatively-filled quiches, and bake up an impressive array of homemade desserts that are proudly displayed in the dining room. Try the mile-high lemon meringue "pie" or the oversized *mille-feuille* (Mon-Fri 12:00-19:00, Sat-Sun 10:00-19:00, 3 Rue des Rosiers, tel. 01 42 72 90 61).

**$ L'As du Falafel** rules the falafel scene in the Jewish quarter. Monsieur Isaac, the "Ace of Falafel" here since 1979, brags, "I've got the biggest pita on the street...and I fill it up." (Apparently it's Lenny Kravitz's favorite, too.) Your inexpensive meal comes on plastic plates, in a bustling setting that seems to prove he's earned his success. The €7 "special falafel" is the big hit (€6 to go), but many Americans enjoy his lighter chicken version *(poulet grillé)* or the tasty and massive *assiette de falafel* (€9). Wash it down it a cold Maccabee beer. Their take-out service draws a constant crowd (long hours daily except closed Fri evening and all day Sat, air-con, 34 Rue des Rosiers, tel. 01 48 87 63 60).

**$ La Droguerie,** an outdoor crêpe stand a few blocks farther down Rue des Rosiers, is an option if falafels don't work for you, but cheap does (€5 dinner crêpes, closed Mon, 56 Rue des Rosiers).

## Near Hôtel de Ville

To reach these eateries, use the Hôtel de Ville Métro stop.

**$$ Au Bourguignon du Marais** is a handsome wine bar/bistro for Burgundy lovers, where excellent wines (Burgundian only, available by the glass) blend with a good selection of well-designed dishes and efficient service. The *œufs en meurette* are mouthwatering, and the *bœuf bourguignon* could feed two (€10-14 starters, €20-26 *plats*, closed Sun-Mon, pleasing indoor and outdoor seating, 52 Rue François Miron, tel. 01 48 87 15 40).

**$ L'Ebouillanté** is a breezy crêperie-café, romantically situated near the river on a broad, cobbled pedestrian lane behind a church. With great outdoor seating and an artsy, cozy interior, it's perfect for an inexpensive and relaxing tea, snack, or lunch—or for dinner on a warm evening. Their *Brick,* a Tunisian-inspired dish that looks like a stuffed omelet, has several filling options and comes with a small salad (€15); it left me stuffed (*plats* and big salads–€13, daily 12:00-21:30 except closed Mon Nov-March, a block off the river at 6 Rue des Barres, tel. 01 42 71 09 69).

**$ Pizza Sant'Antonio** is bustling and cheap, serving up €11 pizzas and salads on a fun Marais square (daily, barely off Rue de Rivoli at 1 Rue de la Verrerie, tel. 01 42 77 78 47).

**$ BHV Department Store**'s fifth-floor cafeteria provides nice views, good prices, and no-brainer, point-and-shoot cafeteria cuisine (Mon-Sat 11:30-18:00, closed Sun, at intersection of Rue du Temple and Rue de la Verrerie, one block from Hôtel de Ville).

### Picnicking in the Marais
Picnic at peaceful Place des Vosges (closes at dusk) or on the Ile St. Louis *quais* (described later). Stretch your euros at the basement supermarket of the **Monoprix** department store (closed Sun, near Place des Vosges on Rue St. Antoine). You'll find small **groceries** open until 23:00 at 48 Rue St. Antoine and on Ile St. Louis.

### Nightlife in the Marais
Trendy cafés and bars—popular with gay men—cluster on Rue des Archives and Rue Ste. Croix de la Bretonnerie (closing at about 2:00 in the morning). There's also a line of bars and cafés providing front-row seats for the buff parade on Rue Vieille du Temple, a block north of Rue de Rivoli (the horseshoe-shaped **Au Petit Fer à Cheval** bar-restaurant and the atmospheric **La Belle Hortense** bookstore/wine bar are the focal points of the action). Nearby, Rue des Rosiers bustles with youthful energy, but there are no cafés to observe from. **La Perla** dishes up inexpensive Tex-Mex and is stuffed with Parisian yuppies in search of the perfect margarita (26 Rue François Miron, tel. 01 42 77 59 40).

**$ Le Pick-Clops** bar-restaurant is a happy peanuts-and-lots-of-cocktails diner with bright neon, loud colors, and a garish local crowd. It's perfect for immersing yourself in today's Marais world—a little boisterous, a little edgy, a little gay, fun-loving, easygoing... and sans tourists. Sit inside on old-fashioned diner stools, or streetside to watch the constant Marais parade. The name means "Steal the Cigarettes"—but you'll pay €11 for your big salad (daily 7:00-24:00, 16 Rue Vieille du Temple, tel. 01 40 29 02 18).

*More Options:* The best scene for hard-core clubbers is the dizzying array of wacky eateries, bars, and dance halls on **Rue de Lappe.** Just east of the stately Place de la Bastille, it's one of the wildest nightspots in Paris and not for everyone.

The most enjoyable peaceful evening may be simply mentally donning your floppy "three musketeers" hat and slowly strolling Place des Vosges, window-shopping the art galleries.

## On Ile St. Louis

This romantic and peaceful neighborhood is filled with promising and surprisingly inexpensive possibilities; it merits a trip for dinner even if your hotel is elsewhere. Cruise the island's main street for a variety of options, from cozy *crêperies* to Italian eateries to Alsatian brasseries and romantic bistros. After dinner, sample Paris' best ice cream (described under "Ice Cream Dessert," later) and stroll across to Ile de la Cité to see a floodlit Notre-Dame. These recommended spots line the island's main drag, Rue St. Louis-en-l'Ile (see map on page 442; to get here use the Pont Marie Métro stop).

**$$$ Le Tastevin** is an intimate mother-and-son-run restaurant serving top-notch traditional French cuisine with white-tablecloth, candlelit, gourmet elegance under heavy wooden beams. The romantic setting (and the elegantly romantic Parisian couples enjoying the place) naturally makes you whisper. The *menus*, which start at €31 (two courses) and rise to €40-54 (three courses), offer a handful of classic choices that change with the season (daily, reserve for late-evening dining, fine wine list, 46 Rue St. Louis-en-l'Ile, tel. 01 43 54 17 31, owner Madame Puisieux and her gentle son speak just enough English).

**$$$ Nos Ancêtres les Gaulois** ("Our Ancestors the Gauls"), famous for its rowdy, medieval-cellar atmosphere, is made for hungry warriors and wenches who like to swill hearty wine. They serve up a rustic all-you-can-eat buffet with straw baskets of raw veggies and bundles of sausage (cut whatever you like with your dagger), massive plates of pâté, a meat course, and all the wine you can stomach for €41. The food is just food; burping is encouraged. If you want to overeat, drink too much wine, be surrounded with tourists (mostly French), and holler at your friends while receiving smart-aleck buccaneer service, you're home (daily, 39 Rue St. Louis-en-l'Ile, tel. 01 46 33 66 07).

**$$ La Brasserie de l'Ile St. Louis** is situated at the prow of the island's ship as it faces Ile de la Cité, offering purely Alsatian cuisine (try the *choucroute garnie* or *coq au riesling* for €19), served in a vigorous, Teutonic setting with no-nonsense, slap-it-down service on wine-stained paper tablecloths. This is a good, balmy-evening perch for watching the Ile St. Louis

promenade. If it's chilly, the interior is fun for a memorable night out (closed Wed, no reservations, 55 Quai de Bourbon, tel. 01 43 54 02 59).

**$$ L'Orangerie** is an inviting place with soft lighting and comfortable seating where diners speak in hushed voices so that everyone can appreciate the delicious cuisine and tasteful setting (€35 three-course *menu*, €27 two-course *menu*, Tue-Sun from 19:00, closed Mon, 28 Rue St. Louis-en-l'Ile, tel. 01 46 33 93 98).

**$ Auberge de la Reine Blanche** welcomes diners willing to rub elbows with their neighbors under heaving beams. Earnest owner Michel serves traditional cuisine at reasonable prices. The giant goat-cheese salad is a beefy meal in itself (€20 two-course *menu*, €25 three-course *menu*, daily from 18:00, 30 Rue St. Louis-en-l'Ile, tel. 01 46 33 07 87).

**$ Café Med,** near the pedestrian bridge to Notre-Dame, is a tiny, cheery *crêperie* with good-value salads, crêpes, and €11 *plats* (€14 and €20 *menus*, daily, limited wine list, 77 Rue St. Louis-en-l'Ile, tel. 01 43 29 73 17). Two similar *crêperies* are just across the street.

### Riverside Picnic for Impoverished Romantics
On sunny lunchtimes and balmy evenings, the *quai* on the Left Bank side of Ile St. Louis is lined with locals who have more class than money, spreading out tablecloths and even lighting candles for elegant picnics. And tourists can enjoy the same budget meal. A handy grocery store at #67 on the main drag (open until 22:00, closed Tue) has tabouli and other simple, cheap take-away dishes for your picnicking pleasure. The bakery a few blocks down at #40 serves quiche and pizza (open until 20:00, closed Sun-Mon).

### Ice-Cream Dessert
Half the people strolling Ile St. Louis are licking an ice-cream cone, because this is the home of *les glaces Berthillon* (now sold throughout Paris). The original **Berthillon** shop, at 31 Rue St. Louis-en-l'Ile, is marked by the line of salivating customers (closed Mon-Tue). For a less famous but at least as satisfying treat, the homemade Italian gelato a block away at **Amorino Gelati** is giving Berthillon competition (no line, bigger portions, easier to see what you want, and they offer little tastes—Berthillon doesn't need to, 47 Rue St.

Louis-en-l'Ile, tel. 01 44 07 48 08). Having some of each is not a bad thing.

## In the Luxembourg Garden Area

Sleeping in the Luxembourg neighborhood puts you near many appealing dining and after-hours options. Because my hotels in this area cluster near St. Sulpice Church and the Panthéon (see the Sleeping in Paris chapter), I've organized restaurant listings the same way. Restaurants around St. Sulpice tend to be boisterous; those near the Panthéon are calmer; it's a short walk from one area to the other. Anyone sleeping in this area is close to the inexpensive eateries that line the always-bustling Rue Mouffetard. You're also within a 15-minute walk of the *grands cafés* of St. Germain and Montparnasse (with Paris' first café and famous artist haunts; see "Les Grands Cafés de Paris," later in this chapter).

### Near St. Sulpice Church

The eateries in this section are served by the St. Sulpice, Mabillon, and St. Germain-des-Prés Métro stops. The streets between St. Sulpice Church and Boulevard St. Germain abound with restaurants, *crêperies*, wine bars, and jazz haunts (for this area, use Mo: St. Sulpice). Find Rue des Canettes and Rue Guisarde, and window-shop the many French and Italian eateries—most with similar prices, but each with a slightly different feel.

**$$ Lou Pescadou-Chez Julien** offers a comfortable atmosphere and above-average bistro fare in a zone where every restaurant looks the same (€9 starters, €18 *plats*, daily, some outdoor seating, 16 Rue Mabillon, tel. 01 43 54 56 08).

**$$ Boucherie Roulière** has a dark interior crammed with locals in search of a thick steak or other meat dish (€9 *entrées*, €19 *plats*, closed Mon, 24 Rue des Canettes, tel. 01 43 26 25 70).

**$$ Santa Lucia** draws positive reviews with wood-fired pizza, good pasta, and killer tiramisu (€12-14 pizza and pastas, €22 *plats*, closed Mon, 22 Rue des Canettes, tel. 01 43 26 42 68).

**$ La Crêpe Rit du Clown** cooks up yummy crêpes (Mon-Sat 12:00-23:00, closed Sun, 6 Rue des Canettes, tel. 01 46 34 01 02).

**Chez Georges** is a bohemian pub lined with black-and-white photos of the artsy and revolutionary French '60s. Have a drink as you sit in a cool little streetside table nook, or venture downstairs to find a hazy, drippy-candle, traditionally French world in the Edith Piaf-style dance cellar (cheap drinks from old-fashioned menu, Tue-Sat 14:00-2:00 in the morning, closed Sun-Mon and in Aug, 11 Rue des Canettes, tel. 01 43 26 79 15).

***Near Boulevard St. Germain:*** A five-minute walk from St. Sulpice Church, this venerable boulevard is home to some of Paris' most famous cafés and best pre- or post-dinner strolling (for café recommendations, see "Les Grands Cafés de Paris," later). Consider a light dinner with a table facing the action at Hemingway's **Les Deux Magots** or at Sartre's **Le Café de Flore** (figure about €12 for an omelet and €18-28 for a salad or *plat*). A block north (toward the river), **Rue de Buci** offers a lineup of bars, cafés, and bistros targeted to a young clientele who are more interested in how they look than how the food tastes. It's terrific theater for passersby from 18:00 until late.

**$$ La Cigale Récamier,** near the Sèvres-Babylone shopping area, is a classy place for a quiet meal at reasonable prices with appealing indoor and outdoor seating. It's about 10 minutes west of Place St. Sulpice, on a short pedestrian square a block off Rue de Sèvres (€20 *plats*, à la carte only, closed Sun, 4 Rue Récamier, Mo: Sèvres-Babylone, tel. 01 46 48 86 58).

### Near the Odéon Theater

To reach these, use the Odéon or Cluny-La Sorbonne Métro stops. In this same neighborhood, you'll find the historic Café le Procope, Paris' more-than-300-year-old café (see "Les Grands Cafés de Paris," later).

**$ L'Avant Comptoir** is a little stand-up-only hors d'oeuvres bar serving up a delightful array of French-Basque tapas for €3-6 on a sleek zinc counter. The menu is fun and accessible, it has a good list of wines by the glass, and crêpes are made fresh to go (daily 12:00-23:00, 9 Carrefour de l'Odéon, tel. 01 44 27 07 97).

**$$ Brasserie Bouillon Racine** takes you back to 1906 with an Art Nouveau carnival of carved wood, stained glass, and old-time lights reflected in beveled mirrors. The over-the-top decor and energetic waiters give it an inviting conviviality. Check upstairs before choosing a table. Their roast suckling pig (€19) is a house favorite. There's Belgian beer on tap and a fascinating history on the menu (€18-23 *plats*, €31 *menu*, a few fish options and lots of meat, daily, 3 Rue Racine, tel. 01 44 32 15 60).

**$$ La Méditerranée** is all about seafood from the south served in a pastel and dressy setting...with similar clientele. The scene and the cuisine are sophisticated yet accessible, and the view of the Odéon is *formidable*. The sky-blue tablecloths and the lovingly presented dishes add to the romance (€28 two-course *menus*, €33 three-course *menus*, daily, reservations smart, facing the Odéon at 2 Place de l'Odéon, tel. 01 43 26 02 30).

**$$ Café de l'Odéon** offers a great chance to savor light meals with a classy crowd on a peaceful and elegant square in front of a venerable theater. Though limited, the menu is accessible and decently priced, and you'll feel like a winner eating so well and so reasonably in such a Parisian setting. From May to October, the café is outdoors-only and serves lunch and dinner—or just go for

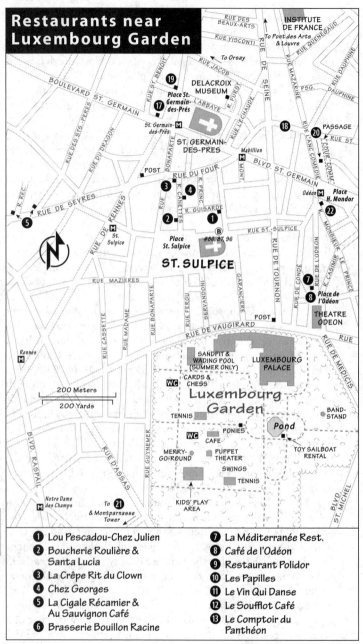

# Restaurants near Luxembourg Garden

1 Lou Pescadou-Chez Julien
2 Boucherie Roulière & Santa Lucia
3 La Crêpe Rit du Clown
4 Chez Georges
5 La Cigale Récamier & Au Sauvignon Café
6 Brasserie Bouillon Racine
7 La Méditerranée Rest.
8 Café de l'Odéon
9 Restaurant Polidor
10 Les Papilles
11 Le Vin Qui Danse
12 Le Soufflot Café
13 Le Comptoir du Panthéon

EATING IN PARIS

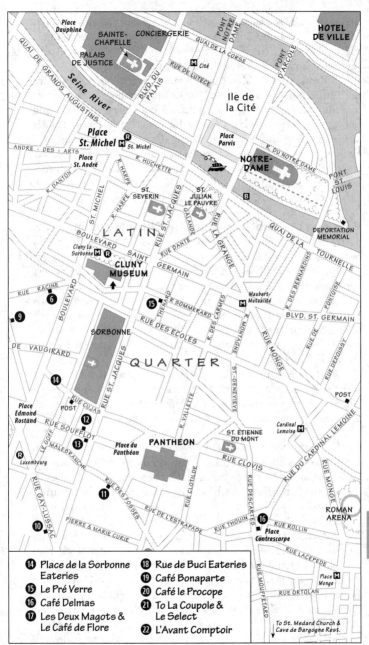

| | | | |
|---|---|---|---|
| ⑭ | Place de la Sorbonne Eateries | ⑱ | Rue de Buci Eateries |
| ⑮ | Le Pré Verre | ⑲ | Café Bonaparte |
| ⑯ | Café Delmas | ⑳ | Café le Procope |
| ⑰ | Les Deux Magots & Le Café de Flore | ㉑ | To La Coupole & Le Select |
| | | ㉒ | L'Avant Comptoir |

EATING IN PARIS

drinks (good €14 salads, €17 *plats* such as salmon and steak tartare; May-Oct daily 12:00-23:00—weather permitting, no reservations, Place de l'Odéon, tel. 01 44 85 41 30). In the winter (Nov-April) they serve lunch only inside the palatial theater lobby.

**$ Restaurant Polidor,** a bare-bones neighborhood fixture since the 19th century, is much loved for its unpretentious quality cooking, fun old-Paris atmosphere, and fair value. Stepping inside, you know this is a winner—noisy, happy diners sit tightly at shared tables as waiters chop and serve fresh bread. The selection features classic bourgeois *plats* from every corner of France; their *menu fraîcheur* is designed for lighter summer eating (€12-17 *plats*, €25-35 three-course *menus*, daily 12:00-14:30 & 19:00-23:00, cash only, no reservations, 41 Rue Monsieur-le-Prince, tel. 01 43 26 95 34).

## Between the Panthéon and the Cluny Museum

To reach these restaurants, use the Cluny-La Sorbonne Métro stop or the Luxembourg RER stop.

**$$ At Les Papilles** you just eat what's offered...and you won't complain. It's a foodie's dream come true—one *menu*, no choices, and no regrets. Choose your wine from the shelf or ask for advice from the burly rugby-playing owner, then relax and let the food arrive. Book this place ahead (€34 *menu*, €16 daily *marmite du marché*—a.k.a. market stew, closed Sun-Mon, 30 Rue Gay Lussac, tel. 01 43 25 20 79).

**$$ Le Vin Qui Danse** is a warm little place serving a good selection of tasty dishes and well-matched wines to appreciative clients (€27 two-course *menu*, add €15 for three wines selected to complement your meal, daily, 4 Rue des Fossés St. Jacques, tel. 01 43 54 80 81).

**$ *On Rue Soufflot with Panthéon Views:*** Facing each other are two cafés—**Le Soufflot** and **Le Comptoir du Panthéon**—that are well-positioned for afternoon sun and soft evening light. A block in front of the Panthéon, they deliver dynamite views of the inspiring dome. Both serve classic café food all day until late and are great for a pensive drink or a light meal—simply choose the one that appeals.

**$ *Place de la Sorbonne:*** This appealing little square surrounds a gurgling fountain and faces Sorbonne University, just a block from the Cluny Museum. It offers several opportunities for a good outdoor lunch or a pleasant dining experience. At amiable Carole's tiny **Baker's Dozen,** you'll pay take-away prices for light fare you can sit down to eat (€5 salads and sandwiches, Mon-Sat until 15:30, closed Sun, tel. 01 44 07 08 09). **Café de l'Ecritoire** is a typical brasserie with salads, *plats du jour,* and good seating inside and out (daily, tel. 01 43 54 60 02). **Patios** serves basic Italian cuisine, including pizza, at decent prices (daily until late, tel. 01 45 38 71 19). **Le Bac de la Sorbonne** is a tad cheaper, but you get what you pay for.

**$$ Le Pré Verre,** a block from the Cluny Museum, is a chic wine bistro—a refreshing alternative in a part of the Latin Quarter mostly known for low-quality, tourist-trapping eateries. Offering imaginative, modern cuisine at fair prices, the place is packed. The bargain lunch *menu* includes a starter, main course, glass of wine, and coffee for €14. The three-course dinner *menu* at €30 is worth every *centime*. They pride themselves equally on their small-producers' wine list, so follow your server's advice (closed Sun-Mon, 8 Rue Thénard, reservations necessary, tel. 01 43 54 59 47).

## On Rue Mouffetard

Several blocks behind the Panthéon, Rue Mouffetard is a conveyor belt of comparison-shopping eaters with wall-to-wall budget options (fondue, crêpes, Italian, falafel, and Greek). Come here to sift through the crowds and eat cheaply. This street stays up late and likes to party (particularly around Place de la Contrescarpe). The gauntlet begins on top, at thriving Place de la Contrescarpe, and ends below where Rue Mouffetard stops at St. Médard Church. Both ends offer fun cafés where you can watch the action. The upper stretch is pedestrian and touristy; the bottom stretch is purely Parisian. Anywhere between is no-man's land for consistent quality. Still, strolling with so many fun-seekers is enjoyable, whether you eat or not. To get here, use the Censier Daubenton or Place Monge Métro stop.

**$$ Café Delmas,** at the top of Rue Mouffetard on picturesque Place de la Contrescarpe, is *the* place to see and be seen. Come here for a before- or after-dinner drink on the terrace, typical but pricey café cuisine, or great chocolate ice cream (open daily).

**$ Cave de Bourgogne,** a young and local hangout, has reasonably priced café fare at the bottom of Rue Mouffetard. The outside has picture-perfect tables on a raised terrace; the interior is warm and lively (€13-16 *plats*, specials listed on chalkboards, daily, 144 Rue Mouffetard—see map on page 411).

## In Montmartre

Much of Montmartre is extremely touristy, with mindless mobs following guides to cancan shows. But the ambience is undeniably fun, so either join in the touristic fray or walk a few blocks away and find a quieter, more authentic meal at one of the places I've listed below. For locations, see map on page 412.

### Near Sacré-Cœur

The steps in front of Sacré-Cœur are perfect for a picnic with a view, though the spot comes with lots of company. For a quieter setting, consider the park directly behind the church. Along the touristy main drag (near Place du Tertre and just off it), several fun piano bars serve mediocre crêpes but offer great people-watching. The options become less touristy and far more tasty as you get away from the top of the hill (skip any place on Place du Tertre). The Anvers Métro stop works well if you're visiting Sacré-Cœur or taking my Montmartre Walk (see those chapters). The Abbesses Métro stop will land you in the heart of the residential Montmartre neighborhood.

**$$$ Moulin de la Galette** lets you dine with Renoir under the historic windmill in a comfortable setting with good prices. Find the old photos scattered about the place (€23 two-course and €29 three-course *menus* at lunch only; €15 starters and €28 *plats* for dinner, daily, 83 Rue Lepic, Mo: Abbesses, tel. 01 46 06 84 77).

**$$ Restaurant Chez Plumeau,** just off jam-packed Place du Tertre, is touristy yet moderately priced, with formal service but great seating on a tiny, characteristic square (elaborate €17 salads, €18-22 *plats,* closed Tue Oct-April and Wed year-round, 4 Place du Calvaire, Mo: Abbesses, tel. 01 46 06 26 29).

**$ L'Eté en Pente Douce** is a good Montmartre choice, hiding under the generous branches of street trees. Just downhill from the crowds on a classic neighborhood corner, it features cheery indoor and outdoor seating, €10 *plats du jour* and salads, vegetarian options, and good wines (daily, many steps below Sacré-Cœur to the left as you leave, down the stairs below the WC, 23 Rue Muller, Mo: Anvers, tel. 01 42 64 02 67).

## Near Place des Abbesses

At the bottom of Montmartre, residents pile into a long lineup of brasseries and cafés near Place des Abbesses, especially along Rue des Abbesses and Rue des Martyrs. The food is average; the atmosphere is anything but. Come here for a lively, tourist-free scene. Rue des Abbesses is perfect for a picnic-gathering stroll with cheese shops, delis, wine stores, and bakeries. In fact, the baker at **Au Levain d'Antan** won the award for the best baguette in Paris in 2011 (Mon-Fri 7:30-20:00, closed Sat-Sun, 6 Rue des Abbesses). Unless another Métro stop is listed, use the Abbesses stop.

**$$ Le Miroir**'s kitchen is run by a young and enthusiastic chef cooking up seasonal French fare. Go for high quality ingredients served to a locals-only crowd. If you enjoyed the wine you had with your meal, cross the street to their wine shop and pick up a bottle to go (€26-33 two or three-course *menus,* Tue-Sat lunch and dinner, Sun lunch only, closed Mon, 94 Rue des Martyrs, tel. 01 46 06 50 73).

**$$ Autour de Midi et Minuit** is a classic French bistro sitting on top of a jazz cellar (see the Entertainment in Paris chapter for concert details). Hot food served upstairs; cool jazz served downstairs (lunch €15, dinner €26-33, closed Mon, 11 Rue Lepic, Mo: Blanche or Abbesses, tel. 01 55 79 16 48).

**$ Le Chinon Brasserie** offers good seating inside and out and is the best bet for café/wine bar ambience and food (daily, 49 Rue des Abbesses, tel. 01 42 62 07 17).

**$ Smooth in the City** provides a much-needed break from rich French fare. For €8.50 you get a fresh fruit smoothie, a healthy salad or veggie-packed sandwich, and a homemade dessert. Order it to go for your walk up the hill, or sit at one of their three outdoor tables (daily 10:00-19:00, 11 Rue des Abbesses, tel. 01 83 56 56 55).

**$ La Fourmi** sits at the bottom of the hill. Open all day, they offer the cheapest coffee and croissants in Montmartre, and simple, affordable lunches (€8-12). In the evening, the place is taken over by hilltop hipsters who come for the inexpensive beer and generous cheese plates (daily, 74 Rue des Martyrs, Mo: Anvers or Pigalle, tel. 01 42 64 70 35).

## Elsewhere in Paris
### Along Canal St. Martin, North of République
Escape the crowded tourist areas and enjoy a breezy canalside experience. Take the Métro to Place de la République, and walk down Rue Beaurepaire to Canal St. Martin. There you'll find a few worthwhile cafés with similarly reasonable prices. **$ La Marine** is a good choice (daily, 55 bis Quai de Valmy, tel. 01 42 39 69 81). In summertime most bars and cafés offer beer and wine to go *(à emporter)*, so you can take your drink to the canal's edge and picnic there with the younger crowd. If the weather's good, the park-like scene along the canal just south of Place de la Bastille is a delight for picnics.

### Dinner Cruises
The following companies all offer dinner cruises (reservations required). Bateaux-Mouches and Bateaux Parisiens have the best reputations and the highest prices. They offer multicourse meals and music in aircraft-carrier-size dining rooms with glass tops and good views. For both, proper dress is required—no denim, shorts, or sport shoes; Bateaux-Mouches requires a jacket and tie for men. The main difference between these companies is the music: Bateaux-Mouches offers violin and piano to entertain your romantic evening, whereas Bateaux Parisiens boasts a lively atmosphere with a singer, band, and dance floor.

**Bateaux-Mouches,** started in 1949, is hands-down the most famous. You can't miss its sparkling port on the north side of the river at Pont de l'Alma. The boats usually board 19:30-20:15, depart at 20:30, and return at 22:45 (€100-155/person, RER: Pont de l'Alma, tel. 01 42 25 96 10, www.bateaux-mouches.fr).

**Bateaux Parisiens** leaves from Port de la Bourdonnais, just east of the bridge under the Eiffel Tower. Begin boarding at 19:45, leave at 20:30, and return at 23:00 (€66-165/person, price depends on departure time, view seating, and *menu* option; tel. 01 76 64 14 45, www.bateauxparisiens.com). The middle level is best. Pay the few extra euros to get seats next to the windows—it's more romantic and private, with sensational views.

**Le Capitaine Fracasse** offers the budget option (€50/person, €80 with wine or champagne; reserve ahead—easy online—or get there early to secure a table; boarding times vary by season and day of week, walk down stairs in the middle of Bir-Hakeim bridge near the Eiffel Tower to Iles aux Cygne, Mo: Bir-Hakeim or RER: Champ de Mars-Tour Eiffel, tel. 01 46 21 48 15, www.croisiere-paris.com).

# Les Grands Cafés de Paris

Here's a short list of grand Parisian cafés, worth the detour only if you're not in a hurry or on a tight budget (some ask outrageous prices for a shot of espresso). Think of these cafés as monuments to another time, and learn why they matter as much today as they did yesterday (see sidebar). For tips on enjoying Parisian cafés, review the "Café Culture" section, on page 424.

## On and near St. Germain-des-Prés

For locations, see the map on page 452. Use the St. Germain-des-Prés Métro stop.

Where Boulevard St. Germain meets Rue Bonaparte you'll find two famous cafés (both open daily). **$$$ Les Deux Magots** offers prime outdoor seating and a warm interior. Once a favorite of Ernest Hemingway (in *The Sun Also Rises,* Jake met Brett here) and Jean-Paul Sartre (he and Simone de Beauvoir met here), today the café is filled with international tourists. **$$$ Le Café de Flore,** next door, feels more literary—wear your black turtleneck. Pablo Picasso was a regular at the time he painted *Guernica.*

Just a block away, **$ Café Bonaparte** offers scenic outdoor seating and the same delightful view for less. Perch here for coffee or a light lunch (on the sunny side of the street, from Les Deux Magots, one block up Rue Bonaparte toward river, tel. 01 43 26 42 81).

Paris' first and most famous, **$ Café le Procope** (1686) was a *café célèbre*, drawing notables such as Voltaire, Rousseau, Honoré de Balzac, Emile Zola, Maximilien de Robespierre, Victor Hugo, and two Americans, Benjamin Franklin and Thomas Jefferson. Have a drink but not a meal. The dining rooms are beautiful, but the cuisine is average (daily 10:00-24:00, 13 Rue de l'Ancienne Comédie, tel. 01 40 46 79 00). To reach it from Café Bonaparte, walk down Rue de l'Abbaye, then continue onto Rue de Bourbon-le-Château.

EATING IN PARIS

## History of Cafés in Paris

The first café in the Western world was in Paris—established in 1686 at Le Procope (still a restaurant today; see listing). The French had just discovered coffee, and their robust economy was growing a population of pleasure-seekers and thinkers looking for places to be seen, to exchange ideas, and to plot revolutions—both political and philosophical. And with the advent of theaters such as La Comédie-Française, the necessary artsy, coffee-sipping crowds were born. By 1700, more than 300 cafés had opened their doors; at the time of the Revolution (1789), there were more than 1,800 cafés in Paris. Revolutionaries from Jean-Paul Marat and Napoleon to Salvador Dalí enjoyed the spirit of freethinking that the cafés engendered.

Café society took off in the early 1900s. Life was changing rapidly, with new technology and wars on a global scale. Many retreated to Parisian cafés to try to make sense of the confusion. Vladimir Lenin, Leon Trotsky, Igor Stravinsky, Ernest Hemingway, F. Scott Fitzgerald, James Joyce, Albert Einstein, Jean-Paul Sartre, Simone de Beauvoir, Gene Openshaw, and Albert Camus were among the devoted café society. Some practically lived at their favorite café, where they kept their business calendars, entertained friends, and ate every meal. Parisian apartments were small, walls were thin (still often the case), and heating (particularly during war times) was minimal, making the warmth of cafés all the harder to leave.

There are more than 12,000 cafés in Paris today, though their numbers are shrinking. They're still used for business meetings, encounter sessions, political discussions, and romantic interludes. Most Parisians are loyal to their favorites and know their waiter's children's names.

Veer left on the picturesque Rue de Buci (more cafés), and turn right on Rue de l'Ancienne Comédie.

### Near Luxembourg Garden

An eclectic assortment of historic cafés gathers along the busy Boulevard du Montparnasse near its intersection with Boulevard Raspail (Mo: Vavin). Combine these historic cafés with a visit to Luxembourg Garden, which lies just a few blocks away, down Rue Vavin (next to Le Select). For locations, see map on page 452.

**$$ La Coupole,** built in the 1920s, was decorated by aspiring artists (Fernand Léger, Constantin Brancusi, and Marc Chagall, among others) in return for free meals. It still supports artists with regular showings on its vast walls. This cavernous café feels like a classy train station, with acres of seating, brass decor, and tuxedoed waiters by the dozen. Bring your friends and make noise. The food is fine; the service can be impersonal, but that's not the reason you came (€28-38 *menus* daily, food served from 12:00 until the wee hours, come early to get better service, 102 Boulevard du Montparnasse, tel. 01 43 20 14 20).

**$$ Le Select,** more easygoing and traditional, was once popular with the more rebellious types—Leon Trotsky, Jean Cocteau, and Pablo Picasso loved it. It feels rather conformist today, with good outdoor seating and pleasant tables just inside the door—though the locals hang out at the bar farther inside (daily, 99 Boulevard du Montparnasse, across from La Coupole, tel. 01 45 48 38 24).

## On Avenue des Champs-Elysées

To reach these two cafés, use the George V Métro stop. These are also described in more detail in the Champs-Elysées Walk chapter.

**$$$ Fouquet's,** which opened in 1899, has played host to coachmen, biplane fighter pilots, artists, today's celebrities...and tourists. Though the intimidating interior is impressive, the outdoor setting is Champs-Elysées great, with pay-for-view €8 espresso (daily, 99 Avenue des Champs-Elysées, tel. 01 47 23 70 60).

**$$ Ladurée,** two blocks downhill, is a classic on Paris' grandest boulevard (Mon-Sat 7:30-24:00, Sun 8:30-24:00, a block below Avenue George V at #75, tel. 01 40 75 08 75).

## On Place de la Concorde

**$$$ Hôtel Crillon's** four-star elegance can be yours for an afternoon. Considered among the most exclusive (and expensive) hotels in Paris, it gives you a taste of royal life that Louis would appreciate. Wear the best clothes you packed, arrive after 15:00, let the bellhop spin the door, and settle into the royal chairs in the *salon du thé*. You'll be surrounded by famous people you won't recognize (about €10 for a pot of tea or double café au lait, about €40 for high tea served daily, €48 if you toss in a glass of champagne, 15:30-18:00, 10 Place de la Concorde, Mo: Concorde).

## Near the Louvre

For locations, see the Louvre map on page 123.

**$$ Café le Nemours,** a staunchly Parisian fixture serving pricey but good light lunches, is tucked into the corner of the Palais Royal adjacent to the Comédie Française. Relish its elegant brass and Art Deco style, along with its outdoor tables that get good afternoon sun. Only two minutes from the pyramid, it's a great post-Louvre retreat (fun and filling €10-12 *croque monsieur* and salads, open daily; leaving the Louvre, cross Rue de Rivoli and veer left to 2 Place Colette; Mo: Palais Royal, tel. 01 42 61 34 14).

**$ Le Fumoir** is another classy place, with brown leather couches perfect for kicking back with a coffee or cocktail (€19 lunch *menu*, daily, 6 Rue de l'Amiral de Coligny, near Louvre-Rivoli Métro stop, tel. 01 42 92 00 24).

## At Gare de Lyon

**$$$ Le Train Bleu** is a grandiose restaurant with a low-slung, leather-couch café-bar area built right into the train station for the Paris Exhibition of 1900 (which also saw the construction of the Pont Alexandre III and the Grand and Petit Palais). It's simply a

grand-scale-everything experience, with over-the-top belle époque decor that speaks of another age, when going to dinner was an event—a chance to see and be seen—and intimate dining was out. Forty-one massive paintings of scenes along the old rail lines tempt diners to consider a getaway. Many films have featured this restaurant. Reserve ahead for dinner, or drop in for a drink before your train leaves (€57 *menu*, €8 beer, €6 espresso, daily, up the stairs opposite track L, tel. 01 43 43 09 06, www.le-train-bleu.com).

## Honorable Mentions

**$ Café de la Mosquée,** behind the Jardin des Plantes and attached to Paris' largest mosque (see map on page 411), beams you straight to Morocco, with outdoor courtyards and an interior room, all in North African tearoom decor with a full menu to match (reasonably priced couscous, daily 10:00-23:00, 39 Rue Geoffroy St. Hilaire, Mo: Place Monge, tel. 01 43 31 38 20). Consider an afternoon tea-and-pastry stop (€2 pastries, eat in or take out).

**$ Café la Palette,** on *le* Left Bank, is across the river and a few blocks from the Louvre. Over 100 years old, this café feels real and unaffected by the passage of time (well-priced drinks, 43 Rue de Seine, Mo: Mabillon). For more on this café, see page 271 in the Left Bank Walk.

**$ Au Sauvignon Café,** the smallest of the cafés described in this section, is perfectly positioned for people-watching near Sèvres-Babylone boutiques (see map on page 452). The interior is vintage Paris, with wall-to-ceiling decor and a fine zinc bar (daily, 10 Rue de Sèvres, Mo: Sèvres-Babylone, tel. 01 45 48 49 02).

# PARIS WITH CHILDREN

Paris works surprisingly well with children—smart parents enjoy the "fine art" of simply being in Paris' great neighborhoods, parks, and monuments while watching their kids revel in the City of Light. After enjoying the city's most family-friendly sights, your children may want to return to Paris before you do.

## Before You Go

Choose hotels in a kid-friendly area near a park. The Rue Cler and Luxembourg neighborhoods are both good. If you're staying a week or more, rent an apartment (see page 416).

If traveling with infants, plan on bringing a light stroller *(pousette)* and a child backpack *(porte bébé)*. Strollers are ideal for neighborhood walks, of course, whereas backpacks are generally better for public transit. Strollers usually work fine on the bus (enter through buses' larger central doors, then park the stroller in the designated *pousette* area...if there's room) but they're tough in the Métro (miles of stairs). Many sights prohibit either strollers or backpacks, but usually not both (some museums that don't allow backpacks even provide strollers).

## Kids' Reading List

Get your kids into the Parisian spirit with books and movies about France. Watch or read the Madeline stories by Ludwig Bemelmans, *The Hunchback of Notre-Dame* by Victor Hugo, *The Three Musketeers* by Alexandre Dumas, or Dumas' *Man in the Iron Mask*.

## Parenting French-Style

Famous for their topless tanning, French women are equally comfortable with public breastfeeding of young babies—no need for shawls or hooter hiders here. Changing tables are nonexistent, so bring a roll-up changing mat and get comfortable changing your baby on your knees, on a bench, or wherever you find enough space.

French grandmothers take their role as community elders seriously and won't hesitate to recommend that you put more sunscreen on your child in the summer, or add a layer of clothing if it's breezy.

For older kids, be aware that the drinking age is 16 for beer and wine and 18 for the hard stuff: Your waiter will assume that your teen will have wine with you at dinner. Teens are also welcome in most bars and lounges (there's no 21-and-older section).

*Anni's Diary of France,* by Anni Axworthy, is a picture-filled book about a young girl's trip; it could inspire your children.

*How Would You Survive in the Middle Ages?* by Fiona MacDonald is an appealing "guide" for kids. Serious kid historians will devour *The Kingfisher History Encyclopedia. Paris,* by Renzo Rossi, is a fun introduction to the city and its history, told mainly through illustrations. *Cathedral,* by David Macauley, re-creates the building of a French Gothic cathedral in detailed pen-and-ink sketches. If your children are interested in art, get your hands on *The History of Art for Young People* by Anthony Janson and *Discovering Great Artists: Hands-On Art for Children in the Styles of the Great Masters* by MaryAnn Kohl. (Also see "Recommended Books and Movies," including some good choices for teenagers, on page 662 of the appendix.)

Bring along plenty of kids' books; they're harder to find and more expensive in Paris. If you run out, visit one of the English-language bookstores listed on page 32.

### Tips

These tips will help your children—and you—have a better trip.
- Give your kids a business card from your hotel, along with your contact information, just in case you get separated.
- Involve your children in the trip. Let them help choose daily activities, lead you through the Métro, and so on.
- Follow this book's crowd-beating tips to the letter. Kids despise long lines even more than you do.
- Eat dinner early, before the sophisticated Parisian crowd dines (aim for 19:00-19:30 at restaurants, earlier at cafés).

Skip romantic places. Look for cafés (or fast-food restaurants) where kids can move around without bothering others. For a review of kid-friendly restaurants, check www.bebeguide. com/restaurants-et-cafes-avec-bebe/2 (though the site is in French, the key information—addresses, prices, and photos—is easy enough to glean). Picnics work well. *Boulangeries* are good places to grab off-hour snacks when restaurants aren't serving.

- To up your toy supply, check large department stores, such as Bon Marché, which tend to have a good selection (see the Shopping in Paris chapter). Visit a bookstore to pick out books together (see page 32).

- Learn and play *boules,* a form of outdoor bowling (for the rules, see the sidebar on page 386). The best thing we did on one trip was to buy our own set of *boules.* We'd play before dinner, side by side with real players at the neighborhood park. Buy your *boules de pétanque* at the Décathlon sports store (Mon-Sat 9:30-20:00, closed Sun, in Commercial les Trois Quartiers mini-mall, 23 Boulevard de la Madeleine, Mo: Madeleine, check their website for other locations, www.decathlon.fr). The *boules* make great (if weighty) souvenirs and also provide entertainment (and memories) once you're back home.

- Check the Paris TI website for hours and prices on children's activities, including shows, museums, and park events (www. parisinfo.com).

- Since school lets out early on Wednesdays, expect Wednesday afternoons to be busy days at parks and other children's sights.

- Consider hiring a babysitter for a night or two—check http:// paris.fr.craigslist.org, or Google "babysitting in Paris." You could also ask your hotelier for a babysitting recommendation.

- Consider visiting an amusement park (such as the one in Tuileries Garden, or Disneyland Paris—both described later) as an end-of-trip reward.

## Top Kids' Activities and Sights

### Parks

Paris's public parks are perhaps your single best source of kid-friendly fun (especially on Wednesdays, when school gets out early). Besides providing an outlet for high-energy kids (and a chance for the whole family to take a sightseeing breather), Parisian parks host a variety of activities, many of them with a quintessentially French flair.

**Marionette shows,** called *guignols* (geen-yohl), can be interesting for children patient enough to sit still. Shows are in French, of course, but have fairly easy-to-follow plots and some internationally understood slapstick (look for them in bigger parks, such as Luxembourg Garden, and check *Pariscope* or *L'Officiel des Spectacles*, under "Marionettes," for times and places). *Boules* are played nearly everywhere (for rules, see page 386). Temporary **amusement parks** pop up in public parks throughout the city; the summer Ferris wheel and rides in the Tuileries Garden are the best—my daughter preferred them to Disneyland Paris. You can rent **toy boats** to sail on a park's pond, or rent real **rowboats** at bigger parks, such as in Versailles' gardens (along the Grand Canal) or in the huge Bois de Vincennes (€12/hour, refundable deposit, Mo: Porte Dorée). Bigger parks can be perfect for a relaxing **bike ride. Pony rides** are offered on certain days in some parks, such as Luxembourg Garden, the Champ de Mars, and the Bois de Vincennes; to learn when and where the ponies are trotting, check www.animaponey.com or call 06 07 32 53 95.

**Luxembourg Garden**—This is my favorite place to mix kid business with pleasure. This perfectly Parisian park has it all—from tennis courts to cafés—as well as an extensive big-toys play area

with imaginative slides, swings, jungle gyms, rope towers, and chess games (see map on page 277). To find the big-toys play area, head to the southwest corner (small fee, entry good all day, many parents watch from chairs outside the play area, open daily, usually 10:00-19:00 in summer, until 16:00 in winter, pay WC nearby). Kids also like the speedy merry-go-round (small fee), the pony rides (by the tennis courts), and the toy rental sailboats in the main pond (activities open daily in summer, otherwise only Wed and Sat-Sun). Near the main building is a toddler wading pool (summer only) and sand pit (both free). A puppet theater hosts *guignol* shows, located in the southwest corner of the park near the children's play area (about €5, Sat-Sun at 11:00 and 15:30, Wed at 15:30, daily mid-July-mid-Aug, in French, 45 minutes, no air-con, tel. 01 43 26 46 47). The park has many shaded paths as well as big, open areas perfect for kicking a ball. Kids can even play in the grass opposite the palace (Mo: St. Sulpice, Odéon, or Notre-Dame-des-Champs).

**Tuileries Garden**—This central park, located between the Louvre and Place de la Concorde, across the river from the Orsay Museum, comes in handy for kid breaks. You'll find the usual children's activities on Wednesdays, Saturdays, and Sundays (toy sailboat rental in pond and pony rides) and fun trampolines in the northwest corner of the park near the Place de la Concorde Métro stop (€2 for 5-10 minutes, 2-12-year-olds only, daily April-Sept 11:00-19:00, closes earlier in off-season, see map on page 63 for specific location). Nearby is a play area with rope towers and slides, and an old-fashioned merry-go-round. The Tuileries Garden also hosts a summer fair with rides, games, and a huge Ferris wheel.

**Jardin des Plantes**—These colorful gardens are a must for gardeners and good for kids. Located on the Left Bank southeast of the Latin Quarter, the park is short on grass but long on kid activities, including several play areas and two kid-friendly natural-science museums (both closed Tue and described below). There's also a zoo, but it has just a few animals in old cages. From the park entrance near the river on Place Valhubert, you'll find these museums lining the left side of the park (Mo: Gare d'Austerlitz or Jussieu).

Young kids enjoy the dinosaur exhibit at the **Galerie d'Anatomie Comparée et de Paléontologie;** there are no English explanations, but they're not really needed (adults-€7, under age 27-free, not covered by Museum Pass, Wed-Mon 10:00-17:00, until 18:00 on April-Sept weekends, closed Tue, busiest on weekends, entrance faces river next to McDonald's).

The **Grande Galerie de l'Evolution,** at the non-river end of the park, is a dazzling museum describing the evolution of animals. It features a giant whale skeleton, tons of dead bugs under glass, all sorts of taxidermied animals, and many other cool exhibits. Pick up the English map and look for the good English explanations (*fiches de lecture)* inserted into wood benches throughout the park (adults-€7, under age 27-free, not covered by Museum Pass, Wed-Mon 10:00-18:00, closed Tue, busiest on weekends, gift shop may have some helpful books in English, tel. 01 40 79 30 00, www.mnhn.fr). On weekends and Wednesdays, you can pay extra to visit the **Galerie des Enfants du Muséum,** a cool series of exhibits within the Galerie de l'Evolution. It's stuffed with animal-centric interactive displays and activities designed for 6- to 12-year-olds, all in English. Visitors are admitted only at 15-minute intervals, and the gallery can fill up fast—consider booking a time slot online a few days ahead (adults-€9—includes Galerie de l'Evolution admission, kids-€7, Wed and Sat-Sun 10:00-18:00, last entry at 16:45, tel. 01 40 79 54 79, www.galeriedesenfants.fr/en).

Turn right out of the Grande Galerie de l'Evolution to leave the park and find the Paris Mosque and the recommended Moroccan-themed Café de la Mosquée (see page 461).

**Parc de la Villette**—This vast area of parks and museums has outdoor concerts, outdoor movies, a playground that's great for summer visits, and grass you're allowed to run around on (a rare treat in Paris). Main attractions for kids are Europe's largest science museum (Cité des Sciences et de l'Industrie), an IMAX theater, a real French submarine, acres of parks, and a working canal (211

Avenue Jean Jaurès, tel. 01 40 03 75 75, Mo: Porte de la Villette, follow Corentin-Cariou or Porte de Pantin signs).

**Cité des Sciences et de l'Industrie:** For families, the best part of this big science-museum complex is **Cité des Enfants,** a fun place that's perfect for simultaneously teaching and exhausting your children. Kids can climb inside a living ant farm, operate a crane (safety vest and too-cute hard hat provided), create whirlpools in the water exhibit, step into a tornado, film themselves driving down the highway in front of a green screen, and much more. Tickets are sold for a specific 1.5-hour time slot, and for one of two sections of the museum: the area designed for 2-7-year-olds, or the one designed for 5-12-year-olds (adults-€8, kids-€6, Mon-Tue starting at 10:00, 11:45, 13:30, or 15:15; Sat-Sun starting at 10:30, 12:30, 14:30, or 16:30; www.cite-sciences.fr). There is a great health-food café on the ground floor, an indoor picnic space, and a bookshop to keep you busy while you wait for your entrance time.

The science exhibit designed for adults, the Expositions d'Explora, is dense—likely to appeal only to hard-core science fans and teenagers on the honor roll (adults-€8, under 26-€6, open same hours as main Cité des Sciences complex: Tue-Sat 10:00-18:00, Sun 10:00-19:00, closed Mon, no specific entrance time required).

A mid-sized 1950s military **submarine** is permanently parked outside the Cité des Sciences. It comes with videos, buttons to press, a working periscope, and tight quarters—even on uncrowded days (€3, closes 30 minutes before rest of Cité des Sciences).

## Biking and Rollerblading

**Biking**—Take your kids out for a bike ride. If the city's streets seem too intimidating, consider heading to one of the parks outside the city center—many of them are great for biking, and even offer rental (such as the gardens of Versailles). **Bike About Tours** has good information and kid-friendly bike solutions (baby seats, tandem attachments, kid-sized bikes). They also offer family tours of Paris and Versailles that include fun activities (€200 for the first 2 people, €25/person after that, 4 hours; for contact information, see page 44).

**Rollerblading**—Remember that Sunday afternoons are fun for skating with locals at your own pace, starting at south side of Place de la Bastille at 14:30 (see page 44, www.rollers-coquillages.org; skate-rental shop nearby).

## Riverboat Rides

A variety of companies offer one-hour Seine cruises on huge glass-domed boats, with departures until 22:30 (best at twilight or after dark). Or hop on a Batobus, a river bus connecting eight stops along the river: Eiffel Tower, Orsay Museum, St. Germain-des-Prés, Notre-Dame, Jardin des Plantes, Hôtel de Ville, the Louvre, and Pont Alexandre III—near the Champs-Elysées. Longer boat trips ply the tranquil waters of a peaceful canal between the Bastille and Bassin de la Villette (see page 46).

## Bus and Car Tours

The double-decker bus tours (see page 45) are a good way to begin your visit. Taking a nighttime tour in a convertible Deux Chevaux is a terrific way to end your trip (page 500).

## Watery Fun

Paris has more than three dozen swimming pools. You can ask your hotelier for the location of the nearest pool, or head for one of the places listed below. Note that boys and men are required to wear Speedo-style (tight) swimsuits at pools *(oh la la!)*; and some public pools require everyone to wear a swim cap (bring one with you, or find them at a local Monoprix or Décathlon sporting-goods store).

**Aquaboulevard**—Paris' best pool/waterslide/miniature golf complex is easy to reach and a complete escape from the museum scene. Indoor and outdoor pools with high-flying slides, waves, geysers, and whirlpool tubs draw kids of all ages. It's pricey (and steamy inside) but a good opportunity to see soaked Parisians at play (kids under 12-€16/6 hours, adults-€28/6 hours, much cheaper rates for more than one visit, daily 9:00-23:00, English-speaking staff, keep a €1 coin for lockers, men's swimsuits sell for €6-10 at the Décathlon store right there, see map on page 476 for location, tel. 01 40 60 10 00, www.aquaboulevard.fr). Ride the Métro to the end of line 8 (Balard stop), walk two blocks under the elevated freeway, veer left across the traffic circle, and find Aquaboulevard in a complex of theaters and shops.

**Joséphine Baker Pool (Piscine Joséphine Baker)**—Housed in a giant barge docked along the Seine, this state-of-the-art floating swimming pool boasts generous wood decks, and views of the city that get even better (though the pool gets more crowded) on sunny days, when the retractable rooftop is opened up (€5 for first 2 hours, then €2.60/hour, daily approximately 13:00-21:00, opens earlier in summer, cabana-type cafés next door, near Gare d'Austerlitz at 8 Quai François Mauriac, Mo: Quai de la Gare or François Mitterrand, tel. 01 56 61 96 50, www.paris.fr).

## Attractions

When it comes to sightseeing with kids, don't overdo it. Tackle one key sight each day (Louvre, Orsay, Versailles), and mix it with a healthy dose of lighter activities. To minimize unnecessary travel, try to match kid activities with areas where you'll be sightseeing (e.g., the Louvre is near the kid-friendly Palais Royal's courtyards and Tuileries Garden). Kids prefer the Louvre after dark, when it's less busy (Wed and Fri only).

Note: At some sights (such as the Army Museum and Arc de Triomphe), Museum Pass-holders must wait in line to pick up their free children's tickets.

**Eiffel Tower and Nearby**—You could fill an entire kid-centric day here. Come early and ride the elevator up the tower before crowds appear, or ride it above the lights at night (✪ see the Eiffel Tower Tour chapter). The **Champ de Mars** park stretches out from the tower's base, with picnic-perfect benches, big toys, sand pits, pony rides, puppet shows, and pedal go-carts. Big toys are located at the non-river end of the park (with your back to the tower, it's to the right). The pony rides, puppet shows, and go-carts are in the center in the park (usually after 11:00 Wed, Sat-Sun, and on all summer days; after 15:00 otherwise, Mo: Ecole Militaire, RER-C: Champ de Mars-Tour Eiffel, or bus #69).

All ages enjoy the view from Trocadéro, across the river from the Eiffel Tower, especially after dark (Mo: Trocadéro). The terrific **National Maritime Museum** (Musée National de la Marine) is docked at Trocadéro, with all things nautical, including wonderful ship models (see listing on page 68; the **Musée de l'Homme** anthropological museum next door is closed through 2013). The **Cinéaqua** aquarium/cinema in the gardens below the Trocadéro boasts 10,000 fish in more than 40 tanks, along with kids' movies—I know, it's an odd combination (students and kids under 12-€12.50, ages 13-17-€16, adults-€20, daily 10:00-19:00, 5 Avenue Albert de Mun, Mo: Trocadéro, tel. 01 40 69 23 23, www.cineaqua.com).

**Notre-Dame**—Paris' famous Gothic cathedral doesn't have to be just old and boring. Replay Quasimodo's stunt and climb the tower (go early to avoid long lines). Kids love being on such a lofty perch with a face-to-face look at a gargoyle. The crypt on the square in front of Notre-Dame is quick and interesting (covered by Museum Pass). Kids can push buttons to highlight remains of Roman Paris and leave with a better understanding of how different civilizations build on top of each other. The small but beautiful park along the river outside Notre-Dame's right transept has sandboxes, picnic benches, and space to run (Mo: Cité). My preteen son loved the traffic-free lanes of the Latin Quarter across the river.
✪ See the Historic Paris Walk chapter.

**Arc de Triomphe and the Champs-Elysées—** This area is popular with teenagers, day and night. Mine couldn't get enough of it. Watch the crazy traffic rush around the Arc de Triomphe for endless entertainment, then stroll Avenue des Champs-Elysées with its car dealerships (particularly Renault's razzle-dazzle café), Virgin Megastore (music), Disney store, and the river of humanity that flows along its broad sidewalks. Take your teenager to see a movie on the Champs-Elysées ("v.o." next to the showtime means it's shown in the original language).

○ See the Champs-Elysées Walk chapter.

**Pompidou Center—**Teens like the Pompidou Center for its crazy outdoor entertainers, throngs of young people, happening cafés, and fun fountains next door (but it's dead on Tue, when museum is closed). Inside, the temporary exhibits and gift shop on the main floor are visually impressive.

The *Star Wars*-esque escalator to the top is a kick for all ages, but it's not free—you need a Museum Pass, a Pompidou combo-ticket, or a €3 Panorama ticket to escalate (Mo: Rambuteau).

○ See the Pompidou Center Tour chapter.

## Near Paris
### Versailles

This massive conglomeration of palaces, gardens, fountains, and forest can be brutal—or a good family getaway if well-planned. Avoid Tuesdays and Sundays, when the place is packed from open to close; the gardens also get crowded on summer weekends, when the fountains are flowing. On other days, arrive around 11:00, and do the gardens first and the interior later, when crowds subside. Note that strollers are allowed in the gardens, but not inside the palace (you'll have to check yours). Rent a bike and let the kids go wild on park paths (bikes of all sizes are available, even toddler bikes with training wheels). Or explore the gardens in a rented golf cart—while pricey (€30/hour), it's great fun and extremely easy.

(For liability reasons, the staff wants only parents to do the driving, but once away from the palace...) Or you can row row row a boat on the Grand Canal. The Domaine de Marie-Antoinette has trails for scampering on, and her Hamlet has barnyard animals up close and personal (keep in mind that the Domaine does not open until noon).

⚙ See the Versailles chapter.

## Disneyland Paris

Europe's Disneyland is a remake of California's, with most of the same rides and smiles. The main difference is that Mickey Mouse speaks French, and you can buy wine with your lunch. My kids went ducky for it.

Disneyland is easy to get to, and may be worth a day—if Paris is handier than Florida or California.

### Getting to Disneyland Paris
**By Train:** The slick 45-minute RER trip is the best way to get to Disneyland from downtown Paris. Take RER line A-4 to Marne-la-Vallée-Chessy (check the signs over the platform to be sure Marne-la-Vallée-Chessy is served, because the line splits near the end). Catch it from Paris' Charles de Gaulle-Etoile, Auber, Châtelet-Les Halles, or Gare de Lyon stations (at least 3/hour, drops you 45 minutes later right in the park, about €8 each way). The last train back to Paris leaves shortly after midnight. When returning, remember to use the same RER ticket for your Métro connection in Paris.

**By Bus and Train from the Airport:** Both of Paris' major airports have direct shuttle buses to Disneyland Paris (every 20 minutes, daily 8:30-20:00ish, €19). Fast TGV trains run from Charles de Gaulle to Disneyland in 10 minutes, but they're less frequent and pricier—the shuttle bus makes more sense.

**By Car:** Disneyland is about 40 minutes (20 miles) east of Paris on the A-4 autoroute (direction Nancy/Metz, exit #14). Parking is about €15/day at the park.

### Dis-Orientation
The Disneyland Paris Resort is a sprawling complex housing two theme parks (Disneyland Paris and Walt Disney Studios), a few entertainment venues, and several hotels. Opened in 1992, it was the second Disney resort built outside the US (Tokyo was first).

With upward of 15 million visitors a year, it quickly became Europe's single leading tourist destination. Mickey has arrived.

**Disneyland Paris:** This park has a corner on the fun market, with the classic rides and Disney characters you came to see. You'll find familiar favorites wrapped in French packaging, like Space Mountain (a.k.a. *De la Terre à la Lune*) and Pirates of the Caribbean *(Pirates des Caraïbes)*.

**Walt Disney Studios:** This zone has a Hollywood focus geared for an older crowd, with animation, special effects, and movie magic "rides." The cinema-themed rides include CinéMagique (a slow-motion cruise through film history on a people-mover, mixing film clips, audio-animatronic figures, and live actors); Studio Tram Tour: Behind the Magic (another slow-mo ride, this time mostly outdoors, through a "movie backlot"); and Moteurs... Action! Stunt Show Spectacular (an actual movie sequence is filmed with stunt drivers, audience bit players, and brash MTV-style hosts). The top thrill rides include the Rock 'n' Roller Coaster (which starts out by accelerating from a standstill to 57 miles per hour in less than three seconds, all while Aerosmith tunes blast in your ears) and the Twilight Zone Tower of Terror (which drops passengers from a precarious 200-foot-high perch).

**Skipping Lines:** The free FASTPASS system is a worthwhile timesaver for the nine most popular rides. At the ride, insert your park admission ticket into the FASTPASS machine, which spits out a ticket printed with your return time—often within 45 minutes (you may only have one FASTPASS ticket at a time). You'll also save time by buying your park tickets ahead (at airport TIs, some Métro stations, or along the Champs-Elysées at the Disney Store, or Virgin Megastore).

**Cost:** Disneyland Paris and Walt Disney Studios charge the same. You can pay separately for each or buy a combined "Hopper" ticket for both. A one-day pass to either park is about €50 for adults and €45 for kids aged 3-11 (check their website for special offers). Kids under 3 are free.

A two-day Hopper ticket for entry to both parks is about €120 for adults (less for kids); a three-day Hopper ticket is about €150. Regular prices are discounted about 25 percent Nov-March, and promotions are offered occasionally (check www.disneylandparis.com).

**Hours:** Disneyland—daily 10:00-19:00, later on weekends, until 23:00 mid-May-Aug, hours fluctuate with the seasons—check website for precise times. Walt Disney Studios—summer daily 10:00-19:00; winter Mon-Fri 10:00-18:00, Sat-Sun until 19:00.

**Information:** Disney brochures are in every Paris hotel. For more info and to make reservations, call 01 60 30 60 53, or try www.disneylandparis.com.

**Avoiding Crowds:** Saturday, Sunday, Wednesday, public holidays, and any day in July and August are the most crowded. After dinner, crowds are gone.

**Eating with Mickey:** Food is fun and not outrageously priced. (Still, many smuggle in a picnic.)

### Sleeping at Disneyland

Most are better off sleeping in the real world (i.e., Paris), though with direct buses and freeways to both airports, Disneyland makes a convenient first- or last-night stop. Seven different Disney-owned hotels offer accommodations at or near the park in all price ranges. Prices are impossible to pin down, as they vary by season and by the package deal you choose (deals that include park entry are usually a better value). To reserve any Disneyland hotel, call 01 60 30 60 53, or check www.disneylandparis.com. The prices you'll be quoted include entry to the park. **Hôtel Santa Fe**** offers a fair mid-range value, with frequent shuttle service to the park. Another cheap option is **Davy Crockett's Ranch,** but you'll need a car to stay there. The most expensive is the **Disneyland Hotel****, right at the park entry, about three times the price of the Santa Fe. The **Dream Castle Hotel**** is another higher-end choice, with nearly 400 rooms done up to look like a lavish 17th-century palace (40 Avenue de la Fosse des Pressoirs, tel. 01 64 17 90 00, www.dreamcastle-hotel.com, info@dreamcastle-hotel.com).

# SHOPPING IN PARIS

Even staunch anti-shoppers may be tempted to indulge in chic Paris. Wandering among elegant and outrageous boutiques provides a break from the heavy halls of the Louvre, and, if you approach it right, a little cultural enlightenment.

In this chapter, you'll find information on shopping for souvenirs, clothing, food, and bargains. Most travelers are interested in finding a few souvenirs and maybe an article of clothing. Here's a simple approach that works for most:

- If you need just souvenirs, find a souvenir shop or consult your neighborhood supermarket for that Parisian box of tea, jam, or cookies—perfect for tucking into your suitcase at the last minute.
- For more elaborate purchases, large department stores provide painless one-stop shopping in elegant surroundings.
- Neighborhood boutiques offer the greatest reward at the highest risk. Clerks and prices can be intimidating, but the selection is more original and the experience is purely Parisian.
- Don't leave souvenir shopping for Sunday, when most stores are buttoned up tight.
- For information on VAT refunds and customs regulations, see page 15.
- Even if you don't intend to buy anything, budget some time for window-shopping. The expression for "window-shopping" in French is *faire du lèche-vitrines*—"window-licking."

## Tips on Shopping

Before you enter a Parisian store, remember the following points:

- In small stores, always say, *"Bonjour, Madame* or *Mademoiselle* or *Monsieur"* when entering. And remember to say *"Au revoir, Madame* or *Mademoiselle* or *Monsieur"* when leaving.

## Key Phrases

| English | French | Pronounced |
|---|---|---|
| Just looking. | *Je regarde.* | zhuh ruh-gar |
| How much is it? | *Combien?* | kohm-bee-ehn |
| Too big/ small/expensive | *Trop grand/ petit/cher* | troh grahn/ puh-tee/sher |
| May I try it on? | *Je peux l'essayer?* | zhuh puh luh-say-yay |
| Can I see more? | *Auriez vous autre chose à me proposer?* | oh-ree-ay vooz oh-truh shohz ah muh proh-poh-zay |
| I'd like this. | *Je voudrais ça.* | zhuh voo-dray sah |
| On sale | *Solde* | sold |
| Discounted price | *Prix réduit* | pree ray-dwee |
| Big discounts | *Prix choc* | pree shock |

- The customer is not always right. In fact, figure the clerk is doing you a favor by waiting on you.
- Except in department stores, it's not normal for the customer to handle clothing. Ask first before you pick up an item: "*Je peux?*" (zhuh puh), meaning, "Can I?"
- For clothing size comparisons between the US and France, see page 667 of the appendix.
- Forget returns (and don't count on exchanges).
- Saturday afternoons are *très* busy and not for the faint of heart.
- Observe French shoppers. Then imitate.
- Stores are generally closed on Sunday, except at the Carrousel du Louvre (underground shopping mall at the Louvre), and some shops near Sèvres-Babylone, along the Champs-Elysées, and in the Marais.
- Some small stores don't open until 14:00 on Mondays.
- Don't feel obliged to buy. If a shopkeeper offers assistance, just say, "*Je regarde, merci.*"

## Souvenir Shops

Avoid souvenir carts in front of famous monuments. You can find cheaper gifts around the Pompidou Center, on the streets of Montmartre, and in some department stores (see page 477). The riverfront stalls near Notre-Dame sell a variety of used books, old posters and postcards, magazines, refrigerator magnets, and other tourist

# Shopping in Paris

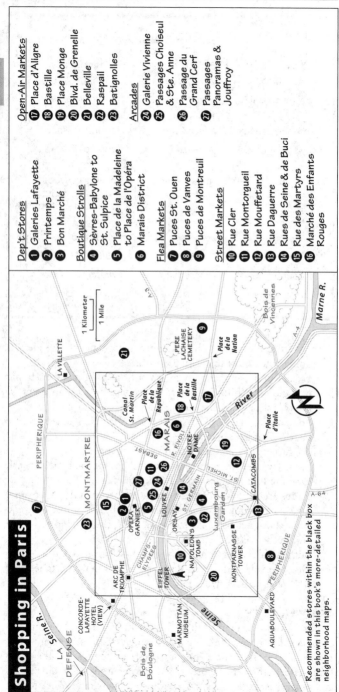

**Dep't Stores**
1. Galeries Lafayette
2. Printemps
3. Bon Marché

**Boutique Strolls**
4. Sèvres-Babylone to St. Sulpice
5. Place de la Madeleine to Place de l'Opéra
6. Marais District

**Flea Markets**
7. Puces St. Ouen
8. Puces de Vanves
9. Puces de Montreuil

**Street Markets**
10. Rue Cler
11. Rue Montorgueil
12. Rue Mouffetard
13. Rue Daguerre
14. Rues de Seine & de Buci
15. Rue des Martyrs
16. Marché des Enfants Rouges

**Open-Air Markets**
17. Place d'Aligre
18. Bastille
19. Place Monge
20. Blvd. de Grenelle
21. Belleville
22. Raspail
23. Batignolles

**Arcades**
24. Galerie Vivienne
25. Passages Choiseul & Ste. Anne
26. Passage du Grand Cerf
27. Passages Panoramas & Jouffroy

Recommended stores within the black box are shown in this book's more-detailed neighborhood maps.

paraphernalia in the most romantic setting; see "*Les Bouquinistes* (Riverside Vendors)" sidebar, later. You'll find better deals at the souvenir shops that line Rue d'Arcole between Notre-Dame and Hôtel de Ville and on Rue de Rivoli, alongside the Louvre.

## Department Stores (Les Grands Magasins)

Like cafés, department stores were invented here (surprisingly, not in America). The stores may seem overwhelming at first, but they generally work like ours, and those listed here are accustomed to wide-eyed foreign shoppers and have English-speaking staff. These stores are not just beautiful monuments; they also offer insights into how Parisians live. It's instructive to see what's in style, check out Parisians' current taste in clothes and furniture, and compare the selection with stores back home.

Parisian department stores begin with their showy perfume sections, almost always central on the ground floor, and worth a visit to see how much space is devoted to pricey, smelly water. Helpful information desks are usually located at the main entrances near the perfume section (with floor plans in English). Stores generally have affordable restaurants (some with view terraces) and a good selection of fairly priced souvenirs and toys. Opening hours are customarily Monday through Saturday from 10:00 to 19:00. Some are open later on Thursdays, and all are jammed on Saturdays and closed on Sundays (except in December).

### Galeries Lafayette and Printemps

You'll find both Galeries Lafayette and Printemps (pran-tom) stores in several neighborhoods. The most convenient and best sit side by side behind the old Opéra, complementing that monument's similar, classy ambience (Mo: Chaussée d'Antin-La Fayette, Havre-Caumartin, or Opéra). Both stores sprawl over multiple buildings and consume entire city blocks. The selection is huge, crowds can be huger (especially on summer Saturdays), and the prices are considered a tad high.

Galeries Lafayette, occupying three buildings, is the must-see store. Enter the main building with the red awnings, and don't miss the sensational belle époque dome (enjoy views from the railing on several floors). Find the champagne-and-coffee bar overlooking the dome just off the central escalator (there are two escalators), then escalate to the grand, open-air rooftop view on the seventh floor (free, climb there from the sixth floor—a workable place for a simple picnic). You'll get a dramatic view of the rear of the Opéra Garnier; see if you can spot beehives on its roof (the honey from these hives is sold in the Opéra gift shop). Fashion shows for the public take place from March through October at Galeries Lafayette on Fridays at 15:00 (call 01 42 82 30 25 or email welcome@galerieslafayette.com to confirm time and to reserve at least one month in advance—they speak English, in auditorium on seventh floor, www.galerieslafayette.com). Beware the *"mode seduction"* on the third floor.

A block to the west, Printemps' impressive facade lures shoppers in search of lower prices and less glitz. The view from its ninth-floor rooftop beats that from Galeries Lafayette; views are possible in all directions, and there's a breezy and reasonable bar/café with interior and exterior seating. Teens and twentysomethings will flip for the Citadium mall of shops on Rue Caumartin, under the walkway between Printemps' two buildings.

Continue your shopping by walking from this area to Place Vendôme (see "Boutique Strolls," next).

## Boutique Strolls

Give yourself a vacation from your sightseeing-focused vacation by sifting through window displays, pausing at corner cafés, and feeling the rhythm of neighborhood life. (Or have you been playing hooky and doing this already?) Though smaller shops are more intimate, sales clerks are more formal—so mind your manners. Here are three very different areas to lick some windows.

### Sèvres-Babylone to St. Sulpice

This Left Bank shopping stroll runs from the Sèvres-Babylone Métro stop to St. Sulpice Church, near Luxembourg Garden and Boulevard St. Germain. You'll sample smart clothing boutiques and clever window displays while enjoying one of Paris' more attractive neighborhoods. This shopping walk ties in well with my Left Bank Walk (and appears on the map on page 72). Some stores on this walk are open Sunday afternoons, though the walk is better on other days.

Start at the Sèvres-Babylone Métro stop (take the Métro or bus #87). You'll find the **Bon Marché** behind a small park. The Bon Marché (means "inexpensive," but it's not) is Paris' oldest department store. It opened in 1852, when fascination with iron and steel construction led to larger structures (like train stations, exhibition halls, and Eiffel Towers). The Bon Marché was the first large-scale store to offer fixed prices (no bargaining) and a vast selection of items under one glass roof, arranged in various "departments." This rocked the commercial world and forever changed the future of shopping. High-volume sales allowed low prices and created loyal customers—can you say "Costco"? But what began as a bargain store has evolved into one of Paris' most elegant shopping destinations.

Start your tour in the center, under the atrium with a high glass ceiling and crisscross elevators. Browse the perfumes, then escalate up to higher floors for a better perspective. Notice the sales clerks seated behind desks rather than standing at counters (at these prices, they seem more like loan officers). Find the less glamorous escalators in the corners of the store to bring you to the very top floor, where you'll find a treasure trove of children's books, toys, and clothing. If you're hungry, there are trendy restaurants in the basement. Or you can graze the gourmet groceries in the store's second building (La Grande Epicerie, behind the main building). It's ideal both for edible souvenirs—such as mustards, teas, and chocolates—and for picnic supplies for the park in front.

From the Bon Marché, walk through the small park and cross Boulevard Raspail. The Hôtel Lutetia to your right was built for shoppers by the Bon Marché's owners. Start down Rue de Sèvres, where you'll find **La Maison du Chocolat** at #19. Their mouthwatering window display will draw you helplessly inside. The shop sells handmade chocolates in exquisitely wrapped boxes and delicious ice-cream cones in season. Parisians commonly offer chocolates when invited over, and no gift box better impresses than one from this store.

Be sure to lick the chocolate off your fingers before entering **Hermès** (next door, at #17), famous for pricey silk scarves—and for the former designer of its fashion house, Jean-Paul Gaultier. Don't let the doorman intimidate you: Everyone's welcome here. This new store, opened in 2011, is housed in the original Art Deco swimming pool of Hôtel Lutetia, built in 1935. Take a spin through this ultra-trendy space, which covers more than 20,000 square feet.

Across the street sits the marvelously old-school **Au Sauvignon Café** (10 Rue de Sèvres, open daily). It's ideal for lunch or a drink (great wine list), and well-situated for watching the conveyor belt of smartly coiffed shoppers glide by. Check in for a hot or cold drink, and check out the zinc bar and picture-crazy interior. If your feet hurt, relief is at hand—a **Mephisto** shoe store is almost next door (Mon 11:00-19:00, Tue-Sat 10:00-19:00, closed Sun).

Continue a block farther down Rue de Sèvres to Place Michel Debré, a six-way intersection. A wicked half-man, half-horse statue (ouch), the *Centaur*, stands guard. Designed by French sculptor César in 1985, it was originally intended for a more prominent square, but was installed here after many deemed it too provocative. The face is of the sculptor himself.

From Place Michel Debré, boutique-lined streets fan out like spokes on a wheel. From left to right: Rue de Grenelle, Rue du Dragon, Rue du Vieux Colombier, and Rue du Cherche-Midi. Each street merits a detour if shopping matters to you.

Definitely make a short detour up Rue du Cherche-Midi (follow the horse's fanny). This street offers an ever-changing but always chic selection of shoe, purse, and clothing stores. Find Paris' most celebrated bread—beautiful round loaves with designer crust—at the low-key **Poilâne** at #8 (Mon-Sat 7:15-20:15, closed Sun). Enter for a sample. Notice the care with which each loaf of bread is wrapped. Next door, the small **Cuisine de Bar** café is a *bar à pains* (bread bar) and serves open-faced sandwiches *(tartines)* and salads with Poilâne bread (generally €9-14; €14 lunch *menu* includes *tartine*, salad, drink, and coffee; Tue-Sat 8:30-19:00, closed Sun-Mon).

Return to the *Centaur* in Place Michel Debré. Check out the **Comtesse du Berry** pâté store, which sells small gift packs. Then turn right and head down Rue du Vieux Colombier.

You'll pass the **Théâtre du Vieux-Colombier** (1913), one of three key venues for La Comédie-Française, a historic state-run troupe. Enter and find the timeline to the right; take a moment to look for names you recognize. How about the playwright Anton Chekov and poet T. S. Eliot—who both wrote plays performed here—or folk singer John Denver? At **Longchamps** (#21) you can hunt for a stylish French handbag in any color. Cross busy Rue de Rennes, gasping at the dreadful Montparnasse Tower, and continue down Rue du Vieux Colombier. Many stores in this area offer just one or two items, but in a variety of colors and patterns. There's **Aubade** for lingerie, **Lola** for ladies' clothes, and **Victoire** for the

## *Les Bouquinistes* (Riverside Vendors)

The used-book sellers *(bouquinistes)* you see along the Seine around Notre-Dame are a Parisian fixture. They've been here  since the mid-1500s, when shops and stalls lined most of the bridges in Paris. In 1557, these merchants were tagged as thieves for selling forbidden Protestant pamphlets during the Wars of Religion (Parisians were staunchly Catholic).

The term *bouquinistes* (boo-keen-eest) probably comes from the Dutch word *boeckin*, meaning "small book." First using wheelbarrows to transport and sell their goods, these hardy entrepreneurs eventually fastened trays to the parapets of the bridges with thin leather straps. After the Revolution, business boomed when entire libraries were liberated from nobles or clergymen and sold cheaply on the banks of the Seine. In 1891, *bouquinistes* received permission to permanently attach their boxes to the quaysides. Today, the waiting list to become one of Paris' 250 *bouquinistes* is eight years.

Each *bouquiniste* is given four boxes, all of a specified size, and rent is paid only for the stone on which the boxes rest (less than €100 per year). The most coveted spots are awarded based on seniority. Maintenance costs, including the required *vert* wagon paint (the green color of old train cars), are paid by the *bouquinistes*. With little overhead, prices are usually reasonable. While these days tourists prefer magnets and posters over vintage books, the city "officially" allows no more than one box of souvenirs for every three boxes of books.

*Bouquinistes* must be open at least four days a week, or they lose their spot. Wednesdays are best (when school is out), and warm, dry days are golden (notice that every item is wrapped in protective plastic). And yes, they do leave everything inside when they lock up at night; metal bars and padlocks keep things safe.

gentlemen. If the man or *petit-garçon* in your life needs a swimsuit, check out **Vilebrequin** (#5).

Spill into Place St. Sulpice, with its big, twin-tower church. **Café de la Mairie** is a great spot to sip a *café crème*, admire the lovely square, and consider your next move. Sightseers can visit St. Sulpice Church (see page 72) or Luxembourg Garden (page 73). Or you can head north on Rue Bonaparte two blocks to Boulevard St.

Germain for more shopping and several *grands cafés* (described on page 458).

Another option is to continue east, exiting the square (with the church on your right) along what is now called Rue St. Sulpice. **Estrella** is a food boutique with excellent teas and coffee beans (including *real* French roast), and a friendly owner, Jean-Claude (closed Sun, 34 Rue St. Sulpice). Pause at **Marie Mercié's** to admire the window display of extravagant and wildly expensive hats (23 Rue St. Sulpice).

Now turn left onto Rue de Seine. What's the best pastry shop in Paris? According to local shopkeepers, it's **Gérard Mulot's** *pâtisserie* (closed Wed, 76 Rue de Seine). That's saying a lot. Ogle the window display and try his chocolate *macarons* and savory quiches—oh, baby. Pick up lunch to go and munch it at nearby Luxembourg Garden. If you need a traditional French picnic knife to cut your quiche, backtrack to the **Tabac** (78 Rue de Seine) for a fine selection of Opinel knives, made in Savoie since 1890. Or if you're missing any other food supplies for the picnic, pop into **Marché Alimentaire St. Germain** (on the next block). The English-language **San Francisco Book Company** is a few blocks east at 17 Rue Monsieur le Prince (see map on page 93).

Stick a *fourchette* in me—I'm done. But if you'd like more, you're in the heart of boutique shopping. Sightseers could take my Left Bank Walk (you're near several points along the route). Or, to reach the Métro, continue up Rue de Seine to Boulevard St. Germain—the Odéon Métro stop is two blocks to the right, and the St. Germain and Mabillon stops are two blocks left.

## Place de la Madeleine to Place de l'Opéra

The ritzy streets connecting several high-priced squares form a miracle mile of gourmet food shops, glittering jewelry stores, four-star hotels, exclusive clothing boutiques, and people who spend more on clothes in one day than I do all year. This walk highlights the value Parisians place on outrageously priced products. The walk links Place de la Madeleine, Rue Royale, Place de la Concorde, Place Vendôme, and Place de l'Opéra. To do it all (with brief stops to shop) takes about 90 minutes and leaves you a block from Galeries Lafayette and Printemps department stores. For most, a shorter one-hour walk—*sans* Place Vendôme and ending on Place de la Concorde—is enough conspicuous consumption. Skip this walk on Sundays, when all shops are closed.

Start at Place de la Madeleine (Mo: Madeleine, see map on page 63). From the Métro, follow *sortie* signs to Place de la Madeleine (sorties 1 or 2), surfacing at the back side of La Madeleine. From here, work counterclockwise around the square.

### Place de la Madeleine

This square is a gourmet's fantasy, lined with Paris' most historic and tasty food shops. Start in the northeast corner at the black-and-white awnings of...

**Fauchon:** This bastion of over-the-top food products has faded from its glory days, and today caters to a largely tourist clientele—though it can still make your mouth water and your pocketbook ache. Fauchon outposts were found all over Paris until competitor Le Nôtre snapped them up. Now the only Fauchon that remains is this mothership store—the place where it all began.

The *Traiteur-Pâtisserie* at #24-26 is like a delicatessen with prepared foods—meats, meals, *pâtisseries* (pastries), breads, and cookies (of course, there are always *madeleines* on this square). Peruse the sumptuous desserts and take-away dinner *plats* that cost more than many restaurant meals (Mon-Sat 9:00-20:30, closed Sun, tel. 01 70 39 38 96). At one end, you'll find a caviar and champagne bar and at the other, the *Boulangerie* with less pricey items and a few barstools for eating *sur place* (Mon-Sat 8:00-18:00, closed Sun, more tables and chairs upstairs plus WCs).

The *Epicerie, Confiserie, Cave* is Fauchon's more impressive shop, across the small street (at #30, Mon-Sat 9:00-20:00, closed Sun). This razzle-dazzle store is all about style, branding, and packaging. Tourists gobble up anything wrapped in pink and black—provided Fauchon's name is emblazoned on it. Stroll downstairs to find the wine bar, a snazzy lunch counter, and cellar. Look for the €5,900 (that's $6,700) bottles of century-old Cognac on shelves—who buys this stuff? Find the elevator and ride two floors up and be tempted by a fashionable café with view tables of La Madeleine (daily 9:00-24:00, tel. 01 70 39 38 39).

**More Shops on Place de la Madeleine:** Turn right out of Fauchon and find **Marquise de Sévígné** next door, where well-coiffed chocolate consultants are just waiting to set you up with the perfect box of chocolate (Mon-Sat 10:00-19:00, closed Sun).

**Hédiard** lies across the square at #21. This older, more appealing, and more accessible gourmet  food shop was founded in 1854 (Mon-Sat 9:00-21:00, closed Sun, tel. 01 43 12 88 88). It showcases handsomely displayed produce and meats, a nifty atrium wine shop, and a smart café above (take the glass elevator up for a coffee or a pricey lunch). The small red containers make good souvenirs, with flavored mustards, jams, coffee, candies, and tea. Anyone can enter the glass doors of the wine cellar, marked *Le Chais*, (find the

€2,500 bottles of Petrus), but you need special permission to access *Les Vénérables* wines.

Two doors down is **La Maison des Truffe** (at 19 Place de la Madeleine, Mon-Sat 10:00-21:00, closed Sun, tel. 01 42 65 53 22). Go inside this small shop to get a look at and a whiff of the product. Ponder how something so ugly, smelly, and deformed can sell for so much (up to €1,000 a pound). The shop also houses a sharp little restaurant serving a variety of dishes, all with truffles (opens at 12:00). The menu is surprisingly reasonable—a truffle omelet for €24, chocolate cake with truffles for €15. You'll also see every possible food that can be made with truffles—even Armagnac brandy—as well as white truffles from Italy that sell for €2,500 a pound. Small jars of black truffles cost €45-70.

Next is **Mariage Frères'** fine teas. Walk in to learn how good tea can smell and to see how beautifully it can be displayed (Mon-Sat 10:30-19:30, closed Sun).

Pass the sparkling **Baccarat** crystal shop and keep going straight, crossing three crosswalks. The vista to your right—of a grand boulevard anchored by a church dedicated to St. Augustine—is a vintage view à la Haussmann. (For more on the man who shaped modern-day Paris, see the sidebar on page 82.)

At #17, **Caviar Kaspia,** you can add Iranian caviar, eel, and vodka to your truffle collection. Find the price list on the counter. The stronger caviars are cheaper (€110 for a small tin). The "finer" caviars sell for up to €12,000 a kilo. (I have a hard time visualizing 2.2 pounds of caviar, and a harder time visualizing paying for it.) The restaurant upstairs serves what you see downstairs—at exorbitant prices (Mon-Sat 10:00-24:00, restaurant from 12:00, closed Sun). A caviar competitor has opened next door (Caviar Prunier), so demand must be strong.

At this point, leave Place de la Madeleine and head south down Rue Royale.

### Rue Royale

Here, we trade expensive food for expensive...stuff. (I'm not sure how Toto landed a storefront here.)

One block down Rue Royale, consider a dip into the classy Village Royale shopping courtyard for a restful pause at **Le Village Café** (closed Sun, tel. 01 40 17 02 19) or to visit the famous chocolatier **Patrick Roger** and his huge chocolate sculptures (Tue-Sat 10:30-19:30, closed Sun-Mon, tel. 01 40 06 99 19).

At Rue du Faubourg St. Honoré, cross Rue Royale to your left—pausing in the middle for a great view both ways—and find **Ladurée** (at 16 Rue Royale) for an out-of-this-world pastry break in a 19th-century setting. Wait for a seat at the busy tea salon, or

pick up some world-famous *macarons* to go (look for the green awning, Mon-Sat 8:30-19:00, Sun 10:00-19:30, tel. 01 42 60 21 79).

You could cut this walk short by continuing two more blocks
down Rue Royale to Place de la Concorde. Browse its crystal and
jewelry shops, then relax at **Hôtel Crillon's** classy café (see "Les
Grands Cafés de Paris," page 458).

To do the entire walk, turn left on Rue du Faubourg St. Honoré and walk several blocks, past numerous clothing boutiques.
Turn left on Rue de Castiglione to reach…

### Place Vendôme

This *très* elegant square is home to the original Hôtel Ritz, opened
in 1898. Hemingway liberated the bar in World War II. Only
upper-crust jewelry stores are allowed on Place Vendôme—Van
Cleef & Arpels, Dior, Chanel, Cartier, and others (if you have to
ask how much…). The square was created by Louis XIV during the
17th century as a setting for a statue of himself. One hundred and
fifty years later, Louis XIV was replaced by a statue of Napoleon.
The column at the center, designed in the style of Trajan's Column
in Rome, was raised by Napoleon to commemorate his victory at
the Battle of Austerlitz. The encircling bronze reliefs were made
from cannons won in this and other battles.

Leave Place Vendôme by walking up Rue de la Paix—strolling
by still more jewelry, high-priced watches, and crystal—and enter…

### Place de l'Opéra

Here you'll find the **Opéra Garnier** and the **Fragonard Perfume
Museum** (described on pages 78-80). You're in the middle of Right
Bank glamor (when you're ready to go, look for the convenient
Opéra Métro stop). If you're not shopped out yet, the Galeries
Lafayette and Printemps department stores are located a block or
two north, up Rue Halévy (see page 477). If you're exhausted from
counting the zeros on outrageous price tags, relax with a drink at
**Café de la Paix** across from the Opéra (daily, 12 Boulevard des
Capucines). It's an appropriately elegant—and pricey—way to end
this tour.

### The Marais

For more eclectic, avant-garde boutiques, peruse the artsy shops between Place des Vosges and the Pompidou Center. Follow the route
suggested for the Marais Walk (see map on page 304), starting at
Place des Vosges and ending where you like. Stick to the west-east
axis formed by Rue des Francs-Bourgeois, Rue des Rosiers, and Rue
Ste. Croix de la Bretonnerie. This area is rich with jewelry, shoe, and
trendy clothing boutiques. On Sunday afternoons, when the rest of
Paris naps, the neighborhood comes alive with shoppers and café

crowds, and enjoys little car traffic. But it's quiet on Saturdays, when the Jewish community rests.

Start by inspecting the galleries under the arcades of Place des Vosges. Consider a daring new piece for that blank wall at home. Exit west via Rue des Francs-Bourgeois and enter a stretch of trendy shops selling clothing, shoes, jewelry, handbags, skin care products, and more. Once you make it down the street, turn left on Rue de Pavée and find the adorable teddy bear shop at #18 (**L'Ours du Marais**), which seems out of place in this trendy area—the friendly owner

wanted to re-create a shop she found in England (Tue-Sat 11:30-19:30, Sun 14:00-19:30, closed Mon). Across the street, the **Mona Lisait** ("Mona was reading") bookstore at #17 bis offers an interesting selection of books and more.

Rounding the corner lands you in the epicenter of Marais hipness and fashion along Rue des Rosiers. Before plunging in, take a break at **Le Loir dans la Théière** at #3, with terrific baked goods, hot drinks, and a welcoming ambience for tired travelers (Mon-Fri 12:00-19:00, Sat-Sun 10:00-19:00). Then walk at a snail's pace along Rue des Rosiers through the heart of Paris' Jewish quarter, where tradition meets fashion in ever-changing forms. The venerable Jewish deli Jo Goldenberg (at Rue Ferdinand Duval) has been transformed into a snappy clothing boutique; notice how the facade doesn't fit the store. If it's lunchtime, pick up a cheap falafel sandwich at **L'As du Falafel** (closed Sat, 34 Rue des Rosiers). At the end of Rue des Rosiers, jog left onto Rue Vieille du Temple, then right on Rue Ste. Croix de la Bretonnerie.

Tea enthusiasts should keep an eye out for the luxurious tea extravaganza at **Mariage Frères,** just off Rue Ste. Croix de la Bretonnerie at 30 Rue du Bourg Tibourg (daily 10:30-19:30, serving tea from 12:00). Don't miss the colorful shopping at **Pylones** (13 Rue Ste. Croix de la Bretonnerie). From here you can continue to the Pompidou Center and find more shops. Le Forum des Halles, a few blocks past the Pompidou Center, is a multilevel underground modern shopping mall.

To experience how much the French love their pets—or to pick up a souvenir for the demanding *chien* in your life—walk a few blocks toward the river and drop into **Un Chien dans le Marais,** where you can peruse the bejeweled doggie collars and clothes (daily 12:00-19:00, 35 bis Rue du Roi de Sicile). And for that item you meant to pack but left behind, stop by the **BHV** (Bazar de l'Hôtel de Ville) department store, which sells just about everything from hardware to lingerie at affordable prices (Mon-Sat 9:30-19:30, closed Sun, at 14 Rue de Rivoli, where Rue de Rivoli meets Rue Vieille du Temple).

## Puces St. Ouen: The Flea Market at Porte de Clignancourt

Paris' sprawling flea markets (*marché aux puces;* mar-shay oh-poos; *puce* is French for "flea") are oversized garage sales. They started in

the Middle Ages, when middlemen sold old, flea-infested clothes and discarded possessions of the wealthy at bargain prices to eager peasants. Buyers were allowed to rummage through piles of aristocratic garbage.

Today **Puces St. Ouen** (poos san-wahn), at Porte de Clignancourt, carries on that tradition. This is the mother of all flea markets, with more than 2,000 vendors selling everything from flamingos to faucets, but mostly antiques (Sat 9:00-18:00, Sun 10:00-18:00, Mon 11:00-17:00, closed Tue-Fri, pretty dead the first 2 weeks of Aug, tel. 01 58 61 22 90, www.st-ouen-tourisme.com and www.les-puces.com).

This market shows off Paris' gritty, suburban underbelly and can be intimidating (in Paris, the have-nots live in the burbs, while the haves want to be as central as they can get). No event brings together the melting-pot population of Paris better than this carnival-like market. Some find it claustrophobic, overcrowded, and threatening; others find French *diamants*-in-the-rough and return happy. (Wear your money belt; pickpockets and scam artists thrive in these wall-to-wall-shopper events—and don't use ATM machines here.) The markets actually get more peaceful the farther in you go. You can bargain a bit (best deals are made with cash at the end of the day), though don't expect swinging deals here.

Space for this flea market was created in the 1800s, when the city wall was demolished (its path is now a freeway), leaving large tracts of land open. Eventually the vacuum was filled by street vendors, then antique dealers. The hodgepodge pattern of the market reflects its unplanned evolution. Strolling the stalls can feel more like touring a souk in North Africa—a place of narrow alleys packed with people and too much to see.

The St. Ouen "market" is actually a collection of individual markets. Most of these are covered alleys, each with a different name and specializing in a particular angle on antiques, bric-a-brac, and junk. You'll find them by walking down the "spine" of

# Puces St. Ouen Flea Market

To M Garibaldi

ST. OUEN

RUE J. FERRY

RUE R. M. BEER

RUE P. CURIE

RUE GAMBETTA

RUE EUGÈNE-LUMEAU

RUE MATHIEU

RUE KLÉBER

RUE LOUIS DAIN

IMP. SIMON

RUE DES ROSIERS

RUE MARIE CURIE

BIRON

L'ENTREPÔT

L'USINE

BONS ENFANTS

R. DE LA GAÎTÉ

RUE PLAISIR

RUE JULES VALLÈS

PAUL BERT

SERPETTE

CAMBO

RUE BIRON

RUE DE LA VILLA BIRON

RUE VOLTAIRE

JULES VALLÈS

ROSIERS

LECUYER

RUE NEUVE P. CURIE

RUE LECUYER

WC

WC

LE PASSAGE

RUE PAUL BERT

ANTICA

VERNAISON

RUE CHARLES SCHMIDT

WC

DAUPHINE

MALIK

MALASSIS

AVENUE MICHELET

RUE JEAN HENRI FABRE

WC

ELEVATED FREEWAY (PERIPHERIQUE)

100 Meters

100 Yards

LE PLATEAU

AVENUE DE LA PORTE DE CLIGNANCOURT

❶ Chez Louisette
❷ Café Paul Bert
❸ La Chope des Puces Bar

▢ MARKET STREETS
▣ COVERED MARKETS

To M Porte de Clignancourt

the market, Rue des Rosiers—look for a map that tries to explain the general character of each (get it at shops or the TI branch just off Rue des Rosiers on Impasse Simon). Here's a brief rundown of the *marchés:* Vernaison (tent-like shops selling a mishmash of stuff), Dauphine (a glass-roofed arcade with quiet shops lining its interior-only lanes), Biron and Serpette (classy antiques), and Paul Bert (open lanes of shops selling a bit of everything, with clean—and free—WCs).

Even if antiques, African objects, and T-shirts aren't your thing, you may still find this market worth the Métro ride. Pretend you just rented a big, empty apartment...and need to furnish it. Come for a reality check—away from the beautiful people and glorious monuments of Paris—and get a dose of life in the 'burbs. Time your trip around lunch; there are many lively and reasonable cafés.

*Eating at Puces St. Ouen:* Buried in Vernaison Market, **Chez Louisette** delivers a great lunch experience. Listen to a latter-day Edith Piaf and eat with a Toulouse-Lautrec look-alike. Madame belts out vintage French *chansons* with an accordion and keyboard to back her up, the ramshackle decor is laced with red garlands and big chandeliers, the jovial crowd sings along, and the prices are cheap. It's popular, so come right at noon or expect to wait (Sat-Mon only, 130 Avenue Michelet, tel. 01 40 12 10 14).

**Café Paul Bert** is where locals come for a traditional brasserie meal. The decor is wonderful inside and out, and the cuisine wins rave reviews (closed Tue-Wed, 20 Rue Paul Bert, tel. 01 40 11 90 28).

**La Chope des Puces** bar is famous for its live Gypsy music concerts on Saturday and Sunday afternoons, complete with a questionable clientele (open 10:30-19:00, 122 Rue des Rosiers, tel. 01 40 11 28 80).

*Getting to Puces St. Ouen:* To get to the Puces St. Ouen, take Métro line 4 to the end of the line at Porte de Clignancourt, then carefully follow *Sortie, Marché aux Puces* signs. Walk straight out of the Métro down Avenue de la Porte de Clignancourt, passing by leather stores and through blocks of stalls hawking trinkets and cheap clothing. Your destination is just beyond the elevated freeway (white bridge). Cross under the freeway—leaving Paris and entering the suburb of St. Ouen—and veer left on the angled street, Rue des Rosiers, the spine that links the many markets of St. Ouen. Avoid the crowds along Avenue Jean Henri Fabre, parallel to the freeway, and you'll do fine. If you're considering buying a large item, be aware that shipping is very expensive (Camard company has the best reputation, tel. 01 49 46 10 82, www.antikaparis.com/camard).

## Other Flea Markets

**Puces de Vanves** is comparatively tiny and civilized, and preferred by many flea-market connoisseurs (Sat-Sun 7:00-17:00, best to arrive before 13:00—when the best stalls close, closed Mon-Fri, Mo: Porte de Vanves). The mega-**Puces de Montreuil** is the least organized and most traditional of them all, with chatty sellers and competitive buyers (Sat-Mon 8:00-18:00, closed Tue-Fri, Mo: Porte de Montreuil).

## Open-Air Markets

Browse these markets for picnics, or find a corner café from which to appreciate the scene. I've listed Paris' most appealing markets below.

## Market Streets

Several traffic-free street markets overflow with flowers, produce, fish vendors, and butchers, illustrating how most Parisians shopped before there were supermarkets and department stores. Shops are open daily except Sunday afternoons, Monday, and lunchtime throughout the week (13:00-15:00).

**Rue Cler**—a wonderful place to sleep and dine as well as shop—is like a refined street market, serving an upscale neighborhood near the Eiffel Tower (Mo: Ecole Militaire; for details, see Rue Cler Walk chapter and the Sleeping and Eating chapters).

**Rue Montorgueil** is a thriving and less touristy market street. Ten blocks from the Louvre and five blocks from the Pompidou Center, Rue Montorgueil (mohn-tor-goo-ee) is famous as the last vestige of the once-massive Les Halles market (just north of St. Eustache Church, Mo: Etienne Marcel; gather a picnic here and take it to the park at Les Halles). Once the home of big warehouses and wholesale places to support the market, these have morphed into retail outlets to survive. Several traffic-free lanes cross Rue Montorgueil—don't miss the nearby covered arcade, passage du Grand Cerf (down Rue Marie Stuart). Check out the irresistible creations at **Pâtissier Stohrer,** where the French expression for "window-licking" *(lèche-vitrines)* must have started (51 Rue Montorgueil, tel. 01 42 33 38 20).

**Rue Mouffetard,** originally built by the Romans, is a happening market street by day and does double-duty as restaurant row at night (see page 455). Hiding several blocks behind the Panthéon, it starts at Place Contrescarpe and ends below at St. Médard Church (Mo: Censier Daubenton). The upper stretch is pedestrian and touristic; the bottom stretch is purely Parisian. Pause for a drink on picturesque Place Contrescarpe, then make your descent down this popular street.

**Rue Daguerre,** near the Catacombs and off Avenue du Général Leclerc, is the least touristy of the street markets listed here (Mo: Denfert-Rochereau; for Catacombs description, see page 76).

**Rue de Seine and Rue de Buci** combine to make a central and colorful market within easy reach of many sights (Mo: Odéon; see also "Les Grands Cafés de Paris," page 458, and my Left Bank Walk).

**Rue des Martyrs,** near Montmartre, makes Paris feel like a village. Consider exploring this lively market scene as part of my Montmartre Walk.

**Marché des Enfants Rouges,** while not really a market street, is a compact, covered market for the northern Marais neighborhood. It's also the oldest covered food market in Paris, built when Louis XIII ruled in 1615. It's named for an orphanage where the children wore red uniforms (the name means "Market of the Red Children"). Here you'll find everything under one roof: lots of organic produce, stands offering wine tastings, and fun, *trés* Parisian lunch options (Tue-Thu 8:30-13:00 & 16:00-19:30, Fri-Sat 9:00-13:00 & 16:00-20:00, Sun 9:00-14:00, closed Mon; a 10-minute walk north from the heart of the Marais at 39 Rue de Bretagne, Mo: Filles du Calvaire or Temple, see the East Paris color map at the front of this book). Find the man making *socca*, a chickpea-flour specialty from Nice. Consider lunch at **L'Estaminet** (daily specials).

## Larger Markets, Usually Morning Only

Every neighborhood has a *marché volant* (flying market), where piles of food stalls assemble on boulevards for one or two mornings each week. Offering cheaper prices and more selection, these markets take over selected boulevards and squares throughout Paris generally 8:00-12:30 (except for Marché Place d'Anvers in Montmartre, open only late Friday afternoon). Expect a lively combination of flea- and street-market atmosphere and items.

**Marché d'Aligre,** 10 blocks behind the Opéra Bastille down Rue de Faubourg St. Antoine, is an intimate open-air market where you'll see few tourists (Tue-Sat 9:00-14:00, closed Sun-Mon, Place d'Aligre, Mo: Ledru-Rollin).

**Marché de la Bastille** is the best of the lot, with a vast selection of products extending more than a half-mile north of Place de la Bastille along Boulevard Richard Lenoir (Thu and Sun until 14:30, Mo: Bastille); consider combining either of these two markets with a stroll through Promenade Plantée park (see page 89) and my Marais Walk.

**Marché Place Monge** is comparatively minuscule, with produce, clothing, and a few crafts (Wed, Fri, and Sun 8:00-13:00; near Rue Mouffetard, Mo: Monge).

**Marché Boulevard de Grenelle,** a few blocks southwest of Champ de Mars park and the Rue Cler area, is packed with produce, nonperishable goods, and Parisians in search of a good value (Wed and Sun 7:00-12:30, between Dupleix and La Motte Picquet-Grenelle Métro stops).

**Marché Belleville** is big and very untouristy (Tue and Fri, Mo: Belleville).

**Marché Raspail,** between Rue du Cherche-Midi and Rue de Rennes, is where the rich and famous shop for food (Tue and

Fri 7:30-14:30, special organic-only market Sun 9:00-15:00, Mo: Rennes).

**Marché des Batignolles** is Paris' largest organic market, located along Boulevard des Batignolles between Métro stations Place de Clichy and Rome (Sat only 9:00-15:00). Saturdays are also big wedding days in Paris: Sneak up Rue des Batignolles to the neighborhood Hôtel de Ville (16 Rue des Batignolles), have a post-market coffee in a café across the street, and watch as the colorful wedding parties stream by.

## Arcaded Shopping Streets *(Passages)*

More than 200 of these covered shopping streets once crisscrossed Paris, providing much-needed shelter from the rain. The first were built during the American Revolution, though the ones you'll see date from the 1800s. Today only a handful remain to remind us where shopping malls got their inspiration, although they now sell things you would be more likely to find in flea markets than at JC Penney. Here's a short list to weave into your sightseeing plan. (They're found on the map in this chapter and on the East Paris color map at the front of this book.)

**Galerie Vivienne,** behind the Palais Royal off Rue des Petits-Champs and a few blocks from the Louvre (ideal to combine with a visit to the courtyards of Palais Royal), is the most refined and accessible of the *passages* (Mo: Pyramides, Bourse, or Palais Royal). Inside this classy arcade, you'll find a chic wine bar (**Legrand Filles et Fils** with a list of five whites and five reds by the glass that change each week, tel. 01 42 60 07 12), tea salon, funky café, and trendy dress shops.

**Passage Choiseul** and **Passage Ste. Anne,** four blocks west of Galerie Colbert and Galerie Vivienne, are fine examples of most Parisian *passages,* selling used books, paper products, trinkets, and snacks (down Rue des Petits-Champs toward Avenue de l'Opéra, same Métro stops).

**Passage du Grand Cerf** is an elegant arcade, easily combined with a visit to the nearby Rue Montorgueil street market described earlier (Mo: Etienne Marcel).

**Passage Panoramas** and **Passage Jouffroy** are long galleries that connect with several other smaller *passages* to give you the best sense of the elaborate network of arcades that once existed (on both sides of Boulevard Montmartre, between Métro stops Grands Boulevards and Richelieu Drouot).

# ENTERTAINMENT IN PARIS

Paris is brilliant after dark. Save energy from your day's sightseeing and experience the City of Light lit. Whether it's a concert at Sainte-Chapelle, a boat ride on the Seine, a walk in Montmartre, a hike up the Arc de Triomphe, or a late-night café, you'll see Paris at its best. Night walks in Paris are wonderful. Any of the self-guided walking tours in this book are terrific after dark.

## Event Listings

### Pariscope

The weekly *Pariscope* (€0.40, comes out on Wed) or *L'Officiel des Spectacles* (€0.35) is essential if you want to know what's going on in Paris. I prefer *Pariscope*: It offers a complete weekly listing of music, cinema, theater, opera, and other special events. Pick one up at a newsstand and page through it. The order of the contents changes periodically, but the basics described below are always there...somewhere.

The magazine, all in French, begins with a listing of "Théâtre" and what's playing at all key theater venues. "Musique" lists each day's events, from jazz to classical to dance (program, location, time, price), including both opera houses if performances are scheduled. Remember that some concerts are free *(entrée libre)*.

A third of the magazine is devoted to *cinéma*—a Parisian forte. While a code marks films as "Comédie," "Documentaire," "Drame," "Karaté," "Erotisme," and so on, the key mark for non-French-speakers is "v.o.," for *version originale* (original-language version)—this means the movie hasn't been dubbed in French. Films are listed alphabetically, by neighborhood ("Salles Paris") and by genre. To find a showing near your hotel, simply look for a cinema in the same arrondissement. "Salles Périphérie" means the cinema is located out in the suburbs. Many cinemas offer discounts on Monday or Wednesday nights.

"Arts" gives hours and locations for gallery showings ("expositions," big and small), and up-to-date hours at museums in and near Paris (*tlj* = daily, *sf* = except, *Ent* = entry price, *TR* = reduced price—usually for students and children).

The "Enfants" section covers a myriad of possible children's activities from *High School Musical* performances to treasure hunts. "Spectacles" are shows (like magic shows); you'll also see many "Marionettes" (puppet) shows and "Cirques" (circuses). These events usually are offered only in French, but they can be worthwhile even for non-French-speakers.

"Promenades et Loisirs" covers outdoor events and sights, including open-air theater, flea markets, sound-and-light shows *(son et lumières)*, key monuments such as the Eiffel Tower and Arc de Triomphe, river cruises, parks, zoos, and aquariums.

For cancan mischief, look under "Paris la Nuit."

## Other Resources

Pick up a copy of the free weekly *A Nous Paris* in the Métro and check out the "Save the Date" section, which is easy to follow even though it's in French. In these pages, this youth-oriented magazine lists what makes their cut for the most interesting event in Paris each day of the week (printed on Mon, www.anous.fr).

If you prefer your event information in English, the *Paris Voice* website has a helpful monthly review of Paris entertainment: www.parisvoice.com. *Time Out's* English website is another good resource, with listings for the city's most talked-about restaurants, reviews of concerts and stores, and ideas for how to enjoy Paris's nightlife and shopping on a budget (www.timeout.fr/paris/en).

## Music

### Jazz and Blues Clubs

With a lively mix of American, French, and international musicians, Paris has been an internationally acclaimed jazz capital since World War II. You'll pay €12-25 to enter a jazz club (may include one drink; if not, expect to pay €5-10 per drink; beer is cheapest). See *Pariscope* magazine under "Musique" for listings, or, even better, the *Paris Voice* website for a good monthly review (www.parisvoice.com). You can also check each club's website (all have English versions), or drop by the clubs to check out the calendars posted on their front doors. Music starts after 21:00 in most clubs. Some offer dinner concerts from about 20:30 on. Here are several good bets:

**Caveau de la Huchette,** a characteristic old jazz/dance club, fills an ancient Latin Quarter cellar with live jazz and frenzied dancing every night (admission about €12 on weekdays, €14 on weekends, €6-8 drinks, daily 21:30-2:30 in the morning or later, 5 Rue de la Huchette, Mo: St. Michel, recorded info tel. 01 43 26 65 05, www.caveaudelahuchette.fr).

**Autour de Midi et Minuit** is a an Old World bistro at the foot of Montmartre, sitting above a *cave à jazz*. Eat upstairs if you like (see page 456 for details), then make your way down to the basement to find bubbling jam sessions on Tuesday and Wednesday and concerts on Thursday, Friday, and Saturday (no cover, €5 minimum Tue-Wed; €16 cover Thu-Sat includes one drink; jam sessions at 21:30, concerts usually at 22:00; no music Sun-Mon; 11 Rue Lepic, Mo: Blanche or Abbesses, tel. 01 55 79 16 48, www.autourdemidi. fr).

For a spot teeming with late-night activity and jazz, go to the two-block-long Rue des Lombards, at Boulevard Sébastopol, midway between the river and the Pompidou Center (Mo: Châtelet). **Au Duc des Lombards** is one of the most popular and respected jazz clubs in Paris, with concerts nightly in a great, plush, 110-seat theater-like setting (admission €20-30, buy online and arrive early for best seats, cheap drinks, shows at 20:00 and 22:00, 42 Rue des Lombards, tel. 01 42 33 22 88, www.ducdeslombards.fr). **Le Sunside,** run for 18 years by Stephane Portet, is just a block away. The club offers two little stages (ground floor and downstairs): "le Sunset" stage tends toward contemporary world jazz; "le Sunside" stage features more traditional and acoustic jazz (concerts range from free to €25, check their website; generally at 20:00, 21:00, and 22:00; 60 Rue des Lombards, tel. 01 40 26 46 60, www.sunset-sunside.com).

For a less pricey—and less central—concert club, try **Utopia.** From the outside it's a hole in the wall, but inside it's filled with devoted fans of rock and folk blues. Though Utopia is officially a private club (and one that permits smoking), you can pay €3 to join for an evening, then pay a reasonable charge for the concert (usually €10 or under, concerts start about 22:00). It's located in the Montparnasse area (79 Rue de l'Ouest, Mo: Pernety, tel. 01 43 22 79 66, www.utopia-cafeconcert.fr).

## Cabaret

**Old-Time Parisian Cabaret on Montmartre: Au Lapin Agile**—This historic little cabaret tries its best to maintain the atmosphere of the heady days when bohemians would gather here to enjoy wine, song, and sexy jokes. Today, you'll mix in with a few locals and many tourists (the Japanese love the place) for a drink and as many as 10 different performers—mostly singers with a piano. Performers range from sweet and innocent Amélie types to naughty Maurice Chevalier types. And though tourists are welcome, there's no accommodation for English speakers (except on their website), so non-French-speakers will be lost. You sit at carved wooden tables in a dimly lit room, taste the traditional drink (a small brandy with cherries), and are immersed in an old-time Parisian ambience. The soirée covers traditional French standards, love ballads, sea chanteys, and more (€24, €7 drinks, Tue-Sun 21:00-2:00 in the morning, closed Mon, best to reserve ahead, 22 Rue des Saules, tel. 01 46 06 85 87, www.au-lapin-agile.com; described in the ❂ Montmartre Walk chapter).

**A Modern Cabaret near Canal St. Martin: Chez Raymonde**—Dinner cabaret is still alive and kicking in Paris. Your evening begins with a good three-course dinner (including apéritif, wine, a half-bottle of champagne, and coffee) in an intimate dining room, where you get to know your neighbors. Around 22:00 the maître d'hôtel and the chef himself kick off the performance with a waltz together. Then it's feather boas, song, and dance—audience participation is encouraged (€85-110/person based on the *menu* you choose, Fri-Sat evenings only, dinner starts at 20:00 when *le chef* greets you in person, performance usually finishes about 23:00, reservations necessary, 119 Avenue Parmentier; Mo: Goncourt, Parmentier, or République; tel. 01 43 55 26 27, www.chez-raymonde. com). On Sunday afternoons, you can also attend a performance over lunch (same prices, starts at 12:30).

## Concerts and Operas
**Classical Concerts**—For classical music on any night, consult *Pariscope* magazine (check "Concerts Classiques" under "Musique" for listings), and look for posters at tourist-oriented churches.

From March through November, these churches regularly host concerts: St. Sulpice, St. Germain-des-Prés, La Madeleine, St. Eustache, St. Julien-le-Pauvre, and Sainte-Chapelle.

**Sainte-Chapelle:** Enjoy the pleasure of hearing Mozart, Bach, or Vivaldi, surrounded by 800 years of stained glass (unheated—bring a sweater). The acoustical quality is surprisingly good. There are usually two concerts per evening, at 19:00 and 20:30; specify which one you want when you buy or reserve your ticket. VIP tickets get you a seat in the first eight rows (€40), Prestige tickets cover the next 15 rows (€30) and Normal tickets are the last five rows (€16). Seats are unassigned within each section, so arrive at least 30 minutes early to get through the security line and snare a good view.

You can book at the box office, by phone, or online. Two different companies present concerts, but the schedule will tell you who to contact for tickets to a particular performance. The small box office (with schedules and tickets) is to the left of the chapel entrance gate (4 Boulevard du Palais, Mo: Cité), or call 01 42 77 65 65 or 06 67 30 65 65 for schedules and reservations. You can leave your message in English—just speak clearly and spell your name. You can check schedules at www.archetspf.asso.fr, but if you want to book online, visit www.classictic.com, which lets you conveniently print out your email confirmation as your ticket.

Flavien from Euromusic offers last-minute discounts with this book when seats are available (limit 2 tickets per book). VIP tickets are discounted to €30 and Prestige tickets to €25. The offer applies only to Euromusic concerts and must be purchased with cash only at the Sainte-Chapelle ticket booth close to concert time.

The evening entrance is at 4 Boulevard du Palais, between the gilded gate of the Palais de Justice and the Conciergerie. You'll enter through the law courts hall, directly into the royal upper chapel, just as St. Louis once did.

**Salle Pleyel:** This concert hall on the Right Bank hosts world-class artists, from string quartets and visiting orchestras to international opera stars. Tickets range from €10 to €150, depending on the artist and seats you choose, and are usually hard to come by, so it's best to order online in advance (252 Rue du Faubourg St. Honoré, Mo: Ternes, tel. 01 42 56 13 13, www.sallepleyel.fr).

**Other Venues:** Look also for daytime concerts in parks, such as the Luxembourg Garden. Even the Galeries Lafayette department store offers concerts. Many of these concerts are free *(entrée libre)*, such as the Sunday atelier concert sponsored by the American Church (generally Sept-June at 17:00 but not every week and not in Dec, 65 Quai d'Orsay, Mo: Invalides, RER: Pont de l'Alma, tel. 01 40 62 05 00, www.acparis.org).

**Opera**—Paris is home to two well-respected opera venues. The **Opéra Bastille** is the massive modern opera house that dominates

Place de la Bastille. Come here for state-of-the-art special effects and modern interpretations of classic ballets and operas. In the spirit of this everyman's opera, unsold seats are available at a big discount to seniors and students 15 minutes before the show. Standing-room-only tickets for €15 are also sold for some performances (Mo: Bastille).

The **Opéra Garnier,** Paris' first opera house, hosts opera and ballet performances. Come here for less expensive tickets and grand belle époque decor (Mo: Opéra). To get tickets for either opera house, it's easiest to reserve online at www.operadeparis.fr, or call 01 71 25 24 23 outside France or toll tel. 08 92 89 90 90 inside France. You can also go direct to the Opéra Bastille's ticket office (open daily 11:00-18:00).

## Evening Museum Visits

Various **museums** are open late on different evenings—called *visites nocturnes*—offering the opportunity for more relaxed, less crowded visits: the Louvre (Wed and Fri until 21:45), Orsay (Thu until 21:45), Pompidou Center (Wed-Mon until 21:00), Grand Palais (Wed until 22:00), Holocaust Memorial (Thu until 22:00), Quai Branly (Thu-Sat until 21:00), Rodin Museum (Wed until 20:45), and Marmottan Museum (Thu until 20:00). The Army Museum may be open Tuesdays until 21:00 (April-Sept).

**Summer Night Spectacle:** An elaborate sound-and-light show (Grandes Eaux Nocturnes) takes place at the Château in Versailles on Saturdays (€23, mid-June-Aug at 21:00, www.chateau versailles.fr).

## Seine River Cruises

Several companies offer cruises after dark as well as dinner cruises on huge glass-domed boats (or open-air decks in summer) with departures along the Seine, including from the Eiffel Tower; see "Dinner Cruises" on page 457 of the Eating in Paris chapter.

## Night Walks

Go for an evening walk to best appreciate the City of Light. Break for ice cream, pause at a café, and enjoy the sidewalk entertainers as you join the post-dinner Parisian parade. Use any of this book's self-guided walking tours as a blueprint, and remember to avoid poorly lit areas and stick to main thoroughfares. Consider the following suggestions; most are partial versions of this book's longer walking tours.

▲▲▲**Trocadéro and Eiffel Tower**—This is one of Paris' most spectacular views at night. Take the Métro to the Trocadéro stop and join the party on Place du Trocadéro for a magnificent view of the glowing Eiffel Tower (see the "Best Views over the City of Light" sidebar on page 80). It's a festival of hawkers, gawkers, drummers, and entertainers.

Walk down the stairs, passing the fountains and rollerbladers, then cross the river to the base of the tower, well worth the effort even if you don't go up (tower open daily mid-June-Aug until 24:00, Sept-mid-June until 23:00). ✪ See the Eiffel Tower Tour chapter.

From the Eiffel Tower you can stroll through the Champ de Mars park past tourists and romantic couples, and take the Métro home (Ecole Militaire stop, across Avenue de la Motte-Picquet from far southeast corner of park). Or there's a handy RER stop (Champ de Mars-Tour Eiffel) two blocks west of the Eiffel Tower on the river.

▲▲**Champs-Elysées and the Arc de Triomphe**—The Avenue des Champs-Elysées glows after dark (✪ see the Champs-Elysées Walk chapter). Start at the Arc de Triomphe (observation deck open daily, April-Sept until 23:00, Oct-March until 22:30), then stroll down Paris' lively grand promenade. A right turn on Avenue George V leads to the Bateaux-Mouches river cruises. A movie on the Champs-Elysées is a fun experience (weekly listings in *Pariscope* under "Cinéma"), and a drink or snack at Renault's futuristic car café is a kick (at #53, toll tel. 08 11 88 28 11).

▲**Ile St. Louis and Notre-Dame**—Take the beautiful ✪ Historic Paris Walk after dinner on the Ile St. Louis (see page 448).

To get to the Ile St. Louis, take the Métro (line 7) to the Pont Marie stop, then cross Pont Marie to Ile St. Louis. Turn right up Rue St. Louis-en-l'Ile, stopping for dinner—or at least a Berthillon ice cream (at #31) or Amorino Gelati (at #47). At the end of Ile St. Louis, cross Pont St. Louis to Ile de la Cité, with a great view of Notre-Dame. Wander to the Left Bank on Quai de l'Archevêché, and drop down to the river for the best floodlit views. From May through September you'll find several permanently moored barges *(péniches)* that operate as bars. Although I wouldn't eat dinner on one of these barges, the atmosphere is great for a drink, often including live music on weekends (daily until 2:00 in the morning, closed Oct-April, live music often Thu-Sun from 21:00). End your walk on Place du Parvis Notre-Dame in front of Notre-Dame (tower open Sat-Sun until 23:00 in July-Aug), or go back across the river to the Latin Quarter.

**Open-Air Sculpture Garden**—Day or night, this skinny riverfront park dotted with modern art makes for a pleasant walk, but it's especially fun on balmy evenings in the summer, when you may encounter rock and salsa dancing. It's on the Left Bank across from Ile St. Louis, running between the Arab World Institute and Jardin des Plantes (free, music around 20:00, very weather-dependent, Quai St. Bernard, Mo: Cardinal Lemoine plus an eight-minute walk up Rue Cardinal Lemoine toward the river).

**Place de la Concorde, Place Vendôme, and Place de l'Opéra**—These three squares tie together nicely for an elegant post-dinner walk (see page 482 in the Shopping in Paris chapter). Take the Métro to Place de la Concorde, and maybe splurge for a pricey drink at one of Paris' most expensive hotels (Hôtel Crillon, see "Les Grands Cafés de Paris" near the end of the Eating in Paris chapter). Get out to the obelisk for a terrific view of the Champs-Elysées and the beautifully lit, Greek-looking National Assembly building (to your left as you are looking up the Champs-Elysées). Then walk up Rue Royale toward La Madeleine, turn right on Rue St. Honoré, then left after several blocks on Rue Castiglione. The sumptuous Place Vendôme makes me wish I were rich. Exit Place Vendôme at the opposite end and walk up Rue de la Paix to find Opéra Garnier, stunning at night (see page 78; Mo: Opéra is right there to take you home).

**Marais**—This artsy neighborhood is a hotbed for nightlife, full of cafés and tiny bars catering to locals and tourists alike. The action centers around Rue Vieille du Temple (Mo: St. Paul), which offers something for every taste and attracts all age groups and sexual persuasions. Look for the Au Petit Fer à Cheval bar and the book-store/winebar La Belle Hortense (daily 17:00-24:00, 31 Rue Vieille du Temple, tel. 01 48 04 71 60), and fan out from there. At the western edge of the Marais, you'll find good boy-meets-girl energy at bars along Rue des Lombards near where it crosses Boulevard de Sebastopol (Mo: Châtelet or Hôtel de Ville, see also "Jazz and Blues Clubs," earlier).

**Place St. Germain-des-Prés and Odéon**—These areas are close to each other and worth combining for evening fun. The church of St. Germain-des-Prés is often lit up and open at night, and Parisians sip drinks at two famous nearby cafés: Les Deux Magots and Le Café de Flore (see page 274; Mo: St. Germain-des-Prés). A few blocks toward St. Sulpice Church, night owls prowl along Rues des Canettes and Guisarde, and a few blocks toward the river, they do the same along Rue de Buci (see "Near St. Sulpice Church" on page 450 of the Eating in Paris chapter). The Odéon, a few blocks away, is home to several movie theaters and still more lively cafés.

## After-Dark Tours

Several companies offer evening tours of Paris. You can take a traditional, mass-produced bus tour for €25 per person, or for a little more (around €100 per couple), take an hour-long, vintage-car tour with a student guide. A pedicab will take you around for €40-50 per hour. Do-it-yourself-ers can save money by hiring a cab for a private tour (€50 for one hour). All options are described below.

Adjust your expectations to the changing times. Paris will always be the City of Light, but it shines a little dimmer these days. In an effort to go green and save money, Paris has toned down the lighting on several monuments, including the Arc de Triomphe and the Louvre's glass pyramid.

### ▲▲▲Deux Chevaux Car Tours

If rumbling around Paris and sticking your head out of the rolled-back top of a funky old 2CV car *à la* Inspector Clouseau sounds like

your kind of fun, do this. Two enterprising companies have assembled a veritable fleet of these "tin-can" cars (France's version of the VW "bug" that hasn't been made since 1985) for giving tourists tours of Paris day and night (**Paris Authentic** and **4 Roues Sous 1 Parapluie**). Night is best. The student-guides are informal, speak English, and are passionate about showing you their city. Appreciate the simplicity of the vehicle you're in. Notice the bare-bones dashboard. Ask your guide to honk the horn, to run the silly little wipers, and to open and close the air vent—*c'est magnifique!* They'll pick you up and drop you at your hotel or wherever you choose. **Paris Authentic** offers many options (€45/person for 2 people for a 1-hour tour, €33/person for 3 people; €160/couple for a 2-hour tour that includes Montmartre and a bottle of champagne, 10 percent tip is appropriate, 23 Rue Jean-Jacques Rousseau, mobile 06 64 50 44 19, www.parisauthentic.com, infos@parisauthentic .com). **4 Roues Sous 1 Parapluie**, which translates to "4 wheels under 1 umbrella," offers comparable tours with candy-colored cars and drivers dressed in striped shirts and berets. Evening tours last 1.5 hours and cost €90 per person for two, €60 per person if you fit three passengers, and €180 if you want the whole backseat to yourself (tel. 08 00 80 06 31, mobile 06 67 32 26 68, www.4roues-sous-1parapluie.com, info@4roues-sous-1parapluie.com)

### Pedicab Tours

Experience the City of Light at an escargot's pace with your private chauffeur pedaling a sleek, human-powered tricycle from TripUp Pedicab Tours. Call ahead, book online, or flag one down; they usually work until about 22:00 (€40-50/hour, mobile 06 98 80 69 33, www.tripup.fr, contact@tripup.fr).

### ▲Nighttime Bus Tours

Below I've listed two different night tours run by the same parent company (Paris Vision). Tickets are sold through your hotel (no booking fee, brochures in lobby) or directly at the Paris Vision office at 214 Rue de Rivoli, across the street from the Tuileries Métro stop.

The nightly **Paris Illuminations** tour is run by Cityrama and connects all the great illuminated sights of Paris with a 100-minute bus tour in 12 languages. The double-decker buses have huge windows, but the most desirable front seats are sometimes reserved for customers who've bought tickets for the overrated Moulin Rouge. Left-side seats are better. Visibility is fine in the rain.

These tours are not for everyone. You'll stampede on with a United Nations of tourists, get a set of headphones, dial up your language, and listen to a tape-recorded spiel (which is interesting, but includes an annoyingly bright TV screen and a pitch for the other, more expensive excursions). Uninspired as it is, the ride provides an entertaining overview of the city at its floodlit and scenic best. Bring your city map to stay oriented as you go. You're always on the bus, but the driver slows for photos at viewpoints (€25, kids-€12.50, 1.75 hours, departs from 2 Rue des Pyramides at 20:00 Nov-March, at 22:00 April-Oct, reserve one day in advance, arrive 30 minutes early to wait in line for best seats, Mo: Pyramides, tel. 01 42 60 30 01, www.pariscityvision.com/en/cityrama/paris-illuminations).

Paris Vision also offers **Paris Illuminations-By Minibus,** which are minivan night tours following a similar route to the bus tours. They will pick you up and drop you off at your hotel (€55, kids-€40, 2 hours, tel. 01 42 60 30 01, www.parisvision.com).

## ▲▲▲Floodlit Paris Taxi Tour

Seeing the City of Light floodlit is one of Europe's great travel experiences and a great finale to any day in Paris. Sunday is by far the best night to go, as there's less traffic—you'll get a better value for the time spent in a taxi. For less than the cost of two seats on a big bus tour, you can hire your own cab and have a glorious hour of illuminated Paris on your terms and schedule. The downside: You don't have the high vantage point and big windows of a bus, and taxi drivers can be moody. The upside: It's cheaper, you go when and where you like, and you can jump out anywhere to get the best views and pictures.

**Tour Overview:** This is a circular, one-hour route—from Notre-Dame to the Eiffel Tower along the Left Bank, then back along the Right Bank. Start at the taxi stand at Notre-Dame or any convenient point along the route (or from your hotel) and make any stops you like. Suggested stops are listed in bold on the list in "Taxi Instructions" (*"petit arrêt"* means "little stop"). To make it more of a party, bring a bottle of red wine and some chocolate to enjoy each time you hop out of the taxi (not in the taxi).

**Taxi Logistics:** Taxis have a strict meter (figure €33/hour plus about €1/kilometer; taxis start with €2.40 on the meter). This suggested loop takes an hour and costs around €45 (more on Sun). If your cabbie was easy to work with, add a 10 percent tip; if not, tip just 5 percent. Traffic can be sparse, and lights are shining between 22:00 and 24:00 every night. Your only timing concern: The Eiffel Tower twinkles for only the first five minutes of each hour after

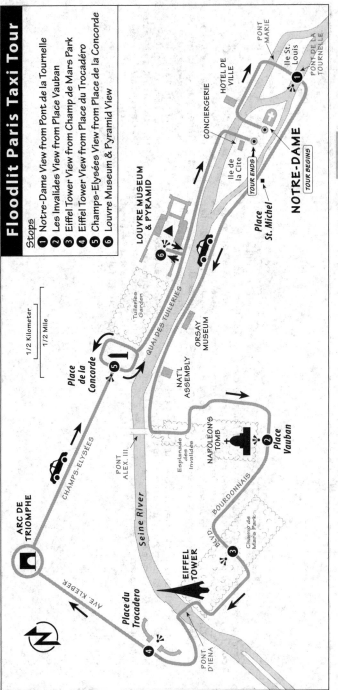

# Floodlit Paris Taxi Tour

*Stops*

1. Notre-Dame View from Pont de la Tournelle
2. Les Invalides View from Place Vauban
3. Eiffel Tower View from Champ de Mars Park
4. Eiffel Tower View from Place du Trocadéro
5. Champs-Elysées View from Place de la Concorde
6. Louvre Museum & Pyramid View

1/2 Kilometer
1/2 Mile

ARC DE TRIOMPHE

AVE. KLÉBER

CHAMPS-ELYSÉES

Place du Trocadéro

PONT D'IÉNA

EIFFEL TOWER

Champ de Mars Park

BLVD BOURDONNAIS

Place Vauban

NAPOLEON'S TOMB

Esplanade des Invalides

PONT ALEX. III

Seine River

NAT'L ASSEMBLY

ORSAY MUSEUM

Place de la Concorde

QUAI DES TUILERIES

Tuileries Garden

LOUVRE MUSEUM & PYRAMID

Place St. Michel

*TOUR ENDS*

Ile de la Cité

CONCIERGERIE

HOTEL DE VILLE

NOTRE-DAME

*TOUR BEGINS*

Ile St. Louis

PONT DE LA TOURNELLE

PONT MARIE

## Taxi Instructions

*Bonjour, Monsieur/Madame. Nous voulons faire un circuit de Paris illuminé d'une heure, avec quelques petits arrêts. Nous paierons le montant indiqué sur le compteur. Nous voudrions suivre la route suivante—combien cela va t-il coûter approximativement? Ça marche?*

Greetings, Monsieur/Madame. We would like a tour of Paris at night for an hour, with a few short stops. We will pay the metered rate. We would like to take the following route—approximately how much will it cost? Can you do it?

1. Notre-Dame
2. Hôtel de Ville
3. Pont Marie
4. **Pont de la Tournelle (arrêt)**
5. Quai de la Tournelle
6. Musée d'Orsay
7. Esplanade des Invalides
8. Invalides
9. **Place Vauban/Eglise du Dôme (arrêt)**
10. **Champ de Mars (Place Jacques Rueff—arrêt)**
11. Tour Eiffel
12. Pont d'Iena
13. **Place du Trocadéro (arrêt)**
14. Avenue Kléber
15. Arc de Triomphe (2 révolutions)
16. Champs-Elysées
17. **Place de la Concorde (1 ou 2 révolutions)**
18. Quai François Mitterrand
19. **Musée du Louvre/Place du Carrousel/Pyramide (arrêt)**
20. Quai du Louvre
21. Notre-Dame

dark. If you start at Notre-Dame at half past the hour, you should be right on time for the sparkles. The driver can take up to four people in a cab, though this is tight for decent sightseeing (with three, everyone gets a window).

Give the driver the instructions printed on the opposite page. Before you go, photocopy it (ask at your hotel), or rip the page out (but trace the route on another map so you can follow along). Make sure the driver understands the plan—and enjoys the challenge. Review with the driver exactly where you hope to stop before you start. Ask him to drive as slowly as possible (say *"Conduisez lentement, s'il vous plaît"*—kohn-dwee-zay lahn-tuh-mahn see voo play) so you can enjoy the ever-changing scene.

And you're on your way. Roll the windows down, learn your driver's name and use it (no first names, use *Monsieur* or *Madame*), and turn the cab light on to read if you like (this is no problem for the driver). Let the cabbie add a few little deviations (which can be great) as long as he understands your general plan. Stop when you want (but remember that the meter runs at about €0.50 per minute when stopped). Some cabbies might speak a little English; if not, learn and use the following key words:

| English | French | Pronounced |
|---|---|---|
| What is your name? | *Comment vous appelez-vous?* | koh-mohn vooz ah-play-voo |
| Slower, please. | *Lentement, s'il vous plaît.* | lahn-tuh-mahn see voo play |
| Stop, please. | *Arrêtez, s'il vous plaît.* | ah-ruh-tay see voo play |
| Wait, please. | *Patientez, s'il vous plaît.* | pah-see-yahn-tay see voo play |
| I love Paris! | *J'aime Paris!* | zhem pah-ree |

**The Tour Begins:** Start at Notre-Dame (taxi stand just in front, on left). Drive over Pont d'Arcole to Hôtel de Ville, then turn right along the Seine (the white stripe of light is a modern bridge connecting the two islands).

Cross the Ile St. Louis on Pont Marie. Stop on the next bridge (Pont de la Tournelle) just after the island, get out, and giggle with delight at the city and illuminated Notre-Dame. Then turn right along the Seine on Quai de la Tournelle, motoring scenically past Notre-Dame.

Drive west along the entire length of the long Louvre—once the world's biggest building (across the river), then under the Orsay Museum (above you, on left). The National Assembly (on left) faces Place de la Concorde (on right). The ornate Pont Alexandre III comes next (on right).

Turn left down Esplanade des Invalides to the gilded dome of Les Invalides, marking Napoleon's Tomb. As you approach the grand building, watch the illusion of the fancy dome sinking behind the facade. Circle clockwise around Invalides for a close-up view. Get out at Place Vauban (behind the dome) and marvel at its symmetry.

Take Avenue de Tourville to Avenue de la Bourdonnais, which runs alongside the Champ de Mars park (former military training grounds that now serve as the Eiffel Tower's backyard). Turn left onto Avenue Joseph Bouvard, leading to a circle made to order for viewing the Eiffel Tower. Get out and gasp.

Pont d'Iéna leads from directly in front of the tower across the Seine to Place du Trocadéro for another grand Eiffel view (get out again and walk toward the tower to get the best photos and to enjoy the night scene here).

Avenue Kléber leads through one of Paris' ritziest neighborhoods to the Arc de Triomphe. Battle twice around the eternal flame marking the Tomb of the Unknown Soldier and Paris' craziest traffic circle: Ask for *"Deux révolutions, s'il vous plaît"* (duh ray-voh-loo-see-yohn see voo play). Notice the rules of the road: Get to the center ASAP, those entering have the right-of-way, and any accidents are no-fault (insurance companies split the costs down the middle). As you circle, notice the uniform boulevards reaching out like spokes from this hub. Try to find the huge and modern La Grande Arche in the distance opposite the Champs-Elysées.

When ready to continue, say the rhyme, "Champs-Elysées, *s'il vous plaît*" (shahnz ay-lee-zay see voo play). Glide down Europe's grandest boulevard—past fancy restaurants, car dealerships, and theaters—to the bold white obelisk marking the former site of the guillotine, Place de la Concorde.

Circle once (maybe twice) around Place de la Concorde, picking out all the famous landmarks near and far. Stop at the center to look up the Champs-Elysées. Then continue east (reminding your cabbie the next stop is "la Pyramide du Louvre") along the Seine on Quai des Tuileries (the two train-station clocks across the river mark the Orsay Museum) and sneak (via a taxi/bus-only lane) into the courtyard of the Louvre for a close look at the magically glowing pyramid. Stop here.

Return to the riverfront along the Right Bank and pass the oldest bridge in Paris, Pont Neuf, and the impressive Conciergerie with its floodlit medieval turrets (this is where

Marie-Antoinette was imprisoned during the Revolution). Turn right on Pont de Notre-Dame and you complete the loop back where you (and Paris) started, at Place du Parvis, facing Notre-Dame on the Ile de la Cité. Or you can ask your cabbie to take you back to your hotel (roughly €15 more).

# PARIS IN WINTER

The City of Light sparkles year-round, but Paris has a special appeal in winter. You'll find inexpensive airfares, fewer crowds, and soft prices for hotel rooms and apartments (rent one for a week or more). Sure, the weather can be cold and rainy (average high in Dec is 44°F), but if you dress in layers, you'll keep warm and easily deal with temperature changes as you go from cold streets to heated museums and cafés.

Paris in winter offers so much to do indoors. Museums, restaurants, and stores stay open as usual; the concert and arts season is in full bloom; and Paris belongs to the Parisians. So go local, save money, and skip the museum lines that confront peak-season travelers. There are worse ways to spend a wintry day than enjoying world-class art, architecture, and shopping during the day and then lingering over a fine (smoke-free) dinner at a cozy corner bistro in the evening. As Cole Porter put it: "I love Paris in the winter, when it drizzles."

Slow down and savor your favorite museums and monuments— spending one-on-one time with Mona and Venus is worth the extra clothes you have to pack. Attend a cooking demonstration, take a short course in art or architecture, or dabble in a wine-tasting class (for details, see the sidebar on page 36). Duck into cafés for a break from sightseeing or shopping, and to warm up. Get on a first-name basis with the waiter at your corner café—just because you can now.

Easter marks the start of the tourist season, when locals find they need to make reservations for their favorite restaurants and can't find seats on the Métro.

This chapter reviews off-season highlights in Paris, but remember—your reward for traveling in winter is the joy of feeling part of a city, like you almost belong here. That's what you'll find on a trip to Paris from November to March.

## November

From late October well into November, **leaves** tumble from Paris' trees, revealing magnificent building facades and turning parks into austere yet romantic places. Winter also brings early sunsets and long evenings, ideal for floodlit neighborhood walks, boat rides, and taxi tours that allow you to view the city of light at a reasonable hour.

Beginning one minute after midnight on the third Thursday of November and running through mid-December, Paris welcomes the arrival of the **Beaujolais Nouveau** with uncharacteristic enthusiasm for such a controlled people. The fresh, fruity wine is rushed from vineyards a bit north of Lyon directly to Paris, where wine bars and most cafés serve it happily, buzzing with news of the latest vintage. The first 24 hours are the most fun and raucous, and it's easy to join the party if you don't mind elbowing your way to the *comptoir* for *un verre*. Cafés and bistros continue the celebration for weeks, many offering special dishes with a glass of the Beaujolais Nouveau.

And speaking of wine, the annual *Salon des Vins des Vignerons Indépendants* (independent winemakers' trade show) is held in Paris on the last weekend of November at the Porte de Versailles exhibition center (Mo: Porte de Versailles, line 12). Here, anyone can sample fine wines from more than 1,000 different stands for about a €6 entry fee.

## December

One of Europe's greatest treats is strolling down the glowing Champs-Elysées in winter. From late November through early January, **holiday lights** adorn city streets, buildings, and monuments, and the Champs-Elysées beams with a dazzling display of lights on the trees that line the long boulevard. The city springs for 1,000 fresh-cut fir trees to put up and decorate around town, 300 of which ring the Rond-Point roundabout at the lower end of the Champs-Elysées. You'll also find cheerful lighting displays on many traffic-free streets, including Rues Cler, Montorgueil, and Daguerre.

Parisians live to **window-shop** (remember that *faire du lèche-vitrines* means "window-licking"). Do some licking of your own along Boulevard Haussmann and view the storefront lights and wild window displays at the grand department stores such as Printemps and Galeries Lafayette. Here you can have your picture taken with Père Noël—France's slimmer version of Santa Claus, dressed in red trimmed with white fur. The  seasonal displays in neighborhood boutiques around Sèvres-Baby-lone and in the Marais (among other areas) are more intimate and offer a good contrast to the shows of glitz around the department stores.

Several **ice-skating rinks** open up in festive locations: in front of the Hôtel de Ville (Paris' main city hall, look also for a small sled run), at the base of the Montparnasse skyscraper, and, in some winters, most spectacular of all—200 feet in the air on the first level of the Eiffel Tower (see photo at the beginning of chapter). The rinks are free to use (around €5 to rent skates, generally open late Nov-Jan from noon into the evening), though for the Eiffel Tower rink, you have to pay the tower admission, of course.

For the kids, there are **Christmas carousels** *(Manèges de Noël)* that whirl at various locations, including the biggies at Hôtel de Ville and the Eiffel Tower. As soon as school lets out, parks come alive with pony rides, puppet shows, and other activities.

The dazzling château **Vaux-le-Vicomte,** an hour south of Paris, opens for Christmas with special holiday decorations (€17, weekends only Dec-early Jan 10:45-18:00; see page 577 for details on the château).

## The Christmas Season

With the arrival of St. Nicholas on December 6, the Christmas season kicks into gear. (Bear in mind, though, that Paris celebrates Christmas with only about 10 percent of the holiday cheer that you'll find in the States.) In mid-December, **Christmas markets** pop up, particularly on the Left Bank (St. Sulpice and St. Germain-des-Prés) and along the Champs-Elysées. At **Notre-Dame,** a big Christmas tree goes up, and they may have a living *crêche* in front. The **Pompidou Center** has an avant-garde tradition: an exhibit of contemporary artists' takes on the Christmas tree. Parisians pick up modest Christmas trees for their homes at flower shops—if you rent an apartment, you could do the same. Be sure to check the *Pariscope* magazine for popular and often free or inexpensive **Christmas concerts.**

## Christmas Eve and Christmas Day

The big event is the Christmas Eve dinner, called **La Réveillon**—
"the awakening"—when Parisians stay awake late to celebrate
the arrival of Jesus. Traditionally, they attend evening Mass (at
Notre-Dame, among other churches), then meet with family and
friends for a big feast. The meal begins with (what else?) escargots, smoked salmon or oysters, and then foie gras. The main dish,

similar to American Thanksgiv-
ing, is turkey, served with a sort
of cranberry sauce, and potatoes
*(gratin dauphinois)*. This evening
is normally celebrated at home
and with family, though some
Paris restaurants (and other
businesses) stay open late to accommodate parties indulging in
raw oysters, cheese, and the Yule

Log *(Bûche de Noël)*—a log-shaped sponge cake iced with chocolate
"bark." After dinner the kiddies leave their slippers next to the fireplace for Père Noël to fill with treats.

On Christmas Day, Paris is very sleepy—make arrangements
ahead of time if you've got a plane to catch, and don't plan on visiting the Louvre (which is closed, along with most museums and
businesses). Visitors looking for **religious services in English** will
find no shortage of churches to attend—choose between the interdenominational American Church, American Cathedral, Unitarian Church, and St. George's Anglican Church (listed in the
appendix). Many of these churches—especially the American
Church—also offer Christmas concerts.

## January

Start the **New Year** off with a bang at the over-the-top fireworks
display at the Eiffel Tower, when thousands of Parisians congregate
on the Champ de Mars before midnight. All of Paris parties on
New Year's Eve, and a table at a restaurant is next to impossible to
land (book early or dine at a café). The holidays aren't over yet—
Paris celebrates the arrival of the Three Kings on **Epiphany** (Jan 6)
with as much fanfare as Christmas itself. The after-Christmas sales
*(soldes)* are an even bigger post-holiday tradition, as locals jam the
boutiques and department stores looking for bargains. These sales,
which last until early February, force stores to keep longer hours.

Parisians celebrate the **Chinese New Year** in a big way (usually falls near the end of January) with parades, decorations, and
fanfare. Ask your hotelier or a TI for parade locations.

PARIS IN WINTER

## Seasonal Foods

Winter is the season for the hunt, when you'll find game birds and venison on restaurant menus. Seventy percent of France's oysters are eaten in the month of December, most of them raw and on the half-shell. Look for busy shuckers outside big cafés, where most oysters are consumed. On street corners you'll hear shouts of *"Chaud les marrons!"* from vendors selling chestnuts roasting on coals. Chocolatiers (including La Maison du Chocolat's five stores) and pastry shops everywhere do a bang-up business during the holiday season, serving traditional treats such as Epiphany cakes (flaky marzipan cakes called *roi de galettes*). Bakeries overflow with these popular cakes starting January 6.

If you like gourmet food, take a spin around Place de la Madeleine, comparing Fauchon's festive displays with Hédiard's, and spring for a truffle omelet at La Maison des Truffles—after all, winter is truffle season (for info on these shops, see page 483 and 484). Just because it's cold doesn't mean that outdoor markets are quiet—*au contraire*, you'll find markets alive with shoppers and vendors no matter what the weather (on Place d'Aligre and along Rue de Grenelle, for example).

One of the great pleasures Paris offers is watching the city bustle while you linger at an outdoor table with a *café crème*, a *vin chaud* (hot wine), or, best, a hot chocolate (simply called *chocolat* and *très* popular in winter). Most cafés fire up the braziers and drape blankets over chairs to keep things toasty outside. And with the strict smoking laws, café and restaurant interiors are wonderfully free of any trace of smoke.

## February and March

These are the quiet months, when Paris is most alone with itself. And though holiday decorations disappear, the City of Light is as beautiful and seductive as ever. Visit Paris in winter and—for a few days—become a Parisian.

# PARIS CONNECTIONS

This chapter covers Paris' two main airports, one smaller airport, seven train stations, and its main bus station. It also includes parking tips for drivers.

Whether you're aiming to catch a train or plane, budget plenty of time to reach your departure point. Paris is a big, crowded city, and getting across town on time is a goal you'll share with millions of other harried people. Factor in traffic delays and walking time through huge stations and vast terminals. At the airport, expect lines at ticketing, check-in, baggage check, and security points. Always keep your luggage safely near you. Pickpockets prey on jet-lagged and confused tourists on public transportation.

## Airports

### Charles de Gaulle Airport (airport code: CDG)

Paris' main airport has three terminals: T-1, T-2, and T-3 (see map). Most flights from the US use T-1 or T-2 (check your ticket, or contact your airline). All three terminals have ATMs *(distributeurs)*, shops, bars, and access to ground transportation into Paris. You can travel between terminals on the free CDGVAL automated shuttle train (departs every 5 minutes, 24/7). Allow 30 minutes to travel between terminals and an hour for total travel time between your gates at T-1 and T-2.

When leaving Paris, plan to arrive at the airport two to three hours early for an overseas flight, or one to two hours for flights within Europe (particularly on budget airlines, which can have especially long check-in lines). For flight info, dial either 3950 from French landlines (€0.35/minute) or, from the US, dial 011 33 1 70 36 39 50, or visit www.adp.fr.

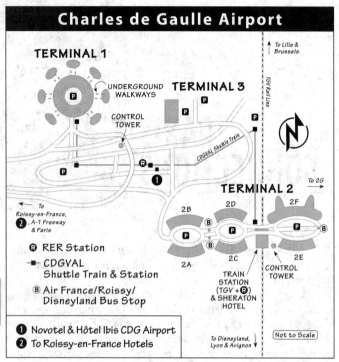

# Charles de Gaulle Airport

TERMINAL 1

UNDERGROUND WALKWAYS

TERMINAL 3

CONTROL TOWER

To Lille & Brussels

TGV Rail Line

CDGVAL Shuttle Train

N

To 2G

TERMINAL 2

2B

2D

2F

To Roissy-en-France, A-1 Freeway & Paris

2A

2C

TRAIN STATION (TGV + Ⓡ) & SHERATON HOTEL

2E

CONTROL TOWER

Ⓡ RER Station

▪■ CDGVAL Shuttle Train & Station

Ⓑ Air France/Roissy/ Disneyland Bus Stop

❶ Novotel & Hôtel Ibis CDG Airport

❷ To Roissy-en-France Hotels

To Disneyland, Lyon & Avignon

Not to Scale

PARIS CONNECTIONS

## Terminal 1 (T-1)

This circular terminal has three key floors—arrival *(arrivées)* on the top floor, and two floors for departures *(départs)* below.

**Arrival Level**—*(niveau arrivée)*: After passing through customs, you'll exit between doors *(porte)* 34 and 36. Nearby are orange information counters with English-speaking staff, a TI (where you can buy a Paris Museum Pass), a café, a newsstand, and an ATM. Walk clockwise around the terminal to find ground transportation: Air France and Roissy buses (door 32), Disneyland shuttles (door 30), and taxis (door 10). Car rentals are at doors 24-30.

**Departure Levels**—*(niveaux départ)*: Scan the departure screen to find out which hall you should go to for check in. Halls 1-4 are on floor 2, and 5-6 are downstairs on floor 1. Also on floor 1 are the CDGVAL shuttle train, cafés, a post office (PTT), pharmacy, boutiques, and a handy grocery. Boarding gates and duty-free shopping are located on floor 3, which is only accessible with a boarding pass.

## Terminal 2 (T-2)

This long, horseshoe-shaped terminal is divided into six halls, labeled A through F. It's a busy place, so take a deep breath and follow signage carefully. The orange information desks are located near gate 6/8 in each hall (ask where to buy a Paris Museum Pass). Taxi stops are well signed. To locate stops for Air France, Roissy, and Disneyland buses—marked on the map on page 514—follow *Paris by Bus* signs. T-2 has a train station, with RER suburban trains into Paris (described later), as well as longer-distance trains to the rest of France (including high-speed TGV trains). It's located between halls C/D and E/F, below the Sheraton Hotel (prepare for a long walk to reach your train).

Car-rental offices, post offices, pharmacies, and ATMs are all well-signed. You can stash your bags at Baggage du Monde, located above the train station in T-2, but it's pricey (€15 for 24 hours), so I'd use a train station's storage instead (tel. 01 34 38 58 97, www.bagagesdumonde.com).

## Transportation Between Charles de Gaulle Airport and Paris

Buses, airport vans, commuter trains, and taxis link the airport's terminals with central Paris. If you're traveling with two or more companions, carrying lots of baggage, or are just plain tired, taxis are worth the extra cost. If you're arriving on a weekday morning, however, taxis are much less appealing, as traffic into Paris can be bad—in that case, the train is likely to be a better option.

### By Bus

**Roissy-Buses** make the 50-minute trip to the Opéra Métro stop in central Paris, arriving on Rue Scribe. From there, it's an easy Métro ride to anywhere in the city. To get to the Métro entrance or nearest taxi stand, turn left as you exit the bus and walk counter-clockwise around the lavish Opéra building to its front (€10, runs 6:00-23:00, 4/hour until 20:45, 3/hour after that, 50 minutes, buy ticket on bus).

For Rue Cler hotels, take Métro line 8 (direction: Balard) to La Tour Maubourg or Ecole Militaire. For hotels in the Marais neighborhood, take line 8 (direction: Créteil Préfecture) to the Bastille stop. A taxi to any of my listed hotels costs about €12 from here.

**"Les Cars" Air France buses** run at least twice hourly from 5:45 until 23:00 (tel. 08 92 35 08 20). **Bus #2** goes to the Etoile stop near the Arc de Triomphe (€16.50, 45 minutes, see map on page 288) and Porte Maillot (with connections to Beauvais Airport, described later). Once at the Arc de Triomphe, catch city bus #92 (one block away) to the Rue Cler area. **Bus #4** runs to Gare de Lyon (45 minutes) and the Montparnasse Tower/train station (€16.50, 1 hour). **Bus #3** goes to Orly airport (€19, 1 hour). Buy tickets from the driver (round-trip tickets or 2 persons traveling together save

# Public Transportation
# to Recommended Hotels

You have many options for traveling between Charles de Gaulle Airport and Paris; which alternative makes the most sense depends not only on your budget, but where you're staying in the city. Here are my tips for getting to recommended hotels, according to the neighborhood they're in. Keep in mind that, at the airport, using buses (and taxis) require shorter walks than taking RER trains.

**Rue Cler Area:** The Roissy-Bus, RER, and "Les Cars" Air France bus all work well for Rue Cler hotels. If taking the Roissy-Bus, ride it all the way to the Opéra stop, then take Métro line 8 (direction: Balard) and get off at the La Tour Maubourg or Ecole Militaire stop. Or hop the RER-B from the airport, change at the St. Michel stop for the RER-C (direction: Versailles Rive Gauche or Pontoise), and, depending on where exactly your hotel is, either change again at the Invalides stop to Métro line 8 (direction: Balard; get off either at La Tour Mauberg or Ecole Militaire), or stay on the RER for one more stop, and get off at Pont de l'Alma. If riding the Air France bus, take it to the Arc de Triomphe, then grab the #92 city bus and hop off at one of the stops along Avenue Bosquet, shortly after crossing the river (for stop locations near the Arc, see the map on page 288; for stop locations on Avenue Bosquet, see page 388).

**Marais and Ile St. Louis:** Take "Les Cars" Air France bus (#4) to Gare de Lyon, find the Métro entry near the bus stop, then take a quick trip on Métro line 1 (direction: La Défense). Get off at the Bastille or St. Paul stops for the Marais, or the Hôtel de Ville stop for Ile St. Louis. Or, take RER-B from the airport to the Châtelet-Les Halles stop and transfer to Métro line 1 (direction: Château de Vincennes; long walk in a huge station), and get off at Hôtel de Ville, St. Paul, or Bastille.

**Luxembourg Garden:** RER-B to the Luxembourg stop.

20 percent) or online, which saves you an additional 10 percent (www.lescarsairfrance.com).

From Paris to the airport, catch Air France buses at Etoile/Arc de Triomphe (on Avenue Carnot—the non-Champs-Elysées side), Porte Maillot (on Boulevard Gouvion-St-Cyr—right side of the Palais des Congres), Gare Montparnasse (on Rue du Commandant Mouchotte—facing the station with the tower behind you, it's around the left side), or Gare de Lyon (in front of #20 Boulevard Diderot—the main street in front of the station).

## By Airport Van

The shuttle vans from Charles de Gaulle work like those at home, carrying passengers directly to and from their hotels, with stops along the way to pick up other passengers. Shuttles work best for trips from your hotel to the airport, since they require you to book a precise pickup time in advance—even though you can't ever know exactly when your flight will actually arrive. Airport vans cost about €32 for one person, €46 for two, and €58 for three. While these vans take longer to reach the airport than a taxi does, compared to taxis they're a good value for single travelers and big families. Have your hotelier book at least a day in advance.

Several companies offer shuttle service; I usually just go with the one my hotel normally uses. Otherwise, try **Paris Shuttles Network** (tel. 01 45 26 01 58, www.shuttlesnetwork.com) or **Airport Connection** (tel. 01 43 65 55 55, www.supershuttle.fr).

**Paris Webservices** actually works well from the airport to Paris, because they meet you inside the terminal and will wait for you if you're late (tel. 01 53 62 02 29, fax 01 53 01 35 84, www.pariswebservices.com, contactpws@pariswebservices.com). For a one-way trip they charge about €30 for one person, or €44 for 2 people. Booking a round trip costs about €160-180 for up to 4 people. Claim a 10 percent discount by mentioning promo code "RSteves77" when you book, then showing your driver a current edition of this book. They also sell Museum Passes with no extra fee (order ahead) and offer excursions (see page 50).

## By Commuter Train

The RER, Paris' suburban commuter train, is your cheapest (though not most convenient) option for getting between the airport and the city center (€9.30, runs 5:00-24:00, 4/hour, 30 minutes to Gare du Nord). It runs directly to well-located RER/Métro stations (including Gare du Nord, Châtelet-Les Halles, St. Michel, and Luxembourg); from there, you can hop the Métro to get exactly where you need to go. It's handy and cheap, but it can require walking with your luggage through big, crowded stations.

From the airport terminal, follow *Paris by Train* signs, then *RER* signs. (If you're landing at Terminals 1 or 3, you'll need to take the CDGVAL shuttle to reach the RER station.) The RER station at T-2 is also a crowded train station, with long ticket-window lines. It's faster to buy tickets from the machines (use the green-colored machines that read *Paris/Ile de France*, coins required, break your bills at an airport shop). Beware of pickpockets; wear your money belt, and keep your bags close. For step-by-step instructions on taking the RER into Paris, see http://parisbytrain.com (see the options under "CDG Airport to Paris").

If you're taking the RER from central Paris out to the airport, allow plenty of time to get to your departure gate (plan for a 10-minute Métro or bus ride to the closest RER station, a 15-minute wait for your RER, plus a 30-minute ride, plus walking time through the stations and airport). At the RER station, make sure the sign over the platform shows *Aéroport Roissy-Charles de Gaulle* as a stop served. (The line splits, so not every line B train serves the airport.) If you're not clear, ask another rider, *"Air-o-por sharl duh gaul?"* Once at the airport, hop out either at T-2 or T-1/3 (where you can connect to T-1 or T-3 on the CDGVAL shuttle).

### By Taxi

The 50-minute trip costs about €65 (more if traffic is bad). Taxis can carry three people with bags comfortably, and are legally required to accept a fourth passenger for €3 extra (though they may not like it). Larger parties can wait for a larger vehicle. Expect to pay a €1/bag handling fee. Don't take an unauthorized taxi from cabbies greeting you on arrival. Official taxi stands are well-signed.

For trips from Paris to the airport, have your hotel arrange it. Specify that you want a real taxi *(un taxi normal)*, not a limo service that costs €20 more (and gives your hotel a kickback). For weekday morning departures (7:00-10:00), reserve at least a day ahead (€5 reservation fee payable by credit card). For more on taxis in Paris, see page 42.

### By Car

Car-rental desks are well-signed from the arrival halls. When returning your car, allow ample time to reach the check-in desks, especially if flying out of Terminal 2—its imperfect signage can make it especially confusing to navigate.

### From Charles de Gaulle Airport to Disneyland Paris

The Val d'Europe (VEA) **Disneyland shuttle bus** leaves from each terminal (€19, runs every 20 minutes 8:30-20:00ish, 30 minutes, www.vea-shuttle.co.uk). TGV trains also run to Disneyland from the airport in 10 minutes, but leave less frequently (hourly) and require shuttle buses at each end—take the shuttle van instead.

## Orly Airport (airport code: ORY)

This easy-to-navigate airport feels small, but has all the services you'd expect at a major airport: ATMs and currency exchange, car-rental desks, cafés, shops, a post office, a TI, and more (for flight info from French landlines dial 3950, from the US dial 011 33 1 70 36 39 50, www.adp.fr). Orly is good for rental-car pickup and drop-off, as it's closer to Paris and far easier to navigate than Charles de Gaulle Airport.

Orly has two terminals: Ouest (west) and Sud (south). Air France and a few other carriers arrive at Ouest; most others use Sud. At both terminals, arrivals are on the ground level (level 0) and departures are on level 1. You can connect the terminals with the free Orlyval shuttle train (departs from Ouest departures level 1 at exit A; from Sud at exit K), or with any of the shuttle buses *(navettes)* that also travel into downtown Paris.

## Transportation Between Orly Airport and Paris

Shuttle buses *(navettes)*, the RER, taxis, and airport vans connect Paris with either terminal.

### By Bus

**"Les Cars" Air France bus #1** runs to Gare Montparnasse, Invalides, and Etoile Métro stops, all of which have connections to several Métro lines. Upon request, drivers will also stop at the Porte d'Orléans Métro stop. For the Rue Cler neighborhood, take the bus to Invalides, then the Métro to La Tour Maubourg or Ecole Militaire. Buses depart from Ouest arrival level exit B-C or Sud exit L: Look for signs to *navettes* (€12 one-way, 4/hour, 40 minutes to Invalides, buy ticket from driver or save 10 percent by booking online, round-trip tickets or 2 persons traveling together save 20 percent, www.lescarsairfrance.com).

The **Orlybus** goes directly to the Denfert-Rochereau Métro stop. From there, you can catch the Métro or RER-B to central Paris, including the Luxembourg Garden area, Notre-Dame Cathedral, and Gare du Nord. The Orlybus departs from Ouest arrival level exit D and Sud exit H (€7, 3/hour, 30 minutes).

A different bus called **"Paris par le train"** takes you to the Pont d'Orly RER station, where you can catch the RER-C to Gare d'Austerlitz, St. Michel/Notre-Dame, Musée d'Orsay, Invalides (change here for Rue Cler hotels), and Pont de l'Alma. Catch this bus at Ouest arrival level exit G or Sud exit F (€7 total, 4/hour, 40 minutes).

The **Orlyval shuttle train** takes you to the Antony RER station, where you can catch RER-B (direction: Mitry-Claye or Aéroport Charles de Gaulle) to Luxembourg and many recommended hotels, Châtelet-Les Halles, St. Michel, and Gare du Nord. Catch the Orlyval at Ouest arrival level exit A or Sud exit K (€11 total, 6/hour, 40 minutes).

### By Taxi

Taxis are outside Ouest arrival level exit B, and to the far right as you leave terminal Sud, at exit M. Allow €40-50 with bags for a taxi into central Paris.

### By Airport Van

Airport vans are a good means of getting from Paris to the airport, especially for single travelers or families of four or more (too many for most taxis; see page 518). From Orly, figure about €23 for one person, or €30 for two people (less per person for larger groups and kids).

### From Orly Airport to Disneyland Paris

The Val d'Europe (VEA) **shuttle bus to Disneyland** departs from Ouest arrival level platform A, exit I; and from the Sud bus station platform 2, exit G (€18, hourly 9:00-19:30, 45 minutes).

## Beauvais Airport (airport code: BVA)

Budget airlines such as Ryanair use this small airport, offering dirt-cheap airfares but leaving you 50 miles north of Paris. Still, this airport has direct buses to Paris (see below) and is handy for travelers heading to Normandy or Belgium (car rental available). The airport is basic, waiting areas are crowded, and services are sparse, but improvements are gradually on the way (airport tel. 08 92 68 20 66—lines open daily 8:00-20:00, www.aeroportbeauvais.com; Ryanair tel. 08 92 78 02 10—lines open Mon-Fri 9:00-19:00, Sat 10:00-17:00, Sun 11:00-17:00; www.ryanair.com).

### Transportation Between Beauvais Airport and Paris

**Buses** depart from the airport when they're full (about 20 minutes after flights arrive) and take 1.5 hours to reach Paris. Buy your ticket (€15 one-way) at the little kiosk to the right as you exit the airport. Buses arrive at Porte Maillot on the west edge of Paris (on Métro line 1 and RER-C). The closest taxi stand is at Hôtel Concorde-Lafayette.

Buses heading to Beauvais Airport leave from Porte Maillot about 3.25 hours before scheduled flight departures. Catch the bus in the parking lot on Boulevard Pershing next to Hôtel Concorde-Lafayette. Arrive with enough time to purchase your bus ticket before boarding (*parking* Pershing ticket booth tel. 01 58 05 08 45, airport ticket booth tel. 03 44 11 46 86).

**Trains** connect Beauvais' city center and Paris' Gare du Nord (20/day, 1.25 hours). To reach Beauvais' train station, take the Beauvais *navette* (€4, 6/day, 30 minutes) or local bus #12 (€1, 12/day, 30 minutes).

**Taxis** run from Beauvais Airport to Beauvais' train station or city center (€14) or central Paris (allow €130 and 1.25 hours).

### From Beauvais Airport to Disneyland Paris

The Val d'Europe (VEA) **shuttle bus to Disneyland** runs three times a day from Beauvais via Charles de Gaulle Airport (€30, 2.5 hours).

## Connecting Paris' Airports

**"Les Cars" Air France bus #3** directly and conveniently links Charles de Gaulle and Orly airports (€19.50, stops at Charles de Gaulle Terminals 1 and 2 and Orly Ouest exit B-C or Sud exit L, roughly 2/hour, 5:45-23:00, 1 hour).

**RER line B** connects Charles de Gaulle and Orly but requires a transfer to the Orlyval train. It isn't as easy as the Air France bus mentioned above, though it's faster when there's traffic (€18, 5/hour, 1.5 hours). This line splits at both ends: Heading to Orly, take trains that serve the Antony stop (direction: St-Rémy-les-Chevreuse), then transfer to Orlyval train; heading to Charles de Gaulle, take trains that end at the airport ("Aéroport Charles de Gaulle-Roissy"), not Mitry-Claye. You can also connect Charles de Gaulle or Orly airports to Beauvais via train. Take the RER-B to Gare du Nord, catch a train to Beauvais, and then a shuttle or local bus to Beauvais Airport (see "Beauvais Airport," earlier).

Three **Val d'Europe (VEA) buses** a day run between Beauvais and Charles de Gaulle, en route to Disneyland (€15, www.vea-shuttle.co.uk).

**Taxis** are easiest, but pricey (about €80 between Charles de Gaulle and Orly, €115 between Charles de Gaulle and Beauvais, €135 between Orly and Beauvais).

## Cheap Flights

If your Paris visit is part of a longer European trip, and you're considering a train ride that's more than five hours long, a flight may save you both time and money. When comparing your options, factor in the time it takes to get to the airport and how early you'll need to arrive to check in.

The best comparison search engine for both international and intra-European flights is www.kayak.com. For inexpensive flights within Europe, try www.skyscanner.net or www.hipmunk.com.

Well-known cheapo airlines include easyJet, which flies out of Charles de Gaulle and Orly airports, and Ryanair, which flies out of Beauvais Airport. Also check Air France for specials. If you're not sure who else flies to your destination, check that airport's website for a list of carriers.

Be aware of the potential drawbacks of flying on the cheap: nonrefundable and nonchangeable tickets, minimal or nonexistent customer service, treks to airports far outside town, and stingy baggage allowances with steep overage fees. If you're traveling with lots of luggage, a cheap flight can quickly become a bad deal. To avoid unpleasant surprises, read the small print before you book.

# Trains

France's rail system (SNCF) sets the pace in Europe. Its super TGV (tay zhay vay; *train à grande vitesse*) system has inspired bullet trains throughout the world. The TGV runs at 170-220 mph. Its rails are fused into one long, continuous track for a faster and smoother ride. The TGV has changed commuting patterns throughout France by putting most of the country within day-trip distance of Paris.

## Schedules

Schedules change by season, weekday, and weekend. Verify train times shown in this book—online, check www.bahn.com (Germany's excellent all-Europe schedule site), or check locally at train stations. The French rail website (www.sncf.com) shows ticket prices and sells some tickets online (worth checking if you're traveling on one or two long-distance trains without a railpass, as advance-purchase discounts can be a great deal).

## Buying Tickets

While there's no deadline to buy any train ticket, the fast, reserved TGV trains get booked up. Reserve well ahead for any TGV you cannot afford to miss. Tickets go on sale 90 days in advance, and the cheapest tickets sell out early; reservations for railpass holders also go particularly fast. To buy tickets online, visit www.tgv-europe.com/en/home; for your pickup option choose any country other than the US and outside western Europe, and you'll be able to print tickets at home or pick them up in the station (if instead you choose "France," the site will be in French, and if you choose "US," you'll be redirected to www.raileurope.com). The US company, RailEurope, delivers tickets to your home, but doesn't always have the lowest rates.

You can buy tickets on the train for a €4-10 surcharge depending on the length of your trip, but you must find the conductor immediately upon boarding; otherwise it's a €35 minimum charge.

## Paris Train Stations

Paris is Europe's rail hub, with six major stations and one minor one, and trains heading in different directions:
- Gare du Nord (northbound trains)
- Gare Montparnasse (west- and southwest-bound trains)
- Gare de Lyon (southeast-bound trains)
- Gare de l'Est (eastbound trains)
- Gare St. Lazare (northwest-bound trains)
- Gare d'Austerlitz (southwest-bound trains)
- Gare de Bercy (smaller station with non-TGV southbound trains)

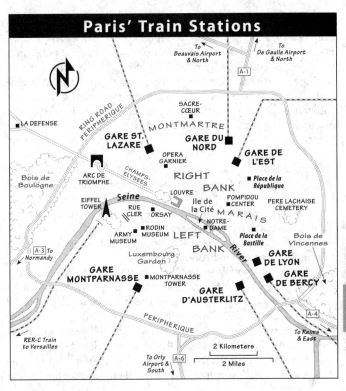

## Paris' Train Stations

All six main train stations have banks or currency exchanges, ATMs, train information desks, telephones, cafés, newsstands, and clever pickpockets (pay attention in ticket lines—keep your bag firmly gripped in front of you). Because of security concerns, not all have baggage checks.

Any train station has schedule information, can make reservations, and can sell tickets for any destination. Buying tickets is handier from an SNCF neighborhood office (see the "SNCF Boutiques" sidebar).

Each station offers two types of rail service: long distance to other cities, called Grandes Lignes (major lines); and suburban service to nearby areas, called Banlieue, Transilien, or RER. You also may see ticket windows identified as *Ile de France*. These are for Transilien trains serving destinations outside Paris in the Ile de France region (usually no more than an hour from Paris). When arriving by Métro, follow signs for *Grandes Lignes-SNCF* to find the main tracks. Métro and RER trains, as well as buses and taxis, are well-marked at every station.

Budget plenty of time before your departure to factor in ticket lines and making your way through large, crowded stations. Paris train stations can be intimidating, but if you slow down, take a deep breath, and ask for help, you'll find them manageable and efficient. Bring a pad of paper for clear communication at ticket/info windows. All stations have helpful information booths *(accueil)*; the bigger stations have roving helpers, usually wearing red or blue vests. They're capable of answering rail questions more quickly than the staff at the information desks or ticket windows. I make a habit of confirming my track number and departure time with these helpers.

## Gare du Nord

The granddaddy of Paris' train stations serves cities in northern France and international destinations north of Paris, including Copenhagen, Amsterdam (see "To Brussels and Amsterdam by Thalys Train," later), and the Eurostar to London (see "To London by Eurostar Train," also later), as well as two of the day trips described in this book (Chantilly and Auvers-sur-Oise).

Arrive early to allow time to navigate this station. From the Métro, follow *Grandes Lignes* signs (main lines) to reach the tracks at street level. Grandes Lignes trains depart from tracks 2-21 (tracks 20 and 21 are around the corner), suburban Banlieue/Transilien lines from tracks 30-36 (signed *Réseau Ile-de-France*), and RER trains from tracks 37-44 (tracks 41-44 are one floor below). Glass train information booths *(accueil)* are scattered throughout the station, and information-helpers circulate (all rail staff are required to speak English).

There's a helpful TI (labeled *Paris Tourisme*) kiosk near track 19 that provides free maps and sells Paris Museum Passes and fast-pass (a.k.a. *"coupe-file"*) tickets. Information booths for the **Thalys** trains (high-speed trains to Brussels and Amsterdam) are opposite track 8. All non-Eurostar ticket sales are at the windows opposite tracks 4 and 12. Passengers departing on **Eurostar** trains (London via Chunnel) can buy tickets and must check in at least 30 minutes early on the second level (climb steps opposite track 17). Check-in is similar to an airline's—you'll fill out a "landing card" and go through security (also see "Crossing the Channel," later). Monet-esque views over the trains and peaceful, air-conditioned cafés hide on the upper level by the Eurostar check-in (find the cool view WCs down the steps in the café). Other WCs are down the stairs across from track 10 (€0.50).

Baggage check and rental cars are near track 3 and down the steps. Taxis are out the door past track 3. Steps down to the Métro are opposite tracks 10 and 19.

**Key Destinations Served by Gare du Nord Grandes Lignes:** **Auvers-sur Oise** (hourly, 1.25 hours with transfer, one direct train April-Oct Sat-Sun only at about 10:00, 35 minutes), **Chantilly-**

Gouvieux (hourly, fewer on weekends, 25 minutes, also served by slower RER-D lines), **Brussels** (about 2/hour, 1.5 hours), **Bruges** (at least hourly, 2.5-3 hours, change in Brussels), **Amsterdam** (8-10/day, 3.5 hours direct), **Berlin** (4/day, 8.25 hours, 1-2 changes, via Belgium, non-Belgium-traversing trains leave from Gare de l'Est), **Koblenz** (8/day, 5 hours, change in Köln, more from Gare de l'Est that don't cross Belgium), **Copenhagen** (7/day, 14-18 hours, 1 night train), and **London** via Eurostar Chunnel train (12-15/day, 2.5-3 hours).

By Banlieue/RER Lines: Chantilly-Gouvieux (3/hour, 50 minutes), **Charles de Gaulle Airport** (4/hour, 45 minutes, runs 5:00-24:00, track 4).

## Gare Montparnasse

This big, modern station covers three floors, serves lower Normandy and Brittany, and has TGV service to the Loire Valley and southwestern France, as well as suburban service to Chartres.

Baggage check *(consigne)* and WCs are on the mezzanine level. Most services are provided on the second (top) level, where the Grandes Lignes and some Banlieue trains arrive and depart. Trains to Chartres usually depart from tracks 10-19, and the main rail information office *(accueil)* is opposite track 15. With your back to the tracks, taxis are to the far left, car rental is to the far right, and Air France buses to Orly and Charles de Gaulle Airports stop outside the exit to the far right. City buses are out the front of the station (down the escalator through the glassy facade). Bus #96 is good for connecting to Marais and Luxembourg area hotels, while #92 is best for Rue Cler hotels (easier than the Métro).

Key Destinations Served by Gare Montparnasse: Chartres (10/day, 65 minutes), **Amboise** (12/day in 1.5 hours with change in St-Pierre-des-Corps, requires TGV reservation; non-TGV trains leave from Gare d'Austerlitz), **Pontorson/Mont St-Michel** (3/day, 3.5-4.5 hours, via Rennes or Dol), **Dinan** (6/day, 4 hours, change in Rennes and Dol), **Bordeaux** (20/day, 3.5 hours), **Sarlat** (3/day, 5.5-6.5 hours, change in Libourne or Bordeaux), **Toulouse** (13/day, 5-7 hours, most require change, usually in Bordeaux or Montpellier), **Albi** (6/day, 6.5-9 hours, change in Toulouse, also night train), **Tours** (10/day, 1.25 hours), **Madrid** (3/day, 12-14 hours, expensive overnight trains from Gare d'Austerlitz), and **Lisbon** (2/day, 21-24 hours via Irun).

## Gare de Lyon

This huge, bewildering station offers TGV and regular service to southeastern France, Italy, Switzerland, and other international destinations. Frequent Banlieue trains serve Melun (near Vaux-le-Vicomte) and Fontainebleau.

# France's Rail System

**Legend:**
- - - - - Rail
━━━━━ Eurostar Rail
━━━━━ TGV High Speed Rail
· · · · · Bus
· · · · · · Boat
✈ Airports (Not All Shown)

**Labels on map:**

ENGLAND
London
Eurostar
Dover
Folkstone
Newhaven
Portsmouth
English Channel
Le Tréport
Dieppe
Le Havre
To Ireland
Cherbourg
Arromanches
Honfleur
Rouen
Roscoff
Mont St-Michel
St-Malo
Bayeux
Caen
Lisieux
Brest
Morlaix
Avranches
Versailles
Lamballe
Dinan
Pontorson
Dol
Chartres
Quimper
Vannes
Rennes
Le Mans
TGV
Orléans
Quiberon
Redon
Angers
Tours
Blois
Amboise
Nantes
Saumur
Atlantic Ocean
Langeais
Chinon
Azay
Tours St-Pierre des Corps TGV Stn.
Vierzon
Poitiers
F R A
La Rochelle
Oradour-sur-Glane
Saintes
Cognac
Limoges
Angoulême
Perigueux
Brive
Libourne
Bordeaux
Les Eyzies
Sarlat
St-Emilion
Le Buisson
Soulliac
Beynac
Cahors
Agen
Montauban
Biarritz
Guernica
St-Jean-de-Luz
Dax
Bayonne
Bilbao
Hendaye
PRIVATE RAIL
Irun
Toulouse
San Sebastián
St-Jean Pied-de-Port
Pau
Lourdes
Miranda de Ebro
Pamplona
Foix
La Tour
Burgos
SPAIN
ANDORRA
To Madrid
To Barcelona

50 Kilometers
50 Miles

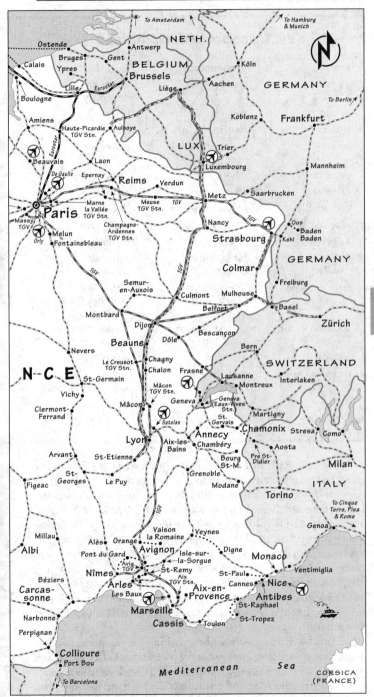

PARIS CONNECTIONS

# Key Transportation Phrases

| French | Pronounced | English |
|---|---|---|
| *accueil* | ah-koy | information/ assistance |
| *niveau* | nee-voh | level |
| *billets* | bee-yay | tickets |
| *réservation* | ray-zehr-vah-see-yohn | reservation |
| *départs* | day-par | departures |
| *arrivées* | ah-ree-vay | arrivals |
| *aller* simple | ah-lay sam-pluh | one-way |
| *aller-retour* | ah-lay ruh-toor | round-trip |
| *a l'heure* | ah loor | on time |
| *fenêtre/ couloir* | fuh-neh-truh/ kool-wahr | window/ aisle seat |
| *fenêtre isolée* | fuh-neh-truh ee-zoh-lay | single seat by window (first class only) |
| *voyageurs munis de billets* | voh-yah-zhoor moo-nee duh bee-yay | travelers with tickets |
| *navette* | nah-veht | shuttle bus |
| *Grandes Lignes* | grahnd leen | major domestic and international lines |
| *RER* | air ay air | suburban lines |

From the RER or Métro, follow signs for *Grandes Lignes Arrivées* and take the escalator up to reach the street-level platforms (Grandes Lignes and Banlieue lines share the same tracks). Grande Ligne trains are divided into two areas: Hall 1 (tracks A–N in the blue area) and Hall 2 (tracks 5–23 in the yellow area). Monitors show either yellow or blue even before the track is posted, so you know which general area your train leaves from. The two areas are connected by the hallway adjacent to track A and opposite track 9. This hallway has all the services. Transilien ticket windows are just inside the hall adjacent to track A *(billets Ile de France)*. Train information booths are opposite tracks A, M, and 11 (others are downstairs).

Don't leave this station without visiting the recommended Le Train Bleu Restaurant, up the stairs opposite track G (see listing on page 461). Its pricey but way-cool bar-lounge works well as a quiet waiting area; otherwise find a seat near the baggage check—from

| French | Pronounced | English |
|---|---|---|
| *Transilien* | trahn-seel-ee-yehn | suburban lines |
| *RATP* | air ah tay pay | Paris' Métro and bus system |
| *SNCF* | es en say ef | France's country-wide train system |
| *TGV* | tay zhay vay | high-speed lines |
| *banlieue* | bahn-lee-yuh | suburban |
| *quai* | kay | platform |
| *accès aux quais* | ahk-seh oh kay | access to the platforms |
| *voie* | vwah | track |
| *retard* | ruh-tar | delay |
| *salle d'attente* | sahl dah-tahnt | waiting room |
| *consigne* | kohn-seen | baggage check (also called *espaces bagages*) |
| *consigne automatique* | kohn-seen oh-toh-mah-teek | storage lockers |
| *première classe* | pruhm-yair klahs | first class |
| *deuxième classe* | duhz-yehm klahs | second class |
| *distributeur* | dee-stree-bew-tur | ATM |
| *PTT* | pay tay tay | post office |

opposite track 13 follow *consigne* signs down one floor (baggage check available daily 6:15-22:00, €4-10).

Taxi stands are well-signed in front of, and underneath, the station. "Les Cars" Air France buses to Gare Montparnasse (easy transfer to Orly Airport) and direct to Charles de Gaulle Airport stop outside the station's main entrance (opposite tracks A-L, walk across the parking lot—the stop is a block down from the Café Européen on the right across from Café Les Deux Savoies; normally at :15 and :45 after the hour; see "By Bus" on page 515).

**Key Destinations Served by Gare de Lyon:** Vaux-le-Vicomte (train to Melun, 2/hour by train, 30 minutes; 3/hour by RER, 45 minutes), **Fontainebleau** (2/hour, 40 minutes; some depart from the Grandes Lignes level, more frequent departures are from one level down—follow *RER-D* signs, and ask at any information booth or ticket window where the next departure leaves from), **Disneyland** (RER line A-4 to Marne-la-Vallée-Chessy, at least 3/hour, 45

# Train Tips

- Arrive at the station with plenty of time before your departure to find your platform (platform numbers are posted about 15 minutes prior to departure), confirm connections, and so on.
- Small stations are minimally staffed; if there is no agent at the station, go directly to the tracks and look for the overhead sign that confirms your train stops at that track.
- Larger stations have platforms with monitors showing TGV layouts (numbered forward or backward) so you can figure out where your *voiture* will stop on the long platform and where to board each car.
- Check schedules in advance if possible. Upon arrival at a station, learn your departure possibilities (don't rely exclusively on online schedules). Large stations have a separate information window or office; at small stations, the ticket office gives information.
- If you have a rail flexipass, write the date on your pass each day you travel (before or immediately after boarding your first train).
- Validate tickets (not passes) and some reservations in yellow machines before boarding. If you're traveling with a pass and have a reservation for a certain trip, you must validate the reservation.
- Reservations for all TGV trains are required and often sell out. You can reserve any train at any station or through SNCF Boutiques (small offices in city centers). A limited number of reservations are allocated for railpass users during peak times—reserve as far ahead as you can for

minutes), **Beaune** (roughly hourly at rush hour but few mid-day, 2.5 hours, most require change in Dijon; direct trains from Paris' Bercy station take an hour longer), **Dijon** (roughly hourly at rush hour but few mid-day, 1.5 hours), **Chamonix** (7/day, 5.5-7 hours, some change in Switzerland), **Annecy** (hourly, 4 hours, many with change in Lyon), **Lyon** (at least hourly, 2 hours), **Avignon** (9/day in 2.5 hours to Avignon TGV Station, 5/day in 3.5 hours to Avignon Centre-Ville station, more connections with change—3-4 hours), **Arles** (11/day, 2 direct TGVs—4 hours, 9 with change in Avignon—5 hours), **Nice** (hourly, 5.75 hours, may require change, 11.5-hour night train possible out of Gare d'Austerlitz), **Carcassonne** (8/day, 7-8 hours, 1 change, night trains leave from Gare d'Austerlitz), **Zürich** (6/day direct, 4 hours), **Venice** (5/day, 10-12 hours with 1-3 changes; 1 direct overnight, 14 hours, operated by private company Thello—which doesn't accept railpasses, important to reserve ahead at www.thello.com; 4 more night trains with changes), **Rome** (3/day, 11-16 hours; 1 night train, 14 hours, may transfer in Milan, operated by

Friday and Sunday afternoons and Saturday mornings.
- Before getting on a train, confirm that it's going where you think it is. For example, if you want to go to Chartres, ask the conductor or any local passenger, *"A Chartres?"* (ah shar-truh, meaning, "To Chartres?").
- Some longer trains split cars en route. Make sure your train car is continuing to your destination by asking, *"Cette voiture va à Chartres?"* (seht vwah-toor vah ah shart-ruh, meaning, "This car goes to Chartres?").
- If a non-TGV train seat is reserved, it'll likely be labeled *réservé*, with the cities to and from which it is reserved.
- If you don't understand an announcement, ask your neighbor to explain: *"Pardon Madame/Monsieur, qu'est-ce qui se passe?"* (kehs kee suh pahs; meaning, "Excuse me, what's going on?").
- Verify with the conductor all of the transfers you must make (*"Correspondance à?"* meaning, "Transfer to where?").
- To guard against theft, keep your bags in sight (direct-ly overhead is ideal but not always possible—the early boarder gets the best storage space). If you must store them in the lower racks by the doors (available in most cars), pay attention at stops. Your bags are most vulner-able to theft before the train takes off and whenever it stops.
- Note your arrival time, so you'll be ready to get off.
- Use the train's free WCs before you get off (but not while the train is stopped in a station).

private company Thello—which doesn't accept railpasses, important to reserve ahead at www.thello.com), **Bern** (9/day, otherwise 4-5.5 hours), **Interlaken** (7/day, 5-6.5 hours, 1-3 changes, 2 more from Gare de l'Est), and **Barcelona** (2/day, 7.5 hours, change in Figueres; night train possible from Gare d'Austerlitz).

## Gare de l'Est

This two-floor station (with underground Métro) serves northeast-ern France and international destinations east of Paris. It's easy to navigate: All trains depart at street level from tracks 1-30. Check the departure monitors to see which section your train leaves from: Departures marked with a yellow square leave from tracks 2-12, while those marked with a blue square depart from tracks 22-30 (suburban Banlieue trains depart from tracks 13-21). A train infor-mation office is opposite track 17, and ticket sales are at each end of the station through the halls opposite tracks 8 and 25. Most other services are down the escalator through the hall opposite tracks

## Coping with Strikes

Going on strike (en grève) is a popular pastime in this revo-
lution-happy country. Because bargaining between man-
agement and employees is not standard procedure, workers
strike to get attention. Trucks and tractors block main roads
and autoroutes (in a movement called Opération Escargot—
"Operation Snail's Pace"), baggage handlers bring airports
to their knees; museum workers make *Mona Lisa* off-limits to
tourists; and Métro and train personnel seem to strike every
year—probably during your trip. What does the traveler do?
You could *jetter l'éponge* (throw in the sponge) and go somewhere less strike-prone (Switzerland's nice), or learn to accept
certain events as being out of your control. Strikes in France
generally last no longer than a day or two, and if you're aware
of them, you can usually plan around them. Your hotelier will
know the latest (or can find out). Make a habit of asking your
hotel receptionist about strikes, or check www.americansin
france.net (click on "Daily Life").

12-20 (baggage lockers, car rental, WC, small grocery store, more
shops, and Métro access). There's a post office at track level, near
the top of the escalators. Access to taxis and buses is out the front
of the station (exit with your back to the tracks).

**Key Destinations Served by Gare de l'Est: Colmar** (12/day
with TGV, 3.5 hours, change in Strasbourg), **Strasbourg** (hourly
with TGV, 2.5 hours), **Reims** (9/day with TGV, 45 minutes), **Verdun** (4/day with TGV, 1.5 hours; 3 hours by regional train with
transfer in Chalôns-en-Champagne), **Interlaken** (2/day, 6.5 hours,
2-3 changes, 7 more from Gare de Lyon), **Zürich** (7/day, 5-6 hours,
1-2 changes, faster direct trains from Gare de Lyon), **Frankfurt**
(5 direct/day, 4 hours; 4 more/day with change in Karlsruhe, 4.5
hours), **Vienna** (7/day, 12-17 hours, 1-3 changes, night train via
Munich or Frankfurt), **Prague** (5/day, 12-18 hours, night train
via Mannheim or Berlin), **Munich** (6/day, 6 hours, most with 1
change, 1 direct night train), and **Berlin** (5/day, 8.5 hours, 1-2
changes; 1 direct night train, 12.5 hours).

## Gare St. Lazare

This compact station serves upper Normandy, including Rouen and
Giverny. All trains arrive and depart one floor above street level.

From the Métro, follow signs to *Grandes Lignes* to reach the
tracks (long walk). Grandes Lignes to all destinations listed below
depart from tracks 23-27; Banlieue trains depart from 1-16. The
ticket office and car rental are near track 27. Train information offices *(accueil)* are scattered about the station. This station has no

baggage check, but it does have a three-floor shopping mall with food, clothing, and more (with your back to the tracks, head a few steps through the halls). Taxis, the Métro, and buses are well-signed.

**Key Destinations Served by Gare St. Lazare: Giverny** (train to Vernon, 8/day Mon-Sat, 6/day Sun, 45 minutes), **Rouen** (nearly hourly, 1.5 hours), **Honfleur** (13/day, 2-3.5 hours, via Lisieux, then bus), **Bayeux** (9/day, 2.5 hours, some change in Caen), **Caen** (14/day, 2 hours), and **Pontorson/Mont St-Michel** (2/day, 4-5.5 hours, via Caen; more trains from Gare Montparnasse).

## Gare d'Austerlitz

This small station provides non-TGV service to the Loire Valley, southwestern France, and Spain. All tracks are at street level. The information booth is opposite track 17, and all ticket sales are in the hall opposite track 10. Baggage check, WCs (with €6 showers that include towel, soap, and the works), and car rental are along the side of the station, opposite track 21. To get to the Métro and RER, you must walk outside and along either side of the station.

**Key Destinations Served by Gare d'Austerlitz: Versailles** (via RER line C, 4/hour, 35 minutes), **Amboise** (6/day direct in 2 hours, 5/day with transfer in Blois or Les Aubrais-Orléans; faster TGV connection from Gare Montparnasse), **Sarlat** (1/day, 6.25 hours, requires change to bus in Souillac, 3 more/day via Gare Montparnasse), **Carcassonne** (1 direct night train, 7.5 hours, plus a decent night train via Toulouse, better day trains from Gare de Lyon), **Cahors** (5/day, 5 hours, at least 1 direct night train; slower trains from Gare Montparnasse), **Barcelona** (1/night, 12.5 hours, make mandatory reservation at least 2 weeks ahead; day trains from Gare de Lyon), and **Madrid** (1 direct night train, 13-14 hours, make mandatory reservation at least 2 weeks ahead, 16 hours via Irun; day trains from Gare Montparnasse).

## Gare de Bercy

This smaller station handles southbound non-TGV trains (Mo: Bercy, one stop east of Gare de Lyon on line 14, exit the Métro station and it's across the street). Facilities are limited—just a WC and a sandwich-fare take-out café.

## To Brussels and Amsterdam by Thalys Train

The pricey Thalys train has the monopoly on the rail route between Paris and Brussels (for a cheaper option, try the Eurolines bus, described later). Without a railpass you'll pay about €65-120 second class for the Paris-Amsterdam train (compared to €50 by bus), or about €40-70 second class for the Paris-Brussels train (compared to €30 by bus). Even with a railpass, you need to pay for train

## SNCF Boutiques

You can save time and stress by buying train tickets or making train reservations at an SNCF Boutique. These small branch offices of the French national rail company are conveniently located throughout Paris, with offices near most of my recommended hotels and museums and at Orly and Charles de Gaulle Airports. Arrive when they open to avoid lines (generally open Mon-Sat 8:30-19:00 or 20:00, closed Sun). For a complete list, see www.megacomik.info/boutiquesncf.htm.

**Historic Core**
- 18 Rue du Pont Neuf, Mo: Pont Neuf

**Marais**
- 2 Rue de Turenne, Mo: St. Paul
- 5 Rue de Lyon, Mo: Gare de Lyon

**Near Major Museums**
- Musée d'Orsay RER station, below Orsay Museum
- Forum des Halles shopping mall, basement sublevel -4, returns office (Salle d'Echanges), Mo: Châtelet-Les Halles

**Champs-Elysées**
- 229 Rue du Faubourg St. Honoré, Mo: St. Philippe-du-Roule

**Farther North on the Right Bank**
- 53 Rue Chaussée d'Antin, Mo: Chaussée d'Antin (near Opéra Garnier and Galeries Lafayette)
- 32/34 Rue Joubert, Mo: Haussman-St. Lazare (near Gare St. Lazare)

reservations (second class-€27-39; first class-€42-62, includes a meal). Book at least a day ahead, as seats are limited (www.thalys.com). Or hop on the bus, Gus.

# Crossing the Channel

## To London by Eurostar Train

The fastest and most convenient way to get from the Eiffel Tower to Big Ben is by rail. Eurostar, a joint service of the Belgian, British, and French railways, is the speedy passenger train that zips you (and up to 800 others in 18 sleek cars) from downtown Paris to downtown London (1-2/hour, 2.5 hours) faster and more easily than flying. The train goes 190 mph both before and after the English Channel crossing. The actual tunnel crossing is a 20-minute, silent, 100-mile-per-hour nonevent. Your ears won't even pop. Get ready for more high-speed connections: Eurostar's monopoly expired at the beginning of 2010, and Germany's national railroad is negotiating to run its bullet trains to London by 2013.

- 71/73 Boulevard Magenta, Mo: Gare du Nord (Gare du Nord)
- 82 Avenue de la Grande Armée, Mo: Porte Maillot (near Hôtel Concorde-Lafayette and Beauvais Airport bus stop)

**Montmartre**
- 27 Rue Lepic, Mo: Blanche

**Eiffel Tower/Rue Cler**
- 80 Rue Saint Dominique, Mo: La Tour Maubourg
- 19 Rue de Passy, Mo: Passy (near Marmottan Museum)
- Invalides Métro/RER station

**Latin Quarter/Luxembourg Garden**
- 54 Boulevard St. Michel, Mo: Cluny-Sorbonne
- 79 Rue de Rennes, Mo: St. Sulpice

**Farther South on the Left Bank**
- 17 Rue Littré, Mo: Montparnasse-Bienvenüe (near Luxembourg Garden and grand cafés)
- 68 Avenue du Maine, Mo: Montparnasse-Bienvenüe (near grand cafés)
- 30 Avenue d'Italie, in Centre Commerciale Galaxie, Mo: Place d'Italie

You'll also find quieter SNCF Boutiques in train stations of the towns I suggest for day trips from Paris, such as Versailles, Fontainebleau, Melun (for Vaux-le-Vicomte), Chartres, Chantilly, Vernon (for Giverny), and Pontoise (for Auvers-sur-Oise).

## Eurostar Fares

Unlike most trains in Western Europe, Eurostar is not covered by railpasses and always requires a separate, reserved train ticket. Eurostar fares vary depending on how far ahead you reserve, whether you can live with restrictions, and whether you're eligible for any discounts (such as those for early purchase or round-trip travel).

A **one-way, full-fare ticket** (with no restrictions on refundability) runs about $400 for first class and $300 for second class. **Discounts** can lower fares substantially (figure $60-160 for second class, one way) for children under 12, youths under 26, seniors 60 or older, and railpass holders. The early bird gets the best price. If you're ready to commit, you can book tickets as early as 6-9 months in advance at www.eurostar.com.

## Buying Eurostar Tickets

Because only the most expensive (full-fare) ticket is fully refundable, don't reserve until you're sure of your plans. But if you wait too long, the cheapest tickets will get bought up.

Once you're confident about the time and date of your crossing, you can check and book fares by phone or online. Ordering online through Eurostar or major agents offers a print-at-home e-ticket option. You can also order by phone through Rail Europe at US tel. 800-387-6782 for home delivery before you go, or through Eurostar (French tel. 08 92 35 35 39, priced in euros) and pick up your ticket at the train station. In Eu-

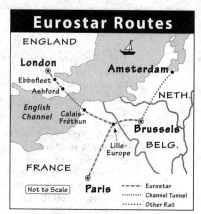

rope you can buy your Eurostar ticket at any major train station in any country, at neighborhood SNCF offices (see the "SNCF Boutiques" sidebar), or at any travel agency that handles train tickets (expect a booking fee). You can purchase passholder discount tickets at Eurostar departure stations, through US agents, or by phone with Eurostar, but they may be harder to get at other train stations and travel agencies, and are a discount category that can sell out.

Remember France's time zone is one hour later than Britain's. Times printed on tickets are local times (departure from Paris is French time, arrival in London is British time).

### Taking the Eurostar

Eurostar trains depart from and arrive at Paris' Gare du Nord. Check in at least 30 minutes in advance for your Eurostar trip. It's very similar to an airport check-in: You pass through airport-like security, fill out a customs form, show your passport to customs officials, and find a TV monitor to locate your departure gate. The currency-exchange booth here has rates about the same as you'll find on the other end.

### Crossing the Channel Without Eurostar

For speed and affordability, look into cheap flights. The old-fashioned ways of crossing the Channel are cheaper than Eurostar (taking the bus is cheapest). They're also twice as romantic, complicated, and time-consuming.

## Buses

The main bus station is Gare Routière du Paris-Gallieni (28 Avenue du Général de Gaulle, in suburb of Bagnolet, Mo: Gallieni, tel. 01 49 72 51 51). Buses provide cheaper—if less comfortable and more time-consuming—transportation to major European cities.

**Driving In France**

ENGLAND

To London ↑

Dover

Calais

English Channel

BELGIUM

Lille

GERMANY

LUX.

Arromanches
(D-Day Beaches)

Honfleur

20m
.5h

45m
.75h

180m · 2.75h

140m · 2.25h

Reims

Verdun

Mont
St-Michel

Bayeux

Caen

80m
1.5h

55m
1h

80m · 1.5h

Rouen

90m · 1.5h

75m · 1.25h

150m · 2.75h

Strasbourg

Paris

305m · 4.5h

Dinan

80m
1.5h

195m · 3h

Chartres

55m
1h

285m · 5.5h

Colmar

50m
1h

40m
.75h

155m · 2.5h

Semur-
en-Auxois

225m · 4.5h

Amboise

85m · 2h

140m · 2.25h

250m · 4h

50m
.75h

165m · 2.5h

50m · 1.25h

Chinon

270m · 5.5h

Beaune

F R A N C E

145m · 2.5h

SWITZ.

m = miles
h = hours

Atlantic
Ocean

360m · 5.25h

220m · 4.5h

135m · 3h

Oradour-
sur-Glane

100m · 2.25h

Lyon

95m · 1.5h

95m · 1.5h

Annecy

55m · 1h

Chamonix

260m · 5h

ITALY

St. Emilion

80m · 2h

Sarlat

30m · 1.25h

Rocamadour

125m · 2.5h

140m · 2h

235m · 5h

Monaco

10m
.5h

St. Jean-
de-Luz

170m · 3h

Albi

70m
1.75h

25m
.5h

Avignon

160m · 2.5h

Nice

20m
.5h

155m · 2.5h

210m · 4.75h

150m · 2.25h

Arles

80m
1.25h

105m · 1.5h

10m
.5h

San
Sebastian

250m · 3.5h

Carcassonne

95m · 1.5h

Cassis

165m · 2.5h

Antibes

SPAIN

ANDORRA

Collioure

Mediterranean
Sea

**Note: Your times may vary based on traffic,
construction, and road conditions.**

PARIS CONNECTIONS

The bus is also the cheapest way to cross the English Channel; book at least two days in advance for the best fares. Eurolines' buses depart from here (tel. 08 36 69 52 52, www.eurolines.com). Look on their website for offices in central Paris.

# Driving

## Parking in Paris

Street parking is generally free at night (19:00 to 9:00), all day Sunday, and anytime in August, when many Parisians are on vacation. To pay for streetside parking, you must go to a *tabac* and buy a parking card *(une carte de stationnement)*, sold in €10, €20, and €30 denominations. Insert the card into the meter (chip-side in) and punch the desired amount of time (generally €1-2/hour), then take the receipt and display it in your windshield. Meters limit street parking to a maximum of two hours. For a longer stay, park for less at an airport (about €10/day) and take public transport or a taxi into the city. Underground lots are numerous in Paris—you'll find them under Ecole Militaire, St. Sulpice Church, Les Invalides, the Bastille, and the Panthéon; all charge about €30-40/day (€60/3 days, €10/day more after that, for locations see www.vincipark.com). Some hotels offer parking for less—ask your hotelier.

# DAY TRIPS

Though there's plenty to see within Paris' ring-road, efficient public transportation expands your sightseeing horizons. The following sights are generally about an hour from central Paris. Do them as day trips, or—for more ambience—stay overnight.

The jaw-dropping Palace of **Versailles**, 12 miles southwest of Paris, was the residence of French kings and the cultural heartbeat of Europe for a century. While Versailles is the grandest of the **Grand Chateaux,** fans of these big palaces have plenty of other options, including Vaux-le-Vicomte (the most beautiful), Fontainebleu (with a pleasant city), or Chantilly (best art). In **Chartres,** an hour southwest of Paris, one of Europe's greatest Gothic cathedrals soars above a pleasant town. Lovers of Impressionism could visit **Giverny** to see Claude Monet's garden, with its pond and lily pads still looking like they did when he painted them. **Auvers-sur-Oise** is a small, plain town that attracted Impressionist painters, and is where Van Gogh died. The city of **Reims** (champagne and cathedral), is 80 miles from Paris, but is an easy day-trip thanks to the high-speed TGV train.

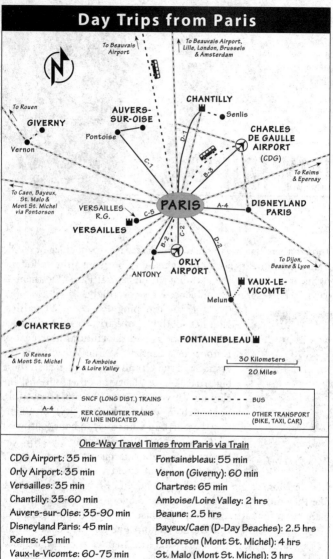

# Day Trips from Paris

SNCF (LONG DIST.) TRAINS          ----- BUS

A-4  RER COMMUTER TRAINS          OTHER TRANSPORT
     W/ LINE INDICATED            (BIKE, TAXI, CAR)

## One-Way Travel Times from Paris via Train

CDG Airport: 35 min

Orly Airport: 35 min

Versailles: 35 min

Chantilly: 35-60 min

Auvers-sur-Oise: 35-90 min

Disneyland Paris: 45 min

Reims: 45 min

Vaux-le-Vicomte: 60-75 min

Fontainebleau: 55 min

Vernon (Giverny): 60 min

Chartres: 65 min

Amboise/Loire Valley: 2 hrs

Beaune: 2.5 hrs

Bayeux/Caen (D-Day Beaches): 2.5 hrs

Pontorson (Mont St. Michel): 4 hrs

St. Malo (Mont St. Michel): 3 hrs

# VERSAILLES

*Château de Versailles*

Every king's dream, Versailles (vehr-"sigh") was the residence of French monarchs and the cultural heartbeat of Europe for about 100 years—until the Revolution of 1789 changed all that. The Sun King (Louis XIV) created Versailles, spending freely from the public treasury to turn his dad's hunting lodge into a palace fit for the gods (among whom he counted himself). Louis XV and Louis XVI spent much of the 18th century gilding Louis XIV's lily. In 1837, about 50 years after the royal family was evicted by citizen-protesters, King Louis-Philippe opened the palace as a museum. Today you can visit parts of the huge palace and wander through acres of manicured gardens sprinkled with fountains and studded with statues. Europe's next-best palaces are just Versailles wannabes.

Worth ▲▲▲, Versailles offers three blockbuster sights. The main attraction is the palace itself, called the **Château.** Here you walk through dozens of lavish, chandeliered rooms once inhabited by Louis XIV and his successors. Next come the expansive **Gardens** behind the palace, a landscaped wonderland dotted with statues and fountains. Finally, at the far end of the Gardens, is the pastoral area called the **Trianon Palaces and Domaine de Marie-Antoinette** (a.k.a. Trianon/Domaine), designed for frolicking blue bloods and featuring several small palaces and Marie's Hamlet—perfect for getting away from the mobs at the Château.

# Versailles

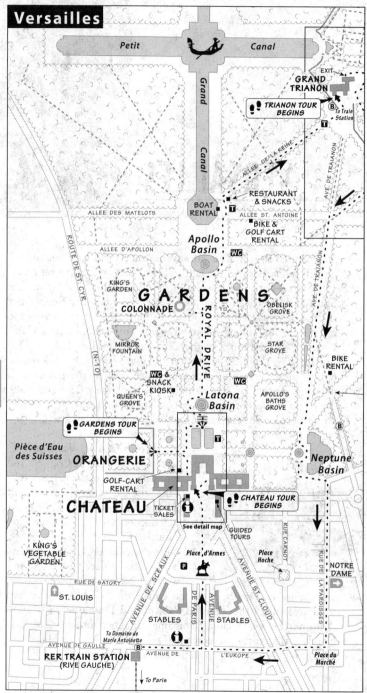

VERSAILLES

Petit Canal

Grand Canal

GRAND TRIANON

EXIT

To Train Station

TRIANON TOUR BEGINS

ALLÉE DE LA REINE

RESTAURANT & SNACKS

BOAT RENTAL

ALLÉE DES MATELOTS

ALLÉE ST. ANTOINE

BIKE & GOLF CART RENTAL

ROUTE DE ST. CYR (N-10)

Apollo Basin

WC

ALLÉE D'APOLLON

AVE. DE TRIANON

KING'S GARDEN

GARDENS

COLONNADE

OBELISK GROVE

ROYAL DRIVE

MIRROR FOUNTAIN

STAR GROVE

BIKE RENTAL

WC & SNACK KIOSK

WC

QUEEN'S GROVE

Latona Basin

APOLLO'S BATHS GROVE

GARDENS TOUR BEGINS

Pièce d'Eau des Suisses

ORANGERIE

Neptune Basin

GOLF-CART RENTAL

CHATEAU

TICKET SALES

CHATEAU TOUR BEGINS

See detail map

GUIDED TOURS

KING'S VEGETABLE GARDEN

RUE CARNOT

NOTRE DAME

Place d'Armes

Place Hoche

ST. LOUIS

AVENUE DE SCEAUX

DE PARIS

AVENUE ST. CLOUD

RUE DE LA PAROISSE

RUE DE SATORY

STABLES

AVENUE

STABLES

To Domaine de Marie Antoinette

AVENUE DE GAULLE

RER TRAIN STATION (RIVE GAUCHE)

AVENUE DE

L'EUROPE

Place du Marché

To Paris

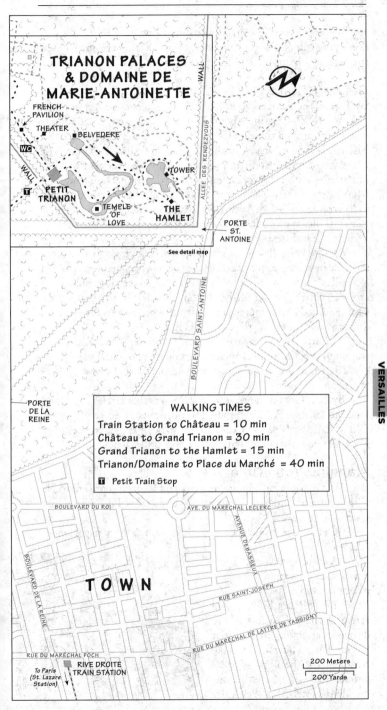

Visiting Versailles can seem daunting because of its size and hordes of visitors. But if you follow my tips, a trip here during even the busiest times is manageable.

## Getting There

**By Train:** The town of Versailles is 35 minutes southwest of Paris. Take the **RER-C train** (4/hour, 35 minutes one-way, €6.50 round-trip) from any of these Paris RER stops: Gare d'Austerlitz, St. Michel, Musée d'Orsay, Invalides, Pont de l'Alma, or Champ de Mars. You can buy your train tickets at any Métro ticket window in Paris—for no extra cost it will include the connection from that Métro stop to the RER. At the RER station, catch any train listed as "Versailles R.G." or "Versailles Rive Gauche" (Rive Gauche is the Versailles station closest to the Château—there are two others). Ride to the last stop.

At the Versailles R.G. train station, exit through the turnstiles by inserting your ticket. Ignore the hawkers peddling guided Versailles tours and tickets. To reach the **palace,** just follow the crowds: Turn right out of the station, then left at the first boulevard, and walk 10 minutes. To return to Paris, all trains serve all downtown Paris RER stops on the C line.

A shuttle bus (see page 565) links the Versailles R.G. train station to the **Trianon/Domaine,** but doesn't go to the palace.

**By Taxi:** The 30-minute ride (without traffic) between Versailles and Paris costs about €60.

**By Car:** Get on the *périphérique* freeway that circles Paris, and take the toll-free A-13 autoroute toward Rouen. Exit at Versailles, follow signs to *Versailles Château,* and park in the huge pay lot at Place d'Armes (€5.50/2 hours, €10/4 hours, €15/8 hours).

## Planning Your Time

Versailles merits a full sightseeing day and is much more enjoyable with a relaxed, unhurried approach. Here's what I'd do on a first visit:

• Get a pass in advance (explained on the next page, under "Passes").

• Avoid Sundays and Tuesdays, when crowds smother the palace interior.

• Leave Paris by 8:00 and arrive at the palace just before it opens at 9:00. Or consider leaving Paris a bit earlier to take advantage of the impressive €9 buffet breakfast at the recommended Hôtel Ibis Versailles (across from the train station). In the morning, tour the Château following my self-guided tour, which hits the highlights.

• Have a canalside lunch at one of the sandwich kiosks or cafés in the Gardens. Spend the afternoon touring the Gardens, Trianon Palaces, and Domaine de Marie-Antoinette. On spring or summer weekends (also on Tue late May-late June), catch the Fountain Spectacles in the Gardens. Stay for dinner in Versailles town (see recommended restaurants at the end of this chapter), or head back to Paris.

• If you need to shorten your visit, skip the Trianon/Domaine, which takes an additional 1.5 hours, plus a 30-minute walk.

• An alternate plan (for late risers) is to visit the uncrowded Trianon Palaces and Domaine de Marie-Antoinette first (opens at noon), then work your way back through the Gardens to the Château, arriving after the crowds have died down. To do this, take advantage of the direct shuttle bus from the Versailles R.G. train station to the Grand Trianon (see the "Getting Around the Gardens" sidebar, later).

In general, allow 1.5 hours each for the Château, the Gardens, and the Trianon/Domaine. Add another two hours for round-trip transit, plus another hour for lunch, and you're looking at an eight-hour day—at the very least.

## Orientation

**Cost:** Buy either a Paris Museum Pass or a Versailles Le Passeport Pass, both of which give you access to the most important parts of the complex (see "Passes" below). If you don't get a pass, buy individual tickets for each of the three different sections.

**The Château:** €15, includes audioguide, under 18 free. Covers the famous Hall of Mirrors, the king and queen's living quarters, many lesser rooms, and any temporary exhibitions. For €1 more, you can get a guided tour of the Château—a great deal (see "Tours," later). Free on the first Sunday of off-season months (Nov-March).

**The Trianon Palaces and Domaine de Marie-Antoinette:** €10, no audioguide available, under 18 free. Covers the Grand Trianon and its gardens, the Petit Trianon, the queen's Hamlet, and a smattering of nearby buildings. Free on the first Sunday of off-season months (Nov-March).

**The Gardens:** Free, except on Fountain Spectacle days, when admission is €8.50 (weekends April-Oct plus Tue late May-late June; see "Fountain Spectacles in the Gardens," later).

**Passes:** The following passes can save money and allow you to skip the long ticket-buying lines (but not security checks before entering the palaces). Both passes include the Château audioguide.

The **Paris Museum Pass** (see page 52) covers the Château and the Trianon/Domaine area (a €25 value) and is the best solution for most. It doesn't include the Gardens on Fountain Spectacle days.

The **Le Passeport** one-day pass costs €18 and covers the Château and the Trianon/Domaine area. The price bumps up to €25 on Fountain Spectacle days.

**Buying Passes and Tickets:** It's best to buy tickets or passes in advance. They're available at any Paris TI or FNAC department store (small fee), or online at www.chateauversailles.fr (print out your pass/ticket or pick it up near the entrance).

In Versailles, passes are sold at the city TI (€2 fee; for TI details, see "Information," later).

Your last option is to buy your pass or ticket at the Château ticket-sales office (to the left as you face the palace). Ticket windows accept American credit cards but have long lines in the morning—avoid the wait by using the ticket machines at the back of the room (you'll need a chip-and-PIN card or bills—which half the machines accept).

**Hours:** The **Château** is open April-Oct Tue-Sun 9:00-18:30, Nov-March Tue-Sun 9:00-17:30; closed Mon year-round.

The **Trianon Palaces and Domaine de Marie-Antoinette** are open April-Oct Tue-Sun 12:00-18:30, Nov-March Tue-Sun 12:00-17:30; closed Mon year-round (off-season only the two Trianon Palaces are open, not the Hamlet or other outlying buildings).

The **Gardens** are open April-Oct daily 9:00-20:30, but may close earlier for special events; Nov-March Tue-Sun 8:00-18:00, closed Mon.

Last entry to all areas is 30 minutes before closing.

**Crowd-Beating Strategies:** Versailles can be packed May-Sept 10:00-13:00. Avoid Tuesdays and Sundays, when the place is jammed with a slow shuffle of tourists from open to close. Ticket and security lines can be long: To skip the ticket-buying line, use a Paris Museum Pass or Le Passeport, buy tickets in advance, or book a guided tour (below). Everyone—including holders of advance tickets and passes—must go through security (longest lines 10:00-12:00). Before queuing up at the security entrance, check for signs that they might have opened up a special, shorter line for passholders (but don't count on it). For strategies once you get into the palace and its grounds, see "Planning Your Time," earlier.

**Pickpockets:** Assume pickpockets are working the tourist crowds.

**Information:** Before you go, check the excellent website for updates and special events—www.chateauversailles.fr. The palace's general contact number is tel. 01 30 83 78 00. Versailles has two information offices. You'll pass the city TI on your walk from the RER station to the palace—it's just past the Pullman Hôtel (daily 9:00-19:00, tel. 01 39 24 88 88). The information office at the Château is on the left side of the courtyard as you face the Château (WCs, toll tel. 08 10 81 16 14). Pick up the free, useful map just inside the Château.

**Guided Tours:** For a basic visit, this chapter's self-guided tour works great. But the 1.5-hour English guided tour gives you access to a few extra rooms (the lineup varies) and lets you skip ticket-buying lines if you came *sans* pass. Ignore the tours hawked as you leave the train station. Book at the guided-tours office in the Château courtyard—it's to your right as you approach the palace (look for *Visites Conferences* signs). You can book a tour online on the palace's website or reserve immediately upon arrival—tours can sell out by 13:00 (€16 includes palace entry—just €1 more than entry alone, €7 if you have pass, tours run about hourly from 9:00-15:00).

**Audioguide Tours:** A free audioguide to the Château is included in your admission (pick up just inside the palace, return as you leave). You can download a free Rick Steves audio tour of Versailles; see page 24. Other podcasts and digital tours are available in the "multimedia" section at www.chateau versailles.fr. The palace audioguide and my audio tour complement one another: Eager students can easily transfer earbuds between devices and listen to both tours as you shuffle through the lavish rooms.

**Baggage Check:** Large bags and baby strollers are not allowed in the Château and the two Trianons (use a baby backpack or hire a babysitter for the day; see page 464); you must use the free baggage check and retrieve your items one hour before closing.

**Services:** There are WCs on either side of the Château courtyard (in the ticket-sales office and in the guided-tours office), immediately upon entering the Château (Entrance H), and near the exit from the Dauphin's Apartments. You'll also find WCs near the Grand Café d'Orléans, in the Gardens near the Latona Basin, at the Grand Canal, in the Grand Trianon and Petit Trianon, and at several other places scattered around the grounds. Any café generally has a WC.

**Photography:** Allowed, but no flash indoors.

**Eating:** To the left of the Château's golden Royal Gate entrance, the Grand Café d'Orléans offers good value self-service meals (€5 sandwiches and small salads, great for picnicking in the Gardens). In the Gardens, you'll find several restaurants, cafés,

# Kings and Queens and Guillotines

• *You could read this on the train ride to Versailles. Relax...the palace is the last stop.*

Come the Revolution, when they line us up and make us stick out our hands, will you have enough calluses to keep them from shooting you? A grim thought, but Versailles raises these kinds of questions. It's the symbol of the *ancien régime*, a time when society was divided into rulers and the ruled, when you were born to be rich or to be poor. To some it's the pinnacle of civilization; to others, the sign of a civilization in decay. Either way, it remains one of Europe's most impressive sights.

Versailles was the residence of the king and the seat of France's government for a hundred years. Louis XIV (r. 1643-1715) moved out of the Louvre in Paris, the previous royal residence, and built an elaborate palace in the forests and swamps of Versailles, 10 miles west. The reasons for the move were partly personal—Louis XIV loved the outdoors and disliked the sniping environs of stuffy Paris—and partly political.

Louis XIV was creating the first modern, centralized state. At Versailles he consolidated his government's scattered ministries so that he could personally control policy. More importantly, he invited France's nobles to Versailles in order to control them. Living a life of almost enforced idleness, the "domesticated" aristocracy couldn't interfere with the way Louis ran things. With 18 million people united under one king (England had only 5.5 million), a booming economy, and a powerful military, France was Europe's number-one power.

Around 1700, Versailles was the cultural heartbeat of Europe, and French culture was at its zenith. Throughout Europe, when you said "the king," you were referring to the French king—Louis XIV. Every king wanted a palace like Versailles. Everyone learned French. French taste in clothes, hairstyles, table manners, theater, music, art, and kissing spread across the Continent. That cultural dominance continued, to some extent, right up to the 20th century.

## Louis XIV

At the center of all this was Europe's greatest king. He was a

and snack stands. Most are located near the Latona Fountain (less crowded) and in a delightful cluster at the Grand Canal (more crowds and more choices, including two restaurants).

In **town,** restaurants are on the street to the right of the parking lot (as you face the Château). Handy McDonald's and Starbucks (both with WCs) are across from the train station. The best choices are on the lively Place du Marché Notre-Dame in the town center (listed at the end of this chapter).

true Renaissance Man, a century after the Renaissance: athletic, good-looking, a musician, dancer, horseman, statesman, patron of the arts, and lover. For all his grandeur, he was one of history's most polite and approachable kings, a good listener who could put even commoners at ease in his presence.

Louis XIV called himself the Sun King because he gave life and warmth to all he touched. He was also thought of as Apollo, the Greek god of the sun. Versailles became the personal temple of this god on earth, decorated with statues and symbols of Apollo, the sun, and Louis XIV himself. The classical themes throughout underlined the divine right of France's kings and queens to rule without limit.

Louis XIV was a hands-on king who personally ran affairs of state. All decisions were made by him. Nobles, who in other countries were the center of power, became virtual slaves dependent on Louis XIV's generosity. For 70 years he was the perfect embodiment of the absolute monarch. He summed it up best himself with his famous rhyme—*L'état, c'est moi!* (lay-tah say-mwah): "The state, that's me!"

### Another Louis or Two to Remember

Three kings lived in Versailles during its century of glory. Louis XIV built it and established French dominance. Louis XV, his great-grandson (Louis XIV reigned for 72 years), carried on the tradition and policies, but without the Sun King's flair. During Louis XV's reign (1715-1774), France's power abroad was weakening, and there were rumblings of rebellion from within.

France's monarchy was crumbling, and the time was ripe for a strong leader to re-establish the old feudal order. They didn't get one. Instead, they got Louis XVI (r. 1774-1792), a shy, meek bookworm, the kind of guy who lost sleep over revolutionary graffiti...because it was misspelled. Louis XVI married a sweet girl from the Austrian royal family, Marie-Antoinette, and together they retreated into the idyllic gardens of Versailles while revolutionary fires smoldered.

**Fountain Spectacles in the Gardens:** On spring and summer weekends, the Gardens charge a mandatory admission fee for these spectacles. Loud classical music fills the king's backyard, and the Gardens' fountains are in full squirt. Louis XIV had his engineers literally reroute a river to fuel these gushers. Even by today's standards, they are impressive.

The fountains run on Saturdays and Sundays from April through October (11:00-12:00 & 15:30-17:30; finale starts at

17:20). They also perform on Tuesdays from late May until late June at the same times. On these "spray days," the Gardens cost €8.50. (Pay at the Gardens entrance; covered by Le Passeport but not Paris Museum Pass.) The calendar of spectacles also includes a few music-only days (on the rare Tue, €8.50) and elaborate sound-and-light displays (Sat mid-June-Aug at 21:00, €23). Check the Versailles website for what's happening during your visit.

**Starring:** Luxurious palaces, endless gardens, Louis XIV, Marie-Antoinette, and the *ancien régime*.

# The Tour Begins

On this self-guided tour, we'll see the Château (the State Apartments of the king and queen as well as the Hall of Mirrors), the landscaped Gardens in the "backyard," and the Trianon Palaces and Domaine de Marie-Antoinette, located at the far end of the Gardens. If your time is limited  or you don't enjoy walking, skip the Trianon/Domaine, which is a 30-minute hike from the Château.

# The Château

• *Stand in the huge courtyard and face the palace, or Château. The golden Royal Gate in the center of the courtyard, nearly 260 feet long and decorated with 100,000 gold leaves, is a recent replica of the original. The ticket-buying office is to the left; guided-tour sales are to the right. The entrance to the Château (once you have your ticket or pass) is through the modern concrete-and-glass security checkpoint, marked* Entrance A. *After passing through security, you spill out into the open-air courtyard on the other side of the golden Royal Gate.*

## The Original Château and the Courtyard

The section of the palace with the clock is the original château, once a small hunting lodge where little Louis XIV spent his happiest boyhood years. Naturally, the Sun King's private bedroom (the three arched windows beneath the clock) faced the rising sun. The palace and grounds are laid out on an east-west axis.

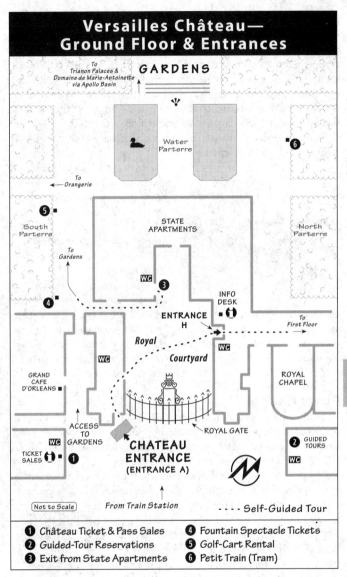

# Versailles Château— Ground Floor & Entrances

GARDENS

To Trianon Palaces & Domaine de Marie-Antoinette via Apollo Basin

Water Parterre

To Orangerie

STATE APARTMENTS

South Parterre

North Parterre

To Gardens

WC

3

INFO DESK

ENTRANCE H

To First Floor

Royal

WC

Courtyard

WC

GRAND CAFE D'ORLEANS

ROYAL CHAPEL

ACCESS TO GARDENS

ROYAL GATE

CHATEAU ENTRANCE (ENTRANCE A)

TICKET SALES

1

2 GUIDED TOURS

WC

Not to Scale

From Train Station

- - - - Self-Guided Tour

1 Château Ticket & Pass Sales     4 Fountain Spectacle Tickets
2 Guided-Tour Reservations    5 Golf-Cart Rental
3 Exit from State Apartments    6 Petit Train (Tram)

**VERSAILLES**

Once king, Louis XIV expanded the lodge by attaching wings, creating the present U-shape. Later, the long north and south wings were built. The total cost of the project has been estimated at half of France's entire GNP for one year.

Think how busy this courtyard must have been 300 years ago. As many as 5,000 nobles were here at any one time, each with an entourage. Riding in sedan-chair taxis, they'd buzz from games to

552 Rick Steves' Paris

parties to amorous rendezvous. Servants ran about delivering secret messages and roast legs of lamb. Horse-drawn carriages arrived at the fancy gate with their finely dressed passengers, having driven up the broad boulevard that ran directly from Paris (the horse stables still line the boulevard). Incredible as it seems, both the grounds and most of the palace were public territory, where even the lowliest peasants could come to gawk—provided they passed through a metal detector and followed a dress code. Then, as now, there were hordes of tourists, pickpockets, palace workers, and men selling wind-up children's toys.

• *Enter the Château from the courtyard at Entrance H—the State Apartments. Inside are an info desk (get a free map), WCs, and free audioguides. Glance through a doorway at the impressive Royal Chapel, which we'll see again upstairs.*

*Just follow the flow of crowds. You may pass through a dozen ground-floor rooms with paintings of Louis XIV, XV, and XVI, and of Versailles at different stages of growth—and may get a peek at the Royal Opera House. (The route and displays change often.) Climb the stairs, passing through more exhibits. Finally, you reach a palatial golden-brown room, with a doorway that overlooks the Royal Chapel.*

## Royal Chapel

Dut-dutta-dah! Every morning at 10:00, the organist and musicians struck up the music, these big golden doors opened, and Louis XIV and his family stepped onto the balcony to attend Mass. While Louis looked down on the golden altar, the lowly nobles on the ground floor knelt with their backs to the altar and looked up—worshipping Louis worshipping God. Important religious ceremonies took place here, including the marriage of young Louis XVI to Marie-Antoinette.

In the vast pagan "temple" that is Versailles—built to glorify one man, Louis XIV—this Royal Chapel is a paltry tip of the hat to that "other" god...the Christian one. It's virtually the first, last, and only hint of Christianity you'll see in the entire complex. Versailles celebrates Man, not God, by raising Louis XIV to almost godlike status, the personification of all good human qualities. In a way, Versailles is the last great flowering of Renaissance humanism and a revival of the classical world.

## Versailles' Royal Opera House

Your tour may include a visit to Versailles' Royal Opera House (Opéra Royale). This 700-seat, oval-shaped theater is a dizzying mix of pink, green, and blue, dazzling with mirrors and chandeliers, and all laced with gold. The entire structure is made of wood, carved to look like Ionic columns or painted to simulate marble. When Marie-Antoinette married the future Louis XVI in 1770, they had their reception here in this building, which was built specifically for the occasion by architect Ange-Jacques Gabriel. It was not only used as a theater, but could also be converted into a ballroom or audience hall quickly by machinery that raised the auditorium floor to the same level as the stage. If you get inside, look up above the double balconies to the chandeliers: It took thousands of candles to light the place for a single night, so performances were rare and treasured.

• *Enter the next room, an even more sumptuous space with a fireplace and a colorful painting on the ceiling.*

## Hercules Drawing Room

Pleasure ruled. The main suppers, balls, and receptions were held in this room. Picture elegant partygoers in fine silks, wigs, rouge, lipstick, and fake moles (and that's just the men) as they dance to the strains of a string quartet.

On the wall opposite the fireplace is an appropriate painting showing Christ in the middle of a Venetian party. The work—by Paolo Veronese, a gift from the Republic of Venice—was one of Louis XIV's favorites, so the king had the room decorated around it. Stand by the fireplace for the full effect: The room's columns, arches, and frieze match the height and style of Veronese's painted architecture, which makes the painting an extension of the room.

The ceiling painting, ringed by a balustrade, creates the effect of a sunroof opening up to heaven. Hercules (with his club) hurries up to heaven on a chariot, late for his wedding to the king of the gods' daughter. The scene echoes real life—Louis XIV

# Versailles Château—First Floor

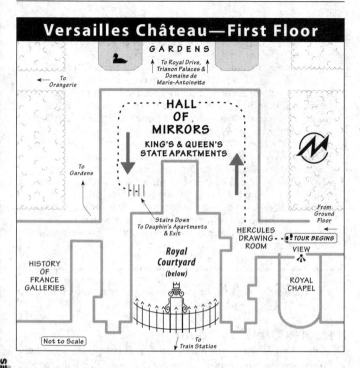

built the room for his own daughter's wedding reception. The style is pure Baroque, a riot of 142 exuberant figures depicted at all angles by Louis' court painter, Charles Le Brun.

• *From here on it's a one-way tour—getting lost is not allowed. Follow the crowds into the small green room with a goddess in pink on the ceiling. The names of the rooms generally come from the paintings on the ceilings.*

## The King's Wing
### Salon of Abundance

If the party in the Hercules Room got too intense, you could always step in here for some refreshments. Silver trays were loaded with liqueurs, exotic stimulants (coffee), juice, chocolates, and, on really special occasions, three-bean salad.

The ceiling painting shows the cornucopia of riches poured down on invited guests. Around the edges of the ceiling are painted versions of the king's actual treasures and royal dinnerware—golden bowls, urns, and gravy boats. The two black chests of drawers are from Louis' furniture collection (most of it was lost in the Revolution). They rest on heavy bases and are heavily ornamented—the so-called Louis XIV style.

Louis himself might be here. He was a gracious host who enjoyed letting his hair down at night. If he took a liking to you, he might sneak you through those doors there (in the middle of the wall) and into his own private study, or "cabinet of curiosities," where he'd show off his collection of dishes, medals, jewels, or...the *Mona Lisa*, which hung on his wall. Louis' favorite show-and-tell items are now in the Louvre.

The paintings on the walls are of Louis XIV's heirs. He reigned for more than 70 years and outlived three of them, finally leaving the crown to his pink-cheeked, five-year-old great-grandson, Louis XV (on the right).

## Venus Room

Love ruled at Versailles. In this room, couples would cavort beneath the goddess of love, floating on the ceiling. One of the ceiling paintings (above the statue, in a rectangular frame) symbolizes the marriage of Louis XIV and Marie-Thérèse, shown in their wedding-limo chariot. Venus sends down a canopy of golden garlands to ensnare mortals in delicious *amour*. Notice how a painted garland goes "out" the bottom of the central painting, becomes a golden garland held by a satyr, transforms into a gilded wood garland, and then turns back into a painting again. Baroque artists loved to mix their media to fool the eye. Another illusion is in the paintings at both ends of the room—the painted columns match the room's real ones, extending this grand room into mythical courtyards.

Don't let the statue of a confident Louis XIV as a Roman emperor fool you. He started out as a poor little rich kid with a chip on his shoulder. His father died before Louis was old enough to rule, and, during the regency period, the French *parlements* treated little Louis and his mother like trash. They were virtual prisoners, humiliated in their home, the Royal Palace in Paris (today's Louvre). There they eked by with bland meals, hand-me-down leotards, and pointed shoes. After Louis XIV attained power and wealth, he made Versailles a pleasure palace, with happy hours held in this room every evening. There was one topic you never discussed in Louis' presence: poverty. Maybe Versailles was his way of saying, "Living well is the best revenge."

## Diana Room

Here in the billiards room, Louis and his men played on a table that stood in the center of the room, while ladies sat surrounding them on Persian-carpet cushions, and music wafted in from next door. Louis was a good pool player, a sore loser, and a king—thus, he rarely lost.

The famous bust of Louis by Giovanni Lorenzo Bernini (in the center) shows a handsome, dashing, 27-year-old playboy-king. His gaze is steady amid his windblown cloak and hair. Young Louis loved life. He hunted animals by day (notice Diana the Huntress, with her bow, on the ceiling) and chased beautiful women at night.

Games were actually an important part of Louis' political strategy, known as "the domestication of the nobility." By distracting the nobles with the pleasures of courtly life, he was free to run the government his way. Billiards, dancing, and concerts were popular, but the biggest distraction was gambling, usually a card game similar to blackjack. Louis lent money to the losers, making them even more indebted to him. The good life was an addiction, and Louis kept the medicine cabinet well-stocked.

As you move into the next room, notice the fat walls that hid thin servants, who were to be at their master's constant call—but out of sight when not needed.

## Mars Room

Also known as the Guard Room (as it was the room for Louis' Swiss bodyguards), this red room is decorated with a military flair. On the ceiling there's Mars, the Greek god of war, in a chariot pulled by wolves. The bronze cupids in the corners are escalating from love arrows to heavier artillery. But it's not all war. Louis loved music and playing his guitar, and enjoyed concerts here in the Mars Room nearly every evening.

Out the window are sculpted gardens in the style of a traditional Italian villa—landscaped symmetrically, with trimmed hedges and cone-shaped trees lining walkways that lead to fountains.

As you wander, the palace feels bare, but remember that entire industries were created to decorate the place with carpets, mirrors, furniture, and tapestries. Most of the furniture we see today is not original, but is from the same period.

## Mercury Room

Louis' life was a work of art, and Versailles was the display case. Everything he did was a public event designed to show his subjects how it should be done. This room may have served as Louis' official (not actual) bedroom, where the Sun King would ritually rise each morning to warm his subjects.

From a canopied bed (like this 18th-century one), Louis would get up, dress, and take a seat for morning prayer. Meanwhile, the nobles would stand behind a balustrade, in awe of his piety, nobility, and clean socks. At breakfast they murmured with delight as he deftly decapitated his boiled egg with a knife. And when Louis went to bed at night, the dukes and barons would fight over who got to hold the candle while he slipped into his royal jammies. Bedtime, wake-up, and meals were all public rituals.

## Apollo Room

This was the grand throne room. Louis held court from a 10-foot-tall, silver-and-gold, canopied throne on a raised platform placed in the center of the room. (Notice the four small metal rings in the ceiling that once supported the canopy.) Even when the king was away, passing courtiers had to bow to the empty throne.

Everything in here reminds us that Louis XIV was not just any ruler, but the Sun King, who lit the whole world with his presence. On the ceiling the sun god Apollo (representing Louis) drives his chariot, dragging the sun across the heavens to warm the four corners of the world (counterclockwise from above the exit door): 1) Europe, with a sword; 2) Asia, with a lion; 3) Africa, with an elephant; and 4) good ol' America, an Indian maiden with a crocodile. Notice the ceiling's beautifully gilded frame and *Goldfinger* maidens.

The famous portrait by Hyacinthe Rigaud over the fireplace gives a more human look at Louis XIV. He's shown in a dancer's pose, displaying the legs that made him one of the all-time dancing fools of kingery (see a photo of this portrait on page 549). At night they often held parties in this room, actually dancing around the throne.

Louis XIV (who was 63 when this was painted) had more than

300 wigs like this one, and he changed them many times a day. This fashion first started when his hairline began to recede, then sprouted all over Europe, and even spread to the American colonies in the time of George Washington.

Louis XIV may have been treated like a god, but he was not an overly arrogant man. His subjects adored him because he was a symbol of everything a man could be, the fullest expression of the Renaissance Man. Compare the portrait of Louis XIV with the one across the room of his last successor, Louis XVI—same arrogant pose, but without the inner confidence to keep his head on his shoulders.

• *Continue into the final room of the King's Wing.*

## War Room

"Louis Quatorze was addicted to wars," and the room depicts his victories—in marble, gilding, stucco, and paint. France's success made other countries jealous and nervous. At the base of the ceiling (in semi-circular paintings), we see Germany (with the double eagle), Holland (with its ships), and Spain (with a red flag and roaring lion) ganging up on Louis XIV. But Lady France (center of ceiling), protected by the shield of Louis XIV, hurls thunderbolts down to defeat them. The stucco relief on the wall shows Louis XIV on horseback, triumphing over his fallen enemies.

Versailles was good propaganda. It showed the rest of the world how rich and powerful France was. A visit to the Château and Gardens sent visitors reeling. And Louis XIV's greatest triumph may be the next room, the one that everybody wrote home about.

## Hall of Mirrors

No one had ever seen anything like this hall when it was opened. Mirrors were still a great luxury at the time, and the number and size of these monsters were astounding. The hall is nearly 250 feet long. There are 17 arched mirrors, matched by 17 windows letting in that breathtaking view

of the Gardens. Lining the hall are 24 gilded candelabra, eight busts of Roman emperors, and eight classical-style statues (seven of them ancient). The ceiling decoration chronicles Louis' military accomplishments, topped off by Louis himself in the central panel (with cupids playing cards at his divine feet) doing what he did best—triumphing. Originally, two huge carpets mirrored the action depicted on the ceiling.

Imagine this place lit by the flames of thousands of candles, filled with ambassadors, nobles, and guests dressed in silks and powdered wigs. At the far end of the room sits the king, on the canopied throne moved in temporarily from the Apollo Room. Servants glide by with silver trays of hors d'oeuvres, and an orchestra fuels the festivities. The mirrors reflect an age when beautiful people loved to look at themselves. It was no longer a sin to be proud of good looks and fine clothes, or to enjoy the good things in life: laughing, dancing, eating, drinking, flirting, and watching the sun set into the distant canal.

From the center of the hall you can fully appreciate the epic scale of Versailles. The huge palace (by architect Louis Le Vau), the fantasy interior (by Charles Le Brun), and the endless gardens (by André Le Nôtre) made Versailles *le* best. In 1871, after the Prussians defeated the French, Otto von Bismarck declared the establishment of the German Empire in this room. And in 1919, Germany and the Allies signed the Treaty of Versailles, ending World War I (and, some say, starting World War II) right here, in the Hall of Mirrors.

• *Midway down the Hall of Mirrors, a short detour to the left circles you through the heart of the palace, to the...*

## King's Bedroom and Council Rooms

Pass through a first large room to find Louis XIV's bedroom. It's elaborately decorated, and the decor changed with the season. On the wall behind the impressive bed, a golden Lady France watched over her king as he slept. The balustrade separated the courtiers from the king. Though this was Louis' actual bedroom, it was also a somewhat public space where he received visitors. The two rooms on either side of the bedroom—right next to where the king slept—were large halls for ambassadorial receptions and cabinet meetings.

Look out the window and notice how this small room is at the exact center of the immense horseshoe-shaped building, overlooking the main courtyard and—naturally—facing the rising sun in the east. It symbolized the exact center of power in France. Imagine the humiliation on that day in 1789 when Louis' great-great-great-grandson, Louis XVI, was forced to stand here and acknowledge the angry crowds that filled the square demanding the end of the divine monarchy.

• *Return to the Hall of Mirrors. Continue to the far end, being sure to enjoy views of the garden. Next is the...*

## Peace Room

By the end of the Sun King's long life, he was tired of fighting. In this sequel to the War Room, peace is granted to Germany, Holland, and Spain as cupids play with the discarded cannons, and swords are transformed into violins. Louis XIV advised his great-grandson to "be a peaceful king."

The oval painting above the fireplace shows 19-year-old Louis XV bestowing an olive branch on Europe. Beside him is his Polish wife, Marie Leszczynska, cradling their baby twin daughters.

The Peace Room marks the beginning of the queen's half of the palace. The Queen's Wing is a mirror image of the King's Wing. The King's Wing was mostly ceremonial and used as a series of reception rooms; the Queen's Wing is more intimate. For instance, on Sundays the queen held chamber-music concerts in this room for family and friends (notice the gilded music motifs).

• *Enter the first room of the Queen's Wing, with its canopied bed. (Note: In 2013, some rooms of the Queen's Wing may be closed for renovation.)*

## The Queen's Wing
### Queen's Bedchamber

It was here that the queen rendezvoused with her husband. Two queens died here, and this is where 19 princes were born. The chandelier is where two of them were conceived. (Just kidding.) Royal babies were delivered in public to prove their blue-bloodedness.

True, Louis XIV was not the most faithful husband. There was no attempt to hide the fact that the Sun King warmed more than one bed, for he was above the rules of mere mortals. Adultery became acceptable—even fashionable—in court circles. The secret-looking door on the left side of the bed was for Louis' late-night liaisons—it led straight to his rooms.

Some of Louis XIV's mistresses became more famous and powerful than his rather quiet queen, but he was faithful to the show of marriage and had genuine affection for his wife. Louis XIV made a point of sleeping with the queen as often as possible, regardless of whose tiara he tickled earlier in the evening.

This room looks just like it did in the days of the last queen, Marie-Antoinette, who substantially redecorated the entire wing. That's her bust over the fireplace, and the double eagle of her native Austria in the corners. The big mahogany chest to the left of the bed held her jewels.

The large canopied bed is a reconstruction. The bed, chair, and wall coverings switched with the seasons. This was the cheery summer pattern.

## Salon of the Nobles

Here, in this mint-green room, the wife of Louis XV and her circle of friends met, under paintings by Boucher—popular with the queen for their pink-cheeked Rococo exuberance. Discussions ranged from politics to gossip, food to literature, fashion to philosophy. All three of Versailles' rulers considered themselves enlightened monarchs who promoted the arts and new ideas. Louis XIV laughed at the anti-authoritarian plays of Molière, and Louis XV gave free room and board here to the political radical Voltaire. Ironically, these discussions planted the seeds of liberal thought that would grow into the Revolution.

## Queen's Antechamber

The royal family dined publicly in this room (also called the Grand Couvert), while servants and nobles fluttered around them, admired their table manners, and laughed at the king's jokes like courtly Paul Shaffers. A typical dinner consisted of four different soups, two whole birds stuffed with truffles, mutton, ham slices, fruit, pastries, compotes, and preserves.

The central portrait is of luxury-loving, "let-them-eat-cake" Marie-Antoinette, who became a symbol of decadence to the peasants. The portrait at the far end is a public-relations attempt to soften her image by showing her with three of her children.

## Queen's Guard Room

On October 5, 1789, a mob of revolutionaries—perhaps appalled by their queen's taste in wallpaper—stormed the palace. They were fed up with the ruling class leading a life of luxury in the countryside while they were starving in the grimy streets of Paris.

The king and queen locked themselves in. Some of the revolutionaries gained access to this upper floor. They burst into this room where Marie-Antoinette was hiding, overcame her bodyguards, and dragged her off along with her husband. (Some claim that, as they carried her away, she sang, "Louis, Louis, oh-oh...we gotta go now.")

The enraged peasants then proceeded to ransack the place as revenge for the years of poverty and oppression they'd suffered. (The stripped palace was refurnished a decade later under Napoleon and eventually turned into a national museum.) Marie-Antoinette and Louis XVI were later taken to Place de la Concorde in Paris, where they knelt under the guillotine and were made a foot shorter at the top.

Did the king and queen deserve it? Were the revolutionaries destroying civilization or clearing the decks for a new and better one? Was Versailles a symbol of progress or decadence?

## Coronation Room

No sooner did the French throw out a king than they got an emperor. The Revolution established democracy, but it was shaky in a country that wasn't used to it. In the midst of the confusion, the upstart general Napoleon Bonaparte took control and soon held dictatorial powers. This room captures the glory of the Napoleon years, when he conquered most of Europe. In the huge canvas on the left-hand wall, we see him crowning himself emperor of a new, revived "Roman" Empire. (Though also painted by the master Jacques-Louis David, this is a lesser-quality version of the famous one hanging in the Louvre.)

Turn and face the windows to see the portrait (between the windows) of a dashing, young, charismatic Napoleon in 1796, when he was just a general in command of the Revolution's army in Italy. Compare this with the adjacent portrait from 10 years later—looking less like a revolutionary and more like a Louis. Above the young Napoleon is a portrait of Josephine, his wife and France's empress. In David's *Distribution of Eagles* (opposite the *Coronation*), the victorious general, in imperial garb, passes out emblems of victory to his loyal troops. In *The Battle of Aboukir* (opposite the window, see photo), Joachim Murat, Napoleon's general and brother-in-law, looks bored as he slashes through a tangle of dark-skinned warriors. His horse, though, has a look of, "What are we doing in this mob? Let's get out of here!" Let's.

# All the King's Horses & Veggies: Lesser Sights near the Palace

Two sights located a few minutes' walk from the Château give a different take on life in royal times. For locations, see the map on page 542.

### The Equestrian Performance Academy (Académie du Spectacle Equestre)

The art of horseback riding has returned to Versailles. On most weekends from May through mid-December, you can either watch a basic training session or enjoy a choreographed performance—including "equestrian fencing"—performed to classical music.

**Cost and Hours:** Training session-€12 (includes a visit of the stables), Sat-Sun and some Thu at 11:15; musical shows-€25, Sun and some Thu at 15:00 plus Sat at 20:00 May-July and at 18:00 Sept-Dec, but schedule is sporadic—check website for closure dates and extra performances; stables (Grandes Ecuries) are across the parking square from the Château, next to the post office; information tel. 01 39 02 07 14, reservations tel. 08 92 68 18 91, www.acadequestre.fr.

### The King's Vegetable Garden (Le Potager du Roi)

When Louis XIV demanded fresh asparagus in the middle of winter, he got it, thanks to his vegetable garden. The 22-acre garden—still productive—is open to visitors. Stroll through symmetrically laid-out plots planted with vegetables both ordinary and exotic, among thousands of fruit trees. The garden is surrounded by walls and sunk below street level to create its own microclimate. Overseeing the central fountain is a statue of the agronomist Jean de la Quintinie, who wowed Louis XIV's court with Versailles-sized produce. Even today, the garden sprouts 20 tons of vegetables and 50 tons of fruit a year, which you can buy in season at the garden shop (same hours as garden).

**Cost and Hours:** €4.50 weekdays, €6.50 weekends, April-Oct Tue-Sun 10:00-18:00, closed Mon, limited hours in winter, 10 Rue du Maréchal Joffre, tel. 01 39 24 62 62, www.potager-du-roi.fr.

VERSAILLES

• *This ends our tour of the Château, but there is more, all described in your free audioguide.*

# The Rest of the Château

On the first floor, you can continue into the History of France rooms, lined with paintings of great men and events; find temporary exhibits to explore; or visit the Salon de Thé Angelina, which serves decadent hot chocolate and luscious pastries (most famous is their Mont Blanc—a chestnut-cream meringue with whipped cream).

• *Stairs lead from the Coronation Room down to the ground floor.*

Downstairs, on the ground floor, are the Dauphin's Apartments. These less-decorated rooms were home to the king's son and daughter-in-law. The crown prince, or "Dauphin," was named for the dolphin on the family crest. During the reigns of Kings Louis XIV-XVI, five different Dauphins played the role of heir apparent without ever becoming king, having been outlived by their aged parents. Also on the ground floor are the Mesdames' Apartments—the rooms set aside for the six daughters of Louis XV.

• *Exit the palace (past a handy WC) into the central courtyard. From there, follow signs to the Gardens* (les Jardins), *located behind the Château.*

*Now might be a good time to break for lunch (see "Eating in Versailles" on page 576). When you're ready for the Gardens, plan your time with the "Getting Around the Gardens" sidebar on the next page.*

# The Gardens

Louis XIV was a divine-right ruler. One way he proved it was by controlling nature like a god. These lavish grounds—elaborately planned, pruned, and decorated—showed everyone that Louis was in total command. Louis loved his gardens and, until his last days, presided over their care. He personally led VIPs through them and threw his biggest parties here. With their Greco-Roman themes and incomparable beauty, the Gardens further illustrated his immense power.

• *Entering the Gardens, with the palace to your back, go to the far left to reach the stone railing. You'll pass through cookie-cutter patterns of shrubs and green cones. Stand at the railing overlooking the courtyard below and the Louis-made lake in the distance.*

# Getting Around the Gardens

**On Foot:** It's a 45-minute walk from the palace, down to the Grand Canal, past the two Trianon palaces, to the Hamlet at the far end of Domaine de Marie-Antoinette. Allow more time if you stop along the way. After enduring the slow Château shuffle, stretching your legs out here feels pretty good.

**By Bike:** There's a bike rental station by the Grand Canal. A bike won't save you that much time (you can't take it inside the grounds of the Trianon/Domaine; park it near an entrance while you tour inside). Instead, simply enjoy pedaling around the greatest royal park in all of Europe (€6.50/hour or €15/half-day, kid-size bikes and tandems available).

**By *Petit Train:*** The fast-looking, slow-moving tram leaves from behind the Château (north side). It stops at the Grand Canal and at the Grand and Petit Trianons (two of the entrance points to the Trianon/Domaine. You can hop on and off as you like (€7, pay driver, free for kids under 11, 4/hour, runs 11:00-18:00). You may laugh at the hokey-pokey tram now, but it looks a lot more attractive at the end of the day when you're faced with the long uphill walk back to the Château.

**By Golf Cart:** This makes for a fun drive through the Gardens, complete with music and a relaxing commentary. But you can't go wherever you want—the cart shuts off automatically if you diverge from the prescribed route. You can't drive it in the Trianon/Domaine, but you can park it outside the entrance while you sightsee inside. Be warned: There are steep late fees. To go out to the Hamlet, sightsee quickly, and get back within your allotted hour, you'll need to rent a cart at the Grand Canal and put the pedal to the metal (€30/hour, 4-person limit per cart, rent down by the canal or at Orangerie side of palace).

**By Shuttle Bus:** Phébus runs a shuttle bus directly between Versailles R.G. train station and the Trianon/Domaine (the shuttle doesn't stop at the Château). This bus can save you 30 minutes of walking time to/from the Trianon/Domaine. It's ideal if you are visiting the Trianon/Domaine first, before the Château. It also works great if you want to return to the train station from the Trianon/Domaine (1-2/hour, runs mid-April-Oct only, €1.70 or one Métro ticket, check current schedule for "Ligne TRI" at www.phebus.tm.fr).

# The Orangerie

The warmth from the Sun King was so great that he could even grow orange trees in chilly France. Louis XIV had a thousand of these to amaze his visitors. In winter they were kept in the greenhouses (beneath your feet) that surround the courtyard. On sunny days, they were wheeled out in their silver planters and scattered around the grounds.

• *Make an about-face and walk back toward the palace. Sit on the top stairs and look away from the palace.*

## View Down the Royal Drive

This, to me, is the most stunning spot in all of Versailles. With the palace behind you, it seems as if the grounds stretch out forever. Versailles was laid out along an eight-mile axis that included the grounds, the palace, and the town of Versailles itself, one of the first instances of urban planning since Roman times and a model for future capitals, such as Washington, D.C., and Brasília.

Looking down the Royal Drive (also known as "The Green Carpet"), you see the round Apollo fountain far in the distance. Just beyond that is the Grand Canal. The groves on either side of the Royal Drive were planted with trees from all over, laid out in an elaborate grid, and dotted with statues and fountains. Of the original 1,500 fountains, 300 remain.

Looking back at the palace, you can see the Hall of Mirrors—it's the middle story, with the arched windows.

• *Stroll down the steps to get a good look at the frogs and lizards that fill the round...*

## Latona Basin

Everything in the garden has a symbolic meaning. The theme of Versailles is Apollo, the god of the sun, associated with Louis XIV. This round fountain tells the story of the birth of Apollo and his sister, Diana. On top of the fountain are Apollo and Diana as little kids with their mother, Latona (they're facing toward the Apollo fountain). Latona, an unwed mother, was insulted by the local peasants. She called on the king of the gods, Zeus (the children's father), to avenge the insult. Zeus swooped down and turned all the peasants into the frogs and lizards that ring the fountain.

• *As you walk down past the basin toward the Royal Drive, you'll pass by "ancient" statues done by 17th-century French sculptors. The Colonnade is hidden in the woods on the left-hand side of the Royal Drive, about three-fourths of the way to the Apollo Basin (you'll spot it off the main path through an opening).*

## Colonnade

Versailles had no pres-
tigious ancient ruins, so
the king built his own.
This prefab Roman ruin
is a 100-foot circle of 64
marble columns support-
ing arches. Beneath the
arches are small birdbath
fountains (imagine them

all spouting water). Nobles would picnic in the shade to the tunes
of a string quartet and pretend that they were the enlightened citizens of the ancient world.

## Apollo Basin

The fountains of Versailles were its most famous attraction, a
marvel of both art and engineering. This one was the centerpiece,
showing the sun god—Louis XIV—in his sunny chariot as he

starts his journey across the sky.
The horses are half-submerged,
giving the impression, when the
fountains play, of the sun rising
out of the mists of dawn. Most
of the fountains were turned on
only when the king walked by,
but this one played constantly
for the benefit of those watching
from the palace.

All the fountains are gravity-powered. They work on the same
principle as blocking a hose with your finger to make it squirt. Underground streams (pumped into Versailles by Seine River pres-
sure) feed into smaller pipes at the fountains, which shoot the water
high into the air.

Looking back at the palace from here, realize that the distance
you just walked is only a fraction of this vast complex of buildings,
gardens, and waterways. Be glad you don't have to mow the lawn.

## Grand Canal

Why visit Venice when
you can just build your
own? In an era before virtual reality, this was the
next best thing to an ac-
tual trip. Couples in gon-
dolas would pole along
the waters accompanied

by barges with orchestras playing *"O Sole Mio."* The canal is actually cross-shaped; you're looking at the longest part, one mile from end to end. Of course, this, too, is a man-made body of water with no function other than to please. Originally, authentic gondoliers, imported with their boats from Venice, lived in a little settlement next to the canal.

These days, the Grand Canal hosts eateries, rental boats, bike and golf-cart rentals, and a *Petit Train* tram stop (see sidebar on page 565).

• *The area called the Trianon Palaces and Domaine de Marie-Antoinette is a 10-minute walk from the Grand Canal. You can enter/exit the Trianon/Domaine at three spots: near the palace known as the Grand Trianon (where we'll enter), near the Petit Trianon palace, or way around back on the far side of the Hamlet.*

*If you're monitoring your time and energy, note that it's a 1.5-hour time commitment to see the whole Trianon/Domaine, plus another 30-minute walk back to the Château. You can take a bike, golf cart, or* Petit Train *(see sidebar on page 565)* as far as the entrance, but you have to walk inside.

*To get to our starting point, the Grand Trianon, start walking up the Grand Canal (see the map on page 542.) About 70 yards past the boat rental (and immediately past the restaurant), veer right. You'll find twin dirt paths flanking a looooong strip of lawn. This leads uphill 500 yards to the Grand Trianon. (Bikers/golf-cart drivers can park their wheels here.)*

## Trianon Palaces and Domaine de Marie-Antoinette

Versailles began as an escape from the pressures of kingship. But in a short time, the Château had become as busy as Paris ever was. Louis XIV needed an escape from his escape and built a smaller palace out in the boonies. Later, his successors retreated still farther from the Château and French political life, ignoring the real world that was crumbling all around them. They expanded the Trianon area, building a fantasy world of palaces and pleasure gardens—the enclosure called Marie-Antoinette's Domaine.

There are many sights to see in the Trianon/Domaine and many paths connecting them. You can either browse with your map, or follow this self-guided route.

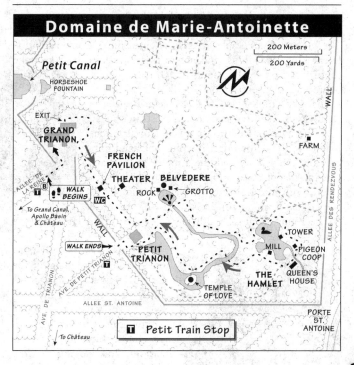

# Domaine de Marie-Antoinette

*Petit Canal*

HORSESHOE FOUNTAIN

EXIT

GRAND TRIANON

200 Meters
200 Yards

WALL

FARM

ALLÉE DE LA REINE

WALK BEGINS

WC

FRENCH PAVILION

THEATER

ROCK

BELVEDERE

GROTTO

ALLÉE DES RENDEZVOUS

To Grand Canal, Apollo Basin & Château

WALL

WALK ENDS

PETIT TRIANON

TOWER

MILL

PIGEON COOP

THE HAMLET

QUEEN'S HOUSE

AVE. DE TRIANON

AVE. DE PETIT TRIANON

TEMPLE OF LOVE

ALLEE ST. ANTOINE

PORTE ST. ANTOINE

To Château

**T** Petit Train Stop

## Grand Trianon

• *To enter the Grand Trianon, you must first pass through a security checkpoint. Pick up the free palace map and follow the one-way route through the rooms.*

## Exterior

Delicate, pink, and set amid gardens, the Grand Trianon was the perfect summer getaway. This was the king's private residence away from the main palace. Louis XIV usually spent a couple of nights a week here (more in the summer) to escape the sniping politics, strict etiquette, and 24/7 scrutiny of official court life.

Louis XIV built the palace (1670-1688) near the tiny peasant village of Trianon (hence the name) and faced it with blue-and-white ceramic tiles. When those began disintegrating almost immediately, the palace was renovated with pink marble. It's a one-story structure of two wings connected by a colonnade, with gardens in back.

## Interior—Left Wing

The rooms are a complex overlay of furnishings from many different kings, dauphins, and nobles that have lived here over the centuries. Louis XIV alone had three different bedrooms. Concentrate on the illustrious time of Louis XIV (1688-1715) and Napoleon Bonaparte (1810-1814). Use your map to find these highlights.

**The Mirror Room (Room 3):** This spacious living room has the original white walls and mirrors of Louis XIV, and the Empire-style furniture of Napoleon (unornamented, high-polished wood, with classical motifs). Napoleon inhabited the Grand Trianon with his second wife, Empress Marie-Louise, and his mother—the women in the left wing, the emperor in the right.

**Louis XIV's Bedchamber (Room 4):** Louis built the Grand Trianon as home for his chief mistress, while his wife lived in the Château. Imagine waking up in this big bed with your lover, throwing back the curtain, and looking out the windows at the gardens. These light, airy, many-windowed rooms were cheery even when skies were gray, a strong contrast to the heavy-metal decor in the mother Château.

Exit into the open-air colonnade (Peristyle) that connects the two wings. Originally, this pink-columned passageway had windows, an enormously expensive luxury that allowed visitors to enjoy the gardens even in bad weather.

## Interior—Right Wing

The Emperor's **Family Drawing Room** (Room 9, immediately to your right upon entering) had many different uses over the years: a theater for Louis XIV, a game room for Louis XV, and Napoleon's family room. After Napoleon was defeated and France's royalty returned, King Louis-Philippe I lived here. Walk through a series of rooms, passing through Louis-Philippe's billiards room, until you reach a room decorated in green malachite.

The **Malachite Room (Room 13)** was Napoleon's living room,

and his library was next door. You'll see the impressive green basin, vases, and candelabras made of Russian malachite given to Napoleon by Czar Alexander I. Another czar, Peter the Great, lodged in the Grand Trianon in 1717, then returned home—inspired to build the Peterhof, a similarly lavish summer palace near St. Petersburg known as the "Russian Versailles."

The **Cotelle Gallery (Room 16),** 170 feet long and painted white, was Louis' reception hall. Later, Marie-Antoinette performed here in theatrical productions for select audiences. The gallery is interspersed with big French doors and lined with paintings of Versailles vistas, peopled by promenading aristocrats. Party guests could admire the gardens in the paintings, then step out into the real thing.

## Gardens

Exit into the gardens and look back. The facade of pink, yellow, and white is a welcome contrast to the imposing Baroque facade of the main palace. The flower gardens were changed daily for the king's pleasure—for new color combinations and new "nasal cocktails."

• *Our next stop is the French Pavilion—find it on your map. To get there from the Grand Trianon gardens, walk clockwise around the perimeter of the Grand Trianon. Make it a tight, 180-degree loop, hugging the palace. When you reach the front (and run into a wall), turn left. Cross a footbridge. Directly ahead, you'll see the French Pavilion.*

## French Pavilion

This small, white building (generally closed) with rooms fanning out from the center was one more step away from the modern world. Inside is a circular room with four small adjoining rooms. Big French doors let in a cool breeze. Here Marie-Antoinette spent summer evenings with family and a few friends, listening to music or playing parlor games. She and her friends explored all avenues of *la douceur de vivre*, the sweetness of living.

• *Up ahead is the large, cube-shaped Petit Trianon palace—that's where our tour will eventually end. Head toward the Petit Trianon, but midway there, turn left, where you can peek into...*

## Marie-Antoinette's Theater

Marie-Antoinette adored the theater and was an aspiring performer
herself. In this intimate playhouse,
far from the rude intrusions of the
real world, the queen and her friends
acted out plays. The soft blue decor
and upholstered walls and benches
give the theater a dollhouse feel.
Though small, it has everything
you'd find in a major opera house:

stage, orchestra pit, balconies, ornate gold ceiling, and raked seating for 100 (photos OK, but no flash).

• *Continue through the oh-so-bucolic gardens until just before the Petit
Trianon. Turn left and follow paths uphill to a pond graced with a tiny
palace.*

## Belvedere, Rock, and Grotto

The octagonal Belvedere palace is as much windows as it is walls.

When the doors were open, it could serve
as a gazebo for musicians, serenading
nobles in this man-made alpine setting.
The interior has a marble-mosaic floor
and walls decorated with delicate, Pom-
peii-esque garlands. To the left of the
Belvedere is the "Rock," a fake mountain
that pours water into the pond. To the
right of the Belvedere (you'll have to find
it) is the secret Grotto.

• *Facing the Belvedere, turn right (east),
following the pond's meandering stream.
Continue gamboling along the paths. In the distance you'll spy a complex
of buildings, with a round, fanciful tower and a smattering of rustic,
half-timbered buildings. Head there to find the Hansel-and-Gretel-like
Hamlet.*

## The Hamlet

Marie-Antoinette longed for
the simple life of a peasant—not
the hard labor of real peasants,
who sweated and starved around
her—but the fairytale world of
simple country pleasures. She built
this complex of 12 thatched-roof
buildings fronting a lake as her
own private "Normand" village.

The main building is the Queen's House—actually two buildings connected by a wooden skywalk. It's the only one without a thatched roof. Like any typical peasant farmhouse, it had a billiard room, library, elegant dining hall, and two living rooms.

This was an actual working farm with a dairy (by the tower), a water mill, a pigeon coop (Le Colombier), and domestic animals. Nearby are the farm and menagerie, where the queen's servants kept cows, goats, chickens, and ducks. The harvest was served at Marie-Antoinette's table. Marie-Antoinette didn't do much work herself, but she "supervised," dressed in a plain, white muslin dress and a straw hat. Though the royal family is long gone, kid-pleasing animals still inhabit the farm, and fat fish swim languid circles in the pond.

• *Head back toward the Petit Trianon. Along the way (in about five minutes), you'll see the white dome of the...*

## Temple of Love

A circle of 12 marble Corinthian columns supports a dome, decorating a path where lovers could stroll. Underneath there's a statue of Cupid making a bow (to shoot arrows of love) out of the club of Hercules. It's a delightful monument to a society where the rich could afford that ultimate luxury, romantic love.

• *And, finally, you'll reach the...*

## Petit Trianon

Louis XV developed an interest in botany. He wanted to spend more time near the French Gardens, but the Summer House just wasn't big enough. He constructed the Petit Trianon ("Small Trianon") at the urging of his first mistress, Madame de Pompadour, and it later became home to his next mistress, Madame du Barry.

This gray, cubical building is a masterpiece of Neoclassical architecture, built by the same architect who created the Opera House in the main palace. It has four distinct facades, each a perfect and harmonious combination of Greek-style columns, windows, and railings. Walk around it and find your favorite.

You can tour the handsome interior (pick up the helpful flier). English explanations are provided in some rooms, as are interactive screens. The Baroque WC was a head of its time.

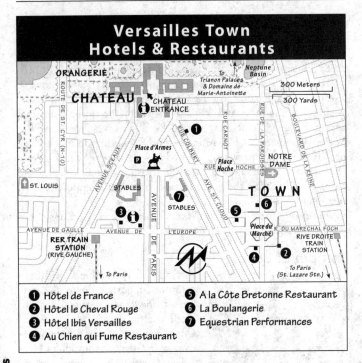

## Versailles Town Hotels & Restaurants

ORANGERIE

To Trianon Palaces & Domaine de Marie-Antoinette

Neptune Basin

CHATEAU

CHATEAU ENTRANCE

300 Meters
300 Yards

ROUTE DE ST. CYR (N-10)

RUE COLBERT

RUE CARNOT

RUE DE LA PAROISSE

BOULEVARD DE LA REINE

**❶**

Place d'Armes

P

Place Hoche

RUE HOCHE

NOTRE DAME

AVENUE SCEAUX

ST. LOUIS

STABLES

AVENUE DE PARIS

STABLES

**❼**

AVE. ST-CLOUD

T O W N

**❻**

**❺**

**❸**

i

AVENUE DE GAULLE

AVENUE DE

L'EUROPE

Place du Marché

R. DU MARÉCHAL FOCH

RIVE DROITE TRAIN STATION

RER TRAIN STATION (RIVE GAUCHE)

**❹**

**❷**

↓ To Paris

To Paris (St. Lazare Stn.) ↓

**❶** Hôtel de France
**❷** Hôtel le Cheval Rouge
**❸** Hôtel Ibis Versailles
**❹** Au Chien qui Fume Restaurant
**❺** A la Côte Bretonne Restaurant
**❻** La Boulangerie
**❼** Equestrian Performances

**VERSAILLES**

When Louis XVI became king, he gave the building to his bride Marie-Antoinette, who made this her home base. On the lawn outside, she installed a carousel. Despite her bad reputation with the public, Marie-Antoinette was a sweet girl from Vienna who never quite fit in with the fast, sophisticated crowd at Versailles. At the Petit Trianon, she could get away and re-create the charming home life that she remembered from her childhood. Here she played, while in the cafés of faraway Paris, revolutionaries plotted the end of the *ancien régime*.

• *The real world and the main Château are a 30-minute* **walk** *to the southeast. If you've had enough walking, you can ride the* **Petit Train** *from here back to the Château. Or, to return directly to the Versailles R.G. train station, go 150 yards up the road to the Grand Trianon to catch the Phébus* **shuttle bus** *(see the "Getting Around the Gardens" sidebar, earlier).*

*For a slightly shorter walk back, and a chance to see the Neptune Basin (an impressive miniature lake with fountains; see map on page 542), walk straight down from the Petit Trianon and turn left on Avenue de la Trianon. (Note that the gate here is closed before Fountain Spectacle shows.) If you stay straight as an arrow, you'll run into the Neptune Basin, where the grand finale takes place on fountain days. Leave Neptune at the far-left corner gate, and you'll pop out onto Rue*

---

## Sleep Code

**(€1 = about $1.30, country code: 33)**
**S** = Single, **D** = Double/Twin, **T** = Triple, **Q** = Quad, **b** = bathroom, **s** = shower only, **\*** = French hotel rating system (0-5 stars). Everyone speaks English and accepts credit cards.

To help you easily sort through these listings, I've divided the accommodations into two categories, based on the price for a standard double room with bath.

**$$** **Higher Priced**—Most rooms more than €100.

**$** **Lower Priced**—Most rooms €100 or less.

Prices can change without notice; verify the hotel's current rates online or by email.

---

*de la Paroisse, the town's main shopping drag, which takes you into the market square. From here a right on Avenue de l'Europe takes you to the Versailles R.G. train station and the RER back to Paris.*

## Sleeping in Versailles

For a less expensive and laid-back alternative to Paris, the town of Versailles can be a good overnight stop, especially for drivers. Park in the palace's main lot while looking for a hotel, or leave your car there overnight (€5.50/2 hours, €14.80/8 hours). Get a map of Versailles at your hotel or at the TI.

**$$ Hôtel de France\*\*\***, in an 18th-century townhouse, offers Old World class, with mostly air-conditioned, appropriately royal rooms, a pleasant courtyard, a bar, and a restaurant (Db-€143, Tb-€180, Qb-€244, Wi-Fi, just off parking lot across from Château at 5 Rue Colbert, tel. 01 30 83 92 23, fax 01 30 83 92 24, www.hotelfrance-versailles.com, hotel-de-france-versailles@orange.fr).

**$ Hôtel le Cheval Rouge\*\***, built in 1676 as Louis XIV's stables, now boards tourists. Tucked into a corner of Place du Marché, this modest hotel has a big, scruffy courtyard with free parking and sufficiently comfortable rooms connected by long, narrow halls (Db-€82-98, Tb-€120, Qb-€130, Wi-Fi, 18 Rue André Chénier, tel. 01 39 50 03 03, fax 01 39 50 61 27, www.chevalrougeversailles.fr, chevalrouge@sfr.fr).

**$ Hôtel Ibis Versailles\*\*** offers a good weekend value and modern comfort, with 85 air-conditioned rooms (Mon-Thu Db-€135, Fri-Sun Db-€90, extra bed-€10, good-value breakfast-€9, Internet access and Wi-Fi, parking-€12, across from RER station at 4 Avenue du Général de Gaulle, tel. 01 39 53 03 30, fax 01 39 50 06 31, www.ibishotel.com, h1409@accor.com).

# Eating in Versailles

In the pleasant town center, around Place du Marché Notre-Dame, you'll find a thriving open market (food market Sun, Tue, and Fri mornings until 13:00; clothing market all day Wed-Thu and Sat) and a variety of reasonably priced restaurants, cafés, and a few cobbled lanes. The square—a 15-minute walk from the Château (veer left as you leave the Château)—is lined with colorful and inexpensive eateries. Troll the intriguing options or try one of these:

**Au Chien qui Fume** is a good choice, with cozy seating inside and out, a playful staff, and reliable, traditional cuisine (€30 *menu*, €16 *plats*, closed Sun, 72 Rue de la Paroisse, tel. 01 39 53 14 56).

**A la Côte Bretonne** is your best bet for crêpes in a friendly, cozy setting. Fluent in English Yann-Alan and his family have served up the cuisine of their native Brittany region since 1951 (€4-10 crêpes from a fun and creative menu, Tue-Sun 12:00-14:00 & 19:00-22:30, closed Mon, fine indoor and outdoor seating, a few steps off the square on traffic-free Rue des Deux Portes at #12, tel. 01 39 51 18 24).

**La Boulangerie** has mouthwatering sandwiches, salads, quiches, and more (Tue-Sun until 20:00, closed Mon, 60 Rue de la Paroisse).

VERSAILLES

# MORE GRAND CHATEAUX

*Vaux-le-Vicomte •*
*Château of Fontainebleau •*
*Château of Chantilly*

The region around Paris (Ile de France) is studded with sumptuous palaces. The city's booming elite class made it the heartland of European château-building in the 16th and 17th centuries. Most of these châteaux were lavish hunting lodges—getaways from the big city. The only things they defended were aristocratic egos.

If you're planning to visit just one palace in all of Europe, it should be Versailles (see previous chapter). But unlike heavily-touristed Versailles, the three châteaux recommended here are quiet (at least on weekdays), letting you enjoy their original pastoral ambience. Consider visiting at least one; they are each very different.

▲▲▲**Vaux-le-Vicomte**—For sheer beauty and intimacy (open daily, closed early Nov-mid-March); described next.

▲▲**Fontainebleau**—For its history, fine interior, and pleasant city (château closed Tue, covered by Paris Museum Pass); see page 581.

▲**Chantilly**—For its beautiful setting and fine collection of paintings (closed Tue, covered by Paris Museum Pass); see page 585.

# Vaux-le-Vicomte

Versailles may be most travelers' first choice for its sheer historic importance, but Vaux-le-Vicomte (voh luh vee-komt) is just flat-out ravishing. With a harmony of architecture, interior decor, and garden design that you won't find anywhere else, it gets my vote for the most beautiful château in all of France.

Compared to Versailles, it's also more intimate, better furnished, and comes with a fraction of the crowds. Though getting to Vaux-le-Vicomte requires more effort, it's an absolute joy to tour.

Located in a huge forest, with magnificent gardens and no urban sprawl in sight, Vaux-le-Vicomte gives me more than a twinge of palace envy.

## Getting There

**By Train:** From Paris, take the RER-D train to Melun from Gare de Lyon, Gare du Nord, or the Châtelet-Les Halles station (direction: Montereau, 3/hour, 45 minutes). Faster SNCF *Banlieue* trains to Melun leave from Gare de Lyon (2/hour, 30 minutes, about €8 one-way).

From Melun's scruffy train station, taxis make the 15-minute drive to Vaux-le-Vicomte (€19 one-way Mon-Sat, €24 eves and Sun, taxi tel. 01 64 52 51 50). Ask a staffer at the château to call a cab for your return, or schedule a pickup time with your driver. Seek others with whom you can split the fare.

On weekends from April to October, Veoila shuttle buses *(navette-châteaubus)* run from Melun's train station to Vaux-le-Vicomte (€3.50 one-way, 4/day Sat-Sun only, 15 minutes, call or check château website for schedule, extra evening trips for candlelit visits). To find the shuttle stop, cross the parking lot in front of the station, walk past the pharmacy, and find the Châteaubus stop in front of the yellow-signed café.

**By Minibus Excursion:** The Paris Vision tour company (also called Cityrama) offers excursions to Vaux-le-Vicomte (www.paris vision.com; see page 45). Some travelers find these worthwhile given the tricky train access.

**By Car:** From Paris, take the A-6 autoroute toward Lyon, then follow signs to Melun. In Melun, follow signs to Meaux, then Vaux-le-Vicomte.

# Orientation

**MORE GRAND CHATEAUX**

**Cost:** €16 covers everything—all floors of the château, gardens, and carriage museum; skip the €14 ticket that doesn't include the top of the château dome; kids 16 and under-€3 less, family deals available, excellent audioguide-€2; not covered by Paris Museum Pass.

**Hours:** Daily mid-March-early Nov 10:00-18:00, closed early Nov-mid-March, tel. 01 64 14 41 90, www.vaux-le-vicomte. com. From April through Oct, the impressive fountains run 15:00-18:00 on the second and last Saturdays of each month. The château reopens for Christmas with special holiday decorations (€17, weekends only Dec-early Jan 10:45-18:00).

**Services:** Parking is easy and free. The excellent gift shop has fine palace guidebooks. Outside the shop is a WC and the reasonably priced L'Ecureuil ("The Squirrel") cafeteria, with a lim-

## Seeing Vaux-le-Vicomte and Fontainebleau

These two châteaux can be combined into a full, though manageable, day trip by car, taxi, or train from Paris (except on Tue, when Fontainebleau is closed). Fontainebleau is 12 minutes by train from Melun or a 30-minute drive from Vaux-le-Vicomte (allow €42 by taxi). If you want to sleep out here, check into one of my recommended hotels in Fontainebleau (listed on page 583).

ited selection (daily 10:00-18:00, until 23:00 during candlelit visits). A leafy restaurant, Les Charmilles, is in the garden beyond the château, serving lunch and afternoon tea.

**Candlelit Visits:** Two thousand candles and piped-in classical music illuminate the palace on Saturday evenings in peak season (€19, early May-early Oct 20:00-24:00, last entry at 23:00). These *visites aux chandelles* re-create a party thrown in Louis XIV's honor in 1661, but note that the gardens are hard to see by candlelight (although it doesn't get truly dark until around 22:00 in late May, June, and July). Buses provide service to and from Melun's train station during these events (described earlier, under "Getting There"; the last train to Paris leaves Melun at about 23:45). On the first and third Saturdays of the month, a 15-minute fireworks display at 22:00 is added to these already light-filled evenings. Fancy dinners are available in the Les Charmilles garden restaurant (*menus* starting at €30, reservations required).

## Visiting the Château

When Vaux-le-Vicomte and Versailles were built, France was slowly heading toward a revolution. Of its 18 million people, 200,000 were clergy ("those who pray"), 150,000 were nobles (those who fight or "carry a sword"), and the rest (17.6 million) were the Third Estate ("those who work"). Of course there was no democracy—just one king and his ministers who ran the show. Somewhat like modern bankers and financiers, these people controlled the workings of the economy, amassing almost unfathomable wealth.

One of them was Nicolas Fouquet, France's finance minister during the reign of Louis XIV, in the 17th century. Vaux-le-Vicomte was his home. A brilliant collaboration between three masters—architect Louis Le Vau, artist Charles Le Brun, and landscape designer André Le Nôtre—this château was the architectural inspiration for Versailles and set the standard for European palaces to come. In fact, after attending Fouquet's château-warming party in 1661, a very young Louis XIV found himself impressed that one man could create such magnificence. He was also curious how one man (other than himself) could pay for it. So, Louis had Fouquet arrested, hired his talented trio, and proceeded to have his bigger and costlier (but not necessarily more splendid) palace of Versailles built.

Monsieur Fouquet's party, and later arrest, feature prominently in the third Musketeer book by Alexandre Dumas (and at least two versions of *The Man in the Iron Mask* were filmed here). From the prison cell where he died, Fouquet wrote longingly of his lost home, "This was the estate I regarded as my principle seat and where I intended to leave some traces of the status I had enjoyed."

If the château feels a bit quirky in the way it's run today, remember it's not national property. It's private. The owner lives on the grounds (but not in the château) and shows it off on his terms.

**Museum of Carriages** *(Musée des Equipages):* Start your tour in the stables, where you can gallop through this fine museum's two long halls, lined with elegant carriages from a time when horses were a big part of daily life. The exhibit begins with a reminder that when the château was built, France had 2.5 million horses (more than 100 horses per thousand people). Today France has 300,000 horses (just 5 per thousand people). While these stables are interesting, the only English info you'll find here is a sign that reads, "This museum is equipped with a permanent alarm system."

**The Grounds:** Next, stroll like a wide-eyed peasant across the stone bridge that spans the ornamental moat facing the palace. Take some time to survey the grand design and admire the symmetry and elegance of the grounds, the outbuildings, and the palace itself. The gardens stretch far beyond the palace, but their main axis runs straight through the center of the château.

**The Palace:** Upon entering, pick up your audioguide. As you wander through Fouquet's dream home, you'll understand Louis XIV's jealousy. Versailles was a simple hunting lodge when this was built. Most of the paintings and furniture you'll see here are not original—Louis confiscated what he liked for Versailles.

The one-way route first takes you through lavish rooms. Then you go upstairs to a simple attic for an exhibition on carpentry and a peek at the wood structure of the building. From here, climb 80 steps between the inner and outer **domes** to a small terrace at the very top, where you can survey the magnificent gardens—the first French formal gardens.

The last rooms on the tour route are among the best, populated with wax figures and explained with concise little histories on the walls. In the **basement,** tour the kitchen, check out the exhibit that sympathetically relates the story of Fouquet's arrest (told as if the present family were related—they're not), and finish with a fascinating exhibit about the gardens of Le Nôtre, including his connection to the Tuileries in Paris, the gardens of Versailles, and Chantilly.

After reading about the gardens, survey them from the palace's back steps. Le Nôtre's first claim to fame, this **garden** was the cutting edge of sculpted French gardens. The designer integrated ponds, shrubbery, and trees in a style that would be copied in palaces all over Europe. Consider the 30-minute walk (one-way) to the viewpoint atop the grassy hill far in the distance. Rentable golf carts (€18/45 minutes, ID and deposit required) make the trip easier.

# Château of Fontainebleau

When it comes to showing the sweep of French history, the Château of Fontainebleau is unrivaled among French palaces. But don't expect Versailles-like unity here. It's a gangly and confusing series  of wings that has grown with centuries of kings.

Its core was built upon a medieval foundation by François I in 1528. It seems every king, queen, and emperor since has loved this place—Louis XIII was born here, Louis XV married here, and Napoleon III was baptized here. And many years later, General George Patton set up headquarters here on his way to Berlin.

Above all, Fontainebleau has more Napoleon Bonaparte connections than any other palace in France. It was here that the pope met Napoleon before the general's 1804 coronation as emperor. And it was from the château's famous horseshoe-shaped staircase that Napoleon gave his stirring abdication speech, trading his rule of France for exile to Elba in 1814.

While Vaux-le-Vicomte and Versailles are French-designed, Fontainebleau was built a century earlier by an Italian. Inspired by his travels through Renaissance Italy, François I hired Italian artists to build his palaces. He even encouraged one artist—Leonardo da Vinci—to abandon his native Italy and settle in France for the last three years of his life.

## Getting There

**By Train:** From Paris, catch a train at the *Grande Ligne* tracks from Gare de Lyon (nearly hourly, 45 minutes, direction: Montereau, €9 one-way) to Fontainebleau-Avon station. Check return train times before leaving the station, as there can be big gaps.

From the train station, take a bus or taxi to reach the château. Bus #1 (direction: Les Lilas) makes the 10-minute trip to the Château stop (3/hour, €1.90, Paris Métro tickets valid). To return to the station, board bus #1 (direction: Les Bouleaux). The station stop is Plateau de la Gare à Avon; confirm when you board the bus by asking: *"Ce bus va à la gare?"* (seh bews vah ah lah gar?).

Taxis from the train station to the château cost about €7; to nearby Vaux-le-Vicomte, it's about €42 (more on Sun and after 19:00, taxi tel. 01 64 22 00 06).

**By Car:** Follow signs to *Centre*, then *Château*. Park across from the château in the big lot (Parking Boufflers) next to the Hôtel Londres. To reach Vaux-le-Vicomte from Fontainebleau (about 30 minutes), follow signs to Melun.

# Orientation

**Cost:** €10, reduced to €5 one hour before closing, free for kids 17 and under, free first Sun of the month, includes audioguide; covered by Paris Museum Pass.

**Hours:** April-Sept Wed-Mon 9:30-18:00, Oct-March 9:30-17:00, closed Tue year-round, last entry 45 minutes before closing, tel. 01 60 71 50 70, www.musee-chateau-fontainebleau.fr.

**Services:** A free bag check is available.

# Visiting the Château

The château's complex floor plan can seem overwhelming, but visitors have little choice when touring the place, so don't struggle to understand the overall design. Find the entry (inside the main gate on the right), and follow the one-way route through the Napoleon I Museum, special exhibit, and royal apartments—these last rooms are beautifully described in the included audioguide.

The **Napoleon I Museum,** while not covered by the audioguide or any English descriptions, is fascinating. The first room features grand portraits of Emperor Napoleon and his first wife, Empress Josephine (painted by Gérard after their coronation). Other rooms—each drenched in the Empire style—are dedicated to Napoleon at war (with his battle coat, tent, and camp gear); his second wife,

Empress Marie Louise (whom he married for her Habsburg heritage, which Napoleon hoped would color his Corsican blood blue); and to their son, the "King of Rome" Napoleon II (who lived in exile after his dad's defeat and died of tuberculosis at age 21).

The hallway is lined with busts and **portraits** of the sprawling imperial family Napoleon created—relatives he put on various thrones across his empire. Looking at the final painting, which depicts Napoleon with symbols of the legal system he gave France, the "Code Napoléon," it's fascinating to consider the mix of ideals, charisma, and megalomania of this leader. This revolutionary hero came out of a movement that killed off the Old Regime—only to create a new Old Regime.

After a swing through the contemporary exhibit, you'll enter the **royal apartments.** The highlights are many. The Papal Apartment was renovated by Napoleon to house Pope Pius VII. The stunning Renaissance hall of François I, which dates from 1528, inspired other royal galleries, including the Hall of Mirrors at Versailles. The opulent ballroom *(salle de bal)* comes with piped-in music and has garden views that evoke royal fêtes. Napoleon's throne room is the only French *salle du trône* that survives with its original furniture. You'll also see the emperor's bathroom, bed, and very important-looking desk.

The palace is slathered in royal and imperial symbolism, and its walls are hung with exquisite tapestries. As you walk its halls, track the artistic shift in style, from Renaissance to Rococo—whose whimsy infuriated the revolutionary mobs—to the more sober, post-revolutionary Neoclassical.

After touring the palace, the **gardens**—designed in the 17th century by landscape architect André Le Nôtre—are worth a stroll.

# Town of Fontainebleau

Everything you need is close. The helpful **TI** is two blocks across from the château, just behind Hôtel Londres. It has hiking maps and rental bikes, and posts train/bus schedules (Mon-Sat 10:00-18:00, Sun 10:00-13:00 & 14:00-17:30, Nov-April closed Sun afternoon, 4 Rue Royale, tel. 01 60 74 99 99, www.fontainebleau-tourisme.com).

An English bookstore, **ReelBooks,** is at 9 Rue de Ferrare—say hi to Sue and Judy. They have a good collection of new, used, and children's books (Tue-Sat 11:00-19:00, closed Sun-Mon, tel. 01 64 22 85 85).

## Sleeping in Fontainebleau

**$$ Hôtel de Londres**\*\*\* is run by gentle Philippe, who rents 15 immaculate rooms, some with views of the château and most with

---

## Sleep Code

**(€1 = about $1.30, country code: 33)**
**S** = Single, **D** = Double/Twin, **T** = Triple, **Q** = Quad, **b** = bath-room, **s** = shower only, **\*** = French hotel rating system (0-5 stars). Unless otherwise noted, English is spoken, credit cards are accepted, and breakfast is not included.

To help you easily sort through these listings, I've divided the accommodations into two categories, based on the price for a standard double room with bath:

**$$  Higher Priced**—Most rooms more than €100.
**$  Lower Priced**—Most rooms €100 or less.

Prices can change without notice; verify the hotel's current rates online or by email.

---

air-conditioning (smaller Db-€130-150, spacious Db with château view-€180, no elevator, Wi-Fi, 1 Place du Général de Gaulle, tel. 01 64 22 20 21, fax 01 60 72 39 16, www.hoteldelondres.com, hde londres1850@aol.com).

**$ Hôtel Ibis Château de Fontainebleau\*\*,** a five-minute walk from the château, is central, clean, and easy (Db-€85-100, Internet access and Wi-Fi, 18 Rue Ferrare, tel. 01 64 23 45 25, fax 01 64 23 42 22, www.ibishotel.com, h1028@accor.com).

## Eating in Fontainebleau

Scads of eating options are in the town center. To reach the center, turn right out of the château courtyard and walk down Rue Denecourt. An appealing collection of pedestrian lanes begins after Place Napoléon Bonaparte. Rue Montebello is restaurant row; you'll find quieter places along the lanes off Rue de la Corne.

**La Taverne** is a happening brasserie with good prices (daily, 23 Rue Grande, tel. 01 64 22 20 85).

**Chez Bernard** has views of the château through its glassy front section and delivers well-respected, traditional cuisine (closed Sun night, 3 Rue Royale, tel. 01 64 22 24 68).

# Château of Chantilly

Chantilly (shahn-tee-yee), 30 minutes north of Paris, floats serenely on a reflecting pond. This extravagant hunting palace delivers great art and formal French gardens with an elaborate moat, but you won't get a feel for château life here. The rooms are 19th-century re-creations and are only visitable on a boring tour—in French.

## Getting There

Taking a train to Chantilly is a breeze, but the last mile and a half to the château is a headache unless you spring for a cab or enjoy a good walk. Leave from Paris' Gare du Nord for Chantilly-Gouvieux (on the Creil line). The RER serves Chantilly, but service is twice as fast on the *Grande Ligne* main lines. Ask at any information desk for the next departure (hourly, fewer on weekends, 25 minutes by train, 50 minutes by RER, about €8 one-way). Upon arrival in Chantilly, confirm return times and whether the trip is via the faster train or slower RER.

*Getting from the Station to the Château:* A free city **bus** (called DUC, Desserte Urbaine Cantilienne) runs infrequently from the station to the château (Mon-Sat, none on Sun, 10 minutes, verify schedule in advance by calling the TI, tel. 03 44 67 37 37). Otherwise, the easiest station-to-château trip is provided by **Taxi One** (about €9 one-way, €18 round-trip, mobile 06 42 05 46 79, or ask at TI). The free shuttle bus and taxis will pick you up at the château gate.

Hikers can **walk** 30 minutes to the château (the TI, next to the station, has maps; see below). Cross the big road in front of the TI and turn right on the dirt path, cross another road, then turn left, following the wooden signs. Walking back to the station, cross the big roundabout above the château, find wooden signs marked *Gare*, and follow them along a dirt path (passing behind the race track).

## Helpful Hints

The **TI** is a block straight out of the train station (Mon-Sat 9:30-12:30 & 13:30-17:30, Sun 10:00-13:30 except closed Sun Oct-April, 60 Avenue du Maréchal Joffre, tel. 03 44 67 37 37, www.chantilly-tourisme.com). A **café** and a small **bakery** with sandwiches and drinks are across from the station. You'll find many cafés and restaurants in the linear town of Chantilly (about a half-mile to the left as you exit the station) and a lively outdoor **market** Saturday until 12:30.

MORE GRAND CHATEAUX

# Orientation

**Cost:** Château and gardens—€14, kids under 18-€5.50; gardens only—€7, kids under 18-€3; good audioguide-€3; covered by Paris Museum Pass.

**Hours:** April-Oct Wed-Mon 10:00-18:00, Nov-March Wed-Mon 10:30-17:00, closed Tue year-round, tel. 03 44 27 31 80, www. chateaudechantilly.com.

**Live Horse Stables** *(Les Ecuries Vivant):* The Prince de Condé believed he'd be reincarnated as a horse, so he built this opulent horse château for his next go-round (it's the huge building to the right as you look out from the château—allow 10 minutes to walk there from the château). The stable museum is closed for renovation in 2013, but the stables, housing 40 horses, are open; riding demonstrations occur at 11:00 and less-frequent but more-elaborate shows at 14:30 (demonstration-€11, full show-€21, generally open April-Nov Wed-Mon 10:00-17:00, Dec Wed-Mon 14:00-18:00, Jan-March Wed-Mon 14:00-17:00, closed Tue year-round, check website or at TI to verify show times, tel. 03 44 27 31 80, www.museevivantducheval. fr).

# Visiting the Château

Lacking the well-preserved and grandiose interiors of other châteaux, Chantilly lays its claim to fame (and the main reason to visit) with its art collection. Because of the social upheaval in France during the Revolution of 1848, the château's owner, Prince de Condé, fled to England. Twenty years later, when blue blood was safe again in France, he returned to his château with a fabulous art collection (800 paintings, including three Raphaels) and book collection. He turned his palace into the museum you see today and willed it to France on the condition that it would be maintained as he left it and the collections would never be loaned to any other museum.

As most of the château was destroyed during the French Revolution, today's palace is largely rebuilt in a fanciful 19th-century style. It's divided into three parts: apartments, art gallery, and library. Skip the unimpressive apartments that require a tour to visit (€6 for 20-minute tour).

The **art gallery and library** are the stars (and are included with your entry). Wander the various rooms of the gallery using handheld explanations provided in each room (hunt for an English version). The audioguide adds meaning and context to your visit. Gallery highlights are paintings by Raphael, Titian, Nicolas Poussin, and Eugène Delacroix. Of the 13,000 books in the prince's library, the most exquisite is the 40-page *Book of Hours* by Jean Fouquet (c. 1460).

The **gardens** immediately behind the château are geometric and austere. Drop down the steps from the château, turn right,

 and follow the signs for 10 minutes to *le Hameau*, where you'll find a sweet little garden café (limited menu features desserts served with real Chantilly cream). This little hamlet of three half-timbered, thatched-roofed homes was the prototype for the more famous *hameau* at Versailles. While the homes are peasant-simple on the outside, they are lavishly decorated within: The prince had certain needs when he played peasant. A shuttle bus circulates through the gardens (€6, leaves hourly from entry gate).

# CHARTRES

Chartres, about 50 miles southwest of Paris, gives travelers a pleasant break in a lively, midsize town with a thriving, pedestrian-friendly old center. But the big reason to come to Chartres (shar-truh) is to see its famous cathedral—arguably Europe's best example of pure Gothic.

Chartres' old church burned to the ground on June 10, 1194. Some of the children who watched its destruction were actually around to help rebuild the cathedral and attend its dedication Mass in 1260. That's astonishing, considering that other Gothic cathedrals, such as Paris' Notre-Dame, took literally centuries to build. Having been built so quickly, the cathedral has a unity of architecture, statuary, and stained glass that captures the spirit of the Age of Faith like no other church.

While overshadowed by its cathedral, the town of Chartres also merits exploration. Discover the picnic-perfect park behind the cathedral, check out the colorful pedestrian zone, and wander the quiet alleys and peaceful lanes down to the river.

## Planning Your Time

Chartres is an easy day trip from Paris. But with its statues glowing in the setting sun—and with hotels and restaurants much less expensive than those in the capital—Chartres also makes a worthwhile overnight stop. Dozens of Chartres' most historic buildings are colorfully illuminated at night (May-Sept), adding to the town's after-hours appeal.

If coming just for the day, leave Paris in the morning by train. Chartres is a one-hour ride from Paris' Gare Montparnasse (10/day, about €13 one-way; see page 525 for Gare Montparnasse details). Jot down return times to Paris before you exit the Chartres train station (last train generally departs Chartres around 21:00).

## Chartres

- **1** Hôtel Châtelet
- **2** Hôtel le Bœuf Couronné
- **3** Hôtellerie Saint Yves
- **4** To Auberge de Jeunesse
- **5** Le Bistrot de la Cathédrale, Le Serpente & Café des Arts
- **6** Le Cloître Gourmand
- **7** Le Pichet Restaurant
- **8** Crypt Tours (via "La Crypte" Bookstore)
- **9** Launderette

- - - - Self-Guided Walk

Upon arrival in Chartres, head for the cathedral. Allow an hour to savor the church on your own as you follow my self-guided tour. Then join the excellent cathedral tour led by Malcolm Miller (1.25 hours; tours usually Mon-Sat at 12:00 and 14:45). Take another hour to wander the appealing old city. On Wednesday and Saturday mornings, an outdoor market sets up a few short blocks from the cathedral on Place Billard.

# Orientation to Chartres

## Tourist Information

At the **TI**, pick up the English brochure with a good map and basic information on the town and cathedral (Mon-Sat 9:30-18:30, Sun 10:00-17:30, in the historic Maison du Saumon building, 10 Rue de la Poissonnerie, tel. 02 37 18 26 26, www.chartres-tourisme. com). The TI has specifics on cathedral tours with Malcolm Miller, and also rents audioguides for the old town (€5.50, €8.50/double set, about 2 hours). The narration, while thin (and providing little

CHARTRES

more information than my self-guided walk), is relaxing and easy to follow. Skip the Chartres Pass, which is sold here.

## Arrival in Chartres

Exiting Chartres' train station, you'll see the spires of the cathedral dominating the town. It's a five-minute walk up Avenue Jehan de Beauce to the cathedral (or you can take a taxi for about €6.50).

## Helpful Hints

**Internet Access:** For a computer and free Wi-Fi, head to the TI (described earlier), or try the Wi-Fi signal at McDonald's (Place des Epars).

**Laundry:** The town has several launderettes. The most central is a few blocks from the cathedral (by the TI) at 16a Place de la Poissonnerie (daily 10:00-13:00 & 14:00-18:00).

**Taxi:** If you need to call for a taxi, try tel. 02 37 36 00 00.

# Sights in Chartres

### ▲▲▲ Chartres Cathedral

The church is (at least) the fourth one on this spot dedicated to Mary, the mother of Jesus, who has been venerated here for some 1,700 years. There's even speculation that the pagan Romans dedicated a temple here to a mother-goddess. In earliest times Mary was honored next to a natural spring of healing waters (not visible today).

In 876, the church acquired the torn veil (or birthing gown) supposedly worn by Mary when she gave birth to Jesus. The 2,000-year-old veil (now on display) became the focus of worship at the church. By the 11th century the cult of saints was strong. And Mary, considered the "Queen of All Saints," was hugely popular. God was enigmatic and scary, but Mary was maternal and accessible, providing a handy go-between for Christians and their Creator. Chartres, a small town of 10,000 with a prized relic, found itself in the big time on the pilgrim circuit.

When the fire of 1194 incinerated the old church, the veil was feared lost. Lo and behold, several days later, townspeople found it miraculously unharmed in the crypt (beneath today's choir). Whether the veil's survival was a miracle or a marketing ploy, the people of Chartres were so stoked, they worked like madmen to erect this grand cathedral in which to display it. The small town built a big-city church, one of the most impressive structures in all

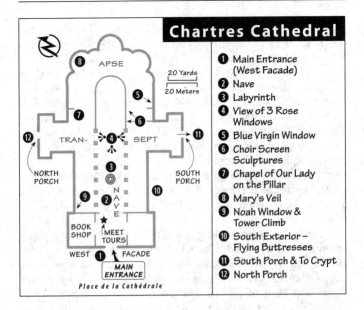

**Chartres Cathedral**

① Main Entrance (West Facade)
② Nave
③ Labyrinth
④ View of 3 Rose Windows
⑤ Blue Virgin Window
⑥ Choir Screen Sculptures
⑦ Chapel of Our Lady on the Pillar
⑧ Mary's Veil
⑨ Noah Window & Tower Climb
⑩ South Exterior – Flying Buttresses
⑪ South Porch & To Crypt
⑫ North Porch

APSE

TRAN- SEPT

NORTH PORCH

SOUTH PORCH

N A V E

BOOK SHOP

MEET TOURS

WEST FACADE

MAIN ENTRANCE

*Place de la Cathédrale*

20 Yards
20 Meters

of Europe. Thinkers and scholars gathered here, making it a leading center of learning in the Middle Ages (until the focus shifted to Paris' university).

By the way, the church is officially called the Cathédrale Notre-Dame de Chartres. Many travelers think that "Notre-Dame" is in Paris. That's true. But more than a hundred churches dedicated to Mary—"Notre-Dames"—are scattered around France. Chartres Cathedral is one of them.

**Cost:** Free, €7.50 to climb the 300-step north tower (free on first Sun of the month and for those under 18).

**Hours:** Church—daily 8:30-19:30; tower—May-Aug Mon-Sat 9:30-12:30 & 14:00-17:30, Sun 14:00-17:30, Sept-April closes daily at 16:30 (entrance inside church after bookstore on left). Mass times vary by season: usually Mon-Fri at 9:00 and/or 11:45; Sat at 11:45 and 18:00; Sun at 9:15 (Gregorian), 11:00, and 18:00 (some services held in the crypt). Call or go online to confirm times given here—tel. 02 37 21 59 08, or go to www.diocese-chartres.com, and click on the *La Cathédrale* (then *Infos Pratiques*, then *Horaires des Messes*).

**Restoration:** The interior is undergoing a multiyear restoration. While you'll encounter some scaffolding inside and out, it affects only about 10 percent of the church.

**Tours: Malcolm Miller,** a fascinating English scholar who moved here 50+ years ago when he was 24, has dedicated his life to studying this cathedral and sharing its wonder through his guided lecture tours. He's still going strong, and his 1.25-hour tours are

**CHARTRES**

riveting even if you've taken my self-guided tour. No reservation is needed; just show up (€10, €5 for students, includes headphones that allow him to speak softly, offered Mon-Sat at 12:00 and 14:45; no tours last half of Aug, Jan-Feb, or if fewer than 12 people show up). Some visitors take two tours on the same day, as every tour is different. Tours begin just inside the church at the *Visites de la Cathédrale* sign. Consult this sign for changes or cancellations. He also offers private tours (tel. 02 37 28 15 58, millerchartres@aol. com). Miller's guidebook provides a detailed look at Chartres' windows, sculpture, and history (sold at cathedral).

You can rent **audioguides** from the bookstore inside the cathedral (near the entrance). Routes include the cathedral (€4.30, 45 minutes), the choir only (€3.30, 25 minutes), or both (€6.40, 70 minutes).

Boring **crypt tours** take you into the foundations of the previous ninth-century church. The only way to see the crypt, this guided tour in French (with English handout) lets you view remnants of the earlier churches, a modern copy of the old wooden Mary-and-baby statue, and hints of the old well and Roman wall (€2.80; April-Oct daily at 11:00, 14:15, 15:30, and 16:30 except no 11:00 tour on Sun; late June-mid-Sept also at 17:15; 2/day Nov-March, 30-minute tours start in the cathedral's other bookstore—La Crypte, located outside church near south porch, tel. 02 37 21 75 02).

**Bring:** Binoculars are a big help for studying the cathedral art. You can rent binoculars cheaply at souvenir shops around the cathedral.

**◉ Self-Guided Tour:** Historian Malcolm Miller calls Chartres a picture book of the entire Christian story, told through its statues, stained glass, and architecture. In this **"Book of Chartres,"** the text is the sculpture and windows, and its binding is the architecture. The complete narrative can be read—from Creation to Christ's birth (north side of church), from Christ and his followers up to the present (south entrance), and then to the end of time, when Christ returns as judge (west entrance). The remarkable cohesiveness of the text and the unity of the architecture are due to the fact that nearly the entire church was rebuilt in just 30 years (a blink of an eye for cathedral building). The cathedral contains the best and most intact library of medieval religious iconography in existence. Most of the windows date from the early 13th century.

The Christian universe is a complex web of heaven and earth, angels and demons, and prophets and martyrs. Much of the medieval symbolism is obscure today. While it's easy to be overwhelmed by the thousands of things to see, make a point to simply appreciate the perfect harmony of this Gothic masterpiece.

• *Start outside, taking in the...*

### ❶ Main Entrance (West Facade), c. 1150

Chartres' soaring (if mismatched) steeples announce to pilgrims that they've arrived. For centuries pilgrims have come here to see holy relics, to honor "Our Lady," and to feed their souls.

The facade is about the only survivor of the intense, lead-melting fire that incinerated the rest of the church in 1194. The church

we see today was rebuilt behind this facade in a single generation (1194-1260).

The right (south) **tower,** with a Romanesque stone steeple, survived the fire. The left (north) tower lost its wooden steeple in the fire. In the 1500s, it was topped with the flamboyant Gothic steeple we see today.

The emaciated column-like statues flanking the three **west doors** are pillars of the faith. These kings of Judah, prophets, and Old Testament big shots foretold the coming of Christ. With solemn gestures and faces, they patiently endure the wait.

What they predicted came to pass. History's pivotal event is shown above the **right door,** where Mary (seated) produces Baby Jesus from her loins. This Mary-and-baby sculpture is a 12th-century stone version of an even older wooden statue that burned in 1793. Centuries of pilgrims have visited Chartres to see Mary's statue, gaze at her veil, and ponder the mystery of how God in heaven became man on earth, as He passed through immaculate Mary like sunlight through stained glass.

Over the **central door** is Christ in majesty, surrounded by animals symbolizing Matthew, Mark, Luke, and John. Over the **left door,** Christ ascends into heaven after his death and resurrection.

• *Enter the church (from a side entrance, if the main one is closed) and wait for your pupils to enlarge.*

### ❷ Nave

The place is huge—the nave is 427 feet long, 20 feet wide, and 120 feet high. Notice the height of the entrance doors compared to the tourists...the doors are 24 feet tall!

The long, tall central nave is lined with 12 pillars. These support pointed, crisscrossed arches on the ceiling, which lace together the heavy stone vaulting. The pillars themselves are supported by

# The Chartres Generation—the 1200s

From king to bishop and knight to pawn, French society was devoted to the Christian faith. It inspired knights to undertake the formidable Crusades, artists to re-create the divine in statues and stained glass, and architects to build skyscraping cathedrals filled with the mystic light of heaven. They aimed for a golden age, blending faith and reason. But misguided faith often outstripped reason, resulting in very un-Christian intolerance and violence.

**c. 1194**  The old cathedral burns down.

**1200**  The University of Paris is founded, using human reason to analyze Christian faith. Borrowing from the pagan Greek philosopher Aristotle, scholars described the Christian universe as a series of concentric rings spinning around the earth in geometrical perfection.

**1202**  The pope calls on all true Christians to rescue the Holy Land from Muslim "infidels" in the Fourth Crusade (1202-1204). This crusade ends disastrously in the sacking of Christian Constantinople.

**1206**  Chartres' cornerstone is laid. The style is *opus francigenum* ("French-style work")—what we now call Gothic. Chartres is just one of several great cathedrals under construction in Europe.

**1207**  Francis of Assisi, a rebellious Italian youth, undergoes a conversion to a life of Christian poverty and love. His open spirit inspires many followers, including France's King Louis IX (a generation later).

**1209**  France's King Philip Augustus, based in Paris, invades southern France and massacres fellow Christians (members of the Cathar sect) as heretics.

flying buttresses on the outside of the church (which we'll see later). This skeleton structure was the miracle of Gothic, making it possible to build tall cathedrals with ribbed walls and lots of stained-glass windows (see the big saints in the upper stories of the nave). Chartres has 28,000 square feet of stained glass. The nave—the widest Gothic nave in France—is flanked by raised side aisles. This design was for crowd flow, so pilgrims could circle the church without disturbing worshippers.

Try to picture the church in the Middle Ages—painted in greens, browns, and golds (like colorful St. Aignan Church in the

**1212** Thousands of boys and girls idealistically join the Children's Crusade to save the Holy Land. Most die in transit or are sold into slavery.

**1220** The external structure of Chartres Cathedral is nearly finished. Work begins on the statues and stained glass.

**1226** Eleven-year-old Louis IX is crowned as *rex et sacerdos,* "King and Priest," beginning a 45-year Golden Age combining church and state. His mother, Blanche of Castile (granddaughter of Eleanor of Aquitaine), serves as his regent during his minority and is his lifelong mentor.

**1230** Most of Chartres' stained glass is completed.

**1244** At age 30, Louis IX falls sick and, while in a coma, sees a vision that changes his life. His personal integrity helps unify the nation. He reforms the judicial system along Christian lines, helping the poor.

**1245** The last Albigensian heretics are burned at Mont-ségur, in a crusade ordered by Louis IX and his mother, Blanche.

**1248** Louis IX personally leads the Seventh Crusade by walking barefoot from Paris to the port of departure. During the fighting he is captured and ransomed. He later returns home a changed man. Humbled, he adopts the poverty of the Franciscan brotherhood. His devotion earns him the title of St. Louis.

**1260** Chartres Cathedral is dedicated. The church is the physical embodiment of the Age of Faith, with architecture as mathematically perfect as God's Creation, sculpture serving as sermons in stone, and stained glass lit by the light of God.

old town, described later). It was full of pilgrims, and was a rough cross between a hostel, a soup kitchen, and a flea market. The floor of the nave slopes in to the center, for easy drainage when hosing down the dirty pilgrims who camped here. Looking around the church, you'll see stones at the base of the columns smoothed by centuries of tired pilgrim butts. With all the hubbub in the general nave, the choir (screened-off central zone around the high altar) provided a holy place with a more sacred atmosphere.

Taking it all in from the nave, notice that, as was typical in medieval churches, the windows on the darker north side feature

Old Testament themes—awaiting the light of Christ's arrival. And the windows on the brighter south side are New Testament. Regardless of which direction they face, the highest windows—way up in the clerestory—are dark from decades of candle soot. As the ongoing cleaning job proceeds, more of the interior will be bright and sparkling like the apse (area behind the front altar).

• *On the floor, midway up the nave, find the...*

### ❸ Labyrinth

The broad, round maze inlaid in black marble on the floor is a spiritual journey. Mazes like this were common in medieval churches. Pilgrims enter from the west rim, by foot or on their knees, and wind inward, meditating, on a metaphorical journey to Jerusalem. About 900 feet later, they hope to meet God in the middle. (The chairs are removed on Fridays. To let your fingers do the walking, you'll find a small model of the maze just outside the gift shop, where the tours begin.)

• *Walk up the nave to where the transept crosses. As you face the altar, north is to the left.*

### ❹ The Rose Windows—North, South, and West

The three big, round "rose" (flower-shaped) windows over the entrances receive sunlight at different times of day. All three are predominantly blue and red, but each has different "petals," and each tells a different part of the Christian story in a kaleidoscope of fragmented images.

Stained glass was created as a way to teach Bible stories to the illiterate medieval masses...who apparently owned state-of-the-art binoculars. The windows were used in many ways—to tell stories, to allow parents to teach children simple lessons, to help theologians explain complex lessons, to enable worshippers to focus on images as they meditated or prayed...and, of course, to light a dark church in a colorful and decorative way.

The brilliantly restored **north rose window** charts history from the distant past up to the birth of Jesus. On the outer rim, a ring of semicircles, ancient prophets foretell Christ's coming. Then (circling inward) there's a ring of red squares with kings who are Jesus' direct ancestors. Still closer, circles with white doves and winged angels zero in on the central event of history—Mary, the heart of the flower, with her newborn baby, Jesus.

## Surviving the Centuries

Chartres contains the world's largest collection of medieval stained glass, with over 150 early 13th-century windows, about 80 percent still the original glass. Through the centuries, much of the rest of France's stained glass was destroyed by various ideologues: Protestant puritans who disapproved of papist imagery (they would never think of it as art), revolutionaries who turned churches into "temples of reason" (or stables), Baroque artists who preferred clear windows and lots of light, and the bombs of World War II.

Chartres was spared many (but not all) of these ravages. During World War II, in anticipation of Nazi destruction, the citizens removed all the windows (burying them in Dordogne cellars) and piled sandbags to protect the statues. Today, Chartres survives as Europe's best-preserved medieval cathedral.

This window was donated by Blanche of Castile, mother of the future King Louis IX (who would build Paris' stained-glass masterpiece of a church, Sainte-Chapelle). Blanche's heraldry frames the lower edge of the window: yellow fleur-de-lis on a blue background (for France) and gold castles on a red background (for her home kingdom of Castile).

The **south rose window,** with a similar overall design, tells how the Old Testament prophecies were fulfilled. Christ sits in the center (dressed in blue, with a red background), setting in motion radiating rings of angels, beasts, and instrument-playing apocalyptic elders who labor to bring history to its close. The five lancet windows below show Mary flanked by four Old Testament prophets (Jeremiah, Isaiah, Ezekiel, and Daniel) lifting New Testament writers (Luke, Matthew, John, and Mark) on their shoulders. (In the first window on the left, see white-robed Luke riding piggyback on dark-robed Jeremiah.) These demonstrated how the ancients prepared the way for Christ—and how the New Testament evangelists had a broader perspective from their lofty perches.

In the center of the **west rose window,** a dark Christ rings in history's final Day of Judgment. Around him winged angels blow their trumpets and the dead rise, face judgment, and are sent to hell or raised to eternal bliss. The frilly edge of this glorious "rose" is flecked with tiny clover-shaped dewdrops.

• *Now walk around the altar to the right (south) side and find the window with a big, blue Mary (second one from the right).*

# GOD = LIGHT

You can try to examine the details, but a better way to experience the mystery of Chartres is just to sit and stare at these enormous panels as they float in the dark of empty space like holograms or space stations or the Queen of Heaven's crown jewels. Ponder the medieval concept that God is light.

To the Chartres generation, the church was a metaphor for how God brings his creation to life, like the way light animates stained glass. They were heavy into mysticism, feeling a oneness with all creation in a moment of enlightenment. The Gospel of John (as well as a writer known to historians as the Pseudo-Dionysus) was their favorite. Here are select verses from John 1:1-12 (loosely translated):

*In the beginning was The Word.*
*Jesus was the light of the human race.*
*The light shines in the darkness,*
*    and the darkness cannot resist it.*
*It was the real light coming into the world,*
*    the light that enlightens everyone.*
*He was in the world, but the world did not recognize Him.*
*But to those who did, He gave the power*
*    to become the children of God.*

## ❺ The Blue Virgin Window

Mary, dressed in blue on a rich red background, cradles Jesus, while the dove of the Holy Spirit descends on her. This very old window (mid-12th century) was the central window behind the

altar of the church that burned in 1194. It survived and was reinserted into this frame in the new church around 1230. Mary's glowing dress is an example of the famed "Chartres blue," a sumptuous color made by mixing cobalt oxide into the glass (before cheaper materials were introduced). The Blue Virgin was one of the most popular stops for pilgrims—especially pregnant ones—of the cult of the Virgin-about-to-give-birth. Devotees prayed, carried stones to repair the church, and donated to the church coffers; Mary rewarded them with peace of mind, easy births, and occasional miracles.

Below Mary (bottom panel), see **Christ being tempted** by a red-faced, horned, smirking devil.

The **Zodiac Window** (two windows to the left) shows the 12 signs of the zodiac (in the right half of the window; read from the bottom up—Pisces, Aries, Gemini in the central cloverleaf, Taurus, Cockroach, Leo, Virgo, etc.). On the left side are the corresponding months (February warming himself by a fire, April gathering flowers, and so on).

• *Now turn around and look behind you.*

### ❻ The Choir Screen—Life of Mary

The choir (enclosed area around the altar where church officials sat) is the heart *(coeur)* of the church. A stone screen rings it with **41 statue groups** illustrating Mary's life. Although the Bible says little about the mother of Jesus, legend and lore fleshed out her life. Take some time to learn about the Lady this church is dedicated to.

Scene #1 (south side) shows Mary's dad hearing the news that Mary is on the way. In #4, Mary is born, and maidens bathe the new baby. In #6, Mary marries Joseph (sculpted with the features of King François I). In scene #7, an angel announces to Mary that she'll be the mother of the Messiah, and (#10) she gives birth to Jesus in a manger. In #12, the Three Kings—looking like the three musketeers—arrive. In #14, Herod orders all babies slaughtered, but Mary's son survives to begin his mission.

Next come episodes from the life of Jesus. On the other side of the choir screen, in #27, Jesus is crucified and, in #28, lies lifeless in his mother's arms. Scene #34 depicts the Ascension, as Jesus takes off, Cape Canaveral-style, while his awestruck followers look up at the bottoms of his rocketing feet. In #39, Mary has died and is raised by angels into heaven, where (#40) she's crowned Queen of Heaven by the Father, Son, and Holy Ghost.

The **plain windows** surrounding the choir date from the 1770s, when the dark mystery of medieval stained glass was replaced by the open light of the French Enlightenment. The plain windows and the choir are some of the only "new" features. Most of the 13th-century church has remained intact, despite style changes, revolutionary vandals, and war bombs.

• *Do an about-face and find the chapel with Mary on a pillar.*

### ❼ Chapel of Our Lady on the Pillar

A 16th-century **statue of Mary and baby** —draped in cloth, crowned and sceptered—sits on a 13th-century column in a wonderful carved-wood alcove. This is today's pilgrimage center, built to keep visitors from clogging up the altar area. Modern pilgrims (including lots of new moms pushing strollers) honor the Virgin by leaving flowers, lighting candles, and kissing the column.

• *Double back a bit around the ambulatory, heading toward the back of the church. In the next chapel you encounter (Chapel of the Sacred Heart of Mary—see map), you'll find a gold frame holding a fragment of Mary's venerated veil. These days it's kept—for its safety and preservation—out of the light and behind bulletproof glass.*

### ❽ Mary's Veil

This **veil** (or tunic) was supposedly worn by Mary when she gave birth to Jesus. It became the main object of adoration for the cult of the Virgin. The great King of the Franks, Charlemagne (742-814), received the veil as a present from Byzantine Empress Irene.

Charlemagne's grandson gave the veil to Chartres in 876. In A.D. 911, with the city surrounded by Vikings, the bishop hoisted the veil like a battle flag and waved it at the invaders. It scared the bejeezus out of them, and the town was saved.

In the frenzy surrounding the fire of 1194, the veil mysteriously disappeared, only to reappear three days later (recalling the Resurrection). This was interpreted by church officials and the townsfolk as a sign from Mary that she wanted a new church, and thus the building began. Recent tests confirm that the material itself, and the weaving technique used to make the cloth, date to the first century A.D., lending support to claims of the relic's authenticity.

• *Return to the west end and find the last window on the right (near the tower entrance).*

### ❾ The Noah Window and Tower Climb

Read Chartres' windows in the medieval style: from bottom to top. In the bottom diamond, God tells Noah he'll destroy the earth. Next, Noah hefts an axe to build an ark, while his son hauls wood (diamond #2). Two by two, he loads horses (cloverleaf, above left), purple elephants (cloverleaf, right), and other animals. The psychedelic ark sets sail (diamond #3). Waves cover the earth and drown the wicked (two cloverleafs). The ark survives (diamond #4), and Noah releases a dove. Finally, up near the top (diamond #7), a rainbow (symbolizing God's promise never to bring another flood) arches overhead, God drapes himself over it, and Noah and his family give thanks.

Chartres was a trading center, and its merchant brotherhoods donated money to make 42 of the windows. For 800 years these panes have publicly thanked their sponsors. In the bottom left is a man making a wheel. More workers are to the right. The panels announce that "these windows are brought to you by..." the wheel-, axe-, and barrel-making guilds.

• *If you'd like to climb the north tower, find the entrance nearby. Then exit the church (through the main entrance or the door in the south transept) to view its south side.*

### ⑩ South Exterior—Flying Buttresses

On the south side, six flying buttresses (the arches that stick out from the upper walls) push against six pillars lining the nave inside, helping to hold up the heavy stone ceiling and sloped, lead-over-wood roof. The ceiling and roof push down onto the pillars, of course,

but also outward (north and south) because of the miracle of Gothic: the pointed arch. The flying buttresses push back, channeling the stress outward to the six vertical buttresses, then down to the ground. The result is a tall cathedral held up by slender pillars buttressed from the outside, allowing the walls to be opened up for stained glass.

The church is built from large blocks of limestone. Peasants trod in hamster-wheel contraptions to raise these blocks into place—a testament to their great faith.

### ⑪ South Porch

The three doorways of the south entrance show the world from Christ's time to the present, as Christianity triumphs over persecution.

**Center Door—Christ and Apostles:** Standing between the double doors, **Jesus** holds a book and raises his arm in blessing. He's a simple, itinerant, bareheaded, barefoot rabbi, but underneath his feet he tramples symbols of evil: the dragon and lion. Christ's face is among the most noble of all Gothic sculpture.

Christ is surrounded by his **apostles,** who spread the good news to a hostile world. **Peter** (to the left as you face Jesus), with curly hair and beard, holds the keys to the kingdom of heaven. **Paul** (to the right of Jesus) fingers the sword of his martyrdom and contemplates the inevitable loss of his head. In fact, all of these apostles were killed or persecuted, and their faces are humble, with sad eyes. But their message prevailed, and under their feet they crush the squirming rulers who once persecuted them.

The final triumph comes above the door in the **Last Judgment.** Christ sits in judgment, raising his hands, while Mary and John beg him to take it easy on poor humankind. Beneath Christ the souls are judged—the righteous on our left, and the wicked on our right, who are thrown into the fiery jaws of hell. Farther to the right (above the statues of Paul and the apostles), horny demons subject wicked women to an eternity of sexual harassment.

**Left Door—Martyrs:** Eight martyrs flank the left door. **St. Lawrence** (second from left) cradles the grill (it looks like a book) on which he was barbecued alive. His last brave words to the Romans were: "You can turn me over—I'm done on this side." **St. George** (far right on right flank) wears the knightly uniform of the 1200s, when Chartres was built and King Louis IX was crusading. Depicted beneath the martyrs are gruesome **methods of torture,** such as George stretched on the wheel. Many of these techniques were actually used in the 1200s by Christians against heretics, Muslims, Jews, and Christian Cathars.

• *Reach the north side by circling around the back end of the church (great views). As you walk, enjoy the peaceful park, fine views over the town, and the church's architecture. Ponder the exoskeletal nature of Gothic design and the ability of medieval faith to mobilize the masses.*

## ⓰ North Porch

In the "Book of Chartres," the north porch is chapter one, from the Creation up to the coming of Christ.

Look between the double doors to see **Baby Mary** (headless), in the arms of her mother Anne, marking the end of the Old Testament world and the start of the New.

History begins in the tiny details in the concentric arches over the doorway. **God creates Adam** (at the peak of the outermost arch, just to the left of the keystone) by cradling his head in his lap like a child.

Next look at the statues that flank the doors. **Melchizedek** (farthest to the left of Mary and Anne), with the cap of a king and the cup of communion, is the biblical model of the *rex et sacerdos* (king-priest), the title bestowed on King Louis IX.

**Abraham** (next to Melchizedek) holds his son by the throat and raises a knife to slit him for sacrifice. Just then, he hears some-

thing and turns his head up to see God's angel, who stops the bloodshed. The drama of this frozen moment anticipates Renaissance naturalism by 200 years.

**John the Baptist** (fourth to the right from Mary/Anne), the last Old Testament prophet who prepared the way for Jesus, holds a lamb, the symbol of Christ. John is skinny from his diet of locusts and honey. His body and beard twist and flicker like a flame.

All these prophets, with their beards turning down the corners of their mouths, have the sad, wise look of having been around since the beginning of time and having seen it all—from Creation to Christ to Apocalypse. Over the door is the culmination of all this history: **Christ on his throne,** joined by Mary, the Queen of Heaven. These sculptures are some of the last work done on the church, completing the church's stone-and-glass sermon.

Imagine all this painted and covered with gold leaf in preparation for the dedication ceremonies in 1260, when the Chartres generation could finally stand back and watch as their great-grandchildren, carrying candles, entered the cathedral.

## Other Sights in Chartres
**International Stained Glass Center (Centre International du Vitrail)**—The low-key glass center (on the north side of cathedral) is worth a visit to learn about the techniques behind the

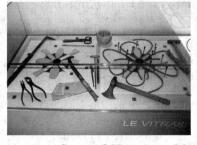

mystery of this fragile but enduring art. Borrow the helpful English booklet (€8 deposit) and take the self-guided tour. A 20-minute video in English describes how glass is made, and a 10-minute French-only video (follow along with the English booklet) explains how it is turned into stained glass.

**Cost and Hours:** €4, Mon-Fri 9:30-12:30 & 13:30-18:00, Sat 10:00-12:30 & 14:30-18:00, Sun 14:30-18:00, 5 Rue du Cardinal Pie, just 50 yards from cathedral, tel. 02 37 21 65 72, www.centre-vitrail.org, secretariat@centre-vitrail.org. The center offers a worthwhile tour and glass-making demonstrations (€6.50-9.50,

1.5 hours) as well as classes lasting from one to seven days; call ahead or email for topics and dates.

## Self-Guided Walk

### Welcome to Chartres

Chartres' old town thrives (except on Sun and Mon) and is worth some exploration. You can rent an audioguide from the TI, or better, just wander, using this walk as your guide.

In medieval times Chartres was actually two towns—the pilgrims' town around the cathedral, and the industrial town along the river, which was powered by watermills. This walk takes you on a 45-minute loop around the cathedral, through the old pilgrims' town, down along the once-industrial riverbank, and back to the cathedral.

• *Begin at the square in front of the church.*

**Cathedral Close:** Around the cathedral was a town within the town. Essentially a precinct run by the church, it was called the "close" of Notre-Dame *(cloître Notre-Dame)*. Looking at the square in front of the church, imagine a walled-in cathedral town with nine gates. It was busy with a hospital, a school (Chartres was a leading center of education in the 12th century), a bishop's palace, markets, fairs, and lots of shops—many of them tucked up against the church between its huge buttresses. Chartres was on the medieval map because of the cathedral and its relic. The town was all about the church. For example, in the medieval mind, the foundation of truth was the number three—the Trinity. Nine (three times three) was also a good number. Chartres consisted of three entities—the town, the close, and the church. And each was sure to have nine gates or doors.

About 20 paces in front of the cathedral's main door, a modern plaque in the pavement points pilgrims to Santiago de Compostela in northwest Spain, home of the tomb of St. James (notice the pilgrim with his walking stick and the stylized scallop shell symbolizing the various routes from all over Europe converging on Santiago). For a thousand years the faithful have trekked from Paris to Chartres and on to Santiago, a thousand miles away. And for centuries, pilgrims have stoked the economy of Chartres.

• *Circle around the cathedral clockwise, passing a fine 24-hour clock at the corner of the church and the striking carvings of the north porch (described earlier). Head under a stately 18th-century wrought-iron gate to the...*

**Bishop's Palace and Grounds:** The bishop essentially ruled from here until the French Revolution secularized the country. This fine building has housed King Henry IV (here for his coronation), Napoleon, and—since 1939—the city's Museum of Fine Arts. An ivy-covered arcade, not quite running from the church to the palace, is all that remains of a covered passageway designed to make the bishop's commute more pleasant. Belly up to the banister as you survey the lower levels of the bishop's terraced gardens and enjoy a view of the lower town. From here you can see why this point has been a strategic choice since ancient times. Beyond the gardens nestles the lower town, which was centered not on the church but on the river, which powered the local industry.

• *From the bishop's garden, continue circling around the cathedral until you reach its south porch (described earlier). Turn left onto...*

**Rue des Changes:** This "street of the money changers" runs south from the cathedral. The layout, street names, and building facades of this historic district all date back to a time when businesses catered to the needs of pilgrims rather than tourists. At Rue de la Poissonnerie (where fish were sold), side-trip half a block left, to a fine old half-timbered building called **Maison du Saumon.** It dates from about 1500, and as you might guess from the carvings, it faced the former fish market. Today it's Chartres' TI.

Back on Rue des Changes, a few more paces brings you to the sky-blue open-air **produce market** on Place Billard (market days are Wed and Sat until 13:00). Chartres' castle stood here until 1802, when it was demolished with revolutionary gusto to make way for the market.

• *From here, Rue des Changes turns into Rue des Grenets. For a detour into a bigger-than-you-thought pedestrian zone of shops, colorful lanes, and café-dappled squares, turn right up Rue de la Pie to Place Marceau (the hub of this network) and Rue Noël Ballay (the main shopping drag). Return to Rue des Grenets, and continue walking away from the cathedral.*

**Rue des Grenets:** Farther down the street is the **Church of St. Aignan.** Squat, crumbling, and unadorned, this is the oldest of Chartres' parish churches. Remember: Locals did not worship in the great cathedral (that was for visitors—like us); they worshipped in the town's simple parish churches. This one is built upon the tomb of a fourth-century bishop of Chartres. Its interior, dating from about 1625, shows how colorful a stone church could be. The vibrant colors, lavish decoration, and vaulted wood ceiling are astonishing, given the plain exterior.

Continue down Rue des Grenets to a tall, skinny **half-timbered house.** As the population grew, so did the fire hazard, and the town required half-timbered buildings to be plastered over for safety. Today, the town government—interested in pumping up the touristic charm—pays folks to peel away the plaster and re-expose those timbers. You can see that this building is one of the oldest—the tilting lintel and the asymmetrical windows are dead giveaways.

Turn left at the house and drop down the *tertre,* a series of **stair-step terraces** that link the upper and lower towns. The well-worn stone benches along the way evoke a day when washerwomen, laden with freshly washed laundry, rested as they climbed the hill after a trip to the river.

• *At the bottom, turn right on Rue St. Pierre, then find the **Church of St. Pierre** (great photo-op of flying buttresses and a delicate yet decrepit interior). Follow Pont St. Hilaire a block below the church, and—bam!— Eure at the river.*

**The Eure River:** This is another photogenic spot, with old buildings, humpback bridges, and cathedral steeples in the distance. Like nearly any industrial town back then, waterwheels provided power. The river was once lined with busy mills and warehouses. The worst polluters were kept downstream (dyers, tanners, slaughterhouses). The names of the riverside lanes evoke those times: Rue du Massacre, Rue de la Tannerie, and Rue de la Foulerie (named for a process of cleaning wool).

When the industry moved out to make room for Chartres' growing population, laundry places replaced the old mills. These were two-story structures—the wash cycle downstairs at the river, then the dry cycle upstairs, where vents allowed the wind to blow through. You can still see some of the mechanisms designed to accommodate periodic changes in the river level. The last riverside laundry closed in the 1960s.

• *Turn left on Rue de la Foulerie, and follow the river back toward the cathedral. The bridge at Rue du Bourg was once the town's main bridge. Cross it and climb uphill. After a block on the left you'll see Queen Bertha's Staircase (Escalier de la Reine Berthe), a one-of-a-kind half-timbered spiral staircase. In a few blocks, you're back at the cathedral. From here, consider stopping by the **International Stained Glass Center** (described earlier, under "Sights in Chartres").*

# Sleep Code

**(€1 = about $1.30, country code: 33)**
**S** = Single, **D** = Double/Twin, **T** = Triple, **Q** = Quad, **b** = bathroom, **s** = shower only, * = French hotel rating system (0-5 stars). Unless otherwise noted, English is spoken, credit cards are accepted, and breakfast is not included.

To help you easily sort through these listings, I've divided the accommodations into two categories, based on the price for a standard double room with bath:

**$$** **Higher Priced**—Most rooms more than €90.
**$** **Lower Priced**—Most rooms €90 or less.

Prices can change without notice; verify the hotel's current rates online or by email.

# Sleeping in Chartres

**$$ Hôtel Châtelet***,** a block up from the train station, is friendly and comfortable. Don't let the facade fool you—inside is a comfy place with a huge fireplace in the lobby and 40 spotless, spacious, and well-furnished rooms. Several have connecting rooms for families and many have partial cathedral views (streetside Db-€115, quiet side Db-€123, Db with cathedral view-€143, add €25/person for Tb and Qb, minibars, air-con, handy and safe parking-€8, 6 Avenue Jehan de Beauce, tel. 02 37 21 78 00, fax 02 37 36 23 01, www.hotelchatelet.com, reservation@hotelchatelet.com).

**$ Hôtel le Bœuf Couronné*** is a vintage two-star hotel, warmly run by Madame Vinsot, with 18 freshly renovated, good-value rooms and a handy location halfway between the station and cathedral (standard Db-€80, big Db-€115, a few good family rooms, no air-con, elevator, Internet access and Wi-Fi, restaurant, 15 Place Châtelet, tel. 02 37 18 06 06, fax 02 37 21 72 13, www. leboeufcouronne.com, resa@leboeufcouronne.fr).

**$ Hôtellerie Saint Yves,** which hangs on the hillside just behind the cathedral, delivers well-priced simplicity with 50 spic-and-span rooms in a renovated monastery with meditative garden areas (Sb-€45, Db-€65, Tb-€75, small but workable bathrooms, breakfast-€7.50, Wi-Fi, TV in the lounge only, 1 Rue Saint Eman, tel. 02 37 88 37 40, fax 02 37 88 37 49, www.hotellerie-st-yves. com, contact@hotellerie-st-yves.com).

**$ Auberge de Jeunesse** (youth hostel), a 20-minute walk from the historic center, is located in a modern building with good views of the cathedral from its terrace (€14/bunk in 4- to 6-bed dorms,

CHARTRES

sheet rental-€2.30, cheap meals, Wi-Fi, kitchen access, 23 Avenue Neigre, tel. 02 37 27 64, fax 02 37 36 75 85, www.auberge-de-jeunesse-chartres.com, auberge-jeunesse-chartres@wanadoo.fr).

## Near Chartres
**$ Chambres d'Hôte Brossollet,** practical only for drivers, is a pleasant haven of tranquility in Saint-Prest, about four miles from Chartres. This spacious property has an enclosed garden, thatched roofs, and two rooms to rent. The kind hosts, Claire and Etienne Brossollet, will prepare dinner in advance upon request (Db-€55, includes breakfast, tel. 02 37 22 25 31, claire. etienne.brossollet@gmail.com). Leave Chartres to the north and follow signs to Saint-Prest. Once in the village, continue straight through on the main road (just over a mile) until you see the thatched roof on the left.

# Eating in Chartres

Dining out in Chartres is a good deal—particularly if you've come from Paris. Troll the places basking in cathedral views, and if it's warm, find a terrace table (several possibilities). Then finish your evening cathedral-side, sipping a hot or cold drink at the recommended Le Serpente.

**Le Bistrot de la Cathédrale** has the best view terrace—particularly enjoyable on a balmy summer evening—and serves reliable, classic French fare. The owner has a thing for wine, so the list is good. He also insists on fresh products (*menus* from €22, *plats* from €14, closed Wed, 1 Cloître Notre-Dame, tel. 02 37 36 59 60).

**Le Serpente** saddles up next door to the cathedral, with view tables on both sides of Rue des Changes, a teapot collector's interior, and cool sling chairs ideal for appreciating the Gothic grandeur. Food is basic bistro, and the prices are fair (daily, 2 Cloître Notre-Dame, tel. 02 37 21 68 81).

**Café des Arts** is one of several places that strings out along pedestrian-friendly Rue des Changes with comfortable indoor and outdoor seating. They are best at good-value €8-12 dinner-size tartines, salads, crêpes, and *plats du jour*; the house wine is a fine value (closed Mon, 45 Rue des Changes, tel. 02 37 21 07 05).

**Le Cloître Gourmand,** facing the cathedral's left transept, boasts a small terrace and an intimate, traditional interior. The young chef loves his meat and prides himself on using only the freshest ingredients (€25 *menu*, closed Mon, 21 Cloître Notre-Dame, tel. 02 37 21 49 13).

**Le Pichet,** just below the TI, is run by endearing Marie-Sylvie and Xavier. This local-products shop and cozy bistro makes a fun lunch stop, with cheap homemade soups and a good selection of *plats*—split the pot-au-feu three ways or try the rabbit with plums (€15 *plats*, Thu-Tue 11:00-18:00, closed Wed, 19 Rue du Cheval Blanc, tel. 02 37 21 08 35).

# GIVERNY AND AUVERS-SUR-OISE

Paris is the unofficial capital of Impressionism, its museums speckled with sun-dappled paintings. But true Impressionist fans will want to do what the Impressionist painters did: don a scarf and beret, and head for the countryside.

At Giverny and Auvers-sur-Oise, you'll follow in the footsteps of Monet, Van Gogh, Pissarro, Cézanne, and others. See the landscapes, flora, and small-town life that inspired these great masters. Little has changed over time, and you'll find pastoral scenes here that still look like an Impressionist painting come to life.

At Giverny, you can visit Monet's home and much-painted garden. (Be warned: the gardens are pretty, but filled with tourists.) Auvers-sur-Oise is a quieter village, with Van Gogh's grave, recognizable settings of several of the artist's paintings, and a multimedia museum on Impressionism. Both places are about an hour's journey from Paris, and easy to reach by public transportation.

## Giverny

Claude Monet's gardens at Giverny are like his paintings— brightly colored patches that are messy but balanced. Flowers were his brushstrokes, a bit untamed and slapdash, but part of a carefully composed design. Monet spent his last (and most creative) years cultivating his  garden and his art at Giverny (zhee-vayr-nee), the spiritual home of Impressionism (1883-1926). Visiting the Marmottan and/or the Orangerie museums in Paris before your visit here, or at least reading the chapters on those museums, will heighten your appreciation of these gardens.

In 1883, middle-aged Claude Monet, his wife Alice, and their eight children from two families settled into a farmhouse here, 50 miles west of Paris (for more on Monet's family, see sidebar on page 259). Monet, already a famous artist and happiest at home, would spend 40 years in Giverny, traveling less with each passing year. He built a pastoral paradise complete with a Japanese garden and a pond full of floating lilies.

In 1912, Monet—the greatest visionary, literally, of his generation—began to go blind with cataracts. To compensate, he used larger canvases and painted fewer details. The true subject of these later works is not really the famous water lilies, but the changing reflections on the pond's surface—of the blue sky, white clouds, and green trees that line the shore.

## Getting to Giverny

Drivers can get in and out of Giverny in a half-day with ease. The trip is also doable in a half-day by public transportation with a train/bus connection, but because trains are not frequent (and less so on the weekend), be prepared for a full six-hour excursion.

**By Tour:** Big tour companies do a Giverny day trip from Paris for around €70. If you're interested, ask at your hotel—but you can easily do the trip yourself by train and bus for about €30.

**By Car:** From Paris' Périphérique ring road, follow A-13 toward Rouen, exit at *Sortie 14* to Vernon, and follow *Centre Ville* signs, then signs to *Giverny*. You can park right at Monet's house or at one of several nearby lots.

**By Train to Vernon:** Take the Rouen-bound train from the Paris Gare St. Lazare station to Vernon, about four miles from Giverny (normally leaves from tracks 20-25, 45 minutes one-way, about €25 round-trip). The train that leaves Paris at around 8:15 is ideal for this trip, with departures about every two hours after that (8/day Mon-Sat, 6/day Sun). Before boarding, use an information desk in Gare St. Lazare to get return times from Vernon to Paris.

*Getting from Vernon's Train Station to Giverny:* From the Vernon station to Monet's garden (4 miles one-way), you have four good options: bus, taxi, bike, or on foot. If you have bags, you can check them at the Café-Tabac de la Gare (a block past the train station bus stop—described below—at 138 Rue d'Albuféra, tel. 02 32 51 01 00).

The Vernon-Giverny **bus** meets every train from Paris for the 15-minute run to Giverny and connects to every return train to Paris (€6.50 round-trip). A bus-and-train timetable is available at

GIVERNY & AUVERS-SUR-OISE

# Giverny

Not to Scale

PARKING LOT

To Museum of Impressionisms & ⑤

RUE CLAUDE MONET

ENTRANCE · EXIT

RUE CLAUDE MONET

HOUSE

RUELLE LEROY

WALLED GARDEN (CLOS NORMAND)

WATER LILY STUDIO GIFT SHOP & EXIT

④

GROUP ENTRANCE

(CHEMIN DU ROY)    D-5 ROAD    (RUE DE FALAISE)

Epte R.

To Bike Path & Vernon

Path

To Gasny

WATER GARDEN

❶ Pedestrian Tunnels (2)
❷ Japanese Bridge
❸ Water Lily Pond
❹ Hôtel la Musardière
❺ To Le Clos Fleuri & Hôtel Baudy
❻ Café/Restaurant & Sandwich/Drink Stand

the station bus stop, the Giverny stop, and on the bus—note return times. To reach the bus stop to Giverny, walk through the station, then follow the tracks—the stop is across from the L'Arrivée de Giverny café. Don't dally in the station—the bus leaves soon after your train arrives. During busy times, a line can form while the driver sells tickets and loads the bus. The bus leaves Giverny from the same stop where it drops you off (see map). Be there at least 15 minutes early to ensure a space (if the bus fills, you may have to wait up to two hours for the next one).

**Taxis** wait in front of the station in Vernon. If you miss the return bus from Giverny, ask any shop, restaurant, or hotel to call a taxi for you (mobile 06 77 49 32 90).

You can rent a **bike** at L'Arrivée de Giverny, the café opposite the train station (€14, tel. 02 32 21 16 01), and follow a paved bike path *(piste cyclable)* that runs from near Vernon along an abandoned railroad right-of-way (figure about 30 minutes to Giverny). Get the easy-to-follow map to Giverny when you rent your bike, and you're in business.

## An Impressionist's Garden

Impressionism was a revolutionary movement and all the rage in European art in the 1880s. Artists abandoned realism  in favor of a wispy style that captured light, glimmers, feelings, and impressions. Committed to conveying subtle atmospheric effects, the Impressionists captured nature as a mosaic of short brushstrokes of different colors placed side by side, suggesting shimmering light. And there is no better nature for an Impressionist ready to paint than Monet's delightful mix of weeping willows, luminous clouds, delicate bridges, reflecting ponds... and lush water lilies.

Hikers can go on **foot** to Giverny (about 1.5 hours one way), following the bike instructions above, and take a bus or taxi back.

**Extension to Rouen:** Consider combining your morning Giverny visit with an afternoon excursion to nearby Rouen—together they make an efficient, workable, and memorable day trip from Paris. From Vernon (the halfway point between Rouen and Paris), it's about 40 minutes by train to Rouen; the return trip from Rouen back to Paris takes 70-90 minutes. Plan to arrive at Monet's garden when it opens (at 9:30), so you can be back to the Vernon train station by about noon. You'll land in Rouen by 13:30 (you'll find a lunchtime train from Vernon to Rouen), and have plenty of time to see Rouen's cathedral and surrounding medieval quarter (Rouen's museums are closed Tue). In Rouen, the TI is a 15-minute walk from the station—pick up their map and audioguide walking tour (or, better yet, get your hands on the Rouen chapter of my *Rick Steves' France* guidebook). If you leave Rouen around 17:30, you'll pull into Paris shortly before 19:00, having spent a wonderful day sampling rural and urban Normandy.

## Sights in Giverny

### ▲Monet's Garden and House

All kinds of people flock to Giverny. Gardeners admire the earthmoving landscaping and layout, botanists find interesting new plants, and art lovers can see paintings they've long admired come to life. Fans enjoy wandering around the house where Monet spent half his life and seeing the boat he puttered around in, as well as the henhouse where his family got the eggs for their morning omelets.

There are two gardens, split by a busy road, plus the house, which displays Monet's prized collection of Japanese prints. The gardens are always flowering with something; they're at their most colorful April through July.

**Cost and Hours:** €9, not covered by Paris Museum Pass, daily April-Oct 9:30-18:00, closed Nov-March, last entry at 17:30, tel. 02 32 51 90 31, www.fondation-monet.com. An audioguide is being developed and may be available when you visit—ask.

**Avoiding Crowds:** Though lines may be long and tour groups may trample the flowers, true fans still find magic in the gardens. Minimize crowds by arriving a little before 9:30, when it opens, or come after 16:00 and stay until it closes. Crowds recede briefly during lunch (12:00-13:30), but descend en masse after lunch. The busiest months here are May and June.

If you can't arrive early or late, buy your tickets online (www.fondation-monet.com) or, for a bit more, at any FNAC store in Paris. Both allow you to skip the ticket-buying line here and use the group entrance.

**Visiting the House and Gardens:** After you get in, go directly into the **Walled Garden** (Clos Normand) and work your way around clockwise. Smell the pretty scene. Monet cleared this land of pine trees and laid out symmetrical beds, split down the

middle by a "grand alley" covered with iron trellises of climbing roses. He did his own landscaping, installing flowerbeds of lilies, irises, and clematis, and arbors of climbing roses. The arched trellises leading to the home's entry form a natural tunnel that guides your eye down the path—an effect exploited in his *Rose Trellis* paintings (on display in Paris at the Marmottan Museum). In his carefree manner, Monet throws together hollyhocks, daisies, and poppies. The color scheme of each flowerbed contributes to the look of the whole garden.

In the far corner of the Walled Garden, you'll find a pedestrian tunnel that leads under the road to the **Water Garden.** Follow the meandering path to the Japanese bridge, under weeping willows, over the pond filled with water lilies, and past countless scenes that leave artists aching for an easel. Find a bench. Monet landscaped like he painted—he built an Impressionist pattern of blocks of color. After he planted the gardens, he painted them, from every angle, at every time of day, in all kinds of weather. Assisted by his favorite stepdaughter, Blanche (also a painter, who married Monet's son Jean, from an earlier marriage), he worked on several canvases at once, moving with the sun from one to the next. In a series of canvases, you can watch the sunlight sweep over the gardens from early dawn to twilight.

Back on the main side, continue your visit with a wander through Monet's mildly interesting **home** (pretty furnishings, Japanese prints, old photos, and a room filled with copies of his paintings). The gift shop at the exit is the actual sky-lighted studio where Monet painted his water-lily masterpieces (displayed at the Orangerie Museum in Paris). Many visitors spend more time in this tempting gift shop than in the gardens themselves.

## Nearby Sights

All of Giverny's sights and shops string along Rue Claude Monet, which runs in front of Monet's house.

**Museum of Impressionisms (Musée des Impressionnismes)**—This bright, modern museum, dedicated to the history of Impressionism and its legacy, houses temporary exhibits of Impressionist art. Check its website for current shows or just drop in. It also has picnic-pleasant gardens in front.

**Cost and Hours:** €6.50, daily April-Oct 10:00-18:00, closed Nov-March; to reach it, turn left after leaving Monet's place and walk 200 yards; tel. 02 32 51 94 00, www.mdig.fr.

**Vernon**—If you have time to kill at Vernon's train station, take a five-minute walk into town and sample the peaceful village. Walk between the tracks and the café across the street from the station, and follow the street as it curves left and becomes Rue d'Albuféra. You'll find a smattering of half-timbered Norman homes near Hôtel de Ville (remember, you're in Normandy) and several good cafés and shops—including the killer Boulangerie/Pâtisserie Rose, which has intense quiche and a good selection of sandwiches (74 Rue d'Albuféra, tel. 02 32 51 03 98).

## Sleeping and Eating in Giverny

(€1 = about $1.30, country code: 33)

**$ Hôtel la Musardière\*\*** is nestled in the village of Giverny two blocks from Monet's home (exit right when you leave Monet's). Carole welcomes you with 10 sweet rooms that Claude himself would have felt at home in, a reasonable and homey *crêperie*-restaurant (€9 crêpes, €26 non-crêpe *menu*), and a lovely yard with outdoor tables (Db-€83-95, Tb-€120-130, Qb-€140, Wi-Fi, 123 Rue Claude

Monet, tel. 02 32 21 03 18, fax 02 32 61 60 00, www.lamusardiere.
fr, resa@lamusardiere.fr).

**$ Le Clos Fleuri** is a family-friendly B&B in a modern house
with three fine rooms, handy cooking facilities, and a lovely garden.
It's a 15-minute walk from Monet's place and is run by charming,
English-speaking Danielle, who serves up a generous breakfast
(Db-€80 for two or more nights, €95 for one night, cash only, Wi-
Fi, 5 Rue de la Dîme, tel. 02 32 21 36 51, www.giverny-leclosfleuri.
fr).

*Eating:* A flowery **café/restau-
rant** and a **sandwich/drink stand** sit
right next to the parking lot across
from Monet's home. Enjoy your
lunch in the nearby gardens of the
Museum of the Impressionisms.

Rose-colored **Hôtel Baudy,**
once a hangout for American Impressionists, offers an appropriately
pretty setting for lunch or dinner
(outdoor tables in front, *menus* from €24, popular with tour groups,
daily, 5-minute walk past Museum of Impressionisms at 81 Rue
Claude Monet, tel. 02 32 21 10 03). Don't miss a stroll through the
artsy gardens behind the restaurant.

# Auvers-sur-Oise

This small, plain town draws
die-hard Van Gogh pilgrims
and those in search of a green
escape from the city. Auvers-
sur-Oise (oh-vehr soor wahz)
is a peaceful place on a bend of
the lazy Oise River, northwest
of Paris. It's a manageable day
trip by car or train. Here you'll
get an intimate glimpse into
life (and death) during the Impressionist era. Hikers will enjoy
stretching their legs between the sights.

Auvers was a magnet for artists in the late 1800s. Charles-
François Daubigny, Jean-Baptiste-Camille Corot, Camille Pissarro, and Paul Cézanne all valued this rural retreat (they were also
unknown at this time). But Auvers is most famous as the village
where Vincent van Gogh shot himself. He had moved here from
southern France to be near his brother Theo (who lived in Paris).

Vincent had talked his way out of the asylum in St. Rémy-de-Provence with assurances that he would be under good care from a sympathetic doctor, Auvers resident Paul Gachet. Gachet advised the artist to throw himself into his work as a remedy for his illness, which he did—Van Gogh spent the last 70 days of his life in this little town, knocking out a masterpiece each day.

Today, this modest little town opens its doors to visitors with a handful of sights and walking trails leading to scenes painted by various artists (some with copies of the paintings posted). Try to arrive before the TI closes for lunch (12:30-14:00) and avoid visiting on

weekends, when Auvers is very busy. Most sights are closed Mondays (some are closed Tue as well) and from November to Easter. Auvers makes a convenient first or last overnight stop for drivers using Charles de Gaulle airport, as it avoids traffic hassles (Auvers is about 20 miles from the airport).

## Getting to Auvers-sur-Oise

**By Train:** Mainline trains to Auvers leave from Gare du Nord and St. Lazare (hourly, 1.25 hours, transfer in Pontoise or St-Ouen, www.transilien.com). On Saturdays and Sundays from April to October, a direct train runs from Gare du Nord (one round-trip per day, 35 minutes, departs Gare du Nord's *Banlieue* tracks at about 10:00, returns from Auvers at about 18:00).

Frequent RER-C trains also run to Auvers with a transfer in Pontoise (2/hour, 1 hour to Pontoise, catch in Paris at St. Michel, Orsay, Invalides, or Pont de l'Alma stops). Pontoise is the end of the line, where it's easy to transfer to Auvers. Ask ahead

at any RER-C station for the best connection for your trip (you can also check www.ratp.fr for RER lines or www.transilien.com for SNCF trains). Service from Pontoise back to Paris is very frequent, with trains to Gare du Nord and St. Lazare, and to points along the RER-C route.

To get from Pontoise to Auvers, a 10-minute ride away, you have three options. You can take the train (direction: Creil) if it's leaving soon (but plan ahead to avoid long waits; before leaving Auvers' train station, jot down return times to Pontoise, as service is sparse but workable). You can catch a bus (stop to the right of the station, runs hourly, look for the posted schedule—you're at "Chemin de la Gare" in Pontoise, and you want the "Marie" stop in

Auvers). Or you can go by taxi (€10; for a bit more money, the same taxi can pick you up in Auvers for the return; tel. 01 30 75 95 95).

**By Car:** Auvers is about 45 minutes northwest of Paris. Take the A-15 autoroute to A-115, and then exit at Auvers-sur-Oise.

# Orientation to Auvers-sur-Oise

The **TI** has good information on all sights; bus, train, and RER schedules; a few picnic tables; and a decent WC (Tue-Sun 9:30-12:30 & 14:00-18:00, Nov-March until 17:00, closed Mon year-round, Rue de la Sansonne, well-signed, tel. 01 30 36 10 06, www.lavalleedeloise.com). Spring for the helpful €1 map showing walking routes, and set the scene for your exploration with the 12-minute video on Auvers-sur-Oise and Van Gogh (€1, English version available).

From Auvers' train station, you can get to the TI by turning left on the main road. There's a handy supermarket on your way into town from the station. For **a taxi** in Auvers, call mobile 06 30 02 19 38 or 09 50 94 13 29.

# Sights in Auvers-sur-Oise

The best way to spend a few hours in Auvers is to wander the streets and paths of the village. Spot locations where well-known paintings were set, stop by the graves of Vincent and Theo, and visit the Château d'Auvers—the town's most worthwhile sight. It's easy to connect Auvers' sights by following my route.

**Musée Daubigny**—This skippable museum, one floor up from the TI, houses a small collection of works by Charles-François Daubigny and other artists who came to work with him. Daubigny was a big supporter of the Impressionist movement.

**Cost and Hours:** €4, Wed-Fri 14:00-18:00, Sat-Sun 10:30-12:30 & 14:00-18:00, closed Mon-Tue, tel. 01 30 36 80 20, www.musee-daubigny.com.

• *Leave the TI following signs uphill for L'Eglise (10-minute walk). You'll recognize the* **church** *(Notre-Dame d'Auvers) from Van Gogh's paintings (interior open 10:00-18:00). Several benches outside with views over the forest make for a good picnic site. From here, follow signs for* Tombes de

Théo et Vincent *up the small street behind the church and walk about 300 yards to the simple cemetery.*

**Vincent's Grave**—Vincent and his caring brother are buried side by side against the cemetery's upper wall about halfway down (look

for the ivy). No one can be sure why Vincent ended his life at 37, but standing at his grave, you can feel the weight of the tragedy and imagine the paintings he might have created. Look for gray dust on the ivy that covers his and Théo's graves: Vincent is wildly popular among the Japanese, some of whom ask to have their ashes spread over his grave. Vincent lies in a coffin made by the same carpenter who built his picture frames.

• *Leave the cemetery and follow the dirt path that bisects a broad* **wheat field** *(any crows swirling on the horizon?), following signs to* Château d'Auvers. *Vincent shot himself out here and died two days later in his bedroom at the Auberge Ravoux (described later). His brother was at his side. His last painting was* Wheatfield with Crows, *painted in this very field in 1890. In about 500 yards, you'll drop down to a street. Turn left when you reach the "T," and pass...*

**La Maison-Atelier de Daubigny**—This well-preserved home/studio once belonged to Charles-François Daubigny, who created the artist colony that Auvers became in the 1880s.

**Cost and Hours:** €6; April-mid-July and mid-Aug-Sept Thu-Sun 14:00-18:30, closed Mon-Wed; closed mid-July-mid-Aug and Oct-March, tel. 01 30 36 60 60, www.atelier-daubigny.com.

• *Past the Maison-Atelier de Daubigny, veer right at signs to the château. You'll soon pass...*

**Musée de l'Absinthe**—This small, one-of-a-kind tribute is to the highly alcoholic, herb-based beverage popular among artists and writers in the late 1800s. Considered dangerously addictive, it was banned in 1915 but is now legal in France.

**Cost and Hours:** €4.50, bottles for sale; mid-June-mid-Sept Wed-Fri 13:30-18:00, Sat-Sun 11:00-18:00, closed Mon-Tue; mid-Sept-mid-June open Sat-Sun only 11:00-18:00; no English descriptions, but staff make an effort to explain displays; tel. 01 30 36 83 26, www.musee-absinthe.com.

• *From here it's a straight, 300-yard shot to...*

▲**Château d'Auvers**—This château has been transformed into a splendid re-creation of life during the Impressionist years. Elaborate and informative multimedia displays use an audioguide, video screens, and lasers to guide you along the Impressionist route that led from Montmartre to the sea, giving you a keen appreciation of life's daily struggles and pleasures during this time. You'll experience the cancan and a mock train ride, and see more than 500 Impressionist paintings. To maximize your experience, bring your own earphones to use with the included audioguide.

**Cost and Hours:** €14, family rates, not covered by Paris Museum Pass; April-Sept Tue-Sun 10:30-18:00; Oct-March Tue-Fri 10:30-16:30, Sat-Sun 10:30-17:30; closed Mon year-round; tel. 01 34 48 48 48, www.chateau-auvers.fr.

• *A short walk beyond the château, Van Gogh enthusiasts can visit the restored home of Dr. Gachet (well-signed).*

**Maison du Docteur Gachet**—It was at Camille Pissarro's suggestion that Dr. Gachet agreed to see Van Gogh, who made an immediate connection with the doctor—"I have found a friend in Dr. Gachet...and something of a new brother, since we are so similar both mentally and physically." The home is furnished as it was when Vincent lived in Auvers, and the garden has medicinal plants that the homeopath Dr. Gachet cultivated and used to treat Van Gogh. You'll also find exhibits of contemporary painters. In addition to being Vincent's personal physician in Auvers, Dr. Gachet was an avid painter and entertained famous artists such as Cézanne, Monet, Renoir, and Pissarro. He inherited all of Van Gogh's works from his time in Auvers (those you see at the Orsay Museum were donated by Dr. Gachet's family). As you tour the doctor's simple home, consider the fact that in 1990, one of Vincent's portraits of Gachet fetched over $80 million at auction. Dr. Gachet is buried at Père Lachaise cemetery in Paris.

**Cost and Hours:** Free, March-Oct Wed-Sun 10:30-18:30, closed Mon-Tue and Nov-Feb, 78 Rue du Dr. Gachet, tel. 01 30 36 81 27.

• *Return to the TI and find...*

**Auberge Ravoux**—Vincent lived and died in an attic room of this inn (also called "Maison de Van Gogh"). Informative English-information plaques in the courtyard explain Vincent's tragic life. The simple room has been re-created to look exactly as it did when he was here (his few furnishings were burned by church officials shortly after his death, as suicide was considered a sin). Wooden steps lead to Van Gogh's room, where staff give some commentary in English and run a 12-minute slideshow.

**Cost and Hours:** €6, March-Oct Wed-Sun 10:00-18:00, closed Mon-Tue and Nov-Feb, tel. 01 30 36 60 60, www.maison devangogh.fr. Food connoisseurs can enjoy a tasty lunch in the *auberge*'s perfectly preserved restaurant (see listing later).

## Sleeping and Eating in Auvers

**(€1 = about $1.30, country code: 33)**
Auvers is a handy first or last stop for drivers using Charles de Gaulle Airport.

**$$ Hostellerie du Nord\*\*\*** is small, friendly, and polished—a treat for those who want to sleep in luxury. It has modern, spacious rooms and a seriously good restaurant that requires reservations (Db-€100-130, suites-€190, *menus* from €60, a block from train station at 6 Rue du Général de Gaulle, tel. 01 30 36 70 74, fax 01 30 36 72 75, www.hostelleriedunord.fr).

*Eating:* The most atmospheric place to eat in Auvers is **Auberge Ravoux,** unchanged (except for its prices) since 1876, when painters would meet here over a good meal (€28-36 *menus*, closed Mon-Tue, on Place de la Mairie, tel. 01 30 36 60 60). Auvers also has grocery stores, cafés, *crêperies*, restaurants, and bakeries with sandwiches. This place was made for picnics.

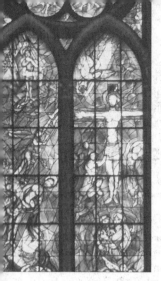

# REIMS

With its Roman gate, Gothic cathedral, Champagne *caves*, and vibrant pedestrian zone, Reims feels both historic and youthful. And thanks to the TGV bullet train, it's just a 45-minute ride from Paris.

Reims (pronounced "rance;" rhymes with France) has a turbulent history: This is where 26 French kings were crowned, where Champagne first bubbled, where WWI devastation met miraculous reconstruction during the Art Deco age (all but 70 buildings were damaged in 1918), and where the Germans officially surrendered in 1945, bringing World War II to a close in Europe. The town's sights give you an entertaining peek at the entire story.

## Planning Your Time

You can see Reims' essential sights in an easy day, either as a day trip from Paris or as a stop en route to or from Paris. Frequent TGV trains make the trip from Paris a breeze. Take a morning train from Paris and explore the cathedral and city center before lunch, then spend your afternoon below ground, in a cool, chalky Champagne cellar. You can be back at your Parisian hotel before dinner. Those continuing to destinations farther east find Reims a convenient place to pick up a car.

To best experience contemporary Reims, explore the busy shopping streets between the cathedral and the central train station. Rue de Vesle, Rue Condorcet, and Place Drouet d'Erlon are most interesting.

# Orientation to Reims

Reims' hard-to-miss cathedral marks the city center and makes an easy orientation landmark. Many sights of interest are within a 15-minute walk from the Reims-Centre train station. Easy-to-use bus routes connect the harder-to-reach Champagne *caves* with the central train station and cathedral. The city has ambitiously renovated its downtown, converting large areas into pedestrian-friendly zones. Citizens are proud of their sleek tram system that connects Reims-Centre Station and Champagne-Ardenne TGV Station.

## Tourist Information

The main TI is located outside the **cathedral**'s left (north) transept (TI open Easter-Sept Mon-Sat 9:00-19:00, Sun 10:00-18:00; Oct-Easter Mon-Sat 9:00-18:00, Sun 10:00-16:00 except March-Easter, when it's open until 18:00; public WCs across street, tel. 03 26 77 45 00, www.reims-tourisme.com). A much smaller, seasonal TI is just outside the Reims-Centre **train station** (mid-April-Dec Mon-Sat 8:30-11:00 & 12:00-18:00, Sun 12:00-17:30).

At either TI, pick up a free map of the town center and a map of the Champagne *caves*. The TI can book a visit to any *cave* that accepts visitors, and can call a taxi to get you there. Note that some of the most popular *caves* require advance booking (for information on reservations and specifics on reaching the *caves*, see "Champagne Tours and Sights," later). The TI also rents audioguides covering the cathedral, city center, and Art Deco architecture (single-€6, each additional set-€4, 1-2 hours each).

## Arrival in Reims

**By Train:** From Paris' Gare de l'Est station, there are three different train routes to Reims. The fastest (and most frequent) is the direct TGV to the recently remodeled **Reims-Centre Station** (9/day, 45 minutes, no baggage check). Check the schedule before booking to avoid slower trains.

To get from the Reims-Centre station to the cathedral, it's a 15-minute walk: Follow *sortie* signs for Place de la Gare (don't use the Clairmarais exit). As you leave the station, walk toward the statue in the gardens and on toward the Grand Hôtel Continental on the pedestrianized Place Drouet d'Erlon. Turn left on Rue Condorcet, then right on Rue de Talleyrand.

To save a little time, you can jump on the tram. Find the tram stop on the square in front of the station (to the left of the statue). Take tram #A (direction: Hôpital Debré) or tram #B (direction: Gare Champagne TGV) two stops to the Opéra stop—the cathedral and TI are behind the Opéra building. For tram and bus info, see "Getting Around Reims," later.

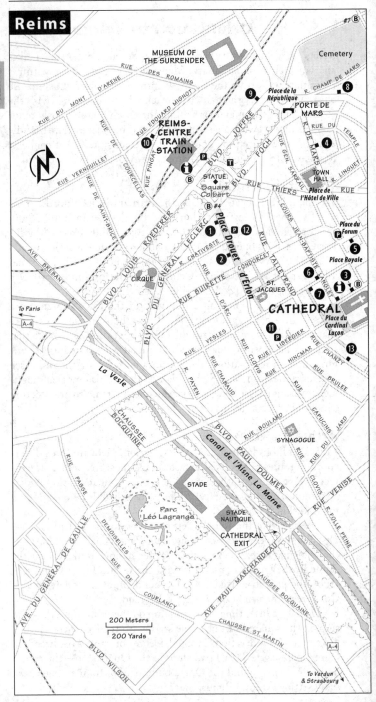

# Reims

MUSEUM OF THE SURRENDER

Cemetery

RUE DES ROMAINS

#7 B

RUE D'ARENE

RUE DU MONT

Place de la République

R. CHAMP DE MARS

8

9

PORTE DE MARS

RUE VERNOUILLET

RUE EDOUARD MIGNOT

RUE DE COURCELLAS

RUE PINGAT

BLVD. JOFFRE

BLVD. FOCH

RUE DU TEMPLE

RUE GEN. SARRAIL

4

RUE DE MARS

REIMS-CENTRE TRAIN STATION

10

P

B

T

STATUE

Square Colbert

BLVD. THIERS

TOWN HALL

R. LINGUET

Place de l'Hôtel de Ville

RUE

RUE DE SAINT-BRICE

B #4

RUE THIERS

N

BLVD. LOUIS ROEDERER

1

P

12

Place du Forum

P

5

Place Royale

AVE. BREBANT

R. CHATIVESTE

2

RUE BUIRETTE

RUE J. D'ARC

Place Drouet d'Erlon

RUE TALLEYRAND

CONDORCET

COURS JEAN-BAPTISTE LANGLET

6

3

ST. JACQUES

i

B

CIRQUE

BLVD. DU GENERAL LECLERC

7

CATHEDRAL

To Paris
A-4

RUE VESLES

RUE CLOVIS

RUE J. D'ARC

Place du Cardinal Luçon

11

P

LIBERGIER

RUE HINCMAR

RUE CHANZY

13

La Vesle

R. PAYEN

RUE CHABAUD

RUE

RUE BRULEE

RUE

RUE CAPUCINS

RUE DU JARD

CHAUSSEE BOCQUAINE

SYNAGOGUE

BLVD. PAUL DOUMER

RUE BOULARD

Canal de l'Aisne La Marne

RUE CLOVIS

RUE VENISE

RUE R. FOLLE PEINE

STADE

Parc Léo Lagrange

STADE NAUTIQUE

CATHEDRAL EXIT

RUE DE DEMOISELLES

RUE PASSE

AVE. DU GENERAL DE GAULLE

RUE DE COURLANCY

AVE. PAUL MARCHANDEAU

CHAUSSEE BOCQUAINE

200 Meters
200 Yards

CHAUSSEE ST. MARTIN

A-4

BLVD. WILSON

To Verdun & Strasbourg

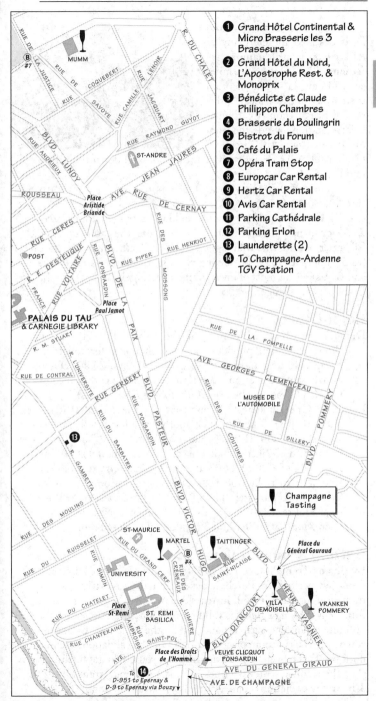

1 Grand Hôtel Continental & Micro Brasserie les 3 Brasseurs
2 Grand Hôtel du Nord, L'Apostrophe Rest. & Monoprix
3 Bénédicte et Claude Philippon Chambres
4 Brasserie du Boulingrin
5 Bistrot du Forum
6 Café du Palais
7 Opéra Tram Stop
8 Europcar Car Rental
9 Hertz Car Rental
10 Avis Car Rental
11 Parking Cathédrale
12 Parking Erlon
13 Launderette (2)
14 To Champagne-Ardenne TGV Station

Other TGV trains from Paris destined for Germany or Alsace stop at the **Champagne-Ardenne** TGV Station five miles away (4/day, 45 minutes). From there, you can take a local "milk-run" (TER) train to Reims-Centre Station, or ride the tram into town (tram #B, direction:

Neufchâtel, walk straight out of the station and down the hill to find the stop).

There are also a few local TER trains that go from Paris through Epernay to Reims (2/day, 2 hours).

**By Car:** Day-trippers should follow *Centre-Ville* and *Cathédrale* signs, and park on the street approaching the cathedral (Rue Libergier) or in the well-signed Parking Cathédrale structure (€1.50/hour). If you'll be staying the night, follow *Reims-Centre* and *Gare* signs for most of my recommended hotels, and park in the Erlon parking garage.

## Helpful Hints

**Department Store: Monoprix,** at the Espace Drouet d'Erlon shopping center, provides one-stop shopping for toiletries, cheap clothing, and groceries (Mon-Sat 9:00-20:00, closed Sun, basement level, 53 Place Drouet d'Erlon, near the recommended L'Apostrophe restaurant, follow *FNAC* signs).

**Laundry:** One launderette is just south of the cathedral (daily 8:00-20:00, 59 Rue Chanzy); another is a few blocks farther south (daily 7:00-21:00, 49 Rue Gambetta).

**Car Rental: Avis** is just outside the central train station at 20 Rue Pingat (tel. 08 20 61 17 05, use the *Clairmarais* exit from the station, turn right, and walk 200 yards). **Europcar** is at 76 Boulevard Lundy (tel. 08 25 04 52 82); **Hertz** is at 26 Boulevard Joffre (tel. 03 26 47 98 78). Rental agencies are usually open Mon-Sat 8:00-12:00 & 14:00-19:00, closed Sun.

## Getting Around Reims

**By Bus or Tram:** Reims has an integrated network of buses and trams (www.citura.fr). Purchase tickets from the bus driver or at any tram-stop machine (€1.60, instructions in English, pay with cash, coins only). A single ticket is valid for one hour and can be used for unlimited transfers, even a round-trip on the same line. Each time you board a bus or tram, place your ticket on the validation machine until you hear a beep (if you skip this step, you might get fined).

The tram system's two lines (tram #A—5/hour, tram #B—2-3/hour; fewer on Sun) connect Reims' two train stations—Reims-

Centre and Champagne-Ardenne TGV—and serve a few key stops in town, including one near the cathedral. To get from either train station to the cathedral and town center, take a tram to the Opéra stop. The cathedral is one block away, around the back of the Opéra building.

# Sights in Reims

### ▲▲▲Reims Cathedral

The cathedral of Reims, begun in 1211, recently celebrated its 800th birthday. It's a glorious example of Gothic architecture, and one of Europe's greatest churches. Clovis, the first king of the Franks, was baptized at a church on this site in A.D. 496, establishing France's Christian roots, which still hold firm today. Since Clovis' baptism, Reims Cathedral has served as *the* place for the coronation of 26 French kings, giving it a more important role in France's political history than Notre-Dame Cathedral in Paris—think England's Westminster Abbey. A self-assured Joan of Arc led a

less-assured Charles VII to be crowned here in 1429. Thanks to Joan, the French rallied around their new king to push the English out of France and finally end the Hundred Years' War. During the French Revolution, the cathedral was converted to a temple of reason (as was Paris' Notre-Dame). After the restoration of the monarchy, the cathedral hosted the crowning of Charles X in 1825—the last coronation in France. During World War I, it was devastated by severe bombing. Then it was completely rebuilt, thanks in large part to John D. Rockefeller...just in time for the start of World War II.

**Cost and Hours:** Free, daily 7:30-19:30.

**❷ Self-Guided Tour:** Stand on the square in front of the cathedral.

**Exterior:** You're admiring perhaps the best **west portal** anywhere, with more than 2,000 statues festooning its walls inside and out. (Medieval churches face east, toward the Holy Land, so you almost always enter through a church's west portal.) Like the cathedrals in Paris and in Chartres, this church is dedicated to "Our Lady" (Notre Dame). Statues depicting the crowning of the Virgin take center stage on the facade. For eight centuries Catholics have prayed to the "Mother of God," kneeling here to ask her to intervene with God on their behalf. In 1429, Joan of Arc received messages from Mary encouraging her to rally French troops against the English at the Siege of Orléans (a statue of Joan is over your left shoulder as you face the church).

Notice the **flying buttresses** soaring from the sides of the church. These massive "beams" are critical to supporting this structure. The pointed arches inside the church push the weight of the roof outward, rather than downward. The "flying" buttresses support the roof by pushing back inward, creating a delicate balance between the two forces. Gothic architects learned by trial and error—many church roofs caved in as they tested their theories and strove to build ever higher. Work on this cathedral began decades after the Notre-Dame cathedrals in Paris and Chartres, allowing architects to take advantage of what they'd learned from those magnificent earlier structures.

Contemplate the lives of the people who built this huge building, starting in 1211. Construction on a scale like this required a wholesale community effort—all hands on deck. Most townsfolk who participated donated their money or their labor knowing that neither they, nor their children, nor their children's children, would ever see it completed—such was their pride, dedication, and faith. Imagine the effort it took to raise the funds and manage the workforce. Master masons supervised, while the average Jean did much of the sweat work. Labor was something even the poorest medieval peasant could donate generously.

**Interior:** The weight of the roof is supported by a few towering columns that seem to sprout crisscrossing pointed arches. This technique allowed the church to grow higher, and liberated the walls to become window frames. Now, look back at the entry wall, with 120 statues filling the niches. The rose window (high above on this wall) contains the best original stained glass in the church (from 1255, removed during World War I to be spared destruction). Most of the windows are clear and newer: 18th- and 19th-century tastes called for more light, and the original, dark stained glass was replaced.

Circulate counterclockwise through the church (find helpful information boards in English). The **south transept windows,** destroyed in World War I, were replaced in 1954 by the local Champagne makers. The windows show the connection of the Champagne industry to this town and its church with scenes portraying the tending of vines (left), the harvest (center), and the time-honored double-fermentation process (right). Notice, around the edges, the churches representing all the grape-producing villages in the area.

The apse (east end, behind the altar) holds a luminous set of **Marc Chagall stained-glass windows** from 1974. Chagall's inimitable style lends itself to stained glass, and he enjoyed opportunities to adorn great churches with his windows. The left window shows

scenes from the Old Testament, and the center features the resurrection of Christ. On the right the tree of Jesse is extended to symbolically include the royalty of France—both affirming the divine power of the monarchs and stressing the responsibility to rule with wisdom and justice. For the cathedral's 800th anniversary in 2011, six modern, abstract windows were installed on either side of the Chagall windows (they aren't working for me).

As you head for the exit, you'll find another Joan of Arc statue standing guard in her chapel.

## Other Reims Sights

**Palais du Tau**—This former Archbishop's Palace, named after the Greek letter T *(tau)* for its shape, houses artifacts from the cathedral (with scant English information, though an audioguide is available at the TI for €6). You'll look into the weathered eyes of original statues from the cathedral's facade (taken in from the acidic open air for their own preservation). A set of precious tapestries, telling stories from the life of Mary, are the originals that warmed the walls of the cathedral's choir in the 16th century. The coronation jewels, vestments, and other garb you see here were mostly made especially for the last French coronation (of Charles X in 1825), since the original finery had been lost a generation earlier in the French Revolution.

**Cost and Hours:** €7.50, May-Aug Tue-Sun 9:30-18:30, Sept-April Tue-Sun 9:30-12:30 & 14:00-17:30, closed Mon year-round, next to cathedral, tel. 03 26 47 81 79, http://palais-tau.monuments-nationaux.fr.

**▲Museum of the Surrender (Musée de la Reddition)**—WWII buffs enjoy visiting the historic room where the Germans

signed the document of surrender of all German forces in the early morning of May 7, 1945. The news was announced the next day, turning May 8 into Victory in Europe (V-E) Day. Anyone interested in World War II will find the extensive collection of artifacts fascinating (particularly the ticker tape with the happy news, old photos, and a worthwhile 10-minute video shown on request). The room of the signing still has the maps with troop positions on the walls and the 13 chairs with name tags, each in its original spot.

**Cost and Hours:** €3, Wed-Mon 10:00-12:00 & 14:00-18:00, closed Tue, 12 Rue Franklin Roosevelt, tel. 03 26 47 84 19.

**Getting There:** It's a 15-minute walk from the central train station, or catch bus #4 in front of the station (direction: La Neuvillette Mairie), go three stops to Mignot, then continue one more block on foot.

**Porte de Mars**—The last vestige of Reims' ancient Roman heritage —an entry gate—is a short walk from the Reims-Centre train station. The Porte de Mars, built in the second century A.D., was one of four principal entrances into the ancient Gallo-Roman town and the only one still standing. Inspired by triumphal arches that Rome built to herald war victories, this one was constructed to celebrate the Pax Romana (a period of peace and stability—after all of Rome's foes were vanquished). Unlike most of the rest of town, the gate was undamaged in World War I, but it bears the marks of other eras, such as its integration into the medieval ramparts. Find the ruts under the arcade that guided chariots, and look for the depiction of the legend of Romulus and Remus (extremely faint on ceiling under left arch), complete with suckling she-wolf, from which Reims gets its name.

**Cost and Hours:** Free, always open, Place du Boulingrin.

▲**Carnegie Library (Bibliothèque Carnegie)**—The legacy of the Carnegie Library network, funded generously by the 19th-century American millionaire Andrew Carnegie and his steel fortune (notice the American flag above the main entrance on the left), extends even to Reims. Built in the flurry of interwar reconstruction, this beautiful Art Deco building still houses the city's public library. Considering that admission is free and it's  just behind the cathedral, it's worth a quick look. Visitors are welcome to admire the mosaics, onyx-laden entrance hall, and Jacques Simon chandelier, but are asked not to enter the reading room (some come here to study). Peek through the reading room door to admire the stained-glass windows of this temple of thought. The gorgeous wood-paneled card-catalogue room takes older visitors back to their childhoods (notice how each card is laboriously typed), or even back to 1928, the year the library was inaugurated.

**Cost and Hours:** Free; Tue-Wed and Fri 10:00-13:00 & 14:00-19:00, Thu 14:00-19:00, Sat 10:00-13:00 & 14:00-18:00, closed Sun-Mon; Place Carnegie, tel. 03 26 77 81 41.

**Art Deco on Place Drouet d'Erlon**—Place Drouet d'Erlon is a long street-like square marking the commercial center of town. (From the central train station, it's directly across the park-like boulevards.) The square's centerpiece, a fountain with a winged figure of victory at the top, celebrates the major rivers of this district. It hasn't worked as a fountain since WWI bombings—a reminder of the devastation brought on this city. All around you'll see the stylized features—geometric reliefs, motifs in ironwork, rounded corners, and simple concrete elegance—of Art Deco. The only hints that this was once a Middle Ages town are the narrow lots that struggle to fit today's buildings. Pop into the Waida Pâtis-serie (closed Mon, 3 Place Drouet d'Erlon) for a pure, typical Art Deco interior. As you stroll about, keep an eye open for "Biscuits Roses"—light, rose-colored egg-and-sugar cookies that have been made since 1756. They're the locals' favorite munchie to accompany a glass of Champagne—you're supposed to dunk them, but I like them dry (most places that sell these treats offer free samples).

## ▲▲Champagne Tours and Sights

Reims is the capital of the Champagne region. While the bubbly stuff's birthplace is closer to Epernay (for more on this town, see page 637), you can tour several interesting Champagne *caves* right in Reims. All charge for tastings and most are open daily. Most have a few daily English tours, but some require a reservation. Call in advance or email from home before your trip for the schedule and to secure a spot on a tour. Martel offers the most personal and best-value tour. Pommery, Taittinger, and Mumm have the most impressive cellars. Villa Demoiselle offers a unique visit inside a mansion. Veuve Clicquot is very popular with Americans and fills up weeks in advance. Bring a sweater, even in summer, as the *caves* are cool and clammy.

Of the *caves* I list, Mumm is easiest to get to. If you don't have a car, the others involve a long **walk** (30-45 minutes) or a **bus** ride (for more, see "Getting There," under "*Caves* Southeast of the Cathedral," later). A **taxi** from either train station to the farthest Champagne *cave* will cost about €15 (many taxis wait at the station). To return, ask the staff at the *caves* to call a taxi for you (tel. 03 26 47 05 05). Warning: The meter starts running once they are called, so count on €5 extra for the return trip.

### Mumm

Mumm ("moome") is one of the easiest *caves* to visit, as it's closest to the central train station (15-minute walk). Reservations are smart, especially on weekends. The basic "Cordon Rouge" visit includes a good 10-minute video, a small museum of old Champagne-making contraptions, and a tour of its industrial-size, modern-feeling chalk cellars where 25 million bottles are stored. The video explains the place's history back to 1827 and the Champagne-making process with the enthusiasm of an advertisement ("Cordon Rouge is dedicated to the audacity and passion of exceptional men and women, with a subtle balance between freshness and intensity"). The tour ends with a glass of bubbly Cordon Rouge. You can pay more for the same tour with extra "guided" tastings.

**Cost and Hours:** One-hour tour with Cordon Rouge tasting-€12, Discovery tasting-€17, Grand Cru tasting-€24; daily 9:00-11:00 & 14:00-17:00, closed Sun; 34 Rue du Champ de Mars—go to the end of the courtyard and follow *Visites des Caves* signs; tel. 03 26 49 59 70, www.mumm.com, guides@mumm.com.

**Getting There:** To walk from the Reims-Centre train station, turn left out of the station and go four very long blocks. It's beyond Place de la République on Rue du Champ de Mars (15 minutes). Or take bus #7 from the station (direction: Béthany) to the Justice stop, turn right (south) onto Rue de la Justice, and then left onto Rue Champs de Mars. To return to the station on bus #7 (direction: Apollinaire), catch the bus at a different Justice stop, at the junction of Rue de la Justice and Rue Champs du Mars. If you are coming from Champagne-Ardenne TGV Station, ride the tram all the way to Reims-Centre Station, transfer to bus #7, and follow the directions above.

### *Caves* Southeast of the Cathedral

Taittinger and Martel, offering contrasting looks at two very different *caves,* are a few blocks apart, about 30 minutes by foot from the town center. These can easily be combined in one visit. Vranken Pommery, Villa Demoiselle, and Veuve Clicquot Ponsardin are a bit farther, require reservations, and are darn pricey—but also have impressive cellars. Pommery and Villa Demoiselle have the same owners and are across the street from each other. Veuve Clicquot is a big draw for American travelers and must be booked in advance.

**Getting There:** From the **town center,** it's a 30-minute walk to Taittinger and Martel—take Rue de l'Université from behind the cathedral's right transept, then Rue du Barbâtre. Pommery, Villa Demoiselle, and Veuve Clicquot are about a 45-minute walk from town. To reach any of these *caves* by bus, take the small Citadine bus #1 (€1.60, 3/hour Mon-Sat, none on Sun, not to be confused with regular bus #1) from the Cathédrale stop (a block to the left behind the cathedral—see map on page 624), and ride 10 minutes (direction: Buirette) to the St. Niçaise stop. The bus drops you close to Taittinger and Martel. It's an additional 10-minute walk to Pommery, Villa Demoiselle, and Veuve Clicquot. To return to the cathedral, catch Citadine bus #2 (around the corner on Rue du Barbâtre, bus stop Salines, direction: Hôtel de Ville), and get off at Royale.

From **Reims-Centre Station,** hop on bus #4 (6/hour Mon-Sat, 2/hour Sun, 20 minutes, direction: Hôpital Debré). Get off at the St. Timothée stop, and ask the driver to point you in the right direction. It's about a five-minute walk to Taittinger and Martel and 15 minutes to the others. To return to the station (or to reach the cathedral by getting off at the Rockefeller or Opera stops), take bus #4 from the St. Timothée stop (direction: La Neuvillette Mairie). You can get even closer to Veuve Clicquot by catching bus #6 from Reims-Centre Station to the Droits de l'Homme stop (4/hour, 20 minutes, direction: ZI Farman). To return to the station, catch bus #6 on Boulevard Dieu Lumière (opposite side of the big roundabout, bus stop Cimitière du Sud, direction: Gare Centre).

If you're coming from the **Champagne-Ardenne** TGV train station, take the tram to the Opéra stop and walk to the cathedral, then transfer to Citadine bus #1 (described earlier). Or take the tram to Reims-Centre station, then transfer to bus #4 (described earlier).

**Taittinger**—One of the biggest and most renowned of Reims' *caves,* Taittinger (tay-tan-zhay) runs a few morning and afternoon tours in English through their vast cellars (show up early or call for times and to reserve a spot, about 20-30 people per tour). After seeing their 10-minute promo-movie (hooray for Taittinger!), follow your guide—mine reminded me of an old-time airline hostess—for 60 chilly minutes and 80 steps down to a chalky underworld of *caves,* the deepest of which were dug by ancient Romans. You'll tour part of the three miles of *caves,* pass some of the three million bottles stored here, and learn all you need to know about the Champagne-making process from your well-informed guide. Popping corks signal when the tour's done and the tasting's begun.

**Cost and Hours:** €16 includes one-hour tour and tasting, tours daily mid-March-mid-Nov 9:30-13:00 & 14:00-17:30 (last tours depart at 11:50 and 16:20), closed weekends off-season, 9 Place St. Niçaise, tel. 03 26 85 84 33, www.taittinger.com, info@taittinger.com.

**Martel**—This offers a homey contrast to Taittinger's big-business style. It's a small operation with less extensive *caves* and is *sans* doubt the best deal in town. Call to set up a visit and expect a small group that might be yours alone. Friendly Emmanuel runs the place with a relaxed manner. Only 20 percent of their product is exported (mostly to Europe), so you won't find much of their Champagne in the US. Their visit focuses on the basics and includes an informative 10-minute film and a tour of their small cellars, which are peppered with rusted old wine-making tools. It culminates with a tasting of three different Champagnes in a casual living-room atmosphere.

**Cost and Hours:** €11 includes 45-minute tour and tasting, tours depart daily 10:00-13:00 & 14:00-18:00, reservations not required but smart, 17 Rue des Créneaux, tel. 03 26 82 70 67, www.champagnemartel.com, boutique@champagnemartel.com.

**Vranken Pommery**—This massive *domaine* is owned by Paul-François Vranken, a Belgian who now has the second-largest Champagne empire in France. While they say reservations are required, it's easy to get a same-day spot on a tour if you call early. Choose between a full tour of the chalk cellars or a shorter Cliffs Notes version. All tours finish with a tasting. The tour starts with a long, regal staircase down into the cool *caves*. Here, thousands of bottles rest in Gallo-Roman chalk quarries, each 100 feet deep, with glass skylights at ground level. These ancient "underground cathedrals" make it easier to endure the robotic tour guide and spiels lauding Pommery.

**Cost and Hours:** €17-21 for one-hour tour, price depends on how many tastings you take, 30-minute tour-€5 less, tour with one glass of the really good stuff-€30; daily 10:00-18:00, closes at 17:00 Nov-March; 5 Place du Général Gouraud, tel. 03 26 61 62 56, www.pommery.com, domaine@pommery.fr.

**Villa Demoiselle**—Across the street from Pommery, this place is also owned by Champagne mogul Vranken, but serves up a different brand. Instead of chalk *caves,* here you'll tour a beautifully restored Art Nouveau home. Built in the early 1900s, it was bought in 2002 by Vranken and has only been open to the public since 2009. Tours in English are fewer here, but all finish in the tasting room veranda.

**Cost and Hours:** €17-25 for one-hour tour, price depends on how many tastings you take, 30-minute tour-€5 less, call or email in advance for the schedule, 54 Boulevard Henry Vasnier, tel. 03 26 35 80 50, www.champagne-demoiselle.fr, villademoiselle@vranken pommery.fr. It's also possible to combine visits to Pommery and Villa Demoiselle (€20).

**Veuve Clicquot Ponsardin**—Because it's widely exported in the US, Veuve Clicquot is inundated with American travelers. Reservations are required and fill up three weeks in advance, so book early (easy via email) before you start your trip. The basic *cave* visit includes a two-flute tasting; other options add on a glass of "La Grande Dame" or pair tastings with cheese.

**Cost and Hours:** €25 for 45-minute tour and tasting, €35 for one-hour tour and "La Grande Dame" Champagne, €90 for 2.5-hour tour and four tastings with cheese; mid-March-mid-Nov Tue-Sat 10:00-12:30 & 13:30-18:00, closed Sun-Mon and mid-

---

## Sleep Code

**(€1 = about $1.30, country code: 33)**
**S** = Single, **D** = Double/Twin, **T** = Triple, **Q** = Quad, **b** = bathroom, **s** = shower only, * = French hotel rating system (0-5 stars). Unless otherwise noted, English is spoken, credit cards are accepted, and breakfast is not included.

To help you easily sort through these listings, I've divided the accommodations into two categories based on the price for a standard double room with bath:

**$$** **Higher Priced**—Most rooms more than €100.

**$** **Lower Priced**—Most rooms €100 or less.

Prices can change without notice; verify the hotel's current rates online or by email.

---

Nov-mid-March; 1 Place des Droits de l'Homme, tel. 03 26 89 53 90, www.veuve-clicquot.com, visitscenter@veuve-clicquot.fr.

### Route de la Champagne
Drivers can joyride through the scenic and prestigious vineyards just south of Reims (the TI has maps). Follow D-9 south to Cormontreuil, then Louvois, then Bouzy, to see the chalky soil and rolling hills of vines that produce Champagne's costly wines. Some of the villages have small hotels if you'd like to sleep surrounded by vineyards, but plan ahead.

## Sleeping in Reims

The first two of my listings are on Place Drouet d'Erlon.

**$$ Grand Hôtel Continental\*\*\*** is a fine old hotel with well-priced, three-star comfort; stay-awhile public spaces; and helpful Maxeme at the desk. Rooms in the new wing are plush and modern, but smaller. Find the framed print of the original historic building before it became a hotel (standard Db-€98, "classic" Db-€129, "traditional" Db-€159-189, apartments for 3-8 available, ask about Rick Steves discount, request a nonsmoking room, air-con, elevator, laundry service, Wi-Fi, parking-€8, 5-minute walk from central train station at 93 Place Drouet d'Erlon, tel. 03 26 40 39 35, fax 03 26 47 51 12, www.grandhotelcontinental.com, reservation@grandhotelcontinental.com).

**$ Grand Hôtel du Nord\*\*** has a welcoming staff and delivers clean and modern comfort at fair rates in surprisingly quiet rooms, despite being right on the square (Sb-€60-70, Db-€70-110, Tb/

Qb-€110-150, free Wi-Fi, elevator, 75 Place Drouet d'Erlon, tel. 03 26 47 39 03, fax 03 26 40 92 26, www.hotel-nord-reims.com).

**$ Bénédicte et Claude Philippon Chambres d'Hôte** is a fine value and a lovely experience. This friendly couple offer two comfortable, homey, and centrally located rooms on Place du Chapitre (#21), 100 yards from the cathedral's north (left) transept. Look for the yellow *Chambres d'Hôte* sign (S-€50, D-€60, T-€75, €5 off for 2-night stays, cash only, includes French breakfast, shared bathroom, third floor with elevator, parking on square, tel. 03 26 91 06 22, mobile 06 77 76 20 13, claude.philippon@sfr.fr).

## Eating in Reims

This is a "meaty" city: Most menus will offer foie gras, raw *tartares* (mostly steak but some fish too), and some dishes you may choose to avoid, such as *rognons, ris de veau, tête de veau, pieds de porc*, and *boudin blanc* (kidneys, sweetbreads, calf's head, pig's feet, and meat sausage, respectively). Find good people-watching opportunities—if not high cuisine—with the scads of restaurants on Place Drouet d'Erlon. All of these recommendations make good lunch or dinner options.

**L'Apostrophe,** an appealing place with a snazzy and cozy interior, offers a well-presented, creative cuisine that draws a loyal clientele (€14-20 *plats,* €22 and €33 *menus,* look for specials, daily, 59 Place Drouet d'Erlon, tel. 03 26 79 19 89).

**Micro Brasserie les 3 Brasseurs** is a rollicking, Alsatian-flavored microbrewery with copper vats and a young, inviting feel. You'll get good brasserie fare and (rare in France) more beer than wine. There's free Wi-Fi with any order—even just a drink (€9-13 salads, €10-13 *plats,* €16 *choucroute,* daily, 73 Place Drouet d'Erlon, tel. 03 26 47 86 28).

**Brasserie du Boulingrin** is the oldest brasserie in town, gushing with Art Deco. A Reims institution, it serves traditional French cuisine (including fresh oysters and a seafood platter) at blue-collar prices (€15-22 *plats,* €18-25 *menus,* closed Sun; 10-minute walk from the Reims-Centre train station at 48 Rue de Mars, not far from the Porte de Mars, tel. 03 26 40 96 22).

**Café du Palais** is appreciated by older locals who don't mind paying a premium to eat a meal or sip coffee wrapped in 1930s ambience. Reims' most venerable café-bistro stands across from the Opéra (€34 *menus,* €20-30 *plats,* daily but closed for dinner Sun-Mon, 14 Place Myron Herrick, tel. 03 26 47 52 54).

**Bistrot du Forum,** an informal and locally popular bistro, has small wooden tables, a cool zinc bar, and view terrace tables. They serve excellent large salads, bruschetta, and burgers, as well as traditional meat and fish dishes (€12-20); check the blackboard for their good-value daily specials. You'll also find a good selection of wines (and Champagne, *bien sûr*) by the glass (daily, 6 Place Forum, tel. 03 26 47 56 58).

For cheap picnic fixings, head to the grocery store at Monoprix (see "Helpful Hints," page 626).

# Near Reims: Epernay

Champagne purists may want to visit Epernay, about 16 miles from Reims (and also well-connected to Paris). Epernay is most famously home to Moët et Chandon, which sits along Avenue de Champagne, the Rodeo Drive of grand Champagne houses.

**Arrival in Epernay:** Trains run frequently between Reims-Centre Station and Epernay (10/day, 30 minutes). From the Epernay train station, walk five minutes straight up Rue Gambetta to Place de la République, and take a left to find Avenue de Champagne. Moët et Chandon (described below) is at #20, and the TI is at #7 (mid-April-mid-Oct Mon-Sat 9:30-12:30 & 13:30-19:00, Sun 11:00-16:00; mid-Oct-mid-April Mon-Sat 9:30-12:30 & 13:30-17:30, closed Sun; tel. 03 26 53 33 00, www.ot-epernay.fr).

**Sights in Epernay:** The granddaddy of Champagne companies, Moët et Chandon offers one-hour tours with three pricey tasting possibilities (€17 for single taste, €24-30 for two tastes, no reservation needed, kids under 18 can join the tour for €11—but no tasting)—daily April-mid-Nov 9:30-11:30 & 14:00-16:30, closed weekends off-season, closed Jan, 20 Avenue de Champagne, tel. 03 26 51 20 20, www.moet.com, visites@moet.fr).

To sip a variety of different Champagnes from smaller producers, stop by the wine bar **C Comme Champagne** (meaning "C like Champagne"). Start with a peek in the wine cellar, then snuggle into an armchair and order by the taste, glass, or bottle. Ask about the ever-changing flight selections (daily 10:00-24:00, 8 Rue Gambetta, tel. 03 26 32 09 55).

*Sleeping in Epernay:* **$$ Hôtel Jean Moët\*\*\*** is a stylish boutique hotel with a cozy lounge, an inviting covered terrace, and 12 pleasant rooms with all the amenities. Ask about their "green" practices (Db-€140-190, suite-€230-270, air-con, free Wi-Fi, 7 Rue Jean Moët, tel. 03 26 32 19 22, fax 03 26 32 50 84, www. hoteljeanmoet.com, contact@hoteljeanmoet.com).

# FRANCE: PAST AND PRESENT

## French History

### Celts and Romans (52 B.C.-A.D. 500)

Julius Caesar conquered the Parisii, turning Paris from a tribal fishing village into a European city. The mix of Latin (southern) and Celtic (northern) cultures, with Paris right in the middle, defined the French character.

**Related Sights:** Cluny Museum (Roman baths), Louvre (Roman antiquities), Paris Archaeological Crypt (in front of Notre-Dame)

### Dark Ages (500-1000)

Roman Paris fell to German pirates ("Franks" = France), and later to the Vikings ("Norsemen" = Normans). During this turbulent time, Paris was just another island-state ("Ile de France") in the midst of many warring kingdoms. The lone bright spot was the reign of Charlemagne (A.D. 768-814), who briefly united the Franks, giving a glimpse of the modern nation-state of France.

**Related Sights:** Cluny Museum (artifacts), Statue of Charlemagne (near Notre-Dame)

### Border Wars with England (1066-1500)

In 1066, the Norman duke William the Conqueror invaded and conquered England. This united England, Normandy, and much of what is today western France; sparked centuries of border wars; and produced many kings of England who spoke French. In 1328 King Charles IV died without an heir, and the Norman king of England tried to claim the throne of France, which led to more than 100 years of Franco-Anglo battles, called the Hundred Years' War. Rallied by the teenage visionary Joan of Arc in 1429, the

French finally united north and south, and drove the English across the Channel in 1453. Modern France was born, with Paris as its capital.

**Related Sights:** Notre-Dame Cathedral, Sainte-Chapelle, Cluny Museum (tapestries), Carnavalet Museum, Sorbonne, Latin Quarter

## Renaissance and Religious Wars (1500s)

A strong, centralized France emerged, with French kings setting Europe's standard. François I made Paris a cultural capital, inviting Leonardo and Mona Lisa to visit. Catholics and Protestants fought openly, with 2,000 Parisians slaughtered in the St. Bartholomew's Day Massacre in 1572. The Wars of Religion subsided for a while when the first Bourbon king, Henry IV, took the throne in 1589 after converting to Catholicism. In 1598, he signed the Edict of Nantes, which instituted freedom of religious worship.

**Related Sights**: Louvre (palace and Renaissance art), Pont Neuf, Place des Vosges, Fontainebleau

## Louis XIV, the Absolute Monarch (1600s)

Louis XIV solidified his power, neutered the nobility, revoked the Edict of Nantes, and moved the capital to Versailles, which also became the center of European culture. France's wealth sparked "enlightened" ideas that became the seeds of democracy.

**Related Sights:** Versailles, Vaux-le-Vicomte, Hôtel des Invalides, paintings by Nicolas Poussin and Claude Lorrain

## Decadence and Revolution (1700s)

This was the age of Louis XV, Louis XVI, Marie-Antoinette, Voltaire, Jean-Jacques Rousseau, Maximilien de Robespierre, and Napoleon. A financial crunch from wars and royal excess drove the French people to revolt. On July 14, 1789, they stormed the Bastille. A couple of years later, the First French Republic arrested and then beheaded the king and queen. Thousands lost their heads— guillotined if suspected of hindering the Revolution's progress. A charismatic commoner promising stability rose amid the chaos: Napoleon Bonaparte.

**Related Sights:** Versailles, Place de la Concorde, Place de la Bastille, Conciergerie, paintings by Watteau, Boucher, Fragonard, and David (Louvre)

## Elected Emperors and Constitutional Kings (1800s)

Napoleon conquered Europe, crowned himself emperor, invaded Russia, was defeated on the battlefields of Waterloo, and ended up exiled to an island in the Atlantic. The monarchy was restored,

## Typical Church Architecture

History comes to life when you visit a centuries-old church. Even if you wouldn't know your apse from a hole in the ground, learning a few simple terms will enrich your experience. Note that not every church has every feature, and a "cathedral" isn't a type of church architecture, but rather a designation for a church that's a governing center for a local bishop.

**Aisles:** The long, generally low-ceilinged arcades that flank the nave.

**Altar:** The raised area with a ceremonial table (often adorned with candles or a crucifix), where the priest prepares and serves the bread and wine for Communion.

**Apse:** The space beyond the altar, generally bordered with small chapels.

**Barrel Vault:** A continuous round-arched ceiling that resembles an extended upside-down U.

**Choir:** A cozy area, often screened off, located within the church nave and near the high altar, where services are sung in a more intimate setting.

**Cloister:** Covered hallways bordering a usually square-shaped, open-air courtyard; traditionally where monks and nuns got fresh air.

**Facade:** The exterior surface of the church's main (west) entrance, generally highly decorated.

**Groin Vault:** An arched ceiling formed where two equal barrel

but rulers toed the democratic line—or were deposed in the popular uprisings of 1830 and 1848. The latter resulted in the Second French Republic, whose first president was Napoleon's nephew. He rewrote the constitution with himself as Emperor Napoleon III, and presided over a wealthy, middle-class nation with a colonial empire in slow decline. The disastrous Franco-Prussian War in 1870 ended his reign, leading to the Third Republic. France's political clout was fading, even as Paris remained the world's cultural center during the belle époque—the "beautiful age."

**Related Sights:** Arc de Triomphe, Baron Haussmann's wide boulevards, Eiffel Tower, Les Invalides and Napoleon's Tomb, Pont Alexandre III, Grand Palais, Petit Palais, Montmartre, Opéra Garnier, paintings by Ingres and Delacroix (Louvre), Impressionist and Post-Impressionist paintings (Manet, Monet, Renoir, Degas, Toulouse-Lautrec, Cézanne, and so on) at the Orsay, Marmottan, and Orangerie museums.

## War and Depression (1900-1950)

France began the turn of the 20th century as top dog, but two world wars with Germany (and the earlier Franco-Prussian War)

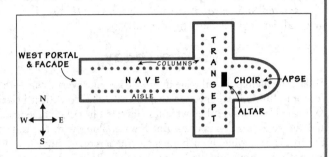

vaults meet at right angles. Less common usage: term for a medieval jock strap.

**Narthex:** The area (portico or foyer) between the main entry and the nave.

**Nave:** The long, central section of the church (running west to east, from the entrance to the altar) where the congregation sits or stands through the service.

**Transept:** In a traditional cross-shaped floor plan, the transept is one of the two parts forming the "arms" of the cross. The transepts run north-south, perpendicularly crossing the east-west nave.

**West Portal:** The main entry to the church (on the west end, opposite the main altar).

wasted the country. France lost millions of men in World War I, sank into an economic depression, and was easily overrun by Hitler in World War II. Paris, now dirt cheap, attracted foreign writers and artists.

This was the age of Pablo Picasso, Maurice Ravel, Claude Debussy, Erik Satie, Igor Stravinsky, Vaslav Nijinsky, Ernest Hemingway, F. Scott Fitzgerald, Gertrude Stein, Ezra Pound, Jean-Paul Sartre, Edith Piaf, and Maurice Chevalier.

**Related Sights:** Picasso Museum (closed for renovation until summer 2013), Deportation Memorial, Holocaust Memorial, Pompidou Center (art from this period)

## Postwar France (1950-Present)

After the war, France reestablished a democracy with the Fourth Republic. But France's colonial empire dissolved after bitter wars in Algeria and Vietnam, which helped mire an already unsteady government. Wartime hero Charles de Gaulle was brought back in 1958 to assist with France's regeneration. He rewrote the constitution, beginning the Fifth (and current) Republic. Immigrants from former colonies flooded Paris. The turbulent '60s, progressive '70s, socialist-turned-conservative '80s, and the middle-of-the-road '90s bring us to the *début de siècle,* or the beginning of the 21st century.

**Related Sights:** Montparnasse Tower, La Défense, Louvre's pyramid, Pompidou Center (modern art)

# France Today

Today, the main political issue in France is—like everywhere—the economy. Initially, France weathered the 2008 downturn better than the US, because they were less invested in risky home loans and the volatile stock market. But France, along with the rest of Europe, is struggling. French unemployment remains high (over 10 percent) and growth is flat-lining. Abroad, the entire eurozone is being dragged down by countries heavily in debt—Greece, Spain, Portugal, Italy, and Ireland. The challenge for French leadership is to address its economic problems while maintaining the level of social services that the French people expect from their government.

France is part of the 27-member European Union (or EU, a kind of "United States of Europe") that has successfully dissolved borders and implemented a single currency, the euro. France's governments have been decidedly pro-EU. But many French are Euroskeptics, afraid that EU meddling threatens their job security and social benefits.

Although France's economy may be one of the world's largest, the French remain skeptical about the virtues of capitalism and the work ethic. Business conversation is generally avoided, as it implies a fascination with money that the French find vulgar. (It's considered gauche even to ask what someone does for a living.) In France, CEOs are not glorified as celebrities—chefs are.

The French believe that the economy should support social good, not vice versa. This has produced a cradle-to-grave social security system of which the French are proud. France's poverty rate is half of that in the US, proof to the French that they are on the right track. On the other hand, if you're considering starting a business in France, think again—taxes are formidable (figure a total small-business tax rate of around 66 percent—and likely to increase). France is routinely plagued with strikes, demonstrations, and slowdowns as workers try to preserve their hard-earned rights in the face of a competitive global economy.

The French political scene is complex and fascinating. France is governed by a president (currently Francois Hollande), elected by popular vote every five years. The president then selects the prime minister, who in turn chooses the cabinet ministers. Collectively, this executive branch is known as the *gouvernement.* The parliament consists of a Senate (343 seats) and the 577-seat Assemblée Nationale.

In France, compromise and coalition-building are essential to keeping power. Unlike America's two-party system, France has a half-dozen major political parties, plus more on the fringes. A simple majority is rare. Even the biggest parties rarely get more than a third of the votes. Since the parliament can force the *gouvernement* to resign at any time, it's essential that the *gouvernement* work with them.

For a snapshot of the current political landscape, look no further than the 2012 presidential elections. The various parties all chose a candidate. Incumbent president Nicolas Sarkozy headed the center-right Popular Movement Union (UMP). He defended his tough-love, carrot-and-stick approach to dealing with the sluggish economy. During his tenure, he cut taxes, reduced the size of government, limited the power of unions, cut workers' benefits, and (most controversially) raised the retirement age from 60 to 62. He also offered tax incentives to those who worked overtime, meaning above the current 35- to 39-hour workweek. Sarkozy also had to defend his flamboyant, materialist, teetotaling lifestyle (which was often criticized as un-French). His wife is Carla Bruni, a sexy Italian model-turned-singer who had previously been linked romantically with the likes of Mick Jagger and Eric Clapton (and one of your co-authors). In 2011, Bruni made her big-screen debut with a blink-and-you'll-miss-her role in the Woody Allen film, *Midnight in Paris.*

Opposing Sarkozy were a host of left-leaning candidates. Francois Hollande, of the center-left Socialist Party (PS), pointed out that Sarkozy's austerity policies were not working. The more-radical Left Front Party (which includes the once-powerful Communists) proposed raising the minimum wage to $2,200 a month and establishing a "maximum wage" of $500,000, beyond which you pay 100 percent taxes. The environmental Green Party (Les Verts) promised to stimulate the economy with half a million new green jobs.

On the far-right was the National Front party (FN), led by Marine Le Pen, daughter of party founder Jean-Marie Le Pen. The FN campaigned on a "France for the French" platform, calling for expulsion of ethnic minorities, restoration of the French franc as the standard currency, secession from the EU, and broader police powers. Ms. Le Pen studiously avoided the kind of anti-Semitic, racist rants that have made her father notorious in France.

After several months and one TV debate (yes, the French election season is that short), François Hollande and the Socialists emerged victorious. And just a month after the presidential election, French voters returned to the polls to select all 577 seats of the Assemblée Nationale. Though it's almost unheard of for a single party to win an outright majority of seats, that's exactly what the

Socialists did, eking out just over 50 percent. Other leftist parties also scored well, giving President Hollande a leftist mandate for change. Nevertheless, Hollande has to work closely with legislators, a strong minority of whom are from opposing parties.

François Hollande is politically moderate and personally modest, even boring. Raised in a suburban Parisian middle-class home, he rose quietly through the ranks: assemblyman from a nondescript *department*, small-town mayor, secretary of the Socialist Party. He's never before held a major elected office. Though Hollande is a "Socialist" (a word that spooks Rush Limbaugh), he's in the mainstream of the European political spectrum. France's "First Lady" is Valerie Trierweiler, a well-known journalist who writes for the glossy magazine *Paris Match* (the French counterpart to *Time*). The first couple is unmarried, and Trierweiler is the first unwed first lady to occupy the Elysée Palace (French White House). *Oh-la-la*—imagine that in your country.

Hollande faces huge challenges. On the sluggish economy, he favors government stimulus rather than austerity: hiring thousands of teachers, building hundreds of thousands of homes, and taxing all income above a million euros at 75 percent. Abroad, he's working closely with Germany to shore up weaker members of the eurozone. One of his first acts in office was to return the retirement age (at least for some workers) to 60.

France must also address immigration, which is shifting the country's ethnic and cultural makeup. Ten percent of France's population is of North African descent, mainly immigrants from former colonies. The increased number of Muslims raises more questions, particularly in tight economic times. The French have (controversially) made it illegal for women to wear a full, face-covering veil *(niqāb)* in public. They continue to debate whether banning the veil enforces democracy—or squelches diversity.

Finally, Hollande must deal with high-profile members of his own turbulent party. In the run-up to the 2012 election, the front-runner was Dominique Strauss-Kahn. He was forced to drop out after being accused of sexual assault in New York City. All charges were later dropped, but the damage was done. (Strauss-Kahn has speculated he was framed by political rivals, and many in France would not find that fanciful.)

Another prominent Socialist is Ségolène Royal. She lost to Sarkozy in 2007, and lost to Hollande in the 2011 primary. As it happens, Royal and Hollande know each other well: They met in college, lived together for 30 years, and raised four children before splitting up in 2007. They never married. French politics makes strange bedfellows.

# APPENDIX

## Contents

## Tourist Information

The website of the French national tourist office, www.franceguide. com, is a wealth of information, with particularly good resources for special-interest travel, and plenty of free-to-download brochures. Paris' official TI website, www.parisinfo.com, offers practical information on hotels, special events, museums, children's activities, fashion, nightlife, and more. (For other useful websites, see page 29.)

TIs are good places to get a city map and information on public transit (including bus and train schedules), walking tours, special events, and nightlife. Unfortunately, Paris' network of TIs—scattered at key locations throughout the city—are otherwise only minimally helpful (for details, see page 28).

While TIs are eager to book you a room, use their room-finding service only as a last resort. They are unable to give hard opinions on the relative value of one place over another. The accommodations stakes are too high to go potluck through the TI. Even if there's no "fee," you'll save yourself and your host money by going direct with the listings in this book.

# Communicating

## Telephones

Smart travelers use the telephone to reserve or reconfirm rooms, get tourist information, reserve restaurants, confirm tour times, or phone home. When spelling out your name on the phone, you'll find that some letters are pronounced differently in French: *a* is pronounced "ah," *e* is pronounced "uh," and *i* is pronounced "ee." To avoid confusion, say "*a*, Anne," "*e*, euro," and "*i*, Isabelle."

This section covers dialing instructions, phone cards, and types of phones (for more in-depth information, see www.rick steves.com/phoning).

### How to Dial

Calling from the US to France, or vice versa, is simple—once you break the code. The European calling chart in this chapter will walk you through it.

#### Dialing Domestically Within France

France has a direct-dial 10-digit phone system (no area codes). To make domestic calls anywhere within France, just dial the number.

For example, the number of one of my recommended hotels in Paris (the Hôtel Relais Bosquet) is 01 47 05 25 45. That's the number you dial whether you're calling it from across the street or across the country.

If you're dialing within France using your US mobile phone, you may need to dial as if it's a domestic call, or you may need to dial as if you're calling from the US (see "Dialing Internationally," next). Try it one way, and if it doesn't work, try it the other way.

Understand the various prefixes. All Paris landline numbers start with 01. Any number beginning with 06 or 07 is a mobile phone, and costs more to dial. France's toll-free numbers start with 0800 (like US 800 numbers, though in France you dial a 0 first rather than a 1). In France these 0800 numbers—called *numéro vert* (green number)—can be dialed free from any phone without using a phone card. But you can't call France's toll-free numbers from America, nor can you count on reaching US toll-free numbers from France.

Any 08 number that does not have a 00 directly following is a toll call, generally costing €0.10 to €0.50 per minute.

## Dialing Internationally to or from France

If you want to make an international call, follow these steps:

• Dial the international access code (00 if you're calling from Europe, 011 from the US or Canada). If you're dialing from a mobile phone, you can replace the international access code with +, which works regardless of where you're calling from. (On many mobile phones, you can insert a + by pressing and holding the 0 key.)

• Dial the country code of the country you're calling (33 for France, or 1 for the US or Canada).

• Dial the local number. If you're calling France, drop the initial zero of the phone number. (The European calling chart lists specifics per country.)

**Calling from the US to France:** To call the Hôtel Relais Bosquet from the US, dial 011 (the US international access code), 33 (France's country code), then 1 47 05 25 45 (the hotel's number without its initial zero).

**Calling from any European country to the US:** To call my office in Edmonds, Washington, from anywhere in Europe, I dial 00 (Europe's access code), 1 (the US country code), 425 (Edmonds' area code), and 771-8303.

## Mobile Phones

Traveling with a mobile phone is handy and practical. Whether you're using a smartphone or a conventional cell phone, the basics for how to make calls and send texts is the same. For specifics on using your smartphone to get online, see the sidebar.

**Roaming with Your Mobile Phone:** Your US mobile phone works in Europe if it's GSM-enabled, tri-band or quad-band, and on a calling plan that includes international calls. Phones from AT&T and T-Mobile, which use the same GSM technology that Europe does, are more likely to work overseas than Verizon or Sprint phones (if you're not sure, ask your service provider). Most US providers will charge you $1.29-$1.99 per minute to make or receive calls while roaming internationally, and 20-50 cents to send or receive text messages. If you bother to sign up for an international calling plan with your provider, you'll save a few dimes per minute. Though pricey, roaming on your own phone is easy and can be a cost-effective way to keep in touch—especially on a short trip or if you won't be making many calls.

**Buying and Using SIM Cards in Europe:** You'll pay much cheaper rates if you put a European SIM card in your mobile phone; to do this, your phone must be electronically "unlocked" (ask your provider about this, buy an unlocked phone before you leave, or get one in Europe—see "Other Mobile-Phone Options," next). Then, in Europe, you can buy a fingernail-size **SIM card,** which gives you

## European Calling Chart

Just smile and dial, using this key:
AC = Area Code, LN = Local Number.

| European Country | Calling long distance within ... | Calling from the US or Canada to ... | Calling from a European country to ... |
|---|---|---|---|
| Austria | AC + LN | 011 + 43 + AC (without the initial zero) + LN | 00 + 43 + AC (without the initial zero) + LN |
| Belgium | LN | 011 + 32 + LN (without initial zero) | 00 + 32 + LN (without initial zero) |
| Bosnia-Herzegovina | AC + LN | 011 + 387 + AC (without initial zero) + LN | 00 + 387 + AC (without initial zero) + LN |
| Britain | AC + LN | 011 + 44 + AC (without initial zero) + LN | 00 + 44 + AC (without initial zero) + LN |
| Croatia | AC + LN | 011 + 385 + AC (without initial zero) + LN | 00 + 385 + AC (without initial zero) + LN |
| Czech Republic | LN | 011 + 420 + LN | 00 + 420 + LN |
| Denmark | LN | 011 + 45 + LN | 00 + 45 + LN |
| Estonia | LN | 011 + 372 + LN | 00 + 372 + LN |
| Finland | AC + LN | 011 + 358 + AC (without initial zero) + LN | 999 (or other 900 number) + 358 + AC (without initial zero) + LN |
| France | LN | 011 + 33 + LN (without initial zero) | 00 + 33 + LN (without initial zero) |
| Germany | AC + LN | 011 + 49 + AC (without initial zero) + LN | 00 + 49 + AC (without initial zero) + LN |
| Gibraltar | LN | 011 + 350 + LN | 00 + 350 + LN |
| Greece | LN | 011 + 30 + LN | 00 + 30 + LN |
| Hungary | 06 + AC + LN | 011 + 36 + AC + LN | 00 + 36 + AC + LN |
| Ireland | AC + LN | 011 + 353 + AC (without initial zero) + LN | 00 + 353 + AC (without initial zero) + LN |

| European Country | Calling long distance within ... | Calling from the US or Canada to ... | Calling from a European country to ... |
|---|---|---|---|
| Italy | LN | 011 + 39 + LN | 00 + 39 + LN |
| Montenegro | AC + LN | 011 + 382 + AC (without initial zero) + LN | 00 + 382 + AC (without initial zero) + LN |
| Morocco | LN | 011 + 212 + LN (without initial zero) | 00 + 212 + LN (without initial zero) |
| Netherlands | AC + LN | 011 + 31 + AC (without initial zero) + LN | 00 + 31 + AC (without initial zero) + LN |
| Norway | LN | 011 + 47 + LN | 00 + 47 + LN |
| Poland | LN | 011 + 48 + LN | 00 + 48 + LN |
| Portugal | LN | 011 + 351 + LN | 00 + 351 + LN |
| Slovakia | AC + LN | 011 + 421 + AC (without initial zero) + LN | 00 + 421 + AC (without initial zero) + LN |
| Slovenia | AC + LN | 011 + 386 + AC (without initial zero) + LN | 00 + 386 + AC (without initial zero) + LN |
| Spain | LN | 011 + 34 + LN | 00 + 34 + LN |
| Sweden | AC + LN | 011 + 46 + AC (without initial zero) + LN | 00 + 46 + AC (without initial zero) + LN |
| Switzerland | LN | 011 + 41 + LN (without initial zero) | 00 + 41 + LN (without initial zero) |
| Turkey | AC (if there's no initial zero, add one) + LN | 011 + 90 + AC (without initial zero) + LN | 00 + 90 + AC (without initial zero) + LN |

APPENDIX

- The instructions above apply whether you're calling to or from a European landline or mobile phone.

- If calling from any mobile phone, you can replace the international access code with "+" (press and hold 0 to insert it).

- The international access code is 011 if you're calling from the US or Canada.

- To call the US or Canada from Europe, dial 00, then 1 (country code for US and Canada), then the area code and number. In short, 00 + 1 + AC + LN = Hi, Mom!

a European phone number. SIM cards are sold at mobile-phone stores, post offices, and some newsstand kiosks for $5-10, and often include at least that much prepaid domestic calling time (making the card itself virtually free). When you buy a SIM card, you may need to show ID, such as your passport.

Insert the SIM card in your phone (usually in a slot behind the battery or on the side), and it'll work like a European mobile phone. Before purchasing a SIM card, always ask about fees for domestic and international calls, roaming charges, and how to check your credit balance and buy more time. This can be tricky to accomplish if you don't speak some French, but the major mobile phone companies—SFR and Orange—usually have English-speaking staff at their stores. (Also, be aware that prompts for voice mail or topping up the card are in French.) When you're in the SIM card's home country, domestic calls average 10 to 20 cents per minute, and incoming calls are free. Rates are higher if you're roaming in another country, and you may pay more to call a toll number than you'd pay to dial it from a fixed line.

**Other Mobile-Phone Options:** Many travelers like to carry two phones: both their own US mobile phone (allowing them to stay reachable on their own phone number) and a second, unlocked European phone (which lets them do all their local calling at far cheaper rates). You could either bring two phones from home, or get one in Europe. If you have an old mobile phone sitting around, ask your provider for the "unlock code" so it can be used with European SIM cards. Or buy a cheap, basic phone before you go (search your favorite online shopping site for "unlocked quad-band GSM phone"). In Europe, basic phones are sold at hole-in-the-wall vendors at many airports and train stations, and at phone desks within larger department stores. Phones that are "locked" to work with a single provider start around $40; "unlocked" phones (which work with any SIM card) start around $60. Regardless of how you get your phone, remember that you'll need a SIM card to make it work.

Car-rental companies and mobile-phone companies offer the option to rent a mobile phone with a European number. While this seems convenient, hidden fees (such as high per-minute charges or expensive shipping costs) can really add up—which usually makes it a bad value. One exception is Verizon's Global Travel Program, available only to Verizon customers.

## Calling over the Internet

Some things that seem too good to be true...actually are true. If you're traveling with a laptop, tablet, or smartphone, you can make free calls over the Internet to another wireless device, anywhere in the world, for free. (Or you can pay a few cents to call from your computer to a telephone.) The major providers are Skype, Google

Talk, and (on Apple devices) FaceTime (all available free for both computers and tablets/smartphones). You can get online at a Wi-Fi hotspot and use these apps to make calls without ringing up expensive roaming charges (though call quality can be spotty on slow connections). You can make Internet calls even if you're traveling without your own mobile device: Many European Internet cafés have Skype, as well as microphones and webcams, on their terminals—just log on and chat away.

## Landline Telephones
As in the US, these days most French do the majority of their phoning on mobile phones. But you'll still encounter landlines in hotel rooms and at pay phones.

**Hotel-Room Phones:** Calling from your hotel room can be great for local calls and for international calls if you have an international phone card (described later). Otherwise, hotel-room phones can be an almost criminal rip-off for long-distance or international calls. Many hotels charge a fee for local and sometimes even "toll-free" numbers—always ask for the rates before you dial. Incoming calls are free, making this a cheap way for friends and family to stay in touch (provided they have a long-distance plan with good international rates—and a list of your hotels' phone numbers).

**Public Pay Phones:** Coin-op phones are virtually extinct in Europe. To make calls from public phones, you'll need a prepaid phone card, described next.

## Types of Telephone Cards
There are two types of phone cards: insertable (for pay phones) and international (cheap for overseas calls and usable from any type of phone). Both types of phone card work only in France. If you have a live card at the end of your trip, give it to another traveler to use—most cards expire 3-6 months after the first use.

**Insertable Phone Cards:** Called *télécartes* (tay-lay-kart), these cards are handy and affordable for local and domestic calls from a phone booth. (Though you can use *télécartes* to call anywhere in the world, they're a bad value for international calls.) They're sold in two denominations—*une petite* costs €7.50; *une grande* €15—at *tabacs* (tobacco shops), newsstands, post offices, and train stations. To use the card, insert it into a slot in the pay phone. Push the flag button on the phone to change the display until you see English, and follow instructions.

**International Phone Cards:** With a *carte international*, phone calls from France to the US can cost less than a nickel a minute. The cards can also be used to make local calls, and they work from any type of phone, including your hotel-room phone or a mobile

# Smartphones and Data Roaming

I take my smartphone to Europe, using it to make phone calls (sparingly) and send texts, but also to check email, listen to audio tours, and browse the Internet. If you're clever, you can do all this without incurring huge fees. Here's how.

Many smartphones, such as the iPhone, Android, and BlackBerry, work in Europe (though some older Verizon iPhones don't). For voice calls and text messaging, smartphones work like any mobile phone (as described under "Using Your Mobile Phone," earlier)—unless you're connected to free Wi-Fi, in which case you can use Skype, Google Talk, or FaceTime to call for free (or at least very cheaply; see "Calling over the Internet," below).

Of course, smartphones also let you get online. This can be handy for keeping in touch, looking up restaurants or concerts, and checking train or bus schedules. To access the Internet with your smartphone, you have two options: Find a Wi-Fi hotspot (see "Internet Access," later), or use your phone for data roaming.

You may have heard horror stories about exorbitant data roaming bills. But avoiding excessive charges is easy: If you know you'll want to access the Internet beyond hotspots, simply call your carrier (or go on their website) before your trip and sign up for an international data roaming plan. Data roaming is always substantially more affordable with a prearranged plan. For example, if you try data roaming without a plan, you'll pay exorbitant rates of about $20 per megabyte

---

phone with a European SIM card. To use the card, dial a toll-free access number, then enter your scratch-to-reveal PIN code.

You can buy the cards at newsstand kiosks and tobacco shops. Ask the clerk for a *"carte international pour les Etats-Unis"* (for the US; cart an-tehr-nah-see-oh-nahl poor lay-zay-tah-oo-nee). Buy a lower denomination in case the card is a dud. Some shops also sell cardless codes, printed right on the receipt.

To make a call, dial the free (usually 4-digit) access number. If the access code on the card doesn't work from your hotel-room phone, try the card's 10-digit, toll-free code that starts with 08. Either way, a voice in French (followed by English) tells you to enter your (usually 12-digit) code. Before or after entering your code, you'll probably need to press (or *touche*, pronounced toosh) the pound key (#, *dièse*, dee-ehz) or the star key (*, *étoile*, ay-twahl). At the next message, dial the number you're calling (possibly followed by pound or star key; you don't have to listen to the entire sales pitch).

Since you don't need the actual card or receipt to use the ac-

(that's around 40 cents per email downloaded, or about $3 to view a typical web page). If you have a plan, the price is closer to 25-50 cents per megabyte (fees vary by carrier).

If data roaming, here are some tips for keeping your costs down: Use free Wi-Fi when possible, and turn on data roaming only when you can't find a hotspot. Manually turn data roaming on and off with each use (look for this under the "Network" settings) to avoid roaming unwittingly when you don't need it. Switch your email settings from "push" to "fetch," so you can choose when to download your emails rather than having them automatically "pushed" over the Internet to your device. Be very clear on your data roaming plan's megabyte limit to avoid inflated overage charges, and be sure to deactivate the plan when you get back  (or set it up to automatically deactivate on your return date). Ask your provider in advance how to keep your data roaming costs reasonable.

Some travelers would rather not bother with data roaming at all. If that's you, simply disable data roaming on your phone (again, under the "Network" settings), and get online only when you find free Wi-Fi (at your hotel, for example). For added security, you can call and ask your service provider to temporarily suspend your data account entirely for the length of your trip.

One way or another, smart travelers are using smartphones to travel more...smartly.

count, you can write down the access number and code and share it with friends.

**US Calling Cards:** These cards, such as the ones offered by AT&T, Verizon, and Sprint, are a rotten value, and are being phased out. Try any of the options outlined earlier.

## Internet Access

It's useful to get online periodically as you travel—to confirm trip plans, check train or bus schedules, get weather forecasts, catch up on email, blog or post photos from your trip, or call folks back home (explained earlier, under "Calling over the Internet").

**Your Mobile Device:** The majority of accommodations in Paris offer Wi-Fi (pronounced "wee-fee" in French), as do many cafés, making it easy for you to get online with your laptop, tablet, or smartphone. Access is often free, but sometimes there's a fee.

Some hotel rooms and Internet cafés have high-speed Internet jacks that you can plug into with an Ethernet cable. A cellular modem—which lets your device access the Internet over a mobile network—provides more extensive coverage, but is much more expensive than Wi-Fi.

**Public Internet Terminals:** Many accommodations offer a computer in the lobby with Internet access for guests. If you ask politely, smaller places may let you sit at their desk for a few minutes just to check your email. If your hotelier doesn't have access, ask to be directed to the nearest place to get online. In small towns outside of Paris, post offices may offer Internet access *(cyberposte)*; buy a chip-card (about the same prices as phone cards) and you're in business.

**Security:** Whether you're accessing the Internet with your own device or at a public terminal, using a shared network or computer comes with the potential for increased security risks. Be careful about storing personal information online, such as passport and credit-card numbers. If you're not convinced a connection is secure, avoid accessing any sites that could be vulnerable to fraud (e.g., online banking).

## Mail

You can mail one package per day to yourself worth up to $200 duty-free from Europe to the US (mark it "personal purchases"). If you're sending a gift to someone, mark it "unsolicited gift." For details, visit www.cbp.gov and search for "Know Before You Go."

The French postal service works fine, but for quick transatlantic delivery (in either direction), consider services such as DHL (www.dhl.com). French post offices are sometimes called PTT, for "Post, Telegraph, and Telephone"—look for signs for *La Poste*. Hours vary, though most are open weekdays 8:00-19:00 and Saturday morning 8:00-12:00. Stamps and phone cards are also sold at *tabacs*. It costs about €1 to mail a postcard to the US. One convenient, if expensive, way to send packages home is by using the PTT's Colissimo XL postage-paid mailing box. It costs €36-45 to ship boxes weighing 5-7 kilos (about 11-15 pounds).

## Local and Emergency Contacts

For tips on making calls, including specifics on dialing toll-free service numbers, see "How to Dial" on page 646.

### Emergency Needs

**Police:** Tel. 17
**Emergency Medical Assistance** (called "SAMU"): Tel. 15
**American Hospital:** Tel. 01 46 41 25 25 (63 Boulevard Victor Hugo, in Neuilly suburb, Mo: Porte Maillot, then bus #82)
**Ambulance:** Tel. 01 45 67 50 50 (message asks for your address and name)
**English-Speaking Pharmacy** (Pharmacie les Champs): Tel. 01

45 62 02 41, open 24 hours every day of the year (84 Avenue des Champs-Elysées, Mo: Georges V)

**English-Speaking Doctors:** For a good list, search on the US embassy's website: http://france.usembassy.gov

**SOS Doctors:** Tel. 01 47 07 77 77 (house calls to hotels or homes, usually €50-70)

**SOS Help:** Tel. 01 46 21 46 46 (anonymous telephone hotline with crisis/suicide prevention listening service in English, daily 15:00-23:00)

**SOS Dentist:** Tel. 01 43 37 51 00 or 01 42 46 11 20

**The American Chiropractic Center:** Tel. 01 45 51 38 38, open Mon-Sat (119 Rue de l'Université, Mo: Invalides, www.chiropractique .com)

**Lost Property** (Bureau des Objets Trouvés, at police station): Tel. 01 45 31 14 80; open Mon-Fri 8:30-17:00, Tue and Thu until 20:00 (36 Rue des Morillons, Mo: Convention, on south end of line 12)

**Collect Calls to the US:** Tel. 00 00 11

### Embassies and Consulates

**US Consulate and Embassy:** Tel. 01 43 12 22 22, (4 Avenue Gabriel, to the left as you face Hôtel Crillon, Mo: Concorde, http:// france.usembassy.gov)

**Canadian Consulate and Embassy:** Tel. 01 44 43 29 00, (35 Avenue Montaigne, Mo: Franklin D. Roosevelt, www.amb-canada. fr). For 24/7 emergency assistance, call collect to tel. 613/996-8885 or email sos@international.gc.ca

**Australian Consulate:** Tel. 01 40 59 33 00 (4 Rue Jean Rey, Mo: Bir-Hakeim, www.france.embassy.gov.au)

### Travel Advisories

**US Department of State:** Tel. 888-407-4747, from outside US tel. 1-202-501-4444, www.travel.state.gov

**Canadian Department of Foreign Affairs:** Canadian tel. 800-267-8376, from outside Canada tel. 1-613-996-8885, www.voyage. gc.ca

**US Centers for Disease Control and Prevention:** Tel. 800-CDC-INFO (800-232-4636), www.cdc.gov/travel

### Tourist Info, Transportation, and Hotels

**Paris Webservices Booking Service** (for hotels, transportation, restaurants, and other tourist activities): Tel. 09 52 06 02 59 (12 Rue de l'Exposition, Mo: Ecole Militaire, RER: Pont de l'Alma, www. pariswebservices.com, contactpws@pariswebservices.com, helpful Gérard)

**G7 Taxis:** Tel. 01 47 39 47 39, www.taxisg7.fr

APPENDIX

## Airports
**Charles de Gaulle and Orly:** Tel. 3950 from French landlines (€0.34/min); from the US dial 011 33 1 70 36 39 50; www.adp.fr
**Beauvais** (serves budget European airlines such as Ryanair, Wizz Air, and Blue Air): Tel. 08 92 68 20 66, www.aeroportbeauvais. com

## Airlines
**Aer Lingus:** Tel. 08 21 23 02 67 (answered Mon-Fri 9:00-17:00)
**Air Canada:** Tel. 08 25 88 08 81 (daily 7:30-15:00)
**Air France:** Tel. 3654 (daily 6:30-22:00)
**Alitalia:** Tel. 08 92 65 56 55 (Mon-Fri 8:00-20:00, Sat-Sun 9:00-19:00)
**American Airlines:** Tel. 08 26 46 09 50 (Mon-Fri 8:00-20:00, Sat-Sun 9:30-18:00)
**Austrian Airlines:** Tel. 08 20 81 68 16 (daily 8:00-20:00)
**British Airways:** Tel. 08 25 82 54 00 (Mon-Fri 9:00-18:00, Sat 9:00-14:00)
**Delta:** Tel. 08 92 70 26 09
**Easy Jet:** Tel. 08 20 42 03 15 (Mon-Fri 8:00-20:00, Sat-Sun 9:00-17:00)
**Iberia:** Tel. 08 25 80 09 65 (24/7)
**Icelandair:** Tel. 01 44 51 60 51
**KLM:** Tel. 08 92 70 26 08
**Lufthansa:** Tel. 08 92 23 16 90 (24/7)
**Royal Air Maroc:** Tel. 08 20 82 18 21
**SAS:** Tel. 08 25 32 53 35 (Mon-Fri 9:00-17:00)
**Swiss International:** Tel. 08 92 23 25 01
**United:** Tel. 08 10 72 72 72 (Mon-Fri 8:00-20:00, Sat-Sun 9:30-18:00)
**US Airways:** Tel. 08 10 63 22 22

## Hotel Chains
**Accor Hotels** (huge chain, including Ibis, Mercure, and Novotel): US tel. 800-221-4542, www.accorhotels.com
**Ibis Hotels:** www.ibishotel.com, tel. 08 92 68 66 86, US tel. 800-221-4542
**Mercure Hotels:** www.mercure.com, tel. 08 25 88 33 33, US tel. 800-221-4542
**Kyriad Hotels:** www.kyriad.com, from US, dial 011 33 1 64 62 59 70
**Best Western Hotels:** www.bestwestern.com, US tel. 800-780-7234
**Country Home Rental:** www.gites-de-france.com or www.gite. com

**Youth Hostels**

Hostelling International, US Office: www.hiayh.org

Hostelling International, Canada Office: www.hostellingintl.ca

## English-Language Churches in Paris

**American Church** (interdenominational): Tel. 01 40 62 05 00, reception open Mon-Sat 9:30-13:00 & 14:00-22:00, Sun 14:30-19:00 (65 Quai d'Orsay, Mo: Invalides, www.acparis.org; for more information, see page 29)

**American Cathedral** (Episcopalian): Tel. 01 53 23 84 00 (23 Avenue George V, Mo: George V, www.americancathedral.org)

**Unitarian Universalist Fellowship:** www.uufp.info

**Scots Kirk** (Church of Scotland): Tel. 01 40 70 09 59 (17 Rue Bayard, Mo: Franklin D. Roosevelt, www.scotskirkparis.com)

**St. George's Anglican Church:** Tel. 01 47 20 22 51 (7 Rue Auguste Vacquerie, Mo: George V or Kleber, www.stgeorgesparis. com)

**St. Joseph's Church** (Roman Catholic): Tel. 01 42 27 28 56 (50 Avenue Hoche, Mo: Etoile, www.stjoeparis.org)

**St. Michael's Church** (Anglican): Tel. 01 47 42 70 88 (5 Rue d'Aguesseau, Mo: Concorde or Madeleine, www.saintmichael-sparis.org)

# Activities

## Classes
### Multi-Subject Classes

**WICE** offers a variety of well-run short- and longer-term classes in English on art, wine, food, and more (joining fee required, 20 Boulevard du Montparnasse, tel. 01 45 66 75 50, www.wice-paris. org).

### French-Language Classes

**Alliance Francaise** has the best reputation and good variety of courses, but also the highest rates; can also help with accommodations (101 Boulevard Raspail, tel. 01 42 84 90 00, www.alliancefr. org).

**Ecole France Langue** provides intensive classes on weekly basis with business-language options (tel. 01 45 00 40 15, www. france-langue.fr).

**Institut Parisien** offers general conversational courses with a maximum of 10 students (tel. 01 42 66 18 08, www.institut-parisien .com).

**Le Français Face à Face** runs intensive French courses with total immersion and full-board options in the town of Angers, in the Loire Valley (tel. 06 66 60 00 63, www.lefrancaisfaceaface. com).

## Cooking Schools and Tours

**Le Cordon Bleu** (tel. 01 53 68 22 50, www.lcbparis.com) and **Ritz Escoffier Ecole de Gastronomie** (tel. 01 43 16 30 50, www.ritz paris.com) have pricey demonstration courses.

These schools are more relaxed:

**La Cuisine Paris** has a great variety of classes in English, reasonable prices, and a beautiful space in central Paris (2-hour classes–€65-90, 4-hour class with market tour–€150, 89 Boulevard St. Michel, tel. 01 40 51 78 18, www.lacuisineparis.com).

**Marguerite's Cooking Courses** offers morning classes with market visits or evening classes with cheese tastings in western suburb of Paris (tel. 01 42 04 74 00, www.elegantcooking.com)

**Cook'n with Class** has convivial cooking and wine-and-cheese classes with a maximum of six students; tasting courses offered as well (located north of Montmartre at 21 Rue Custine, tel. 06 31 73 62 77, www.cooknwithclass.com).

**Susan Herrmann Loomis,** an acclaimed chef and author, offers cooking courses in Paris or at her home in Normandy (tel. 09 51 14 38 94, www.onruetatin.com).

**Edible Paris,** run by Friendly Canadian Rosa Jackson, puts together personalized "foodie" itineraries, and pre-set three-hour "food guru" tours of Paris (www.edible-paris.com).

The chefs at **Le Violon d'Ingres,** the restaurant run by famous restaurateur Christian Constant, also teach cooking classes (see page 439).

## Wine Tasting

I like the friendly sommeliers of **Ô Château** (see page 36 for listing).

## Long-Range Day Trips from Paris

While I don't recommend it, you could arrange longer day trips from Paris to places around northern France, such as the Loire Valley, Burgundy, Mont St-Michel, and the D-Day beaches of Normandy (all beyond the scope of this book, but well-covered in *Rick Steves' France*). Thanks to bullet trains and good local guides who can help you maximize your time, well-coordinated blitz-tour trips to these places are doable, though hardly relaxing. If you do want to see these places in a day, I recommend using a guide from the region who will meet you at the train station (most have cars) and spend the day showing you their region's highlights before making sure you get on your return train to Paris. Book well in advance, though last-minute requests can work out.

**Loire Valley:** Pascal Accolay runs **Acco-Dispo,** which offers good all-day château tours from the cities of Tours or Amboise (from Tours: €21/half-day, €52/day, more if from Amboise; daily, tel. 06 82 00 64 51, www.accodispo-tours.com).

**Burgundy:** For the town of Beaune, contact Canadian **Sarah Bird,** whose tours can include a sample of nearby vineyards and countryside by request (tours available by bike, foot, or car; about €100/1.5 hours, €250/half-day, tel. 03 80 22 06 03, sarah@detours-in-france.com). For tours that focus on vineyards, contact **Colette Barbier** (€230/half-day, €390/day, tel. 03 80 23 94 34, mobile 06 80 57 47 40, www.burgundy-guide.com, cobatour@aol.com), or, for a more youthful perspective, her daughter **Emma** (tel. 06 83 43 50 78 http://burgundy-winetour.e-monsite.com).

**Mont St-Michel and Brittany: Westcapades** runs day-long minivan tours covering St-Malo and Mont St-Michel (€85/day, tel. 02 96 39 79 52, www.westcapades.com, marc@westcapades.com).

**D-Day Beaches by Minivan Tour:** An army of small companies offers all-day excursions to the D-Day beaches from Bayeux or Caen for about €90 per person, or about €475-500 for groups of up to eight, or about €350 to join you in your car (most don't visit museums, but those that do usually include entry fees—ask). **Paul Woodage** is a historian's dream (www.ddayhistorian.com). **Normandy Battle Tours** are led by Stuart Robertson, a gentle Brit who loves teaching visitors about the landings (tel. 02 33 41 28 34, www.normandybattletours.com, enquiries@normandybattletours.com). **Nigel Stewart** is a low-key yet very capable British guide (mobile 06 71 55 51 30, www.dday-guide.com, nigel.normandy@gmail.com). **Victory Tours** offers informal and entertaining tours led by friendly Dutchman Roel (departs from Bayeux only, tel. 02 31 51 98 14, fax 02 72 68 61 66, www.victorytours.com, victorytours@orange.fr). **Normandy Sightseeing Tours** delivers a French perspective (tel. 02 31 51 70 52, fax 02 31 51 74 74, www.normandywebguide.com, fredericguerin@wanadoo.fr). The **Caen Memorial Museum's** "D-Day Tour" package is designed for day-trippers and includes pickup from the Caen train station (with frequent service from Paris), a guided tour through the WWII exhibits at the Memorial Museum, lunch, and then a five-hour afternoon tour in English (and French) of the major Anglo-Canadian beaches. Your day ends with a drop-off at the Caen train station in time to catch a train back to Paris or elsewhere (€111, includes English information book, tel. 02 31 06 06 44—as in June 6, 1944, fax 02 31 06 06 70, www.memorial-caen.fr).

# Resources

## Resources from Rick Steves

*Rick Steves' Paris 2013* is one of many books in my series on European travel, which includes country guidebooks (including France), regional guides (including Provence and the French Riviera), city guides (Rome, Florence, London, etc.), Snapshot guides (excerpted chapters from my country guides), Pocket Guides (full-color little books on big cities, including Paris), and my budget-travel skills handbook, *Rick Steves' Europe Through the Back Door*. Most of my titles are available as ebooks. My phrase books—for French, Italian, German, Spanish, and Portu-

guese—are practical and budget-oriented. My other books include *Europe 101* (a crash course on art and history), *Mediterranean Cruise Ports* (how to make the most of your time in port), and *Travel as a Political Act* (a travelogue sprinkled with tips for bringing home a global perspective). A more complete list of my titles appears near the end of this book.

**Video:** My public television series, *Rick Steves' Europe,* covers European destinations in 100 shows, with nine episodes on France. To watch episodes online, visit www.hulu.com; for scripts and local airtimes, see www.ricksteves.com/tv.

**Audio:** My weekly public radio show, *Travel with Rick Steves,*

features interviews with travel experts from around the world. I've also produced free, self-guided audio tours of the top sights in Paris. All of this audio content is available for free at Rick Steves Audio Europe, an extensive online library organized by destination. Choose whatever interests you, and download it for free via the Rick Steves Audio Europe smartphone app, www.ricksteves.com/audioeurope, iTunes, or Google Play.

## Maps

The black-and-white maps in this book are concise and simple, designed to help you locate recommended places and get to local TIs, where you can pick up more in-depth maps of cities and regions (usually free).

Though Paris is littered with free maps, they don't show all

# Begin Your Trip at www.ricksteves.com

At ricksteves.com, you'll discover a wealth of free information on European destinations, including fresh monthly news and helpful tips from thousands of fellow travelers. You'll find my latest guidebook updates (www.ricksteves.com/update), a monthly travel e-newsletter (easy and free to sign up), my personal travel blog, and my free Rick Steves Audio Europe smartphone app (if you don't have a smartphone, you can access the same content via podcasts). You can even follow me on Facebook and Twitter.

Our **online Travel Store** offers travel bags and accessories that I've designed specifically to help you travel smarter and lighter. These include my popular carry-on bags (roll-aboard and backpack versions), money belts, totes, toiletries kits, adapters, other accessories, and a wide selection of guidebooks, planning maps, and DVDs.

Choosing the right **railpass** for your trip—amid hundreds of options—can drive you nutty. We'll help you choose the best pass for your needs and ship it to you for free.

Want to travel with greater efficiency and less stress? We organize **tours** with more than three dozen itineraries and more than 500 departures reaching the best destinations in this book...and beyond. We offer a seven-day in-depth Paris city tour and an 11-day Paris and the Heart of France tour (focusing on the best of the north), plus a seven-day French Riviera tour, a 13-day Loire to the South of France tour, and a 14-day Wine Regions of Eastern France tour. You'll enjoy great guides, a fun bunch of travel partners (with small groups of around 24-28), and plenty of room to spread out in a big, comfy bus. You'll find European adventures to fit every vacation length. For all the details, and to get our Tour Catalog and a free Rick Steves Tour Experience DVD (filmed on location during an actual tour), visit www.ricksteves.com or call us at 425/608-4217.

the streets. For an extended stay, I prefer the pocket-size, street-indexed *Paris Pratique* or Michelin's *Paris par Arrondissement* (each about €6, sold at newsstands and bookstores in Paris). **Streetwise Paris** maps are popular, as they are rainproof and indestructible (about $8 in the US, www.streetwisemaps.com). Before you buy a map, look at it to be sure it has the level of detail you want.

## Other Guidebooks

If you're like most travelers, this book is all you need. But if you're heading beyond my recommended neighborhoods and destinations, $40 for extra maps and books can be money well spent. If you'll be traveling elsewhere in France, consider *Rick Steves' France* or *Rick Steves' Provence & the French Riviera*.

The following books are worthwhile, though most are not updated annually; check the publication date before you buy.

The scholarly *Michelin Green Guide* is informative if dry. *An Hour From Paris* by Annabel Simms is a well-researched guide for 20 little-known day trips outside Paris. Also recommended are *Paris: The Collected Traveler* (Barrie Kerper) and *The Paris Mapguide* (Michael Middleditch). Of the multitude of other guidebooks on France and Paris, many are high on facts and low on opinion, guts, or personality.

## Recommended Books and Movies

To learn more about Paris past and present, check out a few of these books or films.

### Nonfiction

For a better understanding of French politics, culture, and people, check out *Sixty Million Frenchmen Can't Be Wrong* (Nadeau and Barlow), *Culture Shock: France* (Taylor), *French or Foe,* and *Savoir-Flair!* (both by Polly Platt). *The Course of French History* (Goubert) provides a basic summary of French history, while *The Cambridge Illustrated History of France* (Jones) comes with coffee-table-book pictures and illustrations. *La Seduction: How the French Play the Game of Life* (Sciolino) explains how seduction has long been used in all aspects of French life, from small villages to the halls of government, providing a surprisingly helpful cultural primer.

*A Moveable Feast* is Ernest Hemingway's classic memoir of 1920s Paris. In *I'll Always Have Paris*, Art Buchwald meets Hemingway, among others. *Suite Française* (Nemirovsky) is by a Jewish writer who eloquently describes how life changed after the Nazi occupation. *Is Paris Burning?* (Collins) brings late-WWII Paris to life on its pages. *Americans in Paris: Life and Death under Nazi Occupation* is a fascinating read (Glass). *Paris Noir: African*

*Americans in the City of Light* (Stovall) explains why African Americans found Paris so freeing in the first half of the 20th century.

*Paris to the Moon* is Adam Gopnik's charming collection of stories about life as a New Yorker in Paris (his literary anthology, *Americans in Paris,* is also recommended). *A Corner in the Marais* (Karmel) is a detailed account of one Parisian neighborhood; Diane Johnson's *Into a Paris Quartier* tells tales about the sixth arrondissement. The memoir *The Piano Shop on the Left Bank* (Carhart) captures Paris' sentimental appeal. *Almost French* (Turnbull) is a funny take on living as a Parisian native. Reading *The Flaneur* is like wandering with author Edmund White through his favorite finds. A mix of writers explores Parisian culture in *Travelers Tales: Paris* (O'Reilly).

*The Authentic Bistros of Paris* (Thomazeau), a pretty picture book, will have you longing for a *croque monsieur.* Foodies seek out the most complete (and priciest) menu reader around: *A to Z of French Food, a French to English Dictionary of Culinary Terms* (G. de Temmerman).

### Fiction

Dickens' *A Tale of Two Cities* shows the pathos and horror of the French Revolution, as does Victor Hugo's *Les Misérables* (his *The Hunchback of Notre-Dame* is also set in Paris).

The anthology *A Place in the World Called Paris* (Barclay) includes essays by literary greats from Truman Capote to Franz Kafka. The characters in Marge Piercy's *City of Darkness, City of Light* storm the Bastille. And though it relies on some stereotypes, *A Year in the Merde* (Clarke) is a lighthearted look at life as a *faux* Parisian.

Georges Simenon was a Belgian, but he often set his *Inspector Maigret* detective series in Paris; *The Hotel Majestic* is particularly good. Mystery fans should also consider *Murder in Montparnasse* (Engel), *Murder in the Marais* (Black), and *Sandman* (Janes), set in Vichy-era Paris. Alan Furst writes gripping novels about WWII espionage that put you right into the action in Paris.

For children, there's the beloved *Madeline* series (Bemelmans), where "in an old house in Paris that was covered with vines, lived twelve little girls in two straight lines." Kids of all ages enjoy the whimsical and colorful impressions of the city in Miroslav Sasek's classic picture-book *This Is Paris.*

### Films

*Children of Paradise* (1946), a melancholy romance, was filmed during the Nazi occupation of Paris. In *The Red Balloon* (1956), a small boy chases his balloon through the city streets, showing how beauty can be found in the simplest toy. *The 400 Blows* (1959) and

*Jules and Jim* (1962) are both classics of French New Wave cinema by director François Truffaut. *Charade* (1963) combines a romance between Audrey Hepburn and Cary Grant with a crime story.

*Blue/White/Red* (1990s) is a stylish trilogy of films, each featuring a famous French actress as the lead (*Blue*, with Juliette Binoche, is the best of the three). *Ridicule* (1996), set in the opulent court of Louis XVI, shows that survival depended on a quick wit and an acid tongue. In the crime caper *Ronin* (1998), Robert De Niro and Jean Reno lead a car chase through the city.

*Moulin Rouge!* (2001) is a fanciful musical set in the legendary Montmartre night club. *Amélie* (2001), a crowd-pleasing romance, features a charming young waitress searching for love and the meaning of life. *La Vie en Rose* (2007) covers the glamorous and turbulent life of singer Edith Piaf, who famously regretted nothing (many scenes were shot in Paris). No Disney flick, *The Triplets of Belleville* (2003) is a surreal-yet-heartwarming animated film that begins in a very Parisian fictional city.

For over-the-top, schlocky fun, watch *The Phantom of the Opera* (2004), about a disfigured musical genius hiding in the Paris Opera House, and *The Da Vinci Code* (2006), a blockbuster murder mystery partly filmed inside the Louvre.

Woody Allen's *Midnight in Paris* (2011) is a sharp comedy that shifts between today's Paris and the 1920s mecca of Picasso, Hemingway, and Fitzgerald. If you'll be heading to Versailles, try *Marie Antoinette* (2006), a delicate little bonbon of a film about the misunderstood queen.

## Holidays and Festivals

This section includes festivals in Paris, plus national holidays observed throughout France. Many sights and banks close on national holidays—keep this in mind when planning your itinerary. Before planning a trip around a festival, verify its dates by checking the festival's website or France's national tourism website (www.franceguide.com); www.whatsonwhen.com also lists many festival dates.

In Paris, hotels get booked up Easter weekend (note that Easter Monday is a holiday, and the weeks before and after are also busy), Labor Day, V-E Day, Ascension weekend, Pentecost weekend, Bastille Day and the week during which it falls, and the winter holidays (last half of December). Avoid leaving Paris at the beginning of one of these holiday weekends or returning at the end—you'll be competing with Parisians for seats on planes and trains, or fighting them in traffic on the roadways.

Paris is lively with festivals and events throughout the summer and fall. Kicking off the season in late May or early June is the month-long **Festival of St. Denis** in that Parisian suburb, featur-

# 2 0 1 3

| JANUARY | | | | | | |
|---|---|---|---|---|---|---|
| S | M | T | W | T | F | S |
|  |  | 1 | 2 | 3 | 4 | 5 |
| 6 | 7 | 8 | 9 | 10 | 11 | 12 |
| 13 | 14 | 15 | 16 | 17 | 18 | 19 |
| 20 | 21 | 22 | 23 | 24 | 25 | 26 |
| 27 | 28 | 29 | 30 | 31 |  |  |

| FEBRUARY | | | | | | |
|---|---|---|---|---|---|---|
| S | M | T | W | T | F | S |
|  |  |  |  |  | 1 | 2 |
| 3 | 4 | 5 | 6 | 7 | 8 | 9 |
| 10 | 11 | 12 | 13 | 14 | 15 | 16 |
| 17 | 18 | 19 | 20 | 21 | 22 | 23 |
| 24 | 25 | 26 | 27 | 28 |  |  |

| MARCH | | | | | | |
|---|---|---|---|---|---|---|
| S | M | T | W | T | F | S |
|  |  |  |  |  | 1 | 2 |
| 3 | 4 | 5 | 6 | 7 | 8 | 9 |
| 10 | 11 | 12 | 13 | 14 | 15 | 16 |
| 17 | 18 | 19 | 20 | 21 | 22 | 23 |
| 24/31 | 25 | 26 | 27 | 28 | 29 | 30 |

| APRIL | | | | | | |
|---|---|---|---|---|---|---|
| S | M | T | W | T | F | S |
|  | 1 | 2 | 3 | 4 | 5 | 6 |
| 7 | 8 | 9 | 10 | 11 | 12 | 13 |
| 14 | 15 | 16 | 17 | 18 | 19 | 20 |
| 21 | 22 | 23 | 24 | 25 | 26 | 27 |
| 28 | 29 | 30 |  |  |  |  |

| MAY | | | | | | |
|---|---|---|---|---|---|---|
| S | M | T | W | T | F | S |
|  |  |  | 1 | 2 | 3 | 4 |
| 5 | 6 | 7 | 8 | 9 | 10 | 11 |
| 12 | 13 | 14 | 15 | 16 | 17 | 18 |
| 19 | 20 | 21 | 22 | 23 | 24 | 25 |
| 26 | 27 | 28 | 29 | 30 | 31 |  |

| JUNE | | | | | | |
|---|---|---|---|---|---|---|
| S | M | T | W | T | F | S |
|  |  |  |  |  |  | 1 |
| 2 | 3 | 4 | 5 | 6 | 7 | 8 |
| 9 | 10 | 11 | 12 | 13 | 14 | 15 |
| 16 | 17 | 18 | 19 | 20 | 21 | 22 |
| 23/30 | 24 | 25 | 26 | 27 | 28 | 29 |

| JULY | | | | | | |
|---|---|---|---|---|---|---|
| S | M | T | W | T | F | S |
|  | 1 | 2 | 3 | 4 | 5 | 6 |
| 7 | 8 | 9 | 10 | 11 | 12 | 13 |
| 14 | 15 | 16 | 17 | 18 | 19 | 20 |
| 21 | 22 | 23 | 24 | 25 | 26 | 27 |
| 28 | 29 | 30 | 31 |  |  |  |

| AUGUST | | | | | | |
|---|---|---|---|---|---|---|
| S | M | T | W | T | F | S |
|  |  |  |  | 1 | 2 | 3 |
| 4 | 5 | 6 | 7 | 8 | 9 | 10 |
| 11 | 12 | 13 | 14 | 15 | 16 | 17 |
| 18 | 19 | 20 | 21 | 22 | 23 | 24 |
| 25 | 26 | 27 | 28 | 29 | 30 | 31 |

| SEPTEMBER | | | | | | |
|---|---|---|---|---|---|---|
| S | M | T | W | T | F | S |
| 1 | 2 | 3 | 4 | 5 | 6 | 7 |
| 8 | 9 | 10 | 11 | 12 | 13 | 14 |
| 15 | 16 | 17 | 18 | 19 | 20 | 21 |
| 22 | 23 | 24 | 25 | 26 | 27 | 28 |
| 29 | 30 |  |  |  |  |  |

| OCTOBER | | | | | | |
|---|---|---|---|---|---|---|
| S | M | T | W | T | F | S |
|  |  | 1 | 2 | 3 | 4 | 5 |
| 6 | 7 | 8 | 9 | 10 | 11 | 12 |
| 13 | 14 | 15 | 16 | 17 | 18 | 19 |
| 20 | 21 | 22 | 23 | 24 | 25 | 26 |
| 27 | 28 | 29 | 30 | 31 |  |  |

| NOVEMBER | | | | | | |
|---|---|---|---|---|---|---|
| S | M | T | W | T | F | S |
|  |  |  |  |  | 1 | 2 |
| 3 | 4 | 5 | 6 | 7 | 8 | 9 |
| 10 | 11 | 12 | 13 | 14 | 15 | 16 |
| 17 | 18 | 19 | 20 | 21 | 22 | 23 |
| 24 | 25 | 26 | 27 | 28 | 29 | 30 |

| DECEMBER | | | | | | |
|---|---|---|---|---|---|---|
| S | M | T | W | T | F | S |
| 1 | 2 | 3 | 4 | 5 | 6 | 7 |
| 8 | 9 | 10 | 11 | 12 | 13 | 14 |
| 15 | 16 | 17 | 18 | 19 | 20 | 21 |
| 22 | 23 | 24 | 25 | 26 | 27 | 28 |
| 29 | 30 | 31 |  |  |  |  |

APPENDIX

ing musicians from around the world at various venues (tel. 01 48 13 06 07, www.festival-saint-denis.com).

Paris celebrates the solstice (June 21) with its **Music Festival** (Fête de la Musique), staging concerts throughout the city.

**Bastille Day,** France's National Day (July 14), brings fireworks, dancing, and revelry countrywide (see sidebar on page 306). In late July, the **Tour de France** bicycle race ends on the Champs-Elysées (www.letour.fr; see sidebar on page 298).

From mid-July to mid-August, the **Paris Neighborhoods Festival** features theater, dance, and concerts around the city. At the same time, the fun **Paris Plages,** a riverside ersatz beach, is set up in the middle of the city (see page 60).

**La Villette Jazz Festival** brings a week of outdoor jazz concerts to this Parisian park from late August to mid-September. The first Saturday of October, Montmartre celebrates the **grape harvest** with a parade and festivities. The **Festival of Autumn**

(www.festival-automne.com) runs through fall, with theater, dance, film, and opera performances. If you're in Paris during **Christmas,** see the Paris in Winter chapter for information on things to do. (Christmas week is generally quieter than the week of New Year's.)

For sports events, see www.sportsevents365.com for schedules and ticket information.

Here are some major holidays in 2013:

| | |
|---|---|
| **Jan 1** | New Year's Day |
| **Jan 6** | Epiphany |
| **March 31** | Easter Sunday |
| **April 1** | Easter Monday |
| **May 1** | Labor Day |
| **May 8** | V-E (Victory in Europe) Day |
| **May 9** | Ascension |
| **May 19** | Pentecost |
| **May 20** | Pentecost Monday |
| **July 14** | Bastille Day |
| **Aug 15** | Assumption of Mary |
| **Nov 1** | All Saints' Day |
| **Nov 11** | Armistice Day |
| **Dec 25** | Christmas Day |

# Conversions and Climate

## Numbers and Stumblers
- Europeans write a few of their numbers differently than we do: 1 = 1, 4 = 4, 7 = 7.
- In Europe, dates appear as day/month/year, so Christmas is 25/12/13.
- Commas are decimal points and decimals commas. A dollar and a half is 1,50, one thousand is 1.000, and there are 5.280 feet in a mile.
- When pointing, use your whole hand, palm down.
- When counting with fingers, start with your thumb. If you hold up your first finger to request one item, you'll probably get two.
- What Americans call the second floor of a building is the first floor in Europe.
- On escalators and moving sidewalks, Europeans keep the left "lane" open for passing. Keep to the right.

## Metric Conversions (approximate)
A kilogram is 2.2 pounds, and 1 liter is about a quart, or almost four to a gallon. A kilometer is six-tenths of a mile. I figure kilometers

to miles by cutting them in half and adding back 10 percent of the original (120 km: 60 + 12 = 72 miles, 300 km: 150 + 30 = 180 miles).

| | |
|---|---|
| 1 foot = 0.3 meter | 1 square yard = 0.8 square meter |
| 1 yard = 0.9 meter | 1 square mile = 2.6 square kilometers |
| 1 mile = 1.6 kilometers | 1 ounce = 28 grams |
| 1 centimeter = 0.4 inch | 1 quart = 0.95 liter |
| 1 meter = 39.4 inches | 1 kilogram = 2.2 pounds |
| 1 kilometer = 0.62 mile | 32°F = 0°C |

## Clothing Sizes

When shopping for clothing, use these US-to-European comparisons as general guidelines (but note that no conversion is perfect).

- Women's dresses and blouses: Add 30 (US size 10 = European size 40)
- Men's suits and jackets: Add 10 (US size 40 regular = European size 50)
- Men's shirts: Multiply by 2 and add about 8 (US size 15 collar = European size 38)
- Women's shoes: Add about 30 (US size 8 = European size 38-39)
- Men's shoes: Add 32-34 (US size 9 = European size 41; US size 11 = European size 45)

APPENDIX

## Paris' Climate

| J | F | M | A | M | J | J | A | S | O | N | D |
|---|---|---|---|---|---|---|---|---|---|---|---|
| 43° | 45° | 54° | 60° | 68° | 73° | 76° | 75° | 70° | 60° | 50° | 44° |
| 34° | 34° | 39° | 43° | 49° | 55° | 58° | 58° | 53° | 46° | 40° | 36° |
| 14 | 14 | 19 | 17 | 19 | 18 | 19 | 18 | 17 | 18 | 15 | 15 |

First line, average daily high; second line, average daily low; third line, average days without rain. For more detailed weather statistics for destinations in this book (as well as the rest of the world), check www.worldclimate.com.

## Temperature Conversion: Fahrenheit and Celsius

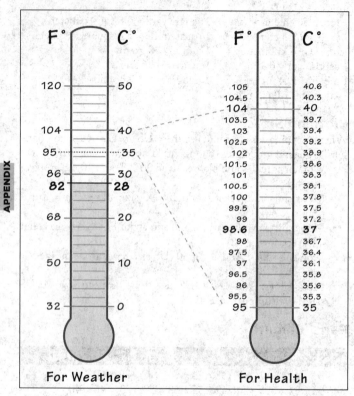

For Weather

For Health

*Europe takes its temperature using the Celsius scale, while we opt for Fahrenheit. For a rough conversion from Celsius to Fahrenheit, double the number and add 30. For weather, remember that 28°C is 82°F—perfect. For health, 37°C is just right.*

# Packing Checklist

Whether you're traveling for five days or five weeks, here's what you'll need to bring. Pack light to enjoy the sweet freedom of true mobility. Happy travels!

- ❏ 5 shirts: long- and short-sleeve
- ❏ 1 sweater or lightweight fleece
- ❏ 2 pairs pants
- ❏ 1 pair shorts
- ❏ 1 swimsuit
- ❏ 5 pairs underwear and socks
- ❏ 1 pair shoes
- ❏ 1 rainproof jacket with hood
- ❏ Tie or scarf
- ❏ Money belt
- ❏ Money—your mix of:
  - ❏ Debit card (for ATM withdrawals)
  - ❏ Credit card
  - ❏ Hard cash (in easy-to-exchange $20 bills)
- ❏ Documents plus photo-copies:
  - ❏ Passport
  - ❏ Printout of airline eticket
  - ❏ Driver's license
  - ❏ Student ID and hostel card
  - ❏ Railpass/car rental voucher
  - ❏ Insurance details
- ❏ Daypack
- ❏ Electronics—your choice of:
  - ❏ Camera (and related gear)
  - ❏ Computer/mobile devices (phone, MP3 player, ereader, etc.)
  - ❏ Chargers for each of the above
  - ❏ Plug adapter
- ❏ Empty water bottle

- ❏ Wristwatch and alarm clock
- ❏ Earplugs
- ❏ Toiletries kit
  - ❏ Toiletries
  - ❏ Medicines and vitamins
  - ❏ First-aid kit
  - ❏ Glasses/contacts/sunglasses (with prescriptions)
- ❏ Sealable plastic baggies
- ❏ Laundry soap
- ❏ Clothesline
- ❏ Small towel
- ❏ Sewing kit
- ❏ Travel information (guide-books and maps)
- ❏ Address list (for sending postcards)
- ❏ Postcards and photos from home
- ❏ Notepad and pen
- ❏ Journal

*If you plan to carry on your luggage, note that all liquids must be in 3.4-ounce or smaller containers and fit within a single quart-size sealable baggie. For details, see www.tsa.gov/travelers.*

# Hotel Reservation

To: _____      _____
             *hotel*                                         *email or fax*

From:_____      _____
             *name*                                         *email or fax*

Today's date: _____ /_____ /_____
                    *day*   *month*   *year*


Dear Hotel _____ ,
Please make this reservation for me:

Name: _____

Total # of people: _____   # of rooms: _____   # of nights: _____

Arriving: _____ /_____ /_____      My time of arrival (24-hr clock): _____
              *day*   *month*   *year*          (I will telephone if I will be late)

Departing: ____ /____ /____
                *day*   *month*   *year*

Room(s): Single____   Double ____   Twin ____   Triple ____   Quad____

With: Toilet ____   Shower____   Bath ____   Sink only ____

Special needs: View____   Quiet____   Cheapest ___   Ground Floor____

Please email or fax confirmation of my reservation, along with the type of
room reserved and the price. Please also inform me of your cancellation
policy. After I hear from you, I will quickly send my credit-card information
as a deposit to hold the room. Thank you.

_____
*Name*

_____
*Address*

_____
*City*                                   *State*         *Zip Code*   *Country*

*Before hoteliers can make your reservation, they want to know the information listed above. You can use this form as the basis for your email, or you can photocopy this page, fill in the information, and send it as a fax (also available online at www.ricksteves.com/reservation).*

## French Pronunciation Guide for Paris

When using the phonetics: Try to nasalize the n sound (let the sound come through your nose). Note that the "ahn" combination uses the "ah" sound in "father," but the "an" combination uses the "a" sound in "sack." Pronounce the "ī" as the long "i" in "light." If your best attempt at pronunciation meets with a puzzled look, just point to the place name on the list.

**Arc de Triomphe** ark duh tree-ohnf

**arrondissement** ah-rohn-dees-mohn

**Art Nouveau** art noo-voh

**Auvers-sur-Oise** oh-vehr-sur-wahz

**Bateaux Mouches** bah-toh moosh

**Bon Marché** bohn mar-chay

**boulangerie** boo-lahn-zheh-ree

**Carnavalet** kar-nah-val-eh

**Champ de Mars** shahn duh mar

**Champs-Elysées** shahn-zay-lee-zay

**Chantilly** shahn-tee-yee

**charcuterie** shar-koo-tuh-ree

**Chartres** shar-truh

**château(x)** shah-toh

**Cité** see-tay

**Cité des Sciences** see-tay day see-ahns

**Conciergerie** kon-see-ehr-zhuh-ree

**Contrescarpe** kohn-truh-scarp

**droguerie** droh-guh-ree

**Ecole Militaire** eh-kohl mee-lee-tehr

**Egouts** ay-goo

**Fauchon** foh-shohn

**Fontainebleau** fohn-tehn-bloh

**fromagerie** froh-mah-zhuh-ree

**Galeries Lafayette** gah-luh-ree lah-fay-yet

**gare** gar

**Gare d'Austerlitz** gar doh-stehr-leets

**Gare de l'Est** gar duh lest

**Gare de Lyon** gar duh lee-ohn

**Gare du Nord** gar dew nor

**Gare St. Lazare** gar sahn lah-zar

**Giverny** zhee-vehr-nee

**Grand Palais** grahn pah-lay

**Grande Arche de la Défense** grahnd arsh duh lah day-fahns

**Hôtel de Sully** oh-tehl duh soo-lee

**Ile de la Cité** eel duh lah see-tay

**Ile St. Louis** eel sahn loo-ee

**Jacquemart-André** zhahk-mar-ahn-dray

**jardin** zhar-dan

**Jardin des Plantes** zhar-dan day plahnt

**Jeu de Paume** juh duh pohm

**La Madeleine** lah mah-duh-lehn

**La Marseillaise** lah mar-seh-yehz

**Le Hameau** luh ah-moh

**Les Halles** lay ahl

**Les Invalides** lay-zan-vah-leed

**Loire** lwar

**L'Orangerie** loh-rahn-zhuh-ree

**Louvre** loov-ruh

**Marais** mah-ray

**marché aux puces** mar-chay oh poos

**Marmottan** mar-moh-tahn

**Métro** may-troh

**Monge** mohnzh

**Montmartre** mohn-mart

**Montparnasse** mohn-par-nas

**Moulin Rouge** moo-lan roozh

**musée** mew-zay

**Musée de l'Armée** mew-zay duh lar-may

**Musée d'Orsay** mew-zay dor-say

**Notre-Dame** noh-truh-dahm

**Opéra Garnier** oh-pay-rah gar-nee-ay

**orangerie** oh-rahn-zhuh-ree

**Orsay** or-say

**palais** pah-lay

**Palais de Justice** pah-lay duh zhew-stees

**Palais Royal** pah-lay roh-yahl
**Parc de la Villette** park duh la vee-leht
**Parc Monceau** park mohn-soh
**Père Lachaise** pehr lah-shehz
**Petit Palais** puh-tee pah-lay
**Pigalle** pee-gahl
**place** plahs
**Place Dauphine** plahs doh-feen
**Place de la Bastille** plahs duh lah bah-steel
**Place de la Concorde** plahs duh lah kohn-kord
**Place de la République** plahs duh lah ray-poo-bleek
**Place des Vosges** plahs day vohzh
**Place du Tertre** plahs dew tehr-truh
**Place St. André-des-Arts** plahs sahn tahn-dray-day-zart
**Place Vendôme** plahs vahn-dohm
**Pompidou** pohn-pee-doo
**pont** pohn
**Pont Alexandre III** pohn ah-leks-ahn-druh twah
**Pont Neuf** pohn nuhf
**Promenade Plantée** proh-mehn-ahd plahn-tay
**quai** kay
**Rive Droite** reeve dwaht
**Rive Gauche** reeve gohsh

**Rodin** roh-dan
**rue** rew
**Rue Cler** rew klehr
**Rue Daguerre** rew dah-gehr
**Rue des Rosiers** rew day roz-ee-ay
**Rue Montorgueil** rew mohn-tor-goy
**Rue Mouffetard** rew moof-tar
**Rue de Rivoli** rew duh ree-voh-lee
**Sacré-Cœur** sah-kray-koor
**Sainte-Chapelle** sahnt-shah-pehl
**Seine** sehn
**Sèvres-Babylone** seh-vruh-bah-bee-lohn
**Sorbonne** sor-buhn
**St. Germain-des-Prés** sahn zhehr-man-day-pray
**St. Julien-le-Pauvre** sahn zhew-lee-an-luh-poh-vruh
**St. Séverin** sahn say-vuh-ran
**St. Sulpice** sahn sool-pees
**Tour Eiffel** toor ee-fehl
**Trianon** tree-ahn-ohn
**Trocadéro** troh-kah-day-roh
**Tuileries** twee-lay-ree
**Vaux-le-Vicomte** voh-luh-vee-kohnt
**Venus de Milo** vuh-news duh mee-loh
**Versailles** vehr-"sigh"

## French Survival Phrases

When using the phonetics, try to nasalize the <u>n</u> sound.

| English | French | Phonetics |
|---|---|---|
| Good day. | **Bonjour.** | boh<u>n</u>-zhoor |
| Mrs. / Mr. | **Madame / Monsieur** | mah-dahm / muhs-yur |
| Do you speak English? | **Parlez-vous anglais?** | par-lay-voo ah<u>n</u>-glay |
| Yes. / No. | **Oui. / Non.** | wee / noh<u>n</u> |
| I understand. | **Je comprends.** | zhuh koh<u>n</u>-prah<u>n</u> |
| I don't understand. | **Je ne comprends pas.** | zhuh nuh koh<u>n</u>-prah<u>n</u> pah |
| Please. | **S'il vous plaît.** | see voo play |
| Thank you. | **Merci.** | mehr-see |
| I'm sorry. | **Désolé.** | day-zoh-lay |
| Excuse me. | **Pardon.** | par-doh<u>n</u> |
| (No) problem. | **(Pas de) problème.** | (pah duh) proh-blehm |
| It's good. | **C'est bon.** | say boh<u>n</u> |
| Goodbye. | **Au revoir.** | oh vwahr |
| one / two | **un / deux** | uh<u>n</u> / duh |
| three / four | **trois / quatre** | twah / kah-truh |
| five / six | **cinq / six** | sa<u>n</u>k / sees |
| seven / eight | **sept / huit** | seht / weet |
| nine / ten | **neuf / dix** | nuhf / dees |
| How much is it? | **Combien?** | koh<u>n</u>-bee-a<u>n</u> |
| Write it? | **Ecrivez?** | ay-kree-vay |
| Is it free? | **C'est gratuit?** | say grah-twee |
| Included? | **Inclus?** | a<u>n</u>-klew |
| Where can I buy / find...? | **Où puis-je acheter / trouver...?** | oo pwee-zhuh ah-shuh-tay / troo-vay |
| I'd like / We'd like... | **Je voudrais / Nous voudrions...** | zhuh voo-dray / noo voo-dree-oh<u>n</u> |
| ...a room. | **...une chambre.** | ewn shah<u>n</u>-bruh |
| ...a ticket to ___. | **...un billet pour ___.** | uh<u>n</u> bee-yay poor |
| Is it possible? | **C'est possible?** | say poh-see-bluh |
| Where is...? | **Où est...?** | oo ay |
| ...the train station | **...la gare** | lah gar |
| ...the bus station | **...la gare routière** | lah gar root-yehr |
| ...tourist information | **...l'office du tourisme** | loh-fees dew too-reez-muh |
| Where are the toilets? | **Où sont les toilettes?** | oo soh<u>n</u> lay twah-leht |
| men | **hommes** | ohm |
| women | **dames** | dahm |
| left / right | **à gauche / à droite** | ah gohsh / ah dwaht |
| straight | **tout droit** | too dwah |
| When does this open / close? | **Ça ouvre / ferme à quelle heure?** | sah oo-vruh / fehrm ah kehl ur |
| At what time? | **À quelle heure?** | ah kehl ur |
| Just a moment. | **Un moment.** | uh<u>n</u> moh-mah<u>n</u> |
| now / soon / later | **maintenant / bientôt / plus tard** | ma<u>n</u>-tuh-nah<u>n</u> / bee-a<u>n</u>-toh / plew tar |
| today / tomorrow | **aujourd'hui / demain** | oh-zhoor-dwee / duh-ma<u>n</u> |

## In a French-speaking Restaurant

| | | |
|---|---|---|
| I'd like / We'd like... | **Je voudrais / Nous voudrions...** | zhuh voo-dray / noo voo-dree-oh<u>n</u> |
| ...to reserve... | **...réserver...** | ray-zehr-vay |
| ...a table for one / two. | **...une table pour un / deux.** | ewn tah-bluh poor uh<u>n</u> / duh |
| Non-smoking. | **Non fumeur.** | noh<u>n</u> few-mur |
| Is this seat free? | **C'est libre?** | say lee-bruh |
| The menu (in English), please. | **La carte (en anglais), s'il vous plaît.** | lah kart (ah<u>n</u> ah<u>n</u>-glay) see voo play |
| service (not) included | **service (non) compris** | sehr-vees (noh<u>n</u>) koh<u>n</u>-pree |
| to go | **à emporter** | ah ah<u>n</u>-por-tay |
| with / without | **avec / sans** | ah-vehk / sah<u>n</u> |
| and / or | **et / ou** | ay / oo |
| special of the day | **plat du jour** | plah dew zhoor |
| specialty of the house | **spécialité de la maison** | spay-see-ah-lee-tay duh lah may-zoh<u>n</u> |
| appetizers | **hors-d'oeuvre** | or-duh-vruh |
| first course (soup, salad) | **entrée** | ah<u>n</u>-tray |
| main course (meat, fish) | **plat principal** | plah pra<u>n</u>-see-pahl |
| bread | **pain** | pa<u>n</u> |
| cheese | **fromage** | froh-mahzh |
| sandwich | **sandwich** | sah<u>n</u>d-weech |
| soup | **soupe** | soop |
| salad | **salade** | sah-lahd |
| meat | **viande** | vee-ah<u>n</u>d |
| chicken | **poulet** | poo-lay |
| fish | **poisson** | pwah-soh<u>n</u> |
| seafood | **fruits de mer** | frwee duh mehr |
| fruit | **fruit** | frwee |
| vegetables | **légumes** | lay-gewm |
| dessert | **dessert** | duh-sehr |
| mineral water | **eau minérale** | oh mee-nay-rahl |
| tap water | **l'eau du robinet** | loh dew roh-bee-nay |
| milk | **lait** | lay |
| (orange) juice | **jus (d'orange)** | zhew (doh-rah<u>n</u>zh) |
| coffee | **café** | kah-fay |
| tea | **thé** | tay |
| wine | **vin** | va<u>n</u> |
| red / white | **rouge / blanc** | roozh / blah<u>n</u> |
| glass / bottle | **verre / bouteille** | vehr / boo-teh-ee |
| beer | **bière** | bee-ehr |
| Cheers! | **Santé!** | sah<u>n</u>-tay |
| More. / Another. | **Plus. / Un autre.** | plew / uh<u>n</u> oh-truh |
| The same. | **La même chose.** | lah mehm shohz |
| The bill, please. | **L'addition, s'il vous plaît.** | lah-dee-see-oh<u>n</u> see voo play |
| tip | **pourboire** | poor-bwar |
| Delicious! | **Délicieux!** | day-lee-see-uh |

For more user-friendly French phrases, check out *Rick Steves' French Phrase Book and Dictionary* or *Rick Steves' French, Italian & German Phrase Book*.

# INDEX

# MAP INDEX

MAP INDEX

# Audio Europe

## Rick's Free Travel App

Get your FREE **Rick Steves Audio Europe**™ app to enjoy...

- Dozens of self-guided tours of Europe's top museums, sights and historic walks
- Hundreds of tracks filled with cultural insights and sightseeing tips from Rick's radio interviews
- All organized into handy geographic playlists
- For iPhone, iPad, iPod Touch, Android

With Rick whispering in your ear, Europe gets even better.

## Find out more at ricksteves.com

# Join a Rick Steves tour

**Enjoy Europe's warmest welcome...** with the flexibility and friendship of a small group getting to know Rick's favorite places and people. It all starts with our free tour catalog and DVD.

**Great guides, small groups, no grumps.**

# Start your trip at

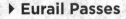

## Free information and great gear to

### ▸ Plan Your Trip

Browse thousands of articles and a wealth of money-saving tips for planning your dream trip. You'll find up-to-date information on Europe's best destinations, packing smart, getting around, finding rooms, staying healthy, avoiding scams and more.

### ▸ Eurail Passes

Find out, step-by-step, if a railpass makes sense for your trip—and how to avoid buying more than you need. Get free shipping on online orders

### ▸ Graffiti Wall & Travelers Helpline

Learn, ask, share—our online community of savvy travelers is a great resource for first-time travelers to Europe, as well as seasoned pros.

## Rick Steves' Europe Through the Back Door, Inc.

# Rick Steves®

## EUROPE GUIDES

Best of Europe
Eastern Europe
Europe Through the Back Door
Mediterranean Cruise Ports

## COUNTRY GUIDES

Croatia & Slovenia
England
France
Germany
Great Britain
Ireland
Italy
Portugal
Scandinavia
Spain
Switzerland

## CITY & REGIONAL GUIDES

Amsterdam, Bruges & Brussels
Athens & the Peloponnese
Barcelona
Budapest
Florence & Tuscany
Istanbul
London
Paris
Prague & the Czech Republic
Provence & the French Riviera
Rome
Venice
Vienna, Salzburg & Tirol

## SNAPSHOT GUIDES

Barcelona
Berlin
Bruges & Brussels
Copenhagen & the Best of
    Denmark
Dublin
Dubrovnik
Hill Towns of Central Italy
Italy's Cinque Terre
Krakow, Warsaw & Gdansk
Lisbon
Madrid & Toledo
Munich, Bavaria & Salzburg
Naples & the Amalfi Coast
Northern Ireland
Norway
Scotland
Sevilla, Granada & Southern Spain
Stockholm

## POCKET GUIDES

Athens
London
Paris
Rome

## TRAVEL CULTURE

Europe 101
European Christmas
Postcards from Europe
Travel as a Political Act

# NOW AVAILABLE:
# eBOOKS, DVD & BLU-RAY

## eBOOKS

*Nearly all Rick Steves guides are available as eBooks. Check with your favorite bookseller.*

### RICK STEVES' EUROPE DVDs

10 New Shows 2011–2012
Austria & the Alps
Eastern Europe
England & Wales
European Christmas
European Travel Skills & Specials
France
Germany, BeNeLux & More
Greece & Turkey
Iran
Ireland & Scotland
Italy's Cities
Italy's Countryside
Scandinavia
Spain
Travel Extras

## BLU-RAY

Celtic Charms
Eastern Europe Favorites
European Christmas
Italy Through the Back Door
Mediterranean Mosaic
Surprising Cities of Europe

## PHRASE BOOKS & DICTIONARIES

French
French, Italian & German
German
Italian
Portuguese
Spanish

## JOURNALS

Rick Steves' Pocket Travel Journal
Rick Steves' Travel Journal

## PLANNING MAPS

Britain, Ireland & London
Europe
France & Paris
Germany, Austria & Switzerland
Ireland
Italy
Spain & Portugal

# Credits

## Researcher
For her help updating this book, thanks to...

### Mary Bouron

Mary caught the travel bug as a child living in London, and later, as an exchange student in France. Born a Seattleite, Mary now confidently calls herself a Parisian. Deeply in love with a Frenchman, and a mother of two, she occupies her free time hunting for the city's best baguette and digging at the root causes of Franco-American cultural miscommunications.